Lecture Notes in Computer Science   3143

Commenced Publication in 1973
Founding and Former Series Editors:
Gerhard Goos, Juris Hartmanis, and Jan van Leeuwen

Wenyin Liu   Yuanchun Shi
Qing Li (Eds.)

Advances in Web-Based Learning – ICWL 2004

Third International Conference
Beijing, China, August 8-11, 2004
Proceedings

 Springer

Volume Editors

Wenyin Liu
City University of Hong Kong, Department of Computer Science
Kowloon, Hong Kong
E-mail: csliuwy@cityu.edu.hk

Yuanchun Shi
Tsinghua University, Department of Computer Science and Technology
Beijing 100084, China
E-mail: shiyc@tsinghu.edu.cn

Qing Li
City University of Hong Kong
Deptartment of Computer Engineering and Information Technology
Kowloon, Hong Kong
E-mail: itqli@cityu.edu.hk

Library of Congress Control Number: 2004109597

CR Subject Classification (1998): H.4, H.3, I.2.6, H.5, K.3, D.2, I.2

ISSN 0302-9743
ISBN 3-540-22542-0 Springer Berlin Heidelberg New York

Springer is a part of Springer Science+Business Media

springeronline.com

© Springer-Verlag Berlin Heidelberg 2004
Printed in Germany

Preface

With the rapid development of Web-based learning and new concepts like virtual class-rooms, virtual laboratories and virtual universities, many issues need to be addressed. On the technical side, there is a need for effective technology for deployment of Web-based education. On the learning side, the cyber mode of learning is very different from classroom-based learning. How can instructional development cope with this new style of learning? On the management side, the establishment of the cyber university imposes very different requirements for the set-up. Does industry-university partnership provide a solution to addressing the technological and management issues? Why do we need to standardize e-learning and what can we do already? As with many other new developments, more research is needed to establish the concepts and best practice for Web-based learning.

ICWL 2004, the 3rd International Conference on Web-Based Learning, was held at the Tsinghua University (Beijing, China) from August 8th to 11th, 2004, as a continued attempt to address many of the above-mentioned issues. Following the great successes of ICWL 2002 (Hong Kong) and ICWL 2003 (Australia), ICWL 2004 aimed at presenting new progress in the technical, pedagogical, as well as management issues of Web-based learning. The conference featured a comprehensive program, including a tutorial session, a keynote talk, a main track for regular paper presentations, and an industrial track. We received 120 papers and accepted only 58 of them in the main track for both oral and poster presentations.

A conference like this can only succeed with an excellent team effort. We would like to acknowledge the great contribution from our program committee members and paper reviewers who helped review submitted papers, select high-quality papers, and provide valuable comments for the authors. We are particularly indebted to Dr. Liu Wenyin, the publication chair as well as the tutorial chair, who did much more than what the roles asked him to. Special thanks go to Guo Ling and Xiang Xin, who did wonderful jobs as the conference secretary and Web master, respectively. Sponsorships from Tsinghua University, City University of Hong Kong, CELTSC, and the Hong Kong Web Society are gratefully acknowledged.

May 2004

Maria Orlowska   Shi Yuanchun
Dennis McLeod   Rynson Lau
Xiaoming Li   Tosiyasu L. Kunii
Qing Li

Organization

ICWL 2004 was organized by Tsinghua University (Beijing, China) in conjunction with the Hong Kong Web Society.

General Co-chairs

Maria Orlowska University of Queensland, Australia
Dennis McLeod University of Southern California, USA
Xiaoming Li Peking University, China
Qing Li Hong Kong Web Society, HKSAR, China

Program Committee Co-chairs

Shi Yuanchun Tsinghua University, Beijing, China
Rynson Lau City University of Hong Kong, HKSAR, China
Tosiyasu L. Kunii Kanazawa Institute of Technology, Japan

Steering Committee Liaison

Joseph S.P. Fong City University of Hong Kong, HKSAR, China

Conference Organization

Organizing Chair
Lizhu Zhou Tsinghua University, Beijing, China

Industrial Stream
Ronnie Cheung Hong Kong Web Society, HKSAR, China

Treasurer
Jianhua Feng Tsinghua University, Beijing, China

Publication
Liu Wenyin City University of Hong Kong, HKSAR, China

Web Master
Xin Xiang Tsinghua University, Beijing, China

Local Arrangements
Li Zheng Tsinghua University, Beijing, China

Publicity
Jianwei Zhang Tsinghua University, Beijing, China

Tutorial Management
Liu Wenyin City University of Hong Kong, HKSAR, China

Conference Secretary
Ling Guo Tsinghua University, Beijing, China

Program Committee Members

Howard Beck	University of Florida, USA
Stephane Bressan	National University of Singapore, Singapore
Wentong Cai	Nanyang Technological University, Singapore
Jiannong Cao	Hong Kong Polytechnic Univ. HKSAR, China
Shi-Kuo Chang	University of Pittsburgh, USA
Elizabeth Change	Curtin University, Australia
Jo Coldwell	Deakin University, Australia
Tharam Dillon	Sydney University of Technology, Australia
Andrzej Goscinski	Deakin University, Australia
John Hughes	University of Ulster, UK
Ali Hurson	Pennsylvania State University, USA
Horace H.S. Ip	City University of Hong Kong, HKSAR, China
Weijia Jia	City University of Hong Kong, HKSAR, China
Qun Jin	Waseda University, Japan
Feiyu Kang	Tsinghua University, Beijing, China
C.-T. King	National Tsinghua University, Taiwan, China
Reggie Kwan	Open University of Hong Kong, HKSAR, China
Tosiyasu L. Kunii	Kanazawa Institute of Technology, Japan
Rynson W.H. Lau	City University of Hong Kong, HKSAR, China
Sue Legg	University of Florida, USA
Clement Leung	Victoria University of Technology, Australia
Guojie Li	Institute of Computing Technology, China
Keqin Li	State University of New York at New Paltz, USA
Qing Li	City University of Hong Kong, HKSAR, China
Xiaoming Li	Peking University, China
Liu Wenyin	City University of Hong Kong, HKSAR, China
Dennis McLeod	University of Southern California, USA
Christine Morin	IRISA/Université de Rennes, France
John Mylopoulis	University of Toronto, Canada
Maria Orlowska	University of Queensland, Australia
Raul Rojas	Free University of Berlin, Germany
Geoff Romeo	Monash University, Australia
Shi Yuanchun	Tsinghua University, Beijing, China
Timothy Shih	Tamkang University, Taiwan, China
Chengzheng Sun	Griffith University, Australia
Changjie Tang	Sichuan University, China
Y.-M. Teo	National University of Singapore, Singapore
Ulrich Thiel	GMD-IPSI, Darmstadt, Germany
A Min Tjoa	Vienna University of Technology, Austria
Zhiwei Xu	Institute of Computing Technology, China
Zongkai Yang	Huazhong Sci. & Tech. University, China
Jianwei Zhang	Tsinghua University, Beijing, China

S.Q. Zheng	University of Texas at Dallas, USA
Lizhu Zhou	Tsinghua University, Beijing, China
Wanlei Zhou	Deakin University, Australia
Zhiting Zhu	Huadong Normal University, China
Yueting Zhuang	Zhejiang University, China

Additional Reviewers

In addition to all members of the Program Committee, the following people were also involved in reviewing the papers:

| Enyi Chen | Quanbin Chen | Jianhua Feng | Ling Guo | Jinyu Li |
| Peifeng Xiang | Xin Xiang | Xin Xiao | Degan Zhang | Nan Zhang |

Table of Contents

e-Learning Platforms and Tools

Learning Resource Deployment, Organization and Management

Practice and Experience Sharing

e-Learning Standards

Pedagogical Issues

Pedagogical Issues

Learning Algorithms
with an Electronic Chalkboard over the Web

Margarita Esponda Argüero and Raúl Rojas

Institut für Informatik, Freie Universität Berlin, Takustr. 9, 14195 Berlin
{esponda,rojas}@inf.fu-berlin.de

Abstract. This paper describes a system for the animation of algorithms on an electronic chalkboard. The instructor teaching an algorithm can enter data directly through a drawing – the algorithm then makes use of this data, for example numbers, or the image of a graph. The drawing becomes alive. The result is a more natural way of teaching and starting algorithmic animations. The paper also describes how to couple a sign and handwriting recognition engine with the animation system. The lecturer can then write programs using her own handwriting, and the programs runs. All animations can be enriched with sound and explanations from the lecturer and can be posted to the Web.

1 Motivation

Algorithmic animations are becoming popular for teaching computer science [1]. There are now many visualizations of algorithmic animations available on-line. Most are used by students, as part of a course, and have been developed by university staff.

We have recently developed an algorithmic animation system called Chalk Animator as an extension for the E-Chalk system. Conventional systems for algorithmic animation handle only computer generated images as building blocks in an animation. Perfect rectangles, circles, arrows, etc. are drawn by the user using a graphical editor or are generated automatically by the system. In this paper we consider a more radical alternative: the generation of algorithmic animations starting from sketches drawn by the user on an electronic blackboard, which is both the presentation tool and the user interface for the lecturer. Not only is this approach time-effective for the lecturer, but also the "look and feel" of animated sketches is very different from computer generated graphics. Sketch animation resembles best the kind of teaching done using a traditional chalkboard. The animations. Once completed, can be see and heard through the Web.

2 The e-Chalk System

The main idea of the E-Chalk system is to provide the functionality of the traditional chalkboard using a large contact sensitive computer screen, but enhanced with all the capabilities of a digital system [7,2,3,4,5]. An electronic blackboard should be as easy to use as a traditional one. The only interface to the electronic board should be a stylus, instead of a piece of chalk.

W. Liu et al. (Eds.): ICWL 2004, LNCS 3143, pp. 1–10, 2004.
© Springer-Verlag Berlin Heidelberg 2004

When an E-Chalk session is started, the server computer starts storing and sending three streams: the board events, the audio channel, and an optional video channel. The three streams can be accessed from a Web page, by starting the E-Chalk client, which is a collection of three client Applets, one for each stream. The streams are synchronized by the audio time stamp. Therefore, an E-Chalk session can be recorded completely, but the quality of the reproduction of the board on the client side is much higher, since the board is repainted with the full resolution of the computer screen. Fig. 1 below shows schematically a teaching scenario: a lecturer teaches to a live audience; the E-Chalk server transmits the audio, video and board streams and stores an archival copy. A remote viewer watches the class using an Internet browser.

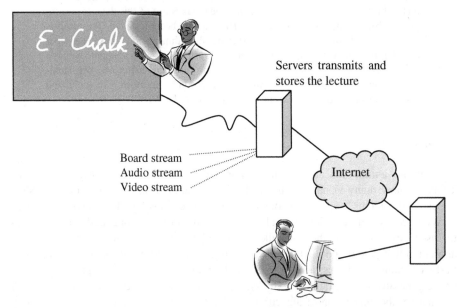

Fig. 1. The E-Chalk system. A lecturer writes on an electronic blackboard. Audio, video, and board contents are stored and are streamed through the Internet. Remote viewers watch a lecture using a Java enabled browser.

Fig. 2 is a screen dump of an actual lecture, as seen by a remote viewer in his browser. The look and feel of the screen is that of a lecture on a good blackboard. The use of color helps to emphasize some important aspects of the lecture.

The main feature of E-Chalk is to go beyond the original blackboard metaphor and provide "intelligence and information on demand". This means, that a series of special programs is running in parallel with E-Chalk and is watching the user interacting with the screen. Certain programs can then become active when certain conditions are met. E.g., a program can observe the handwriting of the user and if a mathematical formula is entered, and if the user writes a special stop symbol, the program can interpret the formula. If it is an equation, it can solve it. This capability has been already implemented in E-Chalk, using Mathematica as the mathematical equation solver [8,9,10].

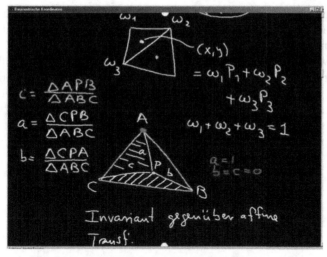

Fig. 2. A real E-Chalk lecture about geometric concepts.

Regarding algorithmic animations there are two things which come immediately to mind as possible extensions of the blackboard metaphor: a) the immediate execution of code written on the blackboard, b) the animation of algorithms started by the lecturer.

3   Executing a Programming Language in e-Chalk

In this section we describe a further educational innovation implemented for the E-Chalk system as. A simple interpreter for the programming language BASIC, was written, and the interpreter was coupled with the handwriting recognition machinery of E-Chalk. The lecturer can now write a BASIC program on the chalkboard and request its immediate execution. This implementation provides a glimpse of what will become possible in the future.

A handwriting recognizer is needed, if code written on the electronic blackboard is to be executed. The E-Chalk handwriting recognizer is a pattern recognition system developed by Ernesto Tapia at the FU Berlin [8].

Symbols are recognized by processing line strokes and extracting relevant features. Such features are, for example, the length of the line stroke, its centroid (in a unitary square), the distance between start and end of the stroke, divided by the total length. Also, the coordinates of a few points along the stroke can be added to the feature vector. The most relevant points for the shape are selected using a shape simplification algorithm. Once a symbol has been transformed into a feature vector, it is given to a neural network or support vector machine, which has been trained previously to recognize this symbol.

As a proof of concept for a programming system based on handwriting recognition, we defined a minimum subset of BASIC, which is nevertheless general purpose and universal. Our own version of BASIC is called *Tiniest BASIC* and consists of only two interpreter commands and six types of instructions.

The two instructions "RUN" and "LIST" can also be entered. RUN starts the program at the first line of code. LIST provides a listing of the current code lines. Nontrivial programs can be written with this language.

Fig. 3 shows JMATH, the program developed by Ernesto Tapia to train the character recognizer [10], coupled with our BASIC interpreter. A Tiniest Basic program has been entered. Each character is surrounded by a box and an identifier of the character which has been recognized. After writing the "LIST" command, the user closes the input by pressing on the B button (BASIC). The window to the lower left shows the output of the Tiniest BASIC interpreter.

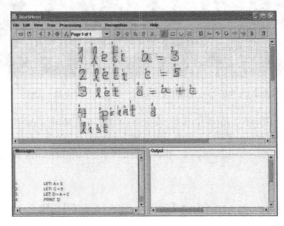

Fig. 3. Screenshot of JMATH, the editor and training program for formula recognition developed by E. Tapia, coupled to the BASIC interpreter.

Fig. 4 shows the same program, but now the command "RUN" has been entered. The output of the program is visible in the lower left window, it is the constant 8.

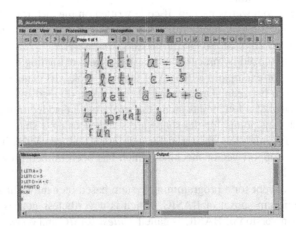

Fig. 4. Screenshot the Tiniest BASIC program after it has been executed.

Many of the options of the JMATH editor will be available in future releases of E-Chalk. Symbols can be erased, for example, by scribbling rapidly on them. Symbols can be moved from their position. If a gap is needed between two lines, the symbols below the first line are selected and moved down. This gesture recognition could allow to edit and annotate programs written in more complex programming languages, as explored in the next section.

4 Interactive Computer Driven Animation of Sketches

In E-Chalk, there is a special color which can be set at the beginning of a session. Strokes drawn with this color are processed by the handwriting recognizer engine. The engine receives all the strokes (as sequences of lines), processes the strokes and gives the result of the recognition to another application (in the case of mathematical formulas, to Mathematica from Wolfram Research). The application processes the input and gives back an ASCII string to E-Chalk or a picture in GIF or JPEG format. This application output (a number, a graph, a drawing, etc.) is pasted to the blackboard.

For our purposes this is not enough. An animation produces multiple frames, which have to be pasted at the same position. If only the history of an algorithm is being drawn, then the handwriting interface is all that is needed, but the output can only be a static image.

There is a way to generate an animation for E-Chalk using its macro recording capability and the handwriting recognizer. In E-Chalk, stroke input drawn with a previously chosen color is always passed to the shape recognition engine. The shape recognition engine groups strokes according to proximity or overlap (some digits, for example, consist of more than one stroke) and recognizes the shape among a library of symbols. This information can be passed to an algorithm animator, not to Mathematica. Our application is an animation engine for E-Chalk, which has loaded an algorithm written in Java. The Java algorithm receives the input from the shape recognition engine, runs the algorithm, and produces an animation script. The animation script is processed as a stream by the animation script interpreter, which in turn produces the code for a macro. After entering the input, the user can then go to the macro menu and start the new macro, which will be played as directed by the animated algorithm. The diagram of Fig. 5 shows schematically the information flow in the E-Chalk system. All steps are transparent for the user, who only has to call the appropriate macro at the end.

The shape recognition engine generates an object library. This is needed, because if we want to reuse the shapes entered by the user, the shapes must be stored by the recognition engine. They are assigned an object number, which can then be used by the animation algorithm generating the script.

5 Examples

After the object library has been defined by the user (by entering its input), the animation algorithm uses this objects in the animation. The instrumented algorithm produces an animation script, which after processing yields a macro file for E-Chalk. The animation runs on the electronic blackboard. Fig. 6 shows the start of the animation and the input written by the user (upper left picture). The upper right side of Fig. 6 shows the progression of the algorithm. The pivot for the comparison is painted red, the other number being compared is painted pink. After a number has reached its final position it is painted green, with a ticker line.

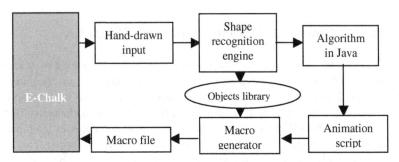

Fig. 5. Information flow for the animation of sketched input.

This experiment is also interesting, since multiple visual cues have been used to reinforce the idea of magnitude. The size of the digits is proportional to their value. The value itself is read by the user. Sorted numbers are shown in green, a color which automatically recalls the association of something being right or correct. The action is taking place at the place where the pivot is, which is painted red to signify work. The position of the two numbers being compared is also marked by two horizontal bars which slide across the array.

The animations produced in this manner can be easily collected as macros and can be replayed by an instructor during class.

In the example above, the separation of the strokes was made by considering only connected objects made of one single stroke sweep. This property is easy to test when given the coordinates of the strokes points.

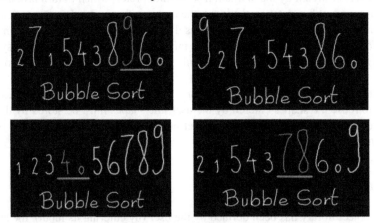

Fig. 6. The bubble sort algorithm running, animated with user input.

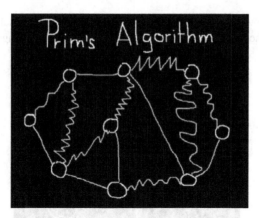

Fig. 7. The user enters the input. Nodes are painted white, edges are green.

The next example is a more spectacular illustration of the kind of animations which become possible once the user is empowered to enter her input using a pen computer. A program which implements the popular Prim algorithm for the computation of a minimum spanning tree was written. A spanning tree is a subset of the graph's edges which touches all nodes of the graph without producing cycles. The minimum spanning tree has minimum total weight (each edge has an associated weight). Fig. 7 shows how the user enters her input: by drawing the nodes and edges of the graph. In this case the extractor program was coded to expect nodes as white elements, edges as green elements. It would have been possible to detect automatically which elements are edges and which circles, but in this case we settled for a simple extractor. The weight of an edge is its total length. The reader can imagine that these are cities connected by roads of different length.

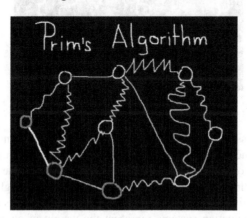

Fig. 8. An edge has been added to the spanning tree (yellow edge). The next node to be visited is painted pink (lower middle).

Fig. 8 shows the further progress of the animation. Nodes in pink have been selected and yellow edges already belong to the spanning tree. The next edge selected is the shortest edge touching the pink nodes. Fig. 9 shows the animation some frames later. The edge to the middle right is being painted yellow after being selected.

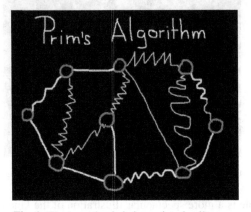

Fig. 9. The last edge is being painted yellow.

Fig. 10 shows the end result. All nodes have been visited and the "road map" is the shortest possible tree connecting all cities.

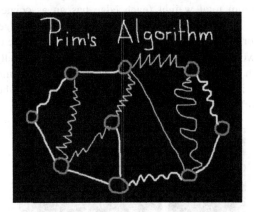

Fig. 10. Final minimum spanning tree.

The more impressive results from the animation are obtained when the user changes the input and the animation runs automatically. Fig. 11 shows four screen-shots of the same algorithm running on a new graph sketched by the user.

In the case of this animation the technique of representing the weight of an edge by its length gives an intuitive feeling for the correctness of the decisions taken at each step. Some algorithmic animation systems represent the weight of an edge sometimes by the width of the edge, but this is the first attempt to represent the weight using a wig-gled line. It is also clear why: other algorithmic animation systems render graphs using lines and circles. It is very difficult to draw esthetically appealing graphs using this convention (length of edge equals weight), but not when the user can sketch on a blackboard. Here we find a definitive advantage of the blackboard compared to simple graph drawing programs. The animation produced by the Chalk animator looks almost like an abstract painting.

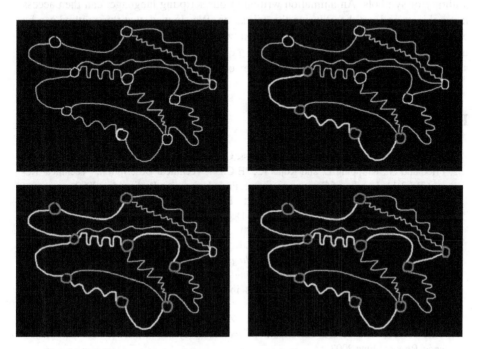

Fig. 11. Prim's algorithm working on another graph (from upper left to lower right).

6 Summary and Discussion

The kind of animations possible with our system has never been tried before: in this paper we have shown how to produce animations directly, using the input possibilities of pen computing. An instructor in a classroom needs a more natural interface with the teaching instrument, i.e. the blackboard, and this is what we have investigated in this paper. Although sketches are used to illustrate algorithms or books, few experiments have been conducted towards coupling sketches and algorithmic animations, the exception being the "low fidelity" algorithms of Hundhausen [6].

Given an electronic blackboard, it is natural to ask if the algorithms could be directly written on the blackboard and could be interpreted by the computer. We have called this "handwriting programming". Our experiment with the Tiniest BASIC interpreter shows that is indeed possible to couple a handwriting recognizer with an interpreter, in order to provide this functionality. The Tiniest BASIC interpreter was written in a few hours. Future work will be oriented towards recognizing pseudocode languages, such as Python.

The second half of the paper deals with E-Chalk and how to implement a two way communication channel between the user and the algorithm to be animated. The E-

Chalk API was modified with this objective, but the same functionality can be obtained through the use of macros. We showed that a user can enter his or her input as a macro, which is then analyzed by a symbol recognizer. The symbol recognizer builds a library of symbols. An animation written in our scripting language, can then access these objects and use them during the animation. We showed, that this method can be extended even to the labels of the animation, which can be produced by text synthesis, that is, by reproducing the handwriting of the algorithm animator. This preserves the sketch form of the diagrams, even when they contain text.

References

1. Brown M., *Algorithm Animation,* MIT Press, Cambridge MA, 1988.
2. Friedland G., Knipping L. and Rojas R., "E-Chalk Technical Description," Technical Report B-02-11, Faculty of Computer Science, Freie Universität Berlin, May 2002.
3. Friedland G., Knipping L., Rojas R. and E. Tapia, "Das E-Chalk System: Stand der Entwicklung," Technical Report B-03-03, Department of Mathematics and Computer Science, Freie Universität Berlin, February 2003.
4. Friedland G., Knipping L., Tapia E. and R. Rojas, "Web Based Education as a Result of AI Supported Classroom Teaching", *Proceedings of the Seventh Conference on Knowledge-Based Intelligent Information & Engineering Systems* (KES), Oxford, England, September 3-5, 2003. To appear in: Lecture Notes in Artificial Intelligence (LNAI) Vol. 2774, Springer-Verlag, Berlin Heidelberg.
5. Friedland G., Knipping L., Rojas R. and C. Zick, "Mapping the Classroom into the Web: Case Studies from several Institutions", *Proceedings of the 12th EDEN Annual Conference*, Rhodos, June 2003.
6. Hundhausen C., Douglas S., "A Language and System for Constructing and Presenting Low Fidelity Algorithm Visualizations", *Proceedings of Software Visualization 2001*, Dagstuhl, Germany, May 20-25, 2001, pp. 227–240.
7. Rojas R., Knipping L., Raffel U. and Friedland G, "Elektronische Kreide: Eine Java-Multimedia-Tafel für den Präsenz und Fernunterreicht", *Informatik: Forschung und Entwicklun,* Vol. 16, No. 3, pp. 159–168.
8. Tapia E. and Rojas R., "Recognition of Handwritten Digits in the E-Chalk System using Support Vector Machines," Technical Report B02-14, Department of Mathematics and Computer Science, Freie Universität Berlin, Oktober 2002.
9. Tapia E. and Rojas R., "Recognition of On-Line Handwritten Mathematical Expressions using a Minimum Spanning Tree Construction and Symbol Dominance," *Proceedings of the Fifth IAPR International Workshop on Graphics Recognition* (GREC), Barcelona, Spain, July 30-31, 2003. To appear in *Lecture Notes in Computer Science*, Special Issue on Graphics Recognition, Springer-Verlag, 2003.
10. Tapia E. and Rojas R., "Recognition of On-line Handwritten Mathematical Formulas in the E-Chalk System," *Proceedings of the Seventh International Conference on Document Analysis and Recognition* (ICDAR), Edinburgh, Scotland, August 3-6, 2003.

The Agile Teaching/Learning Methodology and Its e-Learning Platform

Andy Hon Wai Chun

Department of Computer Science
City University of Hong Kong
Tat Chee Avenue, Kowloon
Hong Kong SAR
andy.chun@cityu.edu.hk

Abstract. The Agile Teaching/Learning Methodology (ATLM) is a teaching/learning methodology designed for higher-education based on the best practices and ideas from the field of software engineering and leveraging upon concepts from agile software methodologies. Although ATLM was designed using concepts borrowed from software engineering, the methodology itself can easily be applied to a wide variety of courses that might require agility in teaching and learning. This paper explains the objectives behind ATLM and the process architecture of the methodology. ATLM emphasizes agility, communication and the learning process. The paper also presents the e-learning platform we have developed to support this ATLM approach to teaching/learning and the technologies behind this platform. The ATLM e-learning platform makes use of a number of modern collaboration and knowledge sharing technologies such as blogging, commenting, instant messaging, wiki and XML RSS.

Keywords: teaching methodology, learning methodology, e-learning platform.

1 Introduction

Agile Teaching/Learning Methodology (ATLM) is systematic approach to teaching/learning that has been successfully applied to the teaching of several Computer Science courses at the City University of Hong Kong [1] for a number of years. Although used for teaching technology-related courses, we believe the methodology itself is general enough to be applied to other disciplines as well. Many other disciplines share the same teaching/learning objectives and goals that are promoted by ATLM. For example, teaching must be agile to cope with changing and diverse learning needs. Learning must be agile to cope with changing research, business, and technology environments. ATLM also encourages communication, knowledge sharing, and the learning process to nurture self-learning individuals. As the ATLM name implies, it is a methodology for teaching as well as a methodology for learning. Teachers need a well-defined approach to teaching just as much as a student needs a well-defined approach to learning. Teaching and learning, of course, go hand-in-hand. ATLM is a balanced methodology that supports both sides of the equation.

W. Liu et al. (Eds.): ICWL 2004, LNCS 3143, pp. 11–18, 2004.

Software Engineering (SE) practitioners have long been well aware of the importance of adopting a well-defined methodology for software development [2]. Software development is a highly complex process and it makes sense to have well-defined steps, tasks and plans as well as an understanding of the dynamics behind the whole development lifecycle and how to deal with expected and unexpected changes, problems and risks.

It turns out that the teaching process is, in many ways, very similar to the software development process. It involves multiple parties with different objectives (sometimes conflicting), a very tight schedule to get things done, a fixed deadline, limited resources and a lot of expected/unexpected changes along the way. Both the teaching and software development processes require detailed planning/scheduling, tracking and management with continuous assessment and feedback from all parties. Getting a software project done correctly and on time is not easy. Making a sure a course is taught properly and on schedule can also be challenging sometimes.

In the past decade, there has been a gradual trend towards favoring a set of "light weighted" software development methodologies called agile processes [3]. These agile processes all follow the same principles as defined in the Agile Manifesto [4] that basically states that for a project to be successful we should value individuals and their interactions rather than rigidly following a process, working software rather than documents and specifications, communication rather than contract negotiation, and responding to changes rather than just following a plan. Agile methodologies put people first and are self-adaptive.

We see a lot of parallels between agile software development and modern teaching and learning. Agile Teaching/Learning Methodology values students/teachers and their interactions rather than a particular approach to teaching/learning, working knowledge rather than rote-learning, communication rather than negotiation, and responding to changes rather than just following a schedule. ATLM emphasizes teacher student communication and stresses the importance of being self-adaptive to cater to changing needs.

2 Key Characteristics

Inspired by these modern agile methodologies for software development, we designed ATLM with three key characteristics – agility, extreme, and independence.

- **Agility** – By agility, we mean the ability for the teacher to quickly adapt and change course pace and possibly structure to suit the needs and abilities of the students. The main objective for teaching is to help students learn. Each and every student is unique. Their learning needs are also unique. Not all students in a class will be able to learn at the same rate or in the same manner. Each time a course is offered, it should not be taught exactly the same way as the students in each class will be different with different learning needs. A teacher will need to ensure that different learning needs are catered to rather than just following a predefined plan. Another way to describe this is "in-sync teaching" – making sure the whole class is in-sync with the material being taught. This is particularly important when there is a mixture of students with different academic backgrounds in the class. We do not want to confuse learning rate with learning capacity. As educators, we need to be sensitive to and facilitate the needs of students from a diverse academic background. It is important to be able to patiently shepherd and encourage weaker students, while showing equal respect and openness.

Agility also means making sure the class, both the teaching and learning aspects, are constantly on track from day one. A good teacher, of course, will need to know the subject well. But, he/she must also know the students well and how they are progressing. Agility enables a self-adaptive teaching/learning process, which adapts to the specific learning needs of each class.

ATLM achieve this type of agility by maintaining a high degree of communication, interaction and feedback between the student and teacher. Teachers need to know how the students are doing and how they like/dislike the teaching approach. Students need to know what is expected from them. ATLM uses a variety of technologies to open up many channels of communication to achieve agility. Details of our e-learning platform will be explained later in the paper.

- **Extreme** – By extreme, we mean if something is good for teaching/learning, we go to the extreme and do it constantly [5]. If giving feedback to students on their learning is good, we should give feedback each class. Conversely, if getting feedback from students is good, we should allow students to give feedback whenever they want. If students learn better by teaching, they should be allowed to teach and share their knowledge constantly.

  ATLM encourages teachers to solicit student feedback on their teaching constantly and from day one. This should not be a formal teaching assessment but rather an informal and possibly anonymous feedback from the student with the main intent to guide and fine-tune the teaching approach. Formal teaching assessments are usually done towards the end of the semester. By the time teachers get results from them, it will be too late to do anything to help improve the teaching for that class. The ATLM e-learning platform provides many different options and means to solicit feedback.

- **Independent** – One of the aspects of ATLM is to train students on "learning the learning process" and not just learning the course content. One of the objectives of ATLM is to gradually take the role of the teacher "out of the loop." With each iteration in the ATLM teaching/learning cycle, the student grows more confident of self-learning so that ideally at the end of the course, the students will be confident in continuing the learning process on their own. This is extremely important for disciplines that are constantly changing, such as Computer Science. Some of the technologies student learn in school can become obsolete in a short time; students need to constantly update themselves and learn on their own. Empowering students with skills for life-long learning is important aspect of ATLM.

3   Iterative Teaching/Learning Cycles

Like other modern software development methodologies [2], ATLM is also an iterative methodology. This means the cycles of the methodology are performed over and over again in iterations; each iteration may progressively have slight variations to be

self-adaptive. For teaching, each lecture or lecture/tutorial combination is one iteration. In ATLM, since we are dealing with both teaching and learning, there are two
cycles that operate in parallel in each iteration – one for the teacher and one for the
student:

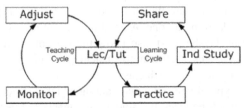

The Teaching Cycle (on the left of the diagram) is for the teacher to follow, while
the Learning Cycle (on the right) is for students. Both the Teaching and Learning
Cycles share the Lecture/Tutorial task:

- **Lecture/Tutorial** – this is the standard lecture and tutorial components of a class.
  In ATLM, we assume each iteration is the time between two lectures; usually a
  week. The role of the teacher-led lecture/tutorial will be greater at the beginning of
  the course and will gradually diminish towards the end when the students are confident in the course material and can begin to learn independently on their own, using
  skills and techniques learned in the course.

In addition, the Teaching Cycle has the following tasks:

- **Monitor** – As one of the key characteristics of ATLM is agility in meeting student
  needs, the teacher must constantly monitor student progress as well as feedback
  from students on their own teaching progress/performance. Student progress can
  easily be monitored, for example, by providing a simple weekly quiz that might or
  might not be counted as part of the official student assessment. Quiz results should
  be provided to students immediately after the class/tutorial. Statistics on quiz results will help students understand learning expectations and also identify weaknesses that need more work. Some teachers do not like giving weekly quizzes, even
  if they are informal quizzes. The result is a less agile class. Teachers will have to
  wait until the first assignment has been collected and graded to see how well students are doing. This may take several weeks. For a semester, this latency is too
  slow and not efficient.
  In addition to student performance, the teacher will also need to monitor his/her
  own teaching performance as perceived by the current group of students. This can
  be done through feedback forms, surveys as well as forums that students are encouraged to participate on an on-going basis. The feedback can be anonymous. The
  main point is for the students to understand that these are not teacher assessment
  exercises but rather a way to allow the teacher to adapt his/her teaching approach to
  cater to current students learning needs. As you can see, feedback is taken to the
  "extreme" in ATLM and is done constantly at each iteration.

- **Adjust/Adapt** – Once student and teaching performance are both understood, the
  teacher should immediately make any necessary adjustments to the course plan,
  schedule or content as well as coursework to help ensure students are "in-sync"
  with their learning. Changes are necessary for agility.

All these three steps are done during each Teaching Cycle. For the Learning Cycle, we have in addition:

- **Practice** – this is the standard coursework component of a class. The nature of the coursework will of course depend on the course being taught. However, ATLM encourages giving students assignments that help reinforce a working knowledge of the course material instead of simply rote-learning. Assignments should also be open-ended with plenty of room for creativity. The creativity aspect also adds an element of competition among the students to create more interesting solution to the assignment problem.

- **Independent Study** – One of the aspects of ATLM is to promote learning skills and prepare students for lifelong learning. Tasks should be given to gradually guide students in learning the learning process and understanding where to find resources to support their learning. ATLM encourages knowledge sharing and collaboration among students as a catalyst for self-learning. Getting students ready for lifelong learning is an important component of ATLM.

- **Knowledge Sharing** – Sharing knowledge is an important part of learning! At each teaching/learning iteration, some time should be allocated for students to talk and share what they have learned during their own studying/research. For example, students may be asked to simply find something interesting from the Web that is related to what is being taught in class and to share that with other students. It should not be a formal presentation and there is no PowerPoint to prepare for. Instead, the student might just open a Website and explains what he thought was interesting, what new concepts he learned and how it relates to the course.

Letting students "teach" greatly enhances their learning experience. Firstly, they learn from others. Secondly, they learn when they prepare for their own presentations. But, most importantly, through the whole process they get to learn one of the most important skills of their life – how to learn on their own!

The classic Learning Pyramid confirms this approach [6]. It charts the average retention rate for various methods of teaching. These retention percentages represent the results of research conducted by National Training Laboratories in Bethel, Maine in 1994. According to that chart, lecture, the top of the pyramid, achieves an average retention rate of only 5%. On the opposite end of the scale, the "teach others/immediate use" method achieves an average retention rate of 90%! ATLM believes that knowledge sharing or "teaching others" is a critical tool in helping students understand the learning process and helps prepare them for lifelong learning. In addition, to sharing in class, ATLM encourages students to share online through the use of several modern collaboration and knowledge management tools such as blogs [7, 8] and wikis [9]. Blogging is currently probably the most common way of sharing knowledge on the Internet. A blog is like an online diary with entries on different topics. The power behind blogging is that others can join in the discussion through commenting [10] or trackback [11] techniques as well as subscribing to blogs. Wiki, on the other hand, is a simple content management system that allows anyone with appropriate logon privileges to add/change and contribute to Web content on-the-fly. Both blog and wiki are powerful technologies that greatly streamline and simplify the process of collaboration and knowledge sharing.

4   Teaching/Learning Best Practices

There are numerous teaching/learning best practices that can be practiced with ATLM.
However, ATLM particularly promotes and emphasizes the following as part of the
methodology:

- **Learn by Sharing** – ATLM makes use of the fact that students learn over an order
  of magnitude better if they also participate in the teaching process. ATLM facilitates this through knowledge sharing exercises.
- **Teach How to Learn** – ATLM emphasizes that, in addition to course content, it is
  important to also teach the learning process. ATLM does this through guided and
  targeted independent study tasks with knowledge sharing and collaboration as motivation.
- **Feedback is Good** – Feedback is what makes ATLM agile. Without feedback, the
  teacher will not be able to improve the course delivery and teaching. Without feedback, students will not know if their work is on track and inline with expectations.
  ATLM facilitates feedback through informal weekly quizzes and feedback forms,
  surveys and online comments.

5   The ATLM e-Learning Platform

Our e-learning platform makes use of an integrated set of innovative technologies to
support the highly dynamic and agile mode of teaching as required by ATLM. The
platform leverages on some of the newest software technologies for knowledge sharing and collaboration. This platform can supplement more traditional technologies
such as forums and blackboards. The following diagram shows the front page of one
of the course websites that uses the ATLM e-learning platform:

Firstly, the e-learning platform makes use of open technologies, standards and
Web-based services. Most of these technologies and services are free. For example,
the whole platform complies to XHTML 1.1 and CSS 2.0 Web standards to ensure the
platform can be displayed on all the popular browsers. In addition, it meets W3C as
well as Bobby 508 and AAA accessibility recommendations. The following is a list of
some of the technologies and services used by the ATLM e-learning platform:

- **Blogging** – Blogging is the newest trend on the Internet. It is like an online diary
  but a lot more. It is tightly linked to other web pages. It allows others to comment
  entries as well as subscribe to diaries. And there are specialized search engines to
  support blog. Blogging is simple and can even be done with a mobile phone! In
  ATLM students use blogs to share what they have learned by writing a small entry
  for each interesting thing they have learned or found through research about the
  topic the class is covering.

- **Wiki** – Wiki is a popular Web-based collaborative tool. It allows content to be
  easily changed on-the-fly. ATLM uses Wiki to allow students to share information
  related to the course. A wiki can also be used for FAQ or to maintain resource
  links.

- **Commenting/Rating** – The platform makes liberal use of commenting technology. Comments can be attached to practically any entry on the course Web site. This greatly improves communication and reduces misunderstanding. In addition, ATLM encourages peer-review through commenting with ranking scores, similar to book ranking in amazon.com.

- **Instant Messaging** – The platform allows students to chat with the teacher online without needing to install any additional software. The convenience of Web-based chat further encourages and promotes communication.

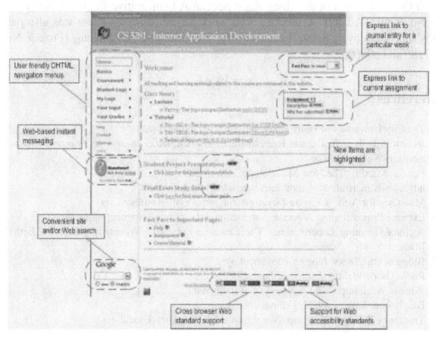

The platform provides shared services that are available on all pages, services such as commenting, instant messaging, search, multi-lingual translations, and updated notifications via XML RSS.

6   Conclusion

We have presented a novel teaching/learning methodology – the ATLM, which we have successful used for teaching technical courses. The methodology focuses on the learning process to ensure students can continue to learn and update their knowledge even after the course has been completed. This is crucial for technical courses, since technologies change so rapidly and what students learn in class may quickly become outdated. However, at the same time, we feel the motivations and objectives behind ATLM might also make it useful for non-technical course content as well. So far, we have applied ATLM and the e-learning platform for several Computer Science courses on programming and software engineering with very good response from students, especially for part-time students who prefer Web-based interactions. We plan to continue to improve the e-learning platform and possibly convert it to a generic framework that can be used by other universities as well.

Acknowledgement

The work described in this paper was substantially supported by a grant from the Research Grants Council of the Hong Kong Special Administrative Region, China (Project No. 9040517, CityU 1109/00E). The work described in this paper was also partially supported by a grant from the City University of Hong Kong (Project No. 7001286 and 6980002).

References

1. The City University of Hong Kong, http://www.cityu.edu.hk
2. Jacobson, I., Booch, G., and Rumbaugh, J., *The Unified Software Development Process,* Addison-Wesley (1999).
3. Fowler, Martin, "The New Methdology," April 2003,
   http://www.martinfowler.com/articles/newMethodology.html
4. Manifesto for Agile Software Development, http://agilemanifesto.org/
5. Extreme Programming: A gentle introduction, http://www.extremeprogramming.org/
6. National Training Laboratories, "The Learning Pyramid," Workshop Materials, Bethel, Maine.
7. Blogger, http://www.blogger.com/about.pyra
8. Radio Userland, http://radio.userland.com/
9. What is Wiki, http://wiki.org/wiki.cgi?WhatIsWiki
10. Blogkomm, http://www.blogkomm.com/
11. Trackback Development, http://www.movabletype.org/trackback/

Activity Theory as Tool
for Analyzing Asynchronous Learning Networks (ALN)

Jerry Zhigang Li and Sharon Elizabeth Bratt

School of Interactive Arts & Technology
Simon Fraser University
jerryli@sfu.ca, bratts@shaw.ca

Abstract. This paper calls on activity theory as tool for analyzing Asynchronous Learning Networks (ALN) to achieve a better understanding of their dynamics. This paper makes some design suggestions for ALN, they are: (1) Provide sufficient training at the beginning; (2) Provide technical support throughout the process; (3) Provide clear guidelines for interaction among students, evaluation criteria for grading, and the deadline for posting to a discussion; (4). Encourage cooperation among students; (5) Designate roles; (6) Provide feedback; (7) Remind students about approaching deadlines; (8) Provide a summary of the discussion at the end.

Keywords: E-learning, web-based learning, Asynchronous Learning Networks, online conference, online discussion, computer-mediated communication, Asynchronous communication, activity theory, instructional design.

1 Introduction

With Internet technology advances, more and more traditional courses are being taught online. In particular, at the Simon Fraser University (SFU) Surrey campus, most undergraduate courses have a significant online component which covers between 33 percent to 100 percent of the course time. Web conferencing via asynchronous communication is the most frequently used technology for online courses. However, the experience at SFU Surrey indicates that some instructors use Asynchronous Learning Networks (ALN) quite effectively, while others do not. Some students enjoy online discussion, while others feel that it adds to their workload, they gain little from it. These varied perceptions of the utility of Asynchronous Learning Networks suggest that there may be factors that can positively affect this medium. These factors could serve as the basis for guidelines to facilitate effective asynchronous conferencing. The goal of this paper is to use Activity theory to analyze ALN and to suggest guidelines for their use.

2 Asynchronous Learning Networks

According to Hiltz [1], "An Asynchronous Learning Network (ALN) is a teaching and learning environment located within a Computer-Mediated Communication (CMC) system designed for anytime/anyplace use through computer networks".

W. Liu et al. (Eds.): ICWL 2004, LNCS 3143, pp. 19–26, 2004.
© Springer-Verlag Berlin Heidelberg 2004

Activity theory conceptualizes all purposeful human activity as the interaction of the elements: subject, tools, object, community, rules, and division of labor among subjects.

"In this model of an activity system, the subject refers to the individual or group whose point of view is taken in the analysis of the activity. The object (or objective) is the target of the activity within the system. Instruments refer to internal or external mediating artifacts which help to achieve the outcomes of the activity. The community is comprised of one or more people who share the objective with the subject. Rules regulate actions and interactions within the activity system. The division of labor discusses how tasks are divided horizontally between community members as well as referring to any vertical division of power and status." [2]

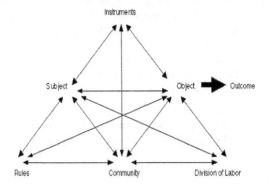

Fig. 1. The structure of human activity [12]

If we use this model to analyze the ALN environment, we can map the elements as follows:

- Subject – Students, instructors.
- Object – knowledge/skills acquisition, project completion, and problem-solving.
- Community – Online virtual community.
- Tools – Networked computers, conference software, Internet.
- Rules – Evaluation criteria, deadlines, rules on message posting.
- Division of labor – Moderator, initiator, follower, concluder, facilitator.

3 Literature Review on ALN with Reference to Activity System

3.1 Subject-Community-Object Mix

ALN allows every student an equal opportunity to participate. Students who are shy or slow processors sometimes find themselves at a disadvantage in the face-to-face classroom environment because they have a tendency to fade into the background as more assertive students dominate the classroom discussion [3]. ALN activity encourages reflection and more complex responses because participants have sufficient time to compose their thoughts before they post their responses [4]. This advantage might be outweighed by several drawbacks to communicating asynchronously in a virtual environment.

Unlike face-to-face discussions, there are no non-verbal or visual cues, no tone or intonation. Students may not feel that they are as involved with a community and its activity, as they would in a traditional face-to-face setting. They may feel isolated by this new setting. Also, discussions may be slow to start due to reluctance by some students to the first one to post [3]. Finally, the time delay between the posting of the question and the responses can be frustrating for some participants [4]

ALN form special communities among the students which are different from the communities formed by other computer mediated communication tools, like ICQ, or MS Messenger, since those communities are likely to consist of friends, co-workers, people with same interests, normally it is to of a social nature, not educational.

3.2 Subject-Tools-Object Mix

Students use networked computers to communicate with each other, and exchange ideas asynchronously to achieve their learning objective or other goal. There are many benefits to this mode of communication. ALN tools enhance collaboration due to increased access. Access to postings can be done from anywhere at anytime therefore participants do not have to coordinate schedules in order to meet. Participants can access the discussion boards to read and respond at their convenience. The ALN tool facilitates peer-to-peer learning as participants frequently have expertise or experiences that will help others in their understanding of a particular subject [4]. In ALN activity, all the responses can be archived for further reference. Electronic posting also improves writing skills. Participants know that their peers, as well as the instructor will read their responses. This raises the bar of quality in their writing [5].

Some students may have substantial prior experience in ALN tools, while others may lack this experience. Therefore the skill level of using the tool may be significantly different. Students are required to learn the ALN tools in order to achieve their learning objective.

3.3 Subject-Tools-Community Mix

ALN tools facilitate economy of communications by allowing the instructor to communicate with the entire class with one posting. This is beneficial for giving feedback or answering questions in a timely manner. Similarly a participant might post a question that others also had. The instructor can post one response to the group so that everyone can benefit from the feedback [5]. These benefits promote a community of learners [3].

Although ALN tools assist students and teachers in forming a community, they inherently constrain these communities by their idiosyncratic features. In other words, the feature set of each tool imposes itself on the community of learners who must adjust their communication style to conform with the tool itself.

3.4 Subject-Rules-Community Mix

A set of protocols is necessary in order to facilitate classroom management and clarify evaluation criteria. This occurs in traditional classroom settings in which an instructors, acting as a moderator manages classroom discussions. Classroom discussions also offer the opportunity for immediate feedback from the instructor. However, in an ALN environment, students can post their messages without waiting for an instructor to bring the discussion to order. The instructor may have to negotiate rules (norms) in writing before the discussion begins.

Another important factor in successful ALN is managing learner expectations. It is important for the student to know whether or not their online activity will be evaluated and what the criteria will be. Students may also benefit from knowing whether the discussions are open-ended or not.

3.5 Subject-Community-Division of Labor Mix

Goodwin indicates "Rather than being the centre of activity, as in the traditional teaching environment, the role of the teacher in the online education process focuses on facilitating, moderating, and working with groups".[6]. Experiences at SFU Surrey also show that role-designation is important for ALN. An instructor may serve in the role as a facilitator to stimulate a student's initiative, and let the student with more skills or experience lead a discussion, or act as moderator. If the discussion is going well and on track, instructor may just stay back, jumping in only when needed. Otherwise, the instructor will be overwhelmed by the information overload. Salmon [7] provides a more detailed explanation of the role of e-moderator in ALN environment.

3.6 Subject- Division of Labor-Object

It is especially useful when the objective is to finish a project or team-based task to design and assign different roles among students based on their subject matter expertise or other attributes. Time is a significant factor in the successful completion of project-based tasks especially when consensus is required. This is made especially problematic in ALNs because decisions are more difficult to make due to the distributed and asynchronous nature of the communication between participants[5]. Clearly defined project roles and deadlines will help participants achieve their objective in a timely manner yet effective manner.

4 Learner Analysis and Design Suggestions

According to activity theory, human activity is carried out through actions. Actions are controlled by the subject's conscious goals, which are the anticipation of the future results of the action. Actions are realized through a series of operations, each accommodated to the concrete physical conditions of the action. Operations describe how the action is realized, adjusted to the actual material conditions of the action. The human activity is guided by anticipation at these three levels. This anticipation is the motive for the activity, the goal of the action and the orienting basis of the operation, respectively [8]. Tensions within and between these elements are termed contradictions, and are considered motivators for development. These can be [9]:

- Subject and Tool: unsuitable tool for student – too restrictive for purpose, maybe too flexible (not enough leverage), too steep a learning curve;
- Subject and Rules: no well-defined rules;
- Subject and Community: inappropriate cultural conditions or organizational structures;
- Subject and Object: conflicting, misunderstood, or contradictory goals;
- Subject and Division of Labor: misaligned distribution of labor.

ALN may give rise to potential tensions based on the contradictions indicated above. A detailed examination of those tensions follows.

4.1 Tension between Subject and Tool

There are many factors that might result in tensions between the participants and the technology. For instance, it is not uncommon for an electronic discussion board to experience some initial discomposure due to the lack of familiarity with the process and procedures of the medium by some of its participants. Some participants may delete others' postings by accident, or make postings in the wrong place. They may not know how to follow the right thread.

Technical difficulties such as disruptions to normal networking operations will have an adverse effect on the timely flow of communications. If the Internet is down, the system may be unavailable for a relatively long period. It may affect the student's ability to post in time to meet the deadline. Instructors must accommodate such circumstances. In other cases the technology is constrained by the compatibility of the user's system configuration. This disparity between the intended design and the end-user's incompatible system may result in the student's inability to complete tasks as required. As can be seen, there will be tensions in this area throughout the whole process. To minimize these tensions, experiences at SFU Surrey suggest that instructor should give students sufficient training and assistance prior to and during the initial stages of the online course. The instructor should also be aware that as discussion continues, and more messages are posted, some students may need technical support for issues such as how to sort messages and how search by key words, name, date, etc.

4.2 Tension between Subject and Rules

According to one study [10], if participation in a discussion board contributes to the final grade then the discussion will be markedly different from non-credit, online discussions. In the first instance, students will be more concerned with the evaluation criteria, such as the number of postings per week, the quality of postings, the difference between starting a new topic and replying to a topic. Therefore, it is recommended that instructors clarify the evaluation criteria as well as keep students on topic, and remind students when the deadline is approaching.

4.3 Tension between Subject and Community

The core concept of ALN is collaboration and sharing knowledge. Salmon indicates that "When participants feel 'at home' with the online culture, and reasonably comfortable with the technology, they move on to contributing" [7]. Students need to get acclimate to the ALN environment before they can exchange information effectively. Primarily, they need to overcome the absence of non-verbal communications such as facial expressions and gestures, tone or intonation in the ALN environment. This may be frustrating at the beginning for some students – especially those who rely on non-verbal cues when communicating in face-to-face conversations. However, there are ways to make up for the weakness of ALN. For example, online socialization can be improved through posting short bios, participants' pictures, using avatars and emoticon that will help to personalize an otherwise faceless virtual community.

Feedback is another important aspect of ALN communication. A participant who posted might feel excluded or ignored if he does not receive any responses [3]. Lack of feedback may result in the participant's anxious speculation about how their posting was perceived by an anonymous audience [4]. Therefore, an instructor should encourage students to participate in the discussions, and give prompt feedback.

4.4 Tension between Subject and Object

As in the traditional classroom, virtual classrooms are populated by students with diverse learning preferences. Since students are invisible in the online environment, these preferences are not as apparent. As such, an instructor should be aware that there are always some silent readers; those students who did not post anything for a particular thread, but did learn something from postings made by others. The instructor needs to motivate those students to actively participate in a discussion.

Sometimes discussions may go off-topic. Sidebar discussions between students that share a rapport may be disruptive to the group. The instructor should remind them of the goal more frequently, in order to keep the discussion topics in focus, but be cognizant of diverse talents and ways of learning [11].

4.5 Tension between Subject and Division of Labor

Participating in an online discussion and providing feedback can be a labor-intensive task for students and instructors. Some students like to post lengthy messages; other students may follow this model because they believe this to be the instructor's preferenc. This misperception leads to an unmanageable amount of content to review and post feedback, especially when messages are posted over a long period of time and the conversation has become disjointed. It will be challenging for an instructor to reply to every posting. One strategy is, to empower a few students to lead each topic. For certain topics, students can be divided into "for" and "against" groups. This role assignment will help management communications, but eventually students will expect the instructor to give a summary or final assessment of the discussion.

5   Conclusion

The advantages of ALN are numerous. The lack of geographic and time constraints, archival properties of the medium, ability to facilitate collaboration and peer-to-peer learning, and supplement to face-to-face instruction make a ALN an additional tool for learning. However, whether the tool of choice is a textbook or a form of computer-mediated communication an effective teacher must employ the correct methods for integrating that tool into the learning design. Technology integration is, after all, both the tools and the methods used in teaching. An astute instructor will select appropriate strategies during the design phase of their course. Some design suggestions which have been discussed in the previous section can be summarized as: (1) Provide sufficient training at the beginning; (2) Provide technical support throughout the process; (3) Provide clear guidelines for interaction among students, evaluation criteria for grading, and the deadline for posting to a discussion; (4). Encourage cooperation among students; (5) Designate roles; (6) Provide feedback; (7) Remind students about approaching deadlines; 8. Provide a summary of the discussion at the end.

This paper offers the reader a basic overview of ALN within the context of Activity theory with the intent of illustrating the advantages and disadvantages of this mode of communication. The brief prescriptives offered here are still at a developmental stage and as such, are incomplete. The next step for this research will be to conduct a more thorough examination of the literature on ALN that address subject, object, tools, community, rules and division of labor in order to provide more detailed prescriptives for effective use of this technology.

Acknowledgements

Thanks to Dr John Nesbit for valuable comments on this paper, and thanks to Sandra McKenzie for editing this paper.

References

1. Hiltz, S. R. and Benbunan-Fich, R.(1997) Supporting Collaborative Learning in Asynchronous Learning Networks, Retrieved March 29, 2004, from
   http://web.njit.edu/~hiltz/CRProject/unesco.htm
2. Mappin, D., Kelly, M., Skaalid, B., & Bratt, S. (2000). Module 15 Activity Theory. Retrieved March 5, 2003, from http://www.quasar.ualberta.ca/edpy597/index.htm
3. Santo, S. A. (2000). Asynchronous Communication Strategies. Retrieved March 13, 2003, from http://www.freecfm.com/s/sas2n/Distance/asynch.html
4. Rossman, M. H. (1999). Successful Online Teaching Using An Asynchronous Learner Discussion Forum. Retrieved March 29, 2004, from
   http://www.aln.org/publications/jaln/v3n2/v3n2_rossman.asp
5. Graham, C., Cagiltay, K., Lim, B.-R., Craner , J., & Duffy, T. M. (2001). Seven Principles of Effective Teaching: A Practical Lens for Evaluating Online Courses. Retrieved March 30, 2004, from
   http://sln.suny.edu/sln/public/original.nsf/0/b495223246cabd6b85256a090058ab98?OpenDocument

6. Goodwin, C. ,Graham, M.,Scarborough, H Developing an Asynchronous Learning Network, Retrieved May 12, 2004, from
   http://ifets.ieee.org/periodical/vol_4_2001/scarborough.html
7. Salmon, G., (2000). E-moderating: The Key to Teaching and Learning Online. London, Kogan Page, 28-30.
8. Bardram, J. E. (1997). Plans as Situated Action: An Activity Theory Approach to Workflow Systems. ECSCW '97, 17-32.
9. Dobson, M (2003), Personal communication.
10. Li, J. (2002). Evaluating Asynchronous Learning Networks (ALN) system. Project for ETEC 600.1.
11. Chickering, A., & Gamson, Z. (1987). Seven principles of good practice in undergraduate education. AAHE Bulletin, 39, 3-7.
12. Engestrom, Y. (1987). Learning by expanding: An activity-theoretical approach to developmental research. Helsinki: Orienta-Konsultit.

An Agent- and Service-Oriented e-Learning Platform

Ivan Madjarov[1], Omar Boucelma[2], and Abdelkader Betari[3]

[1] IUT d'Aix-en-Provence, Département GTR,
Université de la Méditerranée, Marseille, France
ivmad@iut-gtr.univ-mrs.fr

[2] LSIS – CNRS et Université de Provence, Marseille, France
omar@cmi.univ-mrs.fr

[3] Laboratoire d'Informatique Fondamentale de Marseille – CNRS
Université de la Méditerranée, Marseille, France
betari@lif.univ-mrs.fr

Abstract. This paper presents an e-Learning Web-reachable hypermedia system as the foundation of a course content development toolset. Course content, developed in XML, is stored in native XML databases and propagated via Web services. A helper agent delivers the learning objects that compose a course based on a pedagogical strategy pre-defined by the course author. The agent dynamically establishes the learning objects delivery order. The sequencing of Web pages in the proposed system relies on a Petri Net analysis of incoming events such as student responses to exercises.

1 Introduction

This paper introduces an effective agent-oriented approach to drive the implementation of a Web Services-based e-Learning system.

Metadata, the primary building block of the emerging semantic web, will enable computers to understand the nature of information available over the Web hereby driving the coordination of complex Web service assemblies. The e-Learning domain was one of the first to benefit from the definition, among other standards, of LOM (*Learning Object Metadata*) [4]. From another perspective, the distributed nature of the Web suggests that agent technologies will play a key role in leveraging the use of metadata.

For the purpose of this paper, a "*service*" is a component, which handles transactional requests and directs their execution. An "*agent*" is a component, which acts like a mediator between a user and a service. Various interaction configurations are possible including agent-agent, service-service, agent-service, etc. Typical agent architectures have many of the features found in Web Service platforms.

Web Services are self-contained, modular applications that provide a set of functionalities to anyone that requests them. The main characteristic of Web Services is that they interact with the applications that invoke them, using Web standards such as WSDL (*Web Service Definition Language*), SOAP (*Simple Object Access Protocol*)

W. Liu et al. (Eds.): ICWL 2004, LNCS 3143, pp. 27–34, 2004.

and UDDI (*Universal Description, Discovery and Integration*). Leveraging Web standards in an e-Learning environment facilitates the dynamic integration of applications distributed over the Internet regardless of their underlying platforms. Web Services follow the SOAP Protocol to handle communication. The strong reliance of Web Services on XML standards guarantees interoperability so that data manipulated in the proposed learning model becomes readable from any computer. Web Services rely on HTTP (*HyperText Transfer Protocol*) for message transfer and thus have the advantage of being able to flow messages securely through most system firewalls, proxy servers, etc.. Finally, Web Services follow the WSDL protocol to provide the descriptive metadata required to use the services, and UDDI to publicize services on UDDI servers. These combined functionalities facilitate the dynamic integration of applications distributed over the Internet regardless of their underlying platforms.

The organization, classification, encoding and distribution of educational content on the Internet is subject to international standards set forth by the IMS Global Learning Consortium, the Advanced Distributed Initiative (ADL) and the IEEE [7]. A synergy between all these standards is the proposal to organize educational content in *learning objects*, conceived as relatively small chunks of educational material. These objects can be shared among users, reused in different contexts, recombined in different ways to build larger blocks of educational content and create personalized learning paths.

Nevertheless, Web-based educational applications today are still mostly static and based on a generic approach to tutoring that does not take into account individual student needs and scores. An important limitation to consider is that most e-Learning systems available today do not provide personalized and intelligent assistance. A helper agent approach sets forth a major contribution as it comes to taking into account differences among students.

The next section of this paper presents the architecture and implementation of our XESOP system. In the last section, we discuss issues related to the dynamic choosing and sequencing of learning objects that compose a course and how they are delivered to students based on their responses to tests.

2   The XESOP System and the Course Design

Our XESOP system [5, 6] is based on XML technologies and may be used for course development in an e-Learning environment. The structure of a course is subject to a XML Schema (i.e., a grammar) developed according to the most recent standards adopted by the e-Learning community [7]. The system consists of a semantic editor for XML documents with plug-ins that support the description of mathematical equations (MathML) and vector graphics (SVG). Data integrity is preserved via validation rules and by keeping the data structures independent from their presentation. Learning objects created using this system are stored in native type model XML databases [8, 9]. Learning objects include pages of type lesson, examples, exercises or test forms. Presentations are created via targeted selection of relevant document parts. This selection leads to complementary tagging that facilitates automatic content extraction via parsers.

The learning objects representing exercises have a major importance in e-Learning platforms as they make it possible to keep students challenged as they take a course. The exercise concept is therefore an essential ingredient in the assimilation of knowledge. For this reason, we have designed a service and a tool to facilitate the development and execution of remote exercises. The RDS (*Remote Development Service*) can be programmed by course authors to make exercises accessible and actionable at the time and place of delivery. The use of exercises in this environment relies on the creation of a Web Service that provides the necessary functions for the compilation, execution and/or interpretation of these exercises. To facilitate seamless access to the RDS functionality, related development tools are available [6] on a Web-Application Server, where the Web Service resides. This technology is open, leverages the standard Internet protocols (SOAP, TCP/IP), and facilitates access to a native XML database [9] that is responsible for course material integrity.

The system currently runs on the Linux and Windows operating systems. The software, implemented in Java, is an extension of functionalities provided by free and *open source* products. The learning objects structure and design conforms to the LOM specification [4]. Compatibility with IMS [7] standards has been thought through as well to facilitate integration with third party *Learning Management Systems* (LMSs). Our main motivation in implementing the system was to come up with a cost effective portable alternative to expensive commercial LMSs.

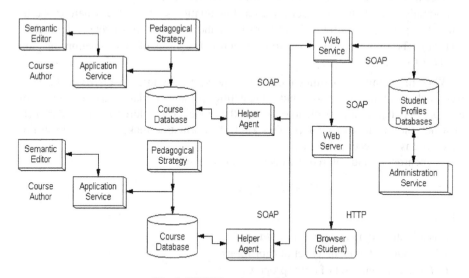

Fig. 1. XESOP system architecture

The realization of a pedagogical strategy relies on facilities for delivering and presenting course learning objects from both *traditional* and *adaptive* ordering viewpoints. Traditional sequencing is most straightforward as the system delivers learning objects according to the order defined by the course author. Adaptive sequencing manages learning objects distribution according to students' answers to exercises. In this case, learning objects' sequencing results from the nature of student answers rather than being based on a pre-established order selected by a course author. In the adaptive approach, sequencing of course pages is never static and is always driven by student capabilities. A *helper agent* is responsible for the guided generation and updating of the content sequence.

3 Helper Agent for Web Page Distribution

We are interested in devising a helper agent responsible for the distribution of course-related Web pages to students according to their tests results. Management of page sequencing is based on an analysis of incoming events via a Petri Net.

Carl Adam Petri introduced Petri Nets in 1962. Petri Nets provide a well-known process modeling technique with formal semantics. Petri Nets have been used to model and analyze several types of systems (i.e.: distributed, asynchronous, synchronous, deterministic or non-deterministic) and processes (i.e. protocols, manufacturing, business) [3].

A Petri Net is a directed, connected and bipartite graph in which each node is either a *place* or a *transition*. The *edges* of this graph connect the *transitions* to the *places* or the *places* to the *transitions*. The places contain *tokens* or marks, which go from place to place by crossing the *transitions* according to *crossing rules*.

Formally [2], a Petri net is defined as a flow relation $< P; T; W >$ where P is a finite set of places, T is a finite set of transitions and W is a set of directed *edges* (flow relation). The flow relation may also be quantified in terms of an evaluation function $W : (P \times T) \cup (T \times P) \rightarrow \{0,1\}$ [3].

When the number of entities modeled in the system is large, the size of the Petri Net quickly becomes enormous and if the entities present similar behaviors, the use of a colored net makes it possible to condense the model. The colored Petri Nets are nets in which the tokens carry colors. This kind of information makes possible to distinguish tokens from each other [1].

A synchronous and colored Petri Net is represented as:

$$R = (P, T, Col, \pi, \lambda)$$ (1)

where:

- P is a finite and non empty set of *places*;
- T is a finite and non empty set of *transitions*;
- Col is a non empty set of *color* properties;
- $\pi \subseteq P x T$,
- $\lambda \subseteq T x P$,
- And we have the property: $P \cap T = \varnothing$.

To address the problem and the solution set forth in this article, we propose to study the management of a Web-based course. As an example, let us assume that a course is composed of three pages and nine exercises. One main exercise is associated to each course page. Upon initial connection, the student receives the content of the first page

(Page 1). After receiving this page, the student goes on to the first exercise (Ex. 1), which corresponds to an event of type *"suite"* which means "next". The student's answer to the exercise represents an event of type *"validate"*. The answer is analyzed and results in a constant from the set {*True, False*}. If the answer is correct, the next course page is sent to the student (Page 2). If the answer is not correct another exercise of the same type as the previous one is sent to the student (Ex. 1-2). If the student's response to the second exercise is correct, the second page of the course is sent to the student, if not the student receives a third exercise of the same type as the two previous ones (Ex. 1-3). The same process applies to all course pages and their corresponding exercises.

The Petri Net associated with this example is represented on Figure 2. Crossing orders are indicated on the corresponding transitions. If the student fails all the exercises corresponding to a course page, a start page is sent back. Similarly, once a student successfully completes the third main exercise, a final page is sent back. For simplification purpose, these ending conditions are not represented in the figure.

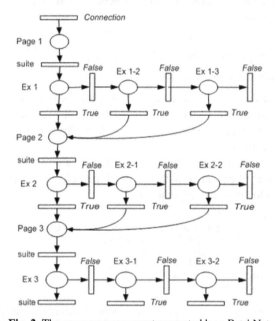

Fig. 2. The course management presented by a Petri Net

According to the Petri Net formalism, a course may be represented as:

$$C = (NC, DC, URI, PN) \qquad (2)$$

where:
- NC is the name of the course,
- DC is the description of the course,
- URI is the Internet address of the course,
- PN is the Petri Net, which models the course management.

The relationship between the basic Petri Net formalism (1) and the course elements is as follows:

- The *P* set represent the set of course pages,
- The *T* set represent the set of events corresponding to the answers,
- The color represents the identity of each student.

In other words, we build the Petri Net by associating a place for each page and a transition to any page changes. To manage the page changes, we analyze the data coming from the student. To carry out the analysis of the answer, we introduce two complementary concepts:

- A *RepEx(a)* function used to defines the type of the data coming from the student machine (*"validation"* or *"suite"*),
- A *μ(a)* function used to analyze a response of type *"validation"*. This function translates the student answer to a constant {*True, False, Suite*}.

The analysis function compares the returned answer with a standard answer. By evaluating their differences, a grade ("note") is generated as an integer value between 0 and 10 ($0 <= note <= 10$):

- $\mu(x) = True$ { $(\text{RepEx}(x) = True) \cap (note(x) \geq 5)$ },
- $\mu(x) = False$ { $(\text{RepEx}(x) = True) \cap (note(x) < 5)$ },
- $\mu(x) = suite$ { $\text{RepEx}(x) = False$ }.

Any transition in the Petri Nets under consideration is ordered according to one single place. This justifies its encoding using a Hash table. The advantage of a Hash table is that the time of insertion and search is $O(1)$. The construction of the Hash table is subject to a collisions control.

The course configuration is described by the author in an XML document using the XML semantic editor [6] provided by the e-Learning platform [5]. The content of this document conforms to the following schema:

```
<?xml version="1.0"?>
<xsd:schema xmlns:xsd="http://www.w3.org/2001/XMLSchema"
targetNamespace="http://www.w3schools.com"
xmlns="http://www.w3schools.com"
elementFormDefault="qualified">
<xsd:element name="valid">
  <xsd:complexType>
    <xsd:sequence>
      <xsd:element name="PlaceE" type="xsd:string"/>
      <xsd:element name="Transition" type="xsd:string"/>
      <xsd:element name="PlaceS" type="xsd:string"/>
      <xsd:element name="URL" type="xsd:string"/>
    </xsd:sequence>
  </xsd:complexType>
</xsd:element>
```

where, *PlaceE* and *PlaceS* ∈ course pages, *Transition* ∈ {*True, False, Suite*}. The key in the Hash table is obtained by concatenating "*PlaceE + Transition*"; the corresponding value is obtained by concatenating "*Places + & + URL*".

The place "*PlaceE*" is the entry point of the transition "*Transition*". For the validation of "*Transition* ", a mark must be present in the place "*PlaceE* ", and the value of the "*Transition*" must correspond to the value of $\mu(x)$. In other words, when a student is in the page corresponding to "*PlaceE*" and "*Transition*" is validated by the event corresponding to the answer, the following page becomes "*PlaceS*".

For student identification and grade attribution, we associate a color property to the mark. This makes it possible to follow the behavior of several students simultaneously, and to memorize the state of users who have visited the course so far. The pair (*id, note*) represents this mark, where:

− *id* is the name of the user,
− *note* is the grade of the student at a given time.

The *color* and *id* fields allow the management of several student sessions at the same time. A Hash table *"Gestion"* (which means "Management") carries out the next stages of several sessions, and is organized as follows:

− The keys of the table correspond to the pages of the course,
− The values represent the marks.

The values of the table *"Gestion"* are modified in the following way: when the user goes from one page to another, which corresponds to going from "*PlaceE*" to "*PlaceS*" by crossing a "*Transition*", its mark is removed from the list "*PlaceE*" and it is added to the list "*PlaceS*". The *"note"* (i.e., grade) of the student is modified as necessary during crossing using the answer analysis function.

At user connection time, two alternatives are possible: upon the first user visit, the user identity must be added to the table *"Gestion"*, if the user already visited this course, its identity is already present in the table. If the student visits the course for the first time a registration procedure is activated (3) and a mark is allotted to him with its identity.

$$(\forall y) \begin{cases} [Conx(y) \supset [AddG(z) \cap (z.id = y) \cap (z.note = 0)]] \\ \Leftrightarrow \\ (\forall x)[\neg InG(x) \cup (x.id \neq y)] \end{cases} \tag{3}$$

where:

− y is a variable that represents the identity of the student who just connected,
− z is a variable that represents the mark (*id, note*) allotted to the student,
− x is a variable that represents a mark,
− the function *AddG* inserts the mark passed as argument in the table *"Gestion"*
− the function *InG* returns *"True"* if the corresponding mark is already present in the table *"Gestion"*, else it returns *"False"*.

The session continuation condition represents the case where the student is already registered in the table *"Gestion"* (4):

$$(\forall x) \begin{cases} [Conx(y) \supset [Cont(z) \cap (z.id = y)]] \\ \Leftrightarrow \\ (\exists x) \vee [InG(x) \cap (x.id = y)] \end{cases} \tag{4}$$

The function *Cont* indicates the place of continuation.

4   Conclusion

The suggested model, with its helper agent, gives the possibility of managing a course in a centralized fashion. It also facilitates the study of various users' behaviors and the sending of different pages according to user tests' results. This model presents a general structure, which can be adapted to other applications or can be generalized. We can easily introduce the concept of time and that of transforming the Petri Net into a time lag net. This would be interesting in cases where time becomes a factor and plays the role of an event in the management of a course. For example, part of the grade (*"note"*) of a student could be allotted based on the time elapsed between the sending of a page to a student and the receipt of the student answer.

References

1. Kurt J. Kurt. Coloured Petri nets: Basic concepts, analysis methods and practical use, volume 1. Springer, (1997).
2. Naquet V., Geniet C. Réseaux de Petri et systèmes parallèles. Armand Colin, (1992).
3. Hamadi R., Benatallah B. A Petri Net-based Model for Web Service Composition. Fourteenth Australian Database Conference, Adelaide, Australia (ADC2003).
4. IEEE. Learning Object Metadata. http://ltsc.ieee.org/wg12. (2003).
5. Madjarov I., Shishedjiev B., Betari A. Remote Development Environment in an e-Learning System, (accepted for publishing in SAER 2004).
6. Madjarov I., Betari A. Un éditeur XML sémantique pour objets pédagogiques stockés dans une base de données XML native, (accepted for publishing in NOTERE 2004).
7. Learning Technology Standards Committee of the IEEE Computer Society, IEEE P1484.1/D8, 2001- 04-06 Draft Standard for Learning Technology – Learning Technology Systems Architecture (LTSA), 2001.
8. Bourret R. XML and Databases. (2003) http://www.rpbourret.com.
9. XML:DB Initiative. Enterprise Technologies for XML Databases. http://www.xmldb.org.

Automatically Generating an e-Textbook on the Web

Jing Chen, Qing Li, Liping Wang, and Weijia Jia

Department of Computer Engineering and Information Technology,
City University of Hong Kong, 83 Tat Chee Avenue, Kowloon, Hong Kong
{jerryjin,itqli,itjia}@cityu.edu.hk, 50095373@student.cityu.edu.hk

Abstract. Nowadays, people tend to learn from the Web because it is convenient, and rich of free information. One significant means of learning on the Web is by submitting a query to a search engine, and browsing through the results to find relevant information. Although in many cases, the search engine works quite well, the results returned are often not appropriate for the learning purpose. In this paper, we propose a novel approach to automatically generate an E-textbook for a user specified topic hierarchy. Such a technology can ease the learning process to a great extent. The validity of our approach is verified through a case study.

1 Introduction

The Web is a vast storehouse of information. People can find information in almost every aspect of life. So is the case for teachers and students. To them, the Web plays an increasingly crucial role in the processes of teaching and learning.

Learning on the Web typically involves the use of a search engine (e.g., Google [6]). However, the experience of learning from search engine results can be very confusing and time-consuming. One of the reasons to this is that Web pages are authored for a variety of purposes. For example, for a keyword/phrase query 'data structures and algorithms', some of the results are the syllabus of a real course 'data structures and algorithms', and such pages often contain links to lecture notes of the course. Others are designed to introduce a book titled 'data structures and algorithms', giving only a table of content with no details and no extra links. Such pages are hardly helpful in the case of learning. Still some others are devised to help people find useful links of implementations of algorithms, which may help those who are familiar with algorithms. With such diversity, computer experts always find what they want, while novices often complain that they hardly get anything reasonable at all.

An ideal solution would be to let people study on the Web as if they were reading through a book. Moreover, learners prefer Web pages with a higher quality of content. High quality Web pages often share several common attributes[1]:

---

[1] In the remaining part of this paper, we shall refer to Web pages with such attributes as 'suitable' pages for learning.

W. Liu et al. (Eds.): ICWL 2004, LNCS 3143, pp. 35–42, 2004.

- Self-Contained: A Web page is self-contained if it contains the maximum of information about the concerned topic. In other words, a self-contained page should not only contain elaborate information about itself, but also enumerate the sub-topics of the concerned topic.
- Descriptive: An informative page should give descriptions and/or definitions of the topic.
- Authoritative: A Web page is regarded as authoritative if it is cited by many reputable 'hub' pages.

In this paper, we advocate a novel approach of automatically generating an E-textbook on the Web for a user specified topic. Our approach starts from a concept tree of the target topic. The approach first generates a query for each node and gets the corresponding candidate Web pages through a search engine. Through mining the URLs and the content of candidate pages, Web pages 'suitable' for the learning process are saved and assigned to the proper node. Thus the E-textbook is completed. With such a challenging yet feasible technology, teachers can resort to the E-book when preparing for their teaching material and students can learn more about interested topics and deepen their understanding.

2   Related Works

Much research efforts have been engaged to bring order to documents in a large document collection. Halkidi [1] devised a system called THESUS using link semantics. They first gather a set of popular Web documents according to Web directories like DMOZ, and adopt a hierarchy of concepts (ontology) and a thesaurus to convert keywords from all pages incoming links to semantics. They then group up documents into semantically coherent subsets and label the subsets for easier browsing. In [2], the author introduces an approach that automatically builds hierarchical word-based summaries for a given set of documents. A language model is used first to characterize documents in the data set, and then a graph-theoretic algorithm is applied to identify the key content-bearing words for the hierarchical summary.

Compared to the achievements in the pursuit of organizing document sets, limited work has been done to distinguish data of higher quality from the massive Web collection, especially for Web learning. To our knowledge, Liu's approach [3] was the first to explicitly point out the task of compiling a book on the Web. In their technique, they first identify the sub-topics or salient concepts of a specified topic, and then find the informative pages containing definitions and descriptions to present to the user. The process is performed in an interactive way, in which users choose the interested salient concepts to further explore. The weakness of their approach is that it lacks an explicit description of the concept structure of the specified topic. In practice, when people read a book, they first look at the table of content and then go on reading the detailed chapters. The table of content helps a reader measure his progress and decide on the subsequent learning plan.

In some occasions, users may know the skeleton of a topic, but they do not have a deep understanding of it. What they need is therefore a tool that can fill the skeleton with the most relevant and important documents automatically. As to be presented in this paper, such a requirement can be addressed by allowing users to specify the topic hierarchy and the system automatically generates the complete textbook for them.

3   Building the e-Textbook

An E-textbook is based on a user specified topic hierarchy, which we call the concept tree. The nodes of a concept tree are labelled with salient concepts of the topic and sub-topics. The root node is the target topic, and its offspring are sub-topics, and then children of these nodes extend the sub-topics further. Figure 1 shows an example of the concept tree corresponding to topic 'data structures and algorithms'. In the following, we first present the definitions and annotations of the concept tree; the data structure and operations to be used in our later algorithms are also introduced.

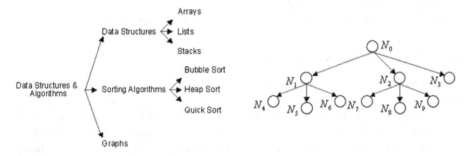

Fig. 1. Example of the concept tree for 'data structures & algorithms'

- N_i denotes the i_{th} node of the concept tree ;
- L_i is the label of N_i, and it characterizes the central concept of a topic or sub-topic by means of a few words;
- Q_i is the query phrase generated for N_i, which is submitted to a search engine to get the candidate Web pages of for the final E-textbook;
- For N_i, there exists a Web page list called $DescriptList_i$. The pages in $DescriptList_i$ mainly come from the retrieved page set of Q_i, but not all the retrieved pages are inserted into $DescriptList_i$. Web pages inserted to leaf nodes are descriptive ones that bear concept definitions of L_i, while those for internal nodes may contain descriptions or overview of L_i and sub-topics of L_i;
- For N_i, $AnchList_i$ is a sorted list of links contained in retrieved pages of Q_i. Each item in $AnchList_i$ is a 3-tuple ($AnchorText_j$,URL_j,$Weight_j$), and the items are in decreasing order of $Weight_j$. The URL links in $AnchList_i$ are used to expand the candidate page set if necessary;

- Retrieved Web pages are stored in *CandidatePool*, awaiting further mining;
- $parent(N_i)$ denotes for the parent of node N_i;
- $child(j, N_i)$ stands for the j_{th} offspring of node N_i.

For a given concept tree, tree nodes are traversed in a width-first order, and for each node, descriptive Web pages are selected from the retrieved document set of the corresponding query. The process of building an E-textbook includes the following three steps:

1. Generate the query phrase for each node and gather the retrieved pages;
2. Mine the Web pages in the retrieved results;
3. Expand the result list for nodes that require more pages.

3.1   Generating the Query Phrase

We use different strategies to generate query phrases for different kinds of concept nodes, and then submit them to a search engine like Google. For node N_i in the concept tree:

- If N_i is a leaf node, $Q_i = L_i$;
- If N_i is an internal node, $Q_i = L_i \cup \{L_j | N_j = child(j, N_i)\}$.

3.2   Mining Retrieved Web Pages

The objective of this step is to mine the Web pages returned by the search engine and keep only those that are 'suitable' for the purpose of learning. In the mining process, Web pages in the result list are first transformed into a tree structure according to their HTML tags, and then a page type is assigned to each Web page. Based on the tree structure and page type, descriptive pages are identified, and unsuitable pages filtered out. Finally, Web pages are sorted according to several factors and highly relevant ones are added to the descriptive list of corresponding tree nodes.

HTML Tag Tree. HTML pages are often represented in a tree structure for manipulation convenience. W3C's Document Object Model (DOM [4]) defines such a structure using HTML tags, called the DOM tree. Compared to that of the typical DOM tree structure, we use a modified tag tree in our approach to denote Web pages, in which more emphasis is put on the organization of page content. A detailed description of the method to generate a modified HTML tag tree is given in [5].

Page Type. How a Web page is handled depends on what type it belongs to. In [5], a two-level identification approach has been proposed to classify Web pages into one of the three categories: topic page, hub page and image page. In our current approach, we make use of topic pages and hub pages, and ignore image pages for simplicity. Topic pages are those that have a main theme, which is described concretely through paragraphs of text. Such pages are quite suitable for an E-textbook, and are kept in the CandidatePool for further processing. Hub pages are those that mainly aim to provide valuable links to other pages. Furthermore, hub pages can be beneficial to our result as well: links contained in hub pages can be used to expand the candidate page set when necessary. Thus links in hub pages and high quality topic pages are extracted and inserted into *AnchList* for deeper mining.

Re-ranking Retrieved Web Pages. As we have discussed, Web pages in the retrieved results of a search engine may not be readily suitable for learning. This problem stems from the way search engines perform a relevance assessment task when they respond to a query. Using Google as an example, its ranking strategy is a combination of PageRank and textual match. PageRank is independent of the query or textual content. It suggests that surfing on the Web is a random walk and defines a measure of prestige over it. Textual match is decided at query time. It takes into account many factors, such as keywords, phrase matches, match proximity and anchor text spamming. The combination shows great flexibility and quality in many cases. But with such a ranking strategy, some Web pages favorable to learning may be ranked rather behind according to the PageRank algorithm.

Our approach intends to tackle this problem by adjusting the rank, which was not suitable for the learning purpose. In our re-ranking process, the following factors are used:

- Cue phrases in URLs and titles:

Some URLs contain terms that imply the content of a page. For instance, URL 'http://www.cs.bu.edu/teaching/cs113/spring-2000/sort/' contains terms like 'edu', 'teaching' and 'sort', from which we may "guess" that it is a Web page generated for educational purposes and its main subject is about sort algorithms. The example indicates two kinds of beneficial terms. The first kind include terms that suggest the writing objective of the author, such as 'teaching' and 'course', which we call $ImplicitKeyItems(IKIs)$. The other kind has terms that include salient concepts in the concept tree, like 'sort'. We can call these terms $ExplicitKeyItems(EKIs)$. Similarly, cue phrases can also be detected in the title of Web pages. Title can be considered an author-given summarization of the Web page. The weight of a URL f_U can be calculated as follows:

$$f_U = \alpha \cdot ImpUrlWt + \beta \cdot ExpUrlWt + \gamma \cdot ExpTitleWt \tag{1}$$

where $ImpUrlWt$ is the number of $IKIs$ in the URL, and $ExpUrlWt$ is the number of $EKIs$. $ExpTitleWt$ stands for the number of $EKIs$ in the title. α, β and γ are parameters to tune the relative importance of the three item types.

- Definitions of concepts:

Definitions are one of the most important manners to explain a concept, so people usually prefer pages that give definition and examples of a concept when they learn knowledge about a topic. Liu's approach [3] gives an efficient routine to identify definitions of concepts. It applies several definition identification patterns to achieve this goal. For example, a Web page is weighted when it contains a sentence like '<concept> is defined as'. Here, <concept> represents a label in the concept tree. We use f_D to denote the number of concept definitions that appear in a Web page.

- The original rank of the pages given by the search engine:

If two pages have the same PageRank value, then the page with a higher topic coverage is generally ranked on the top. In our approach, we use f_R to denote the influence of the original rank value provided by the search engine, given by:

$$f_R = 1/(Rank + \sigma) \tag{2}$$

- Integrating the three factors

Our approach integrates all three factors discussed above, viz., cue phases in URL and anchor text, concept definitions in the page, and the original rank given by the search engine. The pages in the *DescriptList* are ranked according to weight (3):

$$W_i = \lambda_1 \cdot \frac{f_{U_i}}{\sum_{j=1}^{N} f_{U_j}} + \lambda_2 \cdot \frac{f_{D_i}}{\sum_{j=1}^{N} f_{D_j}} + \lambda_3 \cdot \frac{f_{R_i}}{\sum_{j=1}^{N} f_{R_j}} \tag{3}$$

3.3 Expanding Result Lists

Sometimes the *DescriptList* of a node may still remain empty. Under such conditions, the result list of the node needs to be extended. In the expansion process, links in *AnchList* with a higher relevance are crawled from the Web to form a new candidate page set. Then the technologies introduced in section 3.2 are applied to the candidate set to obtain the expanded result. The selection of pages to be inserted into the candidate set relies on the relevance of their associated links in *AnchList*, which makes the relevance measurement a key issue here.

Relevance of URL. In our approach, the relevance of a URL is decided by two factors. The first is the occurrence of cue phrases in the URL and its anchor text. Formula (1) can be used to measure this factor. The second factor is the importance of the page from which the URL is extracted, which is measured by formula (3). This factor depends on the following presumption: links in a more reputable Web page have a higher possibility to be valuable. According to the two factors, the relevance of a link L can be measure by formula (4):

$$f_L = \psi \cdot f_U + (1 - \psi) \cdot W \tag{4}$$

Expansion Algorithm. For a concept node that needs expansion, algorithm 1 outlines the main process. It is guaranteed that URLs with greater relevance and importance will be crawled first. Thus, the construction of the E-textbook is complete.

```
Algorithm 1:
1:   While (Card(DescriptList) < θ && iterative times is less than MaxTimes)
2:   {
3:       Rank the URLs in AnchList according to the W_j (3);
4:       Crawl the pages corresponding to URLs in AnchList with higher weight
5:       and fill the CandidatePool with them;
6:       Mine CandidatePool;
7:       Add resulting pages to DescriptList.
8:   }
```

Fig. 2. Expanding Result Lists

4   Case Study

In this section, we examine our approach along with simple query expansion methods, which were usually used to refine the result of a search engine and compare the results. We first select a concept and generate different query phrases for it. The queries are submitted to Google, and the top 10 results are examined. A Web page is marked as 'suitable' if it accords with the criteria listed in Section 1: self-contained, descriptive and authoritative. Generally, the top 10 results are all regarded as authoritative because the ranking strategy of Google already considers popularity, so authority will not be examined in this case. From their different performances, we can see that simply using different query phrases for a salient concept can hardly satisfy the complex need of learning.

Let us choose 'sorting algorithms' as our target concept:

1. Q_i^1='sorting algorithms';
2. Q_i^2='sorting algorithms bubble sort heap sort quick sort';
3. Q_i^3='sorting algorithms data structures and algorithms'.

Both Q_i^1 and Q_i^2 yielded three 'suitable' Web pages in their top 10 results, and Q_i^3 got the worst results with no 'suitable' pages at all. We choose Q_i^2 as our example since it is also the query chosen by our algorithm. Table 1 shows the top 10 results of query Q_i^2 by Google. In our approach, pages 2, 7 and 8 are successfully identified as 'suitable' and hence are inserted into the descriptive page list of node 'sorting algorithms'.

5   Future Work

As a challenging task to automatically build an E-textbook on the Web, there remains limitations and further issues to be addressed. A main limitation of our work is that the approach mainly targets at identifying descriptive Web pages, while the Web is full of abundant resources such as pictures and animations. To compensate this weakness, we intend to handle multimedia objects in our subsequent research, since a multimedia E-textbook can often serve as a reference of information more effectively.

Table 1. Top 10 results for query Q_i^2 returned by Google

Rank	URL	Descriptive	Hub	Self-contained	Definitions
1	$http://linux.wku.edu/$ $\sim lamonml/algor/sort/$	N	Y	N	
2	$http://linux.wku.edu/$ $\sim lamonml/algor/sort/sort.html$	Y	N	Y	'sorting algorithms'
3	$http://www.cs.hope.edu/$ $\sim alganim/ccaa/sorting.html$	N	Y	N	
4	$http://www.cs.hope.edu/$ $\sim dershem/reu/posters97/$ $brummund/research/ccaa/$ $harrison.html$	N	N	N	
5	$http://www.thinkspot.net/$ $materdei/apcompsci/$ $SearchandSortAlgos/$	N	N	N	
6	$http://www.cs.montana.edu/$ $webworks/webworks-home/$ $links/sorting.html$	N	N	N	
7	$http://www.cs.ubc.ca/spider/$ $harrison/Java/$	Y	N	N	'quicksort'
8	$http://www.devarticles.com/$ $c/a/Cplusplus/Bubble-Sorts-$ $And-C-plus/1/$	Y	N	Y	'sorting algorithms bubblesort heapsort quicksort'
9	$http://www.mcs.csuhayward.edu/$ $\sim simon/handouts/sort/$ $SortDemo.html$	N	Y	N	
10	$http://www.animal.ahrgr.de/en/$ $Animation198.html$	N	N	N	

References

1. Halkidi, M., Nguyen, B., Varlamis, I., Vazirgiannis, M.: THESUS: Organizing Web Document Collections Based on Link Semantics, VLDB J. 12(4): 320-332, 2003.
2. Lawrie, D.J., Language Models for Hierarchical Summarization, PHD thesis, 2003.
3. Liu, B., Chee W. Chin, Hwee T. Ng, Mining Topic-specific Concepts and Definitions on the Web, WWW 2003: 251-260, 2003.
4. DOM, http://www.w3.org/dom/.
5. Zhang, Zh., Chen, J., LI, X., A Preprocessing Framework and Approach for Web Applications, to appear in Journal of Web Engineering Vol.2, No.3: 175-191, 2004.
6. Brin, S., Page, L.: The Anatomy of a Large-scale Hypertextual Web Search Engine, WWW7, 1998.
7. Davison, B.D., Topical Locality in the Web, ACM SIGIR, 2000.

Prioritized Admission Control in Multimedia Network-Based e-Learning

Dali Zhang

Department of Electrical and Computer Engineering
Queen's University
Kingston, Ontario, K7L 3N6, Canada
zhangd@ee.queensu.ca

Abstract. Current network technology has enabled a revolutionary change in teaching and learning. Classrooms and libraries are no longer the only places to study. As more and more information are put on Internet for sharing, web-based e-learning becomes popular. Especially with the advancement of multimedia technology, traditional teacher-centered learning moves to student-centered, with more flexibility in time and place. This paper discusses the network call admission control problem with multimedia network-based e-learning. Many multimedia data are compressed with scalable coding scheme, where different layers of the information have different importance. At the receiver end in decoding, we can adapt the connection between students and teacher in degraded mode, in order to admit more users and achieve higher link utilization. This prioritized adaptation scheme can be greatly useful when network bandwidth is stringent in congested conditions.

1 Introduction

Traditional education method is teacher or classroom centered. This might not be viable in an era of information explosive. The demand of post-education learning has increased very fast, and such methods as night school, radio or TV broadcast find their shortcomings in temporal and/or spatial limitations. Students tend to seek more flexible options in learning rather than traditional centralized ones. In the past decade, the emergence and prosperity of communication network technology has enabled web-based learning, [1] which is highly distributed and flexible for both educational parties. Researches have been carried on to evaluate the learning effects. [4] [6]

In the recent years, we have witnessed a proliferation of multimedia technology in networking area. The study of media streaming aims at such applications as video(audio)-on-demand, online 3D game, net-phone and video-conferencing, etc. A few commercial products have been in use, such as Apple's QuickTime, RealNetworks' Real Player and Real One, and Microsoft Windows Media Player. These applications potentially make e-learning possible in that students can attend classes wherever they have Internet connections (wireline or wireless), and whenever they wish, provided that teachers/schools put the class contents online. Students can choose audio or video mode instead of merely using hypertext

W. Liu et al. (Eds.): ICWL 2004, LNCS 3143, pp. 43–50, 2004.

web page or just download and read. These audio or video courses are flexible to students in that they may pause, rewind or fast-forward according to their own academic background and time schedules. The students also have the option of an interactive mode to participate class discussions by accessing the course website concurrently.

However, most multimedia applications require high bandwidth and low delay and jitter (variance of delays), [8] which place a high demand to current Internet, especially during congested conditions. This paper is to study ways to guarantee quality of services (QoS) with multimedia connections, which directly reflect learning effect. A prioritized admission control scheme is proposed with adaptive transmission.

The paper is organized as follows: section 2 discusses the framework of aforementioned scheme, with an overview of underlying scalable coding algorithms adopted by most multimedia data nowadays; section 3 describes the prioritized admission control algorithm with adaptive transmission; section 4 gives the simulation model and evaluates its performance; section 5 concludes the paper.

2   Framework

Multimedia applications have two properties that distinguish them from traditional network traffic: high bandwidth requirement and delay sensitivity. Normally, audio needs 8Kbps to 128Kbps, and video for 100Kbps up to 15Mbps. These turn out to be main constraints for their transmission on Internet. For example, if a student attends a video or audio course online, any packet loss or delay during network traffic congestion can result in distortion or pause at receiver end. Although the widespread of optical fiber and various efficient source coding methods have alleviated bandwidth requirement more or less, current Internet is still a best-effort network that has no QoS guarantee.

Most current multimedia data are compressed with scalable coding, which is highly adaptive to various transmission environments. Scalability refers to the destination's capability of recovering physically meaningful image or video information by decoding only partial compressed bit streams. The source renders an encoder to compress multimedia data into a cumulative set of layers where information is combined across layers to produce progressive refinement, with each level as an enhancement in quality of the previous one [5]. When one layer fails to get decoded successfully, subsequent layers' data become useless. Therefore, lower-level data, which contain the most essential information of an image/video frame, are placed in base layer. The rest are called enhanced layers. Upon receiving a series of packets, the decoder at the destination can reconstruct video sequence by adding enhanced layers to base layer to refine quality. By assigning higher priority to base layer packets, scalable coding is adaptive to bandwidth constraints and congestion by discarding enhanced layers packets.

In this paper, we assign lower priorities to enhanced layers and high priority to base layer for protection. If network resource is abundant for all layers, they are transmitted in normal mode. Otherwise, one or more enhanced layers are discarded due to congestion (degraded mode) and the audio/video quality at the receiving end is not as well as in normal mode. In order to guarantee the transmission quality, especially base layer's quality, the sender initializes a connection signaling to the destination, reserving resources along its way. Under heavy traffic, if a new connection request would hamper the guarantee to existing services, it is simply rejected(blocked). Therefore, the call/connection admission control (CAC) is a critical step in managing network traffic, in protection of excessive flows' injection.

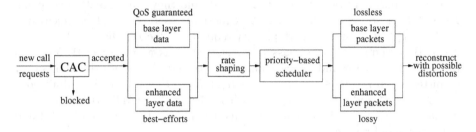

Fig. 1. Block Diagram for Prioritized Adaptation Admission Control.

For most cases of passive e-learning, students are at the receiver end, and they can select the video quality levels before connection request, as shown in figure 1. Because of the burst nature of multimedia data, rate shaper is used to smooth the traffic stream. All data packets are forwarded by routers that can identify their priority, with different scheduling algorithms. Note that distributed passive learning (DPL) [4] is jitter-sensitive and delay-tolerant, while distributed interactive learning (DIL) requires small delay as well as small jitter because of its interactive property.

3   Prioritized Admission Control

In an e-learning platform, it is necessary and important to maintain basic streaming quality (measured with distortion) as well as try to increase the number of concurrent connections (measured with blocking probability). In distributed interactive learning, this can be compared to the class size. As stated in section 2, if we purposely discard one or more enhanced layers for certain streams, then more bandwidth is allowed for new incoming connection requests, and will lead to a lower blocking probability.

Consider a link with capacity c, with each stream demands 1 unit of resource, the maximum tolerable connections is c. Yet, if each stream is able to discard $a\%$ data (enhanced layers' portion), and transmit in degraded mode, then the maximum connections is $\frac{c}{1-a\%}$. Here, $a\%$ is called adaptation percentage. We will show its impact in section 4.

On one hand, the capacity is increased with larger adaptation percentage, on the other hand, it is important to preserve the base layer data, and guarantee their transmission by reserving high priority resource for them. We may not only assign different priorities to different layers, but also classify users into various priority groups. It is possible for high priority users to get all layers of data transmitted while low priority users are blocked because of heavy traffic. Two most well known prioritized admission control algorithms are trunk reservation [3] and maximum threshold. [7]

Trunk reservation (TR) states that a connection will be blocked if cumulative traffic reaches the connection's threshold. For example, in a two-priority traffic system with total resources of T, if high and low priority traffic have threshold t_1 and t_2, (normally we have $1 = t_1 > t_2 > 0$) and they are currently occupying R_1 and R_2 resources, then a class 2 request of resource r will be rejected if $r + R_1 + R_2 > T \cdot t_2$ while a high priority request be blocked when $r + R_1 + R_2 > T \cdot t_1$. By assigning $t_1 > t_2$, class 1 is preferred. Maximum threshold (MT), on the other hand, cares individual traffic class' bound. A low priority call is only admitted when $r + R_2 \leq T \cdot t_2^*$ and $r + R_1 + R_2 \leq T$; class 1 call is admitted if $r + R_1 \leq T \cdot t_1^*$ and $r + R_1 + R_2 \leq T$, where t_1^* and t_2^* are MT's thresholds, and we have $1 \geq t_1^* > t_2^* > 0$. Throughout this paper, t_i and t_i^* are used for TR and MT's threshold respectively.

In this paper, we combine the prioritized admission control algorithm with traffic adaptation. When a audio or video courseware is placed online, students may be able to access it with certain authentication system. By selecting certain level of distortion, the required bandwidth is obtained. Before the stream establishment, a resource reservation request is initialized by the student to server end. If traffic is light, bandwidth is allocated to satisfy all layers and there is little distortion at the user end. Otherwise, resources are given to base layer only, according to the user's priority. This will result in certain distortion at the end user. Further, existing streams can shred their enhanced layers upon congestions so that more students are able to access the courseware. By considering different types of users, differentiated service is provided within a stream or among different streams, and increase the network capacity simultaneously. Section 4 shows the results with simulation. Besides, it is intuitive that the differentiated service will lead to a more complicated network pricing scheme.

4 Simulation Results

Current Internet adopts optical fiber in backbone networks, whose capacity are counted in gigabit per second and allow large degree of multimedia stream multiplexing. Therefore, the performance bottleneck tends to shift to access networks, with various topologies and access methods. In order to eliminate the routing algorithms' impact, a single link model is considered in the following simulation. We assume the traffic arrivals conform to Poisson process with rate λ, and each stream's service time is exponentially distributed with average $1/\mu$. Two-priority classes are considered, with equal arrival rate, in first-come-first-serve, non-preemptive manner. Also assume each request is demanding the same share of resources. In order to make full use of available resources, let trunk reservation's high priority threshold $t_1 = 1.0$ and maximum threshold $t_1^* = 1.0$.

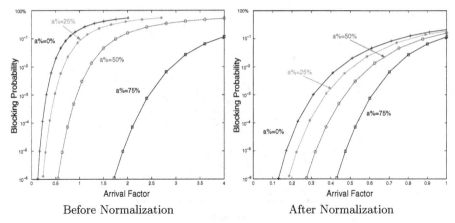

Fig. 2. Blocking Probability with Different Adaptation Percentages. c=10.

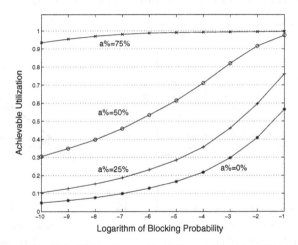

Fig. 3. Achievable Utilization with Different Blocking Rate. c=10.

Let's first investigate how adaptation percentage affects blocking probability. As deduced in section 3, the capacity c becomes $\frac{c}{1-a\%}$ in degradation mode. Without prioritized request, the blocking probability is shown in figure 2. With the same arrival factor, larger adaptation percentage would lead to much lower blocking probability. The arrival factor on the right figure is normalized with $\frac{1}{1-a\%}$, and shows that a larger degree of multiplexing can greatly reduce blocking rate itself. Figure 3 indicates that higher link utilization could be achieved as adaptation percentage increases. Specifically, arrival factor f is the normalization of system arrival rate λ, with service rate μ and link capacity c, $f = \frac{\lambda}{\mu \cdot c}$.

Figure 4 investigates MT threshold's impact on blocking probability. As t_2^* decreases, the available resource for low priority class shrinks, leaving more resource to high priority traffic, and thus leads to higher blocking probability for class 2 and lower rejection rate for class 1. The simulation of trunk reservation

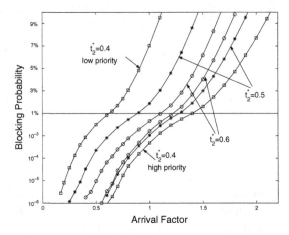

Fig. 4. Blocking Probability with Different t_2^*. a%=50%, c=10.

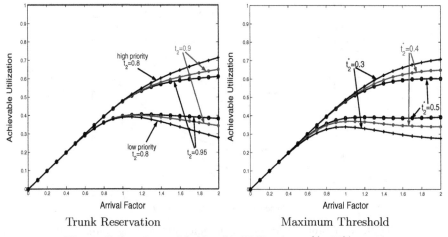

Trunk Reservation   Maximum Threshold

Fig. 5. Comparison of Achievable Utilization. a%=50%, c=10.

demonstrates a similar trend. Therefore, by adjusting threshold, we can control various traffic class' blocking rate. When traffic is light, we may allow most enhanced layers get transmitted, in order to increase the audio/video quality at the receiver end; during heavy traffic, threshold is tuned to a value that provide more opportunities to high priority users.

Also, it is interesting to compare the resource allocation by trunk reservation and maximum threshold, illustrated in figure 5. Both algorithms demonstrate that as arrival factor increases, more resources are assigned to high priority. Yet, it is worth noticing that the resource allocation for maximum threshold tends to converge to certain ratio between the two classes, while in trunk reservation, high priority traffic tends to take dominant resource and deplete low priority class.

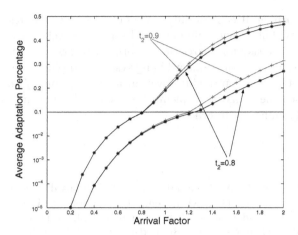

Fig. 6. Average Adaptation Percentage for TR with Different t_2. a%=50%, c=10.

Each traffic class has the same adaptation percentage $a\%$, indicating to what degree their requested bandwidth can be degraded. However, when the traffic is light, almost all sessions can get full bandwidth. As arrivals increase, more sessions are getting degraded or even blocked. When different traffic priorities are mixed together, it would be interesting to study their average adaptation percentage (AAP), which indicates the QoS they get. AAP is lower-bounded by 0%, and upper-bounded by the traffic class' adaptation percentage $a\%$.

Figure 6 describes AAP change with increment of traffic. Since we are aiming to give class 1 high priority, in our scheduling algorithm, we always first perform degradation to low priority traffic, so that allowing more bandwidth to high priority. This phenomenon, when reflected on the figures, shows that class 1 has much smaller AAP than class 2 even when the traffic is light, and lasts for all arrival factors. The upper bound for both traffic types are 50%, which is a system parameter. Therefore, when the traffic is heavy, all curves are approaching 50%, but high priority is much slower.

AAP, when combined with blocking probability, can evaluate a system's performance, because blocking probability denotes the rejected percentage and AAP describes the admitted sessions' transmission quality.

When applying these CAC algorithms in the framework described in section 2, we will be able to maintain QoS and increase system capacity concurrently. As long as an end user's request is admitted, we can guarantee basic QoS for his whole transmission. For schools who provide web-based e-learning platform to students, a low blocking probability is especially desirable to allow more concurrent users and thus larger class size.

5   Conclusion

This paper proposed prioritized admission control algorithms integrated with adaptation for multimedia applications on Internet, and can be very suitable for web-based e-learning. It can not only make fully use of system resource, increase system capacity, but provide differentiated service as well. By assigning different priorities, it is easy for source or network operators to render their pricing scheme, and results in a subsequent billing system. The end users (receivers) are able to select transmission quality level, measured by audio/video distortions. Besides, this scheme is easy to implement and control, and can provide powerful support to e-learning via Internet.

References

1. Bruning, R., Horn, C. A., PytlikZillig, L. M.: Web-based learning : what do we know? where do we go? Greenwich, Conn.: Information Age Pub., 2003
2. Garrison, D. R., Anderson, T.: E-learning in the 21st century: a framework for research and practice. New York: Routledge Falmer Pub., 2003
3. Kelly, F. P.: Routing and capacity allocation in networks with trunk reservation. Mathematics of Operations Research, 15:771-793, 1990
4. Khalifa, M., Larn, R.: Web-based learning: effects on learning process and outcome. IEEE Trans. on Education, vol. 45, No. 4, 2002
5. McCanne, S. R.: Scalable compression and transmission of internet multicast video. Ph.D. Thesis, University of California, Berkeley, 1996
6. Mehlenbancher, B., Miller, C. R., Covington, D., Larsen, J. S.: Active and interactive learning online: a comparison of web-based and conventional writing classes. IEEE Trans. on Professional Communication, Vol. 43, No. 2, 2000
7. Ross, K. W.: Multiservice loss models for broadband telecommunication networks. Springer-Verlag, Inc., London, U.K., 1995
8. Tanenbaum, A. S.: Computer networks, 4th ed. New York: Prentice Hall Pub., 2003

CUBES: Providing Flexible Learning Environment for Virtual Universities

Peifeng Xiang, Yuanchun Shi, Weijun Qin, and Xin Xiang

Key Lab of Pervasive Computing, Computer Science Department,
Tsinghua University, Beijing 100084, P.R.China
xpf97@mails.tsinghua.edu.cn

Abstract. To enable an online virtual university, a learning environment covering the entire spectrum of the learning and management process is required. However, constructing such an environment remains a hard work. One of the problems is to integrate heterogeneous software modules from different providers. In addition, these modules must constantly evolve. In this paper, we propose CUBES, an e-learning enabling system that focuses on the integrity, evolvability and extensibility. In CUBES, a special data exchange module(DEM), along with a global authentication module and a core user information management module, forms a basic supporting platform for the integration of upper educational application modules(EAMs), e.g. a large scale real-time interactive virtual classroom and a dynamic learning quality monitor. A universal portal helps to configure the integrated EAMs, providing a seamless learning environment for users. With the help of the supporting system and the universal portal, EAMs are easily combined together like cubes. Besides, popular e-learning standards, such as SCORM[1] and CELTS[2], are adopted in CUBES to facilitate the sharing of learning resources, the interoperation of user information and also the integration of software modules.

1 Introduction

During the last decade, numerous web-based learning systems, such as Blackboard[3] and WebCT[4] have been developed to provide learning environments for virtual universities. Most of these systems are intended to implement a number of software modules to support the entire online learning and management process. Many systems, especially those used in universities for distance learning, are developed on a collaborative basis: some modules are from other organization, others have to be developed by universities themselves to meet the special demands. In addition, these modules must constantly evolve. How to integrate these heterogeneous software modules into a seamless learning environment has become a big challenge.

One possible solution is the standardization of the system architecture. In recent years, many research efforts are focused into this area, e.g. IEEE's LTSA[5], IMS's ongoing Abstract Framework[6], CMU's service-oriented LSA[7], MIT's OKI[8] and ADL's SCORM. These proposed standardized architectures can undoubtedly facilitate the integration. However, they are still insufficient in terms of:

W. Liu et al. (Eds.): ICWL 2004, LNCS 3143, pp. 51–58, 2004.
© Springer-Verlag Berlin Heidelberg 2004

- To define a widely accepted and practical architecture proves a hard work. IEEE's LTSA, although widely accepted, is a high-level conceptual architecture and insufficient in the practical implementation. Some others, such as MIT's OKI, IMS's Abstract Framework and CMU's LSA, are intended to define the architecture in more details. But they differ in many aspects from each other and are not widely accepted enough. SCORM is probably the most popular e-learning standard nowadays, but it only covers part of the system architecture.
- To thoroughly define each module in the e-learning system architecture is even more difficult. For example, the goal of IMS's Abstract Framework is to define the required applications, services and components in the learning environment, however a long way before accomplishment.
- Standards can hardly cover those newly developed modules, for example the real-time interactive virtual classroom and some adaptive learning tools.
- There are still legacy modules that have to be integrated.

So, based on e-learning standards, efforts still have to be made on the integration. In this paper, we propose CUBES, a standard-based e-learning system. The design and implementation of CUBES focus on the integrity, extensibility and evlovability of heterogeneous software modules. We adopt those mature e-learning standards, e.g. CELTS[2](a localized version of selected standards in IEEE, AICC, ISO etc.) and SCORM[1]. An 1+N+1 three layered architecture is chosen: the first 1 means one basic supporting platform, providing common services such as authentication, core user information management and data exchange for the upper educational application modules(EAMs); N means the EAMs, including those commonly used such as courseware on-demand system, learner management and our newly developed virtual classroom[11] and dynamic learning quality monitor; the other 1 is the universal portal. Compared with other proposed architectures, CUBES has a special data exchange module(DEM) that acts as the mediator between EAMs. CUBES is now served in Webschool Tsinghua Univerity[9], a virtual university regularly attended by more than ten thousand of users.

2   System Architecture

The 1+N+1(which mentioned above)three layered architecture of CUBES is shown in Figure 1. We assume the EAMs, including the common standardized modules, and the legacy ones and those for special purpose, are developed by different organizations. And most of them probably need to evolve and extend in the future. Some of the EAMs are: courseware on-demand system, quiz and test system, learner management, virtual classroom, quality monitor etc. In fact, that's the practical problem we met when starting to build an advanced virtual university for Tshinghua University.

As illustrated in Figure 1, the EAMs are integrated through the interfaces provided by the supporting platform and the universal portal. There is hardly any direct interaction between EAMs. DEM acts as the mediator between different EAMs, providing data exchange services so that the EAMs can provide data, request data, publish events and subscribe to events through DEM. DEM is also responsible for the data access control. When an EAM is modified or a new EAM is added, the modification focuses on the interaction between this EAM and DEM. With the help of DEM, we do not need to modify the interaction between EAMs one by one. As such the efforts on integration and evolution are effectively reduced.

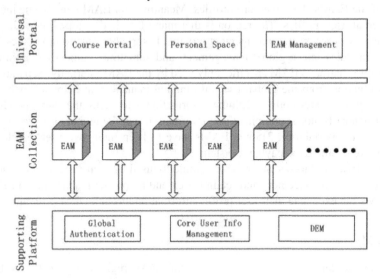

Fig. 1. Overall Architecture of CUBES

2.1 Global Authentication

The global authentication module provides a cookie-based single sign-on service. After the user logins at the universal portal, the global authentication module returns a temporary ticket residing in the user's browser. When the user navigates through different EAMs, this ticket is used as the credit automatically. The ticket will update after a period of time, for example every 6 hours.

It is also responsible for authorization. So it gathers required credential from the integrated EAMs or administrator's configurations, manages a list for each user to indicate his authorization for all of the EAMs integrated in CUBES. When the user navigates into an EAM, the EAM will query the global authentication for the user's authorization.

EAMs can also have their own internal authentication, because there are, indeed, situations when the user needs to be authenticated more than once in a session. For example, our global authentication relies on userid/password, while the integrated payment system requires an X.509 certification for a higher level of assurance. This guarantees the flexibility for multilevel security.

2.2 Core User Information Management

It defines the data structures of a learner's profile and provides services for accessing and manipulating these profiles. At present, there is only one profile for each user, called the core profile. The information stored in this profile is those defined in widely accepted e-learning standards for user information, such as IEEE's PAPI and CELTS-11(a localized version of IEEE's PAPI for Chinese).

All of the EAMs share the core profiles. Meantime, an EAM can also maintain its own internal user profiles. The reason is that many EAMs developed individually do have their own user profile management module. It's troublesome to move these management modules into a global management, and sometimes impossible: 1)Some of the user information is EAM specific, only used by the EAM internally. Separating the user information from the global user information management helps to improve the evolvability and extensibility. 2)Some information still lacks the corresponding e-learning standards, not to combine these information into the global user profile helps to improve the portability. 3)Some EAMs have to keep their own user profile management, for example the payment system.

So, we draw out those standardized, commonly used user information into the core user information management and retain the extending profile management in EAMs. The EAMs can exchange their user profile information through DEM if required.

2.3 DEM

DEM provides data exchange services to all the EAMs registered so that these EAMs can provide data, request data, subscribe to events, publish events, and respond to requests through DEM. It also provides access control to determine which EAM has access to which data. These EAMs may reside in the same server, or in the same LAN(Local Area Network), or even across the internet.

When an EAM is integrated into CUBES, firstly, it must register at DEM with the information about the data it requires from other EAMs and the data it can provide. DEM configures the data interaction processes between EAMs with some additional services such as the data type matching, transforming and caching. From the view of an EAM, it only communicates with the DEM, unaware of the existence of other EAMs. The advantages of having such a DEM are:

- Reducing the cost of integration. When an EAM is modified or a new EAM is added, most of the modification focuses on the interaction between this EAM and DEM. By the help of DEM, we do not need to modify the interaction between the EAM and the others one by one.
- Convenient to optimize the process of data exchange. We can introduce services such as data caching for all the EAMs.
- Having a centralized security model. DEM can provide various communica- tion protocols over which data may be transferred, such as HTTPS, to ease the implementation details of guaranteeing encryption and authentication require- ments. In addition, access control allows the administrator to configure which EAM is allowed to access which data.
- Easy to integrate EAMs developed in different languages. We provide c/c++, java and web service interfaces to ensure the integration of various EAMs.

2.3.1 Design Principles

DEM is designed to make the upper EAMs loosely-coupling, meantime, not losing too much efficiency in runtime. We conclude the design principles as four points:

- REST[10] like interfaces. The interfaces compose of verbs and documents. Four verbs are used in DEM: SEND, STORE, QUERY and REGISTER. The documents appending to the verbs are semantically rich and self-descriptive. When an EAM talks to the DEM(and vice versa), it organizes the transferred data into a self-descriptive document and tags the document with one of the above verbs. REST like interfaces prove flexible and are widely used for integration.
- Stateless. Communications between DEM and EAMs are stateless, such that each request from EAM to DEM(and vice versa) must contain all of the information necessary to understand the request. Each data exchange session composes of one request and one response. This feature improves visibility, reliability and scalability[10].
- Caching. DEM must have a caching mechanism to improve network efficiency.
- Asynchronous communication model. In order to ensure scalability and reliability, the request/response and publish/subscribe communication models should be asynchronous.

2.3.2 Communication with EAMs

The data exchanged through DEM is defined using a series of data objects, along with the schemas that define the semantics of the data. An EAM registers the data objects it provides at DEM.

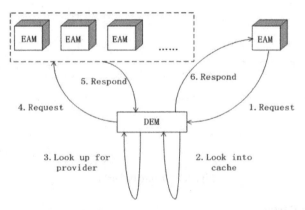

Fig. 2. Process of Data Exchange

The data exchange between DEM and EAMs is in a request and response model. When an EAM requires data, it sends a request message to DEM. DEM is responsible to collect the required data. Firstly, DEM looks into its own cache. If the data in cache is absent, it looks up the registered EAMs to find the data provider, and then sends a request message. When the data is ready, DEM sends it to EAM as a response. The exchange process is illustrated in Figure 2.

EAMs can also subscribe to DEM for notification about data. When an EAM makes a change in the data registered at DEM, it should generate a message to notify DEM. As such the DEM can update its cache and notify other EAMs that subscribe to the changed data.

2.3.3 Structure of DEM

The Structure of DEM is illustrated in Figure 3. The **Interaction Controller** accepts requests and events from EAMs, calls the services provided by other components in DEM, sends requests if the data required is not in the **Database for Cache**, and responses to EAMs when the data is ready. The **Information Manager** stores various information about the data objects for exchange, and provides services to access, modify, add, and delete the stored information. Some of the most important information is: access control to determine which EAM has the access authorization, EAMs as the providers, index of the related data adaptors, schema of the data object used in data type matching, cache information, and events related to the data object from EAMs. These information is organized in a tree based structure and implemented using an LDAP(Lightweight Directory Access Protocol) server. The **Mass Data Handler** divides the exchanged large data into small pieces to reduce the response time and limit the RAM in use. Currently, the size of data in one response is limited to 1M bytes, but it's configurable in runtime. **Data Adaptors** are used to transform the data being exchanged, e.g. from XML to a java object.

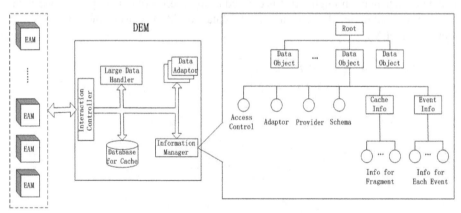

Fig. 3. Structure of DEM

2.4 Universal Portal

The universal portal helps to provide a seamless learning environment for all of the users, including learners, teachers and administrators. The portal determines how the various features and services provided by the underlying EAMs are presented. In the universal portal, users only have a view of various integrated services without the concept of the individual EAM. Some of the important modules or tools provided in the portal to help constructing such an environment are: course portal, personal space and EAM management.

3   Constructing a Learning Environment

To construct a learning environment covering the entire spectrum of online learning and management process, we have integrated the following EAMs into CUBES:

- Large scale real-time interactive virtual classroom[11].
- Courseware on demand system.
- Resource management system for the metadata of learning materials.
- Quiz and test system.
- Payment system.
- Learner management system.
- Dynamic learning quality monitor.
- Assignment deliver and management system.
- Question and answer system based on BBS.

Table 1. Application of CELTS in EAMs

	CELTS -3	CELTS -11	CELTS -13	CELTS -9	CELTS -17
Virtual Classroom	✓			✓	✓
Courseware on demand	✓			✓	✓
Resource Management	✓			✓	✓
Payment System		✓	✓		✓
Learner Management		✓	✓		✓
Learning Quality Monitor		✓	✓		✓
Assignment	✓			✓	✓
Question and Answer	✓			✓	✓
Quiz and Test	✓	✓	✓	✓	✓

Some of the EAMs above conform to CELTS(a localized version of selected standards in IEEE, AICC, ISO etc.) and SCORM(version 1.2). SCORM is applied in the courseware on demand system and the resource management system. The binding with CELTS is illustrated in Table 1.

4   Webschool Tsinghua University Based on CUBES

CUBES is currently deployed in Webschool Tsinghua University[9], a virtual university regularly used by more than ten thousand of users all over China. It provides about 150 online curriculum, ranging from mathematics, computer technology, English to law, art design and economics. We are now trying to improve the use of the large scale real-time interactive virtual classroom for more online real-time courses. Some of the EAMs, such as the learner management system and dynamic learning quality monitor are being evolved according to the feedback from practical use.

5 Conclusion and Future Works

In this paper, we have presented CUBES, an e-learning system providing flexible learning environment for virtual universities. Our system focuses on the integrity, evolvability and extensibility. A basic supporting platform including DEM(data exchange module) and a universal portal are designed to effectively reduce the efforts on integrating and evolving heterogeneous EAMs(educational application modules). In CUBES, we can conveniently add, modify and remove EAMs to construct an appropriate learning environment. Currently, CUBES is deployed as a distributed system in a local area network. In the future, we plan to test CUBES as an internet scale distributed system. As such we can share the valuable EAMs which maybe spread over different universities and institutions.

References

1. SCORM [Online]. Available: http://www.adlnet.org
2. CELTS [Online]. Available: http://www.celtsc.edu.cn
3. Blackboard [Online]. Available: http://www.blackboard.com
4. WebCT [Online]. Available: http://www.webct.com
5. IEEE's LTSA [Online]. Available: http://ltsc.ieee.org/wg1/index.html
6. IMS Abstract Framework [Online].
   Available: http://www.imsglobal.org/specifications.cfm
7. CMU's LSA [Online]. Available: http://www.lsal.cmu.edu/lsal/site/
8. OKI [Online]. Available: http://web.mit.edu/oki
9. Webschool Tsinghua Univerity [Online]. Available: http://www.itsinghua.edu.cn
10. REST Fielding. Architectural Styles and the Design of Network-based Software Architectures: PhD thesis. UC Irvine (2000).
11. Shi, Y., Xie, W., Xu, G., Xiang, P.&Zhang, B. Project Smart Remote Classroom Providing Novel Real Time Interactive Distance Learning Technologies. International Journal of Distance Education Techonologies. vol 1. no 3. (2003) 28-45.

Dinosys:
An Annotation Tool for Web-Based Learning

Emmanuel Desmontils[1], Christine Jacquin[1], and Ludovic Simon[2]

[1] LINA CNRS FRE 2729, Université de Nantes
2, rue de la Houssinière, BP92208,
F-44322 Nantes Cedex 3, France
{desmontils,jacquin}@lina.univ-nantes.fr
[2] SII Nantes, Immeuble Concorde
1, rue Charles Lindberg
44344 Bouguenais Cedex, France
lsimon@sii.fr

Abstract. The main function of freeform annotation systems is to improve exchange, communication and interoperability on the Web. The purpose of this paper is on the one hand, to make a synthesis of the characteristics of the annotations and architectures of annotation systems, and on the other hand to propose a new architecture for an annotation system which is easy to use, lightweight, efficient, non-intrusive, scaleable, shared and platform-independent. The use of this tool within the e-learning framework is also studied.

Keywords: Annotation, Freeform Annotations Systems, Annotation tools, E-learning, Dinosys, Web

1 Introduction

Collaborative working environments as Lotus Notes exist. They are usually used by little groups of people working often together on a specific area. They share a common vocabulary and have their own practices. However, what is possible with this type of collaborative environments is not anymore possible in the Web framework. The Web enables millions of people to communicate together. They have different centers of interest, different practices, and different cultures. On the Web, the information is distributed. In this context, it is usefull to propose tools and methods for understanding, processing and sharing documents in order to implement relevant and efficient services. To answer to this need, the Web annotation systems were born. Their purpose is to improve, on the one hand, the understanding of HTML documents and on the other hand, the communication and the interoperability on the Web.

The freeform annotations systems (FAS) on the Web make it possible to associate reading notes to documents, to share information and to write documents in a collaborative way. In this context, a reader becomes a writer. These kinds of tools can be used in a lot of domain. Typicaly, e-learning domain is

W. Liu et al. (Eds.): ICWL 2004, LNCS 3143, pp. 59–66, 2004.

an interesting application field. FAS make it possible for the learning platforms to become interactive. For instance, the learner can use the system to visualize the courses and to work on them in a more natural way [1]. In this context, the system also helps the tutor to annotate learner's works. Indeed, the systems can store commentaries and can automatize a part of the evaluation process. Consequently, the tutor spends less time on learners's works [2] and the use of such systems improves the evaluation quality and the correction duration [3]. In this paper, we firstly present what annotations are and what their roles are in the communication between the reader and the writer (section 2 and 3). Then, we present our annotation system according to existing systems (section 4). Finally, we present the role which can play our system in e-learning applications.

2 Annotations

An annotation is a graphical or textual information attached to a document and often placed in this document. This place is given by an anchor. Annotations can be linked to various entities: a documents set, a document, a paragraph, a sentence, a term, a word, an image... Annotations were mainly studied by C. C. Marshall [4]. Annotations can be characterized according to several dimensions. We give here a quick overview of these dimensions:

- *formal/informal dimension*: At the formal end of the spectrum, the note can be metadata that follow structured standard. This level of formality ensures interoperability (for instance LOM [5]). Toward the informal end of the spectrum we find note written in natural language.
- *explicit/tacit dimension*: An explicit annotation can be understood by every people while a tacit one requires other knowledge to understand it.
- *function dimension*: This concerns annotation functions during the reading or writing process. We argue that annotations can be used to:
  1. *inform, illustrate, extend the document*. When the reader adds annotations, he/she becomes a writer.
  2. *forum*. The FAS enables the readers to discuss about the document content.
  3. *operationnalize data*. Semantic annotations make it possible to operationalize data embedded into documents. They are used by computers (in opposite to natural language based annotations or to symbole based ones) to disambiguate a document for an automated process.
  4. *help the writing process*. Annotations enable the writer to build his/her document (correcting parts, moving information...).
  5. *help the reading process*. Annotations enable the reader to commune with his/her document. The annotation makes it possible the appropriation of the text by the reader.
  6. *to evaluate a work*: For instance, annotations enable the tutor to evaluate and to correct the work of a learner.

- *role dimension*: This concerns the level of document reading. Some notes make it possible to have a quick reading of documents (hyperlink for example), on the contrary, others give more information on the document in order to improve understanding.
- *temporal dimension*: An annotation can be permanent or transitory.
- *the writer/reader communication dimension*: An annotation can be either private or public. When an annotation is public, there are many degrees: the working group, the institute... The writer's and reader's behaviors lead to "one-to-many" systems (a writer dedicates his document to one or several readers) or lead to "many-to-many" systems (a readers and writers are working in a collaborative way). The FAS on the Web tend to become "many-to-many" systems [6].

3   Freeform Annotations Systems on the Web

The FAS have to take into account several constraints and features of the Web: the client and server are distributed, the communication is supported by a network, FAS are multi-user systems, the communication protocol (HTTP) is poor, HTML data or XML data are not always easy to manage. The systems usually respect the same architecture (figure 1) [7]. An intermediary agent traps the transaction between a Web client and a Web server. This agent acts on the request, on the received pages and sometimes on events which occur on the Web browser. Its main functions are to intercept requests and/or HTML pages and to associate annotations to documents. There are two classes of FAS: proxy-based systems and systems where the intermediary is located on the client side.

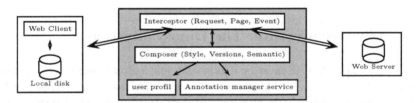

Fig. 1. Overview of a Web annotation tools [7]

3.1   Proxy-Based Systems

Intermediaries based on proxy systems are neither on the client side, nor on the server side [8–10]. The proxy server observes all requests sent by the client and manages the pages which have annotations linked to them and which belong to its database. The main problem of such systems is the confidentiality. Indeed, the proxy server observes all client transactions and modifies Web documents. This also emphases the problem of copyright. To avoid these problems, [10] (CritLink) proposes a system based on optional proxies. In this context, a person uses the FAS only when he needs it (confidentiality) and the Web pages can be consulted without the annotations. But this type of system highlights other problems:

- it is not possible to annotate local documents;
- adding annotations implies a page reload and a specific dialog;
- the system does not manage dynamic pages;
- the system is slow (a bottleneck) because it has to process all received requests;
- the original document is modified (notes are inserted into the document).

But, these systems have several advantages: they are easy to install, the annotations sharing is easy to perform, they are independent of the operating system and of the Web browser used.

3.2 Systems Based on Client Intermediary

These systems are installed on the client side [11–13, 1, 14]. Consequently, they are totally dependent of the operating system and of the Web browser used. Managing shared annotations is not easy. Moreover, some systems propose a protocol to send annotations by electronic mail or to use an annotation server. The latter solution reintroduces the bottleneck problem. The best advantage of these systems is the flexibility of the creation and visualization of the annotations. As the annotation system is integrated into the Web browser, it accesses to the DOM structure of the document and to events which occur. But the problems of confidentiality and of copyright remain. The problem of scalability is not either resolved. A partial solution consists in duplicating the servers (with all the problems relating to distributed databases). The great number of failures shows that all the problems are not yet solved and they need to be more studied. For more precise comparatives see [15, 1, 16, 17, 7, 6].

4   A New Architecture: The Dinosys System

According to [7], Web FAS must be lightweight, efficient, non-intrusive, platform-independent, and scaleable. Moreover, the capability to support collaborative working becomes increasingly necessary. In fact, in the context of people working together and simultaneously, the system has to manage annotations update in real time. But, all capabilities previously stated are rarely properties of existing systems. We propose here a new architecture which tends to answer to these criteria. This architecture takes advantages of the two existing types of architecture, but also brings a new concept which is the distribution. Our system called *Dinosys*[1] (DIstributed NOtation SYStem) is divided into three parts (figure 2): a client (like systems based on intermediary clients), a portal and a set of identical proxy servers (like the systems based on intermediary proxies).

The client visualizes the annotated pages and manages the annotations (creation, deletion, update...). It interacts with the other components of the system in a non-intrusive way for the user. This client is downloaded from the portal

---

[1] http://www.dinosys.org

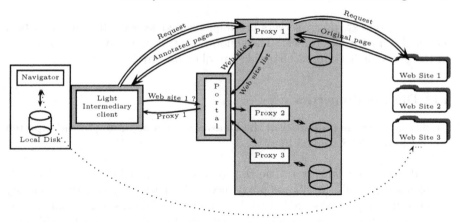

Fig. 2. The Dinosys system architecture

when the user begins to use the system or when a new version is available. The update is also made without user needing (easy to use and transparent).

The portal plays several roles in our system. It enables new users to subscribe to the system and to download the client. Then, when a user has to annotate a page, the client accesses through the portal to the proxy server which manages the page. It also enables the administrator to insert or to configure a new proxy server in the system. Finally, it makes it possible for the different users (administrators, users) to configure their own environment and their own user profil.

Each proxy server manages the annotations of a set of pages. The sets of pages are constituted according to different criteria (the pages belong to the same semantic domain, in order to distribute the system load...). A proxy server has different functions:

- interception of pages requested by a user client and insertion into them of the annotations present in the database;
- interception of new annotations sent by a user client and storage of them in the database;
- management of collaborative working (information of users connected to the same page, dynamic sending to all page used of new/updated annotations).

Dinosys system comprises two types of actors: the users and the administrators. The users consult annotated pages and can add or modify annotations. The users are structured in group in order to take into account the confidentiality needs. Indeed, a user of a group can annotate documents for himself, for his group or for the general group (public group). Every proxy server is supervised by an administrator who decides what the pages the server manages. The Dinosys system is supervised by a general administrator who manages the users (controlling of user and use of the system, nomination of proxy-administrators). It also manages the proxy servers (Web site allocation to the proxy servers, load distribution, including of new proxy servers).

In this context, proxy servers are implemented as servlets associated to a servlet/JSP motor like Tomcat. The annotations which are XML data are stored on the proxy server into database like mysql or postgresSQL.

4.1   Dinosys Properties

We discuss here the properties of the Dinosys system according to the expected properties of a FAS studied by [7].

- *a distributed architecture:* The Dinosys architecture is based on the concept of geographically distributed proxy servers. It guarantees services availability even if proxy servers are halted, because of breakdowns or of maintenance. This architecture also ensures a convenient load distribution by making it possible to set up new proxy servers when necessary. As the response time is improved, the application also becomes more attractive for the end user. The distribution gives two properties to the system: scalability and efficiency.
- *operating system independent, non-intrusive and lightweight*: The client side of the system is implemented by a java applet. The client application is then operating system independent. Moreover, the automatical download of new updates of the client application is non-intrusive for the user.

Another property of our FAS is to take into account the collaborative working. Dinosys system makes it possible to automatically update the annotations and has its own chat. This latter will be used during a collaborative annotations session in "forum" mode. The exchanges are then more direct.

5   Dinosys and e-Learning

The Dinosys system is a distributed FAS that can be used for various e-learning applications. Thanks to Dinosys System, a student can work on a Web document, as if it was a classical paper document. He can annotate the Web documents with informal notes (explicit or tacit). These annotations are especially reading supports. They eventually can be shared by other students. The annotation role is essentially the course appropriation. They focus essentially on document passages and they have a rather long lifespan (a six-month period for example).

Another kind of annotations are those affixed to documents by a tutor according to a pedagogical strategy. These notes can be: course complements (like notes into book), answers to student, remarks, FAQ... These annotations are informal and explicit. They are public and dedicated to students (a writer and several readers). Their role is to illustrate and to extend documents. Their lifespan varies according to their role. They can be persistent (notes, remarks...) or transitory (error...).

The system can also be used in the context of the evaluation of a student works (project, practical works...) by a tutor. In the context of the Web, this use of such annotations is a new concept. The tutor can insert remarks and notes into a student document as if it was a classical paper document. This kind of annotations is private, has an unlimited lifespan and is explicit.

Another application of Dinosys system is the management of the student's collaborative work on a same project. The system makes it possible to insert into documents remarks intended for the other one. Moreover, combination of annotations managed in real time and of an instantaneous message service makes it possible to work directly on documents. These annotations help to write documents or can be used for interactive talk as in a forum. They are transitory and intended essentially for the project members.

The annotations can also be used for the communication between tutors. They can be used to discuss on the course, on the proposed exercises... In this context, the annotations are essentially a forum support. They are dedicated to a group of tutors. They are transitory, explicit and generally informal.

The main originality of our system, compared to the existing FAS dedicated to e-learning [2, 18], is its capability to annotate documents in real time in a multi-user context. The system is also operating system independent. The nearest project is Web-Notes [19]. This system is dedicated to e-learning and makes it possible to insert pre-formatted annotations into HTML pages. The annotation server (servlet) is centralized. Two applets make it possible on the one hand to visualize the notes on the Web browser and on the other hand to edit them. The system manages groups and identification.

6   Conclusion

FAS make it possible to have collaborative working environments where every members can be writer or reader. But, a lot of developed systems either are commercial failures [14, 11] or stopped research projects [10, 8, 1]. These failures are due, on the one hand to a bad annotations understanding and, on the other hand to unsuited system architectures. We have presented a new architecture of FAS which is lightweight, efficient, non-intrusive, platform independent and scaleable. These properties are very important in the context of e-learning applications and are in agreement with the features enumerated by [20]. Indeed, according to J. A. Finins, an environment of e-learning must offer any, or all, of the following devices:

- A communication facility which may be synchronous/asynchronous, tutor-student, student-tutor and/or student-student;
- A shell for interactive/multimedia course materials;
- A collaborative working environment, e.g. a communication facility plus shared file space for group assignments;
- ...

The proposed system is based on proxy server technology (proxy servers are distributed) and on intermediary client technology (in our system the role of the intermediary client is to communicate with portal and with the proxy server which manage documents that will be annotated). A first version of the system was implemented. It will be used in the framework of an e-learning course (International e-mi@ge²).

References

1. L. Denoue and L. Vignollet. An annotation tool for web browsers and its applications to information retrieval. In *RIAO*, pages 180–195, Paris, France, 2000.
2. M. Holmes. Approaches to marking electronic texts. In P. Liddel, editor, *FLEAT III*, pages 107–122, 1998. Markin.
3. L. Desmarais. La persévérance dans l'enseignement à distance - une étude de cas. *ALSIC*, 3(1):49–59, juin 2000. http://www.alsic.org.
4. C. C. Marshall. Toward an ecology of hypertext annotation. In *ACM Hypertext*, pages 40–49. ACM Press, June 1998.
5. IEEE Learning Technology Standards Committee. Standard for learning object metadata. IEEE 1484.12.1, 2002.
   http://grouper.ieee.org/LTSC/wg12/index.html.
6. R. Zohar. Web annotation - an overview. Technical report, Dept. of Electrical Engineering, Israel Institute of Technology, 1999.
7. V. Vasudevan and M. Palmer. On web annotations: Promises and pitfalls of current web infrastructure. In *HICSS-32*. IEEE Computer Society Press, 1999.
8. Jacob Palme. Web4groups, 1998.
   http://www.dsv.su.se/jpalme/w4g/web4groups-summary.html.
9. I. Ovsiannikov, M.A. Arbib, and T.H. McNeill. Annotation technology. *Int. J. Human-Computer Studies*, 50:329–362, 1999.
   http://www-hbp.usc.edu/Projects/annotati.htm.
10. K.-P. Yee. Critlink. In *Fifth Foresight Conf. on Molecular Nanotechnology*, 1997.
11. M. Roscheisen, C. Mogensen, and T. Wonograd. Commentor.
    http://hci.stanford.edu/commentor/doc/, 1994.
12. M.-R. Koivunen, J. Kahan, R. Swick, and E. Prud'hommeaux. Annotea project. http://www.w3.org/2001/Annotea/, 2001. W3C.
13. Imarkup. Imarkup. http://www.imarkup.com/, 2002.
14. Inc ThirdVoice. Thirdvoice 2000, 2000.
15. J. Garfunkel. Web annotation technologies.
    http://look.boston.ma.us/garf/webdev/annote/software.html, 1999.
16. R. M. Heck, S. M. Luebke, and C. H. Obermark. A survey of web annotation systems. Technical report, Dep. Of Math. and Computer Science, Grinnell College, USA, 1999.
17. P. Perry. Web annotations. http://www.paulperry.net/notes/annotations.asp, 2001.
18. Inc. WebCT. WebCT. http://www.webct.com/entrypage, 2000.
19. M. Ronchetti. Why web pages annotation tools are not killer applications? a new approach to an old problem. In P. Isaias, editor, *IADIS Int. Conf. WWW/Internet*, pages 735–738, Lisboa, Portugal, 2002. http://www.iadis.org/.
20. J. A. Finins. Learning technology: The myths and facts.
    http://www/twinisles.com/dev/research/learntech.htm, 2003.

---

² Concerning a software engineer training on Information Systems for Companies Management (see http://www.e-miage.org).

Web-Based Multimedia Authoring and Presentation Framework for Children's Art Cultivation

Hao-Tung Lin, Yi-Chun Lai, Kuo-Yu Liu, and Herng-Yow Chen

Department of Computer Science and Information Engineering, National Chi-Nan University
1st University Rd., Pu-Li, Nan-Tou County, Taiwan 545
{haotung,iclai,caspar}@mclab.csie.ncnu.edu.tw
hychen@csie.ncnu.edu.tw

Abstract. This paper proposes a web-based multimedia authoring and presentation framework to facilitate online pieces creation, sharing, and reuse in e-learning applications. Through the easy-to-use interface of the customized tools, students are allowed to create their own pieces online and then share with friends in a very easy way. To make the presentation of the piece more interesting, the authoring tool provides the capturing mechanism that records all significant authoring steps as synchronization information: temporal and spatial relations between composed objects. Synchronization module in rendering function enables users (author and receiver) to replay a vivid, animated multimedia presentation in a form of as close as possible to the original sense. A prototype has been implemented in a website especially designed for young student art learning, which has being conducted by the Military of Education, Taiwan, since 2003. The experimental results show that this hands-on experience in creating and sharing indeed benefits the efficacy of web-based e-learning.

Keywords: Multimedia authoring, XML

1 Introduction

With the rapid advance in web and e-learning technologies, learning a variety of knowledge on the Web, such as from language leaning (e.g., ESL) to professional domain knowledge (e.g., computer science), have been very popular for many years. In contrast, e-learning systems focusing on art domains and especially for kids or teenagers are few published. Compared with technologies needed for more general purpose knowledge, cultivating children's art through e-learning technology needs much more edutainment ingredients – interesting, interactive, and multimedia. Realizing this kind of e-learning well is really a challenge, not only from a pedagogical viewpoint (the first ingredient) but technical ones (the latter two ingredients).

In 2003 the Ministry of Education in Taiwan started to plan an art learning website (http://arts.edu.tw) for young people (elementary, junior, and senior school students) that integrates learning of four different art aspects with a humanity sense – literature, music, visual art, and performance art. Active learning and easy-to-sharing are two key principles that the site obeys. At the same time our research group, the multimedia and communication Lab of NCNU, was invited to join this e-learning project and

W. Liu et al. (Eds.): ICWL 2004, LNCS 3143, pp. 67–74, 2004.

assist in technical development and implementation. In this paper, we describe how our framework design for online authoring and presentation works. The goal of this framework is to provide a universal platform that enables students to learn more actively, through sharing their own pieces easily with other learners. Peers and teachers can comment students' work for further discussion or instruction [1].

To this end, multimedia authoring and presentation tool named "My e-card" (http://media.csie.ncnu.edu.tw/haotung/myecard/) has been designed to allow students to combine different media objects (such as painting object, typing object, and music object) into a time-ordered, synchronized multimedia document (i.e., animated sound painting). Students can reuse any existing media objects in cyberspace through Universal resource locator (URL) or create new ones by different kinds of supporting tools, such as static painting, writing essay, and composing music. We use XML format to describe multimedia objects and their temporal, spatial relationship metadata because of its high extensibility and flexibility [2][3]. Students can resume their work at other place. They don't have to worry about data integrity, and presentation consistency of the unfinished work that are deposited in the server. At any stage, current piece work can be played out with synchronization to preview the result.

Research has indicated that both competence and confidence are keys to the success of active learning [4][5]. Experimental results show that our present work enforces the highly interactive creation process, which involves acts of media creating and further authoring – an approach leads to personal competence. Moreover, playing composite multimedia work with a synchronized manner and sharing the great work with friends reinforce personal confidence.

The remainder of this paper is organized as follows. We describe the framework of our system in Section 2. Section 3 states that how we make our system interesting for children. Implementation issues and experimental results are shown in Section 4. Section 5 describes the future work. Conclusion remarks are given in Section 6.

2   System Framework

Fig. 1 illustrates the proposed framework over existing web architecture, which is basically a client-server architecture: clients for authoring and presentation, servers for metadata storage and format exchange. The customized multimedia authoring and presentation program will be downloaded from the server into the client's browser and automatically executed. The program should provide users (e.g., students, teachers, experts, and other people) with most friendly multimedia authoring functions and presentation experiences. All the authoring results will be transmitted to the server for storage and sharing. The server-side application gateway should maintain the meta-information of the composed, submitted artist work and handle the content exchange necessary for different presentation tool (e.g., SMIL player). The XML-based metadata describing how different source of media objects are composed mainly consists of three types of information: the URL of media objects (where to locate), temporal information (when to display), and spatial information (where to place). The rendering function of the presentation program needs those meta-data to make a best performance to users. With the help of web technology, the framework can easily reuse a variety of existing multimedia object resources (such as images, video and audio URLs), which needn't be stored in our server.

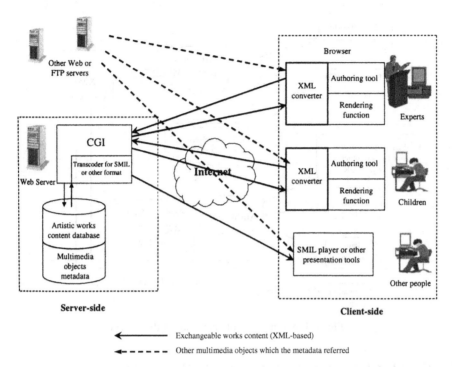

Fig. 1. The web-based multimedia authoring and presentation framework

Fig. 2 shows the detailed components of the client-side tool that consists of several modules: authoring interface, rendering function, XML converter and synchronization module. The authoring interface takes different types of user operations as inputs, including painting, creating objects, modifying objects and options about music or presentation.

The detailed composed actions and necessary information for later presentation are maintained as the internal data structure. The appearances of objects being updated are then monitored to display by the rendering function, under the control of synchronization module. This mechanism naturally integrates the authoring tool with rendering module to achieve "WYSIWYG" capability. Because of the performance consideration, we use the internal data structure for on-the-fly synchronized rendering rather than using the XML format. On the other hand, once the composed results are going to be submitted to the server, the internal data structure used to record the relationship of composed objects will be converted into an XML format for the sake of compatibility and flexibility.

Cooperated in rendering function, the synchronization module enables the whole presentation process to be viewed as a kind of authoring process reconstruction. The details of the painting actions will be rendered step by step and accompany the associated music playback simultaneously. Users can decided in the authoring stage what types of painting/music integrated scenarios are used in the playback stage: background music mode, introduction music mode, and synchronization mode. Other students will learn to understand how peer students made their pieces effectively through this vivid presentation.

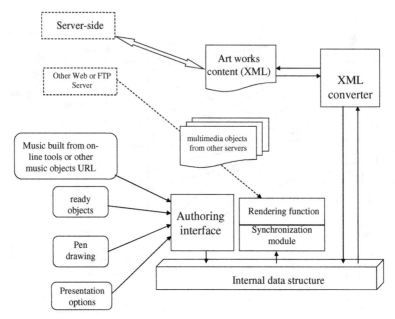

Fig. 2. The framework of client-side of the system

3   Enable Children to Be Interested in Our System

The environment and tools supported by the system may help children to cultivate their art capacity. However, how to attract children to use them actively is an important topic. It decides whether the system is worthy or not. We apply the following guidelines that can attract children to join this site actively.

Children's works should be able to be shared and viewed very easily. Because it's an environment that everyone can learn through viewing other people's work, the web site exhibits all the works created by children. Children can send their work as an E-card to their relatives and friends. Through this web-based system, people can see their works anywhere, anytime.

Children can get feedback about their work from others. Art appreciation is sometime very subjective. Many people may have different answers to the question "Is this piece a good work?" Everyone wish to get feedback from other people, especially good comments. For this reason, some experts in arts are invited as online reviewers who from time to time examine online works and comment them through web interface or email.

Online contest with voting encourages children to perform themselves. We encourage registered students to take part in my e-card contest on the basis of some specific topics. In addition to reviewers, web visitors can vote for the work they think the best. Children must hope that their work can be a popular one. This drives contesters to keep improving their own piece continuously.

4   Implementation

We use the Apache [6] as our HTTP server incorporated with the PHP language [7] as the server-slide Common Gateway Interface (CGI). A large number of web users can view Flash-based web content in their browsers [8]. The Macromedia Flash technology [9] has been as a de facto platform because of its highly interactive capability and multimedia (such as gif, jpg, wav and mp3) format support. To provide interface for end-users as lovely as possible, the Flash technology incorporated with the JavaScript Dynamic HTML control (DHTML) [10][11] are used to develop the authoring and presentation program.

The Flash-based programs are packaged as the SWF format, which is a format patented by Macromedia Flash Co. to deliver the streamable graphics, animation and sound over the Internet. However, some media type, like the MIDI format, cannot be processed by Flash. This is a shortcoming because MIDI possesses low bit rates and high flexibility especially for web-based music composition application. We solve this problem by passing through MIDI format to another player (e.g., Microsoft Media Player) and making MIDI presentation and Flash presentation under a synchronization control of a middle-ware, which is implemented by JavaScript. Namely, both Microsoft Media Player and Flash player can be embedded into an HTML file and controlled with a JavaScript code inside.

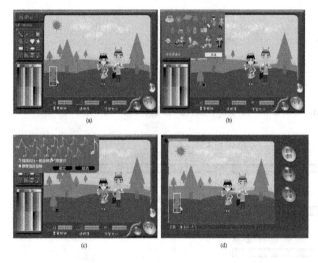

Fig. 3. Some examples of the operation in My E-card. Fig. 3.(a) is the main interface of My E-card. Fig. 3(b) shows the ready-objects chooser. Children can choose the ready-objects to compose a scene. Fig. 3(c) shows the function of music chooser and synchronization configuration. Fig. 3(d) shows the animated presentation process in the presentation interface. A slide bar on the top of the view indicates the presentation time. A virtual moving pen over the currently rendered object is for reality

Fig. 3 shows some examples of the operation in My E-card, the major authoring tool in this system. And Fig. 4 illustrates how the rendering function presents the children's work. There are two major media in this presentation – visual appearance and audio (music). The music can be played in several modes. The music can just be a background music and be repeated again until the end of presentation. It can also be an introduction music in this presentation and be played just in the beginning. In the third mode, the animated painting actions should be finished by the end of the music, so the rendering function normalize all the timestamps of the significant painting actions and fit them into the time scale of the music. The painting objects appear one by one according to the time stamps, as shown in Fig. 5.

The presentations of the art works are very vivid and interesting. It reflects the painting process step by step and with sound effect. The scenarios of presentation looks like a painter who is painting the draw on-the-spot accompanying the music playback. We got many positive feedbacks from online visitors since the web site was announced in 2003. Those people created their art works through the proposed tools and operate them well. The quality of the works they made is quite good and some-time beyond our expectation. Even some adult told us that they think that the tools we proposed are very funny and willing to visit the site more frequently.

Using XML-based format to represent the meta-data makes the integration of different types of media in different presentation platforms much easier. The cost of storing a large number of multimedia objects can be decreased, and the multimedia objects created by different authors can also be reused easily.

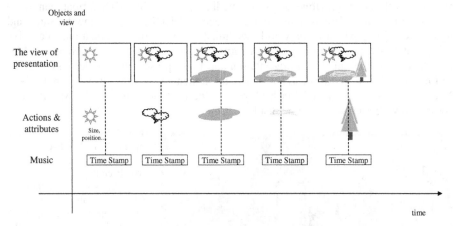

Fig. 4. Logical view of the development rendering function

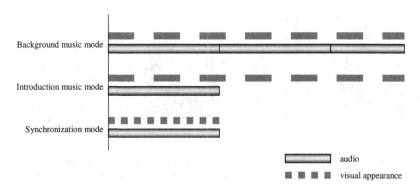

Fig. 5. The diagram of the presentation modes

5   Conclusions and Future Work

In this paper, we described a web-based learning environment for cultivating children's art capacity. A prototype has been implemented in a website especially designed for young student art learning, which has being conducted by the Military of Education, Taiwan, since 2003. The proposed web-based multimedia authoring and presentation framework can facilitate online pieces creation, sharing, and reuse in e-learning applications. Through the easy-to-use interface of the customized tools, students are allowed to create their own pieces and share with friends easily. To make the presentation more interesting, synchronization module in rendering function re-play a vivid, animated multimedia presentation in a form of as close as possible to the original sense.

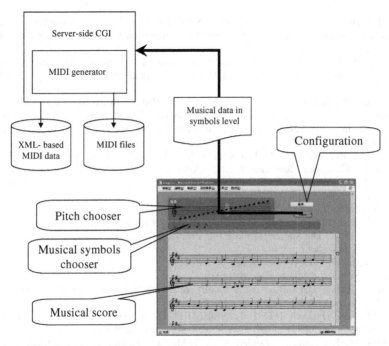

Fig. 6. A simple music generation tool in our system – MIDI composer

In our current system, we have supported some authoring tools and the player. The works which children made are stored in XML format. The XML format is easy to distribute, share and reuse, so our authoring tools and players can integrate and pre-sent the different types of the works easily. The definition of the XML tag we used has been designed for our tools. If the data can be converted into SMIL format or other standards, the works would be distributed and shared with others more easily [12,13].

The presentation in My E-card includes the painting actions and music playings, in the future work, we will try to show the painting actions progress according to the rhythm or other features of the music.

On the basis of the proposed framework, we can develop more interesting author-ing, production tools for different types of art learning and cultivation. For example, the MIDI composer shown in Fig. 6 is a kind of music generation tool we are cur-rently developing. The tool generates MIDI data, which are saved as XML-based format. Our authoring tools can import the finished product, the MIDI date described. Then, children can touch more types of art.

To advance the worth of the framework and the system, we are inviting artists and professionals in different art or education domains to assist us in designing an objective evaluation mechanism. The results of evaluation will offer us more aspects of system promotion.

References

1. M. Pinheiro, J,. Lima, N. Edelweiss, Nabil Layaïda, Tayeb Lemlouma: An Open E-Learning Authoring Environment, Spezielles Seminar im WS 2002/2003 - E-Learning.
2. Extensible Markup Language (XML). Available in: http://www.w3.org/XML/
3. L. Villard, C. Roisin and N. Layada: A XML-based multimedia document processing model for content adaptation, Digital Documents and Electronic Publishing (DDEP00), LNCS, 2000.
4. C. Koutra, N. Kastis, G. Neofotistos, Starlab, M. Panayi: Interactive Learning Environments for Children: User interface Requirements for a Magic Mirror and Diary Composer Environment, Proceedings of One-day Workshop on Interactive Learning Environments for Children
5. Jeremy M. Roschelle,Roy D. Pea, Christopher M. Hoadley, Douglas N.Gordin, Barbara M.Means: Changing How and What Children Learn in School with Computer-Based Technologies, The Future of Children and Computer Technology Vol. 10 • No. 2 – Fall/Winter 2000.
6. The Apache Software Foundation. Available in: http://www.apache.org/
7. PHP: Hypertext Preprocessor. Available in: http://www.php.net/
8. OpenSWF.org – The Source for Flash File Format Information. Available in: http://www.openswf.org/
9. Macromedia Flash Developer Center. Available in: http://www.macromedia.com/devnet/mx/flash/
10. Dynamic Drive DHTML(dynamic html) & JavaScript code library. Available in: http://www.dynamicdrive.com/
11. DHTML Lab: Dynamic HTML Tutorials, DHTML Scripts, Programming, Tools, Code, and Examples. Available in: http://www.webreference.com/dhtml/
12. S. Boll, W. Klas, and J. Wandel: A Cross-Media Adaptation Strategy for Multimedia Presentations, In ACM Multimedia '99 Proceedings, pages 37{46, Orlando, Florida, October 30 - November 5, 1999. Addison Wesley Longman.
13. H. Martin and P. Mulhem: A Comparison of XML and SMIL for on the fly generation of Multimedia Documents from Databases, SCI Conference 2000, USA, July 2000.

A Progressive Content Distribution Framework in Supporting Web-Based Learning

Frederick W.B. Li[1] and Rynson W.H. Lau[2]

[1] Department of Computing, The Hong Kong Polytechnic University, Hong Kong
[2] Department of CEIT, City University of Hong Kong, Hong Kong

Abstract. Web-based learning offers many benefits over traditional learning environments, where it eases auto student-tracking, active content updating, in addition to provide a time, class size and geographical location independent learning platform to students. In recent years, many web-based courses and educational applications have been developed. In particular, the incorporation of 3D content in web-based learning systems allows students to visualize various types of complicated structures or certain difficult conceptual ideas. This eases the learning processing of students. However, as the volume of 3D content is generally much large in size than traditional textual and image based information, a smart content distribution strategy should be employed to fit the limited resources condition of general users. In this paper, we propose a progressive content distribution framework to support web-based learning using 3D content. We also present two prototype web-based learning platforms.

1 Introduction

The World Wide Web (WWW) provides a rich environment for constructing interactive, intelligent, active and collaborative learning environment [1]. It offers certain distinguished advantages over the traditional learning environment. For instance, under traditional learning environment, students are required to gather at certain time and place to attend a lesson. In contrast, web-based learning allows students from geographical separated locations to join a lesson without physically travel. On the other hand, web-based learning natively supports the presentation of various types of media, such as 3D graphics, animation and sound, to help students to visualize and understand certain context or idea with different aspects. For example, traditionally, a medical student needs to mentally process and correlate lots of MRI images to "visualize" possible defects of a patient's internal organ. However, since techniques for constructing 3D graphics models from the MRI images [2] have been available, the learning processing of the medical student could then be speeded up significantly, as they are now be able to visualize and understand medical problems in a straight forward way. Moreover, by adopting web-based learning, students are facilitated to learn actively, since instead of passively perceiving information of the education materials, students are allowed to experience those materials in depth through some simulated environments.

W. Liu et al. (Eds.): ICWL 2004, LNCS 3143, pp. 75–82, 2004.
© Springer-Verlag Berlin Heidelberg 2004

Although 3D enriched web-based learning systems could offer many advantages, as education materials of such systems are likely large in data size, it poses significant content distribution problem. For example, we consider a virtual urban simulation system, which is designed for students to study urban development. There are many geometry models, including models of buildings, cars and people ... etc, for students to download for starting the simulation. Downloading such materials through the Internet can be very time consuming even for students equipped with broadband network connections. More seriously, in most developing countries, where there may be a large population of potential users of web-based learning systems, the majority, however, may still be using 56K modems for connecting to the Internet. Such users are therefore likely hesitated to make use of such learning systems. To facilitate the keen requirement of 3D enriched web-based learning systems, we present a progressive content distribution framework. The framework is based on a client-server architecture, in which the contents of a courseware are distributed from the server to each individual users in an incremental and a need-to-know manner. Although techniques developed in a number of distributed virtual environment (DVE) systems [3–5] also support similar feature, their approaches usually pose to download excessive information to users, which may cause unnecessary long delays to users with slow network connections.

In this paper, we present a content delivery scheme to allow system content to be delivered in different priority according to their importance. In addition, we allow a system to adjust the amount of information to be sent according to the network connection of individual client. The rest of this paper is organized as follows. Section 2 provides a survey on the related work. Section 3 presents the overview of the progressive content distribution framework. Section 4 and 5 present our method for prioritized content and progressive content object delivery, respectively. Section 6 shows our prototype web-based learning platforms and experimental results of our method. Finally, section 7 concludes the work presented in this paper.

2   Related Work

We note that researchers working in *distributed virtual environments* (DVE) are facing similar research problems. They have proposed different approaches [6, 7, 3, 4] for distributing system objects of a virtual environment (VE) to their users. Broadly speaking, such approaches can be classified into *region-based* and *interest-based*.

Systems including DIVE [6] and CALVIN[7], have adopted the region-based approach. They divide a whole VE into a number of pre-defined regions. In particular, a user could work in such system by connecting to a selected region, the system would then require the user to download full content inside the connected region before the user could start to work in the system. However, as the content of a region may be very large in data size, such approach may pose a long download time problem to users. A consequence of this is that, whenever a user switches to other regions, the undesirable long downloading process would then happen again.

In contrast, systems adopting the interest-based approach [3, 8] would dynamically determine the current interest of a user and distribute the relevant content to the user accordingly. Systems adopted this approach include NPSNET [3], MASSIVE [4] and NetEffect [5]. Although such approach generally reduces the content download time significantly, it is still not a complete solution. For instance, as individual system object is needed to download as a whole, certain large system objects, such as the 3D MRI models as discussed, may still occupy the available network bandwidth for a considerable period of time during their transmissions. This would cause jittering experience to the system users.

3   Progressive Content Distribution Framework

The proposed framework adopts the client-server architecture to support progressive content transmission. The server may be a single or a group of machines [9] to manage contents of the web-based learning system. It handles requests from users for content retrieval. In particular, it determines and schedules the required system contents with optimal details to transmit to the users. Figure 1 shows the architecture of our framework.

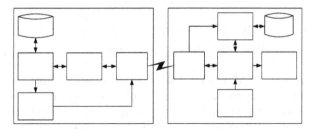

Fig. 1. The architecture of the proposed framework.

In summary, the server module contains 5 components. The *Server Manager* coordinates all components at the server. It processes requests from users and delivers relevant information to them via the network agent. The *Model Manager* determines the required system contents and their appropriate details for transmission to the system users. The *Model Database* stores the complete system content. All the object models of the system content converted beforehand into transmission-ready format and are retrieved by the model manager for transmission. The *Content Delivery Manager* arranges selected system contents in appropriate priorities for delivery. Finally, the *Network Agent* handles all communications among the users and the server, including system content delivery, user status and updates.

The client module represents the client machine of a user, it contains 6 components. The *Client Manager* coordinates all components at the client machine of a user. It processes both updates from the server and user requests. The *Model Manager* maintains the system content received from the server for local display and performs cache management to maximize the content availability at the local storage. The *Local Storage* is the accessible storage space at the user for the model manager to maintain the content received from the server. The *Action Manager* reads commands from the users and converts them into appropriate requests to the server. The *Graphics and Sound Engines* are responsible for rendering visual output and generating the audio in a time critical manner. Finally, the *Network Agent* handles all communications with the server, including receiving system contents and updates from the server. It also sends updates and requests of the user to the server.

4   Prioritized Content Delivery

To perform content delivery, the server selects required system contents from the system database and determines their priority and quality for delivery to users, based on their requirements, such as Area-of-Interest. However, due to network latency, when these objects are received by the user, it may already be too late for them to be useful. To resolve such a problem, we have developed a prioritized content delivery method. Figure 2 expresses the conceptual view of the interest of a user on certain system contents in the system. The white wedge i.e., $Q1$, collects the current interested contents of the user, while $Q2a \bigcup Q2b \bigcup Q3$ collects the potentially interested contents of the user. $Q3$ collects the least interested contents of the user. For content delivery, three queues, $Q1$, $Q2$ and $Q3$ are setup for each user, where $Q2 = Q2a \bigcup Q2b$. The priorities of the three queues for transmission are: $Q1 > Q2 > Q3$. Objects placed in a lower priority queue may be considered for delivery to the user only if all higher priority queues are empty. Within a queue, we further prioritize the system contents by certain visualization importance parameters. For instance, we may sort the system contents by their angular distances from the user's viewing vector, and then by their distances from the player.

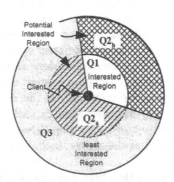

Fig. 2. Visible and potential visible regions.

5   Progressive Content Object Delivery

The prioritized content delivery scheme helps the server efficiently identify the appropriate system contents to deliver to the users. However, as the geometry data of individual 3D content object of the education materials may still be large in size, sending it as a whole may occupy the network bandwidth of the user connection for a significant period of time. This problem may seriously affect the interactivity of the user to the system because some other content objects that are waiting to be sent may not arrive in time for visualization. To address this, we organize the data structure of such kind of content objects into a format to support progressive transmission, i.e., they are arranged to send in parts, and the partially received information may be incrementally refined to improve their qualities at the user during visualization.

In particular, individual 3D content object U is encoded as *progressive meshes* [10], which may be represented as a tuple of a *base record* U^0 and an ordered list P of *progressive records* $\{p_1, p_2, \ldots, p_{|P|}\}$. The base record U^0 contains the minimal and most critical information for a content object U to be visualize at the client. By applying each progressive record p_n, for $1 \leq n \leq |P|$, one by one onto U^0 using the function $\Omega(u, p)$, a series of approximated representations of U, $\{U^0, U^1, U^2, \ldots, U^{|U|}\}$, are obtained, where $U^n = \Omega(U^{n-1}, p_n)$. Each U^n in the series improves the quality or the detail of U^{n-1} with a finite amount and the final $U^{|P|}$ in the series is implicitly equivalent to U, i.e., $U = U^{|P|}$. When transmitting a U to a user, we first transmit the base record U^0. Such record may alert the user for the existence of that content object. Whenever it is necessary, the subsequent progressive records may be transmitted progressively to the user to enhance the visual quality or detail of the object.

6   Results and Discussions

6.1   Prototype Web-Based Learning Platforms

We have implemented the proposed framework in C++. Based on this framework, we have also developed two prototype web-based learning platforms to demonstrate our work. The first one is a city walkthrough system as shown in figure 3. It allows users to study the urban development of a city. It is particularly useful for students to understand and visualize the process of urban planning and design. In such a system, the number of objects, such buildings, roads and trees, is likely very large. This is especially true for systems simulating a well developed city. Our content delivery scheme would help a user to visualize a city with a short startup time. In particular, at the beginning of navigation, only visible objects are first transmitted to the user based on his/her initial navigation position. The other contents of the city would then be progressively sent to the user according to his/her navigation path.

The second prototype web-based learning platform is the *Moai* study system as shown in figure 4, where Moaiare are the famous huge stone carved figures standing on the Easter Island. We build a virtual island and place Moaiare on

(a)   (b)

Fig. 3. Screen shots of our urban walkthrough system.

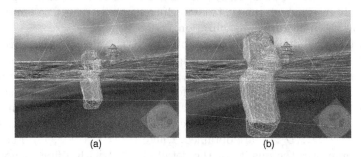

(a)   (b)

Fig. 4. Screen shots of our *Moai* study system.

it, for students to study and visualize Moaiare. Figure 4(a) shows a Moai in a low level of details when a user is located at a considerable distance from it. Figure 4(b) shows the Moai when the user moves near to it. At this moment, more details of the Moai are progressively transmitted to the user and the Moai is then refined to provide more details for visualization. This learning platform is a kind of virtual museum application. However, instead of placing the sculptures (in our case, *Moaiare*) in glass cupboards as in real museums, we could put the sculptures in a virtual environment, which simulates the place where the sculptures are originally located. Such arrangement would allow students to study actively, in which they may *experience* the materials along with their correspondences, such as located environment, culture and history. Such a system obviously offers much advantages over the passive exhibition approach as adopted by the real museums. Of course, the reason for real museums not to build associated environment for each historical sculpture is that, they are most likely lacking of physical space. The web-based learning system is just a good fit solution to this problem.

6.2   Experiment on Content Delivery

In this experiment, we test the efficiency of our content delivery method. During the experiment, a user navigated in a virtual environment of a web-based learning system with a circular path, and the user looked around freely to visualize interested content objects during the navigation. There were about 150 visible content objects located around the user's navigation path. They are all in compressed format with an average size of 124KBytes. We define the *perceived visual quality* as the percentage of the required model data received by the user in terms of the data size. We compare the perceived visual quality by the user during the navigation using different model transmission methods: Method **A** is the full implementation of our content transmission method, Method **B** is our method but without progressive content object transmission, Method **C** is the progressive content object transmission method but without prioritized content delivery, and Method **D** only transmits the base record of each model to the user.

We performed the experiment with a 1.5Mbps broadband connection. (However, only 60% of the bandwidth was available for the experiment. The rest was used by the test program for collecting the statistics.) The result of the experiment is shown in figure 5. For methods with progressive content object trans-

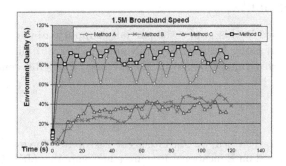

Fig. 5. Performance of various content delivery methods.

mission, i.e., methods **A** and **C**, the server would transmit the current visible content objects to the user up to their optimal qualities. Hence, a user is said to perceive a 100% visual quality if the user receives all such objects in their optimal qualities. For methods without progressive transmission, i.e., method **B**, a user could visualize a content object only if the complete object model is received by the user. Hence, the user could perceive a 100% visual quality only if all current visible objects are completely transmitted to the user. From figure 5, we observe that our method (method **A**) offers a significant superior perceived visual quality to the users then those of the other methods on both network conditions. When compared to method **C**, our method could provide 20% to 70% higher perceived visual quality. When compared to method **B**, our method may even provide 80% higher perceived visual quality occasionally. As a control, we performed an addition test by forcing the server to transmit only the base records of the objects requested (method **D**). Here, a user is said to be satisfied with a visible content object only if the minimal displayable information of such object is completely transmitted to the user. In other words, a user would perceive a 100% visual quality of a visible content object if the base record of the object is completely transmitted to the user. The quality difference between our method (method **A**) and method **D** indicates room for system designer to perform further tuning on the value of optimal perceived visual quality of visible content objects to the users. This provides flexibility for systems fit the limited resources condition of general users.

7 Conclusion

In this paper, we have proposed a progressive content distribution framework to support web-based learning through on-demand transmission of 3D content. We have also presented two prototype web-based learning platforms that we are developing. Our experiment results demonstrate that our method offers a very efficient content distribution performance in supporting 3D enriched web-based learning systems.

Acknowledgments

The work described in this paper was partially supported by a SRG grant from City University of Hong Kong (Project Number: 7001285) and a CERG grant from the Research Grants Council of Hong Kong (RGC Reference No.: CityU 1080/00E).

References

1. Shang, Y., Shi, H., Chen, S.: An Intelligent Distributed Environment for Active Learning. Journal on Educational Resources in Computing (JERIC) **1** (2001) 4
2. Lorensen, W., Cline, H.: Marching Cubes: A High Resolution 3D Surface Construction Algorithm. In: Proceedings of ACM SIGGRAPH '87, ACM Press (1987) 163–169
3. Falby, J., Zyda, M., Pratt, D., Mackey, R.: NPSNET: Hierarchical Data Structures for Real-Time Three-Dimensional Visual Simulation. Computers & Graphics **17** (1993) 65–69
4. Greenhalgh, C., Benford, S.: A Multicast Network Architecture for Large Scale Collaborative Virtual Environments. In: Proc. ECMAST'97. (1997) 113–128
5. Das, T., Singh, G., Mitchell, A., Kumar, P., McGhee, K.: NetEffect: A Network Architecture for Large-scale Multi-user Virtual World. In: Proc. ACM VRST. (1997) 157–163
6. Hagsand, O.: Interactive Multiuser VEs in the DIVE System. IEEE Multimedia **3** (1996) 30–39
7. Leigh, J., Johnson, A., Vasilakis, C., DeFanti, T.: Multi-perspective Collaborative Design in Persistent Networked Virtual Environments. In: Proc. IEEE VRAIS. (1996) 253–260
8. Chim, J., Green, M., Lau, R., Leong, H., Si, A.: On Caching and Prefetching of Virtual Objects in Distributed Virtual Environments. In: Proc. ACM Multimedia. (1998) 171–180
9. Ng, B., Si, A., Lau, R., Li, F.: A Multi-Server Architecture for Distributed Virtual Walkthrough. In: Proc. ACM VRST. (2002) 163–170
10. Hoppe, H.: Progressive Meshes. In: Proc. ACM SIGGRAPH '96. (1996) 99–108

Technologies to Support Collaborative Learning over the Multimedia Home Platform

Martín López-Nores, Yolanda Blanco-Fernández, Ana Fernández-Vilas,
Rebeca P. Díaz-Redondo, José J. Pazos-Arias, Alberto Gil-Solla,
Jorge García-Duque, Belén Barragáns-Martínez, and Manuel Ramos-Cabrer

Department of Telematic Engineering, University of Vigo, 36200, Spain
{mlnores,yolanda,avilas,rebeca,jose,agil,jgd,belen,mramos}@det.uvigo.es

Abstract. T-learning – the provision of educational services over Interactive Digital TV – is regarded as a complement to e-learning solutions, whose scope is limited due to the *digital divide*. The increasing connectivity, together with the fact that IDTV users are no longer passive spectators, permits to start thinking on highly interactive services that support fluid communication among users and service providers. This may enhance the prospects of learning at home, as long as the current offer is mostly based on broadcast content, with scarce use of return channels for feedback. This paper proposes an extension to the Multimedia Home Platform standard, aimed at providing better support for collaborative learning services. We describe an architecture for such services and a selection of freely available technologies for their implementation. We also discuss the possible market implications of our approach, as the ideas presented here contribute to openness in the field of IDTV services.

Keywords: Interactive Digital TV, t-learning, peer-to-peer architectures.

1 Introduction

In recent years, there has been growing interest for distance education systems, in order to overcome the main lacks of traditional learning. This has led to a significant development of Web-based learning initiatives (*e-learning*) [1]. But the increasing use of the Internet has revealed some shortages, related to difficulties in the use of computers for some social sectors, limited penetration of computers in homes and uneven presence of broadband infrastructure, among others. Thus, some initiatives are being taken to port educational services to other mediums than personal computers. These are *t-learning*, supported by Interactive Digital TV (IDTV), and *m-learning*, based on the use of modern mobile devices [10].

Progress is being done towards convergence of these mediums, by promoting interoperability of applications and contents, adaptation to different devices and integration of heterogeneous networks [4]. So, it is not a question of the computer taking over the television or vice versa: it is a question of how the different services and models converge, increasing value to the consumer [8]. This will set

W. Liu et al. (Eds.): ICWL 2004, LNCS 3143, pp. 83–90, 2004.

the foundations for continuous and ubiquitous learning, even though the users' habits and expectancies vary greatly for each particular medium. As a result, the situation today suggests that different solutions should be crafted to adapt the characteristics of each medium, while keeping the goal of convergence in mind.

Our working group has been involved with IDTV architectures and services for several years. Recently, we presented an approach to developing educational applications, that addressed the specifics of broadcast services [7]. According to pjb Associates [11], such services play a significant role at the initial stage of t-learning in which we are today. However, it is commonly agreed that the pedagogical value of t-learning will be greatly enhanced by supporting higher levels of interaction among users and service providers.

The goal of this paper is to anticipate the needs of the future range of services, introducing a framework for the development and deployment of distributed educational services. Our work is based on the *Multimedia Home Platform* (MHP) standard [5], which is the most important normalization initiative in the IDTV field nowadays. In its current version, the mechanisms offered to handle the return channel are still rather simplistic, only adequate by themselves for limited feedback from single users. In response to this, we propose an extension to the standard that improves its support for *real interactivity* and *collaborative work*.

In the following section, we comment past and future trends of t-learning, pointing out its most important peculiarities. Section 3 presents our architecture for distributed t-learning services, with Sect. 4 describing the technologies we consider most adequate for its implementation and some additional details. Finally, in Sect. 5, we discuss the relevance of our work regarding learning and business opportunities, and also suggest future lines of work.

2   t-Learning Experiences and Promises

As a learning platform, IDTV is considered a key to reach the widest audiences, for there is at least one television in nearly every household, while the average penetration of personal computers is not expected to go beyond 70% in the short term (see [10]). Moreover, IDTV is easy to use and well known for everybody, meeting the socially important need to offer online learning services to people who cannot afford to buy a computer, do not have Internet access or lack the knowledge to use such technologies. This is remarkable in the background of a global economy, where access to knowledge is regarded as the best way to maintain a region's competitiveness. As a result, t-learning is getting the attention of governments interested in developing nationwide distance education plans [11].

In the migration from analogical to digital TV, it was soon envisaged that t-learning could help fulfill the emptiness in the set of applications that TV users are willing to pay for (see [10]). So, broadcasters started to provide simple, pioneering services as a complement to their channel offerings [2]. At this initial stage, educational services have been mostly based on broadcast contents (one-way communication, with little use of feedback mechanisms), providing means for *simulated interactivity*, i.e., interaction only with elements available in the broadcast streams. The emphasis was placed on informal learning through *edu-tainment* (*education and entertainment*), coherent with the consideration of TV as a medium for entertainment and the passive habits of the users.

The importance of broadcast services is stressed by the fact that their interactive features are driving users towards *more active profiles* in the use of TV, not being passive spectators anymore. This, together with the increasing availability of high-quality bidirectional networks, makes it possible to start thinking on highly interactive services, based on the profuse exploitation of return channels.

The increased interactivity (referred to as *real interactivity*) brings up opportunities for more engaged learning. By allowing users to actively interact with others, it contributes to mitigate the feeling of *isolation* that is typical in distance education. Moreover, it sets the basis for new ways of *collaborative learning*, promoting the creation of *virtual learning communities* [3] that gather together people with common interests and learning needs. As argued in [11], this is more likely to widen participation in learning than just focusing on the interactive offerings through broadcast-based services.

The Peculiarities of t-Learning. The extensive research done in the e-learning field since the mid 1990s gives some useful theoretical insight for t-learning [8], as well as powerful standards for content management and student monitoring (like SCORM or IMS), which are also applicable to t-learning. Despite, there is unavoidable work needed to accommodate the peculiarities of the IDTV environment [6], that range from the limited resources available at the receivers (set-top boxes) to the complexities of the information distribution mechanisms.

Another major issue is that, while e-learning courses have text and graphics as a central axis, t-learning ones should be naturally based on audio and video. This demands great interrelation capabilities between contents and a temporal reference, and suggests a distinction between *user-driven* and *media-driven* strategies for interactivity [7]. In user-driven strategies, applications respond to the users' actions; in media-driven ones, the evolution of a piece of media controls the flow of applications, so that users take part in a reduced number of decisions. Which approach is most suitable for a given service depends on the role that users are expected to play: user-driven strategies are recommended for active roles, and media-driven strategies for more passive ones. Particularly, media-driven strategies are the best option for edutainment.

3   A Scheme for Distributed t-Learning Services

The work we presented in [7] addresses the needs of broadcast-based t-learning services, offering mechanisms to efficiently exploit simulated interactivity. The extension to real interactivity and collaborative learning that we propose here demands additional solutions: services are conceived as distributed ones and, as commented in Sect. 2, mechanisms are needed to control the way users interact and self-organize into virtual learning communities. This also requires means to differentiate *roles* among users, group management capabilities, etc.

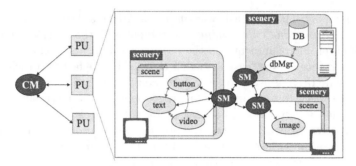

Fig. 1. The structure of a course and the internals of a pedagogical unit

We have devised a simple and flexible structure for educational services (referred to as *courses*). A course is a set of *pedagogical units* (PUs), which define most of the service's logic. PUs are the primary level for contents organization, and they can be arbitrarily complex, containing any kind of elements (media clips, user interface widgets, etc.). As illustrated in Fig. 1, those elements can be laid out in multiple *sceneries* and *scenes*, and several types of interrelations can be established among them. The sceneries determine how the logic of a PU is distributed among a number of different machines – those of users and service providers (*spatial organization*). On the other hand, scenes provide for the *temporal organization* of activities (including content presentation).

Scenes were already introduced in [7], but sceneries are a specific need of distributed courses. Besides supporting distribution, they provide for the definition of *roles* among users. For example, in a remote lecturing service, the lecturer and his audience run different sceneries, so that only the lecturer is given elements to control the sequencing of the slides. In a given PU, there exist as many types of agents as sceneries have been defined, and how an user is assigned a given role is service-dependent: it may be decided by the user himself, by other users, etc.

The composition of a course defines the ordering of its PUs and the *conditional access* dependencies among them. These dependencies can be used, for example, to reject access to one PU until some knowledge has been proved on the preceding ones. At any moment, a PU can be *locked* (access forbidden) or *unlocked* (access granted), and this state can be changed in response to events of any kind. Conditional access is controlled by an entity called the *Course Manager* (CM in Fig. 1). Actually, because of distribution, the CM is not an unique entity, but a replicated object running on every machine inside a virtual community where the course is active. This makes it possible for access conditions to be evaluated for every single user, for all the members of a community as a whole, for those who form a given subgroup in the community, etc.

Every scenery runs a *Scenery Manager* (SM in Fig. 1), which centralizes communication with the CM and other machines. It is also in charge of sequencing the scenes, and controls the synchronization of multiple pieces of information. For this task, we intentionally avoid standards for multimedia synchronization available to Web services, like SMIL, because they are too resource-demanding for set-top boxes and do not fit well within MHP. The alternative we presented in [7] solved the coordination of multiple informational sources within a single set-top box; for the new distributed environment, we have extended it to support synchronization among different sceneries. In the remote lecturing example, this permits all the members of the audience to follow the explanations of the lecturer as he browses a slide show, by automatically keeping their screens up-to-date.

4   Technological Details

This section details the technological framework we propose to support the architecture presented in Sect. 3, with the foundations of the MHP standard.

MHP defines two application models: DVB-HTML, based on Internet technologies, and DVB-J, based on the Java language. As argued in [7, 9], DVB-J has several advantages, because it is more flexible, extensible and suited for the limited resources of a set-top box. Thus, we chose DVB-J for our implementation, and completed the framework with several freely available technologies that fit well within it: XML, JavaBeans and JXTA.

We use XML for many different purposes, such as to communicate with IMS databases and content repositories, to define the message types needed for an application, and to express all those entities with a predefined structure, like the composition of a course in terms of its PUs. On another hand, we resort to JavaBeans as the simplest way to construct applications, because it defines an architecture of components (*beans*) that greatly facilitates development. This can be done in an entirely visual way, provided that a sufficiently rich set of beans is available, together with a suitable environment for their composition.

Both XML and JavaBeans were introduced in the context of broadcast-based t-learning services in [7], and their use is slightly enhanced for distributed ones. But the leading role in the extension presented here is played by JXTA, an open-source initiative aimed at providing a thin layer on top of which peer-to-peer (P2P) applications and services can be built. This technology fulfills the needs of the sceneries approach for distributed logic commented in Sect. 3.

4.1   JXTA Virtual Networks as Virtual Communities

P2P technologies are suitable for the purposes of collaborative t-learning, because they promote *decentralization*, in a way that end users and devices are given much more relevance than in classical client-server architectures. In this regard, JXTA defines a set of protocols that make it possible to establish *virtual networks* on top of Internet and non-IP networks. This technology is network and language-independent, and can be used on a wide range of devices (including PersonalJava-compliant ones, such as MHP set-top boxes).

In our approach, a virtual network maps directly to a virtual learning community, with all the agents in it being treated as peers (Fig. 2). The ways peers discover each other, self-organize into virtual communities, find resources and communicate, etc. are all part of JXTA technology.

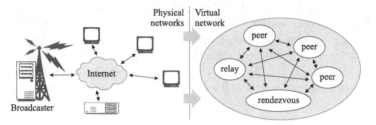

Fig. 2. Mapping physical networks into a virtual one

All the entities in a JXTA virtual network (communities, services...) are published by means of *advertisements*, which are XML descriptors following a given syntax. The mechanism used for discovery is based on *rendezvous super-peers*, i.e., peers in well-known locations designed to cache advertisements. Due to the limited computing power of set-top boxes, we propose to use service providers' computers as rendezvous nodes (Fig. 2), making them also responsible for complex tasks such as group management and searching in the virtual network.

JXTA defines a second type of super-peers – *relays* – to deal with heterogeneous networks and protocols, allowing applications to exchange messages with no concern about the networks they traverse. We exploit this idea to introduce *broadcast relays*, which provide for the combined use of broadcast and IP networks for communication inside a virtual community. Broadcasting is a natural option for information flows that should be served to all the members of a community, as it happens with the explanations of the speaker in the remote lecturing example. This benefits from the robustness and high quality of service of broadcast networks, and avoids squandering Internet bandwidth. By the way, remark that most of the current set-top boxes (including MHP ones) do not support audio or video streaming through the return channel, so any audiovisual content generated by an user should always be sent to a broadcast relay for others to access it. The broadcast relay forwards the messages it receives onto the broadcast networks, addressed to the corresponding virtual community.

JXTA over MHP. As specified in [5], broadcast in MHP is based on MPEG-2 transport streams, and the return channel is mostly operated by means of the TCP/IP suite of protocols. Following the ideas above, we have implemented a JXTA communications layer to make transparent use of broadcast networks and return channels (see Fig. 3, where the gray arrows only exist in broadcast relays).

Regarding the return channel, our communications layer uses the TCP and UDP protocols. As for broadcast, it uses MPEG-2 sections for streaming audio and video content, object carousels for files, and UDP over Multiprotocol Encapsulation for messages due to bindings between elements in different sceneries (remember Section 3). Thus, all the messages exchanged among peers are subject to being broadcast – especially when they are targeted to many others –, taking advantage of the inherent capabilities of broadcast networks for multicas-

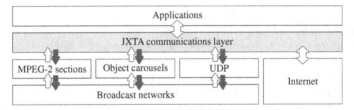

Fig. 3. Our JXTA communication layer

ting. Which mechanism to use is decided considering developers' guidelines and traffic conditions, in order to use the available networks the best possible way.

4.2   Integration in a Development Environment

We have integrated the technologies commented in the preceding sections, coming up with a CASE tool for the development of distributed t-learning services. This is actually an extension of the tool we presented in [7] as the first environment specific for t-learning services. The new version implements the sceneries approach, and provides several new wizards to cope with the needs of distributed services. One such wizard is used to define scripts to dynamically access databases and content repositories. Another one allows defining *interaction patterns* among the peers in a virtual community, taking into account the diverse roles they may take up. It is particularly easy to state that some users can see the effect of actions done by others, or that a particular action can only take place if all the users with a given role agree on it.

5   Discussion and Future Work

In this paper, we have presented an architecture for distributed IDTV services, and a selection of free technologies suitable for its implementation. This comes as an extension to the return channel mechanisms of the MHP standard. Our proposal is based on peer-to-peer technologies, as they natively provide for the establishment of virtual communities of people with shared interests. We also discussed the convenience of establishing a virtual network on top of the physical ones, where the use of broadcast networks for multicast inside a community is a very interesting feature, particularly when dealing with multimedia content.

The introduction of P2P technologies may have a significant impact on the IDTV business models. T-learning initiatives have been so far controlled by mainstream broadcasters, keeping the educative community apart. Because P2P promotes decentralization in networks and services, our approach contributes to *openness in the educational market*, leaving place for private enterprises, and even individual users, to offer learning services (advertising them is just part of the P2P framework). This opens several new ways for broadcasters to make business: hiring their broadcast networks to provide high-quality streaming of multimedia content; hiring computational power and storage capacity for complex computations and large databases; or giving access to content repositories that store numerous selected pieces of learning or audiovisual material.

Our future work will deal with *personalization* and *convergence*. Personalization is a need in order to handle the increasing amount of information available, and also to target services and products to users who may be interested in them. In this regard, the TV-Anytime Forum is working on solutions for the definition of user profiles and mechanisms for the markup, storage and retrieval of multimedia content. On the other hand, the desired convergence of IDTV with other mediums requires further advances in interoperability of software and content. The most relevant roles here will surely be played by the Java language, XML and the MPEG-4 standard. Particularly, MPEG-4 is called to revolutionize the creation, distribution and use of multimedia content. Its foreseeable inclusion in MHP set-top boxes will cause some changes in the way of doing things, extending the focus in development to *media authoring tools*. However, frameworks like ours will still be needed, for example, to deal with distribution, content management, the definition of roles among users, and any other additional logic.

References

1. Alexander, S. E-Learning Developments and Experiences. *Education and Training*, 43:240–248, 2001.
2. Atwere, D. et al. *Interactive TV: a Learning Platform with Potential.* Learning and Skills Development Agency, available at
   http://www.lsda.org.uk/files/pdf/1443.pdf, 2003.
3. Caro, J. et al. E-learning and Virtual Communities. In *Proceedings of the Philippines Computing Science Congress*, 2000.
4. Chiariglione, L. Standardisation in a World of Converging Technologies: the Audio-Visual Case. Audiovisuel et autoroutes, Rennes, France, June 1996.
5. Digital Video Broadcasting Consortium. The Multimedia Home Platform Standard. http://www.mhp.org, 2001.
6. Gil-Solla, A. et al. Exploring T-learning in the MHP Context. In *Proceedings of the IADIS International Conference WWW/Internet*, Lisbon, Portugal, 2002.
7. López-Nores, M. et al. A Mixed XML-JavaBeans Approach to Developing T-learning Applications for the Multimedia Home Platform. In *Proceedings of MIPS 2003*, Naples, Italy, November 2003.
8. Lytras, M. et al. Interactive Television and E-learning Convergence: Examining the Potential of T-learning. In *Proceedings of ECEL 2002*, Brunel, UK, 2002.
9. Morris, S. et al. The MHP Tutorial. http://www.mhp-interactive.org.
10. pjb Associates. Development of Satellite and Terrestrial Digital Broadcasting Systems and Services and Implications for Education and Training. http://www.pjb.co.uk, 1999.
11. pjb Associates. A Study into TV-based Interactive Learning to the Home. http://www.pjb.co.uk/t-learning, 2003.

Proposal for KML Designer
with Web-Based Environment

Chia-Hung Chen[1], Jun-Sing Jwo[1], and Chih-Chi Wang[1]

[1] Department of Computer Science and Information Engineering
Tunghai University
Taichung, Taiwan
G912835@student.thu.edu.tw, jwo@mail.thu.edu.tw

Abstract. Web-based learning has been a major topic of increasing interest for education and business training. The unlimited resources on the Internet are linked as hypertext. However, for learning purpose a knowledge-based modeling of the learning materials is the key to success. KML is the vehicle for modeling the knowledge of the learning material. Using KML on top of web-based learning, it makes users easy to understand the learning strategy without too much external support. KML provides solution to help a user model and reuse his/her learning as a visualized knowledge map.

Keywords: KML, SCORM, e-Learning, knowledge management, visualized knowledge-based

1 Introduction

With the emerging of new technology, *e-Learning* has gradually improved the accessibility, timeliness, and quick distribution when comparing with traditional training techniques. Accessibility provides a learning environment which users can learn anytime, anywhere. Timeliness saves a lot of time to learn. Quick distribution allows users to find the solution in short terms. In addition, with e-Learning, repeated training saves a lot of resources because users can access the teaching materials repeatedly without wasting more human source.

Recently, using information and telecommunication technologies to support synchronous and/or asynchronous e-Learning is an important issue to study. The educational use of computer and Internet has evolved from numerical calculation, spreadsheets, word processor, and information searching to multimedia and web-based applications [2]. In fact, web has become one of the most promising technologies to implement e-Learning. In the past, industrial and educational parties used tapes, VHS, and floppy disks to pass out their knowledge. However, with Internet, comparing with the above media, using web-based technology becomes much easier and more economic.

Learning includes all kinds of information and materials, and somehow some of them are related to each other. For web-based e-learning, these contents are transferred into different types of multimedia documents that can be published on the web. These multimedia documents are linked in hypertext structure. However, for learning purpose, a *visualized knowledge-based* representation of the learning materials is the

W. Liu et al. (Eds.): ICWL 2004, LNCS 3143, pp. 91–97, 2004.
© Springer-Verlag Berlin Heidelberg 2004

key for successful e-learning. In this paper, we use *KML* (*Knowledge Modeling Language*) [4] to model the e-learning contents. KML is a fully visualized modeling language that can represent all kinds of knowledge KML is not only good for *knowledge management*, but also is good for organizing various learning contents. By using KML, users can easily reuse the learning resources without too much external support. In this paper, as an example, we show how to utilize KML to build a Java e-learning map by following SCORM's standard [3].

2 Backgrounds

Applying visualized modeling language to design computer software is one of the major trends for modern software development. Among the visualized modeling technologies, *UML* (*Unified Modeling Language*) is the de-facto one []. UML is quite useful for modeling software systems, but it is hardly to model human knowledge. On the other hand, KML (Knowledge Modeling Language) is the visualized language for modeling the knowledge similar to the one stored in our brain. By using KML, people can easily represent and manage their knowledge.

The building blocks of KML include *knowledge objects*, *relationships* and *diagrams* [5]. There are four types of knowledge objects as shown in Figure 1. They are *topic*, *case*, *content* and *decision*. Topic represents the abstraction of the knowledge and it is denoted as a circle. Case represents a special example that can be treated as the knowledge not yet analyzed and it is in ellipse shape. Content represents the information or resource that related to some knowledge and it is denoted as rounded rectangle. Decision represents the judgment between the knowledge objects and it is in diamond shape.

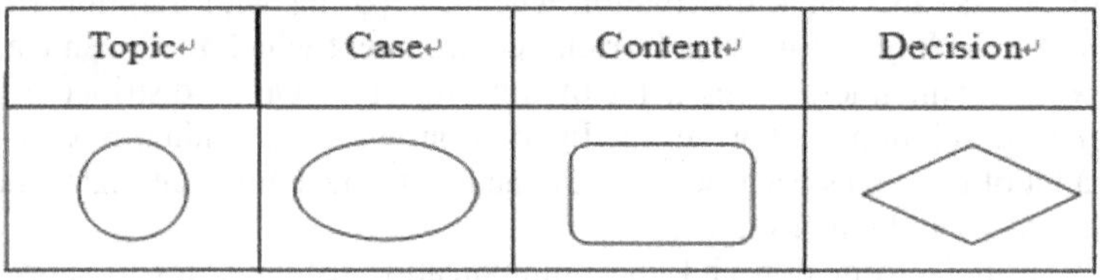

Topic	Case	Content	Decision
◯	⬭	▢	◇

Fig. 1. Types of knowledge objects.

Knowledge objects can have a set of attribute components to further decorate the objects. As given in Figure 2, they are:

1. *State*: there are two different states, namely, *permanent* and *transient*. Permanent state means an unchangeable object; transient state means the state of the object is changeable. They are represented as solid boundary and non-boundary, respectively. It is also possible to add special meaning to a knowledge object by setting its color or changing its size.
2. *Knowledge*: for each knowledge object, knowledge attributes can be added. *Comment* is used to append more information to the knowledge object. For those related multimedia documents, they can be put into the *attachment* attribute. Furthermore, highlight and time stamp also are part of the knowledge attributes.

State	permanent	transient
Knowledge	comment	attachment

Fig. 2. Attribute components for knowledge object.

Relationship in KML is used to build the relationship among knowledge objects. There are ten different relationships in KML. They are *association, generalization, dependency, aggregation, constitution, classification, reference, sequence, extension,* and *interpretation* [5]. Figure 3 has shown four of them which are frequently used for building e-learning map.

In KML, diagram represents the usage of the language. There are two different diagrams that can be used for e-learning. They are *structure* diagram and *activity* diagram. Structure diagram mainly is used to organize knowledge fragments and to show the whole picture of the knowledge. It includes association, generalization, dependency, aggregation, constitution, classification and reference relationships. Activity diagram is to record the knowledge about procedure or operation flow. It includes sequence, synchronization and interpretation relationships.

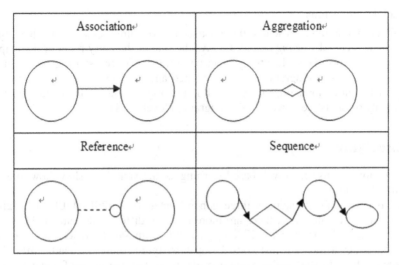

Fig. 3. Four frequent used relationships in e-Learning.

3   KML in e-Learning

By using KML and SCORM's standard, we can model e-learning materials as KML diagrams. These diagrams can further be reused through the web. However, In order to build a good model for e-learning, some of the guidelines should be followed. First of all, *naming* the knowledge objects is very important since names are the knowledge that users will retrieve at the very beginning. Secondly, the *readability* of the knowledge map will affect the learning effect. A very simple map can easily show the whole idea of the knowledge. However, its readability is too simple to show enough knowledge. A very complicated knowledge map can provide better contents. However, its readability is too complicated to see the whole picture. Another issue related to modeling knowledge is the *scope* for each knowledge object. A scope of an object is the contents stored in its attachment. With more contents stored in the attachment, the map becomes simpler and with fewer contents the map becomes more complicated.

The following steps are the process for using KML to build and maintain KML diagrams.

1. Initial modeling:
    A. List out all of the possible knowledge objects that are related to the learning topics. Build the relationships among these objects.
    B. From user's point of view, reconsider the knowledge objects and their relationships. Try to put them into some order in the diagram. After this step, an initial diagram is built.
    C. If a knowledge object aggregates many cases or contents and it makes the diagram complicated, we can put these objects into the attachment. By doing this, the case and content objects should have no effect on the main structure of the diagram.

2. Model decomposition:
    A. In each diagram, basically there exists a most important knowledge object which is called *starting object*. It plays the role of the entry point of the map. If there are too many objects that can be correlated to the starting object in the diagram, a new diagram should be created and this new diagram becomes the attachment of some object that is still in the original map. The diagram in level-n only presents the objects in the diagram in level-(n+1).

4   Case Study

In this section, we use Java web-based learning as an example to show how to apply KML to e-learning.

For Java learning, it includes three general categories: J2SE, J2EE, and J2ME. Under these three categories, there are more than ten different domains [11]. Using J2SE as an example, as shown in Figure 4 which is from *Sun*®, the learning materials and contents are a lot. By just considering this figure, users are really difficult to understand where to start with. Figures 5 and 6 are the examples of using KML to model the maps for Java e-learning. Figure 5 shows the relationship among Java's three major categories. Figure 6 is the learning map for J2SE. Since J2SE contains a lot of contents, we use model decomposition rule to simplify the map. In this map, it shows the sequence between Java syntax, swing, AWT, networking, and I/O are considered as the advanced topics when learning Java technology. With this modeling, we can improve the readability of the map. In fact, we can further set color and change size to emphasize the objects and the relationships in the map.

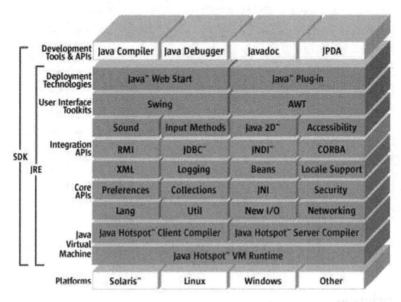

Fig. 4. Java 2 Platform, Standard Edition v1.4 from *Sun*®.

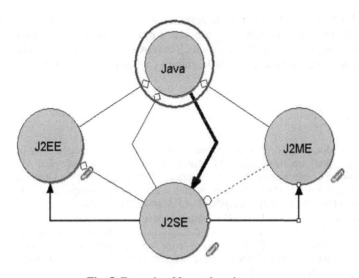

Fig. 5. Example of Java e-learning map.

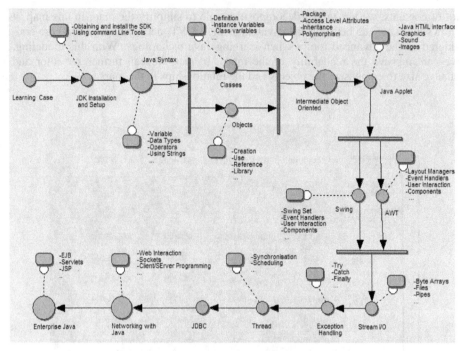

Fig. 6. Example of J2SE e-learning map.

5 Conclusion

Applying KML to model e-learning materials as a learning map is what we propose in this paper. Using KML on top of web-based learning, it makes users easy to understand the learning strategy without too much external support. KML provides solution to help a user model and reuse his/her learning as a visualized knowledge map.

Reference

1. Arapi, P., Moumoutzis, N., Christodoulakis, S.: Supporting interoperability in an existing e-learning platform using SCORM, Advanced Learning Technologies, The 3rd IEEE International Conference on Advanced Learning Technologies (2003), Greece 388 – 389
2. Braham, R.: Knowledge Evaluation in Online Educational Systems, ACS/IEEE International Conference on Computer Systems and Applications (2003)
3. Digital Think: SCORM™ : The E-Learning Standard,
   http://www.digitalthink.com/difs/downloads/products_services/wp_standards.pdf
4. Huang W., Hacid, M.S.: Contextual knowledge representation, retrieval and interpretation in multimedia e-learning, Information Reuse and Integration, IEEE International Conference (2003), USA 258 – 265
5. Jwo, J.S., Wang, C.H.: Knowledge Modeling Language, draft (2003)

6. Liu, C.C., Don, P.H., Chen, K.L., Liu, B.J.: Reusing web learning portfolios by case-based reasoning technology to scaffold problem solving, Computers in Education, Vol. 2. International Conference (2002), New Zealand 1216 – 1217

7. Liu, X.Q., Wu, M., Chen, J.X.: Knowledge aggregation and navigation high-level Petri nets-based in e-learning, Machine Learning and Cybernetics, Vol. 1. International Conference (2002), China 420 – 425

8. Mei, Q., Shen, J.: A knowledge flow driven e-learning architecture design: what is its stratification and how is it personalized, Computers in Education, Vol.2. International Conference (2002), New Zealand 1307 - 1308

9. Pettersson, R., Svensson, G., Wærn, Y.: On Web Based Learning –Experiences from Teaching and Learning Online, The 2002 International Visual Literacy Association, the 34th Annual Conference of the International Visual Literacy Association, Breckenridge, Colorado, USA (2002)

10. Sunye, G., Guennec, A.: Design Pattern Application in UML, Springer-Verglag Berlin Heidelberg (2000) 44-62

11. Sun Microsystem, http://java.sun.com

12. Tao, Y.H., Gu, S.M.: The design of a web-based training system for simulation analysis, Vol. 1., Simulation Conference (2002), Taiwan 645 – 652

13. Vossen, G., Westerkamp, P.: E-learning as a Web service (extended abstract), 7th International Database Engineering and Application Symposiuml (2003), China 242 – 249

AI-Based Teaching Package
for Open Channel Flow on Internet

Kwokwing Chau and Yiuhung Sze

Department of Civil and Structural Engineering, Hong Kong Polytechnic University,
Hunghom, Kowloon, Hong Kong
cekwchau@polyu.edu.hk

Abstract. During the past decade, the trend to couple the World Wide Web (WWW) in teaching and learning has been gaining momentum rapidly. Learning availability over the Internet is expanding and gradually constitutes a usual means of education and training. In this paper, the development and implementation of an AI-based interactive teaching package for open channel flow on Internet is depicted. The latest expert system shell and web production software are used for the development of this system. It is demonstrated that various theories on open channel flow, design, and interactive "What-if" analysis on various design parameters can be performed using this package through an active and dynamic learning environment. It is shown that, with its intrinsic advantages, the WWW has the potential for effecting fundamental changes in the design of learning processes and the education system.

1 Introduction

Within the prevalent educational systems and amongst the population of students that these systems serve, quite a wide ranges and variations among students can be detected. Moreover, the current demand for higher education at different age groups has been increased, particularly in adult age group. There exists a trend that the society increasingly requires people of better educational quality so as to enhance the productivity. Hence if the adults desire to earn more to improve living conditions, they have to upgrade themselves through various channels. But time constraints and places where they were living usually impeded them [1]. Furthermore, the traditional teaching system offers no facility in tracking student's progress or keeping courseware up to date. It is not enough just to supply materials to the students. In order to overcome these problems, new teaching paradigm is entailed.

Nowadays, the society has entered into the information age. The linked material in Internet could be in a variety of formats including picture, sound, video, 3-D modeling, animation or application. As a result of technological advancements in the fields of computer technology, artificial intelligence technology, education and instructional technology, web-based learning (WBL) has been becoming somewhat common place traditional higher educational settings [2]. Many schools try to conduct a minimum of some types of web-based instruction. WBL provides a flexible and cost-effective means and opportunity of access to lifelong educational opportunities and allows people work at their own pace from different locations. The web-based interactive system, which provides the opportunity for interaction from the learners, allows a student to dip-in and dip-out of the different course sections and allows progresses of

W. Liu et al. (Eds.): ICWL 2004, LNCS 3143, pp. 98–104, 2004.
© Springer-Verlag Berlin Heidelberg 2004

students to be monitored and recorded. WBL has also been used in some organizations so as to raise the effectiveness of their education and training operations for the ultimate goal in enhancing the productivity.

Moreover, a knowledge-based system (KBS) has been demonstrated to have the capability of encapsulating systematically the heuristic expertise and knowledge. Successful applications of KBS have been undertaken in different fields including interpretation; design; diagnosis; education; and planning [3-20]. In this study, an AI-based interactive teaching package for open channel flow on Internet is developed and implemented, by employing the latest KBS technology and web production software. By using custom-built interactive graphical user interfaces, it is able to assist learners by furnishing with knowledge in this domain.

2 Web-Based Tools

Recently, the rapid development of the internet-based learning from a text-only medium to an expanding multimedia communication system has increased and diversified delivery mechanisms of quality education. Internet-based learning tools that are commonly used include e-mail, listservs, web-based bulletin boards, chat, online courses, electronic performance support system, static web pages and interactive web pages. The numbers of items to be added on the web page depend on the expected requirement of the users. Among them, it is worthwhile to emphasize the interactive web pages since they include the ability to search a database, ask questions, customize the look and feel of the site, and perform other types of interaction and online web-based course. It is noted that the interactive web pages are still not yet as common as static web pages, yet the number of sites deploying interactive web pages continue to grow.

3 Developing Environment and Tools

It is not easy to compile an ideal web page if one is just using single web design software to create a web site. As such, in this case, several professional software are employed. Moreover, artificial intelligence techniques have been incorporated in the design of the underlying WBL framework.

3.1 KBS Shell with Blackboard Architecture

In order to facilitate development of the knowledge base on open channel flow, expert system shell containing specific representation methods and inference mechanisms is employed. This system has been implemented with the aid of a microcomputer KBS shell Visual Rule Studio, which is a hybrid application development tool under object-oriented design environment. This shell acts as an ActiveX Designer under the Microsoft Visual Basic 6.0 programming environment. In addition, Visual Rule Studio is compatible with Active Server Pages and Microsoft Internet Information Server. The ruleset components can be deployed as part of a web server based application so that, with a web browser and Intranet or Internet access, it may virtually reach any users.

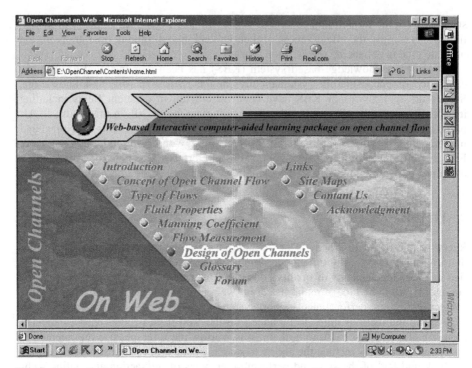

Fig. 1. Screen displaying the opening menu of the computer-aided learning package on open channel flow

Blackboard architecture has been developed to furnish a problem-solving model with contribution from a multitude of knowledge sources at different levels by integration into a single system [21]. A variety of specialized expertise or knowledge sources are grouped into separate modules by employing both rules and frames and, sometimes under object-oriented programming environment. Blackboard system encapsulates information sharing through the common data structure called a blackboard, which compiles the data entries as well as acts as the communication link among various knowledge sources. The blackboard acts as the global system context, which stores the current state of the solution, including problem data, intermediate parameters and final outputs of the design. Both production rules and procedural methods are employed to represent standard and heuristic knowledge on fluid mechanics. Rules are isolated as component objects, which are separated from both objects and application logic. Rule development becomes a natural part of the component architecture development process. Under the declarative knowledge representation environment, objects are used to encapsulate knowledge structure, procedures, and values. Object behavior is tightly bound to attributes in the form of facets, methods, rules, and demons. By defining various types of windows as different classes, such as Check Box, Option Button, List Box, Command Button, Text Box, etc., they can inherit common characteristics and possess their own special properties.

3.2 Web-Development Tools

The frames of the web pages are built by using the software Dreamweaver. Java programs are employed to illustrate interactive open channel design calculations. It provides different combinations of variables in the governing equations for users to design their own channels. JavaScript is used in the search function to provide multiple web site searching so that the user can easily select the web site from the pull down menu. Moreover, it is used to add some functions such as the timer in the web page. Flash is used to effect the animation effects in the home index of the package, making the web page more active and alive. Photoshop is employed to edit all the pictures and graphics in the web page of the package. PhotoImpact is used to perform some special effects in the pictures.

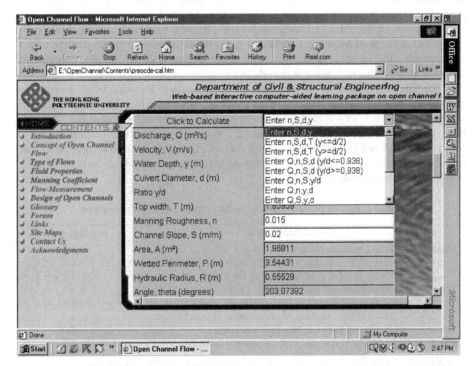

Fig. 2. Screen displaying interactive analysis of circular culvert that can demonstrate the effect of variation of various design parameters on the result

4 Interactive Teaching Package

Broadly speaking, the web pages are grouped into three parts. The first part provides the basic concept of open channel flow [22] to the users, which is a one-way information transfer from the webmaster to the users. The second part provides some design exercises and interactive "What-if" analysis about open channel flow for the users to test how they understand the domain topic, which is a two-way information transfer.

The final part provides some functions to allow the users more direct contacts with the application designer through sending electronic message and the other users through discussion forum. Figure 1 displays the opening menu of the computer-aided teaching package on open channel flow. The structures of the web pages are divided into thirteen headings which include introduction, concept of open channel flow, type of flow, fluid properties, Manning coefficient, flow measurement, design of open channels, glossary, forum, links, site map, contact us, and acknowledgments.

The introduction section outlines the basic characteristics of open channel flow. The classification of open channel into either natural or artificial channel is then explained. The section on concept of open channel flow is divided into four subheadings, namely, general approach, energy principle, velocity distribution, and hydraulic jump. It covers the assumptions taken and the derivation of the governing equations. Under the section on type of flow, the basic concepts of uniform flow and gradually varied flow are articulated. The section on fluid properties shows the general properties of the fluid and summarizes the common values of various fluid properties. The section on Manning coefficient gives the roughness properties of the channel material. In the section on flow measurement, most of the design calculation methods in open channel flow are introduced.

Knowledge on design of channel with various shapes is included in the section on design of open channels. Interactive analysis is employed to relieve the intensive computational work for the analytical solution in the design of open channel. Through the graphical interface as shown in Figure 2, "What-if" analysis can be performed by setting various design parameters. Different computational options are provided, namely, rectangular open channel, circular culvert, triangular channel with or without using end depth method, respectively.

Table 1. Results of the feedback questionnaire survey by the learners

Questionnaire item	Average rating#
Users are proficient in using computer.	3.7
Users can actively control the pedagogical process via the tool.	4.0
The package is very helpful in understanding the topic.	4.2
The system is interactive and user-friendly.	4.1
The package is easy to comprehend and greatly accessible.	4.3
The material with multiple formats of presentation is interesting.	4.1
The tool greatly arouses their interest in this subject.	4.0
The presented material is relevant to the domain subject.	4.2

#5 = Strongly Agree, 4 = Agree, 3 = Neutral, 2 = Disagree, 1 = Strongly Disagree

5 Evaluation of Package

In order to gauge the effectiveness of the system, 103 learners of varied technical backgrounds and experiences are required to complete a questionnaire with 8 questions that evaluate the presented system after their use. The feedback and written evaluations of the users on the scope and effectiveness of the system comprise several useful points. Table 1 shows the results of the user feedback questionnaire survey on using the system. Owing to the inherent variability in user rankings, only extreme rankings, such as exceeding a rank of '4-Agree', are considered significant. From the results, it is delighted to notice that no aspect of the system receives an unfavourable ranking. The tool is considered to be easy to comprehend, interesting, interactive, and relevant to designers. More importantly, the users find that it is extremely helpful and that the tool greatly arouses their interest in this domain subject. Moreover, during this semester, the student tracking records show that the average number of hits for the site per student is 497 times whilst the average time of hit averages at 2.8 minutes per hit. This proves its capability as well as usefulness in serving the purpose of pedagogical support.

6 Conclusions

A prototype AI-based interactive teaching package for open channel flow on Internet is presented. It is shown that the hybrid knowledge representation approach applying object-oriented programming technique with various latest software is viable for this domain problem. The flexibility and open infrastructure of Internet have been demonstrated to be able to act as a media for developing learning application. Through this package, the domain knowledge on open channel flow can be understood easily. Besides, practical design of open channel flow can be enhanced using the interactive analysis.

References

1. Kearsley, G.: The World Wide Web: Global Access to Education. Educational Technology Review **5** (1996) 26-30
2. Maddux, C.D.: The World Wide Web: Some Simple Solutions to Common Design Problems. Educational Technology **38(5)** (1998) 24-28
3. Albermani, F., Chau, K.W.: Web-Based Knowledge-Based System on Liquid Retaining Structure Design as Instructional Tool. Lecture Notes in Computer Science **2436** (2002) 95-105
4. Chau, K.W.: An Expert System for the Design of Gravity-type Vertical Seawalls. Engineering Applications of Artificial Intelligence **5(4)** (1992) 363-367
5. Chau, K.W.: Internet-Based Interactive Package for Diagnostic Assessment on Learning of Fluid Mechanics. Lecture Notes in Computer Science **2783** (2003) 287-296
6. Chau, K.W.: A Prototype Knowledge-Based System on Unsteady Open Channel Flow in Water Resources Management. Water International **29(1)** (2004) 54-60
7. Chau, K.W.: Knowledge-Based System on Water-Resources Management in Coastal Waters. Journal of the Chartered Institution of Water and Environmental Management **18(1)** (2004) 25-28
8. Chau, K.W., Albermani, F.: Expert System Application on Preliminary Design of Liquid Retaining Structures. Expert Systems with Applications **22(2)** (2002) 169-178
9. Chau, K.W., Albermani, F.: Knowledge-Based System on Optimum Design of Liquid Retaining Structures with Genetic Algorithms. Journal of Structural Engineering ASCE **129(10)** (2003) 1312-1321
10. Chau, K.W., Albermani, F.: A Coupled Knowledge-Based Expert System for Design of Liquid Retaining Structures. Automation in Construction **12(5)** (2003) 589-602

11. Chau, K.W., Albermani, F.: Hybrid Knowledge Representation in a Blackboard KBS for Liquid Retaining Structure Design. Engineering Applications of Artificial Intelligence **17(1)** (2004) 11-18
12. Chau, K.W., Anson, M.: A Knowledge-Based System for Construction Site Level Facilities Layout. Lecture Notes in Artificial Intelligence **2358** (2002) 393-402
13. Chau, K.W., Chen, W.: An Example of Expert System on Numerical Modelling System in Coastal Processes. Advances in Engineering Software **32(9)** (2001) 695-703
14. Chau, K.W., Cheng, C., Li, C.W.: Knowledge Management System on Flow and Water Quality Modeling. Expert Systems with Applications **22(4)** (2002) 321-330
15. Chau, K.W., Cheung, C.S.: Knowledge Representation on Design of Storm Drainage System. Lecture Notes in Computer Science **3029** (2004) 886-894
16. Chau, K.W., Ng, V.: A Knowledge-Based Expert System for Design of Thrust Blocks for Water Pipelines in Hong Kong. Water Supply Research and Technology - Aqua **45(2)** (1996) 96-99
17. Chau, K.W., Yang, W.W.: Development of an Integrated Expert System for Fluvial Hydrodynamics. Advances in Engineering Software **17(3)** (1993) 165-172
18. Chau, K.W., Yang, W.W.: A Knowledge-Based Expert System for Unsteady Open Channel Flow. Engineering Applications of Artificial Intelligence **5(5)** (1992) 425-430
19. Chau, K.W., Yang, W.W.: Structuring and Evaluation of VP-Expert Based Knowledge Bases. Engineering Applications of Artificial Intelligence **7(4)** (1994) 447-454
20. Chau, K.W., Zhang, X.Z.: An Expert System for Flow Routing in a River Network. Advances in Engineering Software **22(3)** (1995) 139-146
21. Hayesroth, B.: A Blackboard Architecture for Control. Artificial Intelligence **26(3)** (1985) 251-321
22. French, R.H.: Open Channel Hydraulics. McGraw-Hill, New York (1985)

Efficient Methods for Skimming the Web-Based Synchronization Multimedia Lectures

I-Chun Lai, Kuo-Yu Liu, Hao-Tung Lin, and Herng-Yow Chen

Department of Computer Science and Information Engineering, National Chi-Nan University
1st University Rd., Pu-Li, Nan-Tou County, Taiwan 545
{iclai,caspar,haotung}@mclab.csie.ncnu.edu.tw
hychen@csie.ncnu.edu.tw

Abstract. With the development of streaming technologies and e-learning platforms, more and more multimedia lectures integrating different media are accessible on the web. The massive multimedia lectures with huge and lengthy media decrease the learning efficiency. In this paper, two access modes are provided to help users to search significant information in multimedia lectures rapidly. We apply the temporal relationship among multimedia to search information in different granularities, and detect the significant segments by the analysis concerning the intonation and navigation events of lecturers to offer the user an abridged version of to comprehend a multimedia lecture. The integration of these two modes has been practically applied to Web-based Synchronization Multimedia Lecture system for facilitating the access and browse of multimedia lecture.

1 Introduction

The flourishing development of multimedia lecturing system [1-4] caused a revolution in the pattern of traditional chalk-and-board teaching mode in real classrooms. The multimedia lecturing systems apply speech/video, texts, and various navigation events to simulate live instruction process. Additionally, they enable the learners to attend the lecture anytime anywhere. However, with the rapid growth of multimedia e-learning lectures, the less efficiently the learners retrieve the information of interest. Compared with browsing a static document, skimming a multimedia lecture is much more difficult because of its temporal characteristics. Therefore, it is necessary to develop tools that enable the learners to spend less time on searching the significant content.

Marking the significant segments (and the structure) by instructors manually is an intuitional but most accurate method to help the learners to catch the general point of a lecture. This method, however, is an inconvenient job for instructors and may distract them from their lecturing. Manual-based lecture summary usually needs additional manpower after class.

Time compression [6] is a typical skimming technology to shorten a whole multimedia lecture into a summarized version. The method increases the playback speed of speech with almost no pitch distortion. However, there is a compressed limit to this method because of human perception. Research [8] indicated that people's comprehension declines rapidly when the speech rate is more than 275 wpm (words per min-

W. Liu et al. (Eds.): ICWL 2004, LNCS 3143, pp. 105–112, 2004.

ute). Thus depending on the speech speed, the approach can save at most 1.5 to 2.5 times of the original time.

In this paper, on the basis of Web-based Synchronization Multimedia Lectures (WSML) system (http://english.csie.ncnu.edu.tw) [1], we propose the modes, multilevel access mode and the compression mode (http://english.csie.ncnu.edu.tw/skim/), to support users to locate the significant segments rapidly. In the multilevel access mode, the system supplies a hierarchical access structure of multimedia lectures by analyzing temporal meta-information captured in recording stage or computed in speech-text alignment process. The learners can find out the content they want step by step, from the outline to the details as though they read books – They look up the table of contents and then jump to the section for further read. However, those who just intend to preview the significant segments in a short time still have to find out the significant segments by themselves. Thus, we provide the second mode, the compression mode, to complement the weakness of the multilevel access mode. In the compression mode, the system identifies the significance of each segment by analyzing the instructor's speech and navigation events. Other insignificant segments are hidden during the presentation stage. What the user gets is an abridged version of the original information. With the integration of these two modes, browsing the multimedia lectures in an e-learning platform will become much easier.

2 WSML System

The Web-based Synchronized Multimedia Lecture system integrates audiovisual lectures, HTML slides, and navigation events to provide a synchronized presentation. When the teachers use this system to produce a teaching material, the oral explanation and the navigation events accompanying the lecture will be recorded. In presentation stage such the navigation events as pen strokes, highlight, dynamic annotation, virtual pointer (cursor), and window scrolling will be triggered automatically at appropriate time and spatial positions. Fig. 1 shows an example of the synchronous presentation on the student side. Because of the synchronization mechanism, the learner can experience as vivid on-demand instruction as possible.

3 The Proposed Framework

The integration of various media streams really enriches multimedia lectures, but the large quantities and the temporal distribution of multimedia makes a lecture browser with skimming function inefficient and difficult to design. Fig. 2 illustrates that traditional multimedia system supports synchronization presentations of speech and slide-based lecture. The users can seek the content of interest through the slide-change control bar. However, this unitary access mode only enables the users to select roughly and seek for parts of multimedia lectures. Hence, we propose a framework to solve the problem above. In our framework, the multiple-data-analysis method that considers instructor's speech, navigation event, and the result of speech-text alignment is designed with the provision of two browsing modes: multilevel access mode and compression mode, to meet different access granularity and browsing needs.

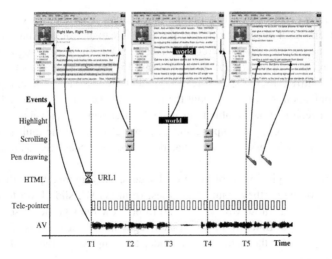

Fig. 1. An example of synchronous presentation on the student side. The AV and HTML URL1 are loaded respectively at T1. The embedded AV player in the browser then starts playing the AV lecture, and the HTML page is rendered at the same time. At T2, a scrolling offset event is triggered to show the content out-of-screen. Then, a highlight event over some important words ("world") is invoked at T3. A scrolling event is triggered again at T4. At T5, a sequence of pen drawing events is driven to show an ink stroke

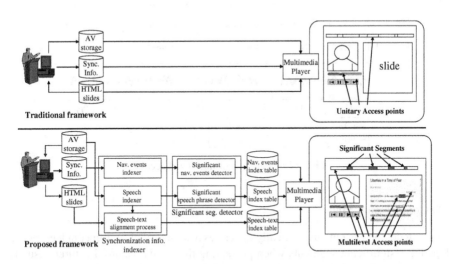

Fig. 2. Comparison of the traditional framework and the proposed framework

3.1 Multilevel Access Mode

In this mode, we offer a multilevel access mechanism to satisfy the users' need of retrieving information in different granularities. During the process of recording, the temporal synchronization information of all the captured navigation events is analyzed by the navigation event indexer to build the index table. After the index table is build, navigation event level access is set, and the user is capable of clicking on any high level events, such as the strokes, to retrieve the corresponding speech segments.

Furthermore, the implicit temporal relationship [5] between the speech and the lecture texts is identified by the speech-text alignment process [11]. The computed temporal synchronization information about the relation between the speech and the text is stored in the speech-text index table to provide the users sentence level access. By way of these analyzing processes, temporal indexes are delivered to the multimedia player to generate efficient access points so that the users can access the data at different levels.

Fig. 3 shows the logical view of multilevel access. This figure depicts that the users can find the information they want by degrees, from HTML slide level to navigation events level. However, those who just intend to preview the significant segments in a short time still have to find out the significant segments by themselves. Thus we provide the second mode, the compression mode, to complement the weakness of the multilevel access mode.

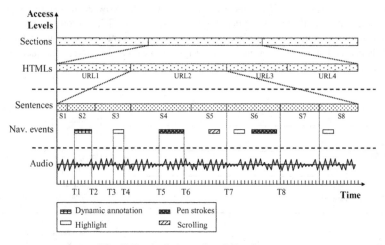

Fig. 3. Logical view of multilevel access

3.2 Compression Mode

In this mode, the system automatically generates a summary of multimedia lecture and skips the insignificant segments when presenting the media lecture. Lecturers usually stress the significant information by means of changing their intonation, pitch, speech rate, volume, pauses and applying some navigation events. Research [9] considering the speech application indicated that the emphasized segments can be used to generate summaries of speeches successfully. Therefore, our system detects the significant segments of multimedia lectures according to concerning the intonation and navigation events of lecturers. The result is delivered to the multimedia player to generate an abridged version of the original information.

In the following we describe how to detect the emphasized speech segments and the significant navigation events, and how to combine these two kinds of data into the summary of multimedia lecture.

Emphasized Speech Segment Detection. The emphasized speech segment detector uses the algorithm proposed by the researchers [7] to compute the pitch activity of each segment delineated by silence with duration of more than 200ms, and then uses the pitch activity of each segment to detect the emphasized portions of the speech. The algorithm works as follows:

1. The whole speech is segmented into frames of 10 ms.
2. For each frame, the pitch value is computed.
3. The threshold is set to select the frames with the top 1% of pitch values.
4. For measuring the pitch activity of each speech segment, the number of frames in each speech segment whose pitch values are over the threshold is counted.

The emphasized speech segment is associated with high pitch activity. The pitch activity of each speech segment is recorded in the speech index table.

Significant Navigation Events Detection. The significant navigation events detector evaluates the significance of neighbor speech phrases according to the types of events. The navigation events are classified into three types: (1) Key events, like pen strokes, dynamic annotations and highlights, have explicitly semantic information and can directly map to important concepts. The speech segments temporally close to key events are usually significant. Besides, the more key events appear in a segment, the more important it is. (2) Breakpoint events such as slide change events and scrolling events often occur at the topic boundaries. Speech segments following breakpoint events are usually significant segments because they are usually the introductions of new topics. Moreover, these types of events are suitable to help segment lectures. (3) Auxiliary events like virtual pointers help present smoothly but do not have obvious semantic information. By way of computation we may extract some high level information from auxiliary events. For example, the pointer moves around a particular region in a short time may represent that the speaker want to emphasize significant concepts. In this paper, how to extract some high level information from auxiliary events are not investigated, and the significance of auxiliary events are not discussed.

The events spatially and temporally close to each other are called "key event group" here. They are usually used to emphasize related and even the same information (Fig. 4 shows an example). Every key event belonging to the same group cannot be segmented temporally, and the range affected by it is the same with the range affected by its group. Therefore, the significant navigation events detector applies grouping technique [10] to identify those key events whose temporal and spatial distance are under a certain threshold to be of the same key event group, and adjusts the affected range of every key event of the group. The significant navigation events detector evaluates the significance of neighbor segments according to the types of events and the affected ranges. The data of each event such as its significance score, affecting speech segments and which key event group it belongs to are stored in the navigation event index table.

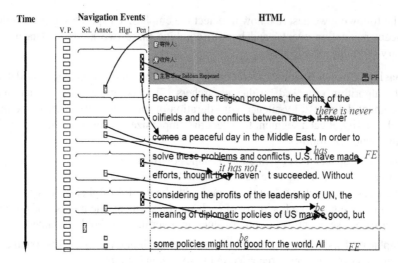

Fig. 4. The events spatially and temporally close to each other usually user to emphasized related and even the same information should be grouped

Compression. After analyzing speech segment and navigation events, the emphasized speech segment detector and the significant navigation events detector generate some time slots marked by significance scores. These data are delivered to the multimedia player to decide the hidden segments. The whole compression process is divided into two phases. In the first phase of compression, silence level compression, the multimedia player deletes those silences less than 500ms among the speech, and reduces the rest silence to 500ms. Why we do not delete all the silence is because some silence is regarded as important cues to listeners to begin speaking [7]. To avoid deleting the key events appearing during silence, we change the timestamp of these key events to make them happen earlier within the period of the nearest speech (Fig. 5 shows an example). After the first compression phase, the whole multimedia lecture is obviously divided into segments surrounded by silence.

In the second compression phase, the multimedia player computes the significance scores of each segment generated in the first compression phase. The significance score of the segment x of the multimedia lectures is as follows:

$$S(x) = S(x_{\text{speech}}) + \alpha S(x_{\text{navigation events}})$$

$S(x_{\text{speech}})$: The sum of the significance score of all the speech segments in this multimedia lecture segment

$S(x_{\text{navigation events}})$: The sum of the significance score assigned by all the navigation events in this multimedia lecture segment

α : Constant weighting

After the significance score of each segment is computed, the segments whose significance scores are more than a certain threshold are picked up. For speech, it takes at least 8 seconds to express complete information. Hence, if the duration of a chosen segment is less than 8 seconds, its neighbor segments will be grouped into the chosen segment until the duration of this segment becomes more than 8 seconds. The multimedia player only presents these chosen segments. Because the amount of significant ranges in every multimedia lecture is different, the compression rate of every multimedia lecture is also different.

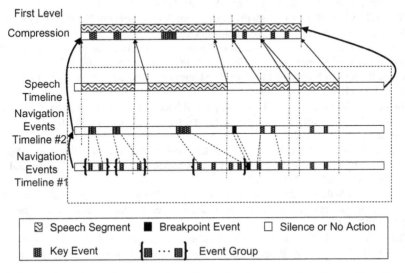

Fig. 5. In the first phase of compression, silence level compression, the multimedia player deletes those silence less than 500ms among the speech, and reduce the rest silence to 500ms. To avoid deleting the key events appearing during silence, we change the timestamp of these key events to make them happen earlier within the period of the nearest speech

4   Conclusion

In this paper, the multilevel access mode and the compression mode are investigated to help users locate the significant segment in multimedia lectures efficiently. These two access methods discussed in this paper are practically applied to the WSML system, a multimedia lecturing system primarily used in SLE (Second Language Education) of our university. We apply the temporal relationship among multimedia to search information in different granularities in a short time, and detect the significant segments by the analysis concerning the intonation and navigation events of lecturers to offer the user an abridged version a multimedia lecture. The integration of these two modes makes the access and browse of multimedia lecture much easier.

References

1. Chen, H.Y., Chen, G.Y., and Hong, J.S.: Design of a Web-based synchronized multimedia lecture system for distance education. Proceedings of International Conference on Multimedia Computing and Systems, vol. 2. (1999) 887-891

 2. Brotherton, J.A., Bhalodia, J.R., and Abowd, G.D.: Automated Capture, Integration and Visualization of Multiple Media Streams. Proceedings of International Conference on Multimedia Computing and Systems. (1998) 54-63
 3. Mukhopadhyay, S. and Smith, B.: Passive Capture and Structuring of Lectures. Proceedings of ACM Multimedia. (1999) 477-487
 4. Roccetti, M. and Salomoni, P.: A Web-based Synchronized Multimedia System for Distance Education. Proceedings of ACM SAC. (2001) 94-98
 5. Chu, W.T., Chen, H.Y.: Cross-Media Correlation: A Case Study of Navigated Hypermedia Documents. Proceedings of ACM Multimedia. (2002) 57-66
 6. Arons, B.: Techniques, Perception, and Applications of Time-Compressed Speech. Proceedings of 1992 Conference, American Voice I/O Society. (1992) 169-177
 7. Arons, B.: Speech Skimmer: Interactively Skimming Recorded Speech. Ph.D. thesis. MIT Media Lab. (1994)
 8. Foulke, E.: The Perception of Time Compressed Speech. Ch. 4 in Perception of Language, edited by Kjeldergaard, P.M., Horton, D.L., and Jenkins, J.J. Charles E. Merrill Publishing Company. (1971) 79-107
 9. Chen, F. R. and Withgott, M.: The Use of Emphasis to Automatically Summarize Spoken Discourse. In Proceedings of the International Conference on Acoustics, Speech, and Signal Processing, IEEE. 1992, pp. 229–233
10. Chiu, P., and Wilcox, L.D.: A dynamic grouping technique for ink and audio notes. Proceedings of the 11th annual ACM symposium on User interface software and technology. (1998) 195-202
11. Chu, W.T., Hsu, K.T., and Chen, H.Y.: Design of an Alignment System for Synchronized Speech-Text Presentation. Proceedings of Distributed Multimedia Systems. (2001) 86-93

Web-Based Collaborative Learning Focused on the Study of Interaction and Human Communication

Xinyu Zhang, Nianlong Luo, DongXing Jiang, Huifen Liu, and Wenyi Zhang

Computer and Information Management Center, Tsinghua Univ., China, 100084

Abstract. The purpose of this study is to explore the interaction and human communication on a Web-Based Collaborative Learning Environment (WBCLE). WBCLE is an integrative, interactive and collaborative learning environment for web based courses. With optimized learning materials, WBCLE also provides interactive functions such as login, students' works upload the instructor's comment feedback, Real-time chat Room and discussion forum and provides collaborative functions such as group management, group collaborative learning, shared resources. Based on the investigations of web courses in WBCLE, the paper analyses the interactive and collaborative functions and web learning patterns, and the impact of human communication. Learning technology can not completely take place of instructor's supervision and communication with students. Strategies for collaborative learning and human communication can improve the educational effectiveness, and they include enhancing message flows among students and the instructor, creating communities in the course, and providing more interactive functions and supervision to the students.

1 Introduction

In terms of the rapid change of information technology (IT) and advancement of instructional technology, the roles of teachers in teaching and students in learning are changed. In previous research, web based courses may lack an important quality that fosters positive student attitudes toward instruction: teacher immediacy, or behaviors that enhance physical and psychological closeness. Teacher immediacy is operationally defined to include both verbal and non-verbal behaviors, and is positively correlated to student satisfaction with both the course and the instructor [1]. Verbal behaviors such as praising students, addressing them by name and using humor in class may evoke immediacy. But most of the existing research focuses on nonverbal immediacy resulting from teacher behaviors such as adopting a relaxed body position, varying one's vocal expression, moving around the classroom, smiling and looking at the class. Immediacy was also related to Student scores, notably including measures that might address the likelihood of taking future courses such as overall perceived value, the quality of instruction and interest in the subject area [2].

In this article, we attempt to analyze the interactive function and human community in a web-based collaborative learning environment. Web courses are clearly at a disadvantage in terms of their immediacy, and web courses of the "computer managed" variety may lack both verbal and nonverbal cues entirely. Computer mediated communication is a selective process in which partners who want to work together do so,

W. Liu et al. (Eds.): ICWL 2004, LNCS 3143, pp. 113–119, 2004.

and the partners are students and instructors as well. Interactive function patterns result in message flow on the web, and it's a new kind of human communication. How to create an interactive web leaning environment that enable more message flow and human communication easily and conveniently? What are strategies that enhance message flow and collaborative learning? Online, Instructors may "talked" more than students [4]. Is it necessary? And how efficient it is to enhance physical and psychological closeness, and the student satisfaction with both the course and the instructor?

2   The Structure of WBCLE

As a case study of multimedia design and implement courses, a web course was developed in 2001, and first it was assistance for face-to-face class. Later, the interactive function has been improved greatly and the collaborative function was required for the group study, and it's used as a web-based course. Now the Web Based Collaborative Learning Environment (WBCLE) is an interactive learning environment. The structure of WBCLE is show in Fig. 1, and there are three kinds of authorized users who can login. The highest are administrators who manage courses, teachers and students, and the secondary are teachers controlling their own course, and students register on at least one course in WBCLE.

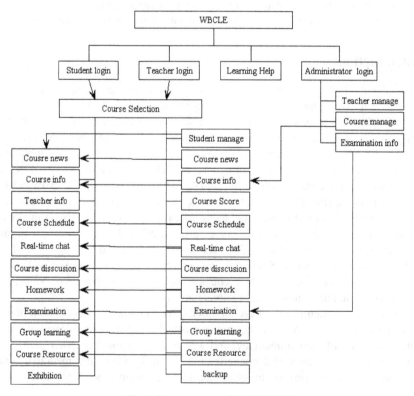

Fig 1. The structure of the WBCLE

One instructor may have more than one course at the same time. Before the course, the instructor can publish the Instructor's Information, Introduction and Schedule of the course, by filling the forms provided by WBCLE. E-books or learning materials can be uploaded and the instructor can manage students' registration ID.

When registered at a course in WBCLE, a student can login with his ID, and he can know the instructor and the outline of the course through Instructor's info. and Introduction of the course. Usually, the Introduction explains the syllabus, prerequisite, learning method, expected object, the way of test and so on. Thus the student may have more motivation and take part in the web learning positively. Also, students ought to provide their basic information by filling the forms in student's info. , so the instructor can know his students better. According to the Schedule, the student should finish reading part of the E-books or Online Materials, and he/she could discuss with instructor and others in Chat room, Discussion forum or by E-mail. After reading and discussion, he/she ought to finish a kind of work (a paper, or a graphic design work, etc.) in the form of web pages. Students upload their works to the Works where the instructor can make comment and mark the work. In WBCLE, every one can visit other's work and instructor's comment, and check his total score that is summed up and put on the web automatically. The instructor can publish News, new Online Materials at any time according to the learning process. In this way, the course goes on.

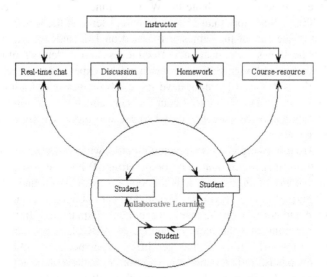

Fig. 2. The interactive functions in WBCLE

3   Interactive Functions and Message Flow in WBCLE

The interactive function of WBCLE includes a synchronous chat room, an asynchronous discussion forum, works area and learning materials' area. (Fig. 2). The discussion forum is an asynchronous public bulletin board where everyone can post message or reply other's post at any time, and the post is shared for others. It's a good way for students to ask questions for other students, or instructor to answer. The chat room is a synchronous way of communication that people must be online at the same time to share message, and the message will no longer exist after they exit.

In works, there is 100MB space for every student to upload and manage his multimedia works with html format. When a student login to the system, he can only enter into and manage his own work space. After a work file is uploaded in everyone's work space, it will be linked to the system automatically, and the instructor can then makes comments and mark each student's work. As a reference, everyone can visit others work and its comments from instructor.

In learning resource, both instructor and students can provide useful online materials to share with others. Students can also contact with instructor by e-mail. In this interactive environment, students could share and discuss such things as texts, images, and multimedia.

4 Strategies for Collaborative Learning and Human Communication

As the development of WBCLE and web courses since 2001, there were investigations at the end of every semester to evaluate the WBCLE function and its educational effectiveness. In 2003, while more than 150 students registered at the web based course, the investigation at the end of the semester is based on 142 students' valid data, and some of the statistic shows the educational effectiveness and student's attitudes to this new way of learning. Although 89% students have no experience of web learning, 87% agree that the web based learning have more advantages than traditional class, and 89% will register further web based courses. This conclusion is similar with the former investigation and proves the web based course was more effective than comparable face-to-face class.

But the web based learning is a self-directed module, which encourage independent scholarship far more than traditional classroom setting. When the instructor present text or publish demand of the works, it is as points for discussion and as a starting point. It doesn't purport to be everything. The students are obliged to review the materials on their own and not rely on the instructor and only explanation. In the investigation, most students think that the main advantage of WBCLE is everyone can learn what is needed for oneself. This way they get different perspectives and can choose – learning is in their hands, and students' most important achievement is the improvement of their ability of self-study. To encourage this self-directed module, WBCLE should have not only enough materials for students to looking for and refer to, but also enable more message flow among instructor and students.

4.1 Enhance Message Flows in Works

Works in WBCLE is one of the places where everyone visits most often. During the learning process, a student will study issues one by one prearranged by instructor, and he will refer to comment and score from the instructor, for every issue finished. He can also visit other's work to see how other's doing so as to adjust his own leaning. The comments to every student's works are individual; it will enhance the closeness with the student. At the other side, all works and comments are shared resources and the excellent works are good reference and inspiration to all the students. During the course, some of the students will improve they works voluntarily, after the instructor's comments and referring other's excellent work.

4.2 Creating Community in Discussion Forum

Discussion forum is another way of enhance message flow and communication. At the course in 2003, there are two sessions at discussion forum; one is for free topics and the other for a special topic prearranged by instructor. 48% students attended free session and the average first post per person was 3.9 pieces. There was at least one reply for every post, and 70% of the replies were from instructor. More students (70%) attended the special session, and the average first post per person was 2 pieces. The replies were 146% and all by students. As one to one communication, 33% students used e-mail and there were average 2.4 mails to instructor per student (Tab. 1).

Table 1. Human communication

E-mails to inst.		Free session in Discussion Forum			Special session in Discussion Forum		
Stud.	Mails/pe	Stud.	First posts/per.	Replies by inst.	Stud.	First posts/per.	Replies by stud.
33%	2.4	48%	3.9	70%	61%	2.1	146%

Web based course can increases student engagement. In a face-to-face classroom, students can sit back and not participate. Online there is no way to maintain a presence unless you are posting and participating. For those who aren't active in face to face classroom because of the learning disability or shyness or whatever, they would login onto the discussion forum and ask questions that they could not have asked in class. For active students, they can answer or reply other's questions the discussion forum. In a face-to-face course, the instructor may say one thing to everybody, the class discussion takes place, and it's over. With a discussion forum, the comments keep coming in every day. Online, class time never stops, as opposed to the classroom where it's contained. In the special session, one first post got 10 replies and it has been read totally 115 times.

Compared with 2002, discussion forum has been improved greatly. In the investigation of 2002, 36.8% students thought their main difficulties in web learning was "short of interaction and guidance to resolve the problem", and 35.3% was "short of supervision to follow the learning schedule", 35.3%. While in 2003, the rate changed to 16% and 59% respectively. It shows the impact of human communication and learning community to web based learning.

Based on the interactive function patterns, the instructor can enhance online participation by creating community and encouraging students' engagement. For example, acknowledging good posts to the discussion forum, and good works uploaded. Another way of community is to encourage collaboration. For example, encourage students to use the discussion forum for questions instead of email, because other students might like to know the answer, too. So, when receives an interesting question via email, the instructor puts the question and its answer on the web, with the questioner's name deleted. In discussion forum, if the instructor answers a question, no one else will continue, as the situation in free session (form 1). While for a special topic prearranged, students can discuss and answer other's question with great interesting, as the situation in special session. So, sometimes the instructor should wait and encourage other students to answer and discuss the question.

4.3   Provide More Interactive Functions and Supervision

And still, there are those "traditional" students who are used to set and learn to the instructor in face-to-face classroom, and to wait for more supervision from instructor, even if there is a better interactive environment. At the other side, the instructor should make a new relationship with the students and encourage their interaction and engagement. Computer mediated communication has other ways to enhance physical and psychological closeness between instructor and students, similar to teacher immediacy. During the semester, there were prearranged discussions in chat room for two times. Many students log onto the chat room at the same time and it's proved basically as a form of emotional communication. There were 33% students contacted with instructor by e-mails, among them 50% also attended discussion forum. 38% students agree that they are easier to express themselves frankly in WBCLE, and 46% agree that WBCLE enhance the communication with instructor. Usually, those are active and "non-traditional" students.

In the investigation of "the best way of learning at college", only 18% chose completely online learning (no face-to-face class at all), 48% chose web based learning (face-to-face three times), and 21% chose web assistant learning (face-to-face once a week). Now the web based course includes face-to-face class three times at the beginning, the middle and the end of the semester. It shows the importance of communication in person which can enhance the closeness between instructor and students, especially for those traditional ones.

For students who are not participating, the instructor should contact them via email and ask if everything's okay, and this should be done automatically by WBCLE. Also, except instructor's comment, students should be able to make comment for other's work, so as to increase the cooperation and communication between students. Therefore, the WBCLE should be improved further more to enhance the interactive functions and increase the educational effectiveness.

5 Conclusion

Learning technology is the basic for web based learning. As the improvement of technical application in WBCLE, the impact of interaction and human communication become an important issue. The interactive functions and web learning patterns can not completely replace instructor's supervision and communication with students. The self-directed module of WBCLE is a great challenge both for traditional students and instructor. By enhancing message flows in works, creating community in discussion forum, and providing more interactive functions and supervision, the strategies for interactive learning and human communication can improve the educational effectiveness.

References

1. Hackman, M.Z. & Walker, K.B. Instructional communication in the televised classroom: the effects of system design and teacher immediacy on student learning and satisfaction. Communication Education 39 (July), 196-206.
2. Moore, A. Masterson, J.T., Christophel , D. M. & Shea, K.A. College teacher immediacy and student ratings of instruction. Communication Education 45(1), 1996
3. McGee, P. A., & Boyd, V., Computer-mediated communication: Facilitating dialogues, 1995, http://curry.edschool.virginia.edu/aace/download/site/HTML1995/173.HTM
4. Harris, Judi.Jones, Greg.A descriptive study of telementoring among students, subject matter experts, and teachers: message flow and function patterns. Journal of Research on Computing in Education v. 32 no1 (Fall 1999):36~53
5. Barab, S. A., J. G. Makinster, et al. (2001). "Designing and Building an On-line Community: The Struggle to Support Sociability in the Inquiry Learning Forum." ETR&D 49(4): 71-96.
6. Bruckman, A. S. (1997). Construction, Community, and Learning in a Networked Virtual World for Kids. the Program in Media Arts and Sciences, School of Architecture and Planning, Massachusetts Institute of Technology: 185.
7. Jonassen, D.H. (1999, September). Constructivist learning environments on the Web: Engaging students in meaningful learning. Information Communication and Technology Conference, Malmö, Sweden. (Invited keynote)
8. Corole A. RICHARDSON, Elizabeth A.HANSEN. Building E-Learning Communities: Using Online Collaborative Tools to Reduce Student Isolation. SCI2002:p208-p211
9. Rika Yoshii. Interactions in computer Aided Instruction Systems to Meet The Changing Goals of Higher Education. ICCE (2002): p1530-p1531
10. Scardamalia, M., & Bereiter, C. (2002). Knowledge building. In Encyclopedia of education, second edition. New York: Macmillan Reference, USA.
11. Zhang XY, Luo NL, Jiang DX, Wu XC. Synchronous Graphic-Interaction in CSCL, ICWL 2003.

PKUSpace:
A Collaborative Platform for Scientific Researching

Ming Zhang[1], Dong-qing Yang[1], Zhi-Hong Deng[1], Ying Feng[2], Wen-qing Wang[2],
Pei-xiang Zhao[1], Sai Wu[1], Shu-an Wang[1], and Shi-Wei Tang[1]

[1] School of Electronic Engineering and Computer Science,
Peking University, Beijing, 100871, China
{mzhang,ydq,zhdeng,pxzhao,wsai,wsa,tsw}@db.pku.edu.cn
[2] Administrative Center for China Academic Library & Information System
{fengy,wangwq}@calis.edu.cn

Abstract. This Paper introduces PKUSpace - a collaborative platform for scientific learning and researching. Supported by efficient automated metadata extraction and powerful text classification modules, PKUSpace provides users with a very helpful and interactive procedure to upload e-resources. We use heuristic methods and regular expression matching techniques to mine different patterns and extract relevant metadata. Upon the well-organized e-sources, we builds a uniform retrieval interface with multi-function to provide taxonomy navigation, full-text search, structural search in the metadata level and meta-searching module with novel result-merging method. Combining two on-line scoring methods: scoring with exponential distribution and metadata scoring, we achieve an effective merging result of matched documents. Furthermore, PKUSpace provides an academic forum for students and professional users in every community to discuss their ideas and research work freely.

1 Introduction

The rapid progress of Internet promoted communication in learning and researching. Meanwhile, resources which used to be accumulated separately by different researchers can now be shared on the Internet. It is urgent to build an open platform for students and researchers to share their resources, and ideas, especially resources that used to be accumulated separately by different researchers.

So far, many digital libraries have been set up to collect and index digital resources and published CD resources, and some content management systems have emerged as well. Citeseer [1] and DBLP [2] are famous for gathering and providing bibliographic information of computer science papers, journals and proceedings. RefWorks [3] is a Web based bibliographic management software, with which users can create their own personal database by importing references from online databases and use these references to write papers. The ARIADNE Knowledge Pool System [4] and LRMMS [5] are systems to collect, share and reuse the dispersed learning resources, and present the end-user a uniform interface to search, just like a meta-searcher. While laying much stress on the metadata, these systems pay no attention to the maintenance, management and share of e-resources. IBM DB2 Content Manager [6] aims at working

W. Liu et al. (Eds.): ICWL 2004, LNCS 3143, pp. 120–127, 2004.
© Springer-Verlag Berlin Heidelberg 2004

for E-Business processes. It provides an enterprise-wide storage system that can capture, create, tidy and manage key business content and dynamically access all information about customers. However, it is not suitable for academic activities. TRS CKM [7] is the first Chinese knowledge management toolkit including several Chinese processing components with functions restricted to Chinese text mining for single-user. MIT's Dspace [8], which can capture, preserve, describe, retrieve, and distribute digital works, offers web-accessible service for academic research communities for the first time. But it still requires users to spend much time on typing in metadata when uploading an item, i.e., a paper, and completely lacks an open way for people in the same group to cooperate and share ideas.

From all foresaid systems or toolkits, we can see that they avoid researchers' trivial work in some degree, but they cannot provide an open and complete platform for students and scientific researchers to safely and conveniently share e-resources without users' extra burden. Aiming at solving this problem, this paper brings forth a collaborative platform for scientific learning and researching – PKUSpace. Although built on the basic resource management capability of MIT's DSpace system, this platform modifies and enhances the functionality so as to make it more feasible and useful for users. The most impressive characters of PKUSpace are as follows:

(1) Convenient exchange and share of e-resources

PKUSpace provides users with a very helpful and interactive procedure to upload e-resources. One of the helpful functions is the automated metadata extraction function that automatically exacts metadata from an uploading PDF paper. Another hidden secret is that PKUSpace develops a powerful text classification subsystem, which can automatically classify an uploading document according to a classification schema such as ACM classification and Mesh classification [9].

(2) Uniform information retrieval

PKUSpace integrates several retrieval methods: traditional full-text and structure searching in both English and Chinese; searching under the guide of subject classification schemes; meta-searching module.

(3) Academic forum and publishing information for scientific researching

PKUSpace provides an academic forum for students and professional users in every community to discuss their ideas and research work freely.

The remainder of the paper is organized as follows. Section 2 describes the three layers architecture and main technologies of PKUSpace. Section 3 describes the automated metadata extraction and text classification method adopted in PKUSpace. Section 4 describes the meta searching module. Section 5 demonstrates a case study. We summarize our works and discuss some future work in section 6.

2   Architecture

Like DSpace and most of the web-based applications today, PKUSpace platform is distinctly divided into three layers: the storage layer, service layer and application layer (showed in Fig 1). This implements the widely used MVC (Model-View-Control) pattern [8]. The upper layer relies simply on the lower one, without any knowledge about the internal details. With this logic separation, the whole system is more reliable and maintainable, for both researchers and developers.

Supported by PostgresSQL database system, the storage layer manages all the data, including the metadata and the content data.

The service layer implements all business logic of the system. Each module in this layer works on the fundamental storage API, and also provides common APIs accessible to other modules in service layer as well as the application layer.

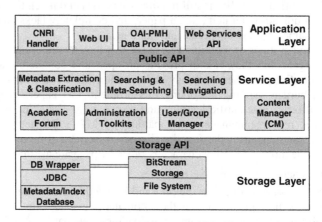

Fig. 1. The architecture of PKUSpace

The Searching & Meta-Searching module is based on a simple but powerful index/search toolkit Lucene [8]. This enables PKUSpace system to perform some simple search operations on content data, as well as advanced search with metadata and Boolean queries. The metadata of scientific journals such as title, author, keywords, reference etc. are extracted by the Metadata Extraction & Classification module and the corresponding file is classified to the subject classification hierarchy.

The Content Manager (CM) is a fundamental part, which managers all digital resource and user profiles. CM distributes a unique identifier to every article, bit stream, image and other forms of resources.

We add an online academic forum to support academic communication. Besides the forum, we provide special guiding information for each scientific research domain, including the knowledge structure of the domain, some fundamental corpora, current research focus, some important conferences and famous scholars.

We afford the system super user perfective administration toolkits, which can be divided into three parts: user toolkit, resource toolkit and handle toolkit. The user toolkit provides the function of management of the community, group and person. The resource toolkit changes the priority for the resource. And the handle toolkit manages the naming method of the handle server.

To feed needs under different circumstances, we provide different interfaces in application layer. The WebUI is the basic interface for researchers to manipulate the whole system. OAI-PMH is a very popular protocol in the digital library domain, which can harvest metadata in a platform-independent way [10]. The OAI-PMH data provider module publishes the metadata of the resources as XML data streams according to OAI http requests from other servers [10]. In the system we adopt WSDL interface descriptions to wrap important functions into Web Services, such as information retrieval, and metadata extraction, and deploy those web services on an Apache SOAP server. PKUSpace uses Handles primarily as a means of assigning globally unique identifiers to digital objects, in order to locate and access the objects. PKUSpace uses CNRI Handle System [11] and our handle naming rule is:

<Handle>:= [<ACM Category Number>].<The last name of the first author>.< An auto-increasing integer>

3 Automatic Metadata Extraction

In order to facilitate the organization and management of large volumes of scientific papers, the first important task is to extract metadata precisely and automatically from text. Our metadata is adapted from Dublin Core [12], with two expended elements: reference block and appendix.

After transforming PDF or PS papers into XML files, we use heuristic methods and regular expression matching techniques to mine different patterns and extract relevant metadata elements. Users can choose those authoritative metadata patterns such as ACM [13], Elsevier [14] and PubMed [15] to guide the metadata extraction or customize their own patterns. The metadata extraction rule database helps us to separate extraction rules from specific extraction procedures

ScientificJournal ::=	Title 'RT' AuthorBlock 'RT' [AbstractBlock] 'RT' [KeywordsBlock] 'RT' Content 'RT' ReferencesBlock 'RT' [Appendix]
AuthorBlock ::=	(AuthorName ',')* AuthorName 'RT' ((AuthorAffiliation ',')* AuthorAffiliation)* 'RT' (AuthorEmail ',')* AuthorEmail 'RT'
AbstractBlock ::=	('Abstract'| 'Abstracts') Description 'RT'
KeywordsBlock ::=	('Key words' | 'Keywords') (SubjectKeyword ',')* SubjectKeyword 'RT'
Content ::=	('Introduction'|'Overview'|Background'|'Motivation') 'RT' Body
ReferencesBlock ::=	(RefBody 'RT') +
Appendix ::=	('Appendix') Description 'RT'
RefBody ::=	(AuthorName ',')* AuthorName Title Publication Volume Page Webpage

Fig. 2. A common case of a metadata pattern

The following are major heuristic methods we used during extraction procedure:

(1) Different metadata elements have different characteristic key words. Identifying these key words accurately may have a positive effect on metadata extraction. Fig 2 shows a common case of a metadata pattern expressed in Backus Normal Formula.

(2) Extract elements with much certainty and little difficulty before those with much uncertainty. Some metadata elements, such as abstracts, key words, content, can be extracted easily at first.

(3) Address Database, Organization Name Database and Domain Name Database are efficient to differentiate related metadata from others. During the extraction procedure, we could use these useful information stored in databases.

(4) The extraction rules representing related metadata patterns are independent of specific journals and can be edited and revised by users. In this way, more extraction rules will be accumulated and more patterns be generated, therefore more papers with different metadata formats may be matched and processed with much higher precision.

Another important task is to assign scientific papers to predefined categories, which is finished by the classifier CRF, a linear text classification algorithm developed by our group [9].

An evaluation was carried out to study the effectiveness of automatic metadata extraction. From 1430 new scientific papers, 290 papers were eliminated during the preprocessing procedure and the remaining 1140 papers were transformed into XML files. The percentage of coarse granularity extraction is above 95% and the percentage of fine granularity extraction is above 83.3%, which is quite promising. This result is as high as, or higher than OpCit [16] conducted by Cornell Digital Library Group.

4 Meta-searching

Meta-searcher, such as SDARTS [17] implemented by Columbia University, is helpful for searching over many databases at once. A critical task for a meta-searcher is to merge results from many databases into a united list. So far, CORI algorithm [18] and other well-known algorithms are based on one premise that the result given by the databases should be scored. But this premise is unpractical, so we design our own algorithm according to our observation.

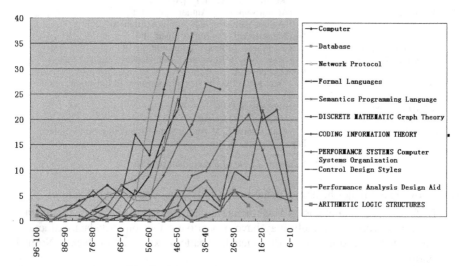

Fig. 3. Score distribution of querying results

Fig 3 is the score distribution diagram of the querying results in Elsevier [14]. X-axis represents the score while Y-axis represents the number of querying results of a certain score range. Thus, the diagram shows the relation between score and the number of results in that score range with each curve in the diagram showing the score distribution of a query. Therefore, we draw two conclusions:

1. The curve approaches an exponential distribution, as discussed in [19]

$$y = \lambda \cdot e^{\lambda \cdot x} \qquad \qquad ①$$

2. Different query has different λ, and the more matched documents are got from a certain query, the bigger the value of λ is. The integral of ① is

$$i = e^{\lambda \cdot b} - e^{\lambda \cdot a} \qquad \qquad ②$$

in which a and b are scores and i is the number of documents scores between a and b. Besides, we find that the scores of the matched documents at the end of querying lists usually approach 0. Hence, giving a query with N matched documents, we can assume that the score of document No. N+1 is 0.

$$N + 1 = e^{\lambda \cdot Max} - e^{\lambda \cdot 0} \qquad \qquad ③$$

Max is the highest score in the result list. If the document No. i got scores x, here we have

$$e^{\lambda \cdot x} - e^{\lambda \cdot 0} = i \qquad \qquad ④$$

From ③ and ④, we get the normalized score of document No. i :

$$score = 1 - x / Max = 1 - \log(i+1) / \log(N+2) \qquad ⑤$$

From this function, we conclude that the score is decided by the number of matched documents N only. This is the first scoring method (**Method 1**), which adjusts λ according to the number of results N.

Now, we make a scoring experiment on a scored database Elsevier [14]. The query words used in the experiment come from the classification subjects of ACM [13]. We evaluate the effectiveness of the scoring methods according to the variance between the scores got through On-line Scoring and the original scores offered by Elsevier. After our experiment, exponential distribution with various λ related to N is proved to be the most effective.

Scoring method	Linear distribution from 1 to 0.55	Exponential distribution with a fixed λ	Method 1 (Exponential distribution with various λ related to N)
Average variance	0.11554	0.044304	0.0298702

Fig. 4. The average variance of different scoring methods

For most databases, the score of the querying results and the times of query words appearing in the metadata of the results show a linear relation. And thus, by analyzing the term frequency of a query word in the metadata, we can estimate the score distribution. The process is assigning a respective weight to title, author and abstract in the metadata, and then scoring them according to the term frequency of the query word. By putting the normalized scores into equation ④, we can get an average λ. This **Method 2** makes up for the limitation in the first method.

Algorithm	Exponential distribution with a fixed λ	Scoring Method 1	Scoring Method 1&2 with weight (0.8/0.2)
Proquest	0.104218	0.083125	0.058568
20 groups	0.090804	0.0708434	0.067529
Stability	not Good	Good	Very Good

Fig. 5. The average variance of the first ten results of different scoring methods

We make some experiments on scoring and result merging on database Elsevier, Proquest and 20 News Groups using the regression method proposed in [20]. Without score of results from latter two resources, we find that by combining **Method 1** (exponential distribution changing with the number of results) and **Method 2** (metadata scoring), we can achieve a more effective merging result.

5   Case Study:
Search under the Guide of Subject Classification Scheme

Currently, there are more than 30,000 papers with PDF form in our system, most of which are free resource mainly from some famous universities and research institutes such as MIT, Stanford, CMU, UC Berkley, Microsoft, IBM and so on.

When all papers are well classified, we build a multi-function search engine that provides taxonomy navigation, full-text search (keyword search), structural search in the metadata level and composition of the three methods.

For the user who knows exactly what he needs, the full-text search is more helpful. Just as the current popular search engine, the user submits his query as some keywords and then the system will find and return the results relative to the keywords. We also accept Boolean expressions such as AND, OR and NOT.

As one of our system's character, we allow the user submit his query in the metadata layer. If the user knows the paper's author, keyword or other metadata, he can easily find his need. He can even use some complicated Boolean expressions to describe his query more precise.

A user will always get a lot of results at his first search. To achieve his goal, he can select the three kinds of search methods to search again in the results. Thus all the search methods are combined together. This is more flexible and convenient.

As an example of the use of the combinatorial search method, we post several queries (some famous authors' names) to the system in different ways (Fig 6). There are obviously more documents returned in the full-text search than in the author only search. In the domain-specific search, before the colon is the classification identifier of ACM and the number after it shows how many documents are retrieved in the domain corresponding to the classification identifier. As we can see, we will get 9 results of the author "Tom M. Mitchell" in the class I which means the domain of Computing Methodologies. And if we narrow the domain to I.2 which means the domain of Artificial Intelligence, sub-domain of I, only 5 results are returned. The user can come more and more closer to his request in this way.

6   Conclusion

In this paper, we have presented our ideas about a collaborative platform for scientific learning and researching. We have built up a prototype – PKUSpace, which can be conveniently utilized by people in different research areas to retrieve information, upload and share resources, get important information in their areas, and exchange academic ideas. We kept the three-layer software architecture and information-management functions of DSpace and added more important characters to it to make our system more powerful and convenient for online users.

Query Keywords	Full-text Search Results	Author Only Search Results	Domain-Specific Search Results	
Abraham Silberschatz	195	24	H.3: 1	B: 2
Jiawei Han	39	21	H: 1	K: 1
Tom M. Mitchell	66	14	I: 9	I.2: 5

Fig. 6. Example of searching in PKUSpcace

Up till now, the PKUSpace has been a prototype used in part of the computer science and biomedicine areas. We would like to apply this system to more disciplines with more platform-independent Web services at Peking University. Furthermore, we will improve our automated techniques, such as metadata extraction, classification, meta-searching in the future.

References

1. http://citeseer.ist.psu.edu
2. http://dblp.uni-trier.de/
3. www.refworks.com
4. Erik Duval, Eddy Forte. The Ariadne Knowledge Pool System. Communications of the ACM, May 2001, Volume 44 Issue 5.
5. Zhongnan Shen, Yuanchun Shi, Guangyou Xu. A Learning Resource Metadata Management System Based on LOM Specification. Computer Science Department, Tsinghua University. 2002
6. http://www-900.ibm.com/cn/software/products/db2/content_manager.shtml
7. http://www.trs.com.cn/products/trsir-ckm/ckm/index.jsp
8. Michael J. Bass, Margret Branschofsky, etc. DSpace - A Sustainable Solution for Institutional Digital Asset Services - Spanning the Information Asset Value Chain: Ingest, Manage, Preserve, Disseminate. March 1, 2002
9. Zhi-Hong Deng, Shi-Wei Tang, Dong-Qing Yang, Ming Zhang, Xiao-Bin Wu, Meng Yang. A Linear Text Classification Algorithm Based on Category Relevance Factors. In Proceedings of the 5th International Conference on Asian Digital Library (ICADL2002), Singapore, December 2002. LNCS 2555, Springer-Verlag.
10. Shu-an Wang, Ming Zhang, Ai-hua Wang, Dong-qing Yang. Constructing an Interoperable Digital Library Metadata Service Based on the OAI Protocol. In Proceedings of the 19th National Conference on Data Bases, Zhengzhou, China. Aug. 2002. (In Chinese)
11. Robert Kahn and Robert Wilensky, A Framework for Distributed Digital Object Services, May, 1995,
12. http://dublincore.org/
13. http://www.acm.org
14. http://www.elsevier.org
15. http://www.pubmed.nl
16. Kristie Seymore, Andrew McCallum, and Roni Rosenfeld. Learning hidden Markov model structure for information extraction. In AAAI 99 Workshop on Machine Learning for Information Extraction, 1999.
17. Panagiotis G. Ipeirotis and Luis Gravano. Distributed Search over the Hidden Web: Hierarchical Database Sampling and Selection. 28th VLDB Conference.
18. J.P. Callan, Z. Lu, ,and W.B. Croft, Searching Distributed Collections with Inference Networks. In SIGIR '95: Proceedings of the 18th Annual International ACM SIGIR Conference on Research and Development in Information Retrieval, pages 21-28, 1995.
19. R.Manmatha, T.Rath and F.Feng. Modeling Score Distributions for Combining the Outputs of Search Engines. SIGIR 2001
20. Luo Si and Jamie Callan. Using Sampled Data and Regression to Merge Search Engine Results. SIGIR 2002

Learning by Seamless Migration –
A Kind of Mobile Working Paradigm

Degan Zhang, Yuanchun Shi, Enyi Chen, Guangyou Xu, and Hongliang Gu

Key Lab of Pervasive Computing, Computer Science Department,
Tsinghua University, Beijing 100084, P.R.China
gandegande@mail.tsinghua.edu.cn

Abstract. In this paper, we propose a kind of mobile learning paradigm –
learning by seamless migration, which has the capability that task for learning
dynamically follows the learner from place to place and machine to machine
without learner awareness or intervention. Our key idea is this capability can be
achieved by architecture of component platform and agent-based migrating
mechanism. In order to study this learning paradigm, a description of pervasive
computing task for learning and migrating granularity of task of learning has
been suggested, firstly. Then, the architecture for seamless migration has been
proposed, a kind of mechanism of seamless migration has been adopted, including solving several sub-problems. Finally, the validity evaluation of this kind of
mobile working paradigm is shown by an experimental demo. Suggested learning paradigm by seamless migration is convenient to learn during mobility and
is useful for the busy or mobile learner.

1 Introduction

Nowadays, many ambitious projects have been proposed and carried on to welcome
the advent of pervasive computing. There are a bunch of branch research fields under
the banner of it, such as Seamless mobility [Satyanarayanan 2001]. For seamless mobility [Danny 2001], the history and context of computing task will be migrated with person's mobility, and the computing device and software resource around this task will
make adaptive change. The chief function requirement of seamless mobility is on the
continuity and adaptability of computing task. The continuity is that the application
can pause and continue the work without the loss of the current state and the running
history. The adaptability is that the application is not restricted by computing device
and context of service but adaptable to its environment.

Apparently, this function of seamless mobility is suitable for mobile learning paradigm [Takasugi 2001] [Takasugi 2003] [Michael 2002]. For learner, it is necessary and
accessible when he/she can NOT complete his/her learning task/courseware, such as
video, audio, text, picture, etc., in one specified scene, he/she can go on learning the
uncompleted task/courseware in other spots by seamless mobility based on the Web.
In our opinion, this is a kind of mobile working paradigm – learning by seamless migration with computing task. But when seamless migration for computing task of
learning is realized on PC, laptop, or PDA, there are several difficult problems to be

W. Liu et al. (Eds.): ICWL 2004, LNCS 3143, pp. 128–135, 2004.

solved: 1) Meet different networked Web environment, such as different OS platform. 2) Manage the seamless-service among multiple machine devices. 3) Descript computing task of learning and only migrate the relative parts of task interested by learner in order to reduce the delay produced by migrated data.

In this paper, we propose a test bed of learning by seamless migration for mobile learning, which can be suitable for the required dynamic changes to the network and environment without learner awareness or intervention, and the condition of only sitting in front of the desktop PC for mobile learning is unnecessary. The structure, mechanism, result of experimental evaluation of the test bed is reported. It makes the ultimate mobile system possible by dynamically implementing the changes required to follow the learner from place to place and machine to machine.

The rest of this paper will be organized as follows. Firstly, we give formal description of task of learning and migrating granularity of task of learning. And then, we propose the architecture of test bed for learning by seamless migration, design a kind of mechanism of seamless migration. Finally, we evaluate the validity of our test bed for mobile learning and draw a conclusion.

2 Description Method for the Task of Learning

In order to explain and realize how to transfer computing task among different computing environments, firstly, a formal description and types of task are required. To meet the environment of pervasive computing, a universal description language for task should to be used. Nowadays, the description languages for workflow or task are mainly based on stationary computing environment [Simmons 2001]. But the computing environment of seamless mobility is dynamic and parallel, the description language should be able to express the time topological structure. So we adopt SMIL (Synchronized Multimedia Integration Language), released by W3C is a standard for compound multimedia integration and description and is supported by the industry currently.

3 Migrating Granularity of the Task of Learning

According to integrity of transferred contents of the task of learning, the migrating granularity of task of learning may be divided into "Strong Transfer", "Weak Transfer". The mode of transferring may be obeyed "Travel Schedule/Plan". Strong transferring means that total information involved in the current task of learning must be transferred, after reaching the target terminal, the task can execute continuously from snapshot point. But in mobile WWW, it is difficult to collect total information of current task, to describe and record the executed status and necessity of task of learning under the high bandwidth network, so the burden of this mode is very heavy and complex. Generally, weak transferring is done for partial executing status and data, its speed is much faster then that of strong transferring, and its delay is much shorter then that of strong transferring. Under weak transferring, a certain MAS has adopted random command, such as Aglet, Mole, and so on. Of course, weak transferring has its shortcomings, for instance, the total historical executing status of task is difficult to be restored. So it is decided only by detailed scenario that which mode should be adopted in the application.

4 Architecture of Test Bed of Learning by Seamless Migration

The architecture of our test bed of learning by seamless migration is divided into four layers. From bottom to top, Networked hardware devices layer, including wire/wireless networked PC, laptop, or PDA.OS layer, including Linux, Windows 2000&XP, Win CE. Middleware layer, which may be divided into 3 sub-layers, from bottom to top, communication component layer for merging OS, container layer for organization and coordination, ADK (Agent development kits) layer for application development. Application layer, including seamless migration manager for computing task of learning, other managers and applications. Here, the focus of our work is in application layer.

Our seamless migration manager for learning is also a MAS including fixed or mobile agents. It runs upon networks-connected PC, laptop, or PDA, masking the boundary of the involved devices and providing a uniform running environment and highly structured communication models for the software modules run on it. In the MAS model, each constituent module has its own execution process, which matches the nature of runtime environment. Now we introduce the manager. The runtime environment is composed of four kinds of components, which are Human-computer interaction interface, Task manager, Continuity manager and Service manager. The introduction of them is as follows.

1) *Human-computer interaction interface* including agent interface and relative controlling. The agent interface is used as defining the attributes of agent, such as ID of agent, Name of agent, Type of agent (such as TA, SA, UA, VA, EA, DA, and so on), Current status of agent (one of five status are "Ready", "Waiting", "Transferring", "executing", "Dead" or "Destroyed"), Association relationship of agent (including relationship between agent and task of learning, relationship between agent and agent).

2) *Task Manager*. It is for application service, which manages the application/task array, including task description of learning, task analyzing, mapping or binding between task and service, loading, executing, planning schedule of task of learning, etc.

3) *Continuity Manager*. It is for preparing "Migrating travel plan/schedule" of task of learning, sensing context, suspending of task, historical status (including log, configuration, etc.) recording, agent management, addressing of target node, determining of transferring granularity which is for avoiding the transferring failure, reducing the remainder dependency & contracting the transferring delay, resume of task of learning, and so on.

4) *Service Manager*. It manages the registration of service, service discovery [Garlan 2002], lookup of service, service selection/association, and mapping or binding between task and service.

These components can communicate each other, and may be controlled by human-computer application interaction interface including agents and relative control, which is individual interface for PC, laptop, PDA. The fixed or mobile agent is the basic encapsulation of the software modules in the system for management of seamless migration. Each device in the runtime environment will host a dedicated process called Container, which provides system-level services for the agents that run on the different devices and manages them as well. The details of other parts of the system are transparent to agent. In our test bed, there is one global dedicated process in the runtime environment, which mediates the "delegated communication" between agents and provides services such as directory service, dependency resolution.

In the following, we emphasize the mechanism of learning task by seamless migration based on agent for *Continuity Manager*. The research for *Service Manager* can be found in [Chen 2003].

5   Mechanism of Seamless Migration Based on Agent

The mechanism of seamless migration is focused on the application level of our test bed of learning, which is different from seamlessness of networking connection on IP (such as smoothly switch among regions, seamless roaming, etc.) and data mobility of workflow. In this paper, we deal with the problems of addressing, seamless migrating/transferring method, etc. Now we discuss a new efficient mechanism of seamless migration for learning task suggested by us.

If the transferred amount of data of learning task is partial, and this part of information must be transferred firstly so that the task can restore the runtime environment and run continuously on the target node for learner, this part of information is regarded as "Key Set", so we can divide the migrated information into several chunks, such as executing code chunk, running status chunk, and so on. For resuming, the "Key Set" chunks must be merged, otherwise it is impossible to go on running continuously.

According to the classification of agent in our test bed of learning, we make the following rule:

1) Navigation Agent (VA) need NOT do direct relative works with the task, which is familiar with the topological structure of Internet/subnet of target node and addressing in the network. The Data Structure of VA may be divided into two parts: one is itself "function body", another is MessageBox (MB, mark as) used as loading moved object and transferring in the Internet/subnet node.

2) Task Agent (WA) does detail jobs, which includes executing the code, managing the data and environmental status, and so on. It can transfer with the Navigation Agent (VA) in the network and need NOT know the structure of Internet/subnet.

3) When migrated/transferred, WA seeks relative VA and joins in its **MB** firstly, and then sent to target node by VA.

For the sake of convenience to explain the method of migration/transfer, we give the following hypothesis:

One TA wants WA on the logic node PA_2 to be transferred to another logic node PA_3, according to the time-topological relation of transferred object, the "TRAVEL SCHEDULE /PLAN" which is a kind of DATA STRUCTURE independent of agent has been made. The current scenario is that the TA is connected with logic node PA_1 which is connected to logic node PA_2 through double direction link, the arrow shows the connected direction and solid line with arrow shows WA can transit the logic link.

The designed and adopted algorithm of seamless migration by us in the test bed includes eight main steps:

1) According to the prepared TRAVEL SCHEDULE/PLAN for migrating/transferring, logic node PA_2 lets VA begin addressing in the network according to the address supplied by logic node PA_3, when the connection is successful, VA sends instruction "TransferNode" to Logic node PA_3 as target node, VA+$\boxed{WA}$ transfer to PA_3 after packing, the packet consists of the recorded structure of WA, the association relationship between WA, the space occupied by WA, the type of WA, the information of VA for task transferring and "Messenger" information for scheduling all Agent (including VA, EA and DA), the state of arrived Messenger is not "Executing" but "Waiting" and storing in the queue of PA_3.

2) Logic node PA_3 sends instruction "UpdateLinking" to all logic nodes connected to PA_2, such as logic node PA_1. The instruction includes the information modifying the link address, such as link ID, IP and Port of two ends. During the transferring, the Messengers to PA_3 store in the relative queue and wait for executing unless the Key Set or the total task is finished to be transferred.

3) When PA_1 has received the instruction "UpdateLinking", it creates the association to new link, and sends instruction "LinksUpdated" to logic node PA_2.

4) When PA_2 has received all expected message "LinkUpdated", and then sends instruction "ActiveNode" to logic node PA_3. The message includes the list of all arrived Messenger. At the same time, PA_2 delete the transferred VA+$\boxed{WA}$.

5) When PA_3 has received the message "ActiveNode", received Messenger from PA_2 listed in the tail of the queue. According to the topological relationship, under the rule of FIFO, PA_3 activates the Messenger, up to now, the transferring work is finished.

6) When all Messengers are activated, each WA will restore running environment and do instruction "ExecuteTask".

7) During the executing of each WA, on the one hand, the historical snapshots will be recorded and saved (including the structure of WA, the association relationship between WA, the space occupied by WA, the type of WA, the information of VA for task transferring and Messenger information for scheduling all Agent (including VA, EA and DA), the state of Messenger for scheduling), on the other hand, VA do the instruction "ListenTask" continuously and get the next transferring instruction "TransferSignal".

8) During the executing of WA, VA checks the prepared TRAVEL SCHEDULE/ PLAN, if another new migrating plan is checked, the "TransferSignal" instruction will be sent to WA. If no instruction "TransferSignal" is received by WA, it will execute its task continuously until the task is completed, otherwise, it will stop executing, and Goto 1 for preparing the new migrating/ transferring.

In our test bed, the addressing mode of VA can select one of three kinds: Registration addressing, Message dispatching, Broadcast addressing.

Registration addressing is to look for the target through registering the IP address or the ID of DNS. The classic representative protocol is Mobile IP protocol, especially, MIPv6. In fact, mobile IPv6 influences the route of data package, but independent of route protocol, such as RIP, OSPF, et al. The operation of IPv6 in Mobile IP includes home Agent registration, triangle route, route optimization, binding management, mobile checking and home Agent discovery. When mobile node connects to foreign chain, besides home address, it can communicate by one or several care of address. The association between home address and care of address of mobile node is named "binding".

Message dispatching is that there is the address of next node on the current transferring road of Agent, the message for Agent can send the target Agent along the double direction cycle link. In this method, MAS let Agents set a Virtual Proxy in the starting point, if the sender of message gets the Virtual Proxy of Agent, it can find the current position of Agent along this pointer.

Broadcast addressing is broadcast query message in all nodes of MAS for addressing. This is a kind of distributed addressing mechanism purely, which is a simple addressing mode in the LAN, but in the WAN, simple broadcast can NOT complete the reliable transmission, distributed snapshot idea can overcome the shortcoming in a certain degree.

Three kinds of addressing mode have their advantages and shortcomings, select them according to different application scenario. As a kind of standard addressing mode, we often adopt the registration addressing as default, because message-chasing cases may exist in Message dispatching, broadcast addressing is not adapted for Mobile learning.

6   Evaluation of the Test Bed for Mobile Learning

Currently, It includes the seamless migration for computing task on PC, laptop, or PDA under dynamic changes to the network and environment without user awareness or intervention. It supplies the function that the task dynamically follows the user from place to place and machine to machine. For example, just like Fig.1, the video-playing task for learning may follow me from my house to other places, such as my office, stadium, coffee house, park, airport, etc., and vice versa [Zhang 2004].

As demo, a kind of the task of learning is described partially by SIML in the following:

```
<smil>
  <head>
   <layout>
   <root-layout background-color="#D3DD86" width="640" height="480" />
   <region id="videoregion" top="0" left="0" width="320" height="240" />
   <region id="textregion" top="0" left="321" width="320" height="159" ->
   </layout>
  </head>
  <body>
```

```
<seq><par>
  <video src="Pervasiv.avi" region="videoregion" begin="0.6s" />
  <audio src="IloveChina.mp3" begin="2.6s" />
  <textstream src="Pervasive.txt" region="textregion" begin="5s"
  end="9000s" />
  </par></seq>
</body>
</smil>
```

The above task of learning has three sub-tasks of learning: Playing *Pervasiv.avi*, playing *IloveChina.mp3*, reading *Pervasive.txt*. They will be done according to the time-sequence in parallel mode based on algorithm mentioned above. With the learner's movement from one station (such as House) to another station (such as Airport), these uncompleted sub-tasks of learning can seamlessly migrate from PC of his /her house to laptop, or PDA with him/her in Airport and go on learning (watching, listening and reading) continuously by mobile agent. In our experiments of mobile learning, the deployment is the CPU frequency, RAM of PC and laptop are 1.2GHz, 256MHz,respectively, and 450MHz、64MHz RAM are for PDA, the speed of wire network and wireless network is 10M/100MHZ, 1-3MHZ, respectively. The experimental nodes are shown in Fig. 1. The nodes were connected by wireless and wired network. PC, laptop, or PDA may join in. Based on the above test bed of learning, one snap-shot comparison result of experiments for seamless migration from PC to PC, laptop and PDA is shown in our experiments.

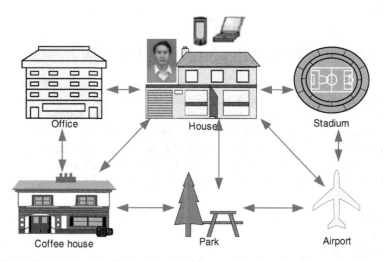

Fig. 1. Task of learning follows me from place to place based on above algorithm

From experiment's results, we can see the delay time from PC to PC is the shortest under the same evaluation framework, but the delay time from PC to PDA is the longest. The reason is discussed in the following: 1) When PCs are connected by wired network, but the laptop, or PDA is connected by wireless network, the result is easy to be accessible or apparent. 2) When PC, laptop, or PDA are connected by WLAN (wireless local area network), the PCs are not mobile and have enough cache buffer, the migrating granularity of task is bigger, the remainder dependency during migrating is less or void, so the same migrated data amount may be transferred in shorter time. But PDA is on the contrary. The cache buffer, the migrating granularity of task and the remainder dependency during migrating of laptop is between PC and PDA. In mobile WWW, it is also apparent to laptop and PDA. Of course, the advantage of PDA is well known.

7 Conclusions

In order to meet the application requirements of mobile learning, we have proposed a kind of novel learning paradigm–learning by seamless migration with computing task, which supplies the function that the task of learning dynamically follows the learner from place to place and machine to machine, so it is convenient to learn during mobility, and is useful/helpful for the mobile learner. Our key idea is this capability can be achieved by layering architecture of component platform and agent-based migrating mechanism. In this paper, we have given the formal description of task of learning, discussed the migrating granularity of task of learning, proposed the architecture of test bed of learning by seamless migration, designed a kind of mechanism of seamless migration, including solving these problems, such as addressing, method of seamless migrating, shortening migration delay, avoiding migration failure and remainder dependency. The validity of the test bed for mobile learning has been evaluated by the demo.

References

[Satyanarayanan 2001] Satyanarayanan M. Pervasive Computing: Vision and Challenges[J]. IEEE Personal Communications, August 2001, 10-17.
[Michael 2002] M.K Kozuch, M.Satyanarayanan, Internet Suspend/Resume[C]. WMCSA 2002.
[Takasugi 2003] K Takasugi. Seamless Service Platform for Following a User's Movement in a Dynamic Network Environment [C]. PerCom'03.
[Takasugi 2001] K Takasugi, Minoru Katayama. "Adaptive System for Service Continuity in a Mobile Environment", IEEE APCC 2001, Tokyo, Japan, Sep. 2001.
[Simmons 2001] Simmons R. A Task Description Language for Robot Control[C]. Proceedings Conference on Intelligent Robotics and Systems, New York, Oct 2001, 138-147.
[Chen 2003] Enyi Chen, Degan Zhang. A Programming Frame-work for Service Association in Ubiquitous Computing Environments [C]. IEEE PCM, Singapore, 2003, 12.
[Shi 2003] Yuanchun Shi. The Smart Classroom: Merging Technologies for Seamless Tele-Education, IEEE Pervasive Computing Magazine, April-June 2003, Vol. 2, No. 2.
[Zhang 2004] Degan Zhang, Guangyou Xu, Yuanchun Shi, Enyi Chen. Moblie agents with intrusion detection during sealess transfer[C]. Pervasive 2004: DC, April 18-23,2004.

XML-Based Agent Communication in a Distributed Learning Environment

Elvis Wai Chung Leung and Qing Li

Department of Computer Engineering and Information Technology
City University of Hong Kong, Kowloon, Hong Kong SAR, China
{iteleung,itqli}@cityu.edu.hk

Abstract. A dramatic increase in the development of technology-based teaching and learning has been witnessed in the past decade. Distributed Learning Environments (DLEs) have emerged rapidly, which blend traditional and IT-based learning with the aid of distributed environments and learning communities. In this paper, we address the issues of collaborative agent communication in DLEs through describing 1) a multi-agent architecture supporting DLEs, 2) agent communication policies to govern the conversation among agents, and 3) XML-based language facilities and algorithms to facilitate communication among agents in DLEs.

Keywords: Distributed Learning Environments, Multi-agent communication architecture, XML

1 Introduction

A dramatic increase in the development of technology-based teaching and learning has been witnessed in the past decade. Many universities and corporations started rethinking the design and implementation of learning systems as well as their environments. *Distributed Learning Environments (DLEs)* have emerged rapidly, which blend traditional and IT-based learning with the aid of distributed environments and learning communities [1].

DLEs allow the flexibility in using either simple sequential access or a more complex high-level interaction between students and instructors. The approaches may be generally categorized as *broadcast*, *online* or *collaborative*. The collaborative learning allows students to interact with peers, while the broadcast approach is more of one-way learning. A combination of broadcast and collaborative approaches can sometimes be more than desirable [1]. Some current examples are Blackboard [4], WebCT [5], and IBM Lotus Learning Management System [6]. Common tools embedded in these systems are electronically warehousing course content and disseminating static lectures and materials. Technology that supports case-based and collaborative pedagogies remains, however, scarce. [2, 3].

Currently, high student dropout rate and low satisfaction with the learning processes remain to be the drawbacks. Not surprisingly, failing to consider students' attributes and instructional strategies seems to cause ineffectiveness even with the technologically advanced DLEs being developed. In response to the above-mentioned issues in the IT-based learning, we have engaged in developing a *Personalized eLearning System (Peels)* over the last couple of years [17, 18]. In this paper, the aims are to address the issues of collaborative agent communication in DLEs.

W. Liu et al. (Eds.): ICWL 2004, LNCS 3143, pp. 136–146, 2004.
© Springer-Verlag Berlin Heidelberg 2004

The rest of this paper is organized as follows: The related work of the current agent communication languages is reviewed in section 2. The specific features of the proposed policies and algorithms are detailed in sections 3 to 5. The final section concludes this paper and makes suggestions for further research.

2   Related Work

In this section, we review some agent communication languages that are closely related to our research. The Agent Communication Language (ACL) concept has its origin in the work of the Knowledge Sharing Effort (KSE) [10, 11]. In the early 1990's the KSE work gave birth to Knowledge Query and Manipulation Language (KQML) and influenced the FIPA (Foundation for Intelligent Physical Agents) standard body ACL [12]. The goal of FIPA is to make available specifications that maximize interoperability across agent-based systems. Many different groups have designed and built multi-agent systems that used KQML for inter-agent communication [8, 9].

Both languages assume a basic non-commitment to a reserved content language. The two languages have the same syntax - that means, a KQML message and a FIPA ACL message look syntactically identical except for their different names for communication primitives. At the level of what constitutes the semantic descriptions, the two languages differ semantically. They also differ at the definitions of the modalities they employ and the level of the choice. In theory, the similarity in basic assumptions and syntax among existing ACLs means that only the communication primitive-specific code should change according to the choice of ACL.

Nowadays, both FIPA and KQML are evolved to use XML as one of the communication languages in their specifications. On the other hand, the incorporation of links of XML into the ACL message takes a significant step toward addressing the problem due to the pointing links to objects and/ or definitions. Thus, ontology technology can be used in ACL which can assist agents to understand the "word meaning" easily. In section 5, we shall discuss the use of FIPA ACL in our prototype as the standard to transfer conversations among multi-agents.

3   Agent Architecture

3.1   Agent Abstraction

An *agent* is an encapsulated computer program that is situated in some environments and is capable of flexible, autonomous actions in that environment in order to meet its design objectives. In particular, an agent has the following characteristics [14,15]:

i.   Clearly identifiable problem solving entities with well-defined boundaries and interfaces;

ii. Situated (embedded) in a particular environment – they receive inputs related to the state of their environment through sensors and they act on the environment through effectors;

iii. Designed to fulfill a specific purpose – they have particular objectives (goals) to achieve;

iv.   Autonomous – they have control both over their internal state and over their own behavior;
v.   Capable of exhibiting flexible problem solving behavior in pursuit of their design objectives – they need to be both reactive and proactive.

   Accordingly, if we denote the environment by S as a set of external states without imposing any constraints on the structure of the elements in the set, then the description for an agent $\mathcal{A}$ is a 3-tuple as follows:

$$\mathcal{A} = (Db, E^S, Act) \tag{1}$$

where Db is a database that contains the agent's acquired knowledge, $E^S = \{e_1,...,e_x\}$ ($x > 0$) is a set of partitions of the environment S which constitute the possible perceptions of the agent, and $Act = \{act_1,...,act_y\}$ ($y > 0$) is a set of possible actions of the agent. According to (1), an agent can determine how the state of the environment is perceived based on E^S. Moreover, the best action for a current request can also be derived based on $Db \times E^S$. Finally, the agent also updates its internal knowledge base according to the newly received perceptions $e_i \in E^S$.

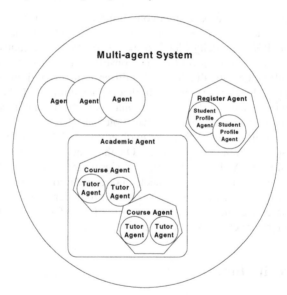

Fig. 1. A multi-agent system abstraction

3.2   Multi-agent Architecture

A *multi-agent system* can be considered as an ensemble of agents acting and working autonomously, each representing an independent focus of control of the whole system [20]. Moreover, it is a loose network of problem-solver entities that work together to find answers to problems which are beyond the individual capabilities or knowledge of each entity [16]. In many cases, agents are required to communicate with each other for collecting information. During the conversation, the goal of each agent is dependent on each communication topic. Normally, in response to the communication topic, the agents are relayed on some pre-defined rules (to be explained in section 4).

Meanwhile, the concept of *agent's facilitator* is employed in the multi-agent system. In particular, a facilitator is an agent that is responsible for coordinating agent communications and cooperative problem solving.

Abstractly, a multi-agent environment $MultiA$ has a formularization of the relationships among the agents in the system as a 4-tuple given below:

$$MultiA = (GE, GAct, A, Act) \tag{2}$$

where $GE = \{ge_1, ..., ge_m\}$ ($m > 0$) is a set S of the environments which constitute the possible perceptions of the agent system, $GAct = \{gact_1, ..., gact_n\}$ ($n > 0$) is a set of possible actions of the agent system, $A = \{a_1, ..., a_z\}$ ($z > 0$) is a set of agents in the agent system, and $Act = \{act_1, ..., act_y\}$ ($y > 0$) is a set of selected actions that are assigned to each action of $GAct$ by A. Thus, the best action $gact_i$ ($1 \leq i \leq n$) for a request can be derived based on $GE \times GAct$ and the selected best action act_j ($1 \leq j \leq y$) will be preformed based on $A \times Act$.

In our proposed system, we introduce a **natural group concept** that is based on the organizational hierarchy working relationship to organize a team for completing a task. As shown in Figure 1 there are two examples of natural groups as discussed below:

- *Tutor Agent, Course Agent, and Academic Agent as one natural group.* A Tutor Agent is responsible for the student learning matters such as presenting personalized learning materials. It needs to communicate with the facilitator, Course Agent, to receive the course materials, and through the Course Agent to talk to other agents if it cannot identify the relevant agents.

- *Student Profile Agent and Register Agent as another natural group:* The main responsibility for the Student Profile Agent is to record the student information such as personal details, course enrolment, and so on. The Register Agent's responsibility is to manage the Student Profile Agents and assigns a new agent when a new student has completed the registration.

To ensure the agents to cooperate efficiently, we will proceed in next section to discuss the communication policies and algorithms.

4 Agent Communication Policies

In order to build up an efficient and effective mechanism for the agents' communication, implementation of the internal communication policies is a core element. During a conversation among agents, we need to manage the related agents, contents, and the rules of the conversation process. In order to coordinate this process, a **Communication Schema** CS can be defined as follows:

$$CS = (Agt, ComAct, Rule) \tag{3}$$

where $Agt = \{agt_1, ..., agt_p\}$ ($1 < p \leq z$) is a set of agents involved in the conversation; $ComAct = \{comact_1, ..., comact_q\}$ ($q > 0$) is a set of packets of conversation ("communicative acts") performed by each agent in Agt ; $Rule = \{rule_1, ..., rule_r\}$ ($r > 0$) is a set of rules for conducting the conversation (ref. *Policy 3* below). The possible result out of the conversation is derived from $Agt \times ComAct \times Rule$. In the following, three natural communication scenarios are shown in Figure 2.

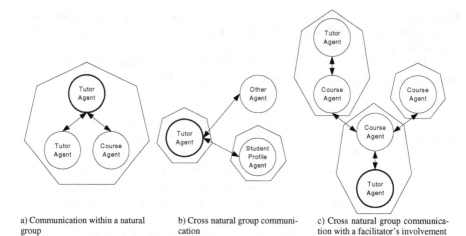

a) Communication within a natural group

b) Cross natural group communication

c) Cross natural group communication with a facilitator's involvement

Fig. 2. Agent communication scenarios

a) ***Communication within a natural group.*** For example, a Tutor Agent communicates with another Tutor Agent for helping two students' discussion on the same topic. A Tutor Agent may also communicate with its facilitator, Course Agent, to receive relevant course materials for designing personalized course materials.

b) ***Cross natural group communication.*** For example, a Tutor Agent communicates with the Student Profile Agent to get a student's information to understand the student workload for designing his study plan. A Tutor Agent may also communicate with another agent for cooperation of a task.

c) ***Cross natural group communication with facilitator involvement.*** For example, a Tutor Agent wants to communicate with other course's Tutor Agent for knowing a student's current study performance so as to design his learning materials. However, it does not have the information about courses enrollment in the current year. Thus, it communicates to the facilitator, Course Agent, to find the student's record in other enrolled courses.

To look further inside the above-mentioned communication scenarios, we notice that there is a common factor for any agent to specify, namely, the *target* it needs to communicate with. In case no such target is specified, the agent will have to seek its facilitator's advice to identify the target. Afterwards, the communication channel is established.

Policy 1: An agent must identify another agent as the target before sending out a message. It can ensure the message to be passed to the target agent and can also reduce the cost of network traffic by avoiding broadcast of the request within the entire multi-agent system. The policy is enforced by Algorithm 1.

1. **If** the *target receiver* is known **then**
2.   ***Send***(*Message, target receiver*)
3. **Else**
4.   ***Inform***(*Message, facilitator*)   *// the sender inform its own facilitator to redirect the message to its target receiver*
5. **End if**

Algorithm 1. Identifying the target agent for communication initialization

Policy 2: Conversations among the agents must be governed by the CFA (Conversation For Action) protocol [19].

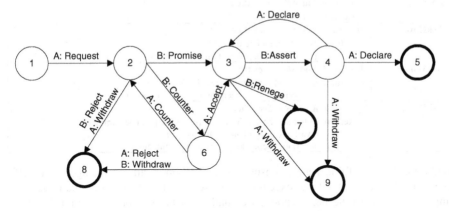

Fig. 3. Conversation for Action (CFA) protocol

Due to its definition clarity on the communication interoperations, the *Conversation for Action* (CFA) protocol [19] is adopted and incorporated in our system as a core communication policy. Through CFA, the agents can communicate with each other and students can also make requests to the agent system smoothly (see the "state-transition diagram" of CFA in Figure 3). Since an agent fulfills its commitments by negotiating with others, additional conversations may be generated during the process for clarification. Referring to the example in Figure 3 if agent B accepts A's initial request, a promise from B should be sent back to A; and if B does not want to fulfill its commitment at any time, it should send a renege message to A. The details of the algorithm are provided in the next section.

For each agent, all knowledge is stored in a database so that it can communicate with or answer questions from other agents. To facilitate the storage mechanism, *Db* in formula (4) is denoted as a repository for storing agent knowledge:

$$Db = (T, F, Skey, L) \tag{4}$$

where T is a set of tables $\{t_1...t_g\}$ $(g>0)$ in *Db*, F is a set of fields $\{f_1...f_h\}$ $(h>0)$ in T, *Skey* is a set of keys $\{skey_1...skey_k\}$ $(k>0)$ for searching data from T, L is a set of links $\{l_1...l_s\}$ $(s \geq 0)$ for joining T together in *Db*. In a particular conversation, an agent (sender) sends a *message* to another agent (receiver). The message includes two types of information: 1) what is required (i.e. the required data), and 2) how to select the data (i.e. selection criteria). If we denote the required data by *RD* as a set of data fields $\{rd_1...rd_u\}$ $(u>0)$, and selection criteria by *SC* as a set of criteria $\{sc_1...sc_v\}$ $(v \geq 0)$, then the receiver needs to check *RD* and *SC* with *Db*. If the checking is successful, the required data will be sent to the sender; otherwise, clarification or rejection will be sent to the sender. To perform the conversation, some pre-defined rules are necessary as stipulated in the following policy.

Policy 3: The predefined rules given in Table 1 are used as guidelines to ensure sound communication among the agents smoothly.

Table 1. Pre-defined rules as "guidelines"

Name	Rule Body
EXE	**If** $RD \subset F$ **And** $SR \subset Skey$ **then** **Return** the result
AskHow	**If** $RD \not\subset F$ **And** $SR \subset Skey$ **then** **Return** "How to complete the [x]?" [x] - a variable dependent on the question
AskWhich	**If** $RD \subset F$ **And** $SR \not\subset Skey$ **then** **Return** "Which [y] is required? E.g. [y]" [y] - a variable dependent on missing parameters
AskWhat	**If** $RD \not\subset F$ **And** $SR \not\subset Skey$ **then** **Return** "What are the selection criteria for the [x]?The parameters may be [y]" [x] - a variable dependent on the question [y] – a variable dependent on missing parameters

While the rules of Table 1 are to ensure correct responses among the agents, the efficiency of the enforcement and execution of these rules is dependent on the underlying implementation. In the next section, we shall describe the communication language and algorithms that actually implement all the communication policies.

5   Agent Communication Language and Algorithms

5.1   Communicative Acts and XML-Based Communication

Based on the *communication schema* and the *communication policies* introduced in the previous section, the agents' *communicative acts* can be defined in terms of the following messages:

> *Request(Sender, Receiver, Query)*
> *Accept(Sender, Receiver)*
> *Reject(Sender, Receiver, [Explanation])*
> *Clarification(Sender, Receiver, Query, [Explanation])*
> *Done(Sender, Receiver, Result)*

where *Sender* is the agent sending the message, *Receiver* is the agent receiving the message, *Query* is the content of the message, *Explanation* is an optional message for explaining the reason of getting **Reject** () or **Clarification** (), *Result* is the answer to the *Query*. Normally, an agent (sender) makes a request to another agent (receiver) through **Request()**. If the receiver can provide the requested information (i.e., result), it will send out **Accept()** for confirmation and return the result through **Done()** subsequently. Otherwise, it will send out **Clarification()** for receiving further explanation or **Reject()** for termination. To implement the above communicative acts, an algorithm (as shown in Algorithm 2) is introduced whose design is based on the CFA protocol.

Meanwhile, to facilitate the transfer of the conversation through XML in a distributed learning environment (DLE), the standard of FIPA ACL (XML message representation specification) is adopted [7]. Table 2 and Figure 4 show, respectively, the *scenario* of multi agents dialogues along with the *subsequent actions* based on the policies and algorithms, and a sample XML-based message for the **Request()** communicative act from Tutor Agent.

```
1. Request (Sender, Receiver, Query);
2. The Receiver performs the required action based on the parameters;
3. If   Perform(Receiver, Query) is successful then
4.                Accept(Sender, Receiver);
5.                Done(Sender, Receiver, Result)
6. Else
7.                Clarification (Sender, Receiver, Query, Explanation);
8.                If  no further reply from the Sender  OR reject message is received then
9.                        Reject(Sender, Receiver, Explanation)
10.              Else   // Reprocessing the request based on the new info from the agent's reply
11.                      Request(Sender, Receiver, Query)
                 End
12.       if
13. End if
```

Algorithm 2. Agent communication algorithm

```xml
<?xml version="1.0" ?>
<message act="Request" conversation-id="000001">
<receiver>
 <agent-identifier>
  <name id="Student Profile Agent" />
  <addresses>
   <url href="http://foo.com/receiver" />
  </addresses>
 </agent-identifier>
</receiver>
<sender>
  <agent-identifier>
   <name id="Tutor Agent" />
   <addresses>
    <url href="http://foo.com/sender" />
   </addresses>
  </agent-identifier>
</sender>
<content>
 Please provide a list of enrolled course for student A.
</content>
 ...
   </message>
```

Fig. 4. XML-based message for the Tutor Agent's Request()

Table 2. Sample agents dialogues with communicative acts and actions

Participant	Messages contents	Communicative act	Response action based on Policy 3
Tutor Agent (TA)	M1 = "Please provide a list of enrolled course for student A"	Request(TA,SPA, M1)	
Student Profile Agent (SPA)	M2 = "Which years? (E.g., 2002/2003, 2003/2004, or all?)"	Clarification(SPA,TA,M1, M2)	The rule of Ask-Which
Tutor Agent (TA)	M3 = "Please provide a list of enrolled courses for student A in 2003/2004"	Request(TA,SPA,M3)	
Student Profile Agent (SPA)	R = "CS5125 Database; CS5130 Networking"	Accept(SPA,TA) Done(SPA,TA,R)	The rule of EXE

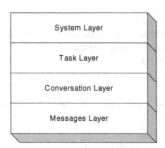

Fig. 5. A layered conceptual model for agents

5.2   Prototype Implementation

As part of our research, we have also been developing a prototype system which adopts a *layered conceptual model* (LCM) for building up the multi-agent system. Specifically, the *LCM* has *4 layers* as shown in Figure 5. The operations of an individual agent $\mathcal{A}$ are designed according to this LCM as follows:

The *system layer* is to monitor $\mathcal{A}$'s cooperation with other agents for accomplishing a specific task and the internal operation.

The *task layer* is to process the requests from a user or other agents in the agent system. It maps an individual request into specific sub-tasks, and sends the subtasks among the agents in the system. The possible actions and rule-based knowledge are stored in a central database (viz., *Db*) so that the task layer can retrieve the best solution based on the actual situation.

The *conversation layer* is to manage the communication among agents for a specific service/request. With respect to these conversations, the flow of messages among agents is based on the proposed conversation algorithm described in section 4.

The *messages layer* is to handle the information passed among the agents during a conversation. The structure of a message is based on the XML specification of FIPA [13], with the detailed algorithm as explained in the previous section.

Our elearning prototype system (called *Peels*) being developed is based on this 4-layered LCM and the agent communication algorithms given in section 4. Figure 6a illustrates a sample screen shot depicting a student requesting a Tutor Agent to get his personalized course materials, and Figure 6b shows the resultant course notes obtained from our prototype system implementing the agent communication algorithms.

6   Conclusion and Future Work

Distributed Learning Environments (DLEs) have emerged rapidly in recent years, which blend traditional and IT-based learning with the aid of distributed environments and learning communities. In this paper, we have addressed the issues of collaborative agent communication in DLEs through describing: 1) a multi-agent architecture supporting DLEs, 2) agent communication policies to govern the conversation among agents, and 3) XML-based language facilities and algorithms to facilitate communication among agents in DLEs. In our subsequent work, we plan to make our system Web-enabled so as to collect real user comments and perform user analysis on the Internet for consolidated research.

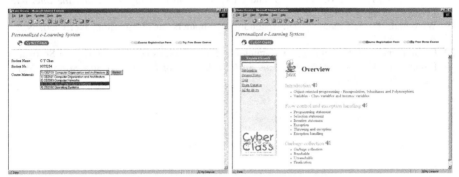

(a) Course selection   (b) Personalized course materials

Fig. 6. Prototype screen shot

References

1. Alavi, M, Distributed learning environments, *IT Systems Perspectives,* 2004
2. Webster, J., Hackley, P., Teaching effectively in technology-mediated distance learning. *Acad. Management J.* 40(6) pp.1282-1309, 1997
3. Alavi, M., Leidner, D. E., Research commentary: technology-mediated learning – a call for greater depth and breadth of research, *Information Systems Research*, Vol. 12, No. 1, pp.1-10, 2001
4. Blackboard, http://blackboard.net
5. WebCT, www.webct.com
6. IBM Lotus Learning Mgt. Sys., www.lotus.com/lotus/offering6.nsf/wdocs/homepage
7. FIPA Message Specification, www.fipa.org/specs/fipa00071/XC00071B.doc
8. Labrou, Y., Standardizing agent communication, *Multi-Agent systems and Applications*, LNAI 2086, pp.74- 97,2001
9. Grosof, B. N., An Approach to Using XML and a Rule-based Content Language with an Agent Communication Language, *IBM Research Report*, RC 21491 (96965)
10. Neches, R., Fikes, R., Finin, T., Gruber, T., Patil, R., Senator, T. and Swartout, W., Enabling technology for knowledge sharing, *AI Magazine*, 12(3):36-56, 1991
11. Patil, R. S., Fikes, R. E., Patel-Schneider, P. F., Mckay, D,m Finin, T., Gruber, T., and Neches, R., The darpa knowledge sharing effort: progress report, *Readings in Agents*, 1997
12. FIPA, www.fipa.org
13. FIPA XML Specification, www.fipa.org/specs/fipa00071/XC00071C.html
14. N. R. Jennings, On Agent-Based Software Engineering, *Artificial Intelligence*, 117 (2), pp.277-296, 2000.
15. M. Wooldridge, Agent-based software engineering, *IEE Proc. Software Engineering* 144(1), pp.26-37, 1997
16. Durfee, E.H., Lesser, V.R. and Corkill, D.D. Trends in Cooperative Distributed Problem Solving. In: *IEEE Transactions on Knowledge and Data Engineering*, TKDE-1(1), pp. 63-83, March 1989

17. Leung, E. and Li, Q., Media-on-demand for Agent-based Collaborative Tutoring Systems on the Web. *Proceedings of the 3rd IEEE Pacific-Rim Conference on Multimedia*, LNCS 2532, pp.976-984, 2002
18. Leung E., and Li Q., Agent-Based Approach to e-Learning: An Architectural Framework, in Kim, W., Ling, T.W., Lee, Y.J. and Park, S.S., *The Human Society and the Internet*, LNCS 2105, pp.341-353, 2001.
19. Winograd, T., & Flores, F. Understanding Computers and Cognition., Norwood, N.J.: Ablex., 1986
20. F. Zambonelli N. R. Jennings, A. Omicini and M. Wooldridge, Agent-Oriented Software Engineering for Internet Applications, in *Coordination of Internet Agents*, Springer Verlag, pp.326-346, 2001

Hook and Screen Division Based Screen Compression for the Real-Time Multimedia Transformation of e-Learning System

Shengjun Li and Rui-min Shen

Computer Science Department Shanghai Jiaotong University
{Shengjunli,rmshen}@sjtu.edu.cn

Abstract. Real-time multimedia transfer is critical for E-learning application. Efficient compression technology should exist to transfer the teaching white board from the main classroom to the student's PC or the distance classroom, along the limited network bandwidth. We assume that the teachers use MS PowerPoint or MS Word in the main classroom for teaching, and we record the screen with our compression technology and transfer the screen video to the distance classroom or students' PCs, the compression uses hook technology to trace the changed area of the screen and divided the screen into 16 small rectangles, and it selectively compressed the changed area of the screen with lossless and lossy compression methods, and use a long motion compensation history buffer to further reduce the time redundancy. The compression method can get a pretty high compression ratio and very good quality of the text and simple icons that are more important; besides, the CPU utilization is also pretty low.

Keywords: Hook and Screen Division, Screen Compression, real-time multimedia transformation, lossless compression, lossy compression, E-Learning

1 Introduction

Currently, real-time E-Learning is a hot topic both in the research committee and industry. Real-time E-Learning should transfer the teaching video in the main classroom to the students' PCs or distance classrooms in real-time.

To transfer the teaching process vividly, the teaching whiteboard (such as PowerPoint played in the teacher's PC) should be recorded and transfer with good quality and in real-time.

At the same time, the video should be compressed with high efficiency for the following reasons. Firstly, the students are geographically distributed, so the teaching video should be transferred across the internet, for the bandwidth dynamic of the network, and the limited bandwidth of the student's PC (some students have ADSL access, but some others used ISDN or even modem), the video should be compressed efficiently so that it can be transferred relatively smoothly across the network. Secondly the compression mythology should not be very complex for we use the PC on which the teachers display PPT for their teaching, the record program should be run on the background and it should not occupy a lot of CPU utilization so as not to influence the teaching process of the main class.

We found out that almost all the teachers use the MS PowerPoint or Word for their class, the playing of PPT is pretty different from the movies which is compressed with Mpeg-2 or Mpeg-4, for the teaching PPT is played more slowly and regularly, and the

W. Liu et al. (Eds.): ICWL 2004, LNCS 3143, pp. 147–154, 2004.

objectives in the PPT page are mostly simple text and GUI icons, though sometime are complex pictures. And some teachers like to jump from one page of PPT to another. So In order to compress the teaching screen efficiently, special compression technique is needed.

For the forenamed reasons, we develop the hook and screen division based screen compression technology. The basic idea is that we divide the screen in to 16 small rectangles (four times four), and use hook technology to capture the change area of the screen. For simplify, we use the out-wrap rectangle of the changing area instead of the precise region. And we map the change rectangle to the 16 screen rectangles, if one rectangle is affected, it should intersect with the changed rectangle and get an intersected rectangle. Iterate the process, we can get at most 16 small changed rectangles if all the divided screen rectangles are affected. And no small changed rectangle can be got if no change on the screen at all. We record all the changed rectangles' size and location, and only compress the data of the changed rectangles and send them out as the compressed video.

To compress the data efficiently, we use both loss compression algorithm such as JPEG for complex pictures in PPT and lossless compression algorithm such as LZW for text and simple icons for they are the most important things in the teaching PPT. To further compress the video, we also use motion compensation technology with a frame buffer of longer history (store eight frames).

And our technology can also save the video data to the local computer disk so that the file can be used for non-real-time E-Learning.

The rest of this paper is organized as follows: Section 2 reviews the related works of the screen compression technology. Section 3 presents the hook and screen division based screen compression technology. Section 4 is the comparison of this technology with other methodologies. Section 5 discusses the application of the technology in the real E-Learning systems. Section 6 concludes the paper and points out the future work.

2 Related Works

Screen compression methods have been researched for a few years; in paper [1] the author introduced LAN-based e-learning system and the key techniques in the multimedia compression in the e-learning system. Paper [2] introduced one IP based video stream system, and the authors mainly introduced the system model and protocol model. Their protocol is RTP/RTCP protocol and RTSP and SDP, Which are all based on IP-layer. Paper [3] discussed the problem of the network video transfer and one solution based on video layer division technology. And they specifically proposed how to use the video layer to reduce the data loss of motion vector's influence on the video quality.

Furthermore, the screen compression has been used for practice for several years. The main screen compression and share technologies are divided into the four following g categories.

2.1 Microsoft's NetMeeting SDK

Microsoft's NetMeeting SDK [4] is a mature technology for the screen sharing; it uses unicast to delivery the desktop to the remote customer for sharing. But it has the following limits: The screen color is too limited (it can support only 256 kinds of colors), and it cannot support multicast so the number of connections is limited by the bandwidth, and the screen video cannot be saved etc.

2.2 Videoconference Technology

With videoconference technology, the screen data is collected from a video camera head. The method is straightforward, but the quality depends on the videoconference system itself rather than the screen's PC. To get high video quality, the video collection card should have very high resolution and the screen video have the un-avoided flash phenomena.

2.3 Screen Capture and Lossless Compression

Software tool PC Anywhere [5] is a remote monitor tool; its function is like a remote terminal. The working principle of PC Anywhere is that the screen is copied and compressed as a picture and sent to the clients. PC Anywhere uses the lossless compression method for the screen data, lossless compression is good for the text or simple icons, but it is not powerful enough for the color-abundant pictures.

2.4 Screen Capture and Lossy Compression

This kind of technology is similar to the technology of screen capture and lossless Compression, except that it uses lossy compression instead of lossless compression, the classical lossy compression is JPEG [6], but JPEG is designed for the compression of colorful pictures, it is not very suitable for the simple pictures such GUI and text which is the most important things in the teaching process.

Our methodology tries to combine all the advantage of the existing methodologies and overcome their deficiency.

3 Hook and Division Based Screen Compression

In this section, we introduce our technology in detail. Note that we use MS Visual C++ to develop the screen compression software on the platform of Windows 2000.

3.1 Hook and Screen Capture

Hook technology is used to capture the changed area of the screen. In our technology, system hook and API hook is installed simultaneously.

The System hook is a technology that can capture the MS window's system messages. The system hook will deal with the following messages such as window refresh, window location change, window size change, menu display, menu exit etc, every message is related to a corresponding window change and the changed area is considered as the out-wrap rectangle for simplicity, collect all the information of the rectangles and combine all of them to one region, when the window-move message comes and is captured, the information of the new window can be got.

The API hook is a trap technology that can capture the system API calls. In the API hook, we process the following API calls: TextOut, Bitblt, StretchBlt, SetDib-

Bits, every API is related to a specific picture display area, the area is got by analyzing the called parameters. By capturing the API calls, API hook can get the management of the APIs, and work out the calls' influence to the screen picture.

With the two hooks, we only analyze the changed area of the screen and not do any other process. In the compression step, we only compress the changed areas (rectangles), if no changes happen, no extra steps are needed to compress the data. By this method, we can reduce the amount of data for video processing, and reduce the CPU utilization and the bandwidth demand for the video data transfer.

The data of the changed screen image is captured from the video card. Firstly, we use GDI function CreateDIBSection to create one bitmap with the same size as the screen, and select the bitmap to a screen compatible device HDC. GDI function BitBlt is used to copy screen image from the video card to the system main memory. By setting the right parameters, using BitBlt function can read any changed rectangle's data. By dividing the changed area to a few rectangles, the changed area can be read by using BitBlt multiple times (each time for one rectangle).

3.2   Compression Process

In our system, the screen is divided into 16 rectangles (four rows and four columns). And we map the changed area to the 16 rectangles. Then we can get the small changed area in every rectangle. For simplicity, we use the out-wrap rectangle of the small changed area in every divided rectangle instead of the precise region. So the changed area can be divided into at most 16 small changed rectangles. And we only process the changed rectangles. The screen area move is shown in Figure-1. And the map of changed area to the divided rectangles is shown in Figure-2.

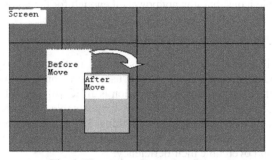

Fig. 1. The screen changed area move

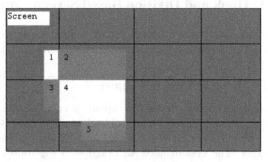

Fig. 2. Map the changed area to the divided rectangles. The change area is mapped to five divided rectangles, and five small changed rectangles are got, numbered from 1 to 5

If one divided rectangle has one small changed rectangle, we will encode the small changed rectangles, also record the location and the size of the small changed rectangle.

To encode the data of one small changed rectangle, we use too kinds of compression techniques, lossy compression method and lossless compression method. Lossy compression method such as Jpeg is used for the complex pictures, and the lossless compression method LZW [7] is used for the simple text and icons. The selection of the compression method depends on a color change threshold, we use a simple and straight forward method to distinguish text and icon from complex pictures, if the color changes in a small macro block is beyond the threshold (in our system we use 24 as the threshold), the data is considered as the data of the pictures, otherwise it is considered as the data of simple text and icons. By using both the lossy and lossless compression methods, we can get very good quality of the video especially of the text and icons, at the same time we can get very good compression ratio.

Furthermore, we use a pretty simple motion compensation strategy to reduce the time redundancy between the frames (or corresponding rectangles), we use a history frame buffer for the previous frames, at most the buffer can store eight most recent previous frames, if the small change rectangle is the same as some rectangle of previous frames, we can only save the index of the rectangle and need not record the data of it, we can further compress the data in this way. After compression, we record the location and the size of the small changed rectangle and the length of compressed data. For the divided rectangle that has no small changed rectangles, we need not record its image data at all.

3.3 Video Data Transfer and Local Data Record

To transfer the reordered data, we use unicast and multicast methods.

Under unicast, the screen-recording program listens to one port (such as port 900), and the remote client using TCP protocol to connect with the recording program. The recording program transfers the compressed data to the client after connection. The application of unicast is limited by the bandwidth and the performance of the re-cording machine, so that multicast should be used for the large-scale E-Learning sys-tems.

Under multicast, the recording program only need to send the compressed data to a multicast server (such as 218.7.7.7), and the clients who join in the multicast group can get data from the server. Multicast can support much more clients, and it will not influence the workload of the recording computer. But the multicast has been limited by the network topology and the package loss problem, so we use both unicast and multicast strategies.

To save the data to the local computer, we use two kinds of file formats to save the video data *.AVI file and our self-defined file *.SR file. For AVI file, we use the API function AVIFileOpen to create AVI file. And use AVIFileCreateStream to create screen stream, and set up the compression flag (AVIStreamSetFormat) that is defined by ourselves.

The *.SR file uses the format which is similar to AVI file but it is much simpler, we throw away the unnecessary file trunk from the AVI files, so the *.SR file is much simpler and a little smaller compared with the corresponding AVI file.

3.4 Decompression Process

The decompression process is a contrary process of compression.

Firstly, the remote client receives IP data package, every data package has the data of a frame of the screen video, one frame consists of a few small rectangles, and we decompress them according to predefined order. Firstly, we receive one video frame data package, and read the location and size of the rectangle in the screen, and then decompress the data, move the data to the corresponding area of the screen, then decompress the second rectangle data, till all of the rectangles (at most 16) are decompressed.

To display the screen image to the preferred window, we use GDI style to display the image; firstly we can the device context of the window (GetDC), and display the screen data to the device (SetDIBBitsToDevice). And then release the device (ReleaseDC).

4   Comparisons and Evaluation

To evaluate the performance of our algorithm, we compared it with other methods. Firstly, we compared it with the other screen compression algorithms. We compare our compression tool SjtuRecorder with other three tools CamTasia [8], Media Encoder [9], and TeachingRecorder.

The test machine is one PC with Pentium III CPU and 256 M memory. And we displayed one teaching PPT and record it with the different tools, respectively. We compare the CPU utilization, the colorDepth and the average bandwidth of the tools. The test result is shown as the following table – table-1.

Table 1.

Encode Tool	SjtuRecorder	CamTasia	MediaEncoder	TeachingRecorder
AudioEncoder	8kbpsDivx	8kbpsDivx	8kbpsWmv	8kbps
CPU utilization	8%	30%	80%	10%
ColorDepth(bits)	16	16	16	16
Average Screen Data(Byte per Sec)	1.6KBps	2KBps	3.1KBps	10.3KBps

From the table, we can find out that our tool SjtuRecorder can get the lowest CPU utilization and the lowest average screen data (Byte per Second).

The reason that CamTasia's performance is poorer than our SjtuRecorder is because that CamTasia use Tscc that is one lossless algorithm as the compression algorithm, and it can only reduce the redundancy between the former and the current frames. It can lead to huge data increase if it meets complex pictures and in the PPT page jump. But in our SjtuRecorder, we use both lossy and lossless compression methods so the data will not increase too bursty even meet complex pictures, and at the same time, our history buffer has stored the data of the most previous eight frames rather than only one, so it can reduce more time redundancy.

The following curve is the comparison between SjtuRecorder and CamTasia.

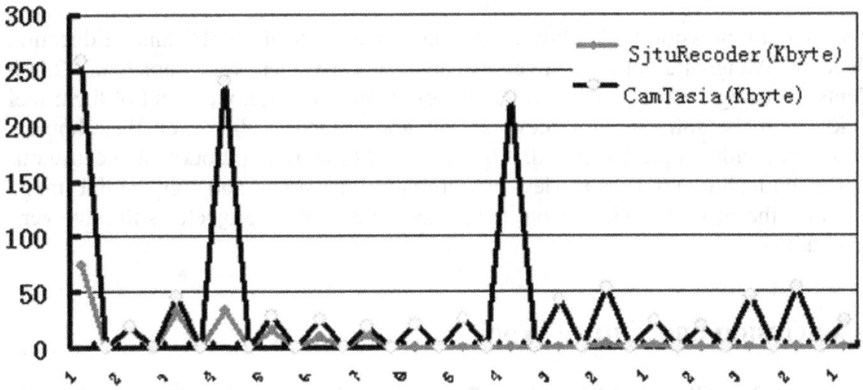

Fig. 3. The X-axis is the sequential numbers of PPT pages, and the Y-axis is the size of the screen data after the compression

This figure shows one interesting thing, if we play the PPT from page 1 to 7, and then play from 6-1,we find out that in the second half of the playing time, the SjtuRecorder's data created is pretty little, this is because the long motion compensation buffer (recall we store most recent eight frames in the buffer), but the CamTasia's data needed is still high which is because it only reduces the time redundancy between the current and former frames, totally only two frames. Also, we find when the CamTasia meet complex pictures, the data will increase suddenly but the increase in the data of SjtuRecorder is not that obvious, this is because Camtasia uses lossless compression for all the screen but SjtuRecorder uses lossy compression for the complex pictures.

To explain why we use 16 as the screen division granularity, we want to say that it is got from the tradeoff between process complexity and the screen division precision. If the granularity is too fine, the process will be too complex and the CPU utilization will be higher, on the contrary, if the granularity is too gross, the data will be bigger and we will lose the usage of screen division.

The following table is one comparison between three screen division granularities.

Table 2.

Division Granularity	2 *2	4*4	8*8
CPU Utilization	6%	8%	11%
Average Screen Data (Byte per second)	2.1KBps	1.6KBps	1.4KBps

We found out that finer granularity than 4*4 can make the average screen data a little smaller, but the CPU utilization is more than 10%, and grosser granularity than 4*4 can get lower CPU utilization (six percent), but the average screen Data is higher than 2 KB per second, so we choose 4*4 for the tradeoff.

5 The Application of the Technology

Our screen compression tool SjtuRecorder have been used in the Distance Education College of Shanghai Jiaotong University, and currently there are more than 12,000 students are using the tool for real-time classes. More than eighty percent of them feel satisfied with the software, for they can get good video quality even their home's network bandwidth is pretty limited. Also, we would like to point out that because our compression technology uses lossless compression for the text and simple GUI image such icons, the projected video from the remote classrooms' projector still have very good quality.

6 Conclusion and Future Work

In this paper, we introduce one new technology to record the screen video for distance E-Learning, the technique divided the screen into 16 small rectangles, and used hook technology to trace the changed area of the screen and map the changed region into the 16 small rectangles, for the small changed rectangles, we use both lossy method (for complex pictures) and lossless compression method (for simple text and icons), and at the same time we use long history buffer for motion compensation (buffer eight frames).This method can get very low CPU utilization and high compression ratio compared with other screen compression and sharing tools.

At the same time, our compression tool can record the video to the local machines.

The limitation of our algorithm is that it cannot compress the movies that are played on the screen; also the compression of natural scenery image is poorer than MPEG.

In the future, we would extend the compression tool with Layered Scalable Coding to fit the network bandwidth variation.

References

1. Yong Liu, Xiao Luo, Critical Issues in the Screen Compression and Transfer Demonstration Systems", Journal of Southwest Technology University, Vol18, No.3, 2003.9
2. Renxiang Yan, Yuan Gao, "Design and Implementation of IP-Based Video Streaming System", Computer Engineering, Vol.27 No.5, 2001.5
3. Jie Li et.al. "Layered Coding for Video Over Network", Computer Engineering and Application, 1998.8
4. URL, http://www.microsoft.com/windows/netmeeting/
5. URL, http://www.symantic.com/pcanywhere/
6. URL, http://www.jpeg.org/
7. URL, http://datacompression.info/Compression.shtml/
8. URL, http://www.techsmith.com/products/studio/default.asp
9. URL, http://www.microsoft.com/windows/windowsmedia

Design for a Learner-Oriented Tracking

Lily Sun, Jude Lubega, and Shirley Williams

Department of Computer Science, The University of Reading, UK
{lily.sun,j.t.lubega,shirley.williams}@reading.ac.uk

Abstract. Learning Management Systems (LMS) in e-learning have functionality for monitoring learning activities. The statistics generated from learning performances can be processed for tutors and a group of learners to improve their quality of teaching and learning. However the current LMS are not designed to facilitate personalised learning support for an individual learner, e.g. adaptive delivery, constructive feedback on assessment and real-time learning activities monitoring. This paper presents a *learner- oriented tracking* approach for one-to-one support. Technical components of this approach can be embedded in the LMS to effectively facilitate learning experience of the individual learner and quality of learning content design. A learner-oriented tracking model relies on the information from a *Learner's Profile* and educational requirements. This determines initially suitable learning content (learning objects) and delivery methods and also provides monitoring information about learners' experiences.

1 Introduction

With the current trend of e-learning environments, a personalized learning can be fostered by adaptive delivery learning content, assessment and generating personalized feedback to learners. Those are major issues to the paradigm shift. Many educational institutions have been adapting the use of technology to deliver content during the learning process; it is increasingly demanding to design systems that can offer dynamic support based on their competence, profile and educational requirements (curriculum). Much of the instructional design to date has concentrated on delivery of the content within Learning Environment to offer an online learning at any time, any where and at a desired time. However they lack instructional designs that integrate educational requirements, learner profile that can generate a real time feedback. In this paper we describe a model to demonstrate how we can integrate the missing bits of instructional design to enhance learner real time support.

Tracking ability is considered as an important function in e-learning. Learning Management Systems (LMS), e.g., Blackboard [1], WebCT [2], Lotus Learning Space [3], and TopClass [4], have functionality of monitoring learning activities. The typical tracking functions of the LMS include: recording log files, duration of visit, learning unit visited by learner/time/frequency and assessment results. The statistics generated from the learning behaviour are processed for tutors and learners to improve the quality of teaching and learning. The tutor uses the statistical information to analyse learner's performance from two dimensions: vertical dimension at single learning unit in one subject area; and horizontal dimension at multiple learning units across subject areas. This can only provide a general evaluation of quality on content design and delivery, but no constructive information about specific improvements is

W. Liu et al. (Eds.): ICWL 2004, LNCS 3143, pp. 155–162, 2004.
© Springer-Verlag Berlin Heidelberg 2004

provided. The LMS supports learners by an assessment record keeping. The learner has a real-time access to only their grades in automatically marked assignments. There is a lack of feedback on other achievements and learning experiences gained during the learning process.

The common functions of tracking in the current LMS are designed based on a learning unit-oriented approach. This approach has some constraints that it is difficult to generate specific information to support individual learners for their self-directed and self-managed learning; and it is impossible to capture and monitor each learner's learning activities. We propose in this paper a learner-oriented tracking approach which fundamentally changes design principles for tracking functions. Information of learning requirements and learning activities during learning processes are captured and monitored that in turn generate constructive feedback for improvements. Technical components of this approach can be embedded in the LMS to effectively facilitate learning experience of the individual learner and quality of learning content design.

2   Knowledge Construction and Learning Process

Learning is a process of knowledge construction within which learners achieve their learning goals by carrying out a number of activities, e.g. attending learning content and assessment, and participating in interactions to reflect their understanding. As Constructivism states, learners play an active role and take on responsibility to construct their own knowledge and meaning [5], [6], [7], [8], [9]. Learners reflect their understanding based on the use of cognitive structure to select and transform information, construct hypotheses, and make decisions. The Semiotic paradigm [10], [11] emphasises that understanding is a subjective process where the prior knowledge affects the interpretation of a given sign in the social setting. Signs can be a verbal language, pictures, literature, motion pictures, theatre, body language, and more. Different learners would interpret meaning of the signs differently and construct knowledge at different levels. They also prefer different ways by which information is presented to them, because this would affect them to receive and respond to the information based on their prior cultural and personal coding - knowledge is not an entity to be acquired but a process of how we come to know. Within the constructivist realm, knowledge is constructed through interaction with the environment.

It is also noted from these theories that learning is subjective. There is no single objective reality; knowledge construction is a process of personal interpretation of the perceived world and the negotiation of meaning. The process of semiosis [12] enables us to structure our experiences and reveal the nature and culture of our understanding. Constructivism advocates that there are no cause-effect relationships between the world and the learner; learning to a large extent depends on the subjective view of the learner. Learning should be collaborative - learning is negotiated from multiple perspectives. Semiotics promotes educational strategies that emphasise many sign systems, or many ways of knowing. Constructivism emphasises that learning emerges from the human organism in ways which conserve adaptation and organisation - learning is to apply some sort of conceptual system upon the phenomena and to bring forth a world including those phenomena. Learning is situated, and it should occur in realistic settings. Signs as codes of experience, according to semiotics, are related to social settings where learning takes place; learning is never a private act. The constructivist approach notes that living systems survive by fitting with one another and with other aspects of the surrounding medium.

Adopting semiotics and constructivist paradigm would have a tremendous impact on designing of an e-learning environment. An e-learning environment should facilitate learners to interpret the multiple perspectives of domain context, guide learners to conduct and manage their personalised learning activities, and encourage collaborative and cooperative learning for critical thinking and problem-solving. We concentrate on two interesting features: 1) instructional design for courseware that meets individual learning requirements; 2) tracking learning activities at each appropriate stage to improve learning performance by providing constructive feedback. These two features share one fundamental issue which is learners requiring just-in-time personalised learning materials, engaging their learning with preferred styles, and enjoying their learning experience to achieve personal learning goals. To satisfy personalised learning, learning requirements are determined by both educational requirements and personal learning requirements. Our research work has developed an instructional design model [13] and a method for articulation of personalised learning requirements [14]. The instructional design model aims to represent learning content design to meet the educational requirements in Higher Education (HE). The method for personalised learning requirements processes personal learning styles and their prior knowledge in a subject domain into a set of computable variables which in turn can be mapped onto instructional design strategies for packaging learning content.

It is recognised that a well designed personal learning package would not entirely assure learners to successfully achieve their learning objectives. A real-time support on learning activities may enforce effective learning. A tracking model to support personalised learning is being developed that monitors learners' achievements at the different stages within their learning process. The information about learner's learning requirements and performance will be used to generate constructive feedback where appropriate for improvements for both the design of learning content and learning achievements.

3   Information Management for Tracking

An effective tracking of learning performance requires various kinds of information about learners, e.g., preferences, prior knowledge, competencies, activity plan, learning status, learning states and achievements at different learning stages.

Preferences refer to learning styles that assist individual learners' learning. The learning styles can be described by the characteristic of cognitive, affective, and physiological factors that serve as relatively stable indicators of how a learner perceives, interacts with, and responds to the learning environment [15]. There are three widely recognised dimensional learning methods for knowledge construction, perception of information (Visual, Auditory, and Tactile), response to information (active, sensing, reflective, and intuitive), and access information (sequential, global). These learning styles of individual learner may be indicators of measuring learning achievement [16] suggests that research of learning styles enables instructional designers to identify clusters of people with similar patterns for perceiving and interpreting situations and to adjust learning environments making them more efficient and successful places for each cluster.

Prior knowledge of a learner indicates a level of knowing of a subject before engaging in learning. This information will assist a content designer to make decision on selecting the suitable learning content which will keep learners' interest and motivation when the learning content is being constructed. Prior knowledge can be measured in a range of None, Slight, Modest, Enough. Prior knowledge together with the learning styles forms the personal learning requirements.

Competence presents tangible achievements (e.g., distinction, merit, pass and fail) of overall learning objectives. These measurable results can be aggregated to reflect learners' performance at each stage in the learning process. An activity plan consists of activities carried out on content and assessment by learners, e.g., learn concepts before doing something, study examples while confirm the understanding of principles, frequency to visit content, duration of a visit on learning content. This information can be used to create a learning pattern and support learners more proactively. Furthermore, the learning activities reflect an actual learning behaviour which will evaluate and recommend the learning style to improve learning.

Learning status is a control of the learning activities that indicate levels of completion of activities, e.g., completed, pending, uncompleted. Based on this information, a necessary adjustment can be generated which can prevent falling behind situation. An achievement records a grade of the individual and overall assessment.

These types of information are structured and encapsulated in a *Learner's Profile* which is associated with individual learners. They are required by a learner-oriented tracking for personalised support.

4   A Learner-Oriented Tracking Model to Support Personalised Learning

A learner-oriented tracking approach relies on the information from a *Learner's Profile* and educational requirements which determine initially a suitability of learning content (learning objects) and delivery methods and also provide monitoring information about learners' experiences. Fig. 1 presents a learner-oriented tracking model.

Learners participate in their learning process from the very beginning before the learning content is packaged. Learners are provided with an opportunity to express their *personal learning requirements*. Personal learning requirements consist of the parameters of both learning styles and prior knowledge. We use a pre-test technique to capture information from

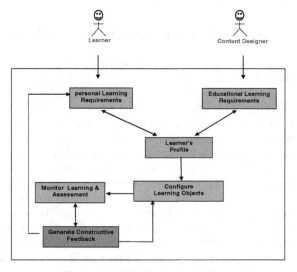

Fig 1. A learner-Oriented tracking model

learners concerning their learning preferences. An example of the pre-test adapted from [18] shows the types of questions in relation to the learning styles:

1. I understand something better after I? (testing for Active/Reflective learner)
   (a) Try it out (b) Think it through (c) None of the above
2. I would rather be considered (Sensing/ Intuitive learner)
   (a) Realistic (b) Innovative (c) None of the above
3. I prefer to get new information in? (Visual, Auditory, Tactile learner)
   (a) Pictures diagrams, graphs and maps (b) Oral direction or verbal information
   (c)   Within direction
4. It is more important to me that an instructor
   (a) Lay out the material in clear sequential steps (b) Give me an overall picture and relate the material to other subjects (c) None of the above
5. Have used C programming language before
   (a) To solve a simple problem (b) To solve a more complex problem (c) I have never used it

The test results are articulated and represented in a preference set

$P(y) = \{R, A, P, PK\}$ where:

Response $(R) = \{$Visual, Auditory, Tactile$\}$
Access $(A) = \{$Sequentially, Globally$\}$
Perception $(P) = \{$Active, Reflective, Sensing, Intuitive, Active/Intuitive, Active/Sensing, Intuitive/Reflective, Sensing/Reflective$\}$ and
Prior Knowledge $(PK) = \{$None, Slight, Modest, Enough$\}$

If the value $P(y)$ is

$$P(y) = \{\text{Active/Intuitive, Visual, Global, Slight}\} \tag{1}$$

It indicates that the learner will be offered the learning content which is packaged according to these requirements [8]. The *Learner Profile* includes $P(y)$, which will be evaluated at the different stages of the learning process where the tracking functions are performed.

Educational Learning requirements (*ELS*) are represented by learning objects (at a module level). A structure of the learning object at the conceptual level is described in Figure 2 [13].

The *Overview* offers general information about the module, such as the module code, level, aims, pre-requisites, co-requisites, learning outcomes, indicative content, assessment strategy, and credits (see figure 2). In this template, the attribute of *Indicative Content* is associated with information objects representing a set of selected topics at appropriate granularities. The attribute of *Assessment Strategy* is embodied

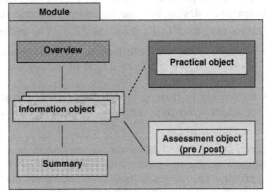

Fig 2. Learning Object representing a module

in *Assessment Objects*. This information can be obtained from module descriptors that are academically accredited and institutionally recognised across Schools in a university. The *Overview* is useful to various stakeholders, e.g., content providers, subject tutors, students, and accreditors, to share information consistently. In our course design, the *Overview* component is built within the ontology for subject disciplines to provide semantics for discovering and comparing relevant content and packaging the degree courses.

The *Information Object* component is the place where the core content is contained. The pedagogical and technical considerations will determine the quality of the Information Object, hence directly affect learning. An information object represents a topic in the module learning object, e.g., algorithm design in a Programming module. The attributes of the *Information Object* have respective *content objects*, such as *Introduction*, *Concept/Principle*, and *Illustration*. The content object *Illustration* includes a number of examples which demonstrate how the concepts can be applied in a context. These content objects aid knowledge construction in solving real world problems. The content object *Illustration* is therefore domain specific and is related to the social and culture context; because the applications of the principles must incorporate rules and constraints which are derived from the context. An *Illustration* object should perform personalised learning functions which allow students to engage interaction and self-reflection while they are learning. *Assessment Objects* are integrated with the corresponding Information Objects. The Assessment Objects are used as a mechanism to generate feedback of learners' performance and to determine sequencing of *Information Objects* during a learning process. Form the experience of our module design, we use quiz in the form of self-assessed questions associated with each *Information Object*. The results are statistically analysed and used for personalised tracking and support.

The *Summary* component concludes the module to review the subject which will assist students in self-assessment and self-reflection on understanding of the topics and applying knowledge and skills for problem solving at large. Recommendation on related areas may be provided to guide students to extend their knowledge for deep-learning. These related areas are offered in the form of learning objects which are associated with the defined aims and learning outcomes rather than general reading.

The *Configure Learning Objects* performs the functions of instructional design for courseware, e.g., selecting the learning objects and associated information objects and assessment objects, and sequencing these objects with instructions. A decision on the instructional design is made based on instructional strategy which is formulated by transforming the $P(y)$ (1) and the ELS. The instructional strategy determines

- selection of suitable information objects, content objects, practical objects and assessment objects, i.e., visual type of the content objects and the right difficult level for the information objects;
- sequencing of these objects to embed the instructions in *global* manner which encourages *active/intuitive* way to response the learning content.

The instructional strategy for a construction of learning content may change when there is a need for improvement suggested by constructive feedback after assessments. Tracking this information may proactively prevent learners falling behind.

Monitor Learning and Assessment will track the learning activities and measure the achievement against the learning objectives by assessments. The learning activities are monitored at both levels of information objects (i.e., subject topics) and learning object (i.e., module level). The assessment results are analysed for a single learning object and multiple learning objects from which the learning pattern can be created to form personalised support. In [18] example of analysed assessment learning objects result has been done. The analysis has been used to show their impact on students' learning as measured by exam results.

Generation of constructive feedback generates feedback reports dynamically by taking the analysis information from *Monitor Learning and Assessment*. There are two types of reports required by tutors and learner respectively. The report for learners contains feedback in different categories which include:

- Encouragement feedback that informs them how good their learning process was and how they could make it better. This encouraging feedback can be in different forms, e.g. all students with a mark less 40% are assumed to have failed attaining their learning objectives and those above 40% to have attained their learning objectives. Dynamic feedback on the grade above 40% depends on the performance. However if the leaner has very poor results (failed) under certain circumstances, the report suggesting for recreation of profile is offered. This implies that initial learning requirements are not adequate or offline consultation is needed e.g. meeting in person with the tutor.
- Feedback suggesting improvements in specific areas, concepts not well mastered e.g. loops in C programming, applications not well understood, skipped area content that was useful for the learning process, are offered. This feedback helps the learners to reflect on their previous learning process and then carry out the suggested improvements.

Tutors receive feedback on the quality of learning content and delivery scheme. This information will assist tutors to improve the method of facilitation and learning support. The feedback also gives tutors an understanding how students achieve the educational requirements.

5   Conclusions and Future work

A learner-oriented tracking model has been proposed that relies on the information from a *Learner's Profile* and educational requirements. This will determine initially a suitability of learning content (learning objects) and delivery methods. Monitoring of the learning process activities and offering of personalised real-time feedback will be carried out by agent and workflow technology.

A personalised tracking agent for each learner will be developed for use in LMS. This agent will be able to extract data from each individual learner's learning process in form of profile. Monitoring of this learner profile within the learning process will be carried using the workflow technology. The multi agent and the workflow technology will be adopted to offer a personalised real-time feedback about the learning process to the learner and tutor. Related work that will design a method for generating learner profile and also one for creating learning objects repositories are underway.

Reference

1. Blackboard.: Blackboard 6.0. http://www.blackboard.net/ (2004)
2. WebCT.: http://www.webct.com/ (2004)
3. Lotus Learning Space.: http://www.lotus.com (2004)
4. TopClass.: http://www.wbtsystems.com/ (2004)
5. Fosnot, C.: Constructivism: A Psychological theory of learning. In C. Fosnot (Ed.): Constructivism: Theory, perspectives, and practice, (pp.8-33). New York: Teachers College Press (1996)
6. Steffe, L.P., & Gale, J. (Eds.): Constructivism in Education. Hillsdale, NJ: Erlbaum (1995)
7. Schunk, D., & Zimmerman, B.: Self-regulated learning: from teaching to self-reflective practice, New York, The Guilford Press (1998)
8. Peter, E.D., & William, G.C.: Constructivism: The Career and Technical Education Perspective. Journal of Vocational and Technical Education, Vol. 16 No. 1, (Fall 1999)
9. Honebein, P.C., Duffy T. and Fishman B.: Constructivism and the Design of Learning Environment: Context and Authentic Activities for Learning, in T.M. Duffy, J. Lowyck and D. Jonassen (eds.), Design Environments for Constructivist Learning, Springer-Verlag, NY, (1993) pp. 87-108.
10. Peirce, C.S.: Collected Papers of Ch.S, Peirce, 1931–1935: Edited by Hartshorne, C. & Weiss, P. Cambridge, Mass (1960)
11. Liu, K.: Semiotics in Information Systems Engineering. Cambridge: Cambridge University Press (2000)
12. Peirce, C.S., (1932-35) Collected Papers of Ch.S, Peirce, 1931 - 1935, edited by Hartshorne, C. & Weiss, P. (1960) Cambridge, Mass.
13. Sun, L. and Williams S.: An Instructional Design Model for Constructivist Learning, Association for the Advancement of Computing in Education (AACE), Finland, in review (2004)
14. Sun, L., Williams S., Ousmanou K and Lubega J.: Building Personalised Functions into Dynamic Content Packaging to Support Individual Learners. 2nd European Conference on e-Learning 2003, Glasgow, Scotland (2003), ISBN: 0-9544577-4-9
15. Keefe, J. W.: Learning style: An overview. In NASSP's Student learning styles: Diagnosing and prescribing programs Reston, VA: National Association of Secondary School Principals (1979) (pp. 1-17)
16. O'Connor, T. O.: Using Learning Styles to Adapt Technology for Higher Education, (1999) at: www.indstate.edu/ctl/styles/main.html
17. Solomon A. Barbara and Felder M. Richard: Index of learning styles questionnaire (2004) at: http://www.engr.ncsu.edu/learningstyles/ilsweb.html
18. Adams, A., Lubega, J., Walmsley, S., and Williams, S.: The Effective of Assessment Learning Objects Produced Using Pair Programming, submitted to EJEL (2004)

Web-Based Adaptive Collaborative
Learning Environment Designing

Yonggu Wang[1], Xiaojuan Li[2], and Rong Gu[1]

[1] College of Vocational and Technical Education, Zhejiang University of Technology
Hangzhou, Zhejiang, China, 310032
wyglxj@sohu.com
[2] Humanities School, Zhejiang University of Finance and Economics
Hangzhou, Zhejiang, China, 310012
lxj@zufe.edu.cn

Abstract. Traditional open web-based collaborative learning environment has two disadvantages. One is the blindness of selecting learning companion; the other is the imbalance of learning burden. However, web-based adaptive collaborative learning environment is composed of discussion forum and one-on-one peer help, user model, collaborative strategy model and adaptive component. It is able to reason and justify logistically, provide learners with appropriate companion list, and limit the number of help requirements that a student receives at one time. Therefore, it can get rid of the disadvantages of traditional open web-based collaborative learning environment, and improve the quality and efficiency of learning.

1 Introduction

Traditional open web-based collaborative learning environment has asynchronous and synchronous collaborative learning tools. Asynchronous collaborative learning tools include BBS, email, news group. And collaborative learning tools comprise a few tools, such as chat room, peer to peer chat software(ICQ), video conferencing system, and so on.

Investigations and Researches have found out that traditional open web-based collaborative learning environment has two disadvantages [1]. One is blindness of selecting learning companion; in the traditional open web-based collaborative learning environment, learners cannot access the cognitive characteristic information, and acquaint himself with the cognitive levels, abilities and styles of his companions. Thereby, the student may select blindly his learning companions from so many companions. On the other hand, there are imbalances on burden of collaborative learning. If one learner has a better learning performance, she or he will receive too many help requirements and have too many learning tasks to deal with, which will pull down the quality of learning.

But web-based adaptive collaborative learning environment is able to reason and justify logistically, provide the learner with companion list, and limit the number of help requirements that a student receives at one time. Therefore, it can get rid of the

W. Liu et al. (Eds.): ICWL 2004, LNCS 3143, pp. 163–168, 2004.

disadvantages of the traditional open web-based collaborative learning environment, and improve the quality and efficiency of learning.

2   Essential Elements of Learning Environment

Web-based adaptive collaborative learning environment is composed of discussion forum and one-on-one peer help, user model, collaborative strategy model and adaptive component. As illustrated in Figure 1. The Tutor and learning companions are participants of collaborative learning activities. Their identities are relative, and can be exchanged under a certain condition. Discussion forum and one-on-one peer help are the specific organizing patterns of collaborative learning activities, are the main channels getting learning companions' characteristic information and the main interface executing adaptive actions. User model records and formulates characteristics of actors who take part in adaptive collaborative learning activities, reasons and justifies the relative characteristics of them, and provides adaptive components with information that is the basis of adaptive action. Collaborative strategies model stores all kinds of collaborative learning strategies and evaluating methods. The adaptive component is the component that execute adaptive actions, the middle component that relates the learning Interface, user model, collaborative strategies model, and the data-bus that circulate learning information.

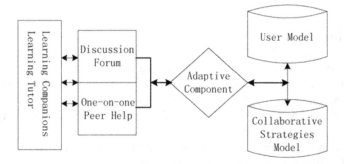

Fig. 1. Essential Elements of Web-based Adaptive Collaborative Learning Environment

2.1   Discussion Forum and One-on-One Peer Help

Discussion forum and one-on-one peer help are the specific organizing patterns of collaborative learning activities. The Research on Instruction based Web has found out that the two patterns are suitable to different types of interaction [2].

The topics of Learning are classified in the discussion forum. Students can bring forward some questions in different discussion forum areas, and can reply the questions that others put forward from different point of view. An experiment shows that, students prefer to post some easier question that can be answered as soon as possible.

The duties of tutors are posting some heuristic and arguable questions, which can inspire students to take part in the discussion, facilitate interactive collaboration and share their knowledge each other. Moreover, tutors should be responsible for supervising the process of collaborative learning, bringing forward some guiding question in time, and preventing the student from deviating from the learning target.

One-on-one peer help is more suitable for intensive collaborative learning activities between participants. A tutor and a student or two students can take advantage of the interactive type.

2.2 User Model

Characteristic information of students includes knowledge level, learning interests and hobbies, cognitive styles, cooperative consciousness, cooperative ability and learning actions data [1].

Generally, the sources of collecting characteristics of student are listed in the Table 1.

Table 1. The Sources of Collecting Characteristics of Student

Characteristics	Sources			
	Learner	Companion	One-on-one Peer Help	Discussion forum
Knowledge Level	✓	✓		
Learning Interests and Hobbies	✓			✓
Cooperative Consciousness	✓		✓	✓
Cooperative ability	✓	✓	✓	✓
On-line			✓	✓
Cognitive Styles	✓		✓	
Accepted Companion	✓			
Rejected Companion	✓			
Accepted Topics	✓			
Cooperation Burden	✓		✓	

2.3 Collaborative Strategies Model

The adaptive collaborative rules which are stored in the collaborative strategies model, are the guarantees to complete adaptive actions in the adaptive collaborative environment. There are five rules in the collaborative strategies model, such as establishing learning topics, announcing knowledge levels, detecting learner online, evaluating cooperative consciousnesses and assessing cooperative abilities, and so on.

Establishing Learning Topics. In a certain discussion forum, A student can establish a learning topic in which he is interested [3]. When a question about the topic is posted, the student will receive an email which notify him a new question posted in the discussion forum. Then the student can login into the discussion forum to browse the answer of the question, or answer the question in a different point view. The fact that the student activates the function of email notification is not only a characteristic of the student, but also that of his companion. For only the questions of his companions are useful for the student, he would activate the email function about the topic.

Announcing Knowledge Levels. The collaborative learning activities of students are active and controllable in adaptive collaborative learning environment. In discussion forum, students can announce their knowledge levels. If one student does not like to answer some questions of a topic, he is entitled to refuse communication with other students. In one-on-one peer help, A student can utter his cooperative willingness. For example, a student can announce the learning characteristics of his companion and the largest number of requests for help that he can accept. And the student can also reject the requirements from his disliked companions. Above all, Learners can configure some parameters and variables in the user model, which represent the social tropism of building user mode.

Detecting Learner Online. It is necessary to detect learner online when designing a adaptive collaborative learning environment. If a companion is online and not in heavy learning burden, a student can send request for help to him, and invite him to their peer-to-peer help. As a result, the student can get immediate feedback. If the companion is offline, the student only can send email or post questions in the discussion forum. And she or he will receive a delayed help. But sometimes, the student cannot get any answer to his questions.

Evaluating Cooperative Consciousnesses. Evaluating cooperative consciousnesses is the reasoning result of user model and the behaviors of his learning action. Researches have found out that there are four facts that can account for evaluating cooperative consciousnesses [4].

- Frequency of logging in discussion forum.
- The number of posting, reading and answering questions in discussion forum.
- The spending time of dealing with his companions' learning troubles.
- The Percentage of rejecting helping requirements.

Assessing Cooperative Abilities. In the same way, the methods assessing cooperative abilities of students are listed below.

- Learner can register his cooperative abilities by himself.
- The companions can evaluate the cooperative abilities of the student in one-on-one peer help.
- There is voting mechanism in discussion forum; students can vote the best companions.
- Other students read the questions and their answers that the student put forward.

2.4 Adaptive Component

In order to help learners select the appropriate learning companions, The adaptive component communicates information with user model and collaborative strategies model, completes a part of data reasoning work, then adapts the actions of learning system. The work procedures of adaptive component are below [5]:

- Abstracting the characteristics of learners from their behaviors.
- Reasoning based on collaborative strategies in collaborative strategies model.
- Selecting the companions from user model that are suitable for the present student.
- Creating the cooperative session between the student and his companion.

Some factors must be considered when the adaptive component selects companions from user model. The factors are listed below [6].

- The companion must master the learning topics.
- The learning styles of the learning companion are similar to those of the student.
- The requests of the student are the standards selecting his companions.
- The cooperative consciousnesses and abilities are stronger.
- The burden of cooperation is relative small.
- The first student who answers questions will be the companion in one-on-on peer help

3   Conclusion

The framework of adaptive collaborative learning environment described in this paper includes discussion forum and one-on-one peer help, user model, collaborative strategies model and adaptive component. It is important to research the relations among the four elements and execution procedures of each element. The research is the most important approach to improve interactive ability of learning environment. The future research is how to integrate learning course material into the adaptive collaborative activities of learners.

References

1. Amy Soller, Bradley Goodman, Frank Linton, and Robert Gaimari. (1998). Promoting Effective Peer Interaction in an Intelligent Collaborative Learning System. In Proceedings of the 4th International Conference on Intelligent Tutoring Systems (ITS 98). San Antonio, TX, 186-195.
2. Amy Soller, Alan Lesgold, Frank Linton, Brad Goodman. (1999). What Makes Peer Interaction Effective?Modeling Effective Communication in an Intelligent CSCL. Proceedings of the 1999 AAAI Fall Symposium: Psychological Models of Communication in Collaborative Systems, Cape Cod, MA, 116-123.
3. McManus, M, & Aiken, R. (1995). Monitoring computer-based problem solving. Journal of Artificial Intelligence in Education, 6(4), 307-336.

4. Amy Soller, Renata Guizzardi, Alessandra Molani, (2004). the 6th International Conference of the Learning Sciences, Santa Monica, CA, 2004. Copyright © 2004, International Society of the Learning Sciences (ISLS).
5. Rich, E. (1989) Stereotypes and user modeling. *User models in dialog systems,*, ed. Kobsa A. and Wahlster W., Springer-Verlag, Berlin, p.35-51.
6. Brusilovsky, P., Schwarz, E., Weber, G. (1996) ELM-ART: An intelligent tutoring system on World Wide Web. *Proc. Third International Conference on Intelligent Tutoring Systems, ITS-96* (Lecture Notes in Computer Science, v.1086) C. Frasson, G. Gauthier, & A. Lesgold (eds.) Springer-Verlag, Berlin, p. 261-269.

A CATV and Internet Combined Framework
for Distance Learning*

Zimin Mo, Wei Xing**, and Dongming Lu

College of Computer Science & Technology, Zhejiang University, Hangzhou, China
`momatin@163.net`, {`wxing,ldm`}`@zju.edu.cn`

Abstract. Web based learning enables more students to have a chance to access the distance learning resources. However, the early experience of using this new learning method in China exposes a few problems, among which the low quality video service is a serious one. This is caused by the difficulty to transfer high quality real-time video on the Internet because of the basic design of the Internet. In this paper, we present a CATV and Internet combined framework to tackle such problems. The framework allows students not only to have a high quality real-time video service, but also to interact with teachers via an interactive question-and-answer system. The main virtue of the framework is that it enables students to access distance learning anytime anywhere with both QoS guarantee and interactive capability. A prototype system based on this framework has already implemented and deployed for more than a year, and a full scale system will be put into running in the near future.

Keywords: distance learning, real-time class, interactive question-and-answer system, framework, high quality video service

1 Introduction

As distance learning becomes more popular, many universities provide distant learning services. Two good examples are Virtual-U [1] and Web-CT [2]. They offer the entire of the learning process, these systems have implemented a number of fundamental components such as synchronous and asynchronous teaching systems, course-content delivery tools and polling and quiz modules, virtual workspaces for sharing resources, whiteboards, grade reporting system, and assignment submission components. These systems enable large group of dispersed individuals to interact and learn on the Web.

As the process of distance learning is going forward, the text-based distance learning system becomes unsatisfactory and people realize the importance of body language, facial expression and voice intonation [6]. To satisfy the requirements of real-time learning, teachers need to transfer the video carrying real-time classroom to the students who want to have a experience of immersion and participation. However, it is very difficult to transmit good quality video on the Internet on which the quality of service (QoS) is not guaranteed. On the other hand, a traditional CATV network has consistent delivery capacity though it lacks the ability to support interaction without

---

* The work of this paper is supported by the Science and Technology Bureau of Zhejiang, PRC under the contracts No. 2003C13021 and No. 021103720
** To whom all author correspondence should be addressed

bi-direction reconstruction. A good way to build a distance learning service platform is combining the two into one network seamlessly.

In this paper, we exert the virtues of both the Internet and the CATV network to create a combined distance learning system. That system is already used in the Distance Education College of Zhejiang University, PRC. The system makes it possible for students to learn anytime anywhere, and meanwhile gives them a good experience as in a real class. It also provides teachers an easy teaching environment where teachers can help students to solve problems in learning.

2   Overview of the System Architecture

The system consists of three parts: a teaching part, a delivery center and a learning part. The teaching part is located in the distance education college, where teachers make courseware, teach in the classrooms and answer students' questions. It is the responsibility for teachers to make courseware, upload the courseware to the delivery center, and arrange the delivery schedule. All these work can be done by a set of general or special tools including the courseware making tools, upload tools and schedule arrange tools in this system. Using these tools, teachers translate the content of a class – the video record, the electronic slides, and materials on the electronic whiteboard – into a courseware, then upload the courseware to the delivery center. These courseware are later delivered to students via CATV network according to the schedule. Meanwhile, the system also supports real-time delivery of the class to students.

The second part is the delivery center that locates at the CATV broadcast center. The service provider receives the real-time video stream and the courseware from the teaching part, convert them into a compatible transfer form for CATV, and deliver immediately or according to the schedule later. There are many kinds of delivery servers such as data servers, stream servers, schedule server, and authentication and authorization server in the delivery center.

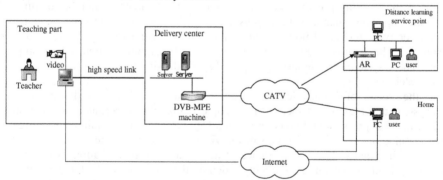

Fig. 1. The system architecture

The last part is the learning part, which is located in students' area such as the student's home or the points of distance learning service. In this part, students receive the learning materials from CATV and interact with the teacher through the Internet. A student can not only take part in a real-time class, but also learn the courseware later by himself if he missed the class. If the students have any problems in their learning, they can enter the pre-scheduled question-and-answer classroom to ask for helps from the teachers. Fig. 1 illustrates the system architecture.

3 Some Components and Features of the System

3.1 Educational Administration Management System

The Education Administration Management System (EAMS) plays a very important role in making the teaching activities going smoothly. The EAMS contains three parts: courseware making and management, schedule making and management, and student management.

Everyday teachers make their class materials into courseware on-the-fly or after class, then upload the courseware to a huge capacity disk storage array. The courseware are classify according to the subjects - such as English, Chemistry - and stages. Because of the increasing volume of courseware, we index each courseware in a database to ease the search and retrieval.

Schedule making and management subsystem is used to arrange the real-time class, the question-and-answer session, and the courseware delivery schedule. Meanwhile it informs students about the schedule. Teachers are given an interface similar to a traditional classes arrangement to set up the teaching schedule, and the system translate such an arrangement automatically into an actual delivery schedule concerning IP channels and time allocation. Schedules upload module uploads the delivery schedule to the delivery center.

Student management subsystem offers the functionality including registration management, tuition fee management, and learning information management.

3.2 High Quality Real-Time Class Service

The CATV network is a broadcast network with guaranteed QoS. It has a simpler architecture and mechanism than the Internet. This makes it very easy to forecast the video quality received in the learning part at the end user site, providing that we get a good quality video at the headend in the delivery center. This can be easily achieved by using high quality video cameras and encoders at the classrooms and a dedicated fiber link between the teaching part and the delivery center.

In the classroom, a teacher gives the lecture in a traditional way, presents some electronic slides (e.g. in Microsoft Powerpoint format), and writes something on the whiteboard now and then. A video camera and a microphone capture the teacher's action and speech, transmitting the signal to a real-time encoder to generate multimedia stream in IP packets. The slides and the contents on the whiteboard are also delivered in JPEG stream through a JPEG transformer.

When the streams get to delivery center through a bandwidth guaranteed network link (e.g. a dedicate fiber link, or a leased line), a stream server receives the streams, converts them to multicast streams and retransmits them to a DVB-MPE packetizing machine.

The approach mentioned above enables students to have a real experience of class. High quality video service is very important to the courses that contain many practical and operational classes, especially in the vocational education. By using our system, a teacher can demonstrate how to do things without worrying about blurry or broken video at the students' learning site. It's also easy for students to follow teacher's instruction and demonstration.

The contents on the whiteboard are always the teacher's teaching materials. Only video and audio of the teacher cannot make the class complete and informative. In our system, the slides and whiteboard contents are captured, encoded, transferred, and finally displayed on the student's PC screen synchronously with the teacher's video and audio stream. The playback is clear in any resolution screen without any visible font distortion. The playback of the teacher's video, slides and whiteboard contents is synchronized to the actual scene in the original classroom.

3.3 Interactive Question-and-Answer Service

Students who take part in distance learning may have such problem as that they cannot solve some problems by themselves when they learn some courses alone. Question-and-answer service is required in this circumstance. Teachers should open question and answer classes periodically, which is already arranged into schedule. The information of the class will be informed students in advance. Students can ask the questions in email before the class begins. The teacher will choose some common questions to prepare before class. In class, the teacher can answer the questions by sound or text, and students can also ask questions for helps. This service use both networks, students ask questions to teachers through Internet and the teacher answers them through CATV.

Fig. 2. A Question-and-Answer Session

In a typical session, a student inputs his name and his password to enter into the class. Teacher can see how many students in the classroom and the students' problems and then choose the proper ones to answer. After the class, the teacher can still choose some good questions not answered from the question list, and make the answers into a courseware that can be downloaded by the students later.

There are other question-and-answer systems, such as Content Based Index and Rerieval (CBIR) question-and-answer system which is used in the Network Education

College of Shanghai Jiao Tong University [3], and so on. The highlight of our system is the ability to offer reliable high quality teacher's video service to the students.

This question-and-answer service is very useful in going over a course before an examination. The teacher can also emphases hotpoint in the course and explain it in detail by this service, which is friendly to all of the students. Fig. 2 gives the view of a typical question-and-answer interface.

3.4 Download-then-Learn Service

Students in distance learning most likely have different life styles. Some of them work in daytime and self-learn after work in the evening or in holidays. Therefore they may miss some important classes. The system makes it very easy for teachers to transfer the contents of the class into a courseware. Afterwards teachers can use upload tools to upload courseware to the delivery center and arrange the delivery schedule.

In the delivery center, servers send courseware to DVB-MPE packetizing machine according to the schedule. Students can download the courseware at home or on a service point of distance learning.

Because of one direction transmission of the CATV network, the download service cannot make use of reliable TCP transfer. Our system use reliable UDP scheme instead. The scheme contains Forward Error Correction (FEC), Asynchronous Layered Coding (ALC) construction blocks.

3.5 Access Methods

Students can access the distance learning service in two ways.

The first way to access the service is proper for a single student at his home or office. The student's PC should be equipped with a DVB receiving card. Such a card receives data from the DVB encapsulated transfer streams, and extract the original IP data. The card acts like an ordinary network adapter.

The second choice for a student is to learn at a distance learning service point. Students can learn together or learn by oneself. It is usually expensive for a distant education site to equip each PC with a DVB receiving card. To adapt this circumstance, we make a machine named Access Router (AR). Such a router receives data from the DVB encapsulated transfer streams, retrieves the original IP data and multicasts the data to the LAN on which each end user's PC attaches. This router can block data not belonging to this education site to save the bandwidth of the LAN. Meanwhile, the router supports access to the Internet.

3.6 Program Guide Service

Students will have a requirement to know when the class begins and which courseware can be downloaded. To meet this requirement, we achieve the function named program guide service (PGS). We use Session Announcement Protocol and Session Description Protocol (SAP/SDP) to manage multicast sessions. By this service, students can know what is being delivered and what will be distributed soon.

3.7 The Protocol Stack of the System

Because resources are transferred on the CATV, the protocol stack of system is different from usual TCP/IP protocol stack. In our system stack, there are two data link layers and two physical layers.

According to ISO/OSI Reference Model, Digital Video Broadcasting (DVB) technology [4] is the main standard for transferring IP data on the CATV, which is originated from Europe and adopted in many areas of the world for transferring digital video. There are many encapsulation standards in the DVB architecture. We choose one of them which is called DVB-MPE (Multi-Protocol Encapsulation). MPE technology enables IP data to be injected into DVB data as its payload. Therefore, we can use traditional IP tools to generate IP data, and send them to the DVB-MPE packetizing machine which can encapsulate IP data to DVB data in order to transfer on CATV network. At the receiving end, students' PC use a DVB card to extract the original IP data from DVB streams. Fig. 3 gives the system protocol stack.

Application Layer	
TCP/UDP	
IP	
Internet data link layer	DVB-MPE
Internet physical layer	CATV physical layer

Fig. 3. The protocol stack

4 Application of the System

A prototype system of the combined framework is implemented and deployed for nearly a year. The teaching part is located in the Distance Education College of Zhejiang University, PRC. There are six real-time classrooms and one question-and-answer classroom equipped with video cameras, microphones and real-time encoders in the college. The teachers there use a special software to make the content of the class into the courseware, upload courseware by content-upload tool and arranges the schedule by the schedule-making tool.

A dedicated fiber links the teaching site to the delivery center, which is deployed at the broadcast and transfer center of Zhejiang GuangLian Information and Network Corporation. There are various servers including data servers, stream servers, the program guide server, the authorization server, the database server to form a broadcasting platform. These servers send education material according to the schedule in IP packets that are encapsulated later by a DVB-MPE packetizing machine. All the data are transferred to more than half of the area of Zhejiang province via DS3 backbone, and later distributed to end user via local CATV network. As of the date this paper was written, six governmental areas out of the total eleven areas of Zhejiang Province can get this service. These areas are Ningbo, Lishui, Huzhou, Jinhua, Shaoxing and Hangzhou. Hundreds of sample students have accessed the service, and most of them find the system very fresh and enjoyable.

Recently, the Distance Education College of Zhejiang University and Zhejiang GuangLian Co. have budgeted first term over ten million RMB (about 1.2 million US dollars) to put this system into actually use. The expected enrollment is estimated very conservatively over ten thousand students in the first year.

5 Conclusions

In this paper, we present a platform combining CATV and the Internet that support distant learning service. High quality real-time class video service and interactive question-and-answer service are the highlights of this system, while the traditional download-then-learn service is also provided. It is very convenient for students to follow the teacher's demonstration by clear video, and it is very interesting and attractive to students by giving them question-and-answer class.

In the future, we will apply and deploy the system to more distance education service providers, and cover more education types such as elementary education, high education, adult education, professional training, and vocational and technical education. Meanwhile, we will collect more data from realistic environment and improve the reliability, scalability, and performance of this system.

References

1. C. Groeneboer, D. Stockley, T. Calvert: Virtual-U: A collaborative model for online learning environments, In: Proceedings of the Second International Conference on Computer Support for Collaborative Learning, Toronto, Ontario, December 1997.
2. WebCT: http://www.webct.com
3. Ruimin Shen, Peng Han, Fan Yang,Qiang Yang, Joshua Zhexue Huang An Open Framework for Smart and Personalized Distance Learning ICWL2002.
4. ETSI Secretariat,Digital Video Broadcast(DVB);Specification for conveying ITU-R System B Teletext in DVB bitstream(EN 300 472 V1.2.2) 1997-8.
5. Alessi, S. M., & Trollip, S. R., Multimedia for learning: Methods and development. Needham Heights, MA: Allyn & Bacon, 2001.
6. Vrasidas, C., & McIsaac, M. S., "Principles of pedagogy and evaluation for Web-based learning", Educational Media International, 37(2), 2000, pp. 105-111.
7. Wilson, P., & Coghill, G., "Student learning issues: Factors to consider prior to designing computer-assisted learning for higher education", Proc. of the International Conference on Computers in Education, November 2000, pp. 576-584.

MPEG-4 Based Interactive 3D Visualization for Web-Based Learning

Qiong Zhang and Jiaoying Shi

The State Key Lab of CAD&CG, Zhejiang University, Hangzhou, 310027, China

Abstract. Interactive 3D based visualization technique can provide additional capacity for e-learning systems. In this paper, we introduce a MPEG-4 standard based interactive 3D visualization system with potential applications in web-based learning. The major features of this prototype system include standard-based efficient compression, view-dependent streaming and rendering, flexible animation and synchronized HTML display. Real examples are presented with the introduction of system architecture and main functionalities.

1 Introduction

In recent years, web-based learning methodology and related technology have been applied to various disciplines with tremendous success [1]. Both teachers and learners can benefits from web-based learning systems through learning-on-demand, multimedia presentation, intuitive GUI, and real-time interaction etc.

Among enormous methods that are already used in web-based learning, Interactive 3D based visualization technique still turns out to be one of the most efficient methods in providing information, if oral or written information cannot be fully presented, the matter becomes multifaceted, or an issue should be explained in general or in detail [2]. There're already quite a few research projects that demonstrated the powerfulness and flexibility of 3D interactive visualization techniques [3, 4, 5] used in e-learning systems.

However, due to bandwidth restriction, traditional representation and delivery model for 3D contents prevents the proliferation of 3D applications on the web [6]. Just like rapid progress in audio/video compression and streaming technology results in the exponential growth of multimedia contents on the web, efficiently compression and streaming delivery of 3D scene is crucial in applying interactive 3D visualization in a web-based environment. Furthermore, considering the courseware interoperation and interchangeability between different learning systems, standardized technology should be given much higher preference over proprietary ones.

This paper intends to apply MPEG-4 standard based 3D technology into learning applications. As we know, MPEG-4 is a digital bit stream format associated to protocols for representing multimedia content consisting of natural and synthetic audio, visual, and object data. A key part of MPEG-4 Systems called BIFS (BInary Format for Scene description) which specifies a coded representation of interactive audio-visual scene description information [7]. Although a BIFS based method for streaming large virtual environment was already proposed in [8], it is primarily concerned about efficiently streaming animation. Specifically, the aim of this paper is to demonstrate how BIFS based interactive 3D visualization techniques can fulfill the requirements of web-based learning applications. The rest of paper is organized as follows.

W. Liu et al. (Eds.): ICWL 2004, LNCS 3143, pp. 176–183, 2004.

Section 2 provides analysis of the suitability to implement BIFS based 3D visualization system serving web-based learning, based on the introduction to the related part of the standard. A BIFS based interactive 3D visualization system is introduced together with several examples in Section 3, followed by a brief conclusion in Section 4.

2   MPEG-4 BIFS and Interactive 3D Visualization

If used as the scene representation in an interactive 3D system, a typical BIFS scene will consist of an encoded hierarchical tree of nodes with attributes and other information, such as routes for describing event routing relation from sources to targets. Leaf nodes in this tree often correspond to 3D geometry data, whereas intermediate nodes group its children to form 3D object, and perform grouping, transformation, and other such operations on those objects. The scene description can evolve over time by using scene description updates. While an MPEG-4 BIFS scene has, for the most part, a structure inherited from VRML [9], its explicit bit stream representation is completely different. Moreover, MPEG-4 adds several distinguishing mechanisms, which make itself very appealing to web based learning system:

1. Data streaming

The BIFS scene description, as well as the mesh data for 3D object, both can be streamed due to the intrinsic properties of their encoding schemes. BIFS scene structure is actually a hierarchical acyclic graph and the encoding process follows depth-first order, i.e., children or sub-nodes of a node are present in the bit stream before its siblings. As a result, it allows a client to start to decode and render part of scene as they arrive. Also, 3D mesh data can be represented with `Hierarchical3DMesh` node [7]. The `Hierarchical3DMesh` means polygonal models with multiple levels of detail (LOD) and smooth transition between consecutive levels. The encoding of `Hierarchical3DMesh` node is part of Synthetic Natural Hybrid Coding standard in ISO/IEC 14496-2:1999 and largely based on Topological Surgery and Progressive Forest Split schemes [6]. The encoded bit stream can be progressively delivered, decoded and rendered.

The streaming feature of MPEG-4 BIFS is a notable contrast with the VRML where a scene is first completely transferred from the server to the client and then rendered, leading to long latency.

2. Scene update

Once a scene is in place, the server can further modify it by using BIFS' scene update mechanism, called BIFS command [7]. BIFS command conveys commands for the replacement of a scene, addition or deletion of nodes, modification of fields, and so on, at certain instant. A very useful application for this mechanism is to progressively transmit large scenes, thus reducing bandwidth requirements.

When the source of animation is a live one, or when better compression is sought, MPEG-4 provides an alternative way to stream animation to the scene with the BIFS animation frame [7]. BIFS animation enables optimal compression of the animation of all parameters in a scene: 3D positions, rotations, normals, colors, scalar values, etc.

3. Compression

BIFS scene description, BIFS command and BIFS animation all can be encoded and quantized, thus reduce the bandwidth requirement. Compared with VRML, the efficiency of BIFS representation is largely due to binary and context-dependent encoding scheme. Through context-dependent encoding and quantization, there's generally single or double digits compression rate gain dependent on the encoded objects [12].

All those mechanisms make BIFS a very promising candidate to implement interactive 3D visualization system for web-based learning.

3   BIFS Based Interactive 3D Visualization System

The system we designed for web-based learning is based on a client-sever model. The server side is pretty simple and only responsible for sending out data streams. It currently supports three data streams, i.e., BIFS command, BIFS animation and hierarchical 3D mesh data. All the contents are prepared and encoded off line. The scene authoring is based on Extensible MPEG-4 Textual Format (XMT-A) format [10]. It is an XML-based version of BIFS. Primarily, there are two reasons to induce us to choose XMT-A as the authoring format. One reason is that XMT-A is designed in mind to interoperate with other multimedia courseware, such as Synchronized Multimedia Integration Language (SMIL) and the Extensible 3D (X3D) etc. The XML based fact makes it universally accessible to other applications. Another reason is to facilitate validation of the scene structure using XML scheme. Automatic validation is especially important for big and complex courseware. Since the XMT-A provides a straightforward, one-to-one mapping between the textual and binary formats. It is pretty easy to convert an XMT-A file to BIFS stream.

The architecture of client-side 3D BIFS player is illustrated in Fig 1. The number of BIFS decodes and mesh decoders are dependent on the number of BIFS animation and hierarchical 3D mesh streams respectively. Each decode has a corresponding Downloader thread which is responsible for setting up connection with the server, buffering arrived data and so on.

The main task of the 3D composer is scene composition and scene management. There are two main threads running in the 3D composer, one is responsible for updating the live scene whenever it gets newly decoded node, the other is for interaction management and events generation and routing. Besides generating final image, the 3D renderer will also return the identifier of an object visible at a particular image location. The renderer is the only place where this information can be obtained when rendering arbitrary shaped 3D objects. This function is required as support for interactivity between the user and scene.

3.1   View-Dependent Downloading and Rendering of Progressive 3D Mesh Data

3D mesh data can either be encoded directly in a BIFS stream or represented as Hierarchical3Dmesh nodes and progressively streamed in another data stream. We prefer to use Hierarchical3DMesh node for complex 3D objects since it allows us to deliver, decode and render them in multiple LODs, a desired property for 3D applications.

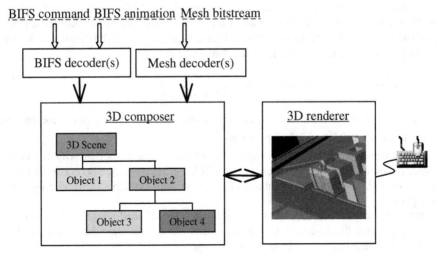

Fig. 1. The architecture of 3D BIFS Player for Web-based Learning

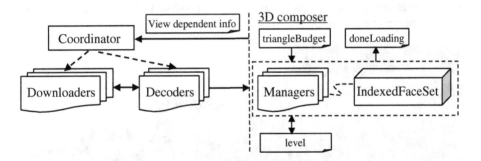

Fig. 2. The implementation details of Hierarchical3DMesh node

As illustrated in Fig 2, the download and management of `Hierarchical-3DMesh` nodes are implemented with a Coordinator thread and three sets of threads including Downloaders, Decoders and Managers at client side. Each `Hierarchical3DMesh` node has its own Downloader, Decoder and Manager threads, which are responsible for downloading, decoding and managing internal data structure of hierarchical 3D meshes respectively. Among them, the Downloader and Decoder threads are instantaneous and will shutdown right after accomplishing downloading and decoding the mesh data. On the contrary, the Manager will persist unless the scene containing the corresponding `Hierarchical3DMesh` node is replaced with another one.

The main task of the Coordinator thread is life cycle management of the Downloader and Decoder threads. After getting `url` information for a new `Hierarchical3DMesh` node, it will spin off a child Downloader and Decoder thread and pair off the newly created Decoder thread with the corresponding Manager thread, which is instead created by the 3D composer. The priority of those threads will be adjusted accordingly based on view dependent information sent from the 3D composer. For simplicity, we currently only consider the distance between the viewer and the object that 3D mesh data represent as the only affecting factor. Roughly speaking, the priority of the Downloader and Decoder thread for a `Hierarchical3DMesh` node is in inverse proportion to the logarithm of the distance, i.e.

$$\text{Priority(Downloader or Decoder)} = \frac{1}{\alpha \log_{10}(d + \beta)} \tag{1}$$

Where d is the distance, α and β are adjustable parameters. In our experiments, α and β are set to 0.9 and 1.1 respectively.

By this way, the closer to the viewer the object is, the higher priority the corresponding Downloader and Decoder thread will have. As a result, 3D objects closer to the viewer will have greater potential to have more data available for rendering in the same period.

Once a Decoder thread accomplishes decoding, it will send an internal message to the Manager and the Manager will in turn send out a `doneLoading` event. This event can be routed to any other node in the scene.

The internal data structure containing all the information necessary to implement smooth transition between different LODs is maintained by the Manager threads. Those threads are in charge of switching LODs responding to the `level` and `triangleBudget` events sent by other nodes.

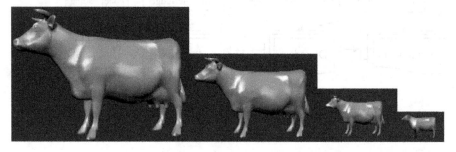

Fig. 3. A cow example illustrating view-dependent rendering of different LODs

As specified by MPEG-4 standard, any `Hierarchical3DMesh` node is seen by the renderer as a read-only `IndexedFaceSet` node as illustrated in Fig. 2. Whether to automatically adjust the polygon numbers in `IndexedFaceSet` node responding to the distance change from the user viewpoint is implementation specific. In our system, we add one more field called `AutoLOD` to `Hierarchical3DMesh` node. This field is an exposed boolean-type field and indicates whether to automatically optimize rendering performance by drawing fewer or simpler polygons when the node is far away from the viewer. If this field is set to true. The corresponding Manager thread is responsible for determining which LOD to use for current viewpoint and dynamically switch between different LODs based on distance change. Technically, the center of the bounding box of a `Hierarchical3DMesh` node will be used to calculate the distance from viewer. Fig 3 shows a cow example, fewer and fewer triangle meshes are used to render the image when the cow moves away from the view. The number of meshes used are 2904, 1591, 768 and 158 respectively at four different distance.

3.2 Interaction and Animation

Large part of the interaction in the system is based on embedded sensor nodes and route definition in the scene. For example, if we want user to see a LOD demo by clicking a 3D object, we can first route events from a `TimeSensor` to an interpolator, a new parameter is interpolated according to the input value, and is then routed to the `level` of the `Hierarchical3Dmesh` node.

Besides, both BIFS command and animation are used as scene update methods to dynamically update scene graph. Generally speaking, BIFS animation provide a more efficiently way to communicate continuous changes in a scene while BIFS command is more suitable for one-time update. For example, if we want to animate disassembly sequence/path for learning purpose and those sequence/path update information is translates into BIFS commands, a sequence of BIFS commands are required to accomplish this task. During this process, some data redundancy will occur since each BIFS command has to specify which node and which field to update. However, BIFS animation can achieve better compression due to the fact that the NodeID and/or fieldID needs not to be specified at each frame and specific quantization, prediction and entropy encoding is used. A real example of mobile phone disassembly using BIFS animation is illustrated in Fig 4, only four frames are shown here. BIFS animation can save around 60 percent bandwidth compared with BIFS command in this example.

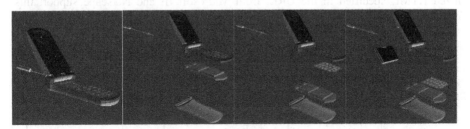

Fig. 4. A mobile phone disassembly example using BIFS animation

3.3 Synchronized HTML Display

Usually, in a web-based learning system, HTML or slide display will be synchronized with multimedia presentation to clearly summarize the points, list references, etc. [11]. For a 3D based system, synchronized HTML display is still useful for providing help or navigation instruction, background information about current selected object, and context explanation.

Basically, there are two ways to achieve synchronized HTML display. One way is to use standard MPEG-4 node `ApplicationWindow`. It can be used to embed an eternal application such as a web browser within the MPEG-4 scene graph. The HTTP link for a HTML page could be passed into `ApplicationWindow` in the parameter field. Following example illustrates how to use this node to launch IE and display a web page when a 3D object is clicked.

```
<Transform translation="100 0 0">
  <children>
    <TouchSensor DEF="tsHTML" />
    <Shape>
      ...
    </Shape>
  </children>
</Transform>
<Transform translation="400 0 0">
  <children>
    <ApplicationWindow  DEF="browser"  url="C:\Program  Files\Internet
Explorer\IEXPLORE.EXE"
      parameter="http://www.icwl2004.org/index.html" size="200,100"/>
  </children>
</Transform>
<Route    fromNode="tsHTML"    fromField="isActive"    toNode="browser"
toField="isActive" />
```

However, this approach is more suitable when the BIFS player is run as an independent application. When the BIFS player is embedded in a web browser, it may have security restriction to launch an external application through `Application-Window` node. As illustrated in Fig 5, by using script in the web page where BIFS player is embedded, there's another way to get around this problem. At first, user action is routed to the 3D composer through the renderer. The composer then updates the scene graph accordingly and fires event to the JavaScript in the same web page of the player. The JavaScript eventually inform the web browser to display the synchronized HTML specified in the URL. Both Microsoft IE and Netscape support this method.

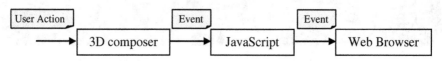

Fig. 5. Event flow for Synchronized HTML Display

4 Conclusion

We have presented a MPEG-4 BIFS based Interactive 3D visualization system. The web-based progressive delivery and rendering of 3D mesh data on a common PC (Pentium 2.8G with nVidia Quadro NVS 280 graphics card) is still acceptable even through a 56k bps channel. It is designed in mind to support interactive learning. With all the necessary capabilities, including efficient compression, view-dependent streaming and rendering, support of various animation methods and synchronized HTML display, it is ready to be used in a web-based learning system. Following are possible future research topics:

1. Integration support of other media, such as audio/video in our system, which needs support of a better time model.
2. Enhancement of synchronization mechanisms – Since our research on BIFS player primarily focuses on 3D scene composition and rendering, there's little work done to support synchronization between different streams.
3. New web-based learning applications – Application development is always important to investigate the suitability and effectiveness of the system.

References

1. A. Aggarwal, Web-Based Learning and Teaching Technologies: Opportunities and Challenges, Idea Group Publishing, Hershey, PA, USA, 2000.
2. F. Klett, Visual Communication in Web-based Learning Environments, Educational Technology & Society, 5(4):38-48, 2002
3. A. Bouras, A. Philopoulos, T. Tsiatsos, e-Learning through distributed virtual environments, Journal of Network and Computer Applications, 24(3):175-199, 2001.
4. Miguel Chover, Óscar Belmonte, et al, Web-based Virtual Environments for Teaching, Eurographics/ACM SIGGRAPH Workshop on Computer Graphics Education, Bristol, UK, 2002.
5. J. Lucca, N. Romano Jr., and R. Sharda, An Overview of Systems Enabling Computer Supported Collaborative Learning Requiring Immersive Presence (CSCLIP), 36th Annual Hawaii International Conference on System Sciences (HICSS'03), Hawaii, USA, 2003.
6. G. Taubin, 3D Geometry Compression and Progressive Transmission, EUROGRAPHICS '99 State of the Art Report, Milan, Italy, 1999.
7. ISO/IEC 14496-1 IS (MPEG-4), Information Technology-Coding of audio-visual objects, Part 1: Systems, 1999.
8. M.Hosseini and N.D.Georganas, MPEG-4 BIFS Streaming of Large Virtual Environments and their Animation on the Web, Proc. ACM Web3D Symposium, pp. 12-25, Tempe, Arizona, USA, 2002.
9. ISO/IEC 14772-1, The Virtual Reality Modeling Language, 1997.
10. M. Kim, S. Wood, and L. Cheok, Extensible MPEG-4 textual format (XMT), ACM Multimedia Workshops 2000, pp. 71-74, Los Angeles, CA, USA, 2000.
11. N. Sharda and A. Hanumanula, Streaming Audio and Video in Web-Based Learning: A Comparative Study of Three Systems, Lecture Notes in Computer Science 2783, pp 206-217, 2003.
12. A. Walsh and M. Bourges-Sevenier, Core Web3D, Prentice-Hall PTR, USA, 2000.

An Adaptive Distance Learning System
Based on Media Streaming[*]

Hao Yin[1], Chuang Lin[1], Jin-Jun Zhuang[1], and Qiang Ni[2]

[1] Department of Computer Science and Technology, Tsinghua University, China
[2] Planete Group, INRIA Sophia Antipolis, France

Abstract. This paper presents the design and development of an adaptive real-time multimedia distance learning system:EasyLearning®, which supports both online learning and courseware on demand through the Internet. By combining the innovative ideas and best features of scalable video coding, screen share algorithm, session control signaling, and TCP-friendly multicast protocol, EasyLearning® is capable of achieving good Quality of Service (QoS) of video and audio, efficiency, and reliability of media delivery. According to the experimental comparison between EasyLearning® and Microsoft media service based system (MMS), Easylearning® provides better performance.

Keywords: Media streaming, distance learning, real-time, QoS, Multicast

1 Introduction

The innovation and development brought by new technologies in our information era has started to appear in education. Distance learning has become a core educational strategy in recent years. The ultimate goal of a real-time multimedia distance learning system is to provide the remote participant with most of the capabilities and experiences that an in-class participant receives. Media streaming, the supporting technique of online learning, typically has bandwidth, delay and loss requirements due to its real-time nature. However, the current Internet does not offer any quality of service (QoS) guarantees to streaming video and audio flows. Furthermore, for video multicast, the intrinsic heterogeneity of the Internet's transmission resource and end systems makes it difficult to achieve both efficiency and flexibility [1]. In addition, the control and signal procedures of the distance learning system are complicated. Thus, distance learning system based on media streaming poses many challenges.

There exists some distance learning systems, notably Stanford-online and Virtual classroom of the University of Washington [2], and various commercial products including those from RealNetworks, Microsoft Media Service [3], and Apple Quicktime. Also, researchers have developed Mbone tools for audio (e.g. vat, rat), video (e.g. vic, nte) and whiteboard (e.g. wt). Our adaptive real-time multimedia distance learning system – EasyLearning® differs in the following aspects from above sys-

---

[*] This work is supported by the National Natural Science Foundation of China (No. 60372019, 90104002, and 60173012), China Postdoctoral Science Foundation (No.2003034152), NSFC and RGC (No. 60218003), the Projects of Development Plan of the State High Technology Research (No. 2001AA112080).

W. Liu et al. (Eds.): ICWL 2004, LNCS 3143, pp. 184–192, 2004.

tems and tools.1) It is based on a quality-adaptive framework to maximize the perceived quality of the delivered multimedia stream up to the level that the available network bandwidth will permit while preventing congestion collapse[4]. 2) A highly efficient screen share algorithm is proposed so that students can view the courseware regardless of its format. 3) A session-layer-protocol considering collaborative work is designed and used in our system, which is based on Session Initial Protocol (SIP).

The paper is organized as follows. In Section 2, we introduce the system architecture of media streaming for our distance learning system. Crucial components of the system, especially, adaptive video encoder, screen compression algorithm and TCP-friendly multicast protocol are introduced in Section 3. In Section 4 we illustrate the framework of Easylearning ®, give a brief introduction to our session control protocol, and provide performance evaluation for Easylearning ®.

2 System Architecture

Fig. 1 illustrates the architecture of media streaming for our adaptive real-time multimedia distance learning system, which offers a flexible environment where applications can maximally exploit the QoS capabilities of supporting networks.

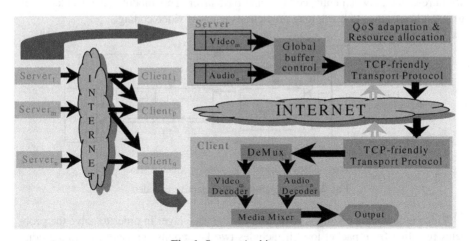

Fig. 1. System Architecture

In this architecture, servers use adaptive encoder to encode raw video and audio. When resource availability or user QoS requirements varies, encoders change the quality of media flows with scalable coding techniques. Then, the TCP-friendly transport protocol packetizes the compressed bit-streams and sends them in a TCP-friendly manner to the Internet. At the receiver side, arriving packets are processed and decoded by the decoder. To present media streams in the same way as originally captured, media mixer is required to achieve synchronization between video and audio presentations.Given the multi-receiver nature of audio and video distribution, we use a TCP-friendly sender adaptive & receiver driven multicast framework.

3 Crucial Components of the System

3.1 Adaptive Video Encoder

Our proposed encoder contains the following three key modules:(1) Compression module, which contains Fine Granularity Scalability (FGS) coding, redundancy source coding and human visual model; (2) Rate shaper module; (3) Resource allocation module. Through a seamless integration, we improve the error resilience and adaptability of our encoder in order to mitigate the packet loss and bandwidth fluctuation. Fig. 2 illustrates the framework of our adaptive video encoder.

At first, raw video is sent to the compression module. This module implements three functions:(1) compressing the raw video into base layer and enhance layer just as FGS [5] encoder does; (2) redundancy source coding of base layer by using multiple prediction threads and inserting Intra-frame (I frame) when the network condition turns worse to limit error propagation derived from packet loss; (3) adapting the quantization step-size based on JND(Just-Noticeable Distortion) model to control the bit rate of base layer [11]. Then, video layers are transmitted to the rate shaper module, which adjusts output bit rate according to network performance. Resource allocation module gets network status from TCP-friendly multicast protocol and allocates bandwidth resource between enhance layer and base layer. This module also decides when to insert key frames to break long prediction chains of video coding.

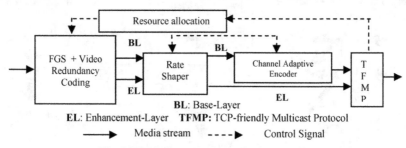

BL: Base-Layer
EL: Enhancement-Layer   **TFMP**: TCP-friendly Multicast Protocol
⟶ Media stream   ----▶ Control Signal

Fig. 2. Block diagram of our adaptive encoder

Video redundancy coding is only used for the base layer in order to solve the problems resulting from packet loss. It includes two key points: 1) using multiple prediction threads; 2) increasing the number of Intra frame to break long prediction chains.

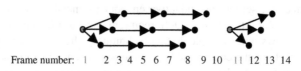

Frame number: 1   2 3 4 5 6 7   8 9 10 11 12 13 14

Fig. 3. Multiple Prediction Thread

As is shown in fig.3, our scheme uses multiple prediction threads to generate the P frame. When the packet loss increases, we can drop one thread's packets. Another solution to packet loss is increasing the intra frame rate, so if one key frame is lost, the bad effect will last shorter.

Rate shaper module is designed to adjust the output frame rate. The previous solution to this problem is to control the frame rate according to the buffer fullness [6]. Obviously the receiver can't get smooth video sequence in this case. Here we propose a new method. As fig.2 indicates, both the base-layer and enhancement-layer are input to the rate shaper module. The base-layer bitstream is divided into multiple groups where I frame and all P frames that involved in the same prediction thread are converged into the same group. When the available bandwidth is small, P frames of a group are dropped. Of course drop all the enhancement bitstreams before that. If the status of the network gets better, firstly recover one group, and then transports the enhancement layer bitstream when bandwidth is richer.

Channel Adaptive Encoder packetizes I-frame of base layer and protects it against packet loss with forward error correction (FEC). Our FEC scheme uses Reed Solomon (RS) codes across packets [11]. In our system, the number of the additional packets is changed with the network status.

According to the available bandwidth and packet loss ratio, resource allocation module periodically updates the quantization parameter of enhancement layer in our video encoder and determines the interval of I frame. It also informs the rate shaper module how to execute frame skipping. On the other hand, in the channel-adaptive encoder, the FEC code rate k/n is adaptively changed with the packet loss ratio.

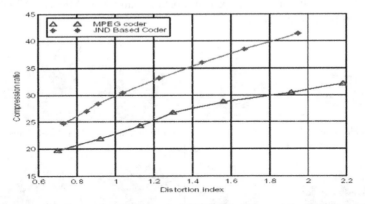

Fig. 4. Performance Comparison between the MPEG-4 Encoder and the JND-Based Encoder

The performance of our JND-based video encoder is compared with the MPEG-4 VM17.0. In Fig.4, the original sequence "Claire" is encoded by MPEG-4 encoder at different scales. The distortion indexes Δ_G [11] of these frames are calculated using spatial-temporal JND profiles. At the same perceptual distortion level, the JND-based encoder provides higher compression ratio than that derived from MPEG-4 encoder. On the other hand, the PSNR of decompressed frames from the MPEG-4 encoder is 1-2 dB larger than that from the JND-based encoder at the same compression ratio. This is a natural result for the JND-based compression scheme. Since with the consideration of JND profile, the irrelevant information for perception is removed, it renders more compression at the same perceptual quality. It renders more numerical error which means less PSNR at the same compression ratio, while keeping the subjective quality superior. Fig. 5 compares the decompressed "Claire" from JND-based encoder and MPEG-4 encoder with almost the same compression ratio. From direct observation we can say that the subjective quality of Fig. 5 (a) is better than that of Fig.5 (b).

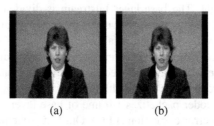

(a)   (b)

Fig. 5. (a) "Claire" from the JND based encoder, Δ_G =0.85, PSNR=36.3dB, Compression ratio=27.0:1; (b) "Claire" I frame from the MPEG-4 VM 17.0 encoder, Δ_G =1.3, PSNR=37.5dB, Compression ratio=26.7:1

We performed many experiments to test the performance of our encoder. Fig. 6 shows the experimental results. In these experiments, available bandwidth for video delivery varies from 256Kbps to 28kbps and packet loss ratio is random from 1% to 5%. It is obvious that our encoder provides better quality than MPEG 4 VM17.0 encoder when network is not good.

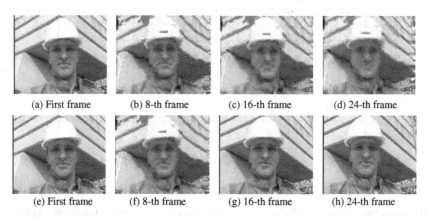

(a) First frame   (b) 8-th frame   (c) 16-th frame   (d) 24-th frame

(e) First frame   (f) 8-th frame   (g) 16-th frame   (h) 24-th frame

Fig. 6. Decompressed foreman sequence (a)-(d): 4 frames from foreman sequence by MPEG 4 VM 17.0 encoder (e)-(f): 4 frames from foreman sequence by RAVE encoder

3.2   Screen Share Module

The main goal of this module is to repeat the screen of teacher's computer to that of client computer. Our approach, illustrated in fig.7, consists of three modules. Captured screen information is divided into 16X16 blocks, compressed by compression module, packetized and sent to clients. In traditional screen share approaches, the screen image (1024*768) contains 2-3M bytes, which is unable to be transferred in real time. So the most important technology is how to compress the image data.

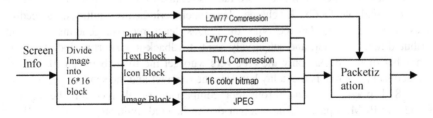

Fig. 7. Illustrate compression algorithm of screen information

The innovation of our compression approach is that according to the color number of the above screen blocks, we divide them into four parts: pure block (only one color), text block (two colors), icon block (three to sixteen colors), and image block (more than sixteen colors). Then, we compress them in different ways. As for pure block, we only need to record the color with 4 bits. Because text block only has two kinds of color, we can look them as foreground and background and use 0 or 1 to represent them. We call it TVL (Two Value Lossless) compression. As for icon block, we reduce color depth, and create a palette to save them. Then, 4 bits are used to store the value of one pixel. This algorithm is just like that used in 16 bits color bitmap. At last image block is compressed by JPEG algorithm. Comprared to JPEG algorithm, our algorthm can provide three times compression-ratio with the same quality.

3.3   TCP Friendly Multicast Protocol (TFMP)

Multicast is a common method for distributing real-time audio and video. Due to the heterogeneity of the Internet, it is difficult to agree with a single transmission rate. It is thus necessary to use multirate video multicast, in which receivers receive video data according to their capabilities. Researchers have proposed sender-based adaptive multicast protocol and receiver-driven layered multicast protocol. However, since the number of layers is practically limited, noticeable mismatches would occur between the discrete set of layer rates and receivers' dynamic rate requirements [8].

We exploit our proposed sender-adaptive & receiver-driven layered multicast protocol (SARLM)[9] to design our TFMP. In TFMP, the sender transforms video streams into several layers and sends each layer to a different multicast group. Each receiver estimates its available bandwidth using TCP throughput formula. As for the estimation approach of the available bandwidth, we have proposed it in [4].

In multicast it is important to avoid feedback implosion. We proposed a statistical approach in [11]. In [9], we introduced a devised Gamma-distributed timer for each receiver, which outperforms other distributed timers when the number of users is very large. The density of the truncated Gamma distributed timer is:

$$f_{z_i}(z_i)=\begin{cases}\dfrac{1}{(e^{\lambda}-1)}\cdot\alpha\dfrac{\lambda}{T^{\alpha}}z_i^{\alpha-1}e^{\frac{\lambda}{T^{\alpha}}z_i^{\alpha}} & ,0\le z_i\le T\\ 0 & ,otherwise\end{cases}$$

where T is a fixed interval, λ and α are factors related to the whole number of receivers. In our scalable feedback scheme, the sender periodically multicasts a feedback request to all receivers. On receiving the request, each receiver generates a Gamma distributed random timer, and selectively sends feedback in a short period. To control the number of feedbacks, only the receivers who get the timer between (0, 0+c) can send feedback, where c is the delay between the receiver and the sender.

Fig. 8 displays the mean throughput comparison of all receivers between our scheme and PLM, a packet pair receiver-driven layered multicast protocol [12]. The figure shows that the mean throughput of our scheme is 150% higher than PLM. According to our simulation, TFMP not only keeps good TCP-friendliness but also prevents feedback implosion.

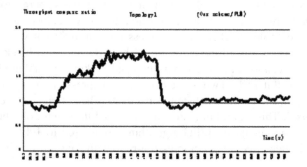

Fig. 8. Mean Throughput compare ratio

4   Evaluations and Conclusions

Fig.9 illustrates the framework of EasyLearning®, which is composed of teacher side, server layer and client side. Teacher side contains main server and screen share server. Main server compresses captured video, audio, image, and text data from the teacher. Some manual management from teacher is also completed in this server. Screen copy server captures and compresses the teacher screen information and sends it to media server. The server layer consists of Video-on-demand (VOD) server, media server, and student management database. VOD server makes synchronized media stream provided by media server into integrated courseware and then stores it into the database for future playback. Student management database maintains students' records and on-line status. Media server marks time stamp on the compressed data to synchronize them and delivers the synchronized stream to VOD server and the clients. Media data can also be submitted from a client to the teacher and other clients through media server in order to take part in video discussion of a group. Client terminal decompresses the stream data from media server and represents them to the student as control signals instructed.

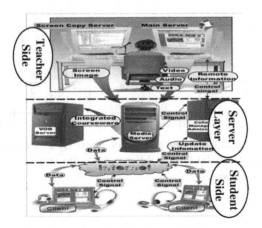

Fig. 9. Framework of EasyLearning® System

To support the control need in distance learning, we present a Session Control Protocol (SCP) based on Session Initiation Protocol (SIP), which is illustrated in fig.10. SCP supports the setup and control of complex multimedia communication services.

There are five kinds of servers and eight control signals in our model. *Administrator Server (AS)* is in charge of giving manual commands. *Resource Server (ResS)* provides either stored or real-time data. *User Agent Proxy (UAP)* acts as intermediary that makes service transparent to the users and reduces the load of other servers. *Redirect Server (RedS)* redirects request of UAP to proper ResS according to the resource which UAP needs. *Registry Server (RegS)* maintains user records.

S1 is resource related control signals from AS to ResS. AS sends *S2* to manage user accounts and get on-line status of users. *S3* includes directives from AS to user and requests from user to AS via UAP. *S4* is used by UAP to get or set user status on RegS. *S5* from RedS tells UAP the location of the resource that UAP needs. *S6* informs resource location to RedS initiatively or passively by RedS. UAP uses *S7* to download or upload data from ResS. *S8* is user's request and instruction for user.

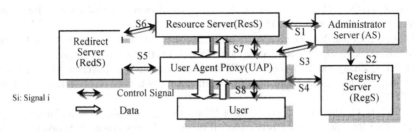

Fig. 10. SCP model

To test the overall performance, a series of comparison experiments between Easylearning® (EL) and Microsoft media service based system (MS)[3] are carried out. 30 persons join the experiment and score the performance with 1 to 5 in different conditions (1 is the worst and 5 is the best). The result is summarized as follows:

	Packet lost: <10%				
	1	2	3	4	5
MS	2	5	10	10	3
EL	1	3	11	11	4

	Packet lost: 20%				
	1	2	3	4	5
MS	5	7	8	8	2
EL	3	5	10	9	3

	Packet lost: 30%				
	1	2	3	4	5
MS	15	9	4	2	0
EL	8	5	9	6	2

	Packet lost: 40%				
	1	2	3	4	5
MS	18	9	3	0	0
EL	8	7	8	5	2

The result shows that our system can provide better QoS of video and audio, transmission efficiency and reliability than Microsoft media service based system, especially in a congestion network.

References

1. D.P.Wu,Y.T.Hou,Y.Q.Zhang and J.Peha, "Streaming video over the Internet: approaches and directions," IEEE Trans. Circuits Syst. Video Technol., vol. 22, no. 3, pp. 282-300, Mar. 2001.
2. Sachin G. Deshpande and J.N. H, "A Real-Time Interactive Virtual Classroom Multimedia Distance Learning System ," IEEE Transaction on Multimedia, Vol.3,No.4, pp.432-444, Dec.2001.
3. Yin Hao, Zhu Guang-xi,Li Xiao-long, Zhu Yao-ting and He Da-an, "Development and Evaluation of a Distance Learning System Based on CSCW," Wuhan University Journal of Natural Sciences,Vol.6,No.1-2,pp.491-494, Mar. 2001.
4. Hao Yin,G-X Zhu,Y-T Zhu,"A New Approach for Available Bandwidth Estimation Based on Improved TFRC Protocol," Proceedings of the International Conference on Fundamentals of Electronics,Comm. and Computer Sci.,2002.
5. Weiping Li, "Overview of Fine Granularity Scalability in MPEG-4 Video Standard," IEEE Trans. on Circuit and Systems for Video Technology, Vol. 11, No. 3, Mar. 2001.
6. D. Wu, T. Hou, W. Zhu, H..J. L, T. Chiang, Y.Q. Zhang, H. J. Chao,"On End-to-End Architecture for Transporting MPEG-4 Video over the Internet," IEEE Trans. on Circuits and Systems for Video Technology, Vol. 10, No. 6, pp. 923-941, Sept. 2000.
7. U. Horn, K. Stuhlmuller, and M. Link et al., "Robust internet video transmission based on scalable coding and unequal error protection," Image Comm., Special Issue on Real-Time Video Over the Internet, Vol. 15, pp. 77–94, Sept. 1999.
8. J.C.Liu, B.Li and Y.Q.Zhang, "A Hybrid Adaptation Protocol for TCP-Friendly Layered Multicast and its Optimal Rate Allocation," Proc. IEEE INFOCOM '02, June 2002.
9. Q. Ni, Q.Zhang,and W.W.Zhu, "SARLM: Sender-adaptive & Receiver-driven Layered Multicasting for Scalable Video," IEEE International Conference on Multimedia and Expo (ICME), Aug. 2001.
10. B. Vickers, C. Albuquerque, and T. Suda, "Source Adaptive Multi-layered Multicast Algorithms for Real-time Video Distribution," IEEE/ACM Transaction on Network, vol. 8, no. 6, Dec. 2000, pp. 720-33.
11. Hao Yin, Zhang Jiang-Shan, Zhu Guang-xi, Zhu Yao-Ting, "Implementation of A Robust Adaptive Video Encoder Based on Human Visual Model," Journal of Electronics, Vol.20 No.2, Mar.2003.
12. A.Legout. PLM:Fast convergence for cumulative layered multicast transmission scheme. Proceedings of ACM SIGMETRICS 2000.

CDAL: A Scalable Scheme
for Digital Resource Reorganization

Chong Chen, Hongfei Yan, and Xiaoming Li

Computer Networks and Distributed Systems Laboratory, Department of Computer Science
and Technology, Peking University, Beijing 100871, PR China
{cc,yhf,lxm}@net.pku.edu.cn

Abstract. In many circumstances, including e-learning, there is a need to reorganize digital resources, scattered in many places, into a coherently accessible repository. This paper introduces a methodology to do the job efficiently. Specifically, the resources that the scheme needs to handle presents the following challenges, 1) mass, 2) various data types, 3) coming out continuously, i.e., the scheme must support incremental reorganization. 4) usually existing with its own directory structures. We describe the scheme in detail, together with considerations for trade-offs. The following features are highlighted: 1) the reorganization of scattered resources is modeled as a tree-merging process, which results in a good trade-off between efficiency and quality. 2) hierarchical storage arrangement with a uniform index at each level ensures scalability. As an application of the scheme, CDAL (Chinese Digital Assets Library) is briefed, which is a TB-scale archive of digital resources on the Web.

Keywords: digital resource, reorganization, tree-merging, storage arrangement, scalability

1 Introduction

In many circumstances, we need to reorganize vast amount of digital resources, scattered over the Internet or different computers, into a coherent fashion, so that people can access them effectively, e.g., digital library, learning material repository.

As we know, many such projects rely on manpower to categorize resource and create metadata. If the way to do so is laborious and ineffective, people would feel the work troublesome and abort the efforts before the collection is built up to a useful size. Ineffective methods usual lead to long time commitment and raise expensive initial cost before the benefit returns.

The scheme proposed here emphasizes cost-effectiveness in terms of human labor time involved. It also illustrates the scalability of the system architecture to accommodate the massive and incremental nature of the collections. Specifically, the resources our scheme needs to handle present the following challenges:

1. The amount of the resources to be reorganized is massive. As the Internet expands, the sharp increment of resource volume makes the conventional method ineffectual.

W. Liu et al. (Eds.): ICWL 2004, LNCS 3143, pp. 193–200, 2004.
© Springer-Verlag Berlin Heidelberg 2004

2. The resources are of various data types, say text, image, audio, video, etc.. Again, a resource may contain files ranging from small text files less than 1KB to large movie files up to 1GB. Such difference in data sizes makes database solution less efficiency. In this paper, we define the term *digital resource* as *a file, or some files (maybe with directory or subdirectories) which represent a certain thing, meaning or entity, and are worthy of treasure in the long term.*

3. The resources to be reorganized are collected as time goes, not come as a whole, namely the scheme must support the incremental reorganization. This requirement is true in digital library, e-learning material repository, and ftp site maintenance.

4. The resources are usually organized within some directory structures. People have to pick them out for reorganization.

Facing these challenges, our scheme and the system under its guidance should allow rapid and incremental inclusion of resources into the system, convenient access of the resources by users, and dynamic configuration without halting.

In what follows, we first give an overview of the scheme and its first successful application, namely CDAL, followed by a presentation and analysis of a tree-merging model for resource reorganization. The hierarchical storage arrangement supporting scalability is then described in section 4. In final section, we list some of related work.

2   An Overview of CDAL Scheme

In July of 2003, with our "Bingle" technology [7], a comprehensive study in [6] discovered more than 6000 public accessible FTP sites, nearly 15 million files in total.

Although what CDAL reorganizes are resources, not respective files, we might as well imagine we want to fetch all the files from the sites and put them together in a centralized location as an archive which is easy to access. How should one go about it? And what's the time cost to accomplish the job?

A brute-force (but reasonable and aggressive) estimation would be, 0.5 minutes is needed to process one file, then 20 million files give 10 million minutes, which results in about 167,000 hours. The question is, can we do it in one fifth of the time or less? This is in fact the direct motivation of CDAL scheme.

Generally, CDAL scheme consists of the following key elements.

1. An overall classification structure to logically reorganize the resources. That is, from users' point of view, the files are all within one big directory tree which presents the classification architecture. (We call it *"big tree"* for convenience). The process of resource inclusion can be modeled as tree-merging, and one can often make pretty good decision about where in the big tree a group of resource files should be moved to, only by examining their original directory names. With suitable storage arrangement strategy speeding up merging, the process time is reduced substantially. Section 3 will analyze this approach in detail.

2. A hierarchical storage scheme to physically accommodate the resources. We deploy resources on distributed storage architecture by replicating the big tree directory structure onto each disk. Each disk holds different resources files in the "tree". All such disks form an extensible coordinate storage units cluster. See section 4.

3. A consistency maintenance procedure for incremental updating and efficient access
by the users. When new resources are physically moved into the system, its presence should be reflected in the big tree as quick as possible. In section 3 and 4, this
issue will be involved.

With careful implementation, we successfully constructed CDAL, a digital resource
archive [8]. As of today, it hosts more than 700,000 files (about 5TB digital resources), a good sample of reusable learning material repository. It took us about 1000
man hours to accomplish. Using this repository, we are able to estimate the ability on
processing the whole ftp files mentioned above much less than one fifth of 167,000
hours. The classification architecture of CDAL, i.e. the big tree, is growing from [5].
CDAL uses DCMI recommendation types as root domain of the big tree. Digital resources of a category could be considered as the leaf nodes of an internal-node the big
tree.

3   A Tree-Merging Model

In our scheme, the time is saved mainly due to two causes, the tree-merging reorganization method and the resource storage arrangement strategy.

3.1   Modeling the Resource Reorganization Process

The resources fetched in advance from the remote ftp sites keep their hosts' file storage structures. The process of picking out a resource from its original storage structure
into a node of the big tree (means some category) is called merging a small tree into
the big tree. *A resource which may consist of its own directory structure or existing as
an independent file* is taken as *a small tree*, comparing with the big tree scale.

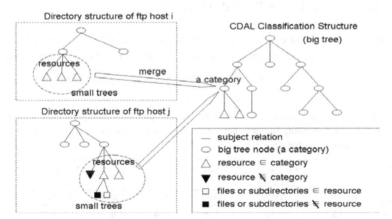

Fig. 1. The process of tree-merging. The figure illustrates 1) the directory structure in each host
represents the owner's view of files organization. The files in one directory are usually on same
subject. I.e., not all resources need to be confirmed, their organization and the file or directory
names give hints to help the manual classification. 2) in tree-merging, the resource could be
wrong-classified or having the wrong-contained components (files and/or its subdirectories)

The tree-merging process composes of two stages, 1) rough classification – a batch of small trees are given a category for each judgment and merged to an internal node in the big tree. The judgment is done by examining the resource names, or at most its superficial structure, instead of looking into its contents. The practice is of course with certain probability of mistake. Yet in this stage, all resources are processed by this means. 2) refining – rectify the wrong-classified resources and wrong-contained components by inspecting the their contents to determine their integrity and to which new categories they belong. This stage will not start immediately after the first stage, but be carried out gradually in the system running by user feedback or check routine. The former right-classified resources will be touched but need not seriously checked. So the time spent for glancing the right-classified resources can be omitted.

Let α is the average number of the resources to be merged to a node in each batch. t_j, the average time cost to determine a resource's category by one judgment. $t_{j'}$, the average time to check the resource content. t_m, the average time to merge resources to the big tree. N, the number of resources to be reorganized. $T_{(1)}$, the time cost to reorganize N resources by tree-merging. P, the accurate probability of judgment. $o(t_j)$ is the time on judging the right-classified resource in refining stage, close to 0.

$$T_{(1)} = [(N/\alpha)t_j + Nt_m] + (1-P)N(t_{j'} + t_j + t_m) + o(t_j) \qquad (1)$$

For comparison, we propose formula (2) which differs from (1) on the check manner–instead of picking out the congener resources as much as possible by briefly judging the resources' name without diving into the inner directory structure to check the resource integrity, the manner in (2) checks each resource's integrity, judging its category, then transferring it into the big tree. This result is considered in ideal accuracy.

$$T_{(2)} = N \cdot (t_{j'} + t_j + t_m) \qquad (2)$$

Comparing the Time Cost in Formula (1) and (2)

1. Parameter estimation

α is usually 3~5 from our experience in classification. P is 0.8~0.9 by post-inspecting the accuracy on classified resource samples (See table 1). t_j is up to the classifier's ability and knowledge. $t_{j'}$ is influenced by the resource integrity. We suppose $t_{j'} = t_j$.

Table 1. The quality of resource classification. The accurate probability P is not the same for different categories, according to our experience. We sample some popular categories of CDAL to present the accurate probability P

Category	Book	Learning reference	Picture	Game	Film	Software	Sound
accuracy	0.879	0.978	0.966	0.956	0.857	0.948	0.88
Samples	132	216	118	114	98	975	50

2. Analysis

The tree-merging system can be built in two choices, first, in pursuit of the ideal classification accuracy; second, in pursuit of quick-to-start and minimizing initial inputs.

We compare $T_{(2)}/T_{(1)}$ in the two cases, let $t_{j'}=t_j$, $P = 0.9$, $\alpha = 3$.

Case1. For ideal classification accuracy. To this end, the refining stage described by formula (1) is necessary. In tree-merging scheme, our resource storage arrangement strategy insures the t_m close to 0, which will be discussed in section 3.2. Let $t_m = 0$, we get $T_{(2)}/T_{(1)} \approx 4$.

Case2. For Quick-to-access All Resources. To this end, the time cost in refining stage may be eliminated from $T_{(1)}$ for comparison, because all resources could be accessed through category browsing or key searching after the first stage. Although there are wrong-classified resources, the accuracy is acceptable. Let $T'_{(1)} = (N/\alpha)t_j + Nt_m$,

$$T_{(2)} - T'_{(1)} = (2-1/\alpha)Nt_j.$$

When $t_m = 0$, $T_{(2)}/T'_{(1)} = 2\alpha$, i.e., $T_{(2)} = 6T'_{(1)}$ if $\alpha = 3$.

Apparently, the result of only rough classification stage can not match up to the quality as that of the formula (2). With later refining, the hitting quality can improve gradually. This scheme helps the system quick to start and minimizes the initial inputs. It is in this manner that CDAL grows from the beginning.

3.2 Evaluating the Resource Storage Arrangement Strategies

There are two choices to in resources storage arrangement. Strategy 1 is to store resources by category. Namely, breaking down the big tree to different category, the resources of same category occupy specific storage units (in CDAL, *a single file system in one physical device, usually a hard disk, is taken as a storage unit*). And strategy 2 is to store resources by big tree. Namely, replicating the big tree directory structure to different storage units; In this case, each unit holds every possible category.

The two strategies have different effectiveness in resource reorganization. We prefer strategy 2, for its only costing the time to update file system index, this time is far less than physically move files from their provenance directory structures to the big tree on storage units. Moreover, the resource is originally stored on units after being fetched from the Web; strategy 2 allows the classification finished in one unit, while strategy 1 does not. When source and the destination are distributing on the network, the time will be unacceptable, even without network failure.

In strategy 2, t_m is the time to move files in one file system of a disk (about 3.0×10^{-6} s/MB, we measure the average time to move files in one storage unit). While, for strategy 1, the average time to transfer files from disk A to disk B on same server is about 0.03s/MB as measured. If the two disks are on different servers, t_m would be longer due to network transformation time. Suppose the size of resources to be transferred is 100MB, the time cost of strategy 1 is at least 3s, while for strategy 2, $t_m \approx 0$.

The Compensation Measures to Strategy 2
Although strategy 2 cuts down the merging time, it has its shortage in other sides.

1. The resources may be reduplicated among disks without being awareness, as the classification is often done respectively by different people in different time.
2. The whole storage system would be searched when accessing only one resource.
3. The whole service system would be involved when updating the service data.
4. The structure changing of the big tree would involve all the disks in storage system.

Yet the compensation costs are affordable. The first two shortages can be remedied by combining the local indexes to a global index and distributing it to each sever. To avoid the efficiency decrease caused by 3, the frequency of updating should be controlled. Fortunately, digital resource repository and accessing service do not require frequent update. And the time spends on the service data updating is not more than 20 minutes in about 5TB resource volumes. For a repository system like CDAL, this duration is acceptable. By scheduling the update routine in idle time, the system can meet the requirement. To save the trouble caused by 4, the big tree in every disk can be modified by automatically mapping the directory structure to new classification.

4   Hierarchical Storage for System Scalability

By designing hierarchical classification structure and mapping it to the big tree, the various mass resources are accommodated in hierarchical storage. This approach brings benefits to system scalability in three aspects, 1) the physical storage scalability; 2) the logical identification scalability; 3) service-providing scalability.

The Physical Storage Scalability. The resources are accommodated by many hard disks. With the big tree replicated onto it, each disk is a small independent repository. The servers only manage resources residing in their units; the data exchange between different servers is nearly unnecessary. Storage servers compose a distributed cluster; each member is of similar function. With the resource volume increasing, the storage capacity of this architecture can be extended by adding new disks, or new servers.

The Logical Identification Scalability. In CDAL system, the physical location of a resource determines its logical identification. The naming space of CDAL is illustrated by the fig. 2. The resource ID consists of the server id, disk id, classification path and the resource directory name. If only the uniqueness is kept in each level respectively, the resources can be identified in hierarchical storage fashion.

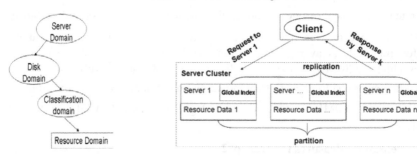

Fig. 2. CDAL hierarchical naming space

Fig. 3. CDAL service-providing scalability

The Service-Providing Scalability. As shown in fig. 3, each server in the cluster functionally includes two parts – resource storage and service-providing. Namely, every member is capable to provide the resource accessing service and share the access workload coming from the Web, except for resource storage. A global index integrating every server's local index is replicated to each of the cluster members. User access requests are distributed to arbitrary server by task scheduler. The indexer finds the target resource location in the global index and delivers the request to the target server. By this means, the system meets the demands of the accessing load balance. If the target storage unit fails to work, the failure would not affect the other units. I.e., during the period in fitting the problem, the whole system keeps function without halting.

5 Final Remarks

We have shown an approach to reorganize a large amount of digital resources efficiently. We have observed several major efforts to collect what exist on the Web into a centralized facility for different purposes. Most notably, Internet Archive has been collecting web pages all over the world since 1997 [1], and IBM web fountain won the unique recognition of IEEE Spectrum [2]. We believe the technique presented in this paper is useful for successively reorganizing non web page materials.

There is one issue which has not been covered above. Why do we use file system, instead of database solution like IBM Content Manager [4] do, to accommodate the resources? R.Grossman in [3] mentioned it is better to select hierarchical storage system for complex object storage management, as well as use lightweight object management component instead of a full-function database in application field like digital resources repository. Except for the reasons put forth by Grossman, the distribution of data storage by database cost much on product purchase and need expensive maintenance cost.

Another issue is searching. As CDAL accumulates more and more resources, browsing through the big tree sometimes is inefficient for a user to locate the resource he needs. Thus, we have also provided filename-based search facility, using "Bingle" technology [7]. For future work, we plan to launch metadata [9] for each resource, which will surely enhance system usability. However, the usual way to create accurate metadata manually costs much, which implies other technique must be invented.

6 Conclusion

In this paper, a tree-merging model on mass digital resource reorganization approach is proposed. We analyses the reason why it could lead to cost-effectiveness on human labor and time cost in three cases. This model also presents a good trade-off between time cost and the service quality under acceptable classification accuracy. The "quick-to-start" property enables many digital resource repository applications to keep the pace with the incremental rate of mass resources with limited initial construction expense. By presenting our terabyte scale archive system CDAL, we illustrate the scalability in storage, identification ability and service-providing.

Acknowledgement

We would like to thank the members of the CNDS lab of PKU for their participation the mass Web digital resources classification in their spare time. Their work is the base of China Web Digital Asset Library. Also, we thank Chen Hua and Wang Jimin for providing Web ftp sites analysis information and "Bingle" technology. We are grateful to Xiang Xin and Peng Bo for their good suggestions to this paper.

References

1. Why the Archive is Building an 'Internet Library'. http://www.archive.org/about/about.php, (2004)
2. IEEE Spectrum. Stephen Cass: The winners, the losers, and the holy grails. IEEE Spectrum. (Jan. 2004)
3. R.Grossman, X.Qin, W.Xu, H.Hulen and T.Tyler.: A Scalable, High-performance Digital Library. Fourteen IEEE Symposium on Mass Storage System, 1051-9173/95 (1995) ISBN: 0-8186-7064-9, Page: 89
4. Content Manager Implementation and Migration Cookbook, IBM Red Books, SG24-7051-00(Jan. 2004). Online at:
   http://publib-b.boulder.ibm.com/Redbooks.nsf/RedbookAbstracts/sg247051.html?Open
5. Dublin Core Metadata Initiative.: DCMI Type Vocabulary, Dublin Core Metadata Initiative. http://www.dublincore.org/documents/dcmi-type-vocabulary/ (2003)
6. Chen Hua, Wang Jimin, Han Jinqiang, and Xie Xin.: FTP Files' Distribution Char-acteristics and Their Implications. Computer Engineering and Applications, Vol.40, No.1, Page: 129-133 (Jan. 2004)
7. CNDS lab at Peking University: Tianwang File Search Engine. http://bingle.pku.edu.cn. (2004)
8. Chinese Digital Assets Library, http://cdal.grids.cn, (2004) (restricted to public access for content copyright)
9. Dublin Core Metadata Initiative.: DCMI Metadata Element Set, Version 1.1: Reference Description, Dublin Core Metadata Initiative. http://www.dublincore.org/documents/dcmi-terms (2003)

An Approach to the Use and Automatic Generation of Web-Based Learning Materials*

Victor Fresno-Fernández, Soto Montalvo-Herranz, Joaquin Pérez-Iglesias,
Jaime Urquiza-Fuentes, and J. Ángel Velázquez-Iturbide

ViDo Group, ESCET – Rey Juan Carlos University, Mostoles, Spain
{v.fresno,smontalvo,joperez,j.urquiza,a.velazquez}@escet.urjc.es

Abstract. This paper presents an approach to the automatic generation
and use of web-based learning materials (WLMs). It consists in three
phases: contents creation, division and browsing. The use of XML in
the creation phase allows achieving independence between contents and
their presentation, in addition to contents reuse. The splitting phase is
an automatic process whose output can be used as WLMs for different
user interfaces. In the browsing phase, the interfaces are generated; we
have implemented two: a user-adaptative interface and a non-adaptative
one. The main features of our approach enables users to create learning
contents without XML technical knowledge and also enables to effectively
navigate the material to their needs.

Keywords: e-learning tools development, web-based education, teaching
materials, electronic documentation.

1 Introduction

Nowadays, Internet has become the main source of information in the world
and its growth results unstoppable. A huge amount of data is accessible at the
Net and several technologies for extraction and sharing of information are being
developed. This is not different in educational environments. In this context,
the development of web-based courses and their materials is growing and it is
more and more important for distance education. This new educational context
exhibits important differences with respect to traditional education [1]. The way
of presenting and creating learning contents must be adapted to several features [13]: *asyncronicity of teaching and learning* (students study at their most
suitable time and place, and the presence of a teacher is not always needed or
possible), *maintenance* (web courses can be updated at any moment, whereafter
the update is directly available to all students), *alternative structures* (hyperlinked, non-linear structures as tree-like hierarchies or graphs), *external links*
(tapping unlimited resources on the Internet using direct links), *integration of
applications* (discussion groups, group learning, peer assessment, etc.).

---

* This work is supported by the Spanish Research Agency CICYT under contract
TIC2000-1413.

W. Liu et al. (Eds.): ICWL 2004, LNCS 3143, pp. 201–208, 2004.

WLMs are mainly based on hyperlinked contents, functional use of interactivity and multimedia components [15]; and they must be tailored to:

1. *Contents exposition.* The contents can be divided according to either *structural* or *semantic* criteria. The structural approach divides contents based on its hierarchical structure and the semantic one divides by concepts. Examples of the structural approach can be found in [5, 11], that generates a division in HTML pages by chapters, (sub)sections or (sub)paragraphs. Examples of the semantic approach can be found in [2, 9, 14].
2. *Learning is not only reading.* Contents that require user interaction (animations, videos, audios, quizzes, etc.) can be made available [14].
3. *Interface and contents customization,* adapting tools to the users [16, 19].

WLMs are made up of static and interactive contents, but they can also be divided into those that do not allow users to modify their contents and interface [8] and those that do it [14, 13, 11]. In the first case, any web browser can be used as the user interface and in the second case, more complex interfaces are needed.

There is a second open question: are students ready to use these new environments effectively? In [1] it is stated that using an electronic environment requires skills and learning processes that are different from those used in a paper-based or face-to-face environments. Other authors claim that difficulties can be found by students adapting themselves to electronic learning methods [10, 18, 4, 12]. Consequently, the learning task can be facilitated by using tools that imitate others that are well known. The "book" metaphor and its implementation as e-books is a good approximation [17] because it allows using, in an electronic environment, a well known and common tool in classical learning. As a result, the potential confussion of hypertext [15] is overcome. One of the main features of the "book" metaphor is that the contents are structured in pages, in addition to chapters, sections, subsections, etc. To simulate a printed book, all the contents in a page will simultaneously be visible without scroll.

Who must divide the contents into pages? Some works [14, 5] consider the author in charge of creating contents that fit the page size of a specific tool. However, we think that the author must center his/her efforts in the production of learning contents and not in splitting pages. In this respect, we will make the production of contents and the division process independent and will separate the contents and its presentation. In this paper, an approach to the use and automatic creation of WLMs is presented. It is made up of three phases:

1. Contents are generated as a semi-structured document.
2. These contents are transformed into a set of pages.
3. The pages are used as WLMs, showing them as an interactive material.

This paper is organized as follows. In section 2, we briefly describe some related works. Our approach will be presented in section 3. The main technical details necessary to implement our approach are described in section 4. Finally, some concluding remarks are made in section 5.

2   Related Work

In this section, some WLMs related tools are described, focusing on the process of contents generation.

CourseGenie [3] is a commercial tool that converts a MsWord document into a set of web pages including navigation and interactive features. First, it uses its own engine to convert a MsWord document into a XML document. Then, it uses an own XSLT engine to transform the XML document into a set of interactive HTML pages. It splits without paying particular attention to the sizes of the resulting pages. EasyGenerator [6] is another commercial application. The author creates contents in separated pages. The application is made up of several tools, helping the author generating learning contents in pages, designing the course final appearance and finally, allowing students to use the course. EasyProf [7] is another commercial tool. It provides an interface for the author to edit, create and format all type of contents and it guides him/her stepwise. In [14] an application to produce electronic course books (ECBs) is presented. Such ECBs consist in a set of HTML pages of two main categories: slide pages and resource pages. The tool has an interface to insert HTML code through different menus, buttons, areas, etc. and does not limit the size of the page. In [11] a tool to manage a course book is presented. The implementation of the course includes several steps: converting the book into HTML through Adobe Frame-Maker; linking the HTML pages with the desired structure; indexing the pages by a search engine; developing interactive components and implementing user authentication and tracking. The division is acomplished by sections of a printed book. All of these tools force the user to pay attention to the appearance of the contents while they are being created. However, we think that the process of creating contents should be independent from their presentation as far as possible. Therefore, the transformation of the contents into the final WLM must be automated. Finally, all the processes must be platform independent.

3   Our Approach

In this section, we describe the different phases to achieve the independent creation and automatic generation of WLMs and their later use.

3.1   Creating Contents

The first phase is the edition of the educational contents. Teachers must generate the contents related to the target subject. These contents will be as much text as images, audio, animations, questions, exercises, etc.

In many cases, educators create educational courseware which is based on proprietary and not compatible formats. As an XML[1] document contains information about contents and structure, but not about appearance, it facilitates

---

[1] Extensible Markup Language. http://www.w3c.org/XML/

information reuse, provided it is a valid document. An important feature is guided edition. An XML editor adequate to WLMs must ensure that the generated XML document is a valid document. It would also be desirable that the document were always valid during the creation process in a way transparent to the author. It is important if we do not assume a widespread knowledge of XML by authors. This asumption is realistic if we put emphasis on usability in the university environment, as much in technical as in non-technical areas.

3.2   Splitting Contents

The input of this phase will be the XML contents. The output must meet two requirements. The first requirement states that the output must be web-based. The second one states that contents must be divided into several pages. Thus, the output of this phase will be formed by these pages and their structure.

The use of HTML will help us to meet both requirements. First, HTML is the language of the Web par excellence. Second, to divide contents into pages we need to know its visual representation on a computer screen and HTML gives us this representation. This phase is made up of two steps: first, transforming XML into HTML contents, then dividing these contents into several HTML pages and extracting the structure of the contents. Figure 1 illustrates these steps.

Fig. 1. Transforming XML contents into HTML pages and extracting its structure

To convert XML into HTML contents we use an XSLT. This transformation could be designed by the author or by others depending on the educational context; for instance, a university could have a general XSL for all of its WLMs. The result of this step will be one HTML page.

Now, the HTML contents can be divided into pages. As every HTML element (texts, images, etc.) has known dimensions, we can group these elements into differents pages, keeping the semantic order. Simultaneously, we extract the hierarchical structure of the contents and pages where they are located.

3.3   Browsing Contents

In this phase, the interface between the user and the contents will be described. Figure 2 illustrates the process. The structure of the contents and the pages where they are located allow the user to know where he/she is at every moment (orientation information), and where he/she can find other contents (contents browsing) [15].

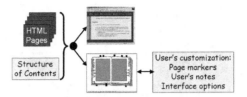

Fig. 2. Two interfaces to access contents

We propose accessing contents in two ways based on the ability to customize interface and contents. A first interface is a non-adaptative WLM, like common websites with navigation aids, menus, tables of contents, etc. The left size of Fig. 3 illustrates this interface. The second interface is a user-adaptative WLM that applies the "book" metaphor allowing the user to add bookmarks and notes, or modify the navigation facilities. The right size of Fig. 3 illustrates this interface.

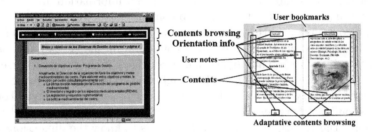

Fig. 3. Adaptative and non-adaptative user interfaces

4 Our Implementation

In this section, the tools developed to implement our approach are described.

4.1 *eXitor*, a XML Editor

eXitor is used for the generation of the contents by authors. Its main aim is to guide the user in the process of edition and creation of always valid XML contents. The tool was developed in Java, given its multiplatform and portability features. A screenshot of *eXitor* is showed in Fig. 4.

The development of this tool is summarized in three steps: first, handling the information about the structure of the document[2]; second, it is needed a persistent structure in memory to store the document and to access the contents; and finally, the interface design is split into two parts: a tree view, to maintain in a visible way the hierarchical structure, and a text view, to edit the textual content. Further information about *eXitor* is available in [20].

---

[2] DTDs or XML-Schema in XML terminology.

Fig. 4. Generation of XML contents with eXitor

4.2 *JoPee*, a Document Splitter

JoPee is a tool to generate web-based learning contents, and it needs: a XML document with the contents, a XSL document and information about elements that show the structural levels in the web contents (structural elements).

As the contents' structure can be diverse, *JoPee* needs information about structural elements, which is given by a configuration file (it can also be generated by an interface). The application must check if the structural elements meet the structure. Each level must have only one style format, because HTML tags are used to know when a new level has started. The XSL document contains the correspondence between elements, structural or not, and the style elements.

To divide the HTML document, *JoPee* needs to know the dimensions of the pages to generate. First, a preprocess step must be done, checking dimensions of images; if they are bigger than the dimensions of pages, new scaled images are created and linked with the original ones; checking lists keeping the number of items in ordered lists and the vignettes of the items in unordered lists. The main process checks the dimensions for each HTML element. If they do not fit the current page, a cut point is established and a new page is created. Simultaneously, an XML document is created, which will have the location of the structural elements in the generated pages.

Nowadays, our prototype uses the DocBook DTD[3] to generate courses in the university. In the same way, it uses a particular XSL for DocBook, where the structural elements are: chapter, sect1 and sect2. However, any schema and its corresponding XSL could be used.

4.3 Browsing Contents with *TasKa* and Web Navigators

With *TasKa* we implement our user-adaptative interface. *TasKa* uses the pages and structure of contents generated by *JoPee* which will be located elsewhere in a web server. Its contents browsing facilities are: access to adjacent items[4], fixed

---

[3] http://www.docbook.org
[4] In Docbook these items are pages, sections, chapters, etc.

bookmarks to the table of contents or the beginning of the current chapter, user defined bookmarks, hyperlinks from/to contents and a record of pages viewed. The orientation information available are: page numbers, page headings and thickness of the sides of the eBook. The user can customize the contents by adding notes to pages and customize the interface by adding bookmarks and configuring the browsing of adjacent items (choosing if he only wants to browse chapters, but no sections, and how many of them). *TasKa* can be used with four different resolutions. *JoPee* splits pages according to these resolutions and saves it in the configuration file. If a user wants to change his resolution, pages must be generated again, but reusing the configuration file in addition to the XML contents, keeping the customization of the users.

For non-adaptative interface, any web browser can be used. In this case, orientation information and the contents browsing facilities must be added to the pages generated. Then a HTML template is applied to struct the previous information with contents of the page. Figure 5 illustrates the template application.

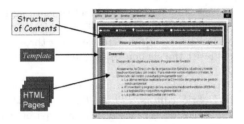

Fig. 5. Non-adaptative material production

5   Conclusions

In this paper, an approach to automatic generation and use of WLMs is described. This approach is a workflow made up of three phases: the contents are created, splitted and browsed.

XML is the language used to create contents, making them independent from its presentation and contents reusing is allowed. A XML editor called *eXitor* is used. It provides guided edition and valid documents generation, so the user do not need a technical knowledge of XML technology. The XML contents are formated and splitted into HTML pages. A tool called *JoPee* is used for it. The contents are processed in an automatic way by: formating, sizewise splitting, structure generating and customization reusing. The web contents are browsed in two ways. Using an user-adaptative interface called *TasKa*, which implements the book metaphor; the contents and browse facilities can be customized. Using any web browser as a non-adaptative interface, the contents can be browsed in the same way a web site is used. JAVA is used to develop *eXitor*, *JoPee* and *TasKa* and so, our WLM implementation is platform independent.

Though we are using this approach to build an eBook about java programming, with compiler and visualizations capabilities, we claim that this approach is general enough to produce other e-documentation, not only WLMs, because the creating and splitting phases can work with any structure of the documents.

References

1. A. Arif. Learning from the web: are students ready or not? *Educational Technology & Society*, 4(4):32–38, 2001.
2. C. Chou. Developing hypertext-based learning courseware for computer networks: The macro and micro stages. *IEEE transactions on Education*, 42(1):39–44, 1999.
3. CourseGenie. http://www.coursegenie.com. Last accessed 29/03/2004.
4. F. Davis. User acceptance of information technology: system characteristics, user perceptions and behavioral impacts. *J. of Man-Machine Studies*, 38:475–487, 1993.
5. N. Drakos. The latex2html translator, 1999. University of Leeds. UK.
6. EasyGenerator. http://www.easygenerator.com. Last accessed 29/03/2004.
7. EasyProf. http://www.easyprof.com. Last accessed 29/03/2004.
8. C. Kohls et al. Using TCL to design interactive e-learning materials. *The Magazine of USENIX & SAGE*, 28(1), 2003.
9. C.M. Boroni et al. Engaging students with active learning resources: Hypertextbooks for the web. In *SIGCSE 2001*, pages 65–69. ACM Press, 2001.
10. G.S. Akerlind et al. Enhancing self-directed learning through educational technology: When students resist the change. *Innovations Education and Training International*, 36:96–105, 1999.
11. I.Fischer et al. An example of generating internet-based course material. In D. Kalpic and V.H. Dobric, editors, *ITI 2000*, pages 229–234. SRCE - UCC, 2000.
12. J. Sheard et al. Challenges of web-based learning environments: Are we student-centred enuf? In *ICWL 2003. LNCS*, pages 1–11. Springer-Verlag, 2003.
13. K. Baas et al. A practical model for the development of web based interactive courses. In *FIE 2001*, 2001.
14. P. Crescenzi et al. A tool to develop electronic course books based on www technologies, resources and usability criteria. In *ITICSE 2003*, pages 163–167, 2003.
15. P. Diaz et al, editor. *Libros Electrónicos*. RA-MA, 1996.
16. P.O. Au et al. A web-based platform for e-learning based on information management system. In *ICWL 2003. LNCS*, pages 46–54. Springer-Verlag, 2003.
17. R. Martínez-Unanue et al. Electronic books for programming education: A review and future prospects. In *ITICSE 2002*, 2002.
18. R.J. Coffin et al. Motivational influences on computer-related affective states. *Computers in Human Behavior*, 15:609–623, 1999.
19. S.S. Ong et al. Experiences in developing and running WebCMS. In *ICWL 2003. LNCS*, pages 55–68. Springer-Verlag, 2003.
20. V. Fresno-Fernández et al. eXitor: a tool for the assisted edition of XML documents. In *ELPUB 2003*, pages 308–315, 2003.

e-Learning Services Provision and Management

Lily Sun[1], Yan Fu[1], Shirley Williams[1], and Tan Sun[2]

[1] Informatics Research Centre and School of Systems Engineering
The University of Reading, UK
{lily.sun,yan.fu,shirley.williams}@reading.ac.uk
http://www.irc.rdg.ac.uk
[2] Library of China Academy of Sciences, China
sunt@mail.las.ac.cn
http://www.las.ac.cn

Abstract. With the rapid development of information technology, learners demand effective personalised learning support, which imposes a new learning paradigm in learning content management. Standards as well as best practice in industry and research community have taken place to address the paradigm shift. With respect to this trend, it is recognised that finding learning content which meet personal learning requirements remains challenging. This paper describes a model of e-learning services provision which integrates the best practice in e-learning and Web services technology so that learning content management is capable of supporting applications of learning services.

1 Introduction

The rapid evolution of information technology has created opportunities to offer various software tools, protocols and standards to support e-learning environment where learners can engage and manage their learning. As a result, learners demand effective personalised learning support that enables them to achieve their learning goals, rather than merely attend learning materials that are largely pre-prepared for them. This significant change in learning requirements imposes a new learning paradigm which needs to enable flexible mode of content configuration, and adaptive delivery and assessment.

In response to the paradigm shift in learning content management, industries as well as research communities have addressed e-learning issues more strategically and innovatively. Open learning objects repositories [4], [5], [6] and digital libraries [7], [8], [9] become general learning resources provisions through the Web. Learning objects, tagged with metadata, and organised based on semantic descriptions (Ontology), can be discovered and accessed. By making learning resources widely available, learning content design becomes more flexible with more options on quality and suitable learning content.

With respect to this trend, it is also recognised that finding learning objects which meet the learning requirements remains challenging. This involves issues about underpinning principles of learning objects design and organisation of learning objects that can support instructional design for satisfying personalised learning requirements. This paper describes a model of e-learning services provision which integrates the best practice in e-learning and Web services technology so that learning content can be effectively managed as learning services.

W. Liu et al. (Eds.): ICWL 2004, LNCS 3143, pp. 209–216, 2004.

2   Learning Resources Management and Instructional Design

Big efforts from SCORM [2], IEEE [1] and IMS [3] have set e-learning standards, which enable content designers to practise learning content design and management in a flexible and customisable manner. A common element in these standards is the concept of learning objects which include a number of characteristics, such as granularity, reusability, interoperability, and aggregation. Cisco [10] has been a pioneer in the development of the e-learning solution architecture and application of learning objects.

From Cisco's view, a Reusable Learning Object (RLO) is a learning object based on learning objectives built from a collection of static or interactive content and instructional practice activities. Each RLO can be mixed and matched to generate personalised courses, lessons, and instructional events. An RLO consists of Overview, Information Objects, Summary, Practice and Assessment which support specific learning objectives [10]. In Cisco's reusable learning object strategy, the guidelines with templates show the practicality of instructional learning content design in the industry.

In Higher Education (HE), however, the approach to instructional design is different from that adopted in industry. It is important that the content design requires learning content having capabilities of being searchable, reconfigurable, reusable and interoperable so that the content design can be self-directed and self-maintained. Furthermore, this capability can enforce satisfaction to meet learning requirements changes. With respect to the Cisco's guidelines, we have adapted and extended their templates for learning content design to meet the educational requirements in HE.

Fig. 1 shows a conceptual model for a module in a degree course that assists instructional design of learning content for e-learning [11]. From educational point of view, a module may be regarded as a learning object, which comprises of five major components: *Overview, Information Object, Practical Object, Assessment Object* and *Summary. Practical Object* is optional depending on the requirements of a subject domain. Each of the components and the objects at their granularity level are tagged by metadata [12] for the content designer to discover and retrieve them from the content repository.

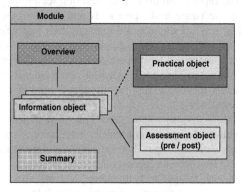

Fig. 1. Template for Module Package

The Overview offers general information about the module, such as the module code, level, aims, pre-requisites, co-requisites, learning outcomes, indicative content, assessment strategy, and credits [11]. The property of Indicative Content is associated with information objects representing a set of selected topics at appropriate granularities. The property of Assessment Strategy is embodied in Assessment Object. The Overview is useful to various stakeholders, e.g., content providers, subject tutors, students, and accreditors, to share information consistently. The Summary component concludes and reviews the subject which will assist students in self-assessment and self-reflection on understanding of the topics and applying knowledge and skills for problem solving at large.

To effectively apply this content design approach for the benefit of individual learners, it requires a large pool of learning content that may be from a number of content providers (e.g., departments, Faculties, or Universities). It, therefore, may involve platforms, applications, and standards that different content providers use.

3   Web Services Technology and e-Learning Services

The e-learning community has been focusing on the ability to discover digital learning resources from heterogeneous repositories by using Web services technology [13]. A Web service is a software system designed to support interoperable machine-to-machine interaction over a network [14]. It has an interface described a service, a set of actions from service providers' and service requesters' point of view, in a machine-processable format (WSDL). Other systems interact with the Web service in a manner prescribed by its description using SOAP-messages, typically conveyed using HTTP with an XML serialisation in conjunction with other Web-related standards. Fig. 2 depicts the Web services architecture.

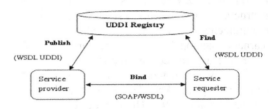

Between business services and clients' requests, a discovery agent (i.e., UDDI – Universal Description, Discovery and Integration) organises services description through business

Fig. 2. Web Services Architecture [14]

registration. A UDDI registry consists of three components: 'white pages' including address, contact and known identifiers; 'yellow pages' including industrial categorisations based on standard taxonomies; and 'green pages', the technical information about services that are exposed by the business [15][16][17]. Fig. 3 illustrates a core data structure of a UDDI registry. A *businessEntity* contains descriptive information about a service provider and its services, each of which is contained in a *businessService* entity. A *bindingTemplate* contained within a given *businessService* provides the

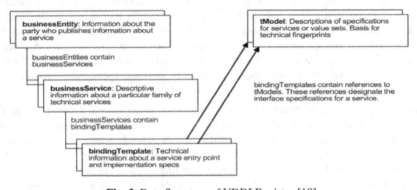

Fig. 3. Data Structure of UDDI Registry [18]

technical description of a Web service. A *tModel* entity, the technical fingerprint, describes services behaviour, conventions, and standards the service complies with.

In e-learning, learning resources, e.g., learning objects, information objects, assessment objects, practical objects, content objects and delivery methods can be defined as learning services which are organised and maintained by learning content providers. In terms of UDDI, learning content providers, e.g., universities can be described by *businessEntity*. Learning services can be represented by *businessService*. In a standard and practical manner, Web services technology provides opportunities for learning content providers to publish, register and share their learning services. Therefore, it has the natural suitability and technicality to support learning content management in e-learning.

4 Learning Services Provision

A model of learning services provision in the e-learning environment is presented including components of *Instructional Design, Content Requestor, Content Provider*, and *Learning Services Registry* (see fig. 4).

Instructional Design. A first stage of instructional design process is learning requirements elicitation where learners' personal learning requirements are articulated and represented as a set of parameters, e.g., learning style and prior knowledge in the subject domain [19]. These requirements together with the educational learning requirements, such as *module level* and *credits* defined in the *Overview* component will form textual

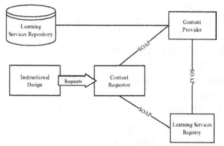

Fig. 4. A Model of Learning Services Provision

requests of appropriate learning content. For example, a learner may enrol on 'Systems Analysis and Design with UML' module. Before the learning content for this module is packaged, the learner can express his/her learning requirements by answering a set of structured questions. The answers will be articulated to identify the learner's learning styles in the categories of 1) means used to perceive information, e.g., visual, audio, or tactile; 2) response type to information, e.g., active, reflective, sensing or innovative; 3) modes preferred to access information e.g., sequential or global; as well as the prior knowledge (e.g., little, modest, enough). The value of the learning style in the categories will determine a selection on information objects, practical objects, and assessment objects, and instructional sequencing to form a learning object. The educational requirements may indicate appropriate module level (e.g., BSc in Computer Science – level 2) and module credit (e.g., 10 CATs).

Content Requestor. A learning content requestor receives textual requests from the instructional design component. The requests are transformed into XML format and sent to a learning services registry to identify a list of candidate services. According to service URIs (Universal Resource Identifiers) available in the registry, the content requestor is directed to the corresponding learning content provider and retrieves appropriate learning services, which match the requests from instructional designers.

Learning Content Provider. A learning content provider, e.g., universities, faculties and schools is an owner of learning services stored in one or more learning services repositories. To support management and discovery of learning content, each learning service in a repository is described by a set of metadata, and an ontology is built to semantically organise the services. An instructional designer makes decisions on service selections from a content provider based on the domain representation by the ontology and individual service description by its metadata.

Learning Services Registry. A learning services registry provides a mechanism to systematically present and manage learning content providers and the learning services in a standard manner. A learning service is identified in a registry either by matching the information of its content provider or the information of services types according to different classifications.

5 Modelling Learning Services Management in UDDI

Two major data structures – *businessEntity* [18] and *businessService* [18] are involved in a service registration in a learning services registry. An instance of the *businessEntity* structure (see fig. 5) describes a learning content provider – The University of Reading, with a *businessKey* property uniquely identified in a registry. *discovery-URLs* lists URLs that point to Web addressable discovery documents of the university, e.g., *http://www.reading.ac.uk*. Simple textual information about the provider is given by its *name – The University of Reading*, and short business *description,* such as *The University of Reading is a top rated research institution,* which indicates the quality and educational level of the provider. *contacts* is a list of single contact information, including the name of the contact person, contact phone number, email address shown in fig. 5 for further enquiries to the content provider. The *identifierBag* contains a list of identifiers, each valid in its own identifier system. For example, The University of Reading is uniquely identified by a nine-digit sequence – *212522689* in the system of D-U-N-S Number [18]. Likewise, the *categoryBag* contains a list of business categories, each of which describes a specific business aspect of the provider. For example, The University of Reading is classified in the category as *Colleges, Universities, and Professional Schools* by NTIS [18]. A provider can be digitally signed for learning service authentication in *Signature* by holding a unique signature key.

   A *businessService* in Fig. 6 allows a learning service – a module of '*Software analysis and design with UML'* to be technically defined. The module *aims* in the *Overview* component forms the *description* of the service. *bindingTemplates* provides technical information to invoke the service, typically a URL (*http://www.rdg.ac.uk /ug/courses/132.html*) and a brief description to indicate the applied protocol (*HTTP*) to the access point. The UNSPSC [18] category system is used to classify the module level (BSc in computer science) as *Undergraduate Programs*. The service can be signed in *Signature* by holding a unique signature key.

   Fig. 7 shows a sample interface of the underlining UDDI data structure. In 'Organization' area, the registry browser captures information about the provider – in this case, The University of Reading. The 'Services' area presents learning services (e.g., *Software analysis and design with UML*), which are categorised in different educational levels (*Undergraduate Programs* or *Postgraduate Programs*). The highlighted 'Service Bindings' gives the data in the *bindingTemplates* to show the access point and protocol of the learning service. Once submitted the registration, the registry automatically generates a unique *Id* number to identify The University of Reading as a learning content provider and a unique *Id* number for the UML learning service.

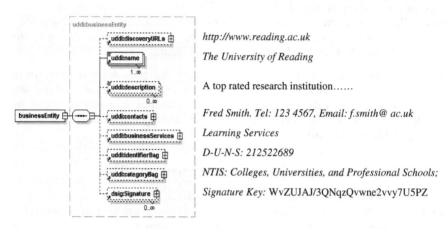

Fig. 5. A Learning Content Provider Registered by *businessEntity*

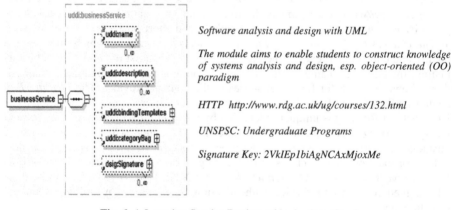

Fig. 6. A Learning Service Registered by businessService

6 Conclusions and Future Work

A model of e-learning services provision and a service management mechanism are presented by integrating the instructional design model of learning content, the Web services technology, and the best technical practices in the research community. Some extensions on content management and retrieval are made to address the needs of HE in order to meet personalised and educational learning requirements. Due to early stage of the work, the retrieval function in learning services registries for different service granularity (e.g., information objects, assessment objects and content objects) needs to be well improved. The ability to locate a content provider who offers a specific learning service involves further collaboration and design work between content requestors and content providers. A design of a learning service ontology will be explicitly devised to manage metadata and learning content, and facilitate intelligent content retrieval.

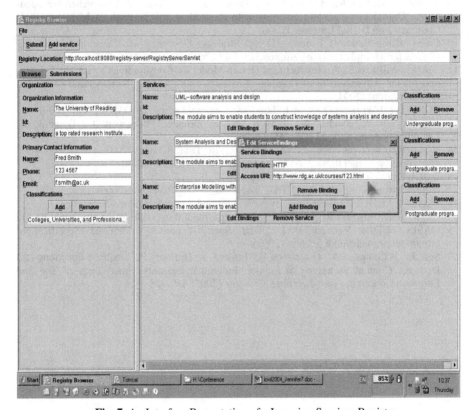

Fig. 7. An Interface Presentation of a Learning Services Registry

References

1. IEEE.: Standard for Learning Object Metadata, Learning Technology Standards Committee (LTSC). http://grouper.ieee.org/LTSC/wg12/ (2003)
2. SCORM.: Best Practices Guide for Content Developers. Learning Systems Architecture Lad.
   http://www.lsal.cmu.edu/lsal/expertise/projects/developersguide/developersguide/ (2003)
3. IMS.: Open Specifications for Interoperable Learning Technology.
   http://www.imsglobal.org/ (2003)
4. IMS.: IMS Digital Repositories Interoperability - Core Functions Information Model Version 1.0 Final Specification.
   http://www.imsglobal.org /digitalrepositories/driv1p0/imsdri_infov1p0.html   (2003)
5. eduSource.: Canadian Network of Learning Object Repositories. http://www.edusource.ca (2004)
6. Duncan, C., Eknekciylu, C.: Digital Libraries and Repositories. *Reusing Online Resource* (ed.), Allison Littlejohn, Kogan Page (2003)
7. Janssen, W., Popat, K.: UpLib: A Universal Personal Digital Library System. DocEng'03, November 20-22, 2003, Grenoble, France (2003)

8. DELOS Working Group 2.1.: Survey on Existing Digital Library Systems. http://www.sztaki.hu/delos_wg21 (2001)
9. Witten, I., McNab, R., Boddie, S., Bainbridge, D.: Greenstone: A Comprehensive open-source Digital Library Software System. In Proceedings of the Fifth ACM International Conference on Digital Libraries (2000)
10. Cisco.: Cisco Reusable Learning Object Strategy: Designing and Developing Learning Objects for Multiple Learning Approaches. http://business.cisco.com/ (2003)
11. Sun, L., Williams S.: An Instructional Design Model for Constructivist Learning. Association for the Advancement of Computing in Education (AACE), Switcherland (Accepted for publication) (2004)
12. LOM.: LOM Working Draft v4.1. http://Itsc.ieee.org/doc/wg12/LOMv4.1.htm (2000)
13. Xu, Z., Yin, Z., Saddik, A.: A Web Services Oriented Framework for Dynamic E-Learning Systems. CCGEI 2003, May (2003)
14. W3C.: Web Services Architecture - W3C Working Draft 8 August 2003. http://www.w3.org/TR/2003/WD-ws-arch-20030808/#whatis (2003)
15. UDDI. Org.: UDDI Technical White Paper. http://www.uddi.org/ pubs/Iru_UDDI_Technical_White_Paper.pdf (2000)
16. Microsoft.: UDDI Business Registry Node. http://uddi.microsoft.com (2003)
17. IB.: MUDDI Business Registry, Version 2. https://uddi.ibm.com/ubr/ registry.html (2003)
18. OASIS.: UDDI Version 3.0.1 UDDI Spec Technical Committee Specification. http://uddi.org/pubs/uddi_v3.htm (2003)
19. Sun, L., Williams, S.A., Ousmanou K., Lubega, J.: Building Personalised Functions into Dynamic Content Packaging to Support Individual Learners. Proceedings of The 2nd European Conference on e-Learning, Glasgow (2003) 439-448

A Modular Approach
to e-Learning Content Creation and Maintenance

Phan Thanh Duc[1] and Peter Haddawy[2]

[1] Mathematics and Informatics Department, Academy of Banking, Hanoi, Vietnam
ducpt@email.com
[2] CSIM, School of Advanced Technologies, Asian Institute of Technology, Thailand
haddawy@ait.ac.th

Abstract. Preparing multi-media rich e-learning content is a labour-intensive process, requiring great time investment from content experts and multi-media designers. This high labour cost is particularly acute in fields in which knowledge changes rapidly. Keeping material current requires periodic review and updating of the material. Thus there is a need for tools to facilitate the updating of asynchronous e-learning material. While much software exists for content creation, content maintenance has received relatively little attention. We present an Learning Content Management System (LCMS) that addresses two aspects of this problem: updating course structure and updating course content. Our approach organizes course material into modular units and externally specifies course structure. We introduce the notion of Updatable Content Unit (UCU). The content author can define such units at content creation time or any time there after. Our system provides functions to search for UCUs, edit them, and integrate them back into the surrounding material.

Keywords: System Architecture, Courseware Building Tool, Management of Learning Resources.

1 Introduction

Of the two basic modes for delivering course material online, synchronous and asynchronous, the latter has gained more popularity due to a number of factors. Among these are: the relatively fixed cost, independent of the number of students; the ability of students to tailor the learning pace and time schedule to their needs; and the ability to use the material for either distance education or to supplement traditional lectures. But this flexibility comes at a price. Preparing multi-media rich learning content is a labour-intensive process, requiring great time investment from content experts and multi-media designers. This high labour cost is particularly acute in fields in which knowledge is changing rapidly. Keeping material current requires periodic review and updating of the material. In the case of rapidly changing areas like e-commerce, this may need to be done on a semester basis. Thus there is a need for tools to facilitate the updating of asynchronous e-learning material. While much software exists for content creation, content maintenance has received relatively little attention. Although content creation tools can be used for content maintenance, the problems are fundamentally different and maintenance requires its own specific set of tools.

W. Liu et al. (Eds.): ICWL 2004, LNCS 3143, pp. 217–224, 2004.

There are two aspects of the content updating process. The first relates to the content structure of the course. Let's take an Electronic-Commerce (EC) course for example. Normally, a course includes some Learning Content Objects (LCOs) – (e.g. course, chapter, lesson). Each of them has a set of resources (assets, physical files) and the sequence among them. Suppose now that some standards for electronic payment are changed, so that the old material must be replaced with updated material. The process of adding the new material is not a very complex task and can be solved with File Transfer Protocol (FTP) applications. However, the major problem is course navigation. Navigation refers to both intra- and inter-LCO navigation. Since objects typically link to other objects, changing from one LCO to another may affect other LCOs. Furthermore, if we introduce a new chapter or lesson, this material must be integrated into the existing navigation scheme.

The second aspect of maintenance involves identifying material in need of updating and then making the changes. For example, in the case of e-commerce, information on things like online sales, the number of online businesses in a given sector, the performance of various high-profile online businesses would ideally be updated every few months. We require support to identify this content and then to make changes to it in such a way that it still fits within the scope of the surrounding material. This problem also arises with localization of material. In web-based training it is not unusual to offer the same course to students in different countries. The teaching material can be more effective if the content is localized to address the particular environment of that country.

In this paper, we describe an implemented system for creating modular e-learning materials that can be easily updated and for supporting the updating process. The technique addresses both aspects of updating discussed above. The problem of updating the navigational structure is solved by explicitly representing the hierarchical and sequential organization of the material and by packaging it as learning content objects. The problem of updating of content is solved by using the concept of "data islands", which are small sections of material that may need to be updated in the future, which the content author can identify during or after the authoring process. These data islands are stored in a database in order to facilitate searching, adding, deleting, editing. Our solution makes extensive use of the Sharable Content Object Reference Model (SCORM) in order to facilitate exchange of material and interoperability with other e-learning software.

2 Related Work

Systems supporting creation and maintenance of e-learning content are known as Learning Content Management Systems (LCMS). Available LCMSs provide functions that allow e-Learning organizations to rapidly author, deploy and manage e-Learning content [3,4,8,9,10]. Although features of LCMSs differ from one system to another, the fundamental components of an LCMS consist of an authoring tool, an administrative application, and a learning object repository or central database. Although it is recognized that one role of an LCMS is to support maintenance of course content [2], little has been done in this area. WebCT [12] has good tools for managing files to update the course content and structure, however, the issue of indexing and updating frequently changing content in a course is not addressed.

Recently, the idea of creating e-Learning courses by combining reusable e-Learning objects has attracted much attention. The SCORM Content Aggregation Model [1] "represents a pedagogically neutral means for designers and implementers of instruction to aggregate learning resources for the purpose of delivering a desired learning experience." But while this standard can be applied to create a modular multi-media e-learning material that facilitates updating, it does not directly address the problem of updating e-learning materials.

3   Modular e-Learning Materials

3.1   Learning Content Model

The Learning Content Model is described as components used to build an LCO from learning resources that can be easily replaced. Also, it defines how these lower-level learning resources are aggregated to compose higher-level units of instruction.

- *Assets:* Assets are electronic representations of learning content.
- *Learning Content Objects (LCO):* This is a collection of one or more assets and is the lowest level of learning resource that will be used by the LCMS.
- *Content Aggregation:* This is a content structure that can be used to aggregate learning resources into a cohesive unit of instruction (e.g. course, chapter, lesson, etc.).

In the past, the tool to control the sequence of learning resource typically embedded, inside proprietary data formats, all of the navigation information that governs which parts of the course the learner will view next. In most cases, authoring tools or systems are defined and applied to designated courses and sometimes used only for a unique course. Using this mechanism, it is difficult to update content.

In our approach, learning resource sequencing is defined in the content structure and is external the learning resource. During run-time, the LCMS is responsible for launching the learning resources in a defined sequence. So the task of content creators is separated into two different parts: developing the learning content objects and specifying their sequence.

3.2   Meta-data

The Meta-data provides a common nomenclature enabling learning resources to be described in a common way. Meta-data can be collected in catalogs or directly packaged with the learning resource. Learning resources described with meta-data can be systematically searched for and retrieved. Meta-data can be classified by their positions within the course manifest file, and according to whether they provide context specific or context independent descriptions.

Context specific meta-data are data specific to a particular course packaged by a manifest file. During the process of creating and updating course structure, context specific meta-data about each LCO such as chapters, lessons are also generated in order to support the process of specifying learning resource sequencing.

Context independent meta-data are data describing individual LCOs or Assets that are independent of a particular course that uses these objects. This information can be used to search the LCOs or Asset for replacement or updating. These might include: LCO or Asset title, general description of an LCO or Asset, the original author of an LCO or asset, keywords associated with the LCO or asset, copyright of the LCO or asset, etc.

3.3 Content Packaging

Figure 1 shows the structure of the Content Packaging. The Content Packaging defines the structure and the intended behaviour of a collection of learning resources and also provides a standardized way to update digital learning resources by using the LCO update tool.

A Content Package contains two major components:

- A special document describing the content organization and resources of the package. This document uses eXtensible Markup Language (XML) to describe the content and is called the Manifest file (manifest.xml). This document is automatically generated based on context specific meta-data about LCOs in the course.
- The physical files (assets) referenced in the Manifest file.

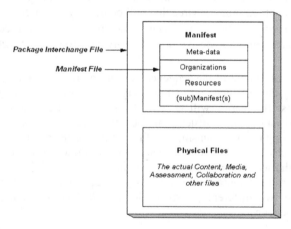

Fig. 1. Content Packaging Conceptual Diagram (Source: SCORM)

3.3.1 Package

A package represents a unit of replaceable content. This may be a part of a course that can be delivered independently as an entire course or as a collection of courses. A package is able to stand-alone; it contains all the information needed to use the packaged contents for learning when it has been unpacked.

3.3.2 Manifest

A Manifest is a description in XML of the resources comprising meaningful instruction. A Manifest can describe a part of a course that can stand by itself outside of a course, an entire course or a collection of courses. So the content developers have to describe their content in the way they want it to be considered for aggregation or disaggregation.

A package always contains a single top-level Manifest that may contain one or more sub-manifests. The top-level Manifest always describes that package and any nested sub-manifests describe the content at the level in which the sub-manifest is scoped, such as a chapter, a learning object, etc.

3.3.3 The Physical Files

The physical files represent the actual files referenced in the resource components. These files may be local files that are actually contained within the content package, or they can be external files that are referenced by a Universal Resource Indicator (URI).

4 Solution

4.1 Updating Course Structure

To manage the whole content of the course, the course structure must be described in a meta-data file – Manifest.xml. Any changes of the course structure shall lead to changes of this file. In order to do that, the LCMS needs to have abilities to generate and update the Manifest file.

The course creator will describe (for a new course) or edit (for an existing course) course structure in a web application. First of all, he/she logs into the LCMS, then he/she will be able to create a new course or update existing courses within his/her authority.

Each course is described by a set of static and dynamic information. The static information describes all the stable data about the course such as course name, course identifier, etc. This data will be kept in static variables based on SCORM standard to ensure the compatibility of the system to the external resources. The dynamic information describes dynamic items of the course such as information about resources of each LCO: chapter, lesson, etc. The course structure is represented according to the following scheme: 1 course – n chapters, 1 chapter – m lessons, 1 lesson – k assets.

This information is not static; it may be changed time after time and we cannot determine the number of variables at the beginning. Therefore, a technique is required to manage the set of static information and dynamic information in the LCMS. The technique which is used in our system is called "dynamic code". It automatically generates blocks of code based on the description of the course creator by using server-side code. However, for efficiency, the combination of the client-side and server-side should be used. As soon as getting all necessary values of the dynamic data, the system will transfer those values to the server to process. This mechanism is also used to easily upload multiple files (assets) from the course creator's computer (client) to the server. The technique to transfer multiple files to self-determine concrete location on the server makes it easier for the course creator to upload files. To avoid the problem of line transferring between client and server when transmitting many files, the process of uploading will be performed with each LCO. Each LCO is uploaded to a suitable directory on the server. Accordingly, all asset files of the LCO are uploaded at the same time.

Example:

An E-Commerce course comprises 2 chapters.

Chapter 1 has 3 lessons: Lesson 1 has 5 assets (files), Lesson 2 has 7 assets

Chapter 2 has 2 lessons: Lesson 1 has 5 assets, Lesson 2 has 3 assets

The Multi-Files-Upload function of the LCMS will create a directory tree as follows:

```
WebServerRoot
  ├─EC-Course
  │       ├──Chapter 1
  │       │        ├── Lesson 1
  │       │        └── Lesson 2
  │       ├── Chapter 2
  │       │        ├── Lesson 1
  │       │        └── Lesson 2
```

And the LCMS performs 8 upload sessions to upload the declared assets for each directory. Figure 2 shows the online course declaration screen of the LCMS.

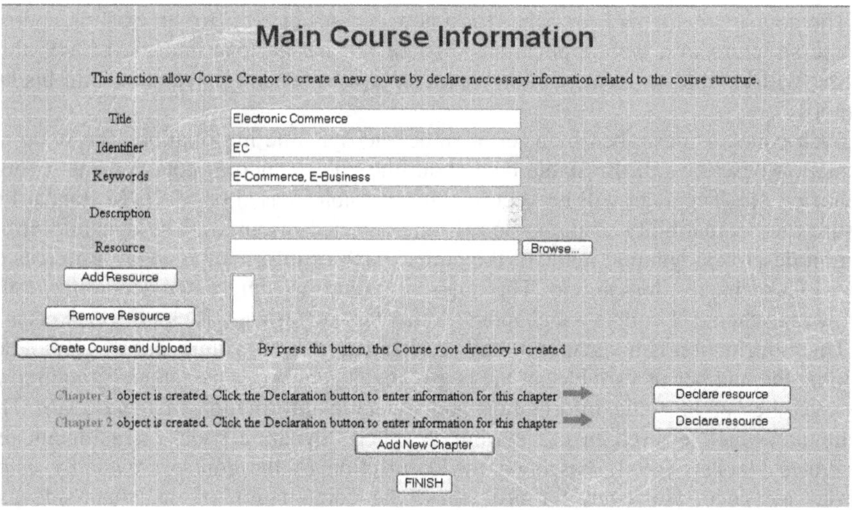

Fig. 2. Course Declaration Screen

After uploading all assets of the LCO in the course, the system will automatically generate a Manifest file. To perform this function, the crucial problem is how to manage all the static and dynamic variables already established during the course structure declaration process. As these variables exist during the time the course creator works with the system, they should be declared as application or session variables.

A Dynamic Menu Tree program is used to read meta-data file (Manifest file) and then generate a tree menu for the course. Each node in the tree menu represents an LCO. Learners can click to each node to move to every part of the course. To move within an LCO, the sequence of the assets in that LCO needs to be declared in advance by the course creator and a module of client-side code will read this information and move within that LCU.

The process of updating contents related to the course structure is solved by reading the Manifest file and allowing the course creator to edit necessary information.

4.2 Updating Course Content

The whole content of the WBT course includes multimedia materials which are embedded in web pages. From web environment point of view, these contents are static information and very difficult to edit. In fact, the frequently changing contents in a WBT course are usually text paragraphs. These paragraphs store contents which possibly change in a short time. In order to manage this kind of information, we propose the concept of Updatable Content Unit (UCU). UCU is a piece of content that is stored in a database. Each UCU can be treated as a record in the database; they are embedded in static web pages and can be converted to static data and vice versa. It has some specific fields to store necessary information to find frequently changing contents in the whole course. For example, an index item to identify the UCU and another item to locate the position (chapter, lesson, etc.) of the UCU in the course. This information will be used to find the UCU in the content update process.

The novelty here is the ability to convert from text to UCU and vice versa. As a result, the LCMS must have necessary functions to convert a static data section to a UCU, to update a UCU, delete or convert a UCU to static data.

We can approach this data from two points of view. From the learner's stance, the appearance of the static data and dynamic data is quite the same. Learners can not distinguish dynamic content from static content. From the course content creator's view, dynamic content can be treated in the following two ways.

First, the course content creator views all course contents in a similar way as the learner by using Dynamic Tree Menu. However, the dynamic contents are represented differently from static contents. They may appear in text boxes with specific colour, etc. The course content creator may edit these contents by selecting sections that need to be edited, calling the edit function to update new content, and saving the modified data.

To convert static content to dynamic content, the course creator selects a text paragraph and calls the convert function to convert the selected paragraph to a UCU. In fact, this function will create a new UCU in the UCU database, copy the selected content to the above UCU, create a connection to the web page and insert the new UCU to current location of the selected paragraph. In practice, each UCU has an index and this index number is used to determine which UCU to locate and in which position of the web page.

In the second way, the content creator can view all existing UCUs in the database and edit necessary UCUs. In this way, the content creator can easily manage all UCUs but can not add or remove any UCU.

5 Conclusion

The issue of maintaining asynchronous e-learning material, while important from the standpoint of cost over the lifetime of the material, has not previously been sufficiently addressed. We have presented an LCMS that addresses two aspects of this problem: updating course structure and updating course content. Our approach builds upon the SCORM standard by organizing course material into modular units and externally specifying course structure. We introduce the notion of Updatable Content Unit. The content author can define such units at content creation time or any time there after. Our system provides functions to search for UCUs, edit them, and integrate them back into the surrounding material.

References

1. Sharable Content Object Reference Model (SCORM) Version 1.2, 2002. (www.adlnet.org/index.cfm?fuseaction=scormabt)
2. Johan Ismail. The design of an e-learning system: Beyond the hype. *The Internet and Higher Education*, Volume 4, Issues 3-4, 2001, Pages 329-336.
3. Click2Learn (http://home.click2learn.com)
4. e-Learning Consulting Co. Ltd (http://www.e-learningconsulting.com)
5. Arnd Steinmetz, Martin Kienzle. "The e-Seminar Lecture Recording and Distribution System". Proceedings of SPIE Vol. 4312 (MultiMedia Computing and Networking 2001
6. Herng-Yow Chen, Gin-Yi Chen, Jen-Shin Hong, *"Design of a web-Based Synchronized Multimedia Lecture system for Distance Education,"* IEEE International Conference on Multimedia Computing and Systems Volume II-Volume 2. 1999
7. Christoph Meinel, Harald Sack, Volker Schillings November 2002. "Course management in the twinkle of an eye - LCMS: a professional course management system". Proceedings of the 30th annual ACM SIGUCCS conference on User services.
8. Ryann K. Ellis "LCMS Roundup" *Learning Circuits*. August 2001. (http://www.learningcircuits.org/2001/aug2001/ttools.html)
9. Jill Funderburg Donello. "Theory & Practice - Learning Content Management Systems" Leadingway Corporation (http://www.leadingway.com)
10. "Making the case for content" - Institute of IT Training and the Training Foundation. (http://www.elearningprofessional.com/index.asp)
11. "The Evolution of the Learning Content Management System". ASTD's Online Magazine about e-Learning. April 2002. (http:// www.learningcircuits.org/2002/apr2002/robbins.html)
12. WebCT (http://www.webct.com)

Using a Knowledge-Based Management to Design a Web-Based Creative Problem Solving System

Lin-Jung Wu and Hsien-Sheng Hsiao

Dept. of Industrial Technology Ed., National Taiwan Normal University
stevie18.tw@yahoo.com.tw, hssiu@ite.ntnu.edu.tw

Abstract. The objective of this research is to analyze the theories, processes, and implementations of Creative Problem Solving (CPS). The combination of electronic learning of the users and knowledge management by the researchers will be studied in a model of web-based CPS module. To what extent and level of enhancement the earning participants can utilize the knowledge-based learning system to support their learning objectives is the main observation for the research. Upon evaluation, learners can create add-on values on knowledge-based management system as it can be used as a platform for subsequent learners' advantage.

1 Introduction

As the public are rampantly adapting to fast-changing technology, creation and innovation are challenging traditional pedagogies and methodologies in realizing human learning potentials. To meet this challenge, learning participants must have the ability to creatively think and solve problems. As the sheer volume of information is increasing at the exponential pace, lifelong learning of consistent learning patterns and persistent learning data has become crucial to one's learning success and information competency. As a result, a new instructional method should be based on problem-solving and thought-process modeling. Instructional methods based on the architecture of information models, such as, peer-to-peer, standalone, file sharing, and client-server. Formulating such concepts from knowledge and content management into usable web-based instructional solutions while not compromising the emphasis on the accumulation and sharing of intelligent capital can be challenging due to the volatile nature of a knowledge-based economy.

As most researches on CPS are limited to the classroom setting, there can hardly any e-learning or web-based knowledge components integrated into the studies. As the need to study CPS with e-learning components in place, we have designed an instructional system as "web-based CPS" which combines knowledge and content management technologies such as learning portfolio database, digital subject database, concept mapping database for building synchronized knowledge integration of the users. As study showed, users of such system do perform better under the assistance of the intelligent learning tools.

2 Background

2.1 Creative Problem Solving (CPS)

According to Torrance (1972), the CPS model developed by Osborn-Pames can improve creativity. Soon, the CPS model has found applications in a variety of fields

W. Liu et al. (Eds.): ICWL 2004, LNCS 3143, pp. 225–232, 2004.
© Springer-Verlag Berlin Heidelberg 2004

such. The research also showed that CPS has a huge efficacy in improving participants' ability in solving problems creatively. Foster (1979) deemed that CPS not only can be used to spark discussions that lead to problem solving of the real life, but it also can be used to formulate solutions in strict academic disciplines. Practising problem solving based on the CPS model regularly motivates participants use CPS model spontaneously to solve problems. The CPS model also helps people make better decisions (Canady 1982) as they think "outside of the box".

Despite the CPS model is broadly used in the classroom settings, very few researchers have focused on how to use multimedia or web-based technology to fully realize the empirical potential of the model. It is proven that the web-based technology did have positive influence on the students using the CPS learning model. In the sense of the three dimensions of information: location, time, and format, students are able to be freed from the traditional constraints of classroom settings that limited where, when, and how they can access the course material and the scope of their coursework. Thus, our research will be focusing on how to design web-based CPS modules with information technologies that facilitate online discussions, file sharing, and peer reviews.

2.2 Concept Mapping with Creative Problem Solving

Concept Mapping is a tool that can help student describe their thought processes and logical patterns. It also shows how an individual defines objects and make inferences to such objects on the topic of discussion. This demonstrates both the implicit and explicit knowledge of the student to the topic.

In the field of cognizance, we not only are able to understand a single concept but also can link concepts with other concepts and identify their relationships much like a web of knowledge networks. Doing so consciously further reinforces our reasoning and analytical capabilities under voluntary control. Furthermore, the process of concept-mapping makes us converge and organize pieces of information from our meta-cognition of the topic. Once we are able to understand and retain the relationships between subjects via the meta-cognition process, it can help us integrate pieces of information, relate and assign significance of the information to the conditions of the problem, and solve the problem by reiterating past conditions for a new solution.

As the model of concept mapping also shows the implicit knowledge of an individual via the demonstration of explicit knowledge of such individual, we can extract such implicit knowledge from the concrete knowledge through abstraction. Thereafter, such abstraction can be formalized and taught to someone else. When a good solution is created and recorded by the previous learner, subsequent learners can create solutions based on the proven solution without going through the trial-and-error stage. More importantly, the subsequent learners will be able to have a chance to observe how the previous learner go about formulating the solution and thus benefit from the logical steps and "insights" from the implicit knowledge of the previous learner.

Current researches on concept mapping also showed it can improve the learning outcome and problem-solving abilities of the learners. Concept-mapping, as an evaluating kit for learning outcome, is worth the effort for the instructors to master.

In terms of group collaboration, concept-mapping can also be used as an assessment tool for CPS since it helps team members map out their solution outputs predominantly. It provides the opportunity for online discussion, learning portfolio assessment, and improved problem-solving teamwork as proven to be more effective than traditional instruction. In the past few years, the Internet technologies and the Web have had rapid growth and popularity among young people whose majority also happens to be students. Thus, building a concept-mapping system on a web-based platform is critical to the learning success for the increasingly computer literate population. Based on the above discussions, we use electronic concept-mapping as the learning kit for web-based CPS instructions to assist learners to think and learn collaboratively.

2.3 Electronic Learning Portfolio

To avoid the loss of the content that was previously learned, electronic learning portfolio becomes a good tool to accrue these learning objects. The main use of the learning portfolio is to record learners' performance and progress during the learning process. Instructors can also use these portfolios to construct profiles for the learners under evaluation to gain a better understanding of the student body and how is the learning taking place. The learning portfolio is not solely for the benefit of the teachers for evaluating students, but it also provides students with a self-development and self-evaluation tool. It can serve as a motivation for students to change passive attitude of receiving course material to actively gathering and organizing materials for the course as they gain a sense of ownership to their own portfolios. Nonetheless, there are still certain challenges such as data accessing, managing searches, storage limitation, and usability to be answered for the learning portfolio to be most effective (Chang & Tung 2000).

The electronic learning portfolio, on the other hand, provides solutions to the challenges of accessing traditional learning portfolios. The digitization of the portfolios with the ease of manipulating data and retrieving information for the users has provided a creative answer to the constraints the traditional learning portfolios confront. Texts, graphs, images, voices, and animations can all be circulated in a LAN (Local Area Network) or in a WAN (Wide Area Network) in the form of multimedia. Thus, software such as database management system can be used to organize data and data warehousing and data mining techniques can be used for learning analysis that incorporates the boundaries that were not possible under the traditional learning portfolio formats. Therefore, the electronic learning portfolios can serve as a decision-support system to the instructor and such benefits made electronic learning portfolios even more valuable.

2.4 Knowledge Management

Knowledge management (KM) is the creation, archiving, and sharing of valued information, expertise, and insight within and across communities and organizations of similar interests and needs, and the goal of which is to build competitive advantage. Knowledge management can be implemented to efficiently obtain valuable output, which is the result from the corporation of people who are in need or interested in sharing their experiences. Knowledge management is an integrated package of methodologies that enables the information supplier to deliver information to the demander in an efficient and lossless manner. Wherever the process of knowledge acquisition takes place, there should be a form of knowledge management system to make passing on of knowledge more productive. Cheng (2001) theorized four steps in knowledge management methodology, namely, Absorption and Classification of Knowledge, Creation of Knowledge, Accumulation and Management of Knowledge, and Sharing and Spreading of Knowledge.

To generalize the concept of knowledge sharing for the purpose of abstraction, we refer to a new model of knowledge sharing as shown in Fig.1. The individuals' implicit (tacit) knowledge is transferred to explicit knowledge of the masses by sharing and essentially branching and reaching out to other people. To simulate such phenomenon, information can be classified into modules and these modules can be accumulated in a knowledge-based management system. Thereafter, the management system can distribute and redistribute the knowledge modules in the proper format to the appropriate audiences in the desired location at the right time. By searching, obtaining, classifying, and absorbing, the explicit knowledge would transform into the learners' tacit knowledge.

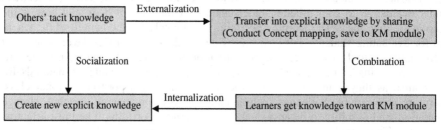

Fig. 1. Knowledge sharing graph

3 Web-Based CPS System Design

3.1 Knowledge Component Database KCDB

The goal and spirit of CPS-based Knowledge Component Database (KCDB) is to provide instructors and learners multiple concurrent services and applications for the purpose of managing knowledge. The database can accumulate and accommodate long-term educational assets such as digitalized learning resource materials and learning portfolios. Learners then can utilize electronic concept mapping to build their CPS knowledge components during their learning processes. As the database grows and becomes more useful, the learners will be able to derive more utilities from it and thus be more interested in learning. The database also provides instructor-led and aggregate functions to push learners to show their co-built CPS concept maps in the form of knowledge products, and could be used as reference for the future-learners.

The implementation of KCDB can be treated as a process of knowledge generation and knowledge management. The implemented product of KCDB would be like a self-regulated online knowledge-generating factory. This is because learners will record their diverging ideas about a problem against their personal concept mappings when they try to solve the problem. Then, through group discussions, the diverging ideas will converge and the reasonable and agreeable ideas will merge to be the model for solving the problem. CPS-based instructional system provides such interaction and online collaboration functions. It can save and store the knowledge components the learners created by collaborative knowledge generation. Built on this concept, KCDB consists of the knowledge gathering, accessing, and broadcasting functions.

Finally, products of learners' collective knowledge generated from CPS learning system would serve as a library for future-learners to access. The efficiency of the eliminating traditional barriers of time, location, and form in resources management can thus provide instructors more add-on values for them to spend quality time on preparing instructional materials. Thus, it raises the level of competitiveness in the educational circles. A simplified diagram of the knowledge component database design is shown in Figure 2.

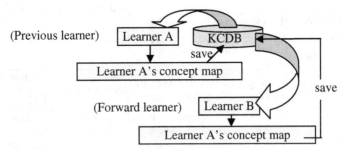

Fig. 2. Knowledge object model

3.2   Instruction System Design

3.2.1 Web-Based CPS Instructional Design
Adopting Osborn-Parnes' six-step CPS model, we developed a web-based CPS instructional process that led to the functionalities of knowledge management, concept mapping, and electronic learning portfolios shown in table 1.

Before meeting for the team discussion, our learning participants, as students, had to complete personalized concept maps using their problem solving ideas and logic. Then, these maps were sent to the instructors and group members for review. After sharing with the group members, the students began a peer assessment session. After the inter-group discussions, each group would generate their unique group concept maps. Then, they could do the peer assessment on the group-basis. Students, at the end of the learning activities, could then modify their personal and group maps.

3.2.2   System Framework
The proposed system includes the following functionalities. The structural design of the system is shown in Figure 3. The upload module is used by Instructors to upload their course syllabi, course contents, and instructional presentations to the system. The learning management module provides the course syllabi, instructional materials, homework/project requirements, group discussion topics, discussion model elucidation, reference resources, learning tools (calculators, translator...), online discussion forum, online-chat room, e-mail, and electronic whiteboard, ...etc. Learning process database can also keep track of the usage and provides an online manpower management to provide other learners with consultation in the form of an online expert system. The theme searching module provides the flexibility of searching previous learners' learning portfolio, concept mapping, and digital theme databases. The concept

mapping module consists of concept mapping editor, concept map file sharing function, collaborative concept mapping tools, and concept mapping grading tools. The learning assessment module provides learners with the functionalities to upload the result of self-assessments and peer assessments for grading. After each assessment, the system stores the scores and comments to leaning assessment database, and then passes the carbon copy of the assessment to the learners and to the instructor.

Table 1. Web-based CPS instruction process

	Instructional process	Main task	Assessment style and require	Compare with Osborn's 6 steps
1	Divide learners into groups	Divide learners into groups by dissimilation		
2	Rule explaining	Clarify learning process and rules		
3	Problem presenting	Convey some valuable problem by graphs, slides, flash, sound…	Understand problem or not?	1-Objective finding (Goal, wish or challenge)
4	Information searching	Learners catch information from chat rooms, discussion forum, online searching engine, online learning material database.	Understand problem or not?	2- Find out the fact (Gather information)
5	Solution planning	Accommodate the information to reduce situation problems to simple questions.	Understand problem or not?	3- Find out the problem (Clarify)
6	Conduct personal CPS concept mapping + uploading for peer assessment	Conduct personal concept mapping, and upload to database. (Peer assessment)	Solve problem or not?	4 -Find out the idea (Generate solution)
7	Within group discussion	Exchange thought with each other by sharing learner's personal concept map.	Solve problem or not?	5-Find out the solution (Select and strengthen)
8	Online expert workshop	Find some evaluation standard to evaluate idea.	Solve problem or not?	5-Find out the solution (Select and strengthen)
9	Generate group's concept mapping	Focus on all kinds of solutions. Evaluate, correct, classified and compare those probably solutions.	Solve problem or not?	5-Find out the solution (Select and strengthen)
10	Final assessment (Groups presentation)	Find out the best solution. And show the solution to other learners.	Answer question or not?	6-Acceptance finding (Action planning)
11	Online questionnaire (Peer assessment)	Make other learners, experts, instructors accept the solution, and conduct appropriate action plan. If people don't accept the solution, learners should correct from beginning.	Answer question or not?	6-Acceptance finding (Action planning)
12	Final self assessment	Learners self-assessment	Self-thinking & growing	

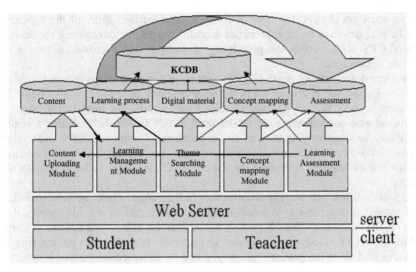

Fig. 3. System Structure

3.2.3 System Prototype Fabrication

We designed the web-based CPS prototype system based on the system framework shown in the instruction design in table 1. System tools are mainly divided into personal learning tools and concept mapping sharing tools. Personal learning tools include "freshman training," "course information," "personal concept tools," "search engine," and "my workshop." Group concept maps sharing tools include "member file sharing," "homework tools," "group concept mapping tools," "discussion forum," "message board," "messenger"…, etc.

4 Conclusion

In the e-learning age, learning activities occur anywhere and anytime. Concept mapping helps people externalize their thoughts and substantiate them in the form of components. Previous learners' learning portfolios along with their concept maps can help the succeeding learners to process learning tasks. By referring to other learners' concept maps and searching for information about topics, learners will gain insights into the topics more easily and quickly to generate different ideas about these topics themselves. To compensate their lack of prior knowledge will avoid low learning efficacy. Previous researches show that the lack of learners' prior knowledge of a subject would affect learner' learning outcome (Wu & Chung 2003) negatively. This proves that individuals' creativity on a subject is based on the knowledge they have on this particular subject. Learners who have wider view of knowledge can efficiently generate learning outcomes with that foundational knowledge. This foundational knowledge is the add-on value that the reusable knowledge components can bring to us.

Secondly, peer assessment within the learning group can help learners jump through the barriers created by their individual bound thoughts. It is helpful to observe others' work to contemplate and to make self-adjustments. In addition, the system can show previously discussed hot topics, help learners think of the topics, and spark helpful discussions in appropriate learning stages for developing the learners' skills of CPS. This avoids the possibility of making the discussion forum a non-academic gossip space.

The electronic learning portfolios can completely record learning process of each learner and assist the instructor on performing assessment tasks. It is also helpful for the learner to take the opportunity to reflect and rethink for their self-growth. The CPS model and concept-mapping model used in our system helps learners improve their ability to creatively think and solve problems. Combining CPS and concept-mapping with knowledge management concepts for the application in e-learning modules allows learners to search for expert advice instantly to learn how to solve problems.

We will continue our system construction in the future. Then, we will include the actual subject instructions to substantiate our research and to provide empirical evidence on the influence of such system to the leaning effect. We believe e-learning combined with knowledge management tools would provide efficient learning performances and their integration will be a trend as an essential part of instructional technology.

References

1. Canady, J. E.: CPS for the educational administrator. The Journal of Creative Behavior, 16(2) (1982) 132-149.
2. Chang, C.-C. & Tung, I.-W.: The construction and implementation of Web-based portfolio system. Tamkang University, Taiwan (2000).
3. Wu, C. L. & Chung, C.Y.: Exploring the relationship between problem solving ability and students' background. Science Education Journal, 245 (2003) 2-10.
4. Foster, K. M.: A guide for teaching creative thinking skills and creative problem-solving in the gifted classroom. San Diego City Schools, Calif. (ERIC Document Reproduction Service NO. ED185 771) (1979).
5. Torrance, E. P.: Can we teach children to think creatively. ERIC Document Reproduction Service NO. ED007089 (1972).
6. Cheng, S.: Using concept mapping in high school biology course. National Chung Shin University, Taiwan (2002).

Context-Based Classification for Link Data*

Yonghong Tian[1,2], Wen Gao[1,2], and Tiejun Huang[2]

[1] Institute of Computing Technology, Chinese Academy of Sciences,
Beijing 100080, P.R. China
[2] Graduate School of Chinese Academy of Sciences,
Beijing 100039, P.R. China
{Yhtian,Tjhuang,Wgao}@ict.ac.cn

Abstract. In Web-based e-learning, an up-to-date catalogue of subject-specific Web resources can effectively offer inexperienced students with an advanced academic portal on the Web. To automatically construct such academic Web resource catalogue, a key issue is how to classify the collected Web pages. However, existing link-based classification methods treat all neighbors equally in the categorization of the target objects. In this paper, we propose a context-based classification approach that can scale well for noisy and heterogeneous link data such as Web pages. We quantitatively measure the contextually topical dependencies between linked objects using the dependence functions, which are then exploited to classify the target objects in the link structure. Experimental results show that the proposed classification model can better capture the link regularities and can facilitate better categorization of linked objects.

Keywords: Management of learning resource, link-based classification, context model

1 Introduction

The Web has become a most important information source and knowledge base for scientific, educational and research applications. In Web-based e-learning, an up-to-date catalogue of subject-specific Web resources can effectively offer inexperienced students with an advanced academic portal on the Web. To automatically construct such academic Web resource catalogues, a key issue is how to classify the collected Web pages. In this paper, Web page categorization is viewed as an application of link-based classification methods, in which the topical correlation between linked pages should be effectively utilized.

In general, the link data can be described by a graph in which the nodes are objects and the edges are links between objects. Links among the objects may demonstrate certain patterns, which may be helpful for classifying the linked objects (e.g., [1], [2]). However, many link data such as Web pages are in essence heterogeneous, often accompanied with much noise, it is important to design link-based classification methods that can scale well in the context of noise and heterogeneity. Existing link-based classification methods treat all neighbors equally in the categorization of the target objects. Obviously, the class information or link features from such noisy neighbors would increase the uncertainty of the categories of the target objects. Ide-

---

* This work was supported by Science and Technology Tackle Key Problem of the National "Tenth Five-year" Plan of China under Grand. 2001BA101A07.

W. Liu et al. (Eds.): ICWL 2004, LNCS 3143, pp. 233–240, 2004.
© Springer-Verlag Berlin Heidelberg 2004

ally, we expect a classifier to recognize such noisy objects and effectively reduce their influence on the classification. Towards this end, we develop a rich context-based probabilistic model to capture the topical dependencies between linked objects.

An innovative aspect of our model is the explicit use of the context. Generally speaking, two objects are said to be contextually dependent if the interpretation of one object is highly related to the other [3]. Therefore, we can model contextual dependencies between objects in the link data. More importantly, we can exploit the learned context models to facilitate classification. In this paper, the contextual dependence is measured by three mechanisms, i.e., class dependency, link structure, and link features. Thus we define a feasible quantitative measure of contextual dependencies, which is called *dependence function*. Using this measure, all linked neighbors are no longer equally treated by the classifier in the categorization of the target objects. Furthermore, we formally describe how to exploit the dependency functions for classification. Experimental results demonstrate that the proposed *context-based link classification* approach can provide better prediction for the attributes of linked objects.

Starting with a simple discussion of the existing linked-based classification models in Section 2, we describe the proposed context-based link classification approach in Section 3. Experimental results are presented in Section 4. We conclude in Section 5.

2   Problem Formulation

Formally, the typical link-based classification problem is modeled as follows: Given the link data represented as an object graph $G = (O, L)$, assign a class label $c_i \in \mathbf{C} = \{c_1, \cdots, c_{|C|}\}$ to $O_i \in O$. For simplicity, this paper uses the same notation O_i for the identity of the object and its content features such as textual keywords.

Generally speaking, for classifying a given linked object, we need to consider its content features and the information from its neighbors. Here we restrict the neighborhood to within a radius of one or two, since exploring larger neighborhoods can be futile and dangerous [1]. Let $\mathcal{N}(O_i)$ to denote the linked neighbors of O_i, $C_{\mathcal{N}(O_i)}$ to represent the set of class values of objects in $\mathcal{N}(O_i)$. Assuming that there is a probability distribution on the link graph, we want to choose c_i to maximize $\Pr[c_i \mid O_i, C_{\mathcal{N}(O_i)}]$ (i.e., *maximum a posterior* estimation, MAP):

$$\hat{c}_i = \arg\max_{c_i} \Pr[c_i \mid O_i, C_{\mathcal{N}(O_i)}]. \tag{1}$$

Under this optimization framework, different probabilistic models are developed to calculate the category posterior probabilities of the target object given its contextual objects, i.e., $\Pr[c_i \mid O_i, C_{\mathcal{N}(O_i)}]$. One oft-used *neighboring-class* model is to assume that given $C_i = c_i$, the content features of O_i are independent of all the classes of all its neighbors $\mathcal{N}(O_i)$ (e.g., [1], [2]). Instead of exploiting the class information from neighbors, Lu and Getoor [4] also proposed a *link-distribution* model that describes the linkage information between an object and a set of its neighbors, and then supports discriminative models describing both the link features and the attributes of linked objects.

In a complex link environment such as in the Web, Web pages often contain many noisy objects and noisy links (e.g., advertisements, navigational bar) that are irrelevant to their main content. In above two models, however, all neighbors are assumed to have the same influence on classifying the target object. Obviously, the class information of the noisy objects would increase the uncertainty of the categorization of the target objects. Ideally, we expect a link-based classifier to recognize such noisy objects or effectively reduce their influence on the classification of the target objects. Towards this end, we need to develop a rich context-based probabilistic model to capture the dependencies between objects, which will be addressed in the next section.

3 Context-Based Link Classification Model

3.1 Modeling Context on Link Graph

Generally speaking, two objects are said to be contextually dependent if the interpretation of one object is highly related to the other. This means there is some *dependence function* between the two objects. In particular, we represent the context of a given object as its most relevant neighbors in the link structure. Based on the linkage information, there are many ways to quantify the dependence function. The simplest way is to set the dependence function value between two linked pages u and v to the constant *one* [8]. To reduce the influence of nepotistic links, Dean and Henzinger [9] showed that connectivity and content analysis should be integrated to capture the more complex correlations among linked objects.

Thus in this paper, we argue that the dependence function should be measured by three mechanisms, i.e., class dependency, link structure and link features. The rationales of the three context parameters are as follows: For the class dependency, we refer it to the correlation between the categories of linked objects. It is naturally measured in terms of the mutual information. By this measure, the higher the mutual information between two objects, the easier it is to estimate the target object given the other object, or vice versa. For the link structure, we consider that two objects (e.g., Web pages) that are close to are generally more informative about each others' categories. Therefore, the link structure can be measured by the link distance between two objects. For the link features, we refer them to the indicators of "*link tightness*" between two objects. For example, a higher weight can be assigned to the neighbor with more links to the target object than that with a single link. More formally, we have:

Definition 1 Given an object graph $G = (O, L)$, a function $\sigma(\cdot, \cdot)$ of two variables is called *dependence function* between two objects $O_i \in O$ and $O_j \in O$ if it satisfies

(1) $\sigma(O_i, O_j) \geq 0$, and

(2) $\displaystyle\sum_{O_j \in \mathcal{N}(O_i)} \sigma(O_i, O_j) = 1$, and

(3) for $\forall O_k \in \mathcal{N}(O_i), O_k \neq O_j$, $I(O_i; O_j) \geq I(O_i; O_k) \Rightarrow \sigma(O_i, O_j) \geq \sigma(O_i, O_k)$,

$$d(O_i, O_j) \leq d(O_i, O_k) \Rightarrow \sigma(O_i, O_j) \geq \sigma(O_i, O_k),$$

$$\varphi(O_i, O_j) \geq \varphi(O_i, O_k) \Rightarrow \sigma(O_i, O_j) \geq \sigma(O_i, O_k),$$

where $I(O_i;O_j)$, $d(O_i,O_j)$ and $\varphi(O_i,O_j)$ are the mutual information, link distance and link feature between O_i and O_j respectively. $I(O_i;O_j)$ can be calculated directly according to the definition of the mutual information [7]. For $d(O_i,O_j)$, we use the Euclidian distance $D_2(O_i,O_j)$. For $\varphi(O_i,O_j)$, we can use the frequency of links between O_i and O_j to the total number of links between O_i and its neighborhood. We call this the **link-count** model. However, this model will induce additional bias since the nepotistic links are rampant on the Web today. To further reduce the influence of such noisy links, we use the frequency of different link modes coexisting between O_i and O_j. In this case, we use the term **mode-count** model. For simplicity, we use $\sigma_{i,j}$ to denote $\sigma(O_i,O_j)$, use σ_i to denote the *dependence vector* of object O_i. Note that for each object O_i, $M_i = |\sigma_i|$.

There are many choices of embodied forms of the *dependence function* between two objects O_i and O_j. Here we use the following form:

$$\sigma_{i,j} = \exp\left(-\beta_1 \frac{d(O_i,O_j)}{\varphi(O_i,O_j)}\right) I(O_i;O_j), \tag{2}$$

where β_1 is a parameter to control the sensitivity of the dependence function value to the ratio $\varphi(O_j,O_j)/d(O_i,O_j)$, which is set as follows: for the mode-count model, $0.8 \le \beta_1 \le 1$; for the link-count model, $0.2 \le \beta_1 \le 0.3$. Thus, instead of using the assumption that the class variables of neighbors are independent given the class label c_i of O_i, we have the following assumption:

$$\Pr[c_i \mid C_{\mathcal{N}(O_i)}] = \sum_{O_{ik} \in \mathcal{N}(O_i)} \sigma_{i,ik} \Pr[c_i \mid C_{ik} = c_j]. \tag{3}$$

Here different neighbors have different influences on the categorization of O_i. Thus the resulting classifier can be written as:

$$\hat{c}_i = \arg\max_{c_i} \Pr[c_i \mid O_i, C_{\mathcal{N}(O_i)}] = \arg\max_{c_i} \frac{\Pr[c_i \mid O_i] \Pr[c_i \mid C_{\mathcal{N}(O_i)}]}{\Pr[c_i]}. \tag{4}$$

3.2 Context Optimization

However, for each $O_i \in O$, there may be a large number of neighbors. A typical academic paper, a patent in the Patent Database, and an average Web page all have typically more than ten citations or out-links [1]. Naïvely restricting the expansion to out-links within the site or domain would miss many valuable links at the same time. Hence to avoid the "context dilution" problem, a more sophisticated method should be used to reduce the objects' contextual space which is often initialized as their neighborhoods.

The context optimization on the link data can be modeled as follows: For a given object O_i in a link graph $G = (O, L)$, find a subset $\mathcal{NC}(O_i)$ of $\mathcal{N}(O_i)$ that minimizes the conditional entropy $H(C_i \mid O_i, C_{\mathcal{NC}(O_i)})$. Here $\mathcal{NC}(O_i)$ denotes the reduced neighborhood of O_i, i.e., its *de facto* context. For simplicity, we use $K_i = | \mathcal{N}C(O_i) |$. In general, $K_i \le M_i$. In this paper, the context optimization problem can be solved using the dependence function. Intuitively, some neighbors with relatively low dependence function values would be removed from the context space of the target object. Formally, the context optimization for a given object O_i is equivalent to find K_i neighbors in $\mathcal{N}(O_i)$ with maximal $\sigma(\cdot,\cdot)$ values, i.e.,

$$\mathcal{N}C(O_i) = \underset{\substack{\mathcal{N}C(O_i) \subseteq \mathcal{N}(O_i), \\ |\mathcal{N}C(O_i)|=K_i}}{\arg\min} H(C_i \mid O_i, C_{\mathcal{N}C(O_i)}) = \underset{\substack{\mathcal{N}C(O_i) \subseteq \mathcal{N}(O_i), \\ |\mathcal{N}C(O_i)|=K_i}}{\arg\max} \sum\nolimits_{O_{ik} \in \mathcal{N}C(O_i)} \sigma_{i,ik} \cdot \qquad (5)$$

Without loss of generality, let $\sigma_{i,i1} \ge \cdots \ge \sigma_{i,iM_i}$, then the optimized context of O_i is $\mathcal{N}C(O_i) = \{O_{i1}, \cdots, O_{iK_i}\}$.

Theoretically, if the neighbor O_{ik} is irrelevant with O_i, then $I(O_i; O_{ik}) \to 0$, which will approximately result in $\sigma_{i,ik} \to 0$. Thus we set a threshold $\sigma_{\perp}$ for the dependence function values, i.e., if $\sigma_{i,ik} \ge \sigma_{\perp}$, then $O_{ik} \in \mathcal{N}C(O_i)$. Furthermore, the threshold can be determined easily. For example, $\sigma_{\perp} = 0.5\bar{\sigma}_i$ or $\sigma_{\perp} = 0.01$.

After the context optimization and the re-normalization of the dependence function values (i.e., let $\sum_{O_{ik} \in \mathcal{N}C(O_i)} \sigma_{i,ik} = 1$), Eq (3) can then be rewritten as

$$\Pr[c_i \mid C_{\mathcal{N}(O_i)}] = \sum_{O_{ik} \in \mathcal{N}C(O_i)} \sigma_{i,ik} \Pr[c_i \mid C_{ik} = c_j]. \qquad (6)$$

The results calculated from this equation instead of from Eq. (3) can be applied in Eq. (4) to assign a new class label to O_i.

3.3 The Classification Framework

Generally, the neighbors of the linked objects may be partly or fully unlabeled. Inspired by the works in [1], [4], this paper also uses the iterative inference procedure. Let $O = O^L \cup O^U$ where O^L and O^U denote the objects in labeled and unlabeled sub-datasets respectively. Firstly, a bootstrap step is used to assign an initial class label to each object O_i in O^U, only using the content features. Then an iterative step is used to refine the classification of the objects in O^U until the algorithm terminates, which includes several sequential operations such as context modeling, influence propagation and termination check. Note that in each iteration step, the dependence vector σ_i for each object O_i will be re-calculated, thus the corresponding context $\mathcal{N}C(O_i)$ will be optimized again, based on the current assignments to linked objects. The framework of the algorithm is as follows:

Algorithm 1. (The Context-Based Link Classification)
Input: Link data $G = (O, L)$, let $O = O^L \cup O^U$.
Given: A predefined class taxonomy $C = \{c_1, \cdots, c_{|C|}\}$ for objects.
Step 1 (Bootstrap): For each O_i in O^U, assign an initial class label to the object O_i only using its content features.

Step 2 (Iteration): Iteratively classify each object O_i in O^U until termination:

Find the initial neighborhood for O_i: $\mathcal{N}(O_i) = \{O_j \mid O_j \in O, \ 0 < d(O_i, O_j) < 2\}$.

2.1 (Context Modeling) Based on the current assignments to linked objects, calculate $I(O_i, O_{ik})$, $d(O_i, O_{ik})$, $\varphi(O_i, O_{ik})$ and $\sigma_{i,ik}$ for all $O_{ik} \in \mathcal{N}(O_i)$.

Select O_{ik} with $\sigma_{i,ik} \geq \sigma_\perp$ to form the current $\mathcal{NC}(O_i)$.

2.2 (Influence Propagation) Calculate the current $\Pr[c_i \mid C_{\mathcal{N}(O_i)}]$ by Eq. (6) using all the class information of its contextual objects $O_j \in \mathcal{NC}(O_i)$, and update the class label of O_i by Eq. (4).

2.3 (Termination Check) If the predefined convergence criteria are met, output final results.

Output: The final class label for each object O_i in O^U.

Several criteria are used to determine whether the iteration process will be terminated, including the convergence of the average entropies over all unlabeled (or target) objects, the consistency of MAP estimates of object categories between two consecutive iterations, and the iteration upper. In this paper, 5 iterations were sufficient to ensure convergence, thus the iteration upper was set to 5.

4   Experiments and Results

Two experiments were designed to evaluate the proposed classification algorithm on the standard WebKB dataset [5], [6]. The WebKB dataset contains approximately 4100 pages from four computer science departments, with a seven-valued attribute representing their types (i.e., faculty, student, staff, department, project, course and other), and 10,900 links between pages. The first experiment dealt with the evaluation of context modeling capability. The second experiment evaluated various link-based classification algorithms with and without context modeling.

As for *context modeling capability*, we denote whether the additional context modeling can reduce the high-dimensional context space (called *dimensionality reduction ability*), and can automatically identify as more linked objects of the same or highly relevant categories as possible from the objects' neighborhood (called *homogeneity*). For simplicity, this paper uses the frequency of contextual objects that are of the same category with the target object to measure the homogeneity of its context space, and uses the ratio between the dimensionalities of context spaces before after context optimization to measure the dimensionality reduction ability.

Figure 1 depicts the curves of the average homogeneity and the curves of the average dimensionality ratio under different $\sigma_\perp / \overline{\sigma}_i$ on WebKB dataset. Here we highlight the curves for the pages with more than 20 initial neighbors in the dataset. Note that the homogeneity ratios without context modeling are only 0.41 and 0.34 respectively for all pages and for pages with more than 20 initial neighbors. And after the context optimization process, these ratios become 0.43 and 0.75. Clearly, the context modeling can significantly increase the context homogeneity and reduce the high-dimensional context space for those pages with relatively more linked neighbors. Namely, we can effectively purify the pages' neighborhood via context modeling and optimization.

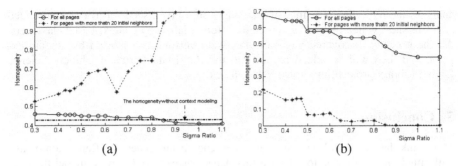

Fig. 1. The curves for (a) the average homogeneity and (b) the average dimensionality ratio of context space under different $\sigma_\perp / \overline{\sigma}_i$ on the WebKB dataset.

Then we tested the conjecture that by link context modeling we can improve the prediction of descriptive attributes. We evaluated the following set of models:

- **Baseline:** The Naïve Bayes model uses only textual features of the page to predict the category of the page. This model is also used for the basic text classification tasks in the following link-based classification procedures.

- **Neighboring-Class Model** [1]: This model equally utilizes the class information of all linked neighbors to predict the category.

- **Link-Distribution Model** [4]: Based on the counts link statistics for in-links, out-links and co-citations, a logistic regression model is built for link features between the target pages and its neighborhood.

- **Context-Based Models:** We may use mode-count model and link-count model to capture the link feature between the target page and each of its neighbors. Hence there are two choices of the context-based classification models.

Table 1. Comparison of average accuracy, precision, recall and F1 scores on each of the classification tasks using different link-based models.

	Without context modeling			With context modeling	
	Baseline (Content-Only)	Neighboring Class Model	Link-Distri. Model	Link-Count Model	Mode-Count Model
Avg. Accuracy	74.3	85.4	86.1	86.6	**89.1**
Avg. Precision	75.3	84.1	85.4	86.7	**88.2**
Avg. Recall	70.6	81.2	82.8	82.3	**82.9**
Avg. F1 Measure	72.9	82.6	84.0	84.4	**85.5**

Table 1 summarizes the average results of 4-fold cross-validation tests using the five classification models on the WebKB dataset. We see that both models of context-based classification significantly improve the average accuracy, precision, recall and F1 scores, although mode-count based models seem to be superior. Hence in the other experiments throughout this paper, the context-based classification utilized the mode-count model to characterize the link features.

In practice, we applied the context-based classification model on the automatic construction of academic Web resource catalogue. In this process, a focused crawler analyzes the hyperlink structure of web pages in a given seed set to find the related pages or sites, which then are assigned to different labels by context-based classifiers. All these newly discovered pages or sites were verified and labeled by domain experts, and then will be added partially to the Phy-Math Portal of Chinese Science Digital Library project (http://phymath.csdl.ac.cn).

5 Conclusion

Many link data such as Web pages are in essence heterogeneous, often accompanied with much noisy information. Hence this paper has explored how to model the contextual dependencies between objects in the link data, and exploited the learned context models to facilitate classification. It should be noted that the link context modeling technique could also be used to other Web-related applications such as enhancing Web search. We plan to further investigate its new applications in the future.

References

1. Chakrabarti, S., Dom, B., & Indyk P.: Enhanced hypertext categorization using hyperlinks. In: Proceedings of SIGMOD'98. Seattle, Washington, USA: ACM Press. (1998) 307-318.
2. Oh, H. J., Myaeng, S. H. & Lee, M.-H.: A practical hypertext categorization method using links and incrementally available class information. In: Proceedings of 23rd ACM Int. Conf. on Research and Development in Information Retrieval (SIGIR-00). Athens, Greece: ACM Press, New York, NY, USA. (2000) 264-271.
3. Brzillon P. Context in problem solving: a survey. The Knowledge Engineering Review, 14(1), 1999, 1-34.
4. Lu, Q. & Getoor, L.: Link-based Classification. In: Proceedings of 12th Int. Conf. on Machine Learning (ICML-2003), Washington DC, AAAI Press, Menlo Park, US. (2003).
5. Craven, M., DiPasquo, D., Freitag, D. McCallum, A., Mitechell, T., Nigam, K., & Slattery, S.: Learning to extract symbolic knowledge from the world wide web. In: Proceedings of the AAAI-98. (Madison, US): AAAI Press (1998) 509-516.
6. Slattery, S., Craven, M.: Combining statistical and relational methods for learning in hypertext domains. In D. Page (Ed).: Proceedings of 8th Int. Conf. on Inductive Logic Programming (ILP-98), no. 1446 in Lecture Notes in Computer Science, (Madison, US), Springer Verlag, Heidelberg, DE. (1998) 38-52.
7. Gray, R. M. Entropy and Information Theory. New York, NY: Springer-Verlag. (1990).
8. Kleinberg, J. Authoritative sources in a hyperlinked environment. Journal of the ACM, 46, 1999, 604-632.
9. Dean, J. & Henzinger, M. Finding related pages in the World Wide Web. In: Proceedings of 8th international World Wide Web Conference (WWW8), Toronto, Canada, Elsevier Science B.V. (1999) 389-401.

Build Presentation Layer for Semantic Contents

Hang Guo, Zhiqiang Zhang, Qi Guo, Lizhu Zhou, and Jianghua Feng

Computer Science Department,Tsinghua University,100084, Beijing, China
{guohang,guoqi00}@mails.tsinghua.edu.cn
{zqzhang,dcszlz,fengjh}@mail.tsinghua.edu.cn

Abstract. Large scale of semantically enriched data is the foundation of the semantic web. We introduce the model used in SESQ* system as the presentation layer of the semantic contents. It is an abstract graph independent of the data storage layer and application layer. Semantic contents of a specified domain are organized as nodes and arcs in the graph. GQML, a manipulation language, is designed for the graph, which is also used as the query language to semantic contents. With this model, the interoperation and integration of different sources will be easier. Now the model has been implemented on Berkley Database System and Relational Database.

1 Introduction

With the rapid growth of the contents on the Internet, it is more and more difficult to locate information with the current search engine techniques. The information on the web is mostly available in human readable forms that lack formalized semantics that would help agent use it [1]. Users can't perform their query just on the attributes they are interested in. Furthermore the presentation structure of the sources is often changed.

Semantic web is believed to have the potentials to facilitate search interoperability, and composition of complex applications by associating meanings with contents [2]. For this purpose, some uniforms have been proposed to structure the contents in semantic web, such as DAML+OIL[3], RDF Schema[4] ,SHOE[5],etc.

In our envisioning, the future semantic web should contain huge amount of semantic contents to satisfy the requirements of users with different interests. However, to use those contents, a unified view of semantic data and a scalable, transparent, persistent store are needed. The reasons can be listed here:

a) The information on the web must be structured to machine-processable format.
b) Content providers may present resources in different formats, e.g. RDF, DAML, OIL etc. If a unified view is provided, applications can query and modify the data of different sources in the same way.
c) The semantic data may be stored in different data repositories, such as relational databases, network databases, hierarchical databases, XML or RDF repositories etc. It will be convenient for the application developers if the storage is transparent to them.

To solve the above problems, we designed a presentation layer as the unified view of different types of structured data. It is a relatively simple graph model with all information defined in the nodes and arcs of a graph. The main features of the layer are:

---

* http://166.111.68.84/sesq

W. Liu et al. (Eds.): ICWL 2004, LNCS 3143, pp. 241–248, 2004.

a) It is independent of the storage layer. In SESQ[6 8], for example, it has been implemented on both Relational Database and Berkley Database System [7].

b) Different data formats can be transformed into the schemas of the model.

c) A powerful language is designed for applications to query and modify the data.

d) It provides an approach for users to define new uniforms for their own data.

To create and maintain the graph, we designed a manipulation language called GQML[8], It is also used as a powerful query language for applications.

The rest of the paper is organized as follows: The next section glances at other proposals to solve the problems. Section 3 gives an architecture that shows how the presentation works. In the section 4, we give the definition of the graph model. Section 5 illustrates the model with a living example. Section 6 introduces the approach to expand the graph with existing sources. In Section 7 we will introduce how to manage the graph and retrieve data from it. Finally, Section 8 presents our future work and conclusion.

2 Related Work

We have found two types of systems that adopt some basic ideas related to our model.

In the first type, e.g. on2broker[9], there exist ontology-based presentation. Data extracted from Web are organized according to the predefined local data schemas (domain ontologies). It is usually difficult, if possible, to integrate data in a different ontology to the system.

In the second type, there exist API-based storage-independent presentation. Sesame [10] is a web-based architecture designed to store and query RDF Data and Schema Information. The local storage of the data is managed by RAL (Repository Abstraction Layer), a set of APIs to manage the repository. The API used in Sesame is something like "Stanford API"[11], which is designed to manage RDF data on different platforms.

Comparing with the first type, our model is more adaptive. Applications can access the data in the same way, no mater in which formats they are and to which domains they belong. By means of GQML statements, applications can perform more complex queries, which will be introduced at Section 7. Except these, Users can design new data format in our model to define their own data.

The interface between our presentation layer and the storage layer is a set of APIs. Like the "Stanford API", they are independent of the local storage layer. Unlike the "Stanford API", they are based on the graph model, not on a single type of resource. The details will be introduced in Section 7.

3 Architecture

In the figure 1, applications first access the presentation layer with GQML statements. Then they are interpreted as strings of atomic operations implemented by the storage layer. Since the data type and storage are transparent to the application layer, applications can access different sites and different storages in the same way. The interoperation between different sites will be much easier.

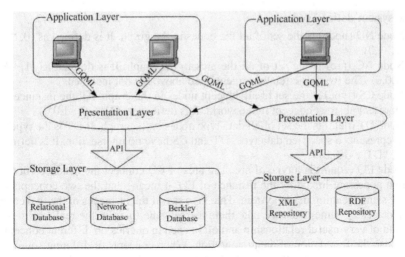

Fig. 1. Presentation Layer in SESQ

4   The Definition of Model

The graph G used in the presentation layer is defined as a two-tuple (N,A) . N is the set of nodes in the graph with some system-defined nodes, which will be discussed in the following part of the section. The nodes in G represent different concepts and their instances. A is the set of arcs. They represent the relationship between nodes. The types of arcs are also defined as nodes, they are treated the same as the other nodes.

In graph G, nodes are defined as (id, text, type, parent, weight). The value of "id" is integer. Every node in the graph has a unique id. The "text" attribute is the label of the node. Most of the information is recorded as regular text in this attribute. Every node in G has a type id, which indicates what kind of node it is. The value of "parent" is the "id" of its parent node. The "weight" attribute shows the degree of importance of the node. The value of it is integer. This attribute is used when the node is evaluated by applications. In our system, if a node doesn't have a "type" or "parent", the value of the attribute will be –1.

In graph G, arcs are defined as (id, type, start, end). The attribute "id" is also the identification of arcs. The attribute "type" indicates what kind of relationship it represents. It points to a specified node, which defined the meaning of the arc.

The attribute "start" and "end" are the ids of nodes connected by the arc. In the graph every arc is directed. Undirected relations, e.g. "Equal" relation mentioned below, can be represented by two directed arcs in the graph.

We define two basic relations between nodes in the graph as the system-defined relations. They are not the elements of A.

a)   Type_Of (n, m) $\Leftrightarrow$ the "type" of m equals to the "id" of n where (m, n $\in$ N)

b)   Parent_Of (n,m) $\Leftrightarrow$ the "parent" of m equals to the "id" of n where (m, n $\in$ N))

If Type_Of (n,m) ,we say that n is the type of m and m is the instance of n. If Parent_Of (n,m) ,we say that n is the parent of m and m is the son of n. They are quite similar to the concepts used in Object-Oriented area. The difference is that their domains are N.

The system-defined nodes are:

a) Node ND (node) is the set of all the nodes in the graph. It is defined as (0, "ND", -1, -1,0).

b) Node AC (arc) is the set of all the arcs in the graph. It is defined as (1, "AC", -1,0,0). The two basic relations mentioned above are not included.

c) Node CS (type) is the set of all concept nodes in the graph. All the instances of it represent abstract concept in the world. It is defined as (2, "CS",-1,0,0).

d) Node DT (data) is the set of all data type nodes in the graph. If DT is the type of n, n represents a specified data type. DT and CS have no intersection. It is defined as (3, "DT", -1,0,0).

e) Node EQ (equal) is a type of arc. The arcs of EQ connect the instances of CS. If two nodes are linked by the instance of EQ, it means that the two concepts have the same meaning in our system. That is to say, if the instances of the two concept nodes carry same texts, we take them as the same thing in the real world. It is a kind of very useful relationship and often used in queries on different concepts. It is also the foundation of data integration. When concepts of different sources are loaded into the graph, the arcs of EQ should be set between similar concepts. It is defined as (4, "EQ",1,-1,0).

f) Node AO (attribute of) is a type of arc. The arcs of AO have two different domains and ranges. It may start from one instance of CS and point to one instance of DT or CS. Or it may start from one instance of the instance of CS and point to one instance of the instance of DT or CS. Obviously in the former condition it connects one concept with its attribute while in the latter it connects one concrete thing with its attribute. It is defined as (5, "AO",1,-1,0). The RDF Definition of the elements in the graph is listed in [12].

5 Example

Now we can use these nodes to define new concepts in a domain. An instance of the graph is shown as Fig 2.

To make it easier to understand, I add red arcs and blue arcs to the example. The former represents the "Type_Of" relation and the latter represents the "Parent_Of" relation. Node No.7 to No.14 are defined by users. Node No.7 and No.8 are the top-level conceptions in the schema. They are not derived from other conceptions. Node No.9 and No.10 are directly derived from them. The dashed arcs and nodes are automatically created by the system. The rules to create them are:

a) When a new node n derived directly from node m is created, all the attributes of m will be replicated and connected to n with arcs of AO.

b) When a new arc is added to the attribute of conception m, all the conceptions derived directly or indirectly from m will have the same arc added to the same attributes.

We keep a copy of the attributes because usually the EQ relation between two conceptions does not affect their upper lever conceptions. As Fig 2 shows, not all men's names are related to papers' author names. Only those who write papers do.

The ids of nodes and arcs are assigned by the system. When a new node or arc is created, a new id will be assigned to it.

It is just a very simple instance. Users can use the system-defined nodes to define their own uniforms and data.

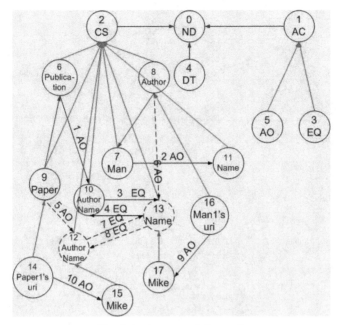

Fig. 2. An instance of the graph

According to Section 4, the graph in Fig 2 is defined as a two-tuple (N,A).

N={(0,ND,-1,-1,0), (1,AC,-1,0,0), (2,CS,-1,0,0), (3,EQ,1,-1,0), (4,DT,-1,0,0), (5, AO,1,-1,0), (6,Publication,2,-1,0), (7,Man,2,-1,0), (8,Author,2,7,0), (9,Paper,2,6,0), (10, AuthorName,2,-1,0), (11,Name,2,-1,0), (12,AuthorName,2,-1,0), (13,Name,2, -1,0), (14, Paper1's uri,9,-1,0), (15,Mike,12,-1,0), (16, Man1's uri,8,-1,0), (17, Mike, 13,-1,0)}

A={(1,AO,6,10), (2,AO,7,11), (3,EQ,10,13), (4,EQ,13,10), (5,AO,9,12) (6,AO, 8,13), (7,EQ,12,13), (8,EQ,13,12), (9,AO,16,17), (10,AO,14,15)}

6   Expend the Graph with Existing Sources

To load data formatted in RDF, DAML, etc, it is necessary to:

a) Map some of the tags defined in the format to the system-defined nodes.
b) Add some new nodes and arcs according to the specification of the format.

Here, we will take RDF as example to present how to transform a specified format to the schema of the model. The RDF tags [4] can be transformed into the graph as Fig 3.

The ND, CS and AC are mapped to "Resource", "Class" and "Property". They play similar roles in their own model respectively. New nodes are created for other resources. The rules are:

a) If resource A is a type of "Resource", "Class" or "Property", create node A and set it as the instance of Node "Resource", "Class" or "Property".
b) If resource A is the subclass of "Resource", "Class" or "Property", create node A and set it as the son of Node "Resource", "Class" or "Property".

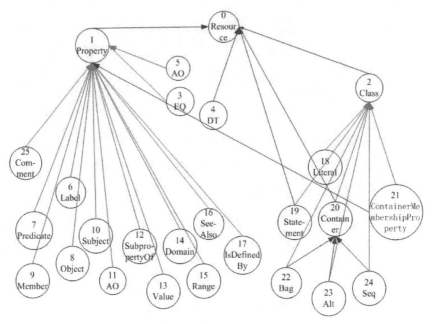

Fig. 3. transform RDF into the graph.

By means of the new nodes and arcs defined in Fig 3., we can transform a RDF document into nodes and arcs in the graph. Since the DAML+OIL vocabulary can be defined with RDF tags [3], the DAML+OIL documents can be handled in the same way.

The semantic meanings of system-defined nodes are simple. Most semantic contents have much more complex structure. So we have to define a lot of new nodes and arcs to describe the structure. Users can define new uniforms for their own data. When several types of documents are loaded, we may map one system-defined node to different tags that have the same meaning. To integrate data in different domains, we can simply define new node "domain" and several instances of it. Then we can group the concept nodes and arcs according to the domains they are in. The "EQ" arc can be used to connect similar concepts in different domains.

7 Manipulate and Query

We have designed a simple language, GQML [12] (Graphic Query and Manipulation Language). As the manipulation and query language of the graph, it is first used to write scripts for the extractor. The extractor builds the graph automatically while the scripts are interpreted.

GQML is a powerful query language. It has two main features:

a) Variables are used in the query predicates. For example, (x)AO(y)EQ(z) & (z)EQ(y) describes the topological characteristic of one sub graph of the model. In the Fig 2, the query will return (9,12,13) and (6,10,13), which are the ids of the result nodes.

b) Regular expressions are used in the query predicate, which are very useful in the queries like "find Mike's ancestors". In GQML, the query may be something like (x)(IsParent)#("Mike"). '#' means the arc is repeated at least once.

As the cost of the powerful query capability, the execution and optimization of GQML is tough. First, a GQML statement is parsed into a string of atomic operations; each of which is mapped to an API independent with the local storage system. Then, the operations are transformed into local manipulation statements, such as SQL statements in the relational database system. The second step should be considered in the implementation of specified the storage platform.

Just as we have mentioned in the Section 3, the interface between the storage layer and the presentation layer is a set of APIs. According to the functions of them, they can be divided into three groups.

a) Add-Remove Group: This part contains the APIs that change elements in the graph. They are used to add nodes and arcs to the graph or remove node and arc from the graph.

b) Modification Group: This part contains the APIs that modifies the attributes of the nodes and arcs. They are used to change the text, type and weight of the nodes or the type of the arcs.

c) Query Group: This part contains the APIs that used to get specified elements in the group. Some of them are used to find nodes and arcs with specified attribute values. Others are used to find nodes according to the specified start or end node and the specified type of arcs that connect them.

Indices are transparent to the interface. Designer of the storage layer is free to adopt any indices he prefers on the local repository. Different indices can be used for different types of resources.

The graph used in SESQ has been implemented with Berkley Database System and Relational Database System (Microsoft SQLServer) .The graph we are using now contains over 100,000 nodes.

8   Future Work and Conclusion

As mentioned in Section 7, the optimization of the GQML is separated into two steps. Both of them are undergoing, especially the second step. And we are planning to test our approach on the relational database first.

We are also planning to implement the model as the global data view with several independently distributed repositories. The distribution of data will be completely transparent to the application developers.

The graph model is a highly adaptive presentation to perform queries and manipulate on different types of structured data. It is independent of the local storage and the processing of semantic contents. Applications can use the data via GQML statements without caring about the difference of data types, domains and storages. Content providers can even define new uniforms for their own data. And if the model can be adopted universally, the integration and interoperation of different semantic data sources will be much easier.

References

1. T. Berners-Lee, J. Hendler, and O. Lassila. "The Semantic Web", Scientific American, 284(5):34–43, May 2001.
2. D. Fensel et al., Spinning the Semantic Web, MIT Press, Cambridge, Mass., 2002
3. I. Horrocks, P. Patel-Schneider, and F. Harmelen. Reviewing the design of DAML+OIL: An ontology language for the semantic web. Technical Report at http://www.daml.org, 2002.
4. D. Brickley and R. Guha. Resource description framework, schema specification 1.0. Technical Report at http://www.w3.org/TR/2000/CR-rdf-schema-20000327,2000
5. S. Luke, L. Spector, D. Rager, and J. Hendler. Ontology-based web agents. In W. Johnson and B. Hayes-Roth, editors, Proceedings of the First International Conference on Autonomous Agents (Agents'97), pages 59–68, Marina del Rey, CA, USA, 1997. ACM Press.W3C Consortium, Mar. 2000.
6. Zhiqiang. Zhang, Lizhu. Zhou etc. "SESQ: An Ontology-based Web Data Engine". Technical Report of SESQ,http://166.111.68.84/sesq, 2003.
7. Margo Seltzer, Keith Bostic, Berkeley Database-Embedded Database System,
   See http: //www.gnu.org /directory/database/admin/BerkeleyDB.html
8. Qi Guo, Lizhu Zhou, Zhiqiang Zhang, Jianhua Feng. A Highy Adaptable Web Information Extractor Using Graph Data Model. The Sixth Asia Pacific Web Conference(APWE B'04),2004
9. Fensel, D., Angele, J., Decker, S., Erdmann, M., Schnurr, H.P., Staab, S., Studer, R., and Witt, A., On2broker: semantic–based access to information sources at the WWW, in World Conference on the WWW and Internet (WebNet99). 1999
10. J. Broekstra, A. Kampman, and F. van Harmelen. Sesame: An Architecture for Storing and Querying RDF Data and Schema Information. In D. Fensel, J. Hendler, H. Lieberman, and W. Wahlster, editors, Semantics for the WWW. MIT Press, 2001.
11. Melnik, S. RDF API Draft. public draft, Database Group, Stanford University. See http://www-db.stanford.edu/~melnik/rdf/api.html, 2000.
12. Hang Guo, Definition Of The Elements In The Graph Model, Tsinghua University. See http://166.111.68.84/sesq/namespace.htm,2004.

e-Learning Content Management
Based on Learning Object

Rui-min Shen, Li-ping Shen[*], and Xin-wei Fan

Computer Science Dept, Shanghai Jiaotong University
{rmshen,lpshen,xwfan}@sjtu.edu.cn

Abstract. In this paper, we propose to organize learning contents into small "atomic" units called Learning Objects so that they could be reused effectively, and then introduce methods to establish Learning Objects repository, finally we give a detail description about a retrieval system based on the latest SWI-Prolog technologies and the packaging of the Learning Objects.

Keywords: Learning Object, Ontology, Modified dynamic Directed Acycline Graph (MDAG), Meta-data, Content Packaging Specification.

1 Introduction

eLearning is now a huge market, a market and technology that encompasses Learning, Training, Marketing, and online Support, and almost everything hitting us electronically can be called eLearning. The management of useable and reusable learning content is vital to deploy efficient and effective eLearning system. Most eLearning contents today are organized in a linear, sequential way, with large number of pages and without any description per se. Such contents couldn't be reused by other authoring tools and content management systems. In this paper, we propose to organize learning contents into small chunks called Learning Objects (LO) – the "atomic" units of knowledge. There are anonyms of LO as Knowledge Object [1] and Sharable Content Object (SCO) [2]. Reusable objects enable us to put appropriate knowledge in the direct path of users. We need to create instructionally sound objects that are usable inside and outside of the traditional learning environment in order to have a significant impact on business performance. It must be flexible and easily managed so that the granules can be reused in different applications and for mass production of content in a team environment. We will introduce how to establish LO repository, how to retrieve individualized LO and then package them together for publish and transfer as a whole.

---

[*] The work of this paper is supported by the National Natural Science Foundation of China under Grant No. 60372078. Rui-min Shen is a committeeman of the Chinese e-Learning Technology Standardization Committee, and a professor of the Computer Science Dept. Shanghai Jiao Tong University, whose research interest lies in Data Mining, e-Learning Technology etc. Li-ping Shen is a lecture of the Computer Science Dept. Shanghai Jiao Tong University.

2 Learning Object Repository Construction

"Building all the courses from scratch is like building kit cars in your garage" [1]. In order to mass-produce and distribute knowledge with high-quality, predictable results with less cost, we should be able to provide a LO Repository, a central database for storing and managing learning content that may be delivered through a variety of medias (Web, CD-ROM, printed materials) either as individual objects or as part of a larger course structure.

First of all, we need to define the contents that will be stored in the repository [3]: the concepts which are to be communicated, and their classification and inter-relation, i.e. the ontology of the content. This description can be performed by a domain expert, and does not require that learning issues are taken into account. For example, the concept "router" is the sub-concept of "networking device", and relates to "switch" and "gateway". We also need to define the dependencies between the concepts, i.e. which are the competencies that are related to each concept in the ontology of the learning material. These competencies serve for encapsulating the "pre-conditions" of learning, i.e. defining the expertise required before presenting a specific concept to the learner. For example, "internet protocol" is the prerequisite of the concept "router". So all the concepts depend on each other with different logic relations and then build up a Modified dynamic Directed Acycline Graph (MDAG) diagram as figure 1.

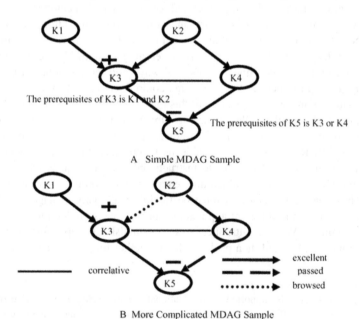

Fig. 1. MDAG Diagram Samples

For each concept in the ontology, we also need to define some questions and tests which determine whether the learner has understood the concept.

Subsequently, we need to compile and define the LOs that are instances of each concept of the ontology. LOs can be available as text files, images, videos, simulations, etc. Each LO is described through meta-data, such as who is allowed to see this information, the style and format it will be presented in, the other LOs that are related to it, and it is "linked" to specific knowledge points (here we regard knowledge point as concept) in the ontology. In order to describe the atomic units of knowledge concisely, we choose a subnet of the China e-Learning Technology Standardization Committee (CELTSC) Learning Object Metadata Specification [7] and add some extensions as figure 2.

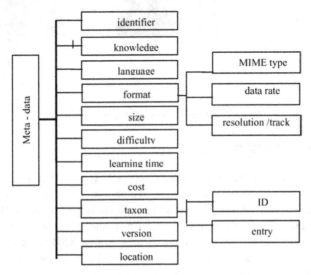

Fig. 2. Metadata Elements

One LO could include one or more knowledge points, so the metadata could have one or more knowledge point elements. The format element is used for Medium-Neutral Delivery. It allows us to select and modify the LO to any designated export format, based on what is most appropriate and cost effective. The sub-element resolution/track indicates the resolution of the figure and video LOs or the tracks of the sound LOs. The version element is used for rapid and automatic online update.

We have developed a suite of Graphic Content Management Tools to construct the learning content Ontology, the DAG and the metadata of the Learning Objects.

3 Learning Objects Retrieval

Figure 3 demonstrates the architecture of the retrieval system. The Fact library is composed of the Meta-data and the Concept DAG Diagram. The explorer submits the logic commands of resource requirements by the end user. Then the Java Servlets reform the logic commands and send them to the inference engine. The SWI-Prolog[4] inference engine calculates out the result and returns back to the user.

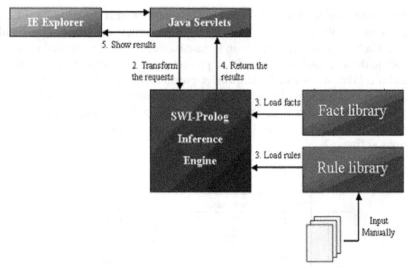

Fig. 3. Retrieval System Architecture

3.1 Core Inference Engine

We use the Meta-data of the LOs and the Concept DAG Diagram to retrieve the appropriate LOs according to the user queries. We choose the SWI-Prolog technologies instead of Flogic in Ontobroker[5] because its core inference engine XSB[6] excels at First-Order Logic Inference and has well-defined interfaces for us to call as free source software. However the most import reason is that XSB has implemented Tabling technologies that can avoid infinite recursions that occur when finding a valid concept chain in our system.

Since the SWI-Prolog is a prolog-like system, server should load both facts and rules during the initialization. Here we designed a set of Java API used to transform the Meta-data files(XML files) and the Concept DAG Diagram into the knowledge based prolog facts. The rules are input manually by the administrator and stored in a document beforehand. Having finished the steps above, the server works as follows:

1. Retrieve the post query from the web explorers via the HTTP port.
2. Send this query to the inference engine via the SWI-Prolog's connection to the XSB.
3. According to the local facts and local rules, retrieve LOs from the repository.
4. Get the results from the inference engine and parse them.
5. Organize the LOs according to the results and send back to the web explorers.

3.2 User Interface

We provide two kinds of interface for the end user, so the system is something familiar with the Ontobroker system. One is a big text area component in the page, which is designed for the expert user. By this way user can input the abstract prolog language. It has drawbacks: the user should not only have a well master of Prolog's syntax, but also be familiar with the predicates and ontology in our system. To remedy these drawbacks, we design another interface where almost every general condition selections are list in the web page such as the destination knowledge point to master, the overall learning period and etc. The system will help to generate the prolog commands and display them in the input field. The users can modify that commands manually as they wish. So not only the rookies could use this system, the experts also could benefit from it.

Except for the conditions listed in rookies interface, we also add some intelligent factors based on the user's purpose. Overall we divide the users into two groups: knowledge point aimed users and efficiency-aimed users. We put emphases on different conditions towards these two groups. For example, users of group one may care more about the content of the knowledge point, so the attention should be focused on how to filter the knowledge points. Users from group two only want to know something quickly in the limited period, and then the learning period will be a main factor. Although there may be no satisfied result meets the requirement, the users could adjust their inputs and try to find a satisfied one.

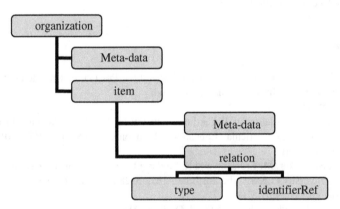

Fig. 4. Extend CELTSC Content Package <item> Element

3.3 Content Packaging

As we discussed how to make a query above, we have to think another question how to deliver and present the results to the end user explicitly and effectively. The system adopts CELTSC Content Packaging Specification[8] to package the LOs. Though CELTSC Content Packaging Specification CD1.6 only defines a hierarchical resource organization, to practise other complex organization structures is encouraged. Here we introduce a DAG-type organization to package the selected LOs. We extend the <organization>.<item> element with adding an optional sub-element <relation> as Figure 4. The <relation> element has two attributes. The type attribute describes the relationship with other LOs, for example prerequisite or subsequent or parallel. The IdentifierRef attribute locate the corresponding LO resources. Each item packages a Learning Object, its metadata and the relationship with other LOs. We provide two kind of final presentation: a DAG presentation that directly lists the knowledge points from the resource deposit and a skeleton presentation that describes the metadata of the learning resource. The first presentation is much more explicit but can not provide the extra information besides the learning resources content while the second one fix up this drawback.

4   Conclusion

In this paper, we give a brief introduction of our efficient learning content management system. It is an effective experiment by establishing learning content repository based on Learning Objects and incorporating knowledge inference engine technologies. There are some advanced design concepts in this system: (1) the schema and ontology constructed can be shared by other applications and agents. (2) The system can be upgraded conveniently by expanding its fact library and rule library. In the future, we will polish the system in the following aspects. Firstly we may integrate content authoring into our system. Secondly we may improve the individualized content delivery to enhance the intelligence.

References

1. J. Z. Li, R. Close: The Promise of eLearning and the Practice of Knowledge System Design. http://www.leadingway.com/eLearning.pdf
2. www.adlnet.org
3. C. Karagiannidis, D. Sampson, F. Cardinali: Integrating Adaptive Educational Content into Different Courses and Curricula. Educational Technology and Society 4(3) 2001
4. www.swi-prolog.org
5. D. Fensel, S. Decker, M. Erdmann and R. Studer: Ontobroker: How to make the WWW intelligent. University of Karlsruhe, Institute AIBE, 6128 Karlsruhe Germany.
6. www.semanticweb.org/XSB/
7. http://www.celtsc.edu.cn/download/CELTS-3.1(CD1.6).zip
8. http://www.celtsc.edu.cn/download/CELTS-9.1(CD1.6).zip

Improving Web-Based Learning: Automatic Annotation of Multimedia Semantics and Cross-Media Indexing

Yueting Zhuang, Congmiao Wu, Fei Wu, and Xiang Liu

The Institute of Artificial Intelligence, Zhejiang University,
Hangzhou, 310027, P.R.China
yzhuang@cs.zju.edu.cn, wu_congmiao@eyou.com,
wufei@cs.zju.edu.cn, lxlotus@sohu.com

Abstract. Multimedia plays an important role in the web-based learning environment. In this paper, we validate management and retrieval of large multimedia collections through high-level semantics. A novel algorithm is proposed for automatic annotation of image based on support vector machine and statistical learning. In addition, we construct cross-media indexing for multi-modal data upon the annotation result to support cross-media search. Experiments show that our algorithm can interpret multimedia semantics accurately and cross-media indexing can support cross-media search effectively.

1 Introduction

As the amount of learning resources available on the Internet grows, there is an increasing need for an effective mechanism to help people find them. Web-based learning emerges, as the times require. It profits from a combination of techniques including computer networks, multimedia, content portals, digital libraries, search engines, etc. Among them, we are particularly interested in the management of multimedia resources. It can facilitate the task of E-learning. For example, when a biology teacher introduces panda, he might use an image to explain how the panda looks like, play a clip of video to show its daily habit, or listen to a sound clip of its bleating. Obviously, the effect of teaching in this way is much better than using simple text and oral explanation only. It also validates cross-media retrieval in a web-based learning environment.

Multimedia resources are required to be managed, retrieved and integrated through high-level semantics, which is traditionally obtained from manual labeling. Well-annotated image collections include Corel image galleries (http://elib.cs.Berkeley.edu/photos/corel/), most museum image collections (http://www.thinker.org), the web archive (http://www.archive.org), etc. However, this approach is liable to subjective, and requires a huge amount of human effort [1]. As new multimedia resources increase dramatically everyday, an automatic annotation method becomes necessary and important. In this paper, we propose a novel approach to automatically annotate image content. First, support vector machine (SVM) is used to classify images automatically; statistical learning method is then adopted to select the most appropriate keywords for an incoming image on the basis of the annotated image collections. An effective cross-media indexing schema is devised upon the annotated results to support cross-media search [2].

W. Liu et al. (Eds.): ICWL 2004, LNCS 3143, pp. 255–262, 2004.

The remainder of this paper is organized as follows. Section 2 summarizes the previous related work. An overview of the proposed annotation algorithm appears in Section 3. Section 4 gives the concept of cross-media indexing. Experiments are done in section 5. Conclusion and future work are given in the final part.

2   Related Work

There has been a lot work on exploiting knowledge from multimedia to support web-based learning [3, 4]. All these work intended to analyze and retrieve multimedia based on low-level features. But people are accustomed to learn through high-level semantics. Some work has been focused on automatically annotating multimedia semantics [5–9].

Machine translation and statistical learning are two widely used techniques to look at the probability of associating words with image regions (or the whole image). Co-occurrence Model [5] is used to compute the probability of words within individual image region. Recently, Translation Model [6] is proposed to describe images using a vocabulary of blobs. Each image is segmented into regions and represented by a certain number of blobs. Translation Model can be viewed as an improvement for Co-occurrence Model. More recently, CMRM [7] is used to evaluate the probability of words with the whole image since regions in one image are always placed into a certain context. For all these work, CMRM is the most similar with our work.

3   Automatic Annotation of Image

In this section, we provide a detailed description of the method we use to automatic annotation of image.

3.1   Semantic Skeleton of Image Collection

Classification is a good way to organize a large collection of images into categories with different semantic meanings. Here, we propose to use *semantic skeleton* to describe the semantics of an image category. Each image within the category is an instance of the *semantic skeleton*.

Suppose we are given an annotated image category C. Each image $I \in C$ is represented by $I = \{w_1, w_2, ..., w_m\}$, where w_i is the keyword. The *semantic skeleton* is defined as *SemanticSkeleton=<ID,Title,KeywordSet,SemanticBlobSet>*, where *KeywordSet* is the union of all annotated keywords; *SemanticBlobSet* is a vocabulary of blobs abstractly representing meaningful image regions of the category. The Normalized Cuts [10] method is implemented to segment images into regions and the blob vocabulary is then constructed according to [6]. The *SemanticBlobSet* is then represented as *SemanticBlobSet=* $\{b_1, b_2, ..., b_n\}$.

3.2   SVM-Based Image Classification

Support vector machines [11] are core machine learning techniques, which have both strong theoretical foundations and excellent empirical successes. SVMs were originally designed for binary classification, and have been extended to solve multi-class classification problems. Here, we adopt the one-against-one method [12] for both of its good performance and easy implementation. For a K-class classification problem, the one-against-one method trains K(K-1)/2 binary classifiers. Each classifier c_{ij} can assign a testing data x into either class i or class j. Voting strategy is adopted to combine the predicting results for all K(K-1)/2 classifiers. If classifier c_{ij} predicts x into class i, the vote for the ith class is added by one. Otherwise, the vote for the jth class is increased by one. Then x is predicted to be in the class with the highest vote.

3.3   Automatic Annotating Image

Suppose there exists a training collection $T = T_1 \cup T_2 \cup ... \cup T_K$, which contains K classes of annotated images. *Semantic skeletons* are constructed for each category. Each image $J \in T$ has a dual representation of words and blobs $J = \{w_1, w_2, ..., w_m; b_1, b_2, ..., b_n\}$. Here $\{w_1, w_2, ..., w_m\}$ represents the annotated keywords and $\{b_1, b_2, ..., b_n\}$ represents blobs corresponding to image regions. The value of n depends on the complexity of the image. m and n in each image need not be equal. For each image $\mathbf{I}$ in the testing collection, $\mathbf{I}$ is first classified into one of the categories. The blob representation $I = \{b_1, b_2, ..., b_n\}$ is computed straightly forward. The task of automatic annotation is reduced to selecting the most suitable words to describe the image content correctly, i.e. to select words that have the highest probability $P(w|I)$.

Since each image in the training collection has a dual representation of words and blobs, automatic annotation can then be treated as a translation procedure which translating the vocabulary of blobs into words. This work is similar to cross-lingual information retrieval [13]. Once a testing image $\mathbf{I}$ is classified into category T_i, the probability $P(w|I)$ can be estimated as follows:

$$P(w|I) = \lambda \cdot P(w|T_i) + (1-\lambda) \cdot \sum_{b \in I} P(b|I)P(w|b) \qquad (1)$$

Where λ is the smoothing parameter. The traditional TF.IDF model [14] is adopted to compute $P(w|T_i)$ and $P(b|I)$:

The conditional probability $P(w|b)$ can be estimated as the expectation over the training images $\mathbf{J} \in T_i$:

$$P(w|b) = \sum_{J \in T_i} P(J) \cdot P(w|b, J) = \sum_{J \in T_i} P(J) \cdot \frac{P(w, b|J)}{P(b|J)} \qquad (2)$$

The prior probability $P(J)$ is kept uniformly over all images in T_i. Considering the dual representation of image $\mathbf{J}$, the probabilities of drawing single blob b and word-blob pair (w, b) from $\mathbf{J}$ are given by:

$$P(b \mid J) = \alpha_i \cdot \frac{f(b,J)}{|J|} + (1 - \alpha_i) \cdot \frac{f(b,T_i)}{|T_i|} \tag{3}$$

$$P(w,b \mid J) = \beta_i \cdot \frac{f((w,b),J)}{|J|} + (1 - \beta_i) \cdot \frac{f((w,b),T_i)}{|T_i|} \tag{4}$$

Where $f(b,J)$ or $f((w,b),J)$ is the number of occurrences of blob b or word-blob pair (w, b) in **J**, $f(b,T_i)$ or $f((w,b),T_i)$ is the number of occurrences of blob b or word-blob pair (w, b) in T_i, $|J|$ is the aggregate count of all words and blobs occurring in image J, $|T_i|$ is the size of T_i, and α_i and β_i are smoothing parameters according to category T_i, respectively.

From equation (1) – (4), we can estimate the probability of one word given a testing image **I**.

4   Cross-Media Indexing

Web-based learning environment already contains large volumes of multimedia resources. However, most multimedia retrieval approaches available at present are dedicated to a certain media type and thus are inapplicable to web-based learning environment. In this paper, cross-media indexing mechanism is devised to integrate multi-modal data into a seamless retrieval system. High-level semantics for multi-modal data is learned through automatic or manual annotation. One type of media object can then be indexed by another type if they have similar semantics. For example, a video that describes a tiger's daily life can be indexed by both an image and an audio when they are all annotated by the keyword "tiger". With cross-media indexing, learning resources with similar semantics can be organized together. Teachers can make multimodal courseware more efficiently. Students can understand learning concepts much easier and funnier with multimodal illustration. All these can improve web-based learning greatly.

5   Experiments and Discussion

We use the dataset[1] in [6] to compare the performance of annotation models in a strictly controlled way. The dataset consists of 5,000 images from 50 Corel Stock Photo CDs. Each CD includes 100 images on one specific topic. We can learn much knowledge from this large image database. Fig.1 shows some sample images about Sweden in 201000# CD.

In the experiments, images are segmented using the Normalized Cuts [10] method. Only regions larger than a threshold are selected. 33 features are extracted from each region. Each image has 1-10 blobs and 1-5 annotated keywords. Details of the above processes are described in [6]. We divide the dataset into two parts. 90 images are

---

[1] http://www.cs.arizona.edu/people/kobus/research/data/eccv_2002

selected from each CD as the sub-training set, the whole training set consists of 4,500 images. The evaluation set contains the remaining images. K-means clustering (K=20 in this paper) is implemented for each sub-training set to construct the corresponding *semantic skeleton*. Overall there are 371 words and 1000 blobs in the training set. In the following subsections, we will compare the experiment results from different annotation models, and demonstrate the effectiveness of cross-media indexing in the cross-media search.

Fig. 1. Sample images from 201000# CD

5.1 SVM-Based Classification

We adopt the RBF kernel $K(x_i, x_j = \exp(-\gamma \|x_i - x_j\|)$ for SVM classifiers. Color histogram (in HSV color space) and Tamura texture are used as image features. The optimal values for parameters C and γ [15] are estimated by cross-validation and grid search method. Finally we obtain 54.5% classification accuracy on the dataset. The reported classification accuracy is not high. One main reason is that Corel image galleries are classified on high-level semantic topics. Fig.1 already shows some sample images with the same topic but diverse low-level features.

5.2 Annotation Model Comparison

We compare the performance of four annotation models – the Co-occurrence Model, the Translation Model, the FACMRM [7] Model and the Model proposed in this paper. We annotate each evaluation image with 5 keywords for Co-occurrence Model, FACMRM Model and Our Model. The Translation Model annotates different images with different numbers of keywords. To evaluate the annotation performance, we retrieve images using keywords from the vocabulary. We treat manual annotation as the ground truth. The recall is defined as the number of correctly retrieved images divided by the number of relevant images in the evaluation set. The precision is defined as the number of correctly retrieved images divided by the number of retrieved images. A query word for which recall and precision are both larger than zero is called an effective word (EW). The Co-occurrence Model, Translation Model, FACMRM Model and Our Model have 19, 49, 66 and 112 EW, respectively. The union of the four EW sets gives a new EW set which has 120 elements. Table 1 shows the mean recall and precision of the four models on this EW union set.

One can learn from Table 1 that the annotation performance of Our Model is much better than the other three models (although the classification accuracy is still not high enough).

Table 1. The mean recall and precision comparison of four models on EW union set

Model	Co-occurrenc	Translation	FACMRM	Our Model
EW number	19	49	66	112
Recall	0.062	0.14	0.22	0.51
Precision	0.040	0.084	0.19	0.25

To compare the model performance more extensively, we evaluate the mean recall and precision of the intersection of different EW sets. Since the Co-occurrence model has only 19 EW, we consider the intersection (which has 41 EW) of other three models' EW sets (see Table 2). It is shown that Our Model still has the highest mean recall and precision. From the two comparison experiments, it could be concluded that Our Model has optimal performance in both annotation accuracy and generality.

Table 2. The mean recall and precision comparison of three models on EW intersection set

Model	Translation	FACMRM	Our Model
Recall	0.37	0.44	0.60
Precision	0.22	0.34	0.36

When the recall is higher than 0.4 and the precision is higher than 0.14, the query word is regarded as a good word (GW). The Co-occurrence Model, the Translation Model, the FACMRM Model and Our Model have 6, 15, 32 and 57 GW, respectively. However, the precision usually decreases when the recall increases. To combine the recall and precision into a single efficient measure, we use F-measure [16]. Table 3 shows the comparison result of the four models on individual GW sets. Our Model has both the largest number of GW and the highest value of the F-measure.

Table 3. Performance comparison of four models on individual GW sets

Model	Co-occurrence	Translation	FACMRM	Our Model
GW number	6	15	32	57
Recall	0.79	0.63	0.59	0.70
Precision	0.26	0.28	0.39	0.36
F measure	0.39	0.39	0.47	0.48

5.3   Cross-Media Indexing Evaluation

We have built a small multi-modal dataset to evaluate the effectiveness of cross-media indexing in cross-media search [2]. The dataset describes five categories of animals including bird, dog, tiger, insect and monkey. Each category has 100 images, 50 videos and 50 audios. The media objects are collected from Corel image galleries and the Internet. Videos are first segmented into shots. Key frames are extracted from shots [17]. Images together with key frames of videos are automatically annotated using our annotation model. Audios are annotated manually. Cross-media indexing is built on annotation results. *Content Coverage* (CC) is used to evaluate the retrieval effectiveness when retrieving multi-modal data. The *Content Coverage* is defined as the number of retrieved relevant media objects divided by the number of retrieved media objects. In our experiment, a query is formulated by randomly selecting a sample media object from the dataset. For each query, the system returns 100 media objects as the results. We generate 5 random queries for each category and conduct 10 rounds of relevance feedback for each query. The average CC for five categories reaches 82.8%, which is a quite satisfying result.

6 Conclusions and Future Work

In this paper, we propose an automatic image annotation algorithm based on SVM and statistical learning. Cross-media indexing is then built upon the annotation result for multi-modal data. Comparison with other annotation models shows that our algorithm surpasses the others in the annotation accuracy and generality. Cross-media indexing constructed from annotation results can well support cross-media search in a multi- modal learning environment, which greatly improves web-based learning.

Future work can be focus on the following topics: (1) Exploit more effective visual features for images to improve the classification accuracy. (2) Automatically annotate videos and audios using their multi-modal property such as text located on video frames and transcribes from audio, etc. (3) Construct a large multi-model learning environment and test cross-media indexing more extensively.

Acknowledgements

This work is supported by the National Natural Science Foundation of China (No. 60272031), 973 Program (No. 2002CB312101), Technology Plan Program of Zhejiang Province (2003C21010), Doctorate Research Foundation of the State Education Commission of China (No. 20010335049), Zhejiang Provincial Natural Science Foundation of China (M603202)

References

1. M.Markkula, E.Sormunen, "End-user searching challenges indexing practices in the digital newspaper photo archive", *Information retrieval*, vol. 1, 259-285, 2000.
2. J.Yang, Y.T.Zhuang, Q.Li, "Search for multi-modality data in digital libraries", *Proceedings of The 2nd IEEE Pacific-Rim Conference on Multimedia*, Beijing, China, pp. 482-489, 2001.
3. Yueting Zhuang, Xiu Liu, "Multimedia Knowledge Exploitation for E-Learning: Some Enabling Techniques", *The 1st International Conference on Web-based Learning*, Hong Kong, China, pp. 411-422, 2002.
4. Yueting Zhuang, Yi Mao, Fei Wu, Yunhe Pan, "3D Model and Motion Retrieval: The Extended Dimensions for Web-Based Learning", *The 2nd International Conference on Web-based Learning*, Melbourne, Australia, pp. 230-240, 2003.
5. Y.Mori, H.Takahashi, R.Oka, "Image-to-word transformation based on dividing and vector quantizing images with words", *In MISRM'99 1st International Workshop on Multimedia Intelligent Storage and Retrieval Management*, 1999.
6. P.Duygulu, K.Barnard, N.de.Freitas, D. Forsyth, "Object recognition as machine translation: Learning a lexicon for a fixed image vocabulary", *In 7th European Conference on Computer Vision*, Copenhagen, Denmark pp.97-112, 2002.

7. J. Jeon, V. Lavrenko, R.Manmatha, "Automatic Image Annotation and Retrieval using Cross-Media Relevance Models", *Proceedings of The 26th Annual International ACM SIGIR Conference*, Toronto Canada, pp. 119-126, 2003.

8. Jia Li, James Z. Wang, "Automatic Linguistic Indexing of Pictures by a Statistical Modeling Approach", *IEEE Transactions on Pattern Analysis and Machine Intelligence*, vol. 25, no. 9, pp. 1075-1088, 2003.

9. Xiang Sean Zhou, T. S. Huang, "Unifying Keywords and Visual Contents in Image Retrieval", *IEEE Multimedia*, April-June Issue, 2002.

10. J.Shi, J.Malik, "Normalized cuts and image segmentation", *IEEE Transactions on Pattern Analysis and Machine Intelligence*, vol. 22, no. 8, pp.888-905, 2000.

11. C.J.C.Burges, "A tutorial on support vector machines for pattern recognition", *Data Mining, and Knowledge Discovery*, vol. 2, no 2, pp.121-167, 1998.

12. C.-W. Hsu, C.-J. Lin, "A comparison of methods for multi-class support vector machines", *IEEE Transactions on Neural Networks*, vol. 13, pp. 415-425, 2002.

13. J.Xu, R.Weischedel, C.Nguye, "Evaluating a probabilistic model for cross-lingual information retrieval", *Proceedings of the 24th Annual International ACM-SIGIR Conference*, New Orleans, LA USA, pp.105-110, 2001.

14. G.Salton, G.Buckley, "Introduction to Modern Information Retrieval", *McGraw-Hill Book Company*, New York, 1982.

15. C.-W. Hsu, C.-C. Chang, C.-J. Lin, "A practical guide to support vector classification", July 2003.

16. C.Van Rijsbergen, "Information retrieval", 2nd edition, Butterworth, London, 1979.

17. Yueting Zhuang, Yong Rui, Thomas S. Huang, Sharad Mehrotra, "Adaptive Key Frame Extraction Using Unsupervised Clustering", *Proceedings of International Conference on Image Processing*, pp. 886-870, Chicago, IL, October 1998.

Multimedia Distance Learning Application on Embedded End Device

Xin Chen, Yongqin Zeng, and Ningjiang Chen

Philips Research East Asia, 38 Floor, Tower 1, 218 Tian Mu Xi Road,
200070, Shanghai, P.R.China
{mylan.chen,yongqin.zeng,james.nj.chen}@Philips.com

Abstract. Distance Learning application is one of the most important and complicated applications of multimedia technologies. Distance learning end devices mainly consist of PC-like devices and embedded end devices, which target on two different groups of users respectively. This paper presents a multimedia distance learning application on an embedded end device, which is based on the Nexperia PNX1300 processor and characterized by low-cost, easy-to-use and stability. A demo system and several technical issues of this application are addressed. A comparison with other distance-learning solutions is also provided.

1 Introduction

There has been a great achievement on multimedia technologies in the past years. Killer applications are the driven force of the technologies towards success. Multimedia Distance Learning (DL) is one of the most important applications in China. Currently DL end devices are mainly PC-like devices including PC, EC (embedded computer), NC (Network Computer), and MMNC (Manageable Multimedia NC).

PC is the most popular device. It requires complex operation skill and has a higher cost than other devices. EC simplifies the hardware of the PC and uses low-power CPU. But its computation power is also less than the PC. EC usually includes an ASIC (Application Specific Integrated Circuit) chip to do the media processing. The idea of NC comes from the Java world. Since NC puts too much burden on the server, it seems not successful. MMNC takes part of the computation load of the server by computing locally. It is operated like a home appliance. But MMNC is not suitable for the distributed user group, since it requires a high bandwidth to access the data on the server.

Now in the market there is very few embedded end devices based on processors for consumer electronics (CE). These devices usually have low power consumption and low cost. The usage of them is very simple. Zero maintenance is possible. They are more like CE devices.

The devices listed above can be categorized into two groups: PC-like devices and embedded devices. They target on different groups of DL users. This paper explores the DL solution on the Nexperia PNX1300, a multimedia processor designed for embedded end devices [1]. This solution provides an easy-to-use, low-cost, and stable DL

W. Liu et al. (Eds.): ICWL 2004, LNCS 3143, pp. 263–270, 2004.

system. The software running on the PNX1300 follows the architecture that is designed for cross-platform development. A lot of available authoring tools can be used to design the courseware for this solution.

To further promote DL applications, it is very important to solve the issue of how to exchange the courseware among different systems. This will free the DL application from limited supports of content providers. General DL standards [2][3][4][5] defined by LTSC (IEEE Learning Technology Standards Committee) and CELTS (Chinese E-learning Technology Standard Committee) cover nearly all the existing specifications and standards of media content, including proprietary ones. It generates barriers for exchanging media content. An open specification for operational components and interoperability [4][5] is preferred to ensure a real interoperability of DL content. With an interface of the open standard for media content, courseware designers have a "many-to-many" relationship with DL systems, that is, designers can create courseware independent of DL systems and platforms while system operators have more resources of courseware. The DL solution in this paper supports the open standard.

This paper is organized as follows: Section 2 introduces a DL system and proposes open formats for DL content. Several technical issues of the DL application on the Nexperia PNX1300-based end device are explored in Section 3. Section 4 presents some results of using our system and draws the conclusions.

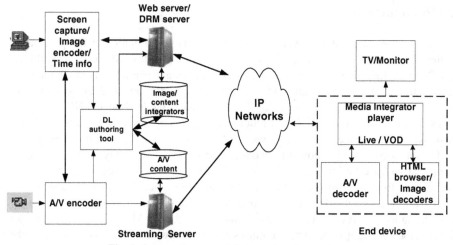

Fig. 1. System diagram of distance learning system

2 Distance Learning System

Figure 1 shows the system diagram of a web-based DL system. The content from the server side is usually composed of two parts: one is a teacher's audio/video stream encoded and stored on the streaming server, the other is the assistant teaching content stored on the web server. These two parts are synchronized and transmitted from the server side to the client side through an IP network. The DL authoring tool is used to generate the courseware automatically with the A/V from a camcorder and screenshots from a PC in a live broadcast and compile the courseware with existing content. At the client side, the content is decoded and rendered on a TV display or a PC monitor.

Other than an IP network, the content can be transmitted via other channels, such as IP over DVB-S/C/T. It can even be distributed through static storage such as optical discs. This system diagram doesn't include the transmission of the audio/video content from the client side to the teacher side or to other clients. This function can be added when the bandwidth of back channel is sufficient.

2.1 Formats Used in Application

The typical DL courseware consists of a teacher's audio/video stream, the assistant teaching content, and a multimedia integration application, which integrates and synchronizes the individual content. The formats of the teacher's A/V streams include MPEG2, ISMA MPEG4, and proprietary formats such as MOV of Apple, RM of RealNetworks and ASF of Microsoft. The assistant teaching content can be A/V streams, texts, images, HTML pages and Flash applications, etc.

To integrate the contents, HTML with JavaScript, SMIL (Synchronized Multimedia Integration Language) [6] and BIFS (BInary Format for Scenes, the system layer of MPEG4) [7] can be used. These techniques enable the synchronization and layout of all types of the content and the interactivity between the users and the courseware.

It can be seen that many choices exist when selecting the formats for a DL application. Content providers and system integrators will play a major role in formats decision. We strongly recommend open formats rather than proprietary ones, since it is important for building up an open DL platform and making the resource sharing among different systems possible. As an example, the formats used in our prototype are: ISMA MPEG4 for A/V, JPEG for images, and SMIL or HTML with JavaScript for integration [8]. Following this open standard of formats, content providers can offer courseware to many system integrators using different platforms, while system integrators can have many choices of courseware. Courseware compatible to the open standard can be shown both on a PC and on an embedded end device.

2.2 Comparison between the Embedded Solution and Other DL End Devices

A PC solution provides powerful functionalities. However, it has the drawbacks of high cost, high entrance requirements and instability. An embedded device solution is featured as low-cost, easy-to-use and easy-to-maintain but less computational power.

A comparison among different types of DL end devices is given in Table 1. Programmable embedded end devices have the advantages of upgradeable functionality and extended product life cycle, which ASIC-based devices do not have. Compared with PCs, embedded devices are cheaper and easier to use and maintain. But PCs have more computational power and developers than embedded devices.

Figure 2 compares the cost per unit (in USD) of different DL end devices. It shows that the embedded end device without HDD (Hard Disk) is cheaper than the PC-based devices. The embedded device is much cheaper than any other device in the models with HDD. In section 3, an example of a DL application on an embedded solution based on the Nexperia PNX1300 is explained in detail.

Table 1. Comparison among different end devices for distance learning

	Advantages	Disadvantages
PC	Flexible, rich computational power and support wide range of format	High cost, difficult to use and maintain for all users, short product life cycle (hardware)
Embedded (Programmable[a])	Upgradeable, flexible, low cost, easy to use and maintain, extended product life cycle	Smaller number of active developers
Embedded (ASIC)	Low cost, easy to use and maintain	Unupgradable, inflexible, support fixed format, short to moderate product life cycle

[a] The programmable embedded device uses a DSP processor, such as the Nexperia PNX1300, different from the ASIC.

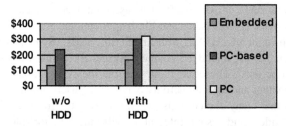

Fig. 2. Cost per unit (in USD) of different end devices for distance learning

3   DL Application on the Nexperia PNX1300-Based End Device

The Nexperia PNX1300 family is developed by Philips Semiconductors for consumer electronics. The PNX1300 is a powerful multimedia processor, which has a DSP CPU of VLIW (Very Long Instruction Word) architecture to accelerate the multimedia applications by scheduling five simultaneous RISC-like operations into one VLIW instruction. The PNX1300 processor also consists of many co-processing units to accelerate processing of audio, video, graphics, control and communication data-streams.

The PNX1300 processor utilizes the software architecture of TSA (TriMedia Software Architecture) / TSSA (TriMedia Streaming Software Architecture) [9] to enable interoperability and reusability of software components. It abstracts layers of hardware peripherals and operating system. Software developed under this architecture can be reused easily on different platforms of the Nexperia family, such as PNX1300, PNX8525, and PNX1500 [1]. The DL application introduced in this paper is programmed according to TSA/TSSA.

3.1   Software Architecture

Figure 3 shows the software architecture of a DL player in a block diagram. This architecture supports two applications, the HTML browser and the SMIL player, both of which can integrate different kinds of decoders including an MPEG4 decoder and an image decoder, etc. According to TSSA, an application consists of one application module and several TSSA modules. In Figure 3, the module at the top is the application module and the rest ones are the TSSA modules, which are grouped for different decoding tasks.

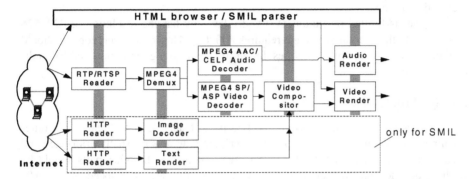

Fig. 3. Software architecture of the player on the Nexperia PNX1300-based end device

Normally every decoding task is started with an input module (e.g. a RTP/RTSP or HTTP reader), then followed by a decoding module (e.g. an Image or MPEG4 A/V decoder) and ended by an output module (e.g. an Audio or Video render). There are three tasks in Figure 3. The first task is MPEG4 decoding. The other two tasks, image decoding and text rendering, are only called by the SMIL player, since the HTML browser comprises these functions. The HTML browser/SMIL parser runs in the application module, which controls all the TSSA modules through control queues shown in the gray lines. The Video render module supports two layers blending, one for the HTML page rendering and the other for the video, image and graphics composing. All the input data comes from the network and the composite output goes to a TV display. Several issues are discussed in the following subsections, which are worth considering in the embedded implementation of a DL application.

3.2 Decoder

A DL application includes different kinds of content. It is inevitable to meet new media formats. Hence the software architecture of a DL player should support new codecs easily. Since the content is usually designed in the form of web pages (in HTML or XHTML etc.) or scripts (in SMIL etc.), different media types are distinguished by the MIME (Multipurpose Internet Mail Extensions) information within a web page or script. Based on the content awareness, the application module will create a new task to process the media data.

A followed issue is how to implement the new task with the codec modules. Fortunately, TSSA is modularized and dynamically configurable. If the new codecs are encapsulated into the TSSA modules, serializing required modules (with the help of a standardized interface in the TSSA) could create a new task in seconds.

3.3 Display

There are two limitations of a TV display for showing multimedia applications. One is screen flicking. Different from the progressive screen of a PC monitor, the TV display is normally interlaced. It leads to screen flicking for static content, such as text, which makes people dizzy. An anti-flicking component in software or hardware is desired to reduce the influence.

The other is limited resolution. A TV display only has the resolution of 720*576 (PAL), while the normal web page requires 800*600. Hence, the web content should be redesigned with an appropriate resolution, if shown to a great number of TV audience properly.

3.4 Synchronization

As mentioned above, synchronization between the teacher's A/V streams and other teaching content must be realized. The teacher's A/V streams is usually prioritized and used as the time base for the whole courseware. It means the other parts should be fetched, decoded and rendered in accordance with the decoding speed of the A/V stream. However, the assistant content could be delayed due to unexpected network congestion.

There are two methods to adjust the rendering time of other parts according to the decoding speed of A/V. One is to query at a certain interval, to get the SMPTE relative timestamp of the decoded A/V content, based on which the integrator decides whether to render the other parts. This method can be implemented with JavaScript in HTML pages, SMIL players, etc. However, it's less efficient because of the uninterrupted querying.

The other method is to trigger the decoding or rendering of other parts. For example, supposing an image needs to be shown when the teacher's A/V stream is played for 10 seconds, instead of querying what's the current time of the decoded A/V content by the integrator, the A/V decoder sends a notification when it decodes to 10 seconds, to the HTML browser or the SMIL player, which will process the notification as defined. Obviously this method is more effective. This method has been implemented by some proprietary technologies such as WMT of Microsoft and RM of RealNetworks, by adding an event stream, which is a text of the required operation, to the binary file of encoded A/V.

A general implementation is to define an object for an event stream, which describes the operation to other parts of the courseware. This event stream is generated at the server side and packed with the A/V package of a corresponding time. When the integrator or synchronizer at the client side receives this package, the event stream is processed directly. This ensures that the binary file of an encoded A/V stream can remain unchanged. Nevertheless, a packaging module and an unpacking module will need to be added to the server and the client, respectively.

3.5 Indexing

When audiences view the DL content in VOD (Video On Demand) mode, they either watch it from the beginning to the end or watch selectively the interested chapters via an index. Sometimes the content includes sub-clips from several video streams. Therefore, the application is expected to be able to play the video streams from any given position. The issue is how to inform the codecs about where to start or stop.

On the Windows platform, the ActiveX control technology is utilized to inform the codecs through control parameters in scripts. However, there is no such a similar technology for an embedded system. One solution is to utilize the CGI-like extension in the HTML language. For example, an extended URL like *rtsp://www.video.com/demo.mp4&x.y.w.h.start-time* can be used to describe the start time (start-time), screen position ((x, y) is the coordinate of left-top point) and screen size (w is the width and h is the height) of an MPEG4 stream. The information after the symbol "&" is parsed by the embedded application but ignored by the PC application.

4   Results and Conclusions

A demo DL application is implemented on a PNX1300 STB (Set Top Box)[10]. Figure 4 shows a screenshot of a piece of courseware. A commercial authoring tool, sofTV.Presenter [11], is used to create the courseware. Learners need only use a remote controller to navigate the courseware. Software can be upgraded by online updating the firmware of the STB. Compared with another demo application running on an embedded computer, the application on the STB is more stable. The same courseware following the open standard of formats (see Section 2.1) can be shown both on the PC and on the STB without modification.

In summary, a DL application on an embedded device was investigated in this paper. Several technical issues were discussed. Further exploration of interactive functionalities is expected to support advanced DL applications. Open formats of the DL content are strongly recommended to enable a rapid growth of DL applications. With its very low cost and zero maintenance, the embedded end device based on the PNX1300 is very suitable for widely deployment, such as in western villages in China.

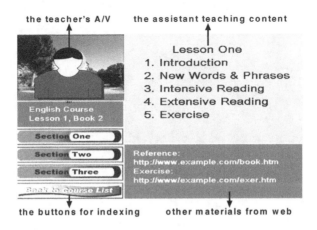

Fig. 4. A screenshot of courseware

References

1. Philips Semiconductors: Nexperia -- Media Processing,
   http://www.semiconductors.philips.com/products/nexperia/media_processing/index.html.
   Philips Semiconductors
2. IEEE LTSC P1484.18: Draft Standard for Learning Technology, Platform and Media Profiles. LTSC (2001)
3. CELTSC-17.1 (CD1.6): Platform and Media Profiles. CELTSC (2002)
4. IEEE LTSC P1484.1: Draft Standard for Learning Technology, Architecture and Reference Model. LTSC (2001)
5. CELTSC-1.1 (CD1.6): Architecture and Reference Model. CELTSC (2002)
6. Jeff Ayars et al.: SMIL 2.0 Specification, W3C Recommendation. W3C (2001)
7. Ningjiang Chen and Yongqin Zeng: Embedded Streaming Player Based on MPEG4-BIFS Interactive Technology. TV Engineering 11 (2003)
8. Yongqin Zeng, Ningjiang Chen, and Xin Chen: Interactive Streaming Multimedia with Scalable Video Streams. ISBT (2003)
9. TriMedia Technologies: TriMedia SDE v2.2 Document. TriMedia Technologies Inc. (2000)
10. Cathay Roxus: SBA2000 CE User Manual. Cathay Roxus (2003)
11. SofTV.net: sofTV.Presenter Technical Guide, version 2.3. SoftTV.net,
    http://www.softv.net (2003)

Web-Based Collaborative Learning System Design for Navigation Education and Training

Cui Xie, Yicheng Jin, Xiuwen Liu, and Yong Yin

Nautical Science and Technology Institute, Dalian Maritime University, Dalian, China
xiecuidlmu@sohu.com
{jycdmu,liuxw}@dlmu.edu.cn
bushyin_dmu@263.net

Abstract. Modeling and system design for a web-based collaborative learning and training system for navigation education and training (NAVIGATION – WCLS) was presented in this paper. The system framework design is based on collaborative learning, visual learning ideas, simulation technology and our newly developed campus-based desktop multifunctional navigation teaching system. The NAVIGATION -WCLS aims to facilitate learning navigation theory and technology anywhere and anytime.

1 Introduction

Main objective of navigation education and training is to foster learners to become qualified and competent for their future work in the maritime industry both afloat and ashore. This requires learners must master basic navigation theory and navigation technology proficiently. However, learners often experience difficulties in learning navigation course, especially in ship maneuvering and collision avoidance curriculum, because they must fully understand maneuvering concepts and principles that are sometimes impossible to master only when they learn by personal experience. Though a full functional marine simulator is the most effective method available for navigation training not only because they can simulate the operational characteristics of many types of ships, but also because they may replicate real world scenarios, we also have to recognize that this is not practical or feasible in all cases. Since the limited accessibility, immobility, the long development cycle, limited application life, expensive cost and system maintenance of the full mission marine simulator, it can not ensure that all seafarers or students have enough time to go into training. In addition, while the university thrives on improved enrollment, it faces the physical limitations of learning environment for curriculum practice. To solve the Problem, based on our finished distributed marine simulation system (V.Dragon 2000)[1] and our newly developed campus-based desktop multifunctional navigation teaching system (see Fig 1), now Dalian Maritime University (DMU) starts developing a web-based learning system fully combining visual learning, collaborative learning, and simulation-based learning strategies to enhance navigation education and training at all levels.

The Web environment offers significant benefits to the developers of collaborative systems. The Key features of Internet-based learning environments [2] include: interaction, global accessibility, availability of online resources, learner-controlled pace, convenience, nondiscriminatory, cost effective, collaborative learning, online evaluations and etc. All these properties make the Web a powerful platform for building

W. Liu et al. (Eds.): ICWL 2004, LNCS 3143, pp. 271–276, 2004.

collaborative applications. Web-based collaborative learning system can be divided into two categories: one is asynchronous system, such as CSILE/Knowledge, Learning Space, WebBoard, and WebCT; the other is synchronous system including Conference MOOS, WebChat Broadcasting System, and Microsoft Netmeeting[3]. Professor Peter Muirhead proposes an idea that student can access online simulation training from anywhere and anytime, not only when on land, but from a ship at sea[4]. InfoWERK began to develop e-learning based marine training courses programs[5]. Naval Postgraduate School (NPS) is conducting research and development of next generation web-based 3D graphics authoring tools to enable rapid development and distribution of 3D content over the World Wide Web[6](Figure 2 depicts the 3D visualization of an AT/FP Scene). NAVIGATION –WCLS will provide an efficient and flexible collaborative learning environment to help learners to learn the navigation theory and perform some training interactively without the restrictions of location or time.

Fig. 1. The primary own-ship bridge of marine simulator (left), multifunctional navigation teaching lab (middle) and multifunctional navigation teaching unit (right)

Fig. 2. An X3D scene from the AT/FP scenario rendered in the NPSNET-V framework

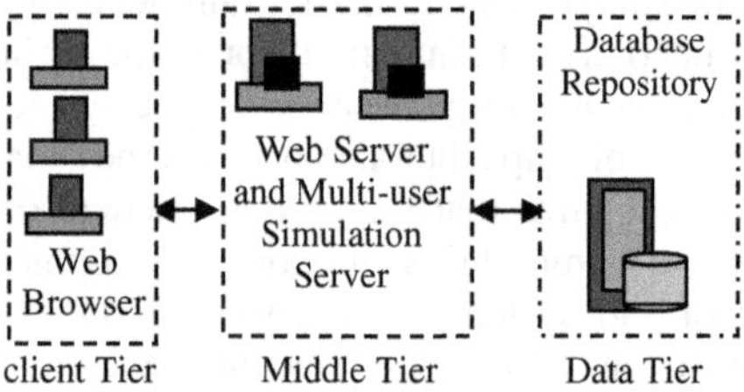

Fig. 3. A three-tier architecture of NAVIGATION–WCLS

2 Overall System Architecture

The governing design goal is to create a layered, loosely coupled object-oriented framework that is easily extensible and modifiable. A three-tier architecture is employed in the development of NAVIGATION -WCLS (Fig. 3), which contains an online database server, a Web server with a multi-user simulation server capability for basic theory learning and marine simulation training, and clients' browsers. Changeable information is managed by an online database management system. The Web server works as middleware to take data from clients and save the data in the database. It also retrieves data from the database and presents it to clients. Static information, which is used for the web site, such as description of learning or training topics, are stored directly on the Web server. The multi-user simulation server is independent from the Web server, which executes the simulation task and takes care of the communication between clients especially important for real-time marine simulation training.

3 NAVIGATION-WCLS Modeling

3.1 The Objective of NAVIGATION-WCLS

The main objective of NAVIGATION -WCLS is to design and implement a flexible and integrated web-based collaborative learning system to facilitate navigation education and training, The NAVIGATION -WCLS focuses on interaction, visualization, collaborative learning, and encouraging emergence decision-making with teamwork. Interaction is achieved by developing multiple multimedia modules covering numerous training topics and collaborative tools. Visualization and collaboration are necessary for creating a positive atmosphere, aiding retention and stimulating learners' interests for navigation learning and training. NAVIGATION-WCLS will provide a strong visual reinforcement and greatly enhance learners' learning experience.

3.2 Strategies and Principles of Systematic Design

Since the NAVIGATION –WCLS is used for supporting navigation education and training, not only design strategies according to [7] but also current standards (including IMO, STCW 1995, SOLAS and etc.) should be considered. Also the Department of Defense Advanced Distributive Learning [8] ideas should be referenced. The main strategies are as follows:

Scalability: The NAVIGATION –WCLS must support dynamic changes of the system scales. It should provide flexible configuration and strong adaptability for various navigation learning or training topics. It should use object-oriented entity presentation method and unified interface criterion to construct system components and facilitate adding new applications.

Hiberarchy: This includes the hiberarchy of software architecture and the whole learning process management. Fine hiberarchy will simplify the system development cycle, reinforce the system maintenance and robustness. Fine hiberarchy is the foundation of the system interactivity, scalability and resource reusability.

Easy Management and Maintenance: Since the NAVIGATION –WCLS is a hiberarchy system composed of many distributed subsystems with interrelation and interaction, which requires proper subsystems integration solution and efficient data storage mechanism. In order to get the coherence presentation of the whole system, we should adopt the multi-dimensional storage format of database, the multi-user inquiry interface and fast indices etc. Expect for the system openness, easy accessibility and efficient assessment method, all the navigation learning and training contents should be rich and tailorable to one's individual will.

3.3 Framework Modeling

The NAVIGATION -WCLS is composed of seven parts – 3D virtual ocean world, Internet-based multimedia modules, database module, collaborative learning and training module (including learner and tutor interface, collaborative learning tools), evaluation module, learner module and teacher module. The main modules are as follows:

Three-Dimensional Virtual Ocean World: The NAVIGATION -WCLS includes a Web-based 3D virtual world. Learners are allowed to perform ship maneuvering, collision avoidance and other navigation training in the 3D virtual ocean world, which including 3D ship models, dynamic ocean surface, docks, ports, building, and etc. Three-dimensional visualization is hard to realize for large-scale scene over the Internet because of heterogeneous computer systems and the bandwidth of the network. But due to the introduction of Virtual Reality Modeling Language (VRML) and its successor, the Extensible 3D (X3D) and other effective simplifying algorithm for 3D models, it has become possible to distribute 3D content over the World Wide Web.

Multimedia Module: Multimedia modules are the key elements of NAVIGATION - WCLS including two sections. One is a curriculum information resource part that explains some specific navigation curriculum topic and the other is a simulation tool that is designed to allow the learner to conduct some marine trainings. Usually, the learner is expected to study the curriculum knowledge and related materials carefully before they start using the simulation since the simulation assumes that the learner has a basic knowledge of the particular topic. The learner can choose any kind of simulation subject, modify multiple valid parameters at one time and manipulate a simulated own-ship across the defined seaway. The results can be obtained through evaluation module and then presented by use of animations, graphics, and tables. The collaborative group training module is another example that allows the learner to conduct collision avoidance exercise or ship maneuvering in a shared virtual ocean world in different locations.

Database Management: The NAVIGATION -WCLS uses multiple databases to manage all static and changeable data. The changeable data include data of learner accounts, data of team accounts, and data of training process and results. To use the NAVIGATION–WCLS, each learner must provide necessary information to create a learner account. If one's account has been created before, it will be used to search the learning history records from learner models database, If one's account cannot be found in learner records database, a new account number will be appended in the learner records database when learner submitted his register form, which is used to form learner model. After creating an account in the database, the learner can log into the NAVIGATION–WCLS, Based on one's knowledge background, the NAVIGATION–WCLS can adaptively provide suggested proper learning or training exercise for learner. Learner can select some learning subject or explore the learning or training modules to do some interested exercises under 3D virtual world or learn some basic navigation theory. Learner's learning history records or his new learning records can be used to form learner model. In order to conduct collaborative training, a shared team account must be created in the database. The team members then can log in the team account and use the same training module to conduct group ship maneuvering exercise such as collision avoidance. Real-time information sharing and real-time manipulation of own-ships can be implemented.

Collaborative Learning and Training Module: The Collaborative learning and training module is the core part to implement the learning of navigation curriculum and the marine training. It implies the interaction with other learners or the teachers by collaborative learning tools: Asynchronous learning tools includes email, presentation tools, bulletin boards, search engine, and etc; Synchronous learning tools includes internet phone, chat room, video conference, seminar room, and etc. These learning tools can be used to facilitate and to enhance learner's learning performance. This module comprised of a client-side learning application, and a server-side multi-user-supporting simulation application. The client-side application performs the curriculum learning or the ship maneuvering training, and the server-side application takes care of communication, simulation and coordination. Computer networking and event process are the foundation of this module. Under the help of collaborative learning tools, an interactive and collaborative learning environment will be constructed to support the basic navigation theory learning and the navigation training over the WWW.

Teacher Module: Teacher in NAVIGATION -WCLS can assess how learners are performing in real time and, when appropriate, prod you to act, suggest alternatives, provide useful information and other assistance similar with face-to-face collaborative learning environment include questioning, task constructing, coaching, modeling, pushing learners to articulate ideas and explore new avenues, and occasional and timely direct instruction. It is also planned that an intelligent teacher will be assigned to every registered learner.

Evaluation Module: Evaluation in NAVIGATION -WCLS is more concerned collaborative learning outcomes and training process. Evaluation is conducted for learning and training respectively. Domain competence is more than domain knowledge, it also comprises a whole range of skills for navigation. Skills based competence is vital, especially the analysis, interpretation, decision-making and the practice experience. Learners training process is recorded in the database, which can be download to local client-side for replay. At the same time, the training results can also be used for skill evaluation by teachers or group members or through automatic evaluation function. Relative evaluation methods on technical progress of learners in ship handling can be found in [9][10].

4   Conclusion and Further Research

In this paper we have presented a design of NAVIGATION –WCLS, which provides a unique set of learning and training subjects accessed easily anywhere and anytime through an Internet browser. NAVIGATION -WCLS embodies the most effective training approach "learn by doing"[11] and collaborative learning strategies [2].

Based on reliable learning theoretical foundation, the system is in the design and analysis phase presently. There are a lot of further works will be done, for example, how to realize systematic framework based on programming, how to ensure the real-time ability and the safety, etc. Since a good navigation learning system requires skillful design more than it requires massive amounts of programming and intricate graphics, building effective web-based collaborative learning system requires careful design and extensive refinement. After the first functional version is up and running, it will be directly used by the students to gather evaluation and feedback information to aid in further development of the system.

References

1. Yin Yong, Ren Hong-xiang, Jin Yi-cheng, Sun Teng-da.: Graphic Technology of Distributed Marine Simulation System-V.Dragon (2000). Journal of System Simulation, Vol.14 No.5 (2002) 617-619
2. Sadhana Puntambekar: An integrated approach to individual and collaborative learning in a web-based learning environment. In Proceedings of the Computer Support for Collaborative Learning (CSCL) 1999 Conference, Dec. PP12-15, (1999)
3. Zhao Jianhua, Li Kedong and Kanji Akahori , Modeling and System Design for Web-Based Collaborative Learning. http://www.eecs.kumamoto-u.ac.jp/ITHET01/proc/084.pdf
4. Muirhead, P.:Broadband Technology and marine Simulation: Why Not Simulator Training Anywhere,Anytime?. Vol.1.International Conference on Marine Simulation and Ship Maneuverability (MARSIM'03) conference proceedings, Japan, (2003), RA-1-1 – RA-1-8
5. Web-based training by infoWERK Developing skills for the future. http://www.infowerk.co.at/spring02/media/infobroschure.pdf
6. Web-Based 3D Technology for Scenario Authoring and Visualization. http://web.nps.navy.mil/~brutzman/Savage/toc.html
7. McConnell, D.: Implementing Computer Supported Cooperative Learning. London, (2000).
8. Morris, J.J., Weisenford, J.,and Boland, W.: Information Technology Advances will Support advanced distributed learning anytime and anywhere. proceedings of the Interservice/Industry Training, Simulation, and Education Conference (II/ITSEC), Orlando, FL, (1999)
9. Kinzo INOUE, Rong MA, Hideo USUI, Cemi YURTOREN.: A Method of Quantitatively Evaluationg on Technical Progress of Students in Ship Handing Simulator Training. Vol.1.International Conference on Marine Simulation and Ship Maneuverability (MARSIM'03) conference proceedings, Japan, (2003) RA-6-1 – RA-6-6
10. Baldauf, M., Benedict, K., Felsenstein, C., Kirchhoff, M.: Computer-based Support for the Evaluation of Ship Handling Exercise Results. Vol.1. International Conference on Marine Simulation and Ship Maneuverability (MARSIM'03) conference proceedings, (2003) RA-5-1 – RA-5-10
11. Kolb, D.: Experiential learning: Experience as the source of learning and development. Englewood Cliffs, NJ: Prentice-Hall. (1984).

Aphasics' Communities Learning on the Web

Marc Spaniol[1,2], Ralf Klamma[1,2], Luise Springer[1,3], and Matthias Jarke[1,2,4]

[1] Forschungskolleg "Medien und kulturelle Kommunikation", Universität zu Köln,
Bernhard-Feilchenfeld-Str. 11, D-50969, Germany
[2] RWTH Aachen, Informatik V, Ahornstr. 55, D-52056 Aachen, Germany
{mspaniol,klamma}@cs.rwth-aachen.de
[3] Universitätsklinikum Aachen, Lehranstalt für Logopädie, Pauwelstr. 30, D-52074
Aachen, Germany
lspringer@ukaachen.de
[4] Fraunhofer FIT, Schloss Birlinghoven, D-53754 Sankt Augustin, Germany
jarke@fit.fraunhofer.de

Abstract. Barrier free learning on the web is one of the greatest challenges for computer science in the future. While the growth of the internet was exponential in the last years, still many communities don't benefit from web technology for their learning issues due to improper tools and constricted communication processes. These problems increase when developing applications for communities of people with special needs. In this paper we present the case study of a cooperative web-learning environment called SOCRATES to overcome difficulties in new media usage. It supports a learning community comprising patients suffering from aphasia (aphasics), therapists, researchers on linguistics, and system developers. Aphasics using SOCRATES are now able to communicate freely among others without having to be afraid that they might get lost in rapid conversation and are now able to meet others over spatial distances while protecting their privacy in an insular virtual community.

1 Introduction

Aphasics suffer from a difficulty of language because of a brain injury, called aphasia, which affects one or more aspects of the complex process of comprehending and formulating verbal messages resulting from newly acquired desease of the central nervous system [Dama81]. Aphasia is the greek word for "without speech", what's only partially correct, since the brain injury might affect speech, understanding, reading, and writing in different degrees. Due to the degree and location of the brain injury, those affects are more or less serious. Aphasics are not mentally handicaped. They can think logically and are able to understand and interpret situations correctly. Since the financial support for therapies is limited both in amount and time, aphasics are organizing themselves in self-help groups and meet in regional centers. Nevertheless, meetings can be organized only several times a year because transportation costs are too high. So, there is a need for additional communication and web-based learning tools. Hence, access to web technologies and online learning has been recognized as an issue of increasing

W. Liu et al. (Eds.): ICWL 2004, LNCS 3143, pp. 277–285, 2004.

importance for the HCI community and the European Community [MKZa02]. Recent research in this area focuses mainly on individuals. So, Holzinger's system offers input assistance by developing touch pads for handicapped or elderly people [Holz02]. Other approaches aim at voice recognition, facing problems due to misrecognition depending on the pronounciation [PVTO02]. Similarly, predictive systems as well as auditive user interfaces, up to now lack reliability in recognition [LaMu02,WPTC02]. Alternatively, Chene and Hoel try to transform the content in their system to increase readibility [ChHo02], but lack usability in interactive systems due to missing input options. However, most of the systems are bound to costly and sensitive equipment neglecting the fact that many communication barriers are best overcome in cooperative learning communities by bringing together end-users, therapists, researchers, and developers.

In this paper we present and discuss our approach in overcoming difficulties in conversations based on settings in digital media. The rest of the paper is organized as follows: In the next section we describe learning and collaboration processes of aphasics' communities and their difficulties in digital media usage. Then we'll describe SOCRATES (Simulation of Oral Communication, Research, Analysis and Transcription Engineering System) as an approach to (re-) combine digital media to foster collaboration in learning communities of aphasics. The paper closes with a summary and an outlook on further research.

2   Learning Processes in Aphasics' Communities

Learning is a social system within the communities of practice [Weng98] and needs a tight interplay between communicative acts and the organization of information. Regarding this, the organization of knowledge is to be found as a structuring element, whereas communicative acts often have discursive nature. Empirical studies [DaLe86,GrKl00] show that even the mental maps of people strongly depend on the media through which they communicate effectively. Bringing together those parts that contradict each other in principle appears to be a challenge for the recombination of digital media in personalized community software. Nevertheless, the problem is that one can't develop concepts separately from the media that are used for communication, especially in barrier free collaboration among learners. Similar to the assumptions by [PLHa02], the knowledge building process can be seen as a combination of Nonaka and Takeuchi's thesis [NoTa95] with the aspects of difficulty triggered knowledge creation (Engeström) [Enge87] and knowledge building communities (Bereiter) [ScBe94].

Figure 1 shows a modification of Nonaka and Takeuchi's cycle of knowledge creation adapted to the requirements of community-oriented learning, showing the continuous spiral of knowledge creation with the four modes of knowledge conversion: socialization, externalization, combination, and internalization. Implicit knowledge is personal knowledge that is hard to formalize or communicate to others. Explicit knowledge is formal knowledge that is easy to transmit between individuals and groups. In this model implicit and explicit knowledges are both important for further knowledge creation by transforming implicit knowl-

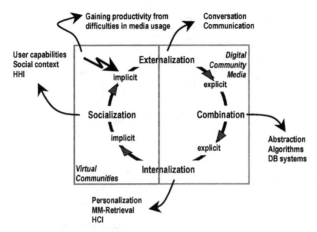

Fig. 1. Communication and learning in aphasics' communities adapted from [NoTa95]

edge into explicit and vice versa, dividing up the process in two sections. On the left hand side, we concentrate on *virtual communities* representing information that is mostly transferred by human human interaction (HHI). *Socialization* means implicit information in the medium man based on the social context. In aphasics' communities, the transfer of implicit knowledge into explicit knowledge is most likely to be affected by difficulties, since user's often have problems in *externalizing* their opinion due to word finding and spelling problems. Consequently, this problem has to be solved and it is up to us to gain productivity from the difficulties, by initiating monitored repair processes in SOCRATES. For therapists and researchers knowledge within the community is *externalized* when conversation protocols are stored in a repository, thus making difficulties in communication accessible for further evaluation. On the right hand side, *digital community* media are located representing structured and categorized information that has been made explicit. *Combinational* operations include storage, transcription, and retrieval of conversation protocols. That is the cutting edge where virtual communities and digital community media meet. Learning as observed by *internalization* has different meanings for the different types of community members. For the patients it is a self or community initiated therapeutical mean possibly amplified by improved human-computer interaction. Therapists gain new therapy concepts by analyzing the transcripts and researchers new insights into the mechanisms of language production. Last but not least, SOCRATES developers learn from the feedback given by the other groups.

3   SOCRATES

Communication difficulties are a common fact in our daily life. They are not only limited to the conversation itself, but are also inherent to the medium. When designing community software, it is necessary to analyze the nature of a difficulty

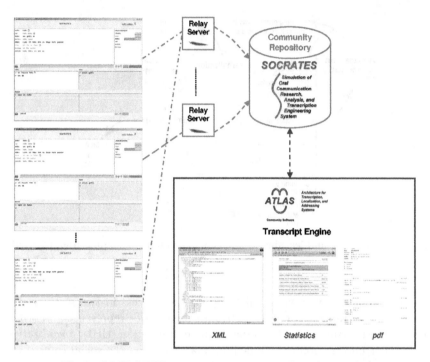

Fig. 2. SOCRATES community support and analysis software

in order to adjust the repair strategies. With respect to aphasics' communities, we are trying to find media mixes that increase their benefits by simultaneously reducing their deficits. SOCRATES combines digital media to make difficulties in single media usage less visible. On the one hand we are creating a meeting point for those people and on the other hand the system can also be used by therapists and researchers for a further analysis on conversation structures. Research in oral aphasics' communities is still in its infancy and this is even more true for simulated orality like in chat boards. For linguistic research and therapy development one of the most interesting features is automatic extraction of time delays between pressed keys because this might indicate the grade of disability.

Figure 2 gives an overview on the SOCRATES community system. On the left hand side are the screendumps of the Java client applets communicating via Apache relay servers. The relay servers are used to coordinate conversations and to enrich them with additional metadata, which is necessary for further computation. In the case of SOCRATES, time delays between letters to be spelled are especially captured. The digital community media are being captured in XML trace files to be placed in the conversation repository. The underlying community software architecture ATLAS (Architecture for Transcription, Localization and Addressing Systems) is a community management system especially handling digital multimedia created by communities using networked information systems [SKJa03]. To evaluate the dialogs, transcripts and statistics are being generated from the XML files, e.g. in pdf format. SOCRATES is similar to Internet Relay Chat (IRC) [OiRe93], which offers a good possibility for a real-time text-based communication in communities. An IRC Server relays all incomming messages to the other participants taking part in the same conversation. Server code has been added to our chat application that is partially located on the relay server. The SOCRATES core is similar to other user interface applications in the IRC area, but adapted for people with concentration deficits. Triggered by user interaction the system creates certain messages that are passed to a dispatcher. The dispatcher invokes a callback function, which processes the message and performs corresponding actions, like creating, cancelling or changing of files.

The SOCRATES clients are thin and only used for presentation and filtering of events generated by the human computer interaction. In case of events requiring the execution of some server code it is being sent to the relay server. The processing of such messages on the server side is similar to what was explained in the section above. The type of the message is checked and the corresponding functions are called and actions are performed if needed. Message processing between client and server is performed asynchronously. This means that client is not blocked after having sent a message but is able to perform other actions like receive other messages as a result of actions of the other users. In addition, the client may discard messages due to a new state of the system. Access to SOCRATES is granted by a login procedure making the system exclusive to those persons suffering from aphasia, their therapists and researchers. So, members are protected from people who might molest or amuse about the aphasic's stories. Even more, the system becomes somewhat unique, since only those are allowed to participate who share a common value. To provide that, passwords are only given to those persons that are active in or known to self-help groups.

3.1   Combining Media for Aphasics' Web-Based Learning

Figure 3 shows a multi-user talk in the SOCRATES Java applet. Its design is similar to convential chat boards, but it allows aphasics to initiate a decoupled conversation of a up to four people in case they encouter difficulties to participate in the chat-board communication. Our approach tries to overcome the word finding and spelling problems of aphasics by invoking the community in their learning process. This process is initiated by an aphasic pushing the button on the right hand side of the applet indicating the interest in starting a "Talkrunde" (eng. multi-user talk). After launching a multi-user talk a screen at the bottom of the Java client applet is highlighted. This screen offers a synchronous communication of up to four persons similar to a face to face talk. In the meantime, all other chatters are informed of the newly initiated multi-user talk by displaying a designated sign behind the aphasic's name. Those chatters willing to join the conversation click on the sign to participate. Due to the synchronousity in a multi-user talk the others are now aware of any difficulties in the spelling process and may help to find the right words by proposing them. The activation of a SOCRATES multi-user talk is described in detail in table 1.

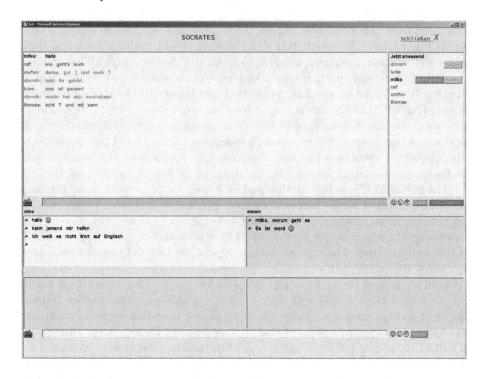

Fig. 3. SOCRATES: Combining chat and multi-user talk (in German)

3.2 Analyzing Community Learning in SOCRATES

Data in SOCRATES is based on XML files capturing all necessary information to cover the context of conversation, which are participants, global time, delays and the conversation itself. By keeping compatibility to XML SOCRATES data can be easily interpreted by applications compliant to the standard. Even more, automatic processing of the files is backed by their hierarchical structure. Hence, queries can be used to access selected elements of a document via XPath/XQuery [BBC*02]. Conversations in SOCRATES can be automatically converted into different output media allowing the therapists to adapt their therapy to the user's individual needs. For a better traceability of the conversation process, the transcripts contain additional information about the spelling process, like delays and repairs. The transcripts are an extension of the analysis standard in linguistics (GAT) [Selt98] for written text pool [Spri04]. An example of an automatically generated transcript from a SOCRATES XML file is shown in figure 4. Every interaction with our chat system is contained in the transcript as well as the delays while typing. In addition, therapists and researchers can replay the whole conversation based on the information contained in the SOCRATES XML transcript. Hence, they can now seek for recurring patterns of spelling problems and monitor the learning process of individuals and their community via a web-form displaying statistical data.

Table 1. SOCRATES activation protocol

1a)	An user pushes the "Gesprächsrunde" (eng. multi-user talk) button.
2a)	The callback function is called by the GUI.
3a)	A new message is prepared and being sent to the relay server.
4a)	The message is received by reading thread and enqueued for further processing.
5a)	A processing thread dequeues the message and passes to the dispatcher.
6a)	The dispatcher checks the type of the message and calls the suitable callback function.
7a)	A new conversation is being created and the user is added as a participant, which means that corresponding records are created in the database.
8a)	A message is sent that contains information on a newly created multi-user talk.
8b)	To all other participants currently active on the chat board a message is sent that a multi-user talk has been started.
9ab)	The client receives the message and processes it.
10a)	The function tries to connect the user to this conversation.
10b)	All other users see the newly started multi-user talk by highliting a corresponding sign.
11a)	If the connection is successful the fields at the bottom of the chat applet get visible and the multi-user talk starts.
12b)	Joining the multi-user talk by others is done by clicking the designated sign.
13b)	The steps 2a)-6a) are executed for users joining the multi-user talk.
14b)	The function tries to add the user to this conversation, since it is limited to up to four participants. If this was successful the last two steps are executed.
15b)	A message is sent to the client containing all relevant information (IDs, port, etc.).
16b)	The last steps are the same as 9a)-11a) but now on helper's side.

Legend:
 a): indicates actions of the user initiating a multi-user talk
 b): indicates actions of users joining the multi-user talk

4   Conclusions and Outlook

In this paper we presented our collaborative learning environment SOCRATES for aphasics' communities. Learning experiences are very promising as one of the participants suffering mild aphasia and severe speech apraxia wrote [Gref04]: "With chat we are all on the same level, and the thing that's important in my eyes is that we are amongst ourselves and understanding each other. [...] As person suffering speech apraxia it's good for me to be able to concentrate on writing and not pronunciation. A chatting side effect is that to keep up you have to be able to read fast. Initially, i had a lot of problems with that, but now it's more or less OK. That's why I think this kind of 'therapy' is a very good idea."

In SOCRATES, the emerging problems of a single usage of digital media - the interrupts based on word finding processes of aphasics - can be made visible and thereby repaired. By making their actions transparent, community members are addressed to participate and collaborate. By coupling the medium of a chat and a talk it becomes possible to make difficulties visible. Even more, tracing of conversations allows to analyze sessions and to customize users' therapies. Due to the options given by the XML based trace-file, therapists can select from versatile media for further analysis. In addition to statistics and replays of face to face talks, SOCRATES offers transcripts in XML, PDF and RTF format. By relying on XML as interchange format we keep flexibility for further developments. The next step will be to develop adaptive user interfaces to make the content presentation dependent on predefined settings and user's needs. Hence, we are researching on optimizing the comfort in human-computer interaction. Hence, we have started joint research projects at our collaborative research center to

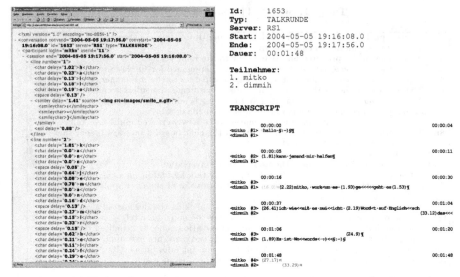

Fig. 4. SOCRATES conversation XML file and its pdf transcript(in German)

improve addressing and personalization in our community software [SKJa03]. We hope to detect a model core common to learning processes, which can be extended to fulfill specific requirements in versatile area of applications.

Acknowledgements

This work was supported by German National Science Foundation (DFG) within the collaborative research centers SFB/FK 427 "Media and cultural communication", SFB 476 "IMPROVE", and by the 6th Framework IST programme of the EC through the Network of Excellence in Professional Learning (PROLEARN) IST-2003-507310. We'd like to thank our colleagues for the inspiring discussions.

References

[BBC*02] Berglund, A. et al.: XML Path Language (XPath) 2.0. *http://www.w3.org/TR/xpath20/* (2002).

[ChHo02] Chene, D., Hoel, M.: Web site accessibility auditing tool for visually deficient persons OCAWA. *Miesenberger, K., Klaus, J., and Zagler, W. (eds.): Proceedings of ICCHP 2002, Linz, Austria* (2002), pp. 27 - 32.

[DaLe86] Daft, R. L., Lengel, R. H.: Organizational Information Requirements, Media Richness and Structural Design. *Management Science, 32, 5* (1986), pp. 554 - 571.

[Dama81] Damasio, A. R.: The Nature of Aphasia: Signs and Syndromes. *Sarno, M. T. (ed.): Acquired Aphasia, New York, Academic Press* (1981), pp. 51 - 64.

[Enge87] Engeström, Y.: Learning by expanding. *Orienta-Konsultit Oy, Helsinki* (1987).

[Gref04] Grefe, U.: 3 + 4 = 8 Vergraben und verschüttet sind meine Worte! 2nd edition, Schulz-Kirchner-Verlag, Idstein (2004) (in German) in print.

[GrKl00] Grote, K., Klamma, R.: Media and Semantic Relations. Comparison of Individual and Organizational Knowledge Structures. Dagstuhl Seminar "Knowledge Management. An Interdisciplinary Approach", Schloss Dagstuhl, Germany, July 9-14 (2000).

[Holz02] Holzinger, A.: User-centered interface design for disabled and elderly people: First experiences with designing a patient communication system (PACOSY). Miesenberger, K., Klaus, J., and Zagler, W. (eds.): Proceedings of ICCHP 2002, Linz, Austria (2002), pp. 33 - 41.

[LaMu02] Lauruska, V., Musteikis, T.: Developing of predictive communication system for the physically disabled people. Miesenberger, K., Klaus, J., and Zagler, W. (eds.): Proceedings of ICCHP 2002, Linz, Austria (2002), pp. 267 - 270.

[MKZa02] Miesenberger, K., Klaus, J., Zagler, W. (eds.): Proceedings of the 8th International Conference on Computer Helping People with Special Needs. ICCHP 2002, Linz, Austria, July 15-20 (2002).

[NoTa95] Nonaka, I., Takeuchi, H.: The Knowledge-creating Company. Oxford University Press, Oxford (1995).

[OiRe93] Oikarinen, J., Reed., D.: RFC1459 - Internet Relay Chat Protocol (1993).

[PLHa02] Paavola, S., Lipponen, L., Hakkarainen, K.: Epistemological Foundations for CSCL: A Comparison of Three Models of Innovative Knowledge Communities. G. Stahl (ed): Computer Support for Collaborative Learning: Foundations for a CSCL community. Proceedings of the Computer-supported Collaborative Learning 2002 Conference, Hillsdale, N.J.; Erlbaum (2002), pp. 24 - 32.

[PVTO02] Privat, R., Vigouroux, N., Truillet, P., Oriola, B.: Accessibility and affordance for voice interactive systems with the VoiceXML technology. Miesenberger, K., Klaus, J., and Zagler, W. (eds.): Proceedings of ICCHP 2002, Linz, Austria (2002), pp. 61 - 63.

[ScBe94] Scaramalia, M., Bereiter, C.: Computer support for knowledge-building communities. The Journal of the Learning Sciences, 3(3) (1994) pp. 265 - 283.

[Selt98] Selting, M. et al.: Gesprächsanalytisches Transkriptionssystem (GAT). Linguistische Berichte, 173 (1998), pp. 91 - 122 (in German).

[SKJa03] Spaniol, M., Klamma, R., Jarke, M.: ATLAS: A web-based software architecture for multimedia e-learning environments in virtual communities. W. Zhou, P. Nicholson, B. Corbitt, J. Fong (Eds.): Advances in Web-Based Learning, Proceedings of ICWL 2003, Melbourne, Australia, August 18-20, 2003, Springer-Verlag, Berlin Heidelberg, LNCS 2783 (2003), pp. 193 - 205.

[Spri04] Springer, L.: Mediendifferenz und Sprachverwendung - Eine emprirische Studie zur medienspezifischen Prozessierung des Sprachwissens bei Agrammatikern und Sprachgesunden. Jäger L. and Linz E. (eds.): Medialität und Mentalität - Theoretische und empirische Studien zum Verhältnis von Sprache, Subjektivität und Kognition, Fink-Verlag, München (2004), pp. 221 - 249 (in German).

[Weng98] Wenger, E.: Communities of Practice - learning, Meaning, and Identity. Cambridge University Press, Cambridge, UK (1998).

[WPTC02] Willis, T., Pain, H., Trewin, S., Clark, S.: Informing flexible abbreviation expansion for users with motor disabilities. Miesenberger, K., Klaus, J., and Zagler, W. (eds.): Proceedings of ICCHP 2002, Linz, Austria (2002), pp. 251 - 258.

Crossing Boundaries with Web-Based Tools for Learning Object Evaluation

Jerry Zhigang Li[1], John C. Nesbit[1], and Griff Richards[2]

[1] School of Interactive Arts & Technology, Simon Fraser University
2400 Central City, Surrey, BC, Canada V3T 2W1
{jerryli,nesbit}@sfu.ca
[2] British Columbia Institute of Technology
Burnaby, British Columbia, Canada, V5G 3H2
griff@sfu.ca

Abstract. Learning object repositories and evaluation tools have the potential to serve as sites for interaction among different cultures and communities of practice. This paper outlines the web-based learning object evaluation tools we have developed, describes our current efforts to extend those tools to a wider range of user communities, and considers methods for fostering interaction among user communities. The approaches considered include establishing shared but differentiated learning object evaluation standards, mapping between local languages, ontologies and practices, and recommending objects across community boundaries.

Keywords: e-learning, reviews, quality, repositories, communities, eLera, LORI, convergent participation, collaboration, professional development

1 The Need for Learning Object Evaluation Across Communities

Learning objects are distinguished from other educational resources by their immediate availability through web-based repositories that are searchable with standardized metadata. Specialized repositories serving different user communities are emerging that are interlinked by metadata and interoperability standards. Within the next five years, the U.S. National Science Digital Library (NSDL) is predicted to grow to include as many as 100,000 specialized collections representing over a million learning objects [1]. As we have claimed previously [2], the effectiveness of most online learning resources is severely limited because they do not follow design principles established by educational research, and have not been subjected to formative user testing. Thus, there is a pressing need for methods and tools to facilitate the development, evaluation and dissemination of high quality resources.

The strategy of specializing learning object evaluation tools for specific user communities clearly offers benefits through more focused support for community needs. However, here we also consider complementary strategies for fostering communication and interaction among these communities. Such strategies are important to avoid the establishment of 'multiple solitudes' in which innovations, solutions and beliefs are not readily disseminated across community boundaries. This paper introduces resource evaluation tools we have developed and describes how we are extending these tools to diverse communities of practice, language and culture.

W. Liu et al. (Eds.): ICWL 2004, LNCS 3143, pp. 286–292, 2004.
© Springer-Verlag Berlin Heidelberg 2004

2   Current Approaches to Evaluation

Current learning object evaluation sites can be viewed as variations on a common model [3,4,5]. Each is formed from a searchable database of resource metadata conforming to the IEEE LOM standard, evaluation criteria in the form of guidelines or an instrument, a process for conducting reviews including restrictions on who can review, and a structured form in which all reviews are published.

In the common model there are often two tiers of evaluation – reviews by individual users and reviews by selected experts or "peers." These mirror the two different types of consumer product evaluation systems found on the Web. For example, at one video game review site (www.pcgamereview.com), any user can register to rate and comment on three quality dimensions of a video game. Similarly, at a general consumer product review site (www.reviewcentre.com), any user can rate products on the two dimensions of "quality" and "value for money", as well as record comments. In contrast to these open evaluation systems, other product evaluation sites present only expert reviews. As with most of the product review sites, the evaluation processes of learning object repositories provide few opportunities for interaction among expert reviewers (e.g. content experts and instructional designers), and even fewer between expert and consumer reviewers (e.g., learners and teachers). Such interactions are potentially important because reviewers have been consistently observed to modify their evaluation of a learning object after being presented with reviews that differ from their own [6, 7].

3   eLera

eLera is a website designed to support a distributed community of teachers, instructors, researchers, instructional designers, and media developers. The initial version of eLera was publicly released in November 2003 at www.elera.net. eLera is a member of eduSource Canada, a network of interoperable Canadian repositories.

Developed in Zope, eLera maintains a searchable database of learning objects and reviews, and provides tools for learning object evaluation. eLera complies with the IEEE learning object metadata standards as interpreted by the CanCore guide [8]. It uses a modified version of the Dewey Classification System as a subject taxonomy. eLera includes evaluation forms and reports, statistical aggregation of ratings, and a "my collection" feature allowing members to assemble frequently used objects. Basic features include a home page listing recently registered members and reviews, and the ability to search other repositories using the eduSource Communication Language [9].

4   Learning Object Review Instrument (LORI)

The eLera website allows users to evaluate resources with the Learning Object Review Instrument [10]. LORI has been iteratively developed through testing with instructional developers and teachers [6]. Version 1.5 of LORI includes nine items shown in Table 1. For each of the nine items, reviewers can enter comments and ratings on a 5-point scale. Reviews are published in eLera as web pages.

Table 1. Dimensions of learning object quality in LORI 1.5

Content Quality	Veracity, accuracy, balanced presentation of ideas, and appropriate level of detail
Learning Goal Alignment	Alignment among learning goals, activities, assessments, and learner characteristics
Feedback and Adaptation	Adaptive content or feedback driven by differential learner input or learner modeling
Motivation	Ability to motivate and interest an identified population of learners
Presentation Design	Design of visual and auditory information for enhanced learning and efficient mental processing
Interaction Usability	Ease of navigation, predictability of the user interface, and quality of the interface help features
Accessibility	Design of controls and presentation formats to accommodate disabled and mobile learners
Reusability	Ability to use in varying learning contexts and with learners from differing backgrounds
Standards Compliance	Adherence to international standards and specifications

5 Tools for Collaborative Evaluation

eLera's tools for collaborative evaluation are designed to support the convergent participation model developed in previous research [6, 7, 11, 12]. In this model, small evaluation panels are formed from participants representing relevant knowledge sets and interests (e.g., subject matter expert, learner, instructional designer). A panel moderator chooses objects for review, schedules the review activity, and invites panel members. Moderators can use eLera's request feature to invite panel members to review an object. Members may choose to accept or reject participation. After the panel members have completed individual reviews, they meet in an online, real-time conference to discuss their evaluations. In this model, reviewers first discuss the items showing the greatest inter-rater variability. The moderator can use statistics calculated by eLera to order items for discussion. Panel members can edit their ratings and comments during the session. The moderator can publish a panel review by automatically aggregating individual reviews authored by panel members.

Two studies [6, 7] have shown that the collaborative review process causes participants' ratings of learning object quality to converge. This research also found that participants believe collaborative evaluation is an effective activity for teaching and learning about learning object quality.

6 Localization and Trans-Localization of eLera

The term *localization* is often used to connote the adaptation of a website to the language and culture of specific linguistically, geographically or ethnically defined groups. Here we also use the term when adapting to communities of practice, such as high school teachers or e-learning professionals. In this section we provide examples of both types of localization of the eLera website. We use the term *trans-localization* to connote methods or practices that promote communication and interaction among communities and cultures.

Internationalization, by which we mean adherence to international standards and avoidance of content or symbols that are heavily laden with idiosyncratic cultural knowledge, is a pre-requisite for both localization and trans-localization. The eLera website was designed to comply with the IEEE standard for learning object metadata. It also avoids reference to local or national institutions, and other knowledge not likely to be meaningful to an international audience.

Table 2. Ratio of web pages to users for different language groups in 2002. Data for pages [16] and users [14] from referenced sources

Language	Web Pages (Millions)	Web Users (Millions)	Pages per User
English	11425	234	48.87
German	156	43	3.63
French	113	23	4.92
Japanese	98	61	1.61
Spanish	60	50	1.20
Chinese	**48**	**78**	**0.62**
Italian	41	24	1.71
Dutch	39	13	2.98
Korean	31	28	1.10
Portuguese	29	19	1.55
Other	168	64	-----

6.1 Localizing Language

Over the last decade, the demographics of the web have seen a dramatic shift toward a more culturally diversified, multilingual user base. The proportion of users accessing the web in English dropped from 49.6% in 2000 [13] to 35.6% in 2003 [14]. The proportion accessing the web in Asian languages (mainly Chinese, Japanese and Korean) increased from 20.6% in 2000 [13] to 29.4% in 2003 [14]. Chinese-speaking web users, the second largest language group after English, increased from 1 million in 1997 to 160 million in 2004, and are expected to number 220 million by 2005 [14].

eLera has been localized to French and Chinese using the Zope localizer tool [15]. Most eLera pages are composed of several elements from different sources, such as navigation menus, page body, and images with text. For every element of the web page, eLera determines in which language it will be shown. The determination is based on an ordered set of languages preferred by the user. If a user prefers French, but also knows some English, then the user can set his or her preference to {French, English}. eLera will show French by default, but if the element is not available in French then it will display in English.

Chinese was selected not only because Chinese speaking users are the second largest language group on the web, but also because they are relatively underserved by available content. Table 2 shows that the ratio of web pages per user is far lower for Chinese than other major language groups on the web.

With learning object metadata and reviews represented in multiple languages in the eLera database, how can users in one language community use the information generated by another language community? Standardized metadata present a lesser problem because standard translations can be developed for all field names and fixed vocabulary values. We used the Canadian CanCore guidelines [8] for mapping such metadata between English and French. We then extended this mapping to the Chinese E-Learning Technology Standard (CELTS) 3.1 [17].

Although numerical ratings require no translation, the evaluative comments entered by users do present a challenge. We are exploring a method in which reviewers are able, for each item of LORI, to select comments from a closed menu in addition to entering free text. Comments selected from menus would be automatically mapped to all supported languages.

6.2 Localizing Ontologies

Leacock, Nesbit and Richards [18] found that teachers working with eLera in professional development workshops expected the subject taxonomy to follow the provincial curriculum structure they work with daily. They found eLera's modified Dewey system somewhat confusing and not availing of the specific needs of their community. For example, instead of the searching for objects with the Dewey subject "genetics and evolution," they would have preferred to use "grade 9 biology." Later versions of eLera will allow localization of subject taxonomies so that members can opt for a taxonomy already established in their community.

With subject terms entered in a local ontology, how can users in one community (e.g., Ontario high school teachers) use the metadata generated by users in another community (e.g., French university professors)? We are planning to use a modified version of the Dewey classification system as a universal subject taxonomy into which a large number of local subject taxonomies can be mapped. Hatala and Richards [19] proposed that, instead of enforcing a full metadata standard, repositories provide a narrow subset of the standard and allow extensions generated by community needs. We intend to follow this principle in localizing subject ontologies.

6.3 Localizing Evaluation Tools

E-learning design communities, unlike consumer communities, require methods for formative evaluation. We are now planning versions of eLera to facilitate workflow within teams that develop learning objects. For example, we may create a review instrument in which items become activated or deactivated as the object passes through defined stages. At the end of the development cycle, when the object is published, the incrementally assembled review can be published as a summative warrant of quality. This enterprise leads immediately to an examination of critical factors influencing learning object quality in design and development: What work is completed in each stage of the development process? Who should monitor quality at each stage? What information must be communicated to assure quality?

7   Recommendation across Boundaries

Through eLera we are researching models for supporting e-learning communities of practice. This research asks how online communities should be structured to foster norms of reciprocity, collective action, identity, and information flow. Key questions at this stage are: How can community members recommend resources and reviews to others? How can they find, and be introduced to, other members with similar or complementary interests? How can they build the identity, interpersonal trust and reputation that are prerequisite to effective collective activity?

At present, eLera provides only rudimentary facilities for recommendation and trust. By default, search results are ordered by average rating so that the most highly rated objects are presented at the top of the list. Users can also choose to order objects by *popularity*, a metric that is incremented whenever an object is placed in a personal collection. To support trust and alliance building, eLera members can create personal profiles detailing their interests and areas of expertise. Thus, decisions about whether to trust and collaborate with a reviewer can be based on the combined knowledge of his or her profile and previous reviews.

As we build on these features we are researching more advanced models of trust and recommendation that will contribute to the nascent research base in this area [20, 21, 22]. For example, we are implementing a "web of trust" – a social network in which members can create a list of highly trusted others. eLera will be able to recommend new members for one's trust list, and objects and reviews associated with those members, by chaining forward through the network of trust lists.

We expect to find relatively dense patterns of trust relationships within communities and sparse connections between communities. This being so, how can relevant objects and reviews be recommended across community boundaries? Recent work on the "six degrees of separation" phenomenon [23] has demonstrated that only sparse connections between node clusters are sufficient to ensure that the distance between any two nodes in a large network is fairly short. This suggests that as long as a few members of a community are connected to other communities, a strategy of recommending objects and reviews associated with near neighbors on the web of trust may ensure sufficient circulation of relevant objects across community boundaries.

8   Conclusion

Although the languages, tools and practices used in evaluating learning objects may need to be specialized for different communities, these communities need not operate as multiple solitudes. On the contrary, methods for recommending objects, and mapping metadata and reviews across languages and ontologies, can sustain substantial communication and interaction among learning object communities.

References

1. Saylor, J.M.: Why Every Digital Science Collection Builder Should Contribute Catalog Information to the National Science Digital Library. Retrieved December 28, 2003 from http://collections.comm.nsdlib.org/cgi-bin/wiki.pl?WhyJoin

2. Nesbit, J.C., Li, J.: Web-Based Tools for Learning Object Evaluation. *International Conference on Education and Information Systems: Technologies and Applications.* Orlando, Florida (2004)
3. Clarke, M.: CLOE Peer Review. Retrieved January 30, 2003, from Co-operative Learning Object Exchange: http://cloe.on.ca/documents.html
4. Merlot Peer Review. Retrieved March 31, 2004 from www.merlot.org
5. Digital Library Network for Engineering and Technology. Retrieved March 31, 2004 from www.dlnet.vt.edu
6. Vargo, J., Nesbit, J.C., Belfer, K., Archambault, A.: Learning Object Evaluation: Computer Mediated Collaboration and Inter-rater Reliability. *International Journal of Computers and Applications* **25** (2003) 198-205
7. Nesbit, J.C, Leacock, T., Xin, C., Richards, G.: Learning Object Evaluation and Convergent Participation: Tools for Professional Development in E-Learning. *7ᵗʰ IASTED International Conference on Computers and Advanced Technology in Education* (2004)
8. Friesen, N., Fisher, S., Tozer, L., Roberts, A., Hesemeier, S., Habkirk, S.: *CanCore Guide for LOM Implementation.* CanCore Initiative. Retrieved January 7, 2004 from www.cancore.ca
9. Hatala, M., Richards, G., Eap, T., Willms, J.: *The EduSource Communication Language: Implementing Open Network for Learning Repositories and Services.* Retrieved January 7, 2004 from www.sfu.ca/~mhatala/pubs/sap04-edusource-submit.pdf
10. Nesbit, J.C., Belfer, K. Leacock, T.: *Learning Object Review Instrument (LORI).* E-Learning Research and Assessment Network. Retrieved January 7, 2004 from www.elera.net
11. Nesbit, J.C., Belfer, K.: Collaborative Evaluation of Learning Objects. In: McGreal, R. (ed.): *Online Education Using Learning Objects.* London: Routledge/Falmer (2004)
12. Nesbit, J.C., Belfer, K., Vargo, J.: A Convergent Participation Model for Evaluation of Learning Objects. *Canadian Journal of Learning and Technology* **28** (2002) 105-120
13. Haynes, J.D.: Internet Management Issues: A Global Perspective *Chapter 5 - International User Interfaces.* Idea Group Publishing (2002)
14. Global Reach: Global Internet Statistics. Retrieved March 28, 2004 from http://www.global-reach.biz/globstats/index.php3
15. David, J.: Localizer. Retrieved March 28, 2004 from http://www.j-david.net/
16. Retrieved March 31, 2004 from http://www.netz-tipp.de/languages.html
17. Xiang, X., Shen, Z., Guo, L., Shi, Y.: Introduction of the Core Elements Set in Localized LOM Model. *Learning Technology*, 5, IEEE Computer Society (2003)
18. Leacock, T., Richards, G., Nesbit, J.C.: Teachers need simple effective tools to evaluate learning objects: Enter eLera.net. *7ᵗʰ IASTED International Conference on Computers and Advanced Technology in Education* (2004)
19. Hatala, M., Richards, G.: Global vs. Community Metadata Standards: Empowering Users for Knowledge Exchange. *International Semantic Web Conference*, Sardinia, Italy (2002)
20. Wiley, D.A., Edwards, E.K.: Online Self-Organizing Social Systems: The Decentralized Future of Online Learning. Retrieved January 4, 2004, from http://wiley.ed.usu.edu/docs/ososs.pdf
21. Recker, M., Walker, A.: Supporting 'Word-of-Mouth' Social Networks via Collaborative Information Filtering. *Journal of Interactive Learning Research,* **14**, (2003) 79-98
22. Recker, M., Walker, A., Lawless, K.: What Do You Recommend? Implementation and Analyses of Collaborative Filtering of Web resources for Education. *Instructional Science* **31** (2003) 229-316
23. Buchanan, M.: Nexus: Small Worlds and the Groundbreaking Theory of Networks. Norton, New York (2002)

Web-Based Handwriting Education
with Animated Virtual Teacher

Howard Leung and Taku Komura

Department of Computer Engineering and Information Technology,
City University of Hong Kong, Hong Kong
{howard,itaku}@cityu.edu.hk

Abstract. Traditionally, in teaching handwriting, the teacher writes a character on the blackboard, and then students try to follow the teacher in order to write the same character. The teacher can check whether a student's handwriting is spatially correct by looking at its shape but he/she is not able to verify if the student is writing in the correct stroke order with the correct number of strokes. As a result, we design a web-based handwriting education system. With our proposed system, students can stay at home to do the exercises for learning the handwriting of characters. A student's handwriting can be captured in digital format with the information in both temporal and spatial domain and the results can be sent to the teacher for evaluation. In addition, we propose to animate a virtual teacher on the student's terminal for demonstrating the handwriting of the characters to give students a sense of presence.

1 Introduction

Studies in Hong Kong [1] have shown that children in the upper kindergarten are quite ready to write Chinese characters. Traditionally, in teaching handwriting, the teacher writes a character on the blackboard, and then students try to follow the teacher in order to write the same character. At home, students may be given homework for tracing the strokes of a character on a copy book or for copying a character for a few times as practice. With this approach, the teacher can only check whether a student's handwriting is spatially correct by looking at its shape. He/she is not able to verify if the student is writing in the correct stroke order with the correct number of strokes. As a result, we design a web-based handwriting education system for teaching people writing characters. With our proposed system, students can stay at home to do the exercises for learning to write characters. A student's handwriting can be captured in digital format with the information in both temporal and spatial domain (coordinates and time stamps of the stroke samples and pen up/down events) and the results can be sent to the teacher for evaluation. In addition, we propose to animate a virtual teacher on the student's terminal for demonstrating the handwriting of the characters to give students a sense of presence.

One research issue of our system is the handwriting analysis. The objective of handwriting analysis is to reduce the workload of the teacher by assisting in the automatic evaluation of the handwritings. Essentially the idea is to make a reliable system

W. Liu et al. (Eds.): ICWL 2004, LNCS 3143, pp. 293–300, 2004.

that can analyze precisely a student's handwriting and then provide accurate feedback to the student about where a character is written wrong. This handwriting analysis problem is different from handwriting recognition. In handwriting recognition, it suffices to find criteria that are just enough to differentiate between the correct character from all other incorrect characters. In handwriting analysis, instead of looking for the most similar character from a set of characters, we need to find out whether and more importantly where the character is written wrong. We aim to train a person to write correctly instead of training the system to ignore mistakes.

Another research issue is the animation of the virtual teacher for writing. While it is possible to capture with a 3-D glove the 3-D motion of the hand during the handwriting and then render the same motion of the hand in the virtual environment, further parameters need to be determined in order to render the remaining part of the body if we want to have a whole body model for the virtual teacher. This can be achieved by applying inverse kinematics to solve for the unknown joint angles of the body.

This paper is organized as follows. Section 2 describes some prior work on the related issues. Section 3 provides a description of our proposed system. The conclusions and future work are given in Section 4.

2 Prior Work

Although pen-based devices become more and more popular to the general public in recent years [2], yet there is no software that can precisely analyze a handwritten character. As a result, no accurate feedback can be provided on whether and where the character is written wrong by considering simultaneously the spatial and the temporal information (coordinates and time stamps of the stroke samples and pen up/down events) captured with the input pen device.

In electronic ink processing, Lopresti et al. [9][10] reported their work on matching hand-drawn pictures which they call "pictograms". This approach has a drawback that it treats the same hand-drawings with different stroke orders as a poor match. In order to make the system less sensitive to the stroke order, Lopresti and Tomkins [11][12] proposed to match the strings block by block. However, poor match may still result if a stroke is drawn in reverse direction (i.e., when the start point and the end point of a stroke interchange). Under these approaches, string matching is performed for the alignment based on the time sequence. As a result, it has the assumption that the strokes are drawn in the correct temporal order. This may not be the case for beginners who just start learning handwriting.

There are some researches about handwriting quality evaluation. Some of them target for the English handwriting by evaluating the shape and slant of the input alphabet [13]. Others target for Chinese characters by extracting some global features to determine how similar they match to a given model [5][6][7][8]. They consider the input handwriting as an image and then extract shape features. However, for a beginner in Chinese handwritings, there may be errors in the spatial (shape) and/or the temporal (stroke order and number of strokes) domain, as a result, in our problem, we need to find an approach that can handle matching with both spatial and temporal variations without an underlying assumption about the correctness in either domain.

In terms of animation with inverse kinematics, Tak *et al.* [3] solved the redundancy problem and then calculated the trajectory of the end effectors so that the posture of the body resembles the posture in the original motion. In contrast to the approach in [3], one of the authors proposed in [4] to extract the feature of the motion at the moment the user controls the model, and apply it to solve the redundancy problem and move the end effectors. Therefore, although the approach by [3] is superior for retargeting motion, our approach in [4] has an advantage in creating new postures that retain the feature of the original motion.

Some researchers work on synthesizing brush-like strokes based on the pen-based input device [18][19]. Their objective is to create beautiful calligraphy using computer that is different from our objective of handwriting education. On the other hand, Solis *et al.* [20] developed a haptic interface with a control system to restrict the user to move along a predefined trajectory. This approach is more intrusive compared with our proposed system.

3   Our Proposed System Description

The block diagram of our system is shown in Fig. 1. There are two parties using the system: the teacher and the student. On the teacher side, there is a terminal with an application to send out exercises to the students and receive the student's submissions in order to monitor the student's progress. In addition, there is a 3-D glove that is connected to the teacher's terminal for capturing the teacher's 3-D hand motion during the handwriting. On the student side, there is also a terminal with an application to display an animated virtual teacher to demonstrate the handwriting to the students. Furthermore, there is a pen-based device that serves as the input device to capture the student's handwriting. Once the handwriting is captured, it is sent to the student's terminal for storage and it is also possible to send it to the teacher's terminal to be evaluated by the teacher.

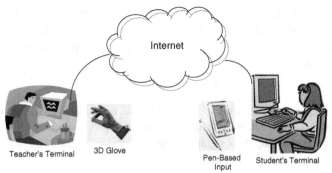

Internet

Teacher's Terminal   3D Glove   Pen-Based   Student's Terminal
                                             Input

Fig. 1. System diagram

3.1   3-D Motion Capture of the Teacher's Writing Hand

A 3-D glove is used to capture the 3-D motion of the hand when the teacher is writing. This information is stored in the teacher's terminal so that it can be loaded next time when the same handwriting demonstration is needed. The 3-D glove only captures the position of several joints of the hand. In order to be able to animate the body of the virtual teacher during handwriting, other joints of the body need to be calculated. The animation process is explained in the next section.

3.2 Animated Virtual Teacher

In order to facilitate a transparent communication between the teacher and the student through the web, we make use of the animation techniques for improving the quality of visual communication in order to give students a feeling of presence when we animate the virtual teacher on the student's terminal. In addition, the bandwidth required to transmit the parameters used to animate a virtual teacher is much less than transmitting the actual video of the teacher. Furthermore, with the animation technique, it is possible for the student to change viewpoint when they are looking at the handwriting demonstration of the virtual teacher in order to get a good look at the characters that students are supposed to learn.

As mentioned in the previous section, the 3-D motion of the hand is captured by the 3-D glove. The captured 3-D motion data is used to animate the hand of the virtual teacher to be displayed on the student's terminal. In addition, the other joint angles of the virtual teacher are calculated based on the inverse kinematics approach proposed in [4]. In this approach, we first assume that the human body has n degree of freedom (DOF) and specify the joint angles of the human body by a vector:

$$\theta = (\theta_1, \theta_1, \ldots, \theta_n) \tag{1}$$

The change in position and rotation of the hand segments (ΔP, ΔQ) and the change in joint angles $\Delta\theta$ are related by the following equation:

$$\begin{pmatrix} \Delta P \\ \Delta Q \end{pmatrix} = J\Delta\theta \tag{2}$$

The problem of finding $\Delta\theta$ given (ΔP, ΔQ) is redundant because the DOF of $\Delta\theta$ is higher than the DOF of (ΔP, ΔQ). As a result, in order to solve for $\Delta\theta$, we use the method proposed in [17] that solves the reudundancy problem by minimizing a quadratic function as follows:

$$\Delta\theta^T W\Delta\theta \tag{3}$$

Where W is a weight matrix, which value can be calculated in a way that the features of the original motion is retained by using the method proposed in [4]. The values of the generalized coordinates that minimize the quaternion in Equation (3) can be obtained by

$$\Delta\theta = W^{-1}J^T (JW^{-1} J^T)^{-1} \begin{pmatrix} \Delta P \\ \Delta Q \end{pmatrix} \tag{4}$$

It should be pointed out that when the animation of the body will look quite different between the cases when the handwriting is in small characters and when the handwriting is in big characters. Often for handwriting education, the handwriting should preferably be big enough for the student to see the details clearly. It is challenging to animate such handwriting motion naturally across the whole body. An example of animating the whole body based on the motion of a hand is shown in Fig. 2.

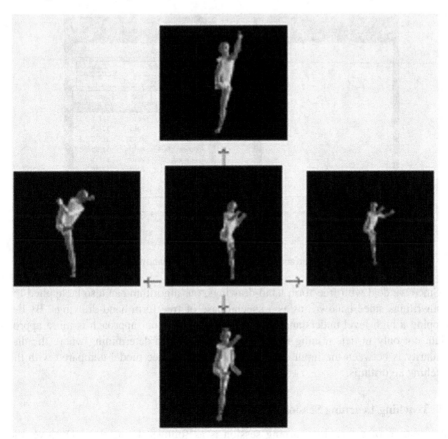

Fig. 2. Using inverse kinematics to animate the body by controlling the left hand

3.3 Capture of Student's Handwritings

A PDA device can be used to capture the student's handwritings. We have implemented an interface to achieve this purpose. As shown in Fig. 3, our interface is able to capture a person's handwriting in vector format, i.e., the information of the strokes that are sequences of 2-D coordinates capturing the positions of the pen during the pen-down events. In this interface, it is also possible to save and load the handwritings in the vector-based format which we call "sketches".

3.4 Handwriting Analysis

We have been conducting research along the area of pen computing [14][15][16]. More specifically we work on the area of sketch retrieval. In this research, a sketch is a free-form hand-drawings that can contain a character, a mathematical symbol or a chemical symbol, etc... The goal of sketch retrieval is to find sketches from the database that are similar to the query sketch.

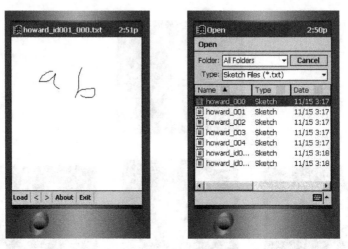

Fig. 3. Interface for capturing student's handwritings

Since we deal with free-form hand-drawings, our algorithm can also be applied for handwritings since handwriting is a special case of free-form hand-drawings. By developing a high level understanding of the handwriting, our approach is more appropriate not only in determining the similarity, but also in determining where the dissimilarity is between the input character and the reference model compared with the matching algorithms.

3.5 Teaching/Learning Session

The scenario of a teaching/learning session is as follows. Using the 3-D glove, the teacher's handwriting can be first captured and then the teacher will assign some writing exercises to the students. When the student initiates a learning session, the virtual teacher is displayed and it will be animated to demonstrate the handwriting of some characters. Afterwards the student is asked to practice the handwriting of those characters with the pen-based input device. The student may see the demonstration of the animated virtual teacher again if he/she is not clear about how to write. Once the student finishes the exercise, the results are sent to the teacher's terminal. Either the handwriting analysis program is used to evaluate the handwriting quality or the teacher performs this task by him/herself in order to monitor the student's progress.

4 Conclusions and Future Work

In this paper, we have presented our design of a web-based handwriting education system for teaching people writing characters. With our proposed system, students can stay at home to do the exercises for learning to write characters. A student's handwriting can be captured in digital format with the information in both temporal and spatial domain (coordinates and time stamps of the stroke samples and pen up/down events) and the results can be sent to the teacher's terminal for automatic evaluation with handwriting analysis or for manual evaluation by the teacher. In addition, we propose to animate a virtual teacher on the student's terminal for demonstrating the handwriting of the characters by using the 3-D hand motion data captured by a 3-D glove and using inverse kinematics to determine the other joint angles of the body.

There are several extensions for this work. First of all, more handwriting samples can be collected in order to improve the performance of the handwriting analysis. Moreover, some user studies can be performed in order to examine the effectiveness of our system and determine what we can do to tune our system. In addition, the correspondence between the 3-D motion data of the hand and the handwritten character will be studied in order to estimate the 3-D motion of the hand for new characters in order to minimize the amount of data collected by the 3-D glove.

References

1. Curriculum Development Council, "A Study on Chinese Handwriting at the Kindergarten Level". Hong Kong: Government Printer, February 1996.
2. Schomaker, L.R.B. "From handwriting analysis to pen-computer applications". IEE Electronics Communication Engineering Journal, Vol. 10, No. 3, pp. 93-102, 1998.
3. S. Tak and H. Ko. "Example guided inverse kinematics", Proceedings of the International Conference on Computer Graphics and Imaging (CGIM) 2000, 2000.
4. Taku Komura, Atsushi Kuroda, Shunsuke Kudoh, Tai Chiew Lan, Yoshihisa Shinagawa, "An Inverse Kinematics Method for 3D Figures with Motion Data" Proceedings of Computer Graphics International 2003, pp 266-271 (CGI2003).
5. Kim, D.-H., Kim E.-J. and Bang, S.-Y. "A Variation Measure for Handwritten Character Image Data Using Entropy Difference". In Pattern Recognition, Vol. 30, No. 1, pp.19-29, 1997.
6. Ozaki, M., Adachi Y., Ishii N. and Koyazu T., "CAI System to Improve Hand Writing Skills by means of Fuzzy Theory", In Proc. IEEE Intl. Conf. on Fuzzy Systems and the Second Intl. Fuzzy Engineering Symposium, pp. 491-496, Vol. 2, March 1995.
7. Chou S.-L. and Yu S.-S. "Sorting Qualities of Handwritten Chinese Characters for Setting up a Research Database", In Proc. Intl. Conf. on Document Analysis and Recognition, pp.474-477, October 1993.
8. Kato T. "Evaluation System for hand-written characters", In Proc. Machine Vision Applications in Character Recognition and Industrial Inspection, pp. 73-82, February 1992.
9. Lopresti D. and Tomkins A. "Approximate Matching of Hand-Drawn Pictograms". In Proc. Third Int. Work. Frontiers Handwriting Recognition, pages 102-111. May 1993.
10. Lopresti D. and Tomkins A. "On the searchability of electronic ink". In Proc. of the Fourth Intl. Workshop on Frontiers in Handwriting Recognition, pp. 156-165, December 1994.
11. Lopresti D. and Tomkins A. "Temporal domain matching of hand-drawn pictorial queries". In Proc. of the Seventh Conf. of The Intl. Graphonomics Society, pp. 98-99. August 1995.
12. Lopresti D., Tomkins A. and Zhou J. "Algorithms for matching hand-drawn sketches". In Proc. of the Fifth Intl. Workshop on Frontiers in Handwriting Recognition, pp. 233-238, September 1996.

13. Kulesh V., Shaffer K., Sethi I. and Schartz M. "Handwriting Quality Evaluation", In Proc. Intl. Conf. Advances in Pattern Recognition, pp.157-165, March 2001.
14. Leung W. H. and Chen T. "User-Independent Retrieval of Free-Form Hand-Drawn Sketches". IEEE Intl. Conf. on Acoustics, Speech, and Signal Processing, Vol. 2, pp. 2029-2032, Orlando, FL, May 2002.
15. Leung W. H. and Chen T. "Retrieval of Sketches Based on Spatial Relations Between Strokes". IEEE Intl. Conf. on Image Processing, Vol. 1, pp. 908-911, Rochester, NY, September 2002.
16. Leung W. H. "Representations, Feature Extraction, Matching and Relevance Feedback for Sketch Retrieval", Ph.D. Thesis, Carnegie Mellon University, June 2003.
17. Whitney, D.E. "Resolved motion rate control of manipulators and human prostheses". IEEE Transactions on Man-Machine Systems 10, 47–53, 1969.
18. Wong H. T. F. and Ip H. H. S. "Virtual Brush: Model-Based Synthesis of Chinese Calligraphy", Computers & Graphics, Vol. 24, No. 1, pp. 99-114, February, 2000.
19. Yamasaki T. and Hattori T. "Computer Calligraphy - Brush Written Kanji Formation Based on the Brush-Touch Movement". IEEE Intl. Conf. on Systems, Man and Cybernetics, pp. 1736-1741, 1996.
20. Jorge Solis, Carlo Avizzano Avizzano, Massimo Bergamasco, "Teaching to Write Japanese Characters Using a Haptic Interface". Symposium on Haptic Interfaces for Virtual Environment and Teleoperator Systems, pp. 255-262, 2002.

From e-Learning to Virtual Learning Community: Bridging the Gap

Naomi Augar, Ruth Raitman, and Wanlei Zhou

School of Information Technology, Deakin University, Melbourne, Australia
{augar,ruth,wanlei}@deakin.edu.au

Abstract. 'Community' has become a buzz word in the E-Learning arena. This paper examines the concept of virtual community, in the context of E-Learning. It defines what constitutes a virtual community and virtual learning community. A model comprising four essential criteria that define a virtual learning community is proposed. These criteria are discussed with relation to Deakin University's E-Learning system. The paper concludes by highlighting the factors that may help bridge the gap between Deakin's present provision of E-Learning to the development of a virtual learning community.

1 Virtual Communities

Virtual learning communities have the potential to solve problems in the distance learning arena. A sense of community can help distance learners overcome feelings of isolation, reduce student attrition rates and enhance their learning experience [1, 2]. This paper examines the definition of virtual community and what constitutes a virtual learning community. The findings are applied to the analysis of Deakin University's current learning management system, to determine how to bridge the gap between Deakin's present E-Learning system and a virtual learning community.

Virtual communities are formed by groups of people who use Internet and computer technology to communicate with one another. The communication may be text or audio based, or may even be facilitated by video conferencing. However, there is more to virtual communities than people interacting with technology. The sharing of a common interest or goal creates a social bond, or sense of community amongst users [3, 4].

Some researchers [5, 6], believe that the definitions of what makes a virtual community are flawed. According to [5] the views held by many researchers are 'technologically deterministic'. He contends that many technologists believe that the outcome of building a group Computer Mediated Communication, CMC system is the creation of a virtual community. However, [5] argues that technology alone can not facilitate a virtual community.

Definitions such as that provided by [7] or [3] highlight the influence of social context on the creation of a virtual community. The social context and the medium cannot be separated, as both are required to facilitate this new kind of community; the virtual community.

W. Liu et al. (Eds.): ICWL 2004, LNCS 3143, pp. 301–308, 2004.

2   Virtual Learning Communities

Virtual learning communities are virtual communities where the shared goal or purpose of the community members is learning. There are varied notions of what constitutes a virtual learning community. The term is used widely, sometimes without clarification. This paper attempts to identify the essential criteria for creating a virtual learning community, and apply them to the analysis of Deakin University's learning management system.

According to [8] a learning community can be defined as:

"Various kinds of individuals interacting in a common location for the purpose of gaining knowledge in, understanding of, or skill in a subject matter through instruction, study, and/or experience by the creation of a social state and condition that nurtures and encourages learners."

The term 'virtual' describes the 'place' where interaction and instruction occurs: the Internet. Rather than a physical classroom, a virtual classroom is created using study materials, bulletin boards and instructors, which are provided in an virtual learning environment [9].

Hence, it can be said that a virtual learning community is a group of learners that interact in a common online environment to gain understanding of subject matter. Learners build on their knowledge by interacting with each other, their instructors and learning materials. By sharing a common learning goal and interacting socially over a period of time learners develop and share a sense of belonging and shared purpose.

We propose four interrelated criteria that must be present for a virtual learning community to evolve: social context, facilitation, technology and a shared learning goal. This model is depicted in Figure 1.

Fig. 1. Criteria critical to the emergence of a virtual learning community.

Social context was identified earlier in the paper as a critical factor in the emergence of virtual community. What does it take to develop social context in a group of learners so community may emerge? Research by [2] contends that for a learning community to develop, the "four related dimensions: spirit, trust, interaction, and commonality of learning expectations and goals" must be fostered within the group. Concepts like spirit, trust and interaction can all be grouped under the heading of social context. Community members must feel confident enough in the virtual environment, to interact with one another and form social bonds.

The emergence of trust between members of learning groups is based on their shared experience and interaction. The instructor must play a key role in helping forge the early bonds that lead to the emergence of trust and group spirit. Each student needs to develop their own social presence. The instructor can aid this process by modeling appropriate interactions during the early stages of group communication [2]. Building trust amongst learners is critical. If community members share individual experiences, a shared history can be cultivated, and trust amongst group members developed [10].

A *shared learning goal* is quite a difficult criterion to meet. One may assume that if students choose to enroll in a subject they will have an interest in the subject matter. However, this is not always the case. As [11] points out each learner has individual learning goals, such as getting a degree, or doing enough to pass. However, their motivation may not include any goals related to working in discussion groups or participating in a virtual learning community. How then do teachers motivate them to do so? As [2] suggests a way to encourage interaction is to make student participation compulsory and subject to assessment based on the "...quantity, quality, and timeliness of their contributions."

Technology is fundamental to the development of any virtual learning community. In a distance learning environment where students have limited access to technical support, technology must be easy to use and reliable to ensure that frustration with technology does not impact on a student's motivation to participate in the virtual learning community. A study by [12] contends that ongoing technical problems can frustrate distance learners and impact negatively upon their learning experience.

Facilitation is critical to the development of virtual learning communities. When instruction and learning materials are offered online, one cannot automatically assume that a virtual learning community will result. Both [13] and [14] believe that just because a group of learners have to work together to produce a learning outcome, does not mean they can automatically be dubbed a learning community. Further, [13] contends that it is difficult to facilitate a sense of community amongst a group of learners in the relatively short time frame of a university semester.

Social context must be developed quickly, in order for a sense of community to emerge in the limited timeframe of a semester. The key to developing social context in a virtual learning environment is effective facilitation. The absence of prompt feedback and clear instruction can frustrate distance learners, and negatively affect their motivation to participate [12]. The work of [11] and [2] discusses the importance of the instructors role in supporting learners, intervening in cases of conflict, and modeling appropriate online behavior. The instructor needs to nurture the emerging sense of community amongst participants and also ensure that the learning task is being completed appropriately [2].

3 e-Learning at Deakin University

Deakin University, in Victoria, Australia offers dual mode delivery of higher education degrees to students. Approximately half of Deakin's student body completes some or all of their degree through distance education [15]. Deakin comprises several campuses throughout Victoria. A given subject may be offered simultaneously at multiple campuses, as well as off campus.

The School of Information Technology has many units that are offered at two campuses and in both on and off campus mode. Inline with University policy to promote online education, students completing a degree in Information Technology must complete an entire subject online [16]. This is achieved through Deakin's learning management system, DSO, Deakin Studies Online [17].

DSO is facilitated by WebCT Vista and provides bulletin boards, synchronous chat rooms, whiteboards and the like for communication and collaboration. Static course content is delivered in HTML, PDF or Powerpoint formats. DSO also provides tools for management of assignments, assessment as well as class management [17]. Deakin is continuously developing its online delivery system to enhance the experience of all distance and on campus learners.

The research presented in this section relates to a recent survey of Deakin students who participated in an online unit as part of their Information Technology Degree. The anonymous survey elicited the attitude of students toward learning and working in asynchronous discussion groups using DSO. The data is discussed with relation to the criteria highlighted in the previous sections of this paper. The discussion and analysis identifies the areas in which DSO fails to meet the criteria for a virtual learning community, and suggests ways to bridge these gaps.

Whilst the basic criteria for a virtual community at Deakin (in terms of enabling technology and participants) exist at present, something is missing. Almost half of the students surveyed for this study reported a negative perception of learning in groups online, as shown in Figure 2. Conversely, just over half felt the experience was satisfactory or at best, good. So how is the current system failing in its ability to satisfy students? If students are not happy to interact and participate in online learning groups using the current technology, a sense of community cannot emerge amongst learners.

3.1 Social Context

Social context was sadly lacking from the interactions in the discussion groups. Critically, developing a social presence was largely left to the learners to manage. They were encouraged to introduce themselves by way of publishing a short 'resume' document in their discussion area as part of the first assessable activity. There were no learning exercises that encouraged the active exchange of personal information or experiences amongst learners. This passive approach to participation, posting one contribution per week or per topic, continued through out the semester.

Students were given discussion topics that spanned several weeks. Some of the topics took the form of scenarios that they had to analyse. They were required to review related literature, and highlight their findings by reporting back to the group. The reporting process was meant to evolve into lively discussion. However, as one student pointed out:

> "...it is called an online discussion, but actually very few discussions evolved. Everyone just attached their own work when they felt it was complete."

3.2 Shared Learning Goal

The unit the participants undertook as part of this study is compulsory. Students cannot attain an Information Technology Degree without completing this subject. As such their motivation to participate is essentially so they can get their degree.

Participation in discussions is worth 10% of the students' final mark for the subject. Therefore, to gain a high mark in the subject, students have to participate in discussions. If the student's goal is only to pass, they may be loath to participate as it takes a considerable amount of time, and is only worth 10% of the final mark. This view is reflected by one student who commented:

> *"...the total online participation mark was only worth 10% of the final grade. This meant there were many students who simply did not bother participating at all during the semester, since they felt the mark 'wasn't worth the trouble'."*

Only 42% of students surveyed indicated that all group members participated in the discussions. This lack of participation may be attributed to the minimal assessment of discussions. It may also be due to a lack of encouragement from online instructors. Of the students that did participate in discussion, almost half joined in on a daily basis, as shown in Figure 3. It is this daily participation that needs to be encouraged to facilitate a sense of community. Whilst 42% of participants contributed weekly, it may be the case that these students were contributing purely to ensure they got marks rather than to aid the discussion and learning process.

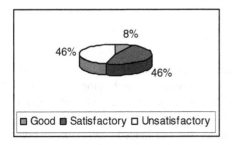

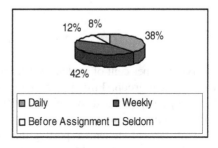

Fig. 2. View of working in groups online.   **Fig. 3.** Dialogue frequency.

3.3 Technology

Many students surveyed expressed frustration with the DSO technology. The current evolution of DSO was first introduced in 2003, and as such was subject to teething problems at the time of the study (the latter stages of 2003). Students were frustrated with the time it took to load content, confusing navigation and server failure that denied them access all together. Some administrative problems occurred during semester whereby the content for the entire subject was mistakenly deleted from DSO resulting in students being unable to participate for a number of days.

Being the first time that DSO was used to facilitate this unit, and the first time students had used the technology at all, some technology related problems were expected.

It is envisaged that by the next running of the subject, most students will be familiar with the technology and network and administrative problems will be overcome. Instructors will also be familiar with common problems experienced by students, and able to rectify them before they become obstacles to the learning process. It is therefore likely that in future, technology problems will not have such a big impact on students' attitude to the subject and its delivery.

3.4 Facilitation

Students were asked to quantify how long it took their instructor to respond to specific questions posed in their discussion group, the results can be seen in Figure 4. For lively discussion to take place most student queries need to be answered promptly, lest discussion stall due to disagreements or lack of clarity about related issues. Whilst the majority of student queries were answered within a couple of days, unfortunately, 17% of questions posed to instructors never received a response.

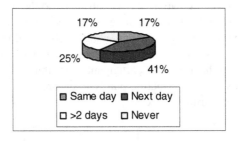

Fig. 4. Instructor response time.

Sixty-two per cent of students reported that instructors had offered unprompted advice to their group. Fifty per cent of students reported the instructor helped with knowledge gaps related to their discussions. When problems emerged in discussion groups instructors were active in mediating group disputes and managing social equality, with 39% of students reporting that the instructor had helped resolve group conflict. These results show that instructors did get involved in guiding discussions. However, a more pro-active approach may help to facilitate active discourse and improve students' perceptions of learning online.

3.5 Overview of Survey Results

Survey results showed that almost half of the students surveyed were unhappy with learning online using DSO. One of the main problems highlighted was student frustration with the technology. The results and comments were similar to those highlighted by [12], and supported the contention that technology problems can have a negative impact on the learning outcomes of a web based learning experience.

Analysis of the data in terms of social context and facilitation highlighted the fact that students need a more interactive way of introducing themselves to other group members, and sharing their experiences and ideas with the group. Whilst instructors played a role in answering direct questions from students, their role should be extended to modeling social presence in the early weeks of semester. Instructors should facilitate dialogue amongst group members by posing questions to individuals and the group as a whole, and encouraging other members to follow suit. Instructors must review discussion groups and offer feedback as often as possible, preferably on a daily basis. If students are expected to participate on a daily basis, they will be frustrated if instructors cannot offer feedback within the same timeframe.

Finally, active participations in group discussions should be rewarded with a higher percentage of the final mark. If students are to take participation seriously, and interact on a daily basis, the marking scheme should be adjusted to reflect importance of their efforts.

4 Conclusion and Future Work

The review of DSO in this paper supports the beliefs of [13] and [14]. Forcing students to work together in an online environment does not automatically create a virtual learning community. Certainly some participants may learn from the experience, but a sense of community can only emerge when students trust one another and share similar learning goals.

Survey results indicate that decreasing technology problems and increasing the assessment weighting for online discussions may enhance the students' motivation to learn online. Students may interact in a more lively fashion if they know their interactions are rewarded with marks. Providing a greater instructor presence in the early weeks of semester to demonstrate social presence may also help to promote lively regular discourse.

Implementing these recommendations will not automatically result in the creation of a virtual learning community. However, it may help bridge part of the gap between the present delivery of E-Learning at Deakin University, and the eventual creation of a virtual learning community.

Further work is planned in relation to students' perceptions of community in an online setting. It is envisaged that future surveys will further explore the factors and criteria outlined in this paper. The use of different collaborative technologies such as wikis is also being explored as a means to encourage collaboration and trust amongst learners.

References

1. Lanham, E. and W. Zhou, *E-Learning: Literature Survey*, Deakin University, Geelong (2002)
2. Rovai, A.P., *Building a Sense of Community at a Distance*, International Review of Research in Open and Distance Learning <http://www.irrodl.org/content/v3.1/rovai.html>, [accessed: 19.02.04] (2002)

3. Chignell, M., J. Ho, and M.C. Schraefel, *Towards an Evaluation Methodology for the Development of Research-Oriented Virtual Communities*, <http://www.dgp.toronto.edu/~mc/papers/WETICE2000-CHSch.pdf>, [accessed: 22.03.2003] (2000)

4. Rheingold, H., *The Virtual Community: Finding connection in a computerized world*. London, Secker & Warbur (1994) 325

5. Jones, Q., *Virtual-Communities, Virtual Settlements & Cyber-Archaeology: A Theoretical Outline*. Journal of Computer Mediated Communication. 3(3) (1997)

6. Weinreich, F., *Establishing a point of view toward virtual communities*, CMC Magazine <http://www.december.com/cmc/mag/1997/feb/wein.html>, [accessed: 20 July 2003] (1997)

7. Jones, S.G., *Understanding Community in the Information Age*, in *Cybersociety Computer-Mediated Communication and Community*, S.G. Jones, Editor. Sage Publications Inc.: California (1995)

8. Saragina, P., *Creating a Virtual Learning Community*, TCC 99 <http://leahi.kcc.hawaii.edu/org/tcon99/papers/saragina.html>, [accessed: 15.03.04] (1999)

9. Oren, A., et al., *LEARNET - A Model for Virtual Learning Communities in the World Wide Web*), Tel-Aviv University, Tel-Aviv (1998)

10. Daniel, B., G. McCalla, and R. Schwier. *A Process Model for Building Social Capital in Virtual Learning Communities*. International conference on Computers in Education. Aukland IEEE Computer Society (2002)

11. Lewis, R. *Learning Communities - old and new*. International conference on Computers in Education. Aukland IEEE Computer Society (2002)

12. Hara, N. and R. Kling, *Students' Frustrations with a Web-Based Distance Education Course*. First Monday. 4(12) (1999)

13. Stump, K., *Can We Really Build One Anyway?* CVC Professional Development Center <http://pdc.cvc.edu/common/article.asp?entry=1&idx=1656>, [accessed: 19.04.2004]

14. NEA, *Teaching and Learning Outside of the Box*, National Education Association of America <http://www.nea.org/he/advo00/advo0006/feature.html>, [accessed: 21.02.2004] (2000)

15. Calvert, J., *Deakin University: Going Online At A Dual Mode University*, International Review of Research in Open and Distance Learning <http://www.irrodl.org/content/v1.2/deakin.html>, [accessed: 19.02.04] (2001)

16. Deakin_University, *Online Technology in Courses and Units*, Deakin University <http://theguide.deakin.edu.au/TheGuide.nsf/WI?OpenFrameSet>, [accessed: 23.02.04] (2003)

17. Coldwell, J. *Mapping Pedagogy to Technology - A Simple Model*, in *Advances in Web-Based Learning ICWL 2003*. Melbourne Springer.(2003)

A Web-Based CAD System for Learning
and Laboratory Purpose

Ying Shan Tai and Wenyin Liu

Dept of MEEM; Dept of Computer Science, City University of Hong Kong
{meystai,csliuwy}@cityu.edu.hk

Abstract. A Web-based CAD system for learning and laboratory purpose is presented in this paper. The system serves as a three-in-one courseware: a pedagogical tool for teaching, an experimental tool for learning and a programming kit for laboratory. As a pedagogical tool, the system can help teachers interactively demonstrate the properties of curves and their associated equations with animations. The same tool can be used by students to play the animations themselves. As a programming kit, the same CAD system allows some CAD functions to be programmable for laboratory purpose. All activities are available on-line through a standard Web browser. A prototype is implemented and a user study is conducted for evaluation of the system. The result shows that the students like the system since it allows them to learn and practice the subject at home.

1 Introduction

Mathematical representation of geometric entities is a main topic in a Computer Aided Design (CAD) course. The teaching of some graphical elements such as Bezier curve and cubic spline has been regarded as a difficult task [1]. In fact, traditional lectures in computer graphics are considered incapable of conveying the complex principles [2]. It is beneficial to provide a graphical tool for teacher to demonstrate and for students to learn the related concepts. Such tool, in the form of a simple CAD System, can demonstrate the curve properties with animations and interactions. A related work called DesignMentor [3] has been found for similar purpose. It is a pedagogical tool for learning B-splines and surfaces, developed by the Geometric Computing and Graphics Group of the Department of Computer Science, Michigan Technological University. It provides an intuitive way, which is non-mathematical, to introduce important concepts and algorithms of B-splines to junior computer science students to minimize the need of lengthy and tedious mathematical discussion. Example features include showing graphically the control points, the control polygon, curvature sphere, etc. These geometric properties can be displayed on-the-fly by moving a tracing point on curves by a sliding bar.

However, DesignMentor is a stand-alone system. It is hard to find such system, which is also Web-based. A Web-based system can allow teacher to demonstrate the CAD system outside a laboratory, e.g., in a lecture theatre equipped with an Internet PC and a projected screen. It can also allow students to access it from home. A stand-alone system requires some installation procedures and most of ad hoc standalone coursewares usually experience the system compatibility problem. Therefore a Web-based system without requiring the users to do tedious job of installation, which is

W. Liu et al. (Eds.): ICWL 2004, LNCS 3143, pp. 309–316, 2004.
© Springer-Verlag Berlin Heidelberg 2004

also platform independent, is desirable. In brief, we need a pedagogical tool, which is Web-based, so that it can be applicable to a lecture, a tutorial or self-learning at home.

Besides lecture and tutorial, there is usually a laboratory session for students to do experiments about programming of geometric functions in CAD systems. An existing Experimental CAD System (ExpCAD) [4] was developed for such purpose by the Department of Manufacturing Engineering and Engineering Management, City University of Hong Kong. It was a programming kit for a laboratory session of a CAD/CAM course (MEEM3007) of the department. Through this laboratory, students can practice CAD programming in geometric transformation and curve point computation. The program was written in C++ and OpenGL. However, students only need to have basic knowledge of C Language because they are required to write only selected subroutines such as vector and matrix multiplications, transformation matrix construction, and curve point computation. All the tasks about graphical representations have been written for them. Students put their codes in the predefined program structure. If a student can write all the subroutines required for a specific CAD function, compile and bind them with the CAD system, the specific CAD function will work.

A programming kit like ExpCAD is very common. The limitation is that it is usually not Web-based. Students' programming skills are very diverse. Some students cannot finish the programming tasks within the provided laboratory time. When they want to practice the programming kit on their own paces, they do not have the resource. Some Web-based learning systems for programming purposes can be found [5], but similar systems that apply to programming of CAD functions are rare. There is a need to put the CAD programming kit on the Web so that students can use the system at any time and any place.

Hence, we develop the Web-based CAD system for learning and laboratory purpose (CADLP), which combines the pedagogical tool and the programming kit. It is actually a 3-in-1 online courseware applicable to lecture, tutorial and laboratory. Users can access the courseware with a standard Web browser with minimal configuration. In this paper, we present design, implementation, and evaluation of CADLP.

2 System Requirements

The CADLP system provides all functionalities in an integrated Web-base interface. End-users of the system include the students and instructors. There are three modes of operations, namely, teaching, learning and laboratory mode.

In the teaching and learning mode, CADLP, like a simple CAD system, provides basic CAD functions such as drawing line, polygon, Bezier curve and cubic spline, performing entity translation, rotation, reflection, deletion, etc. Instructor can use the system to demonstrate the Computer Graphics concepts. The system provides interactive animations to demonstrate various curve properties such as parametric variable, blending functions, control polygon and tangent vectors. There is also real-time generation of curve equations to compare with the graphical elements. In the learning mode, students can use the same system to learn and practice the above topics. Instructor can switch to teaching mode in which the graphic screen displays in larger font and thicker line for classroom projector. As the pedagogical tool is an online CAD system, it is run as a Java applet on the client side. Students use a Web browser with Java Plug-in to run the CAD system. If the client machine has no Java Plug-in already installed, the system will prompt the student to download it on-the-fly.

In the laboratory mode, students can do experiments on the programming of CAD functions in a virtual laboratory environment. They will practice how to write subroutines of entity transformations and curve creations. Students using this system are expected to have basic Java programming skills. Actually, they will only be required to write pieces of Java methods with predefined input and output. Except for a standard Web browser, students do not need to install any Java compiler or Java development environment because the code compilation is done at the server. The conceptual framework is illustrated in Fig. 1. Firstly, the source files are submitted for remote compiling. Secondly, the server compiles the source code on behalf of the client and returns the compilation errors, if any, to the client. Finally, if the source code is compiled without error, the subroutine will be bound with the main CAD program and the whole CAD system will be returned to the client for running test. Students should get aware that their working files are located somewhere in the server under their own accounts. They open, edit, and save remote source files online. In order to allow the students to save their files locally for offline editing, a download function is required. Similarly, a file upload function is required to put their files back to server.

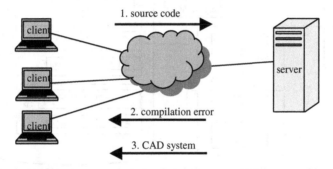

Fig. 1. Conceptual framework of CADLP in the Laboratory Mode

To access the student's individual programming work, file management of students' project files is required. For security consideration, only authorized users can login the system for data input and update, and only the authorized students can access their own files. On the other hand, instructor can access all students' project files and evaluate their work. To this end, password validation and access control procedure are required.

3 System Design

3.1 System Architecture

Fig. 2 below shows the CADLP system architecture in both the teaching/learning mode and the laboratory mode. In the teaching/learning mode, instructors can load the CADLP applet through the web server to demonstrate CAD functions and the curve properties. Students can practice the same demonstration with the same applet and with a little different customization. In the laboratory mode, each authorized user is associated with a project account and has a personal project folder. The server program mainly consists of Java Server Pages (JSPs) and a Java Bean (for the compiler handler). The Database Access handler, through the DBMS, accesses the student directory path from the student account database. The file system handler selects the appropriate folder to serve the client. The compiler handler dispatches the compilation job to the Java Compiler, and the error stream and output stream from the compiler are redirected and returned to the client. The compiled student's codes should be put into the correct student folder assigned by the file system handler. Each student folder has a set of prewritten classes that provides a test version of CADLP applet for testing codes written by students (e.g. Lab1.java and Lab2.java in Fig. 2).

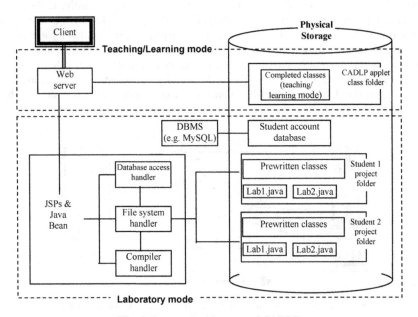

Fig. 2. System Architecture of CADLP

3.2 Screen Design

CADLP uses two types of user interfaces. The teaching/learning mode has a graphical user interface resembling that of an ordinary CAD system. The laboratory mode is a Web-based interface with a layout of a software development environment built up with HTML elements such as buttons, forms and text areas. Each type of user interface has a menu button to switch between each other.

In the teaching/learning mode (Fig. 3), the browser embeds the CAD system in the form of applet. In the applet, the topmost level is the Desktop Pane, which consists of multiple internal frames [6]. The draw frame contains a graphics canvas, a status bar and a coordinate bar. An equation frame is at the bottom to reflect the active curve equation. The parameter frame contains the graph of plotting blending functions against the parametric variable t. A slide bar is also in this frame to adjust the parametric variable. Moving this slide bar can show various animations including the tracing point in the draw frame, the updating equation in equation frame and the varying blending functions in the parameter frame. The teaching mode is the same as learning mode except that some graphical elements and texts are larger in order to provide a clearer display on the projected screen in a lecture theatre.

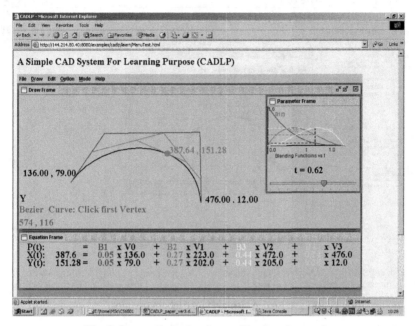

Fig. 3. Screen displaying the teaching/learning mode

In the laboratory mode (Fig. 4), CADLP is mainly a Web-based interface. It consists of a Source Editor Frame for source code editing and a Message Frame for displaying messages from the compiler. Students can save, compile and execute their codes. To test the compiled code, students activate the <Test Code> button. A new pop-up window, which contains the CAD system, is opened automatically as an applet. The applet consists of only a Draw Frame and an Output Frame. The Output Frame displays the user-defined debugging information. To modify the code, the user may close the applet and return to Source Editor Frame. <Download> button allows users to save a copy of the source code to local storage. <Upload> button allows users to replace the source code in the server with one in the local storage. <Next Lab> button is used to switch to next source file. <Folder> button is used to display a list of source files for selection. <Learning Mode> button brings the user to the teaching/learning mode. Finally, the <Logout> button clears the session information and returns to the login page. Some hyperlinks on the right hand side might be used to open lecture notes or lab instructions.

4 Implementation Issues

In the teaching/learning mode, CADLP is just a CAD System in the form of a self-contained applet [7] featured with Java2D API. Java applet is platform-independent and Java2D API, which is sufficient for graphical capability of our system, is also supported by the use of plug-in of a standard Web browser.

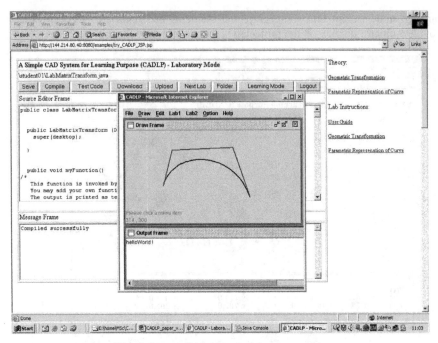

Fig. 4. Screen displaying the laboratory mode

In the laboratory mode, CADLP supports an online programming environment. It applies various Web technologies including HTML, JSP, JavaScript, Java Bean and Applet. The source code editor is simply an HTML Textarea generated by servlet. JSP, as an extension of servlet technology [7], helps to separate the HTML code from the servlet code and relieve the tasks of servlet from HTML formatting. The servlet portions of the JSPs perform central tasks including database access, user authentication, session tracking, file access, and code compilation. JavaScript [7,8] contributes to validate HTML form and for event handling of menu buttons. The server contains a Java Bean [7,8] for executing Java Compiler. It receives the uploaded source code from the client and save it to local storage. The compiler is then called to compile the source code. Any compilation error is redirected to the servlet, which returns the error message to the client. If the code is compiled without error, the object code is bound with the main CAD System and returned to the client as an applet. On the client side, a user usually needs to recompile the applet many times during the coding and debugging process. In order to reload the latest version of code, the Java classloader cache should be disabled from the Java plug-in. Java plug-in also provides a Java console, which can be used as an additional debugging tool for the applet.

On the security issue, as the user's code is running as an applet on user's own machine, there is no security risk to the server.

5 Evaluation

A usability study was carried out to get the feedback from the end-users about the software. Brief instructions were provided for the participants and questionnaires were designed to collect the result. As there is certain complexity of the programming tasks in the laboratory mode (the normal laboratory has three 3-hour sessions), it is not practical for participants to spend so long playing the software. Therefore, they were just required to print a "Hello World" to the output frame of the applet.

There were three participants to the usability test. Two of them had experiences on the traditional programming Lab. The remaining one is an experienced CAD user with basic knowledge of programming. All results were based on a bipolar 5-point rating scale (1=strongly disagree, 2= disagree, 3= neutral, 4= agree, 5=strongly agree), and all are positive questions. The questionnaire result shows that if they had already downloaded the Java plug-in, they had no difficulty to launch the web-based software (4 points). The download speed and page refresh rate when switching between pages were acceptable (4 points). They agreed that it was easy to switch between the learning mode and the laboratory mode (4 points). They inclined to agree that the system helped them to learn curve properties (3.7 points). On the negative side, they inclined to disagree that the programming kit is easy to use (2.6 points). No one agreed that they liked the layout of source editor and message window. In the provided source code, they did not know where to add their code in the right place in the program structure (2.3 points). They felt that it was difficult to configure the Java Plug-in before using the programming kit, though they could finally configure it by themselves (2.3 points). Although there were negative feedbacks on the programming kit, two of them stated that they liked doing the programming labs with this online system rather than in the laboratory room. In open questions, feedback about the system's strengths included "user friendly, convenient" and "easy to use". The weaknesses included "delete function in the learning mode is not sensitive enough" and "the layout of the screen should be well organized". One more general comment was "The guidelines for using the software is not clear enough. I was confused in using (configuring) the Java Plug-in". After the questionnaires, two participants were invited to have personal interviews. One participant said that the command terms on the buttons in the laboratory mode were not self-explanatory. He suggested adding more explanations in the usability test instruction. Another participant said she liked the learning mode but the laboratory mode was difficult. But she added that if the students had attended the lecture just before using the software the result would be better. She also expressed a very good point to advocate this software project that the students need such online tool at home to experiment the programming lab in order to be ready for test and/or examination because they have no resources at home after the dedicated hours of laboratory.

The results of the usability study show that the system help students learn curve properties. It is worth developing such a pedagogical tool and the programming kit, which are web-based, so that students can still use the tool at home beyond scheduled laboratory hours. Users found it easy to launch the system with a standard Web browser provided that a Java plug-in had already been installed. Although there were so many negative comments, the majority of them are due to the immaturity of the user interface. We need to do additional work for improvement. The selection of entities should be more sensitive. The Java plug-in configuration instruction should be more intuitive. Some universal and better command terms for buttons in the laboratory mode should be used. The layout of the laboratory mode should be improved. The readability of the program structure should be improved so that students can easily find the right place to add their codes. One way is to add different colors and add line number for easier debugging. In order to get a more accurate usability test, a larger sample size is required. It is most desirable that a usability test with a group of participants who are students just completing the lecture of the CAD/CAM course be further conducted.

6 Conclusion

An existing experimental CAD system, which originally supports programming experiment in laboratory classes, was wholly rewritten in platform-independent Java so that it can be accessed on-line through the Web. The final prototype, CADLP, adds functionality to turn the on-line CAD system into a pedagogical tool for teaching and learning Computer Graphics concepts. Actually, CADLP becomes a three-in-one courseware applicable to lecture, tutorial and laboratory sessions of a CAD course, supported by teaching, learning and laboratory mode of the system respectively. For example, a lecturer can demonstrate curve properties on projected screen in a lecture theatre, students can do curve animation at home on the Web, and at any time do programming tasks on CAD functions in a virtual laboratory environment. This paper in particular shows how an online programming kit for CAD course can be designed and implemented. The merits of CADLP system are shown in its integrated Web-based environment for all activities mentioned above. End-users do not need to install the software to run the CAD system. Neither do they need to install compiler and software development kit in order to do CAD programming exercises. They only have to use a standard Web browser with Java plug-in. On the security issue, there is no harm to the server even though the system supports user written codes because these codes are running as applet on the client's side. The usability test and personal interviews show that the system fulfills the need to access the pedagogical tool and the programming kit at home. The usability of the system depends on sufficient step-by-step instructions of the software, comprehensive user interfaces and minimal user system configuration.

References

1. Lowther, J., Shene C.K.: Teaching B-splines Is Not Difficult! In: Proc. 34th ACM Annual SIGCSE Technical Symposium, Reno, Nevada, pp. 381-385 (2003)
2. Yang, L., Sanver, M.: Web-Based Interactive 3D Visualization for Computer Graphics Education. Lecture Notes in Computer Science, Vol. 2436 (ICWL), Springer (2002)
3. Design Mentor, Geometric Computing and Graphics Group, Department of Computer Science, Michigan Technological University. (http://www.cs.mtu.edu/~shene/NSF-2)
4. Li E.: CAD/CAM Course: Lab, Dept of MEEM, City University of Hong Kong.
5. Cao, J., Chan, A., Cao, W., Yeung, C.: Virtual Programming Lab for Online Distance Learning. Lecture Notes in Computer Science, Vol. 2436 (ICWL), Springer (2002)
6. Deitel H.M.: Java: How to Program, 4th edition, Prentice Hall (2002)
7. Deitel, H.M., Deitel, P.J., Nieto T.: Internet & World Wide Web: How To Program, 2nd edition, Prentice Hall (2002)
8. Hall, M., Brown, L.: Core Web Programming, 2nd edition, Sun Microsystem (2001)

A Web-Based Teacher Assisting Agent System

Jianhua Ma, Ryosuke Komatsu, and Runhe Huang

Faculty of Computer and Information Sciences,
Hosei University, Tokyo 184-8584, Japan
{jianhua,n00k1015,rhuang}@k.hosei.ac.jp

Abstract. In the conventional teaching, teaching assistances (TAs) play impor-tance roles in supporting a teacher's teaching activities. This paper presents a Web-based teacher assisting agent system in which a set of automated pro-grams, so called agents in this context, is developed. It is described that how the agents are generated, where they reside, and how they work independently or collaborate with each other to assist a teacher. It is emphasized that a later de-veloped working agent can be easily incorporated into the system under the de-veloped system framework. It is addressed that both agent persistency and mo-bility in the system can be achieved by the proposed mechanisms.

Keywords: teacher assistant agent, mobile agent, online teaching.

1 Introduction

For teaching a web-based course, apart from organizing course contents and instruct-ing students, a teacher usually has to prepare an electronic version of the course con-tents and manage the course contents like updating the contents, uploading them to a Web server site, and checking on hyperlinks. For a non-computer science course teacher, it may be not an easy job. However, there are some commercial products like FrontPage, PowerPoint, and Dreamweaver, available for preparing electronic course contents. Moreover, a number of special authoring tools such as the intelligent e-learning system [1] and the multimedia distributed learning environment [2] have been developed for assisting course content preparations. Regarding instruction of remote students, there are many researches published and systems developed. For instances, the personalized multimedia tele-education environment [3] and Internet based teleteaching [4] are for tele-lecturing. GPSS [5] and VCR [6] are for group learning. PdWeb [7] and fill-in-blank program problems [8] are for online assign-ments. SPC table [9, 10] is for evaluation and assessment. Recently the agent tech-nology is also applied to distance learning [11–13].

In contrast, there are a few researches and software tools that are contributed to the content management. Without automatic content management, a teacher has to do it manually like timely control content accessibility, periodically adding assignment solutions, occasionally revising a part of the contents, promptly giving announce-ments, and frequently checking on hyperlinks inside the contents. Though the content management seems trivial, it is important means for teachers to improve their remote teaching quality and reduce avoidable complaining from students. Although some teachers put their course contents online once and never change them, it is sure that alive and dynamically editable/growing course contents can improve teaching quality and achieve the maximum learning effectiveness.

W. Liu et al. (Eds.): ICWL 2004, LNCS 3143, pp. 317–324, 2004.
© Springer-Verlag Berlin Heidelberg 2004

This research is dedicated to a teacher assisting agent system with which the course content can be automatically updated and maintained by a set of incorporated agents. An agent can work independently or collaborate with other agents to assist a teacher for teaching related activities. An agent platform and two build-in agents are developed so as to easily incorporate later developed working agents and efficiently manage working agents. Since an agent in this context is a Java object, when the host where the agent resides is shutdown, the agent will die. To solve this problem, mechanisms for agent persistency and mobility are proposed and implemented.

2   Some Basic Considerations in the System Design

Instead of human TAs, a set of teacher assisting agents are developed to assist a teacher's teaching related activities, in particular, the content management that is focused in this paper. According to the tasks to achieve in the content management, agents roughly fall into three categories: content handling agents, information handling agents, and hyperlink maintaining agents. Since each agent in this three categories is dedicated to a task, let us name it as a working agent. Any agent can work independently or collaborate with others to achieve a task, it becomes very important that all working agents have to be well organized and be able to communicate with each other. Therefore, the administration agent is designated for administration work of all working agents and the command agent is generated for enabling the mobility of working agents and coordinating their communications. All agents are organized in a hierarchy structure as shown in Fig. 1.

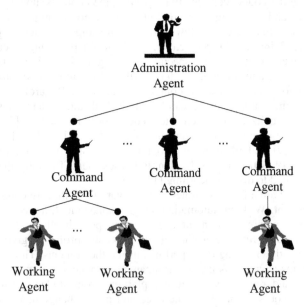

Fig. 1. The agent hierarchy

Both the administration agent and the command agent are build-in agents. The former resides in the teacher host and the latter resides in both the teacher host and the proxy host. Others, the working agents, are generated in runtime and can reside in the teacher host or move to another proxy host as shown in Fig. 2. Their mobility is under a command agent's control. With mobility, a working agent can continue its work without halt due to a shutdown or power off of the teacher host. When knowing that the proxy host is to be shutdown, the working agents can return to the teacher host. In the same principle, any working agent in a proxy host can be moved to another proxy host if it is necessary. Different working agents can move to different proxy hosts as long as the proxy hosts exist and are installed with the agent proxy environment. Agents are java objects, once the teacher host is shutdown, the administration agent and the command agents that reside in the teacher host will die. To keep the administration agent and the command agents persistent, there is a mechanism of marshalling an agent into an XML file and demarshalling the XML file to the agent. Thus, when the teacher host is power on again, the administration agent and the command agents can start from the previous states rather than the initial state. When the teacher host is shutdown and the teacher would like to request an agent to perform a task, the teacher can use an alternative computer or mobile device to simply manipulate the working agents in the proxy host.

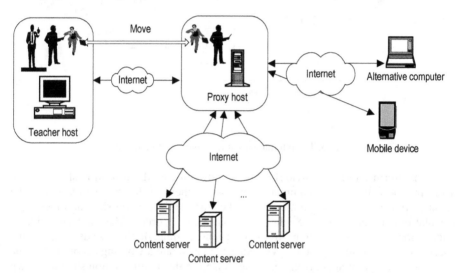

Fig. 2. The residence of agents and mobility of the working agents

3   The Agent Platform

In this paper, we can present only a limited number of working agents to assist teacher work. For sure, any teacher is expecting more and more working agents to support his/her various works related to teaching, which are not only limited to the content management. Therefore, it is natural to come out an idea of having an agent platform with which any later developed agent can be easily incorporated into the system. With this ability, the web-based teacher assisting agent system can become a scalable system that meets different teachers with different requirements. The system size and scale can varies by adding required agent packages to or deleting specified agent packages from the agent module directory in the file system. Having already incorporated agent packages, any requested agents can be generated, registered, and managed on the agent platform.

The agent platform is a package which mainly includes six classes: platform interface, platform initiator, specification repository, administration agent, agent encoder, and agent decoder as shown in Fig. 3.

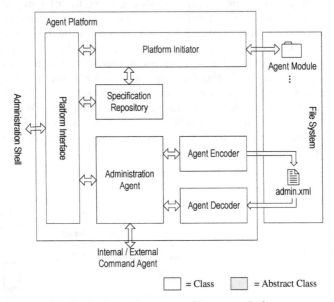

Fig. 3. The internal structure of the agent platform

The platform interface provides a bridge between the administration shell and the agent platform. It receives commands and passes them to the internal classes of the agent platform. It starts when a user launches the administration shell and then calls the platform initiator and the administration agent in order. The platform initiator fetches the agent specifications from the agent module. It then sends them to the specification repository. When a user requests to generate a working agent, that is, the user selects a type of agent from the **action** menu in the administration shell as shown in Fig. 4, the request command is sent to the platform interface that pools related agent specifications from the specification repository and sends them to the administration agent. The administration agent manages all generated working agents in a parent-child tree structure and keeps their latest status. When the host is shutdown, it sleeps by marshalling all its related data to an XML file via the agent encoder and wakes up by marshalling the XML file back to it via the agent decoder and starts it again. The administration agent updates the status of related agents once it receives any reports from a command agent that can be the internal one, that is, the one in the agent environment, or the external one, that is, the one in the agent proxy environment. When it is necessary, a generated working agent can be moved to the proxy host by dragging its name from the agent list on the right to the proxy host in the host list on the left in the administration shell window given in Fig. 4. The command agent in the proxy host is then taking care of the new coming working agent.

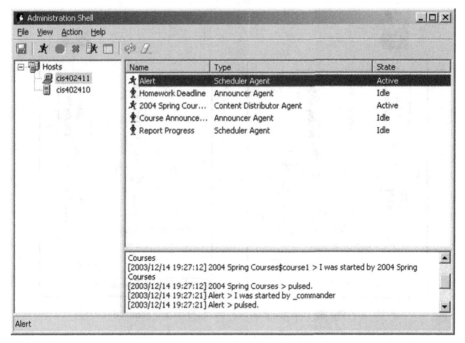

Fig. 4. The administration shell window

4   The Agent Environment and the Agent Proxy Environment

Once generated, the working agents can reside either in the administration host or the proxy host. Therefore, there are two versions of environments in which the working agents are running. The agent environment is installed in the teacher host and the agent proxy environment is installed in the proxy host.

As given in Fig. 5, the agent environment mainly consists of the administration shell, the agent platform, the agent module, and the agent runtime. The agent proxy environment mainly includes the agent access shell, the gateway, the agent module, and the agent runtime. A user usually interacts with the agent environment via the administration shell in the teacher host, he/she, however, can interact with the agent proxy environment via the agent access shell in the proxy host in some cases when the teacher host is shutdown or the user is remote from the teacher host. The agent module contains all classes that are required in the processes of working agent generation and running. It is, therefore, accessed from the agent platform and the agent runtime. Once the proxy host is selected, the agent module is uploaded automatically to the proxy host from the teacher host. Communications between two environments are through the stub in the agent environment and the gateway in the agent proxy environment by SOAP messages. The stub is a class that serializes an agent into an XML file and dispatches it to another agent environment. The tie is a class that de-serializes the received XML file into an agent and the command agent inserts it into the parent-child tree in the command agent.

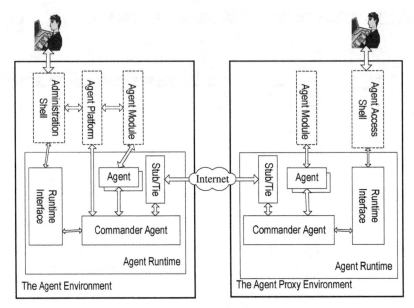

Fig. 5. Two agent environments and their connection

5   The Working Agents

Working agents are developed according to their different tasks. This paper is focused on the content management for which there are three categories of working agents: the content handling agents, the information handling agents, and the hyperlink handling agents. Each category has a set of different type agents for different specific tasks. Some working agents available in the system such as content uploading agent, content revising agent, content appending agent, disable/enable content agent, information advertising agent, course scheduling agent, hyperlink checking agent, and hyperlink repairing agent.

Collaboration among some of them is necessary, for instances, a course scheduling agent may need to send a time event to a disable/enable content agent in a predefined timing (such as when a term starts/ends) so that the disable/enable content agent can link up/off the lecture contents. An advertising agent needs to obtain the scheduled time for popping up/erasing news. Collaboration among the working agents is coordinated by the command agent and communication is through the stub and gateway.

Different type working agents can be designed by different developers as long as they follows a certain design style that is defined in the interface classes, IAgent and PropertySheet, and super classes, Agent and PropertySheetImpl. A working agent, for instances, course scheduling agent, can be defined as follows:

   class SchedulingAgent **extends** Agent **implements** ISchedulingAgent
   class ISchedulingAgent **extends** IAgent
   class SchedulingAgentPropertySheet **extends** PropertySheetImpl
   class PropertySheetImpl **implements** PropertySheet

For those specific propertie related to a type of agent (named as X) can be freely added in XAgentPropertySheet class and those specific jobs for the agent to do can be also freely defined in XAgent class. The finished Java class files together with a-gent.xml are put into the agent module directory. The type of agent is ready for use in generating instant agents which are working in runtime as shown in Fig. 6. The core in the agent runtime is the working agent core package that contains the common classes required to run working agents. A working agent is also able to interact with other agents or external resources via **Sensor** and **Effector**.

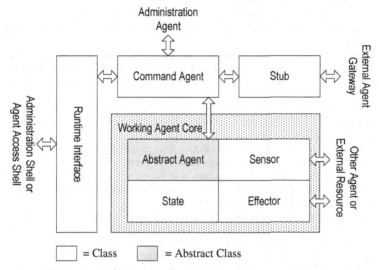

Fig. 6. The agent runtime

6   Conclusions and Future Work

This paper presents a Web-based teacher assisting agent system. Although the current version of the system is focused on working for the content management, it is a piece of practical workable system. Moreover, it is no doubt it can become a complete teacher assisting system since the system framework has been carefully modularized such that it has a distingushed feature, scalability. More and more new type of work-ing agents can be easily designed by any developers and quickly incorporated into the system.

In the current implementation of the system, the serveral standard technologies such as XML and SOAP are applied. Both the agent environment and the agent proxy environment run on Java-based hosts. Java is also used for developing new types of working agents. It may be worthywhile to investigate whether a developed agent in a non-Java language is able to be incorporated into the system and whether a Ja-va-based agent environment host can easily communication with a non-Java agent environment host such as Microsoft .NET framework [14].

Although agents (Java programs) developed have a certain automation, it is ex-pected to develop intelligent agents to really assist teachers with decision making ability. Teachers are expecting to relieve from some of their tedious work since intelligent working agents can work more efficiently and effectively.

References

1. Timothy K. Shih et al, "An Intelligent System with Authoring and Assessment Mechanism", *Proceedings of the 17th International Conference on Adv. Info. Networking and Applications*, Xi'an, China, 2003.
2. Peter Holt et al, "Towards a Multimedia Distributed Learning Environment", *Proceedings of the Seventh International Conference on Distributed Multimedia Systems*, Taipei, Taiwan, 2001.
3. Z. Cheng et al, "An Overview of an Interactive and Personalized Multimedia Tele-Education Environment over Gigabit Network", *The Proceedings of 2000 International Conference on Information Society in the 21st Century*, Aizu-Wakamatsu, Fukushima, Japan, 2000.
4. Frank Imhoff et al, "Internet Based Teleteaching using the IP-based German Broardband Science Network", *Adv. in Edu. Technologies: Multimedia, WWW and Distance Education*, John Wiley & Sons, Inc, 2001.
5. A. Hazeyama et al, "Development of a Group Programming Support System", *Adv. Res. in Computers and Communications in Education*, IOS Press, 1999.
6. Jianhua Ma et al, "Collaborative Teaching and Learning in Virtual Collaboration Rooms over the Internet", *Proceedings of International Conference Assisted Instruction and Internet Computing*, Taipei, Taiwan, 2000.
7. Kenji Kaijiri et al, "Program Diagnosis System on World Wide Web", *Adv. Res. in Computers and Communications in Education*, IOS Press, 1999.
8. A. Kashihara et al, "Making Fill-in-Blank Program Problems for Learning Algorithm", *Adv. Res. Computers and Communications in Education*, IOS Press, 1999.
9. Flora Chia-I Chang, "Automatic Assessment of Student Performance in Distance Learning", *Proceedings of International Conference Assisted Instruction and Internet Computing*, Taipei, Taiwan, 2000.
10. F. C. Chang et al, "Course Authoring and Student Assessment System for Distance Learning", *Proceedings of the Eighth International Conference on Distributed Multimedia Systems*, San Francisco, California, USA, 2002.
11. Marcelo Milrad et al, "Using Intelligent Agents as Tools To Support Collaboration in Distributed Learning Environment", *Adv. Res. in Computers and Communications in Education*, IOS Press, 1999.
12. Fuhua Lin et al, "Design and Analysis of an Agent-based Online Learning System", *Proceedings of the Seventh International Conference on Distributed Multimedia Systems*, Taipei, Taiwan, 2001.
13. Catalin Buiu et al, "Prolog Collaborative Agents for Distance Education", *Adv. Res. in Computers and Communications in Education*, IOS Press, 1999.
14. MSDN .NET, http://msdn.microsoft.com/netframework/.

An Application-Oriented e-Learning System with Self-monitoring and Adaptive Exercises

Joseph Fong[1], Irene Kwan[2], Margaret Ng[1], Ivan Li[1], and S.K. Chan[1]

[1] Department of Computer Science, City University of Hong Kong, Hong Kong
csjfong@cityu.edu.hk
[2] Department of Information System, Lingnan University of Hong Kong

Abstract. eLearning has deficiencies. It is difficult to monitor students' learning progress and verify students' understanding of a topic. Self Monitoring System(SMS) and Adaptive Exercise System(AES) is a solution to the problem. With SMS, students can actively monitor their learning progress for better efficiency. With AES, professors can determine which levels of exercises the student should take for progressive learning. This paper presents a methodology of using sequencing instructions of fixed format case study and free format empirical study for self learning process. The fixed format provides a predefined input and fixed model answer output for students to obtain general concept of the topic. The free format provides a chance for the students to apply their learned knowledge a real life situation. We focus on teaching students how to apply their learnt knowledge in a real life application such as data modeling techniques by eLearning.

1 Introduction

eLearning is growing fast due to the increasing popularity of Internet. Many institutes move courses from classroom to the World Wide Web (WWW) of Internet. Students can learn by themselves on the web using web browser. They do not need to come to school to learn. They can learn at any time and any place where they can access Internet. Institutes do not need to concern classroom space and limited number of student intake. Thus, institutes can save cost from renting classrooms and make more profits from tuition fees.

Although eLearning is a very good learning approach, the quality of eLearning system provided by institutes are different. In addition, there is no standard methodology for implementation of eLearning system. Students have difficulties to determine the quality of eLearning system the institutes provide. They can determine only by trial and error. The following factors are common deficiencies of eLearning courses provided by some institutes:

Problem 1: *It is difficult to monitor students' learning behavior and progress:*

Most of the eLearning courses neglect the learning behavior of the students. eLearning system does not know how much time the students spend on every chapter. When

W. Liu et al. (Eds.): ICWL 2004, LNCS 3143, pp. 325–332, 2004.

students spend too much time on a chapter, the system does not actively inform students their progress and provide recommendations for them.

SMS Solution: For students to achieve the goals and reach the target of the course, SMS actively monitor the learning progress is very important. A great analogy for studying a course is doing a project. To do a project, every project member should keep monitoring the progress of every task and make sure it follows the schedule and reaches every milestone on time. Otherwise, the project would be delayed or failed at worst. When students take a course, especially eLearning courses, students are self-motivated to learn. No teachers take care of their progress. In order to study all items in the syllabus of the course on time, monitoring learning progress is a must. However, rare eLearning courses provide such important tools for students.

Problem 2: *Difficult to verify and ensure students' understanding or level of proficiency:*

Most of eLearning courses provide static learning materials on the web, for example, Microsoft Word document, PDF (Portable Document Format) document and HTML (Hypertext Markup Language). Students learn by studying these materials. No one can ensure how much students understand these materials. Tools like exercises or tests are rarely provided or not adequate for students to verify themselves. Even through exercises or tests are provided, it does not consider the fact that the ability of different students are different. The exercises are not adaptive for all students with different ability. Not all students can get benefit from it.

AES Solution: For student to understand the knowledge of the course taught, AES helps students to verify and ensure that their understanding and proficiency on the learning process are suitable. Since students are aware of what they do not understand, they can concentrate on it and make improvement. They do not waste time on the topics they grasp. High ability students can explore further to more advance knowledge, whereas other students can understand the knowledge they must know at least.

There are theories for the order and organization of learning activities or sequencing of instructions[8]. Sequencing of instruction influences the way information is processed and retained. The theory suggests simple-to-complex sequences, and let students form their own learning sequences or adapt instructions to the experience or interest of learners. Figure 1 shows the architecture of sequencing instructions in the application oriented eLearning system.

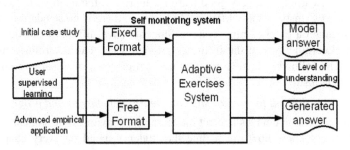

Fig. 1. Architecture of Application oriented eLearning system

2 Related Work

The majority of currently available remote-access laboratories lack a number of key features. These include (1) a coherent consistent overall framework and approach to online experimentation, interface design and site layout; (2) there is no clear and defined procedure for assessing the success of the online coursework carried out by the students [1]. In this paper, we have overcome these deficiencies. Adaptive means the learner needs to go through an initial simple training exercise before an advanced free format exercise. In case the student cannot finish the advanced one, he/she needs to go back to the simple exercise for review.

A factor in developing this system is to ensure that the e-learners experience is a positive one, and the administration is geared to support the e-learners through all aspects of their on-line experience [2]. Adaptive Learning Systems have failed to gain widespread acceptance. A critical factor that determines the popularization of these systems is the possibility of using the standardized data models for exchanging and reusing learning resources [3]. In order to guarantee that the contents and service are acceptable for global users, a standardized data model is introduced.

System Architecture Mode: The Learning Technology System Architecture (LTSA) [4] is used to specify a high level system architecture and layering for students and instructors to use computer-based training, intelligent tutoring, education and training technology.

Data Mode: The system stores relevant information about data requirements of a case study. It combines Java, JDBC, XML, SQL and data modeling using the Extended Entity-Relationship (EER) approach [7].

Course Structures Mode: Moving a course from an educational platform to a different one implies transferring the course contents of (lessons, questionnaires, simulators etc. with their associated metadata and also constructing the way that the contents are structured [5].

Student behavior Mode: Meta-tagging learning elements approach enables the flexible execution of course which depends on the individual learning style of the student [6]. With this mode, a clear procedure is defined for accessing each level of study.

3 Methodology for Self-monitoring System and Adaptive Exercises System

To solve the problems and achieve the objectives as mentioned, two systems are proposed to solve the problems. They are Self-Monitoring System (SMS) and Adaptive Exercise System (AES).

Step 1: Self-monitoring System (SMS)
Self-Monitoring System monitors the learning behavior and progress of students. The eLearning system will let user design and adapt the behavior of students and create a learning environment in favor of the learning style of student individually. In addition,

students can actively monitor their own learning progress, or let the system to inform them the progress automatically. As a result, the overall efficiency for student to learn in web is improved. Principles of using the SMS are:

a) Scheduling: The proper practice is to design a scheduling or time management preference for student to plan their study. First, students study a course may include many parts, for example, the reading course notes, doing exercise and participating discussion. Student can plan their time spent on individual parts. The system keeps monitoring how much time the student spends on individual parts. If the time spent is more than what they prefer, the system will actively alert the student. Beside the planning individual part, overall time spend is also needed. Second, SMS provides checkpoint for student to verify their progress. This checkpoint can be on user-specified time or on a regular time basis. When the time occurs, appropriate status is shown such as schedule and time spent on each exercise.

b) Visualized Status: SMS uses graph to present the checkpoint status of learning progress in order to enhance the learning efficiency of student. The students can find out the learning progress at a glance. System should design to use graph to show the time spent and the scheduled time spent on every individual parts at the same time for easy comparison.

c) Interactive Advice: Interactive advice are provided actively when there has something to advise. Students decide whether they accept or reject that advice. Students can save time to find the problem in their study. The system guides them to complete the course efficiently.

Step 2: Adaptive Exercise System (AES)
An Adaptive Exercise System helps student to ensure their understanding of the eLearming course material in the level of proficiency, and improve the standard of students after taking the eLearning course. AES provides an exercise database for student to practice. The exercises in the database are categorized by topics and levels. Levels are ranged from basic to expert. AES uses adaptive approach to determine which levels of exercise the student should take. That means a more difficult question is given to student if they correctly answered a question, otherwise, an easier question is given to student if they failed to answer a question. In order to ensure that the students can really understand and apply the learnt theories, we divide the exercises into two sequential instructions as follows.

a) Initial Fixed Format Case Study Exercise: This exercise aims to deliver the basic theory of the subject to learn, for example, database design concepts. A case study with a fixed input and model answer will be provided for learning purpose. Student follow the case to design a database system step-by-step. The case study includes the business background, user requirements, model answers, instructions and guidelines. Students complete the eight steps for a database design process. In each step, students answer will be verified against the model answers that will be given to the students for reference.

b) Advanced Free Format Empirical Application Exercise: This exercise is similar to the Fixed Format Exercise except that no data requirement or entity descriptions will be given. It provides the flexibility for student to define their own required data, choose the key fields and the related attributes. Also, it gives an opportunity to student to set the relationship between entities. At the end of the exercise, an Extended Entity Relationship model designed by student will be generated. This exercise allows students to design database system for their own applications. In each step, the evaluation process will be applied on the students entered data, and the understanding level of the students in database design.

4 Prototype of the Application Oriented e-Learning System

A prototype on the application oriented eLearning system was implemented and evaluated by students as:

Step 1: Self-monitoring System (SMS)

The advice page is designed to use colored text like red color text to display message in order to attract student attention. Button is shown under the message to help student redirect to relevant page. The layout of this page is shown in Figure 2[9] which show number of current answer out of total questions to reflect the student's level of understanding of the subject.

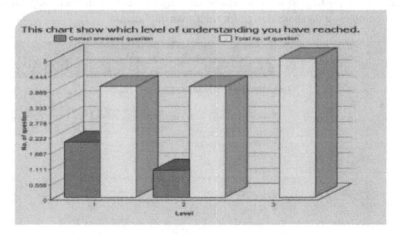

Fig. 2. Monitor the level of understanding

Step 2: Adaptive Exercise System (AES)

There are two kinds of exercises as:

a) Fixed format (Case study)[10] – Figure 3 shows a set of pre-defined data requirement of a case study for the students to complete the design process according to the background and user requirements.

Fig. 3. Instructions of a fixed format case study

b) Free format (empirical application) – A free format system is provided to students to customize their own database design for an empirical study. The student enters an empirical case study data requirements into the eLearning system which generates a well format database design under user supervision interactively. The derived database design will be in the correct format of an Extended Entity Relationship model with data semantics as defined by the students. Figure 4 shows an example for students to enter their own data requirements (which is different from a fixed format that provides predefined data requirements at the beginning) [10][11] The free format verifies the entered data according to data modeling techniques theories in each step until the students complete a database design for their own application.

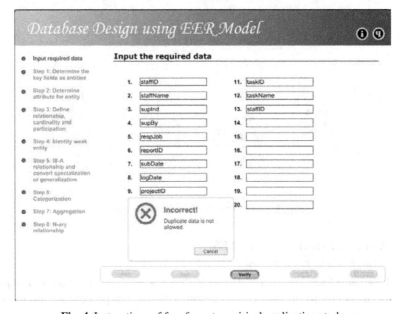

Fig. 4. Instructions of free format empirical application study

In free format data modeling, validation rules are applied to the users data to ensure the resultant database design is theoretical correct, which meets users requirements. Error message will be displayed for invalid users entry in data modeling such as:

Entity is without entity key.
Duplicate entity name exists.
Duplicate relationship name exists.
Same strong entity and weak entity exist..
Weak entity has single attribute key only.
Weak entity does not concatenate strong entity keys.
Superclass and subclass entities do not have the same key.
Attribute appear in both superclass and subclass entities in is-a relationship.
Aggregation entity is not related to any entity.
....

5 Conclusion

Self-Monitor feature improves the learning efficiency of the student, and helps students monitor their learning pace. Whenever they are out of pace, they are notified by the system. Thus, the students can concentrate on the unfamiliar topic without waste time on other things. Adaptive Exercise feature increases average level of standard of the student. Student are trained by the use of exercise according to their level of proficiency. The exercise is tailor-made for their level. They can progressively increase their level of proficiency. As a result, the overall level of standard is increased. The fixed format exercise facilitates the students to learn the basic theories of a subject based on a case study. After that, they can continue the free format exercise to apply what they learnt from an empirical application dictated by the students themselves. In summary, students learn how to apply their learnt theory.

References

1. Callaghan, M.J.; Harkin, J.; McGinnity, T.M.; Maguire, L.P., "An Internet-based methodology for remotely accessed embedded systems", Systems, Man and Cybernetics, 2002 IEEE International Conference on , Volume: 6 , 6-9 Oct. 2002, Pages:6 pp. vol.6
2. Forman, D.; "Cultural change for the e-world", Computers in Education, 2002. Proceedings. International Conference on , 3-6 Dec. 2002, Pages:1412 - 1413 vol.2
3. Santos, J.M.; Anido, L.; Llamas, M.;, "On the use of e-learning standards in adaptive learning systems", Advanced Learning Technologies, 2003. Proceedings. The 3rd IEEE International Conference on , 9-11 July 2003, Pages:480
4. http://edutool.com/ltsa/04/
5. Anido, L.; Llamas, M.;, "A contribution to the e-learning standardization", Standardization and Innovation in Information Technology, 2001 2nd IEEE Conference , 3-6 Oct. 2001, Pages:295 – 309
6. Altenhofen, M.; Schaper, J.;, "Flexible instructional strategies for e-learning", System Sciences, 2002. HICSS. Proceedings of the 35th Annual Hawaii International Conference on , 7-10 Jan. 2002, Pages:342 – 351

7. http://www.cs.cityu.edu.hk/~jfong/cs6401/eLearning.html
8. Martin Blochl, Hildegard Rumstshofer, Wöß,"Individual E-Learning Systems Enabled by a Semantically Determined Adaption of Learning Fragments", Johannes Kepler University Linz, Australia, Proceedings of DEXA 2003, pp.640-645.
9. W M Li, "Effective Web-Based Relational Database Learning System", BSCS Final Year Project Report 2003-2004, Department of Computer Science, City University of Hong Kong, 2004.
10. S K Chan, "Towards Adaptive Web-based Learning for Database Design", BSCS Final Year Project Report 2003-2004, Department of Computer Science, City University of Hong Kong, 2004.
11. http://personal.cityu.edu.hk/~50153621/Start.swf

Methodologies of the Personalized Courseware Construction Tools for e-Learning

Yanhua Cao[1], Xiaoming Li[2], Huisheng Chi[1], and Xihong Wu[1]

[1] National Laboratory of Machine Perception and Center for Information Science
Peking University, Beijing 100871, China
`yhcao@cis.pku.edu.cn`, `chi@pku.edu.cn`, `wxh@cis.pku.edu.cn`
[2] Department of Computer Science, Peking University, Beijing 100871, China
`lxm@pku.edu.cn`

Abstract. The Personalized Courseware Construction Tools (PCCT) are described which are to meet the personalization requirement in e-learning. Teachers can use them to prepare an adaptive courseware in a more efficient way and learners can have a personalized learning environment to optimize their learning. The experimental results have showed that the courseware based on the PCCT is superior and the personalized tutoring is an efficient way to the learner's knowledge acquisition.

1 Introduction

The growing popularity of e-learning has created a need for personalization. Individual differences exist in the learner's learning outcome that depending on learner's ability and preferred learning style in hypermedia environment. Meanwhile, with the development of e-learning technologies, learners can be provided more effective learning environment to optimize their learning. The conventional courseware for e-learning provides the same curriculum structure and content in a page of a courseware to different learners despite individual differences such as knowledge background, learning style and learning speed etc. It can not be met the different needs of learners and is urgent to create a kind of dynamic courseware that can organize the content flexibly and dynamically to adapt the learner's different feedbacks. In this paper, the Personalized Courseware Construction Tools (PCCT) are described for teachers to prepare the adaptive courseware according to different learner's learning outcomes, and for learners to learn in a personalized environment where learners can choose among three learning patterns: Random Learning Pattern, Sequential Learning Pattern and Feedback Learning Pattern. In the following section, the functional structure of PCCT is discussed where the architecture and functions of the system are specified. In the third section, the experiment of the system is discussed in detail, in which the design for the learning experiment is introduced and the results of the experiment are given, which indicate the personalized learning is superior to the general learning. Finally, conclusions and future work are discussed in Section 4.

2 Functional Structure

PCCT is a system for personalized courseware constructing with a graphical interactive interface and personalized learning with an adaptable environment.

W. Liu et al. (Eds.): ICWL 2004, LNCS 3143, pp. 333–337, 2004.

2.1   Architecture of the System

PCCT is composed of four functional components: (a) Instructional Content Compilation, (b) Curriculum Structure Organization, (c) Learning and Testing Planning, and (d) Dynamic Construction. The functional architecture of the system is shown as in Figure 1, and described in the following sub-section.

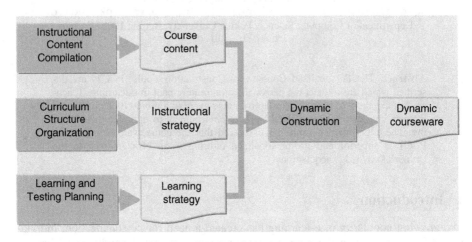

Fig. 1. The functional architecture of the system

2.2   Functions of the System

The Instructional Content Compilation Module. The module is supported by three databases (DB), i.e. Knowledge-Point DB, Test DB and Template DB, using which a teacher can edit the smallest basic knowledge unit into a knowledge-point by choosing an appropriate presentation template, and arrange the corresponding test problems and answers.

The Curriculum Structure Organization Module. In the module, a teacher can represent his or her personalized instructional pattern and strategy by using structural concept map, in which a node expresses knowledge-point, a line linking two nodes expresses the correlation between the knowledge-points, and the layer represents the concepts in the chapters, sections and units of the course.

The Learning and Testing Planning Module. The module is for a teacher to prepare an instructional sequence and related testing, such as Basic-Test – a test before learning, Unit-Test – a test during learning process and Comprehensive-Test – a test after learning, which is used to evaluate the learner's learning outcomes.

The Dynamic Construction Module. This module assembles the instructional strategy, learning strategy and instructional content to construct a dynamic personalized courseware, provides a learning-and-testing environment for a learner in different learning pattern according to his or her background and style, and manages the log recording the learner's learning time, learning pattern and learning score.

3   Experiment

3.1   The Design for the Learning Experiment

First, we design a courseware of Computer Essentials, including two chapters, total six sections, in which 145 knowledge-points are included. Next, we design a corresponding testing database including 60 questions and its answers. Finally, two examination papers are prepared for learners, one is Basic-Test for testing the learner's learning aptitude before using the system, and the other is Comprehensive-Test for evaluating the learner's learning effect. Table 1 shows the detail design of the experiment.

Table 1. The outline of the learning experiment

Experimental purpose	1. Studying the personalized learning outcomes and comparing with different learning patterns; 2. Studying the relationship between the learning effect and the time that personalized learners spend in the learning process.
Experimental object	High school students or freshmen of universities.
Experimental range	1. Volunteer recruited from internet: freshmen, and non-computer specialty; 2. Students from same class: grouping randomly and homogenously.
Experimental organization	1. Recruiting the volunteers; 2. Planning the experimental time table; 3. Experimenting.
Experimental time	Add up to two hours for each learner. 1. Routine training: 10 minutes; 2. Learning on computer: 50 minutes; 3. Testing: 50 minutes (Basic-Test: 10 minutes, Comprehensive-Test: 40 minutes); 4. Feedback: 10 minutes.
Experimental method	1. Grouping the learners into three groups randomly: ten learners in one group, (corresponding to three learning patterns); 2. Learning by using the learning system on computer; 3. Testing before and after learning; 4. Answering the writing questionnaire.
Experimental steps	1. Training the learners for software using (10 minutes); 2. Testing learners before learning (10 minutes); 3. Learning on computer (50 minutes); 4. Testing learners after learning (40 minutes); 5. Answering the questionnaire of the satisfaction degree (10 minutes).

3.2 The Experimental Results

Thirty freshmen take part in the experiment, and are grouped in three groups randomly. First, they finish the Basic-Test, including six questions, which cover basic concepts from every section. Then they learn in the personalized learning environment, in which each group using one of three learning patterns: Random Learning Pattern (RLP), Sequential Learning Pattern (SLP) and Feedback Learning Pattern (FLP). In RLP, the learning objects are organized as a tree of hypermedia and the learners can browse through the knowledge-points with an index tree randomly. In SLP, the learning objects are organized in a default sequence defined by the PCCT and all learners learn the knowledge-points in the same order. In FLP, the learning objects are dynamically organized according to the learner's feedback defined by the PCCT and the learner can choose the different learning path of knowledge-points. Hardly had the learners learned the course, when they attended the Comprehensive-Test, including twelve questions, in which there are one basic and one comprehensive question in each section. The correct rate of test is used to estimate the effect of learning and the correct rate per hour is used to estimate the efficiency of learning. The correct rate of test is defined as the ratio of learner's score to the total of the test. The experimental results are showed in the following figures.

Figure 2 shows the correct rate of Comprehensive-Test, where it is indicated that the learning effect in the FLP group is the best and that in the RLP group is better than that in the SLP group.

Figure 3 shows the average efficiency of Learning, in which learners in the FLP group also achieved the greatest speed of learning and the descending order of the three groups is the same as that in Figure 2: FLP, RLP and SLP. It is out of our expectation before the experiment. Our presumption of the sequence is FLP, SLP and RLP because it is thought that the knowledge organized in context is easy to be acquired for learners.

According to the correct rate of the Basic-Test, we divided the data of Comprehensive-Test into two incorporating groups: High-score group, where the correct rate is higher than or equal to seventy percent, and Low-score group, where the correct rate is lower than seventy percent.

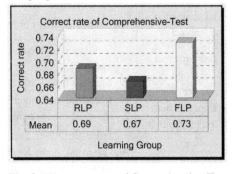

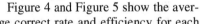

Fig. 2. The correct rate of Comprehensive-Test

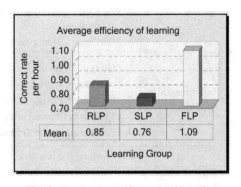

Fig. 3. The average efficiency of learning

Figure 4 and Figure 5 show the average correct rate and efficiency for each incorporating group, in which it is indicated that the FLP groups consistently score better than other groups. Contrasting the RLP and SLP groups in two incorporating groups points out that the learning effects of

RLP is greater than that of SLP in the high-score group, meanwhile, the learning effects of SLP is greater than that of RLP in the low-score group. This result in the low-score group is consistent with our presumption: the learning effect of the FLP group is superior to the others, and that of the SLP group is greater than that of the RLP group. Furthermore, we can derive that learners with SLP in Low-score group make more progresses than that in High-score group in the personalized learning environment, i.e., learners who have no knowledge background progress faster through the instructed uniform learning.

4   Conclusions and Future Works

This paper describes the system of the Personalized Courseware Construction Tools, which provides the tools for teacher to prepare the courseware and an environment for learner to learn in personalized style, and analyzes the experimental results, comparing the different learning pattern in a personal-

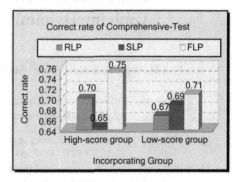

Fig. 4. The average correct rate for incorporating group

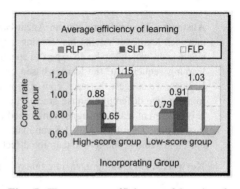

Fig. 5. The average efficiency of learning for incorporating group

ized learning environment. From the analysis, we can derive a conclusion that the personalized tutoring, which can provide interaction between learners and the learning system, is an efficient way for the learner's knowledge acquisition.

Studying other factors such as the numbers of Unit-Test that learners finished, the ratio of testing time to learning time during the personalized learning is ongoing, and we will improve the system to meet more needs of teachers and learners.

Acknowledgments. This paper is funded by the Modern Distance Education Project of China Ministry of Education and Beijing Natural Science Foundation (No. 4002012).

References

1. Abidi, S.S.R., Goh, A.: A Web-enabled Exam Preparation and Evaluation Service: providing real-time personalized tests for academic enhancement, Proceedings of IEEE International Conference on Advanced Learning Technologies, 2001, pp. 441-442
2. Chan, M., Podlaseck, M., Alvarado, N., Schonberg, E.: A Personalized Navigation Tool for Online Listening and Free Browsing: The Glass Engine, Award paper of Education Multimedia, Hypermedia & Telecommunications 2002 (ED-MEDIA 2002), http://www.aace.org
3. Koyama, A., Barolli, L., Tsuda, A., Cheng Z.: An agent-based personalized distance learning system, Proceedings of the 15th International Conference on Information Networking, 2001, pp. 895–899

Agent-Based Web Learning System
Applying Dynamic Fuzzy Petri Net

Yueh-Min Huang[1], Juei-Nan Chen[1], Shu-Chen Cheng[1], and William C. Chu[2]

[1] Department of Engineering Science, National Cheng Kung University,
No. 1, Ta-Hsueh Road, Tainan 701, Taiwan
huang@mail.ncku.edu.tw
nan@www.mmn.es.ncku.edu.tw
n9889101@ccmail.ncku.edu.tw
[2] Department of Computer Science and Information Engineering, TungHai University,
No. 181, Taichung-Kang Road, Sec. 3, Taichung 40744, Taiwan
chu@csie.thu.edu.tw

Abstract. This paper presents an Agent-Based Web Learning System to facilitate each learner achieving his learning target. Agent is a software assistant for single user, which can be an expert in specific domain. The agent can generate a learning sequence to the learner based on DFPN (Dynamic Fuzzy Petri Net). Besides, we suggest that each course should define the study intensity function to normalize different exercise grade criteria. In DFPN, each learner should receive different learning suggestions based on evaluation degree of truth of any proposition. Therefore, ABWLS can make students feel that "everyone is different", and achieve one-to-one learning effect.

Keywords: E-Learning, Dynamic Fuzzy Petri Net, Agent

1 Introduction

Due to the appearance of Internet, many people use computer networks to accomplish a plenty kinds of tasks. Now, Internet is being wide used in various fields such as natural science, political science, psychology, information management and etc. In the field of education, there are various applications to facilitate learner, especially for distance education. However, general learning system usually cannot provide suitable learning materials depending on the learner's learning effect. More and more people try to apply the Artificial Intelligence techniques to the application of distance learning, especially the agent technology.

In this paper, we aim to propose an Agent-Based Web Learning System (ABWLS) which mainly includes four main modules: *LCMS*, *WSMS*, *LMS*, and *Agent*. Furthermore, with regard to the agent's behavior mechanism, we proposed Dynamic Fuzzy Petri Net (DFPN) extended from Fuzzy Petri Net [3] to provide the learning sequence dynamically, and normalize the exercise grade via the study intensity function to keep the flexibility of the course definition.

The rest of this paper is organized as follows. In Section 2, we briefly introduce some researches of the agent used in e-Learning environments. In Section 3, we pro-

W. Liu et al. (Eds.): ICWL 2004, LNCS 3143, pp. 338–345, 2004.

pose a simple e-Learning architecture. Then we aim at how agent provides a suitable learning sequence to each learner in Section 4. Finally, the conclusions are made in Section 5.

2 Software Agents in e-Learning

Despite the recent fall in interest in intelligent agent research, the vision of employing a computer as an agent, called an intelligent tutor, to assist a student to learn has been continuously pursued since Carbonell [1] conducted his pioneering work on simulating a Socratic tutor using a semantic network technique in the early 1970s.

When this intelligent tutor initiated in 1980s, many intelligence techniques were developed and people were looking forward to seeing such an intelligent tutor which understood the needs of students and also provided different strategies in interacting with students. However, in the mid 1980s, some researchers challenged the possibility of implementing such intelligent tutor and the role it might take [4]. Therefore, the role of intelligent tutor, the variety, distribution and the social context of educational agent were further discussed. That is, the view of the intelligent tutor was open up.

Chan and Baskin [2] provided Learning Companion System (LCS) which included three learning protocols between the student and the learning companion. First, working independently and comparing working (competition). Secondly, working collaboratively with one's working and one's watching (suggestion). Thirdly, working collaboratively and sharing responsibility (collaboration). Besides, Chan and Baskin conducted an approach which students themselves can teach the learning companion; in other words, learning how to learn by teaching. The focus on this approach is to let students provide learning companion knowledge and examples and also see how learning companion solves the problems and show whether the solution is correct or incorrect. This "learning by teaching" approach has already examined by researches [7,8].

In addition, Hietala and Niemirepo [5] provided the EduAgent system which has multiple learning companions. There are two strong learning companions and two weak ones. According to the researches, introverts and intelligent students prefer the strong companions which have expert knowledge and rarely make mistakes. In contrast, extroverts and less capable students tend to use weak companions which provide less knowledge and make more mistakes. Researches found that different students prefer different learning companions. Introverts and more capable students prefer the strong companions. Extraverts and less capable students prefer the weak companions. These researchers have suggested that "a group of heterogeneous companion agents the learner's disposal will increase his/her motivation to collaborate with agents."

In brief, the learning companion is a computer-simulated character that has human-like characteristics and act as non-authoritative role in the social learning settings.

3 Agent-Based Web Learning System

ABWLS is an integrated e-learning system [6] that provides teachers creating curriculum contents, utilizing sharable learning resources, and offering students an intelligent web learning environment associated with the diversification of presentation versions to various devices. The system diagram of each module is shown in Figure 1.

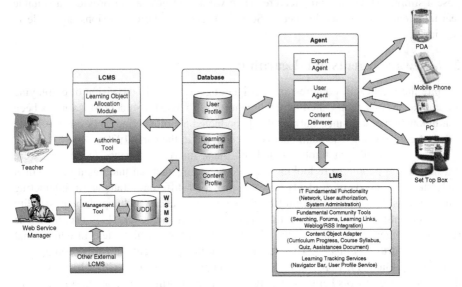

Fig. 1. Agent-Based Web Learning System Architecture

➢ *LCMS (Learning Content Management System)*. The LCMS mainly aims at providing a convenient editing tool for teacher to fabricate an integrated course. Furthermore, in order to utilize all kinds of learning contents in different standards such as IMS [9] and SCORM, [10] it incorporates plug-and-play compatibility. The LCMS can transform the learning contents to fit in the content with SCORM standard via a simple and easy editing tool. Since the learning material can be used by the scenario of SCORM standard, it can correspond with a reusable component to be reused by the other teachers.

➢ *WSMS (Web Services Management System)*. WSMS is for managing Web services resources and provides a consistent and secure mechanism. Through Web services technology, teacher can locate the learning resources from the content provider according to UDDI search results, and then include these learning objects to be parts of curriculum materials (shown in Figure 2).

➢ *LMS (Learning Management System)*. The purpose of LMS is to provide a virtual environment for students with the functions of online learning, online discussion, performing learning activities, taking assessments, recording learning history, showing achieved percentage of scheduled progress, etc. LMS can approximately be classified into four functional modules:(1) IT Fundamental Functionality (Network, User authorization, System Administration), (2) Fundamental Community Tools (Searching, Forums, Learning Links, Weblog/RSS Integration), (3) Content Object Adapter (Curriculum Progress, Course Syllabus, Quiz, Assistances Document), (4) Learning Tracking Services(Navigator Bar, User Profile Service).

➢ *Agent*. In ABWLS, we use *User Agent* to record student's learning behaviors via navigation bar interface. Besides, many people use various computing devices to progress the e-learning activities. We employ *Content Deliverer* to be a translator between the learning resources and the presentation devices. Finally, ABWLS disposes of an *Expert Agent* to serve a student who wants to study this course. The *Expert Agent* will guide the student's learning sequence depending on his learning results.

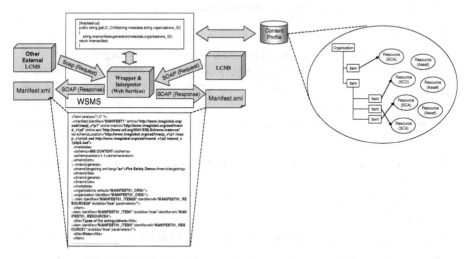

Fig. 2. Web Services Management System Conceptual Diagram

4   Dynamic Fuzzy Petri Net

After introducing the system architecture in Section 3, we now show the mechanism of *Learning Object Allocation Module* (shown in Figure 1) using DFPN, which generates the learning sequence as the *Expert Agent*'s knowledge. The learning process can schedule dynamically and we expect this kind of usage can help users learn more effectively.

4.1 Dynamic Fuzzy Petri Net Definition

In the following, we extend the fuzzy Petri net model [3] and define as Dynamic Fuzzy Petri Net (DFPN). DFPN can increase the flexibility of an agent's behavior to provide the learning sequence when we construct the knowledge. A DFPN is a bipartite directed graph including two types of nodes: places and transitions, where circles represent places and bars represent transitions. Each place in a DFPN may or may not contain a token associated with a truth value between zero and one. Each transition in a DFPN is associated with a certainty factory value and a threshold value between zero and one. In a DFPN, the relationships from places to transitions and from transitions to places are represented by directed arcs. A generalized DFPN structure can be defined as a 9-tuple:

$$DFPN = (P, T, D, I, O, f, \alpha, \beta, \delta),$$

where

$P = \{p_1, p_2, ..., p_n\}$ is a finite set of places;

$T = \{t_1, t_2, ..., t_m\}$ is a finite set of transitions;

$D = \{d_1, d_2, ...d_n\}$ is a finite set of propositions;

$P \cap T \cap D = \phi$, $|P| = |D|$

$I: T \to P^\infty$ is the input function, a mapping from transitions to bags of places;

$O: T \to P^\infty$ is the output function, a mapping from transitions to bags of places;

$f: T \to [0,1]$ is an association function, a mapping from transitions to real values between zero and one;

α: $P \to [0,1]$ is an association function, a mapping from places to real values between zero and one;

β: $P \to D$ is an association function, a bijective mapping from places to propositions;

δ. $T \to [0,1]$ is an association function, a mapping from transitions to real values between zero and one.

If $p_j \in I(t_i)$, then there exists a directed arc from the place p_j to the transition t_i. If $p_k \in O(t_i)$, then there exists a directed arc from the transition t_i to the place p_k. If $f(t_i) = \mu_i$, where $\mu_i \in [0,1]$, then the transition t_i is said to be associated with a real value μ_i. If $\beta(p_j) = d_j$, where $d_j \in D$, then the place p_j is said to be associated with the proposition d_j. If a DFPN contains some tokens in some places, the token in a place p_j is represented by a labelled dot "$\overset{\alpha(p_j)}{\bullet}$", and the token value in a place p_j, $p_j \in P$, is denoted by $\alpha(p_j)$, where $\alpha(p_j) \in [0,1]$. If $\alpha(p_j) = y_j$, where $y_j \in [0,1]$, and $\beta(p_j) = d_j$, then we can see that the degree of truth of proposition d_j is y_j. As shown in Figure 3, if $f(t_i) = \delta_i$, where $\delta_i \in [0,1]$ is a threshold value, then the transition t_i is said to be associated with a real value δ_i.

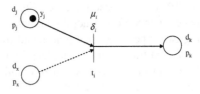

Fig. 3. A Dynamic Fuzzy Petri Net

Case 1: If $y_j \geq \delta_i$, then the agent ignores the dotted line which is associated with transition t_i.

Case 2: If $y_j < \delta_i$, then the dotted line becomes a solid arc of the agent's behavior.

Here we formally define the study intensity function h to retain the elasticity of the course arrangement, because each teacher may give different exercise grade definition of each course. Therefore, the exercise grade should normalize using the study intensity function h which is defined by each teacher before starting DFPN to simulate the expert agent's behavior.

$$
y_j = \begin{cases} 0, & x < a \\ h\left(\dfrac{x-a}{b-a}\right) & a \le x \le b \\ 1, & x > b. \end{cases} \tag{1}
$$

Moreover, X is the universe of exercise grade, $x, a, b \in X = [0, 100]$. a is the lower bound of a course arrangement. If the exercise grade is less or equal to the lower bound a, it means that the learning effect is unfavorable. Oppositely, b is the upper bound both of them are defined by the teacher. If the exercise grade is larger or equal to the upper bound b, it means that the learning effect is beneficial.

The mapping of study intensity function is $h : y_j \to y_j$. y_j is the study intensity degree, where $y_j \in [0,1]$. The higher study intensity degree y_j means more learning result of certain part in a course. The study intensity degree comes into DFPN model is the token. If r proportions are satisfied with a solution, we use h(r) to express the study intensity of a solution. Besides, we know that the study intensity function has numbers of properties to be related. If exercise grade is less or equal than the lower bound of a course arrangement, this part of course has zero satisfaction, h(0) = 0. Oppositely, if exercise grade is larger or equal than the upper bound, this part should have completed satisfaction, h(1) = 1. The more study intensity satisfaction, the more intensity degree, $h(u) \ge h(v)$ if $u > v$. Thus, $h : y_j \to y_j$ is a mapping such that

1) $h(0) = 0$
2) $h(1) = 1$
3) $h(u) \ge h(v)$ if $u > v$.

Figure 4 shows two other examples of study intensity function. In the linear case h(r) = r and in the power case h(r) = r². We note that all of these are particular cases of a whole family of study intensities, $h(r) = r^\omega$ where $\omega \in (-\infty, \infty)$.

4.2 Dynamic Fuzzy Production Rules

We can use DFPN to represent the fuzzy production rules of a rule-based system, as shown in Figure 3. Let PR be a set of dynamic fuzzy production rules, $PR = \{PR_1, PR_2, ..., PR_n\}$. The general formulation of the ith dynamic fuzzy production rule is as follows:

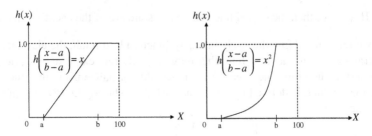

Fig. 4. Study Intensity Function

PR_i : IF $y_j \geq \delta_i$ THEN $PR_i = SPR_i$ (Threshold Value $= \delta_i$)   (2)

ELSE $PR_i = DPR_i$

$$\begin{cases} SPR_i : \text{IF } d_j \text{ THEN } d_k \ (\text{CF} = \mu_i) \\ DPR_i : \text{IF } d_j \text{ AND } d_l \text{ THEN } d_k \ (\text{CF} = \mu_i) \end{cases}$$

where y_j is the token value in d_j; the truth of each proposition is a real value between zero and one. δ_i is a threshold value, which is defined to determine using SPR_i or DPR_i in the DFPN model. SPR_i is the ith Static Production Rule, which is represented by a solid line. It will persistently subsist in these relations; DPR_i is the ith Dynamic Production Rule, which is represented by a dotted line. Depending on the token value y_j and threshold value δ_i, it will turn up dynamically.

d_j and d_k are static propositions, which will persist in these relations; the truth of each proposition is a real value between zero and one. d_l is dynamic proposition, which will be influenced by the threshold value δ_i; the truth of each proposition is a real value between zero and one. μ_i is the value of the certainty factor (CF), $\mu_i \in [0,1]$. The larger the value of μ_i, the more the rule is believed in.

Here we use *DPR* to provide learning sequence more flexible. As a result of the learner sometimes does not acquire appropriate learning result according to the learning map from teacher, the purpose of *DPR* is to provide auxiliary learning material. Dynamic propositions are defined to be the auxiliary learning material, whenever we find out the learner getting poor learning result through estimation. As to *SPR*, it provides stable production rule, which is complete the same with fuzzy production rule proposed by [3]. In this paper, we emphasize to tie in *DPR* to provide more flexible arrangements to each learner.

5 Conclusions

In this paper, we have proposed an Agent-Based Web Learning System which can provide the learning sequence to an individual learner. The agent can guide the learner to achieve his learning target based on the exercise grade. Besides, we improve the work of [3] by presenting a DFPN (Dynamic Fuzzy Petri Net) to model agent's knowledge and provide the learning sequence dynamically. In our future works, we will aim at promoting the learning results based on learner's behavior using data mining methodologies.

Acknowledgment

This research was supported in part by the National Science Council of the Republic of China under Grant NSC 93-2524-S-006-001.

References

1. J.R. Carbonell, "AI in CAI: an artificial-intelligence approach to computer-assisted instruction," *IEEE Transactions on Man-Machine Systems*, 11(4), 1970, pp. 190–202.
2. T.W. Chan, A.B. Baskin, "Learning companion Systems," *Intelligent Tutoring Systems: At the Crossroads of Artificial Intelligence and Education, Chapter 1*, New Jersey: Ablex Publishing Corporation, 1990.
3. S.M. Chen, "Fuzzy Backward Reasoning Using Fuzzy Petri Nets," *IEEE Transactions on Systems, Man, Cybernetics – Part B: Cybernetics*, Vol. 30, No. 6, 2000, pp. 846–856.
4. X. Gilmore, J. Self, "The application of machine learning to intelligent tutoring systems," *Artificial Intelligence and human learning, intelligent computer-aided instruction*, 1988, pp. 179–196.
5. P. Hietala, T. Niemirepo, "The Competence of Learning Companion Agents," *International Journal of Artificial Intelligence in Education*, Vol. 9, 1998, pp. 178–192.
6. [6] Y.M. Huang, J.N. Chen, K.T. Wang, C.H. Fu, "Agent-Based Web Learning System," *Learning Technology Newsletter*, 2004. (To Appear)
7. J.A. Ramirez Uresti, "Should I Teach my Computer Peer? Some Issues in Teaching a Learning Companion," *Intelligent tutoring Systems. Fifth International Conference, ITS'2000*, Vol. 1839 of Lectures Notes of Computer Science, Spring-Verlag, 2000, pp. 103–112.
8. S. Ur, K. VanLehn, "STEPS: A Simulated, Tutorable Physics Student," *Journal of Artificial Intelligence in Education*, 6(4), 1995, pp. 405–435.
9. *IMS Content Packaging Best Practice Guide*, Version 1.1.3 Final Specification, June, 2003 Available at: http://www.imsglobal.org/
10. *SCORM Version 1.3 (2004)*, Advanced Distributed Learning, January 30, 2004 Available at: http://www.adlnet.org/

Design and Implementation of Virtual Computer Network Lab Based on NS2 in the Internet*

Jianxin Wang[1], Bei Peng[1], and Weijia Jia[2]

[1] School of Information Science and Engineering, Central South University,
ChangSha, 410083, China
jxwang@mail.csu.edu.cn
[2] Department of Computer Engineering and Information Technology,
City University of Hong Kong, Kowloon, HongKong
itjia@cityu.edu.hk

Abstract. This paper proposed the design model and implementing method of virtual Computer Networks lab which is based on NS2. In this lab, the client part is implemented with Java Applet, NS2 is used as computing platform, Nam is used as the tool for displaying in the client, and Java RMI is used for communication between the server and the client. The virtual experiment equipments are implemented with Java Bean. The server that uses NS2 as computing platform has powerful simulating capability. The Web-based Virtual Computer Networks lab provides platform between users and NS2, which makes users leave out the trouble of studying NS2.Users can use it to do network simulation experiment and deeply understand the complex behavior in computer networks.

Keywords: Virtual Lab, RMI, NS2, Nam, Java Applet, JavaBeans

1   Introduction

With the rapid development of Internet, remote education as a new teaching mode attracts more and more attention of governments, enterprises and societies. How to implement online experiment is still a totally new and difficult issue, and virtual lab is an efficient way to resolve this problem.

Computer Networks is a newly developed subject in recent decades. We propose the Computer Networks virtual laboratory based on NS2, which is an aid to remote education. In the virtual lab, students can study this subject with a visual interface via Internet. We use NS2, a widely used multi-protocol network simulator, as the computing platform, Nam as the visual tool at the client. NS2 is a huge and complex system. Although the updated NS2 manual improves the situation to some extent, it can't meet the students' demands yet. Our proposed virtual Computer Networks laboratory is developed in Java language, and use RMI (Remote Method Invocation) mechanism to implement the communication between the client and the server. With this virtual laboratory students can conveniently study the Computer Networks course.

---

* This work was sponsored by the China National Science Fund 90304010.

W. Liu et al. (Eds.): ICWL 2004, LNCS 3143, pp. 346–353, 2004.

2   Related Work

Nowadays researching and building work of virtual laboratory system has already been carried on in many organizations. An Internet virtual laboratory, proposed in Ref.[1], is developed in Java language. Its client is implemented with Java Applet and the equipment components are implemented with JavaBeans. Some specific apparatuses and devices in it are programmed as components. Users can design the experiment process visually, and choose or create experimental device object dynamically. A remote virtual laboratory on programming language is introduced in Ref.[2]. Its client is implemented with HTML and Java Applet, and the server is implemented with CGI and Java Servlet. Users write program code in the lab, and the client will send the code to server by text. After receiving the code, server will use the relevant compiler to compile and execute the code, then return the result to the client. A Web-based distributed education virtual laboratory is proposed in Ref.[3]. The component database of the server in this system can be distributed on different hosts. And the server components are developed on LabView. A virtual experimental environment in Ref.[4] can effectively integrate third-part simulation tool, such as MATLAB.

Remote education system of Computer Networks course has been improved a lot. IP networks virtual laboratory in Ref.[5] uses an Ethernet Switch and several PC used Linux as simulation device. Users can remotely input Linux operate command, and the server return simulation result to users. The system's capability of simulation isn't enough, because it can only simulate some network operate commands, can't simulate protocols. Ref.[6] discusses a design of virtual laboratory based on virtual prototype, and proposes the architecture of virtual network laboratory and network experimental system. It also uses NS2 as simulation tool to illuminate some examples, but it only invokes NS2 locally.

Due to the powerful function of NS2, multi-protocol simulator, it can meet the research and education demand. NS2 is always used for simulation and emulation of computer network in research field, but it is difficult for students to use NS2. There are two reasons: (1) NS2 network simulator is complex to install and use, and it's difficult for students to master. (2) NS2 uses source codes to provide all sorts of simulate circumstance, but it's difficult for people who study computer networks course to learn the syntax of NS2 codes. This article builds a bridge between the NS2 network simulator and general students. It makes users save the worry of studying NS2 and users also can use NS2's powerful simulation function. It make easier for users to understand the complex behavior of networks.

3   Design of Virtual Computer Networks Lab

Virtual Computer Network laboratory based on NS2 is mainly composed of two parts: the server and the client. Its architecture is shown in Fig. 1. The server contains the server program entry, and the remote invocation of NS2 simulator. The client contains the implementation of laboratory's virtual devices, the creation of simulation scripts and the local invocation of Nam visual tool.

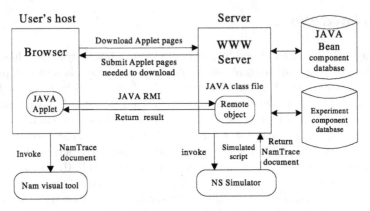

Fig. 1. The architecture of Virtual Computer Networks Lab

The interface of the client is implemented with Java Applet, and the virtual devices are developed with JavaBeans.

User uses browser-supported JAVA to create connection with Web server. After entering the virtual laboratory, browser will download the Applet and Nam code automatically from the server to the client, and the codes are executed on the browser's Java VM. At first user chooses experiment, creates topology, configures parameters, and press button "Start" to submit. Then the system begins to run the simulation. the client uses RMI mechanism to implement the remote invocation of NS2 simulator, and creates TCL script according to the simulating scenario submitted by user. Then the client sends the TCL script as object parameters to the server. Receiving the request, the server creates simulate script according to the received parameter, and invokes NS2 simulator to achieve the request. After simulation is done the server returns the result to the client. According to the NamTrace document the client invokes local Nam visual tool to dynamically demonstrate the simulation process.

RMI is a mechanism of remote method invocation and is developed for the communication of JAVA applications by SUN. By using RMI, a Java program can easily invoke Java objects method of other computers in network. It is useful to develop distributed applications based on Java. This system uses RMI mechanism to implement that the client invokes the NS2 simulator at the server remotely and return experiment data to the client after finishing simulation. After user building a simulated network environment, the client sends the scenario to the server by RMI. Server receives the request,invokes NS2 simulator to do the simulation and returns the results to the client. Flat text is not enough to perfectly describe the properties of the network. So the visual interface is adopted to add a method of presenting network dynamically. And it is helpful for users to study and modify the networks as well. We use Nam as visual interface tool. The events produced in the process of simulation will be shown to users clearly by this tool. By using Nam users will understand the complex behavior in network clearly. In TCL script files generated at client we can set NS2 simulator to generate NamTrace file that is a special format file used by Nam after finishing simulation.

When the server returns data to the client after simulation is done, the client can show the events according to the NamTrace file by using Nam tools. When users save experiment data, system will save the scenario information and Nam-Trace file automatically so that when users do the same experiment system can use NamTrace file to show experiment result and needn't invoke NS2 to simulate.

4   System Implementation

4.1   The Implementation Using RMI

This system uses RMI mechanism to implement that the client invokes the NS2 simulator at Web server remotely. The client should send the simulating scenario to NS2 simulator accurately when invoking the server methods remotely. The mechanism of RMI supports remote parameters delivery conveniently, and can deliver a whole object as parameters or return value that is not a predefined data structure. The client sends experiment objects of scenario type as parameters of getInvokeNS to the server. When server receives this request, it copies these objects, generates TCL scripts, then invokes NS2 simulator to do simulation and send the results back to the client. Fig. 2 shows how the client invokes getInvokeNS method remotely.

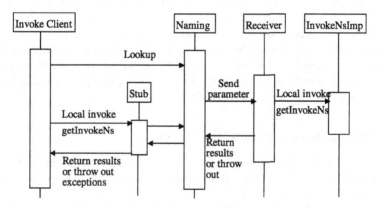

Fig. 2. Remote invocation of getInvokeNS method

Remote objects is defined as interfaces in Java. Remote interface claims every method of remote invocation. The code of interface Invoke is:

public interface Invoke extends Remote;

public String getInvokeNs(Experiment c) throws RemoteException.

The implementation of interface Invoke includes getInvokeNs to invoke NS2 simulator. The server needs to create and install a secure manage program, register a referenced remote object. The code is shown in Fig. 3.

The code of client remote invokes getInvokeNs method is shown in Fig. 4.

```
if (System.getSecurityManager()==null) {
    System.setSecurityManager(new RMISecurityManager());}
InvokeNsImpl obj = new InvokeNsImpl();
Naming.rebind("//localhost/InvokeNsServer", obj);
```

Fig. 3. A referenced remote object registration

```
System.setSecurityManager(new RMISecurityManager());
String url = "rmi://localhost/";
Invoke cl =(Invoke)Naming.lookup(url+"InvokeNsSever");
System.out.println(cl.getInvokeNs());
```

Fig. 4. The client invokes getInvokeNs method remotely

4.2   The Implementation of the Server

The design of the server mainly includes the server program entry, the implementation of object method and the NS2 invocation.

Server program is used for the start-up of RMI register program and registration of remote object. RMI register is a program that simply provides name search service. When the server invokes rebind(), the register will save this relationship. The register is a independent program named rmiregisty which must run before server programs are invoked.

The server should create one or more instances for remote object and wait for the client's invocation. When the server receives remote invoking request, it will generate script files and return results to the client after simulation is done.

The server should implement all the methods claimed in remote interface. Fig. 5 shows how the server invokes NS2.

4.3   The Implementation of the Client

The client includes the implementation of virtual lab equipments, the generation of simulation scripts, the client program for remote service and the local invocation of Nam visual tool.

We use Java Applet to implement the client of the virtual lab. The main functions of the client are to implement user screen. The user screen of the client is shown in Fig. 6. The user screen includes menu bar, toolbar, the edit column of topology property and lab property, experiment operating window, equipment column and experiment column. In lab property column users can choose some experiments such as IP route and TCP etc. in equipment column user can use mouse to drag equipments to construct topology.

In NS2 simulator, the configuration of simulation is regarded as a program instead of a static configuration. A simulation scenario defines an input to the program. A scenario includes a network topology (include the physics connection between nodes and the static feature of links and nodes), communication pattern

```
public class InvokeNsImpl extends UnicastRemoteObject implements Invoke {
public InvokeNsImpl()throws RemoteException {super();}
...
public String getInvokeNs(Experiment c) throw RemoteException
...
    String str=this.invokeNs(String s);
Return str;}
...
public String invokeNs(String s) {
...
try{String str[]=new String[2];
    str[0]="c:/ns2/bin/ns.exe";
    str[1]=s;
    Runtime R=Runtime.getRuntime();
    Process p=R.exec(str);
    StreamGobbler errorGobbler = new
    StreamGobbler(p.getErrorStream(), "ERROR");
    StreamGobbler outputGobbler = new
    StreamGobbler(p.getInputStream(), "OUTPUT");
    errorGobbler.start();
    outputGobbler.start();
    int exitVal = p.waitFor();
    System.out.println("ExitValue: " + exitVal); } catch (Throwable t)
        {t.printStackTrace();}
    String result=this.getResult;
    return result;}}
```

Fig. 5. The server invokes NS2

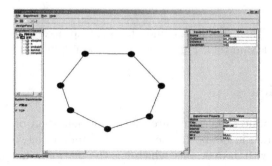

Fig. 6. The user screen of the client

which defines network using pattern and position of sending node, generation of test an network state (the errors of nodes and links).

This virtual lab uses JavaBeans to develop experiments lib. Every experiment JavaBeans generates TCL script by reading the properties of virtual equipments, and sends the script to the server by using RMI remote invocation mechanism. The server generates local script for simulation. Fig. 7 shows the generating process of simulation script.

When initializing the Applet, the client automatically downloads Nam visual tools from Web server. After simulation is done the server sends the NamTrace

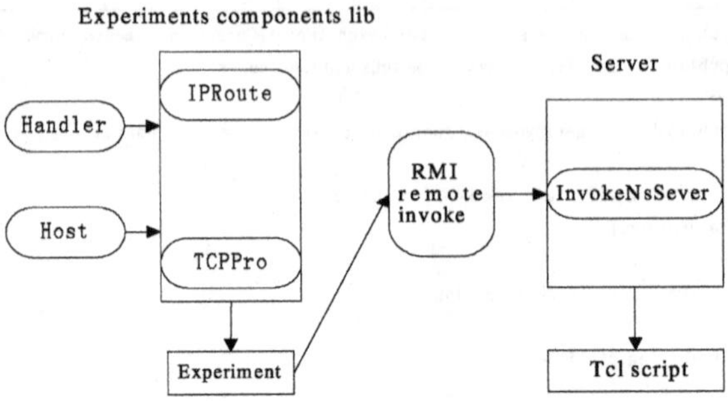

Experiments components lib

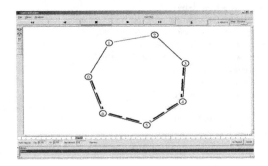

Fig. 7. The generation of simulation scripts

Fig. 8. Nam dynamic demonstration

file to the client. Then the client demonstrates the process of network simulation by invoking local Nam tool. Fig. 8 shows the Nam dynamic demonstration.

5   Conclusion

This paper introduces the structure and implementation of virtual computer network lab system in detail. In the virtual Computer Networks lab, the client is implemented with Java Applet which has the platform independence and security of Java language. This system uses NS2 as the simulator in the server, Nam as the client visual tool, which takes advantage of the powerful functions of the multi-protocol simulator NS2, so this system can support large scale, multi-protocol simulation and overcome the shortcoming that NS2 is difficult for users to study. This system provides a good platform for students to study Computer Networks course remotely. On this platform, user can do experiments at anytime, anywhere, can construct network simulation scenario easily, quickly, economically and efficiently. By using statistics data and the dynamically demonstration of simulating process, students will deeply understand the complex behavior in computer network and master the basic technologies of computer network protocol.

References

1. Wang Jianxin, Chen Songqiao, Jia Weijia, and Pei Huiming, The Design and Implementation of Virtual Laboratory Platform in Internet, Proceedings of The First International Conference on Web-based Learning, P.169-177
2. Jiannong Cao, Alvin Chan, Weidong Cao, and Cassidy Yeung, Virtual Programming Lab for Online Distance Learning, LNCS 2436First International Conference, ICWL 2002 Hong Kong, China, 2002, P. 216-227.
3. L. Benetazzo, M. Bertocco, F. Ferraris, A. Ferrero, C. Offelli, M. Parvis, and V. Piuri, A Web-Based Distributed Virtual Educational Laboratory, IEEE Transaction On Instrumentation and Measurement, 2000, 49(2): 349-356.
4. Wang Jianxin, Lu Weini and Jia Weijia, A Web-Based Environment for Virtual Laboratory with CORBA Technology, International Journal of Computer Processing of Oriental Languages, Vol. 16, No. 4 (2003) 261-274
5. L.Fabrega, J.Massaguer, T.Jove, and D.Merida, A Virtual network laboratory for learning IP network, The 7th Annual Conference on Innovation and Technology in Compute Science Education, June 2002, Aarhus, Denmark.
6. Li Min, Li Renfa, Yang Dashan, Zhang Renqing, Virtual Network Laboratory Based on Virtual PrototypeComputer Engineering and Applications ,38(7):151-153, 2002.

Semantics-Based Answers Selection
in Question Answering System*

Xia Sun and Qinghua Zheng

School of Electronics and Information Engineering, Xi'an Jiaotong University,Xi'an, China
`sx@mailst.xjtu.edu.cn, qhzheng@mail.xjtu.edu.cn`

Abstract. Motivated by the large requirement of Web answer in E-learning, this paper proposes a novel answer selection scheme of NL-WAS. With our scheme, the semantic types of the user's question and the semantic templates were used to implement semantics-based answers selection. The semantic type is identified to reduce the retrieval scope firstly. When the semantic type can't be decided easily, the statistical similarity and the semantic similarity are computed to select the right answers. Otherwise, different strategies are proposed to match answers according to the type of user's question. If the semantic types between the user's question and one candidate's are same, the same parts of their semantic templates are compared. When they have correlative semantic types, the corresponding parts of their semantic templates are compared according to the rules that are used to match different templates. The experimental results show that NL-WAS can answer the most test questions correctly.

Keywords: QA systems, Semantic Similarity, E-learning, Natural Language Process

1 Introduction

Web Answer is one of key issues in E-learning due to the rapid growth of network education. Recently, several research projects have been investigated to study the problem of automatically answering simple questions by identifying and extracting the answers from Web [1]. Unlike traditional information retrieval, these question-answering systems (QA systems) provide direct answers to users' questions, rather than a ranked list of documents. Due to the encouragement of the Text Retrieval Conference (TREC) [2], some QA systems, e.g., PowerAnswer from Language Computer Corporation (LCC) [3], have achieved good performance.

There are two differences between those systems and our question-answering system based on natural language named NL-WAS [4], besides different languages. Firstly, from the viewpoint of applications, NL-WAS is designed for E-learning users to answer their questions during the leaning process of coursewares, in which users' queries would often contain some special terms of various curriculums. In addition, queries are generally complex and specific. Secondly, in terms of implementation, the

---

* Funding for this work was provided by NSF grant 60373105 and 863 advanced tech. project grant 2001BA01A01. Xia Sun, PhD candidate. Qinghua Zheng, Professor. Committee member, Distance Education Technology Collaboration Committee, P.R.China. Committee member, Academy of Microcomputer, P.R.China.

W. Liu et al. (Eds.): ICWL 2004, LNCS 3143, pp. 354–362, 2004.

structure of knowledge base in NL-WAS is different from that of current QA systems. Our knowledge base is composed of a set of files corresponding to the curriculums, and these files are organized in question/answer format (QA pairs) for frequently asked questions and answers. As a result, other than extracting snippets from the documents or segments, NL-WAS matches the user's question against the question portion of a QA pair in knowledge base, and then returns the QA pairs to users.

In this paper, we describe our NL-WAS project that focuses on semantics for answers selection. The basic idea is as follows: the user's question is analyzed for keywords extraction and semantic type identification. When the type of the user's question can't be decided obviously, the statistical similarity and the semantic similarity are computed to select the right answers. Otherwise, the semantic template is filled out. Different strategies are proposed to match answers according to the type of user's question. In the end, NL-WAS outputs the five top-ranked list of QA pairs to the user.

The rest of this paper is organized as follows. Section 2 gives the architecture of the NL-WAS. Section 3 describes the question classification. Section 4 introduces how to match answers. In section 5, experimental results are given and analyzed. Finally, we conclude our work.

2 System Architecture

Most QA systems based on Web document collections exhibit a fairly standard structure: analyze the user's question, locate documents/paragraphs likely to contain an answer from collections, and pinpoint the most likely answer passages. We adopt this typical architecture and incorporate the techniques of information retrieval, information extraction and natural language processing to improve the performance.

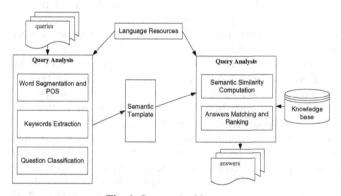

Fig. 1. System Architecture

As shown in Fig.1, NL-WAS's architecture is composed of two modules. The first module is question analysis. It obtains the semantic presentation of the user's question. Since there are no blanks to mark word boundaries in Chinese text, Word segmentation is the first step in computer processing of Chinese language. After segmentation and POS (Part Of Speech) tagging, keywords should also be picked out and finally the question type should be identified. These three operations don't have explicit boundary. Basing on the semantic information collected, we can fill out semantic templates of the user's query. The second module is answers selection. It checks the similarity between a user's question and each candidate one of QA knowledge base. Finally, it outputs the most similar QA pairs to users. In order to save the searching time, similar to the course of users' queries, questions in the knowledge base have already been analysed by another pre-processing program.

In our system, there are two kinds of language resources. One is *Chinese Thesaurus Cilin* [5], which conducts semantic classification for Chinese words in common use (see section 4). The other is the semantic network named SpecNet developed by ourselves, which describes semantic relations between two special terms (see section 4).

3   Question Classification

The experimental results of recent TREC QA-Track show that question classification is of benefit to exactly and efficiently finding the expected answers. Question classification methods analyze a question in order to determine what type of information is being requested so that the system may better recognize an answer. Many systems define a hierarchy of question types. For example, (Ittycheriah et al., 2001) defined 31 original question types in two levels of hierarchical structure. (Harabagiu et al., 2000) also defined a number of hierarchical question types, and (Hovy et al., 2001) defined 141 question types of a hierarchical question taxonomy. Within all of these taxonomies, the given questions have brief phrasal answers (factoids). However, questions that NL-WAS processed are generally involved in knowledge about certain curriculums. So we need adopt a new method to build our own Chinese question classification.

After more than several thousands questions drawn from log files of curriculum learning on the Web were analyzed by some of our coagents, 13 question types were derived, along with one additional question type, *Other*. 13 question types are defined as *Definition, Attribute, Difference, Application, Makeup, Category, Reason, Method, Choice, Time, Place, Person* and *Example*. We don't try to classify all kinds of questions by predefined question types. If we can't recognize the type of a question clearly, this question is defined as *Other*. We make the best of keeping on quite obvious characteristics of every question. Our question taxonomy makes classification an easy task and offers the potential of very high accuracy.

Interrogative word, co-occurrence patterns, characteristics words and the POS tag of subsequent word associated with it are the criterions to distinguish 13 question types. Most natural questions contain Interrogative words. We define 4 kinds of Chinese interrogative words: "why", "who", "where", "how". Each kind of interrogative words has a set of words those are same meaning, such as "为什么, 为何 (why)" etc. Some co-occurrence patterns and characteristics words in given questions may also reflect on the target intention of these questions. Characteristic words are content words and co-occurrence patterns are often several concurrent Chinese characters. For example, "超文本传输协议的定义是什么? (What's the definition of http protocol?)", has a characteristic word, "定义 (definition)" and a co-occurrence pattern, "定义是什么 (what's the definition)". The steps of identifying the question type are as follows: first, makes a shallow parsing based on the words appearing in original query, including word segment and POS tag. Second, decides the question type according to interrogative word. If the given sentence lacks interrogative word, turn next step; third, judge whether co-occurrence patterns exist or not, because co-occurrence patterns are great useful to distinguish the question type quickly. If the given sentence still lacks co-occurrence patterns, it just turns to the next step; at last characteristics words and the POS tag of subsequent word associated with it will give us some hints to identify the question type. We tested 3,780 questions about the topic of computer network, and recognized 304 *Other* type questions. That is to say, 13 question types can cover over 92% test questions.

It is noteworthy that these 13 question types are correlative. For example, a question about "difference between *http* and *ftp*" is related to the other question about definition of *http* and *ftp*, because the user can more or less understand the difference between *http* and *ftp* from their definitions. It is a significant difference between general QA systems and our NL-WAS. We should provide not only an exact answer but also a related answer considering learning knowledge. So we regard not only the sentences with the same question type but also the sentences with relevant type in answer matching phase. This will avoid possibly leaking the expected answers. After analyzing a large number of questions, experts give the correlativity matrix of 13 question types, shown in Table1.

Table 1. Correlativity Matrix of Fractional Question Types

λ	Definition	Difference	Attribute	Reason	...
Definition	1	0.8	0.1	0.1	...
Difference	0.8	1	0	0.7	...
Attribute	0.1	0.7	0	1	...
Reason	0.1	0.7	0	1	...
...	...	...	...	...	...

Questions have different semantic types and the forms of the key information, which expresses main meanings of sentences. For instance, the key information of a question with *Definition* semantic type is special terms or noun phrase. But, the key information of a question with *Reason* semantic type is a syntax, which describes subject, predicate and object. Key information is the object of subsequent semantic match processing. We can calculate the similarity of these two questions as long as compare their key information. According to the characteristics of each question type, we divide 13 question types into 3 kinds of semantic templates.

4   Answers Selection

4.1   Word Similarity

An important measurement of relation of two words is the semantic distance between them. The similarity between words is inversely proportional to their distance, which is shown as the following equation (1):

$$Sim_c(W_{c1}, W_{c2}) = \frac{a}{Dis(W_{c1}, W_{c2}) + a} \tag{1}$$

Where $Sim_c(W_{c1}, W_{c2})$ represents similarity between two common words, denoted by W_{c1} and W_{c2}. $Dis(W_{c1}, W_{c2})$ is the semantic distance between two words. And a is a tunable system parameter.

We utilize the *Chinese Thesaurus Cilin* to conduct the semantic distance between two words in common use. *Cilin* comprises 12 major categories, 94 medium categories, and 1428 minor categories. And the minor categories can be further divided into synsets according to their meanings. Every synset includes several words with the same or similar meanings. This hierarchical classification has embodied synonymous relation and hyponymy relation [6]. There should have only one path between any two nodes in the tree structure of the thesaurus. And the length of this path is viewed as the semantic distance of them. The similarity of two words in common use can be calculated according to equation (1).

NL-WAS is designed for the Web users to answer curricular questions, and users' queries would contain some special terms. In order to compute the similarity between two special words, we adopt a simple estimation shown in equation (2).

$$Sim_s(W_{s1}, W_{s2}) = \begin{cases} k_1 & W_{s1} \text{ and } W_{s2} \text{ are synonymous relation;} \\ k_2 & W_{s1} \text{ is of } W_{s2}\text{'s } father \text{ concept;} \\ k_3 & W_{s1} \text{ is of } W_{s2}\text{'s } son \text{ concept;} \\ k_4 & W_{s1} \text{ is of } W_{s2}\text{'s } brother \text{ concept;} \\ 0 & \text{Otherwise} \end{cases} \quad (2)$$

Where, W_{s1} is a special word in a question from knowledge base, and W_{s2} is a special word in a user's question. The relation between W_{s1} and W_{s2}, such as synonym, *father* concept, *son* concept and *brother* concept, is obtained via consulting SpecNet. $Sim_s(W_{s1}, W_{s2})$ represents similarity between two special words. Moreover experimental parameter k_i is constrained by $0 < k_4 < k_3 < k_2 < k_1 < 1$.

In our previous works, we have constructed a domain knowledge representation framework, SpecNet, which describes Chinese special words senses and relations among them, including synonym, *father* concept, *son* concept and *brother* concept. We don't make a complete description of the SpecNet. Interested reader can refer to [7,8].

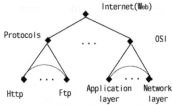

Fig. 2. A Sample Structure in SpecNet

As shown in Fig.2, every node in the structure represents a concrete special term. Words in pair of brackets and the conception that the node represents are synonymously related. For instance, the node for *Internet* and *Web* has synonymous relationship. One words is the ancestral node of the other one, then the former is *father* of the latter and the latter is *son* of the former, such as *protocols* and *http*. If the two words are in different branches of one ancestral node, they have *brother* relationship, e.g. *http* and *ftp*.

At last, a threshold is employed to revise words similarity score. The ultimate $Sim(W_1, W_2)$ is calculated as follows:

1. The value of the word similarity score is equal to 1, if two words are exactly match.
2. In partial matching, if W_1 and W_2 are two common words, we set a threshold to 0.25. In other words, if $Sim_c(W_{c1}, W_{c2})$ is great than the threshold, the value of $Sim_c(W_{c1}, W_{c2})$ is added to the word similarity score. Otherwise the value of 0 is added to the score.
3. In partial matching, if W_1 and W_2 are two special words, $Sim_s(W_{s1}, W_{s2})$ is added to the word similarity score.

4.2 Answers Matching

Once the semantic type of user's question have been identified, two independent matches will be performed:

Semantic Templates Matching. If the semantic type of user's question is one of 13 question types, the following processes will be carried out.

1. Initial candidates are composed of all the questions in the knowledge base that have the same or correlative semantic type with the user's question.
2. If the semantic type of the user's question and a candidate's are same, then the same parts of their semantic templates are compared. Otherwise, their relevant parts of their semantic templates were compared in terms of rules that be used to match different templates. Phrases are elements of the same or relevant parts in semantic templates (see appendix), and phrases comprise words. So using word similarity, we can calculate the similarity between two phrases. Considering the effects of headwords and modifiers in phrases are different, the similarity between two phrases is shown as follows:

$$Sim(P_1, P_2) = \lambda_{qc}(HSim(W_{h1}, W_{h2}) + MSim(W_{h1}, W_{h2})Sim(W_{m1}, W_{m2})) \quad (3)$$

where,

P_1 and P_2 are the phrases in the user's question and in the candidate question, respectively;

W_{h1} and W_{h2} denote headwords in P_1 and in P_2, respectively;

W_{m1} and W_{m2} denote modifiers corresponding headwords in P_1 and in P_2, respectively;

$Sim(W_{h1}, W_{h2})$ is the similarity value of two headwords;

$Sim(W_{m1}, W_{m2})$ is the similarity value of two modifiers;

H and M are weights associated with $Sim(W_{h1}, W_{h2})$ and $Sim(W_{m1}, W_{m2})$, respectively. We set H to 0.7, and M to 0.3 according to experimental results; and

λ_{qc} is a correlative coefficient obtained from the Table1. And it indicates the correlativity between the user's question type and candidate question type.

3. The ultimate match score between query and candidate is accumulation of the similarity of each part in two semantic templates. Then rank the candidates according to this match score and output the first 5 QA pairs.

Vector and Semantic Matching. If the semantic type of user's question is none of 13 question types, statistical similarity and semantic similarity [9] will be computed. The value of statistical similarity is equal to the cosine of the angle between vector representing the user's question and the vector representing the QA pair. The significance value that is term frequency times log of inverse document frequency. Semantic similarity is even accumulation of words similarity between each word in user's question and each word in QA pair. Then we combine statistical similarity score and semantic similarity score in a weighted average to arrive at an overall match score. Finally, rank the candidates and output the first 5 QA pairs.

5 Experimental Results and Analysis

At present, the prototype of NL-WAS has already been developed and applied in the network education. We took *Computer Network* course as an example to verify its performance and validity. There are 1,500 QA pairs in NL-WAS's knowledge base, and we have gathered 100 actual questions to evaluate the performance of the system, 89 test questions that have answers in the knowledge base, the other do not have answers.

First, we scanned each QA pair from knowledge base to match against each test question. As long as a QA pair contributes to that test question, it would be regarded as reasonable answer. So we obtained a set of standard answers to every test question. Next, standard answers and outputs that NL-WAS returned were compared and assessed. This manual evaluation is simplified with the following: none of outputs was in a set of standard answers, and then we judged the response to this test question was *error*. And if NL-WAS returned *NIL*, but answers to the test question did exist in knowledge base, we mark "error" to this test question either. Otherwise, the answers were recognized *right*. Then the experimental results show as Table 2. Scores include the number and percentage of questions that were answered correctly; and the precision and recall for recognizing when there is no correct answer in the knowledge base.

Table 2. Evaluation Scores

Number of test question	100
The number of correct answer	86
Percentage of correct answer	86%
NIL precision	75%
NIL recall	27.3%

The results in Table2 illustrate that NL-WAS can answer the most test questions correctly. Furthermore, we find that there were 27 *definition* questions, 18 *difference* questions and 21 *Attribute* question in test questions, and system correctly answered 26, 16 and 16 questions respectively. This result is exciting. But *NIL* recall of 27.3% is disappointing. It means that system always returns garbage when there is no exact answer in the knowledge base. It can't tell the difference between the good answers and bad answers. So we still need devote our time to the research of natural language understanding in order to improve the performance of Chinese QA system.

A test question often has several reasonable answers. And Fig.3 illustrates distribution of the optimal answer in the ranking returned by system. From the result, we can conclude that most of the first ranked QA pairs are optimal answers, almost occupying 46%; 69 ranked lists of three QA pairs contain optimal answers; and 78% test questions are given optimal answers in the list of five QA pairs. This result shows the most optimal answers appear in the outputs.

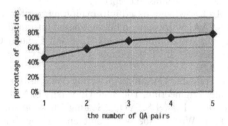

Fig. 3. Distribution of the Optimal Answer in the Ranking

6 Conclusions

In this paper, we have described answers selection in a Chinese QA system from a semantic perspective. Questions type plays a very important role in answers selection. However, building complete question taxonomy requires excessive manual efforts and can not cover all possible cases because there are many ways to put the same question. As a result, we don't try to put all kinds of questions into our question typology. We match these questions that aren't clearly classified against questions in the knowledge base by other means. Other two properties of our system are that correlativity among these question types is built and different strategies are adopted to match answers according as the type of user's question. They effectively increase precision in semantic matching.

Acknowledgements

Funding for this work was provided by NSF grant 60373105 and 863 advanced tech. project grant 2001BA01A01.We also give our thanks to all of the people who have contributed to this research and development, in particular our team member Haifeng Dang and Sujuan Zhang.

References

1. Eduard Hovy, et al.: Toward Semantics-Based Answer Pinpointing. In Proceedings of the Human Language Technology Conference, November 2001.
2. Text Retrieval Conference (TREC). http://trec.nist.gov/
3. Ellen M. Voorhees.: The TREC-11 Question Answering Track Report. National Institute of Standards and Technology, 2002.

4. Qinghua Zheng, et al.: NL-WAS System based on Natural Language. Mini-Micro Systems. (accept)
5. Jiaju Mei.: Chinese thesaurus *Tongyici Cilin*. Shanghai thesaurus Press, 1983
6. Sujian Li, Xiong Huang, Shuo Bai, Qun Liu.: Semantic computation in a Chinese question-answering system. Journal of Computer Science and Technology, 2002
7. Qinghua Zheng, Zhaojing Wang, Xia Sun.: An Approach to Generate Semantic Network of Concept Based on Structural Corpus. Journal of Computer Research and Development. (accept)
8. Xia Sun, Qinghua Zheng.: A Method of Special Domain Lexicon Construction Based on Raw Materials. Mini-Micro Systems. (accept)
9. Robin D. Burke, et al.: Knowledge-based information retrieval from semi-structured text. In Proceedings of the AAAI Workshop on Internet-based Information Systems, 1996
10. Sanda Harabagiu, et al.: Answering Complex, List and Context Questions with LCC's Question-Answering Server. In Proceedings of the TExt Retrieval Conference for Question Answering, 2001
11. Abraham Ittycheriah. Trainable Question Answering Systems. PhD Thesis, Department of Electrical and Computer Engineering, The State University of New Jersey. 2001
12. Cody Kwok, Oren Etzioni, Daniel S. Weld.: Scaling Question Answering to the Web. In Processdings of the Tenth World Wide Web Conference. Hong Kong, 2001
13. Zhiping Zheng.: AnswerBus Question Answering System.. In Proceedings of Human Language Technology Conference. San Diego, CA, 2002
14. Steven Abney, Michael Collins, Amit Singhal.: Answer Extraction. In Proceedings of ANLP. Seattle, WA, 2000

Learning Content Recommendation Service Based-On Simple Sequencing Specification

Li-ping Shen and Rui-min Shen[*]

Shanghai Jiao Tong University, Computer Science Dept.,
Huashan Rd. 1954, Shanghai,200030, China
{lpshen,rmshen}@mail.sjtu.edu.cn

Abstract. A new era of e-learning is on the horizon, hundreds of Learning Contents are created and more and more people begin to acquire acknowledge thru e-learning. The traditional teaching method is already showing its limitations that students from different backgrounds are still given the same contents at the same time, and they may only interest in part of a whole learning content. In this paper, we propose a novel way to organize learning contents into small "atomic" units called Learning Objects so that they could be used and reused effectively. The Learning Objects together with their ontology are systemized into knowledge base. An intelligent recommendation mechanism based on sequencing rules is then introduced with detail, where the rules are formed from the knowledge base and competency gap analysis. Finally we establish a test knowledge base system, using and extending the ontology editor Protégé-2000 and its Protégé Axiom Language.

Keywords: Learning Object, Knowledge Base, Recommendation, Competency Gap Analysis, Sequencing Rule, Protégé-2000.

1 Introduction

A new era of e-learning is on the horizon with a huge market, a market and technology that encompasses Learning, Training, Marketing, and online Support, and almost everything hitting us electronically can be called eLearning, people have accepted e-Leaning to a great extent. And the traditional teaching method is already showing its limitations that students from different backgrounds are still given the same learning contents at the same time, and they may only interest in part of a whole learning content. Most eLearning contents today are organized in a linear, sequential way, with large number of pages and without any description per se. Such contents couldn't be used to provide the exact content to the learners and also couldn't be reused by other authoring tools and content management systems. In this paper, we propose a novel way to organize learning contents into small chunks called Learning Objects (LO) – the "atomic" units of knowledge. There are synonyms of LO as Knowledge Object

---

[*] The work of this paper is supported by the National Natural Science Foundation of China under Grant No. 60372078 and by the Chinese e-Learning Technology Standardization Committee (CELTSC) project. Li-ping Shen is a member of the content based working group of the CELTSC, also a lecture of the Computer Science Dept. Shanghai Jiao Tong University. Rui-min Shen is a committeeman of the CELTSC, and a professor of the Computer Science Dept. Shanghai Jiao Tong University.

W. Liu et al. (Eds.): ICWL 2004, LNCS 3143, pp. 363–370, 2004.

[1], Sharable Content Object (SCO) [2] and Learning Asset [3]. Reusable objects enable us to put appropriate knowledge in the direct path of users. We need to create instructionally sound objects that are usable inside and outside of the traditional learning environment in order to have a significant impact on business performance. It must be flexible and easily managed so that the granules can be reused in different applications and for mass production.

People have made great efforts on research about recommendation systems using content based filtering and collaborative filtering[4]. These systems locate and retrieve information with respect to users' profiles (interests and behaviors). Matching information with user profiles has been extensively studied in information retrieval and recommendation areas [5][6][7]. Most of the existing matching approaches are based on distance and similarity measures or probabilistic methods [6]. Usually, the designer should select several features and design some similarity calculation or evaluation methods beforehand. With these features and methods, users can easily find useful information. However, because user profile(s) or similarity is predefined by the features and computing methods employed. Addition of new features or changes to existing user profiles can involve a significant amount of recomputing. This drawback means that the traditional matching approaches are not well suited to a dynamic environment where the users' preferences are likely to be subject to change. Another problem is that it is not easy to characterize and represent user profiles accurately, or to design correct methods to compute the similarity between information and user profiles precisely. In consequence the resulting recommendations may inevitably include some users with mistaken and uninteresting information.

This paper proposes to recommend learning content based on the expert learning object knowledge base and personal learning progress. The expert learning knowledge base incorporates information about simple sequencing. This recommend mechanism needs not the whole learner profile including interests and preferences, but just needs the information of the learning progress and learner's competency, so avoids the drawbacks explained above. In the following sections we will introduce the recommendation approach in detail. Section 2 introduces the method to establishing Learning Objects knowledge base by using the ontology editor Protégé-2000[8]. The intelligent recommendation mechanism based on the Learning Object Knowledge Base and learner's competency is presented in section 3. We establish a test LO knowledge base by using and extending the ontology editor Protégé-2000 and its Protégé Axiom Language and it is described in section 4. Section 5 concludes this paper.

2   Learning Objects Knowledge Base

What is a Learning Object? How small should it be? During content design and authoring activities, when determining the size of a SCO, thought should be given to the smallest logical size of content that one might desire to have tracked by a LMS at runtime [2]. In order to use and reuse the LO efficiently, we define here a LO is a learning content lasting less than 30 minutes and containing only one knowledge point, i.e. concept.

First of all, we need to define the contents that will be stored in the knowledge base [9]: the concepts which are to be communicated, and their classification and interrelation, i.e. the ontology of the content. This description can be performed by a domain expert, and does not require that learning issues are taken into account. For example, the concept "router" is the sub-concept of "networking device", and relates to "switch" and "gateway". All the concepts interrelated with each other build up a concept graph. In this paper, we only consider simple relationships that link concepts to a tree. We also need to define the dependencies between the concepts, like "prerequisites" i.e. defining the expertise required before presenting a specific concept to the learner. For example, "internet protocol" is the prerequisite of the concept "router". The competencies that are related to each concept in the ontology of the learning Objects are also defined. In this paper we suppose that each concept corresponds to one competency, so all the competencies form a competency tree as its corresponding concept tree. For each competency in the ontology, we define some questions and tests which determine whether the learner has understood the concept and should be granted a specific competency.

Subsequently, we need to compile and define the LOs that are instances of each concept of the ontology (only the leaves of the concept tree have LOs). LOs can be available as text files, images, videos, simulations, etc. Each LO is described through meta-data, such as how much it costs to browse this LO, the style and format it will be presented in, the language it uses, and the specific knowledge points in the ontology it is "linked" to. We leverage the Chinese e-Learning Technology Standardization Learning Object Metadata Specification [10] to describe such information.

3   Recommendation Mechanism

In order to recommend appropriate content to different learner, we need to construct an application Knowledge Base on the LO Knowledge Base. Our recommendation Mechanism bases on competency gap analysis and the IMS simple sequencing specification [11], so we should further define the learner profiles and sequencing rules. We here just define simple learner profiles, for example, name, ID, learning progress, competency, objective competency and preferable language etc.

3.1 Sequencing Rules

The sequencing rules form the basis for the intelligent recommendation system, which define how the learners will navigate the concepts of the ontology, how different LOs are selected for different learners based on the learner profiles and the internal relationship of the concepts. According to the IMS simple sequencing specification [11], the sequencing rules have the following form: if constraints then action. The constraints may be one of (each could add unary operator NOT): satisfied, objective measure greater, completed, time limit exceeded etc., and the action may be: continue, retry, previous, skip and exit. We integrate the rules with competency gap analysis, i.e. before selecting the LO to be presented, system compares the competencies that the learner has acquired (referred as learner competencies following) and the objective competencies, computes the target competency, then thru the competency to concept binding and concept to LOs binding, present the selected target LO to the user. The objective competencies may have multiple competencies and is relatively stable during a learning period. Whilst the target competency is used to determine the next LO to be presented, so only has one competency and is always changing during the learning period. The following exhibits some examples of the sequencing rules.

The initiate rules are used when the user logins to the system and the other rules are used during the learning process.

Initiate rule:
If objective competencies not met then {compute target competency, present LO
                                        binding to target competency}.
If objective competencies met then exit.

Sequencing rules:
If satisfied then {update learner's competencies, compute target competency, pre-
                   sent LO binding to the target competency}.
If failed then present the LO binding to one of the prerequisite.
If objective competencies met then exit.

3.2 Target Competency Computation

The computation of the target competency in the sequencing rules is to find a competency that helps the user gain upon his objective competencies. The method is firstly
to compute the gap competencies thru comparing the learner competencies and objective competencies, then to find a competency in or outside the gap competencies
which will help shorten the gaps. In the competency gap analysis, when the parent
competency is the objective competency and none of its child competencies is among
the learner's competencies, then the parent competency will be included in the gap
competencies, otherwise the remainder child competencies will be included in the gap
competencies. The computation of gap competencies is denoted in equation 1.

$$C_g = \{\, c_{gi} \mid c_{gi} \in C_o \text{ and } c_{gi} \notin C_u \text{ and } \text{child}(c_{gi}) \notin C_u \,\} \in \{\, c_{gi} \mid \text{parent}(c_{gi}) \in C_o \tag{1}$$
$$\text{and } \exists\, \text{child}(\text{parent}(c_{gi})) \in C_u \text{ and } c_{gi} \notin C_u \,\}$$

Let C_u: set of learner competencies
C_o: set of objective competencies
C_g: set of gap competencies
Child(c): the child of the competency c.
Parent(c): the parent of the competency c.

All the gap competencies make up a tree (if the gap competencies construct separate trees, add a root node to connect them). Considering that when defining the concept tree and competency tree, the easy and basic nodes are always put at left side, the
left-most node is apt to be the candidate recommended one. So in the target competency computation, Postorder Search Algorithm could be used. If the prerequisites of
the accessed point have all been acquired by the user and the accessed point has no
child, then this competency will be the target competency, else its first child (the left-
most node) will be the target competency. The pseudo code for the target competency
computation is as following:

```
#define begin

PostSearch (ComTree, ca): process returns the next access
competency after one-step search, returns null when the
search ends. ComTree is the gap competency tree and ca is
present accessed competency.
```

```
Child(c): process returns the first child if c has child,
else returns Null.

ct: the target competency

#define end

Begin

ca=PostSearch (ComTree, Null)

do

  Cp=set of prerequisites of the concept binding to ca

  if Cp ⊆ Cu then

  { if (c=Child(ca) ≠ null) then {ct=c, exit} ct=ca, exit}

while ((ca=PostSearch (ComTree, ca) ≠ null)

ca=PostSearch (ComTree, Null)

Cp=set of the prerequisites of the concept binding to ca

ct=c | c ∈ Cp and c ∉ Cg

End
```

3.3 Rollup Rules

The learner's competency update in the sequencing rules is controlled by rollup rules. If a competency contains sub-competency, the results of the sub-competency should be rolled up into summary result of the parent. The rollup can be controlled by rules such as:

Satisfied if any child is satisfied;
Satisfied if all children are satisfied;

Every parent competency has rollup rules. Whenever a child competency is acquired will invoke the check-up of parent's rollup rule. If the parent competency meets, the parent competency will add to the learner's competencies and all its child competencies will be deleted.

4 Experiment

We use the ontology editor and knowledge base editor protégé-2000[8] developed by Stanford to construct the LO knowledge base. We choose protégé-2000 because it has intuitive and easy-to-use graphical user interface, has extensible plug-in architecture and has well-organized API document to help access the knowledge base. Again the Protégé-2000 has the Protégé Axiom Language (PAL) to extend knowledge modeling environment with support for writing and storing logical constraints and queries about frames in a knowledge base, which we could use to devise the sequencing rules. Our application uses the edu.stanford.smi.protege.model package to access the LO knowledge base and the edu.stanford.smi.protegex.pal package to edit rules. We package the application as web services which could be accessed at different platform. Fig.1 describes the system architecture.

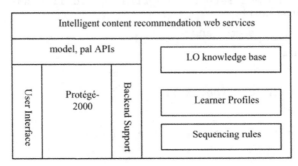

Fig. 1. System Architecture

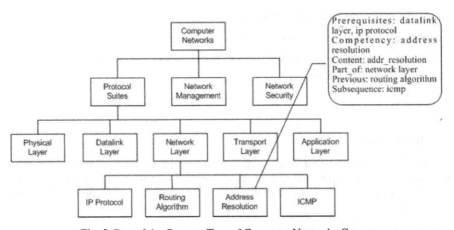

Fig. 2. Part of the Concept Tree of Computer Networks Course

As an example in this paper, we construct a LO knowledge base of Computer Networks course. Fig.2 illustrates the directive, curricular-based and linear structure of part of the concepts of the Computer Networks. We store the concept tree in the LO knowledge base, each concept have slots such as name, competency, prerequisites, content, part_of, has_part, previous and subsequence. The LOs are web contents, and are added to the knowledge base together with their metadata.

The class learner describes the learner profiles, having slots of name, ID, objective competencies, competencies, evaluation results, learning content and control mode. The control mode slot is used to allow the learner to select contents by oneself.

PAL provides a set of special-purpose frames to hold constraints and queries that are added to a Protégé knowledge base, respectively the: PAL-CONSTRAINT and the PAL-QUERY classes. The PAL constraint-checking engine can be run against the knowledge base to detect frames that violate those constraints. PAL is a subnet of Knowledge Interchange Format [12] and is used for writing restrictions on existing knowledge, not for asserting new knowledge. Though, we could use PAL to design sequencing rules. In our system, the action is the same, i.e. to find the target competency and the next LO to recommend or exit. So the sequencing rules could be organized as: if PAL_CONSTRAINT then PAL_QUERY. We define sequencing rules as following:

1. Create a class named Rollup_Rules and two slots for it, one is named condition with PAL_CONSTRAINT type and the other is named type with symbol type. The action of the rules is default and realized in the application program: add the parent node to the learner competencies and delete its child nodes in the learner competencies.
2. Edit instances of Rollup_Rules and apply them to parent competencies.
3. Create an instance of PAL_QUERY class to compute the gap competencies. We could use the AskQueries() method of the PAL.QueryEngine Interface to get all the answers of the PAL_QUERY instance.
4. Create a class named Sequencing_Rules and two slots for it, one is named condition with PAL_CONSTRAINT type and the other is named type with symbol type. Create a subclass of the Sequencing_Rules named Initiate_Rules.
5. Edit instances of Sequencing_Rules. We compose 4 Sequencing_Rules instances,among which the one with type 1 could be used as Initiate_Rules. The actions of the rules are realized in the application program. We could use the CheckKnowledgeBase() method of the PAL.ConstraintEngine Interface to check all the PAL_CONSTRAINT instances.
6. Realize the actions in the program.

For the actions above, the key action is computing target competency. Because the PAL couldn't assert new knowledge and do recursion, we realize this action in the program and use the algorithm as explained in section 3.2.

I tested this simple recommendation system in my class in the Network Education College (www.nec.sjtu.edu.cn) during the course review period. Finally I did a survey about the system. 158 out of the 219 students of my class turned in their feedbacks, most of whom gave me positive remarks and many helpful advices such as "I like the system, it helps me locate the contents that I should spent more time on quickly", "the exercises are too monotone with only one selection type" and "each knowledge point has only one content, it is preferable that each has multiple contents with different difficulties" etc. Thanks for all my students' tests and advices.

5   Conclusion and Future Work

In this paper, we give a detail description of the rule-based recommendation mechanism based on the competency gap analysis, concept tree and LO knowledge base. We test the mechanism with the knowledge base editor Protégé-2000, the PAL and the java program extending the Protégé-2000. The advantages of the system are: zero startup time and machine learning time, and the adequate content granularity – LO makes the adaptive and individualized content recommendation possible.

The method and system introduced in this paper base on simple sequencing rules (only 4 kinds of rules) that still couldn't realize full intelligent recommendation. And we just consider simple concept graph–concept tree which reflects simple relationships between concepts. The knowledge base is less adaptive once it is set up with expertise knowledge, and it's a pity that PAL can't assert new knowledge. There are still many aspects to consider and improve of our system in the future.

References

1. J. Z. Li, R. Close: The Promise of eLearning and the Practice of Knowledge System Design. http://www.leadingway.com/eLearning.pdf
2. P. Dodds: Sharable Content Object Reference Model (SCORM™) Version1.3, the SCORM Content Aggregation Model. January 30, 2004, www.adlnet.org
3. Charalampos K., Demetrios S., Fabrizio C.: An Architecture for Defining Re-usable Adaptive Educational Content. IEEE International Conference on Advanced Learning Technologies (ICAL'01)
4. Zeng C, Xing CX, Zhou LZ: A survey of personalization technology. Journal of Software, 2002,13(10):1952~1961 (in Chinese with English abstract).
5. W. Frakes and R. Baeza-Yates. Information Retrieval: Data Structures and Algorithms. Prentice Hall, 1992 ISBN 0-13-463837-9
6. G. Salton: Automatic Text Processing. Addisom-wesley, 1989. ISBN 0-201-12227-8
7. Resnick P. and Varian H. R.: Recommender Systems. COMMUNICATIONS OF THE ACM, March 1997/vol. 40, No.3.
8. http://protégé.stanford.edu
9. C. Karagiannidis, D. Sampson, F. Cardinali: Integrating Adaptive Educational Content into Different Courses and Curricula. Educational Technology and Society 4(3) 2001
10. http://www.celtsc.edu.cn/download/CELTS-3.1(CD1.6).zip
11. http://www.imsproject.org/simplesequencing
12. Knowledge Interchange Format. Draft proposed American National Standard (dpANS), NCITS.T2/98-004

Learning Object Models and an e-Learning Service Infrastructure for Virtual e-Learning Communities

Gilliean Lee and Stanley Y.W. Su

Database Systems R&D Center
Department of Computer & Information Science & Engineering
University of Florida, Gainesville
FL 32611-6125, USA
{glee,su}@cise.ufl.edu
http://www.dbcenter.cise.ufl.edu

Abstract. In this work, distributed and sharable learning resources are modeled by two types of Learning Objects (LOs): Atomic Learning Object and Composite Learning Object. LOs are uniformly published as Web-services in a constraint-based Web-service registry and are made sharable and reusable. This paper presents the learning object models for the specification of these two types of LOs and an extended Web-service infrastructure, which provides a standard framework for the registration, discovery, binding and invocation of these objects. An Event-Trigger-Rule Server is integrated with a Learning Process Execution Engine to make Composite Learning Objects active, flexible, customizable and adaptive.

1 Introduction

Web-based data and application systems are valuable resources for constructing instructional materials for teaching, training, problem solving and decision support. One approach to make use of these distributed, heterogeneous data and application systems is to apply object-oriented technology and "wrap" them as distributed objects. These distributed objects can then be used to compose learning objects (LOs) for instruction and training purposes.

In recent years, there have been a number of initiatives in developing and standardizing technologies for Web-based learning. The Advanced Distributed Learning Initiative [2], the IMS Global Learning Consortium [12], and the Open Knowledge Initiative [10], are a few examples. The Sharable Content Object Reference Model (SCORM) [1] is a reference model initiated by the Advanced Distributed Learning (ADL) program of the Department of Defense (DoD) and the White House Office of Science and Technology Policy (OSTP). According to the SCORM's specification, it is envisaged that Internet users and heterogeneous LMSs would use the Web as a universal platform for accessing and launching sharable content objects and for establishing close communication, interaction and coordination among content object developers, course authors, users, and administrators. To realize this vision, sharable content objects must be durable, interoperable, accessible and reusable. In order to

W. Liu et al. (Eds.): ICWL 2004, LNCS 3143, pp. 371–378, 2004.

meet these requirements, it is necessary to have a uniform way of modeling, not only learning resources, but also heterogeneous learning tools and LMSs, as well as an information infrastructure to enable the interoperation and sharing of their contents and system functionalities. Also, the aggregation model that defines learning sequences and processes has to be flexible, adaptable and customizable to meet different learners' needs and learning contexts. Our research and development work to meet the above needs is consistent with the vision and the goals of the ADL Program.

A virtual community is a Web site, through which members of the community can share useful information related to their common interests. Virtual educational communities, such as MERLOT [15], EOE [11], and CLOE [8], provide learning object repositories, from and to which people can find and provide useful learning materials. They provide Web-browser-based user interfaces for the registration and search of leaning objects. However, they do not provide application interfaces for programmatic searches and accesses to the learning materials. Such interfaces would facilitate the reuse of learning objects by learning management systems that bind learning objects dynamically at runtime.

In [20], it was envisioned that "building the technological infrastructure to support dynamic, ad-hoc communities of lifelong learners who interact within an environment of learning objects through a creative blend of advanced computing technologies, high performance networks, authoring and collaboration tools". In the same context, it is useful to establish an infrastructure over the Internet to allow people who are interested in specific subjects of learning to form their own virtual communities.

In this work, we model distributed and sharable learning resources by two types of Learning Objects (LOs): Atomic Learning Object and Composite Learning Object. LOs are uniformly published as Web-services in a constraint-based Web-service registry and are made sharable and reusable. This paper presents the learning object models for the specification of these two types of LOs, and an extended Web-service infrastructure, which provides a standard framework for the registration, discovery, binding and invocation of these objects.

The structure of this paper is as follows. Related work, and LO models are presented in Sections 2 and 3, respectively. A virtual e-learning community with an e-learning service infrastructure is introduced in Section 4. A summary is given in the final section.

2 Related Work

Effective delivery of learning contents to learners of different backgrounds and interests in order to maximize the effect of learning is one of the goals of e-learning. Structuring learning contents is directly related to this goal. Learning process models, such as SCORM's Content Aggregation Model [1] and Cisco's Reusable Learning Object [6] are two popular models that organize learning contents/objects for effective delivery. A tree structure, used in SCORM, Cisco's reusable learning object (RLO), L3 [4], and KnowledgeTree [7], is commonly used to model a learning process. A tree node represents a granule of learning object/content to be presented to learners, which can be a course, module or lesson.

SCORM is intended to provide a standard framework for building learning systems that enable the reusability and sharing of learning contents developed by different authoring tools. SCORM's Sequencing Definition Model [3] is a rule-based sequencing model that supports adaptive execution of an Activity Tree using sequencing rules, rollup rules, and the status of learning objectives. The Activity Tree defined by the model is a hierarchical structure of learning activities and their corresponding learning contents.

SCORM's Sequencing Definition Model provides the desirable features described above; however, it has a few limitations. First, it does not have a conceptual model for modeling learning objects. In SCORM, three types of learning resources are distinguished: Asset, Sharable Content Asset and Sharable Content Object. However, what these resources are comprised of has not been explicitly specified. Second, non-leaf activities in an Activity Tree neither present contents nor perform assessment in SCORM. We believe that it is useful to allow a non-leaf node to present an introduction and/or a summary of the contents covered by its child activities. Assessment items for testing the integrated knowledge of the contents presented by the child activities should also be allowed. Third, there is no model or specification for assessments in the sequencing model. We introduce a model-based assessment technique to facilitate flexible assessments.

KnowledgeTree uses learning goals, preferences and knowledge of the individual learner to select the most appropriate learning materials. Our dynamic binding of requests to LOs is similar to their idea of binding learning materials at runtime. However, we leverage standardized Web-services technologies for the registration and discovery of LOs, and add meta-data and constraints in LO specifications.

L3 allows the selection of navigation rules at runtime, and uses meta-tags for describing the knowledge type and the inter-relationships of learning process elements. Our model allows sequencing rules to be attached to each activity at both the design-time and run-time in order to achieve adaptive and flexible learning process execution.

3 Learning Object Model

The concept of "*object*" promotes reusability in that objects of small granularities can be re-used to compose larger objects for use in different learning contexts. In our work, we model a learning object in terms of content items, practice items, and assessment items needed to cover a subject of learning and to conduct an assessment. By including these three types of learning items in an LO specification, the author of the LO can ensure that practice and assessment items presented to learners are consistent with the presented content items. In addition to these three types of items, the meta-data associated with the LO can be added in an LO specification [6] [13]. The meta-data is expressed in terms of a set of attributes and the constraints associated with these attributes. Constraints can be categorized into attribute constraints (i.e., the legitimate values of these attributes) and inter-attribute constraints (i.e., their value relationships). In our work, the constraint specification is used in the registration and discovery of learning objects [17].

3.1 Learning Resource Taxonomy

We distinguish three types of learning resources, and a taxonomy based on the order of their constructions is defined. The lowest resource in the taxonomy is called *learning asset*, which represents the most basic resources available on the Web. A learning asset can be a simple file, such as a text, image, audio, or video clip, or a complicated web page. The next level of resource is called Atomic Learning Object (ALO), which consists of content, practice and assessment items, as well as the meta-data and constraints associated with the ALO. The top level learning resource in the taxonomy is called Composite Learning Object (CLO), which is a tree-structured learning process model containing modeling constructs, such as activities, connectors, and edges. Fig. 1 illustrates the taxonomy and reference/binding relationships among learning resources.

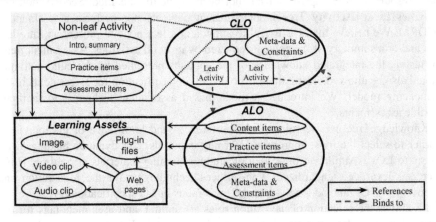

Fig. 1. Taxonomy of Learning Resources and Relationships

3.2 Learning Object Models

A *learning content definition model* is used to model ALOs uniformly in terms of pre-assessment items, content items, practice items, post-assessment items, and meta-data and constraints associated with the objects. Meta-data and constraints include attributes such as *language, targeted age group, prerequisites, cost, etc.* and their allowed values and value relationships.

A *learning process definition model* is introduced in our work to model CLOs. It is based on SCORM's Sequencing Definition Model with several extensions. A CLO is modeled by an activity tree, in which learning *activities* are nodes, *connectors* are used to bridge parent activities with their child activities and to specify the *sequencing control modes* [3] that define the sequencing behavior of child nodes, and *edges* are used to connect activities to connectors, and vice versa. By separating the control information (sequencing control modes) from activity specifications, run-time customization of a learning process instance can be carried out more easily.

Each activity specification contains an activity name, an activity id, a textual description of the activity, learning objectives, and a set of optional condition-action rules, an optional assessment information for assessment execution and problem selections, and a limit on the execution of activity in terms of the time or the number of allowed executions. It can also contain learning items in a non-leaf activity or binding information in a leaf activity, which may include service request information for static binding or constraints for dynamic binding. As shown in Fig. 2, the condition-action rules may contain 1) pre-activity rules, 2) after-pre-assessment rules, 3) drill-down rules, 4) roll-up rules, and 5) after-post-assessment rules. At each of the above five stages of processing an activity, an event is posted to trigger the processing of condition-action rules that are associated with the event. Since the condition parts of these rules may check the user profiles, assessment results, and the progress they made at the stage of processing the activity, it is possible that only some of these rules are applied to a specific learner or a category of learners, and that different learning paths are selected for learners of different competencies and profiles. Triggered rules can even customize the control structure of a CLO run-time instance to alter its control flow, activity specification and sequencing control modes to accommodate learners of distinctively different profiles. To facilitate adaptive and flexible LO binding, the binding information in a leaf activity can reflect the context and constraints (time, language, cost, age, etc.) dynamically as well.

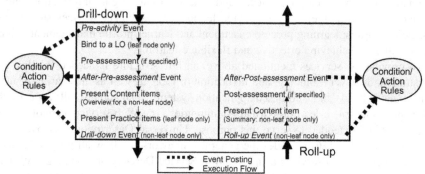

Fig. 2. Tasks in an Activity Node at Runtime

In our learning process model, we allow any activity node to carry out an assessment task on the learning contents covered by the tree that is rooted at the node. The assessment items used in the assessment task can be randomly and proportionally selected from the assessment items of the non-leaf nodes and those learning objects bound to the leaf nodes. The above provision gives a course author a greater flexibility on when and how assessments are to be carried out. Fig. 3 shows an activity tree with several assessments. A quiz will be given after each of its chapters, and only those students who pass less than two of the three quizzes need to take a midterm exam, i.e., the assessment of the first part. To make the midterm assessment optional, a roll-up rule of the Midterm activity can be defined as "*if at least 2 child activities are Satisfied, then regard it as Satisfied*", and the after-post-assessment rule "*if the current activity is not Satisfied, then perform the assessment*". After the midterm, there will be no quiz for the chapters of the second part but there will be a mandatory final exam for the second part. The course will be considered passed only if both midterm and the final exam are passed, which can be specified by a roll-up rule *"if all Satisfied, then regard it as Satisfied"* attached to the root of the activity tree.

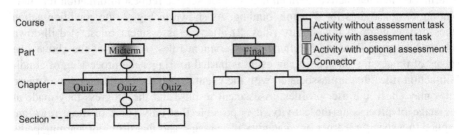

Fig. 3. An Activity Tree with Assessments

4 e-Learning Service Infrastructure for Virtual Communities

The existing virtual e-learning communities provide directory services for the registration and discovery of learning objects, and spaces for exchanging information among members. However, they do not provide learning management services such as assessment, adaptive learning process enactment and learner profile management, which are essential for achieving effective and flexible e-learning.

To provide the services mentioned above, an infrastructure is needed to allow the registration, discovery, binding, and invocation of LOs, as well as the sharing of multimedia data objects and web-based application systems. It should also allow the establishment of multiple e-learning virtual communities. The Web-service technology can be adapted and extended to serve this purpose. Universal Description, Discovery and Integration (UDDI) [16] provides the general framework to allow all types of objects to be defined as Web-services using the Web Service Description Language (WSDL) [19]. However, the existing UDDI does not allow the specification of constraints associated with Web-services. Without this specification capability, an LO can be selected by the registry, but does not satisfy a requestor's requirements.

In this work, we have extended the WSDL and UDDI's capabilities by allowing the specification and processing of constraints associated with learning objects. Requestors' requirements can also be specified as constraints in a constraint specification language. We use a Constraint Satisfaction Processor [9] to store constraints and perform constraint matching to select suitable Web-services.

In our virtual e-learning community, people or organizations play different roles. *Content providers* use authoring tools to define and create learning assets and ALOs. The ALOs are stored and maintained at the providers' local repositories that make use of the Apache Xindice XML database [5]. *Content composers* use a CLO authoring tool to compose CLOs. An *e-Learning Service System,* which includes a Learning Process Execution Engine and an Event-Trigger-Rule Server (ETR) [14], carries out tasks defined in a CLO, such as sequencing activities, performing assessments, etc. The XML documents that describe CLOs are stored at the content composers' local repositories. Meta-data and access points of ALOs and CLOs are registered as Web-services in a *Constraints-based Registry*, which can be browsed and queried by users who play various roles. The Registry leverages the UDDI registry as a back-end to store the access points of LOs. The operations (i.e., behaviors) of these objects are accessible programmatically as Web-service operations by using the Simple Object Access Protocol [18]. Each virtual community has a host site, which provides content brokering, learning process execution and event-trigger-rule management services. The main functions of the *Administrator* at the host site are to administer the activities of the virtual community, maintain the e-learning software systems, and enforce the community's rules and policies. *Content Evaluators*, elected by the virtual community, review, evaluate and rate the ALOs and CLOs that are registered with the registry. They approve or disapprove their inclusion for the community's use as well as their modification and removal. *Content learners* can browse and query the registry to find, bind and launch the desired ALOs or CLOs for execution by the execution engine. The enactment of a CLO will programmatically access and sequence the presentation and assessment of the CLO by binding to and accessing its ALOs and CLOs. Fig. 4 shows the e-learning service infrastructure composed of software components that support the tasks of people and organizations that play different roles in a virtual e-learning community. Due to the space limitation, technical details of the infrastructure that cannot be included in the paper will be given in the conference presentation.

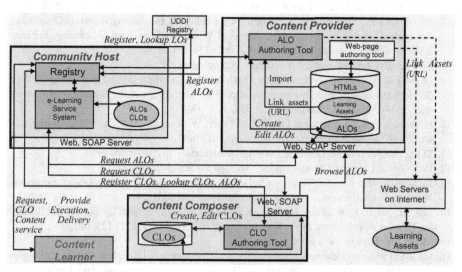

Fig. 4. Web-Service-based E-learning Service Infrastructure

5 Summary

In this paper, we have presented problems and requirements in the design and imple-mentation of LOs. We defined two types of LOs: ALOs that aggregate related Web resources with assessment and practice items, and CLOs that allow the assembly of ALOs and CLOs for adaptive and flexible sequencing of the LOs. The meta-data of

LOs are registered with the Constraints-based Registry and used for their discovery and binding. In this paper, we also presented the concept of virtual e-learning community and the collaborative roles of its members. A Web-service-based e-learning service infrastructure and its key components have also been described. The infrastructure makes use of several components that have been developed for other applications, such as the ETR Server and the Constraint-based Registry. Its authoring tools for designing ALOs and CLOs have also been developed. The integration of these existing components with the newly developed ones is in progress.

References

1. Advanced Distributed Learning (ADL) Initiative: SCORM 1.3 Content Aggregation Model, http://www.adlnet.org/ (2004)
2. ADL Initiative: http://www.adlnet.org/
3. ADL Initiative: SCORM 1.3 Sequencing and Navigation, http://www.adlnet.org/ (2004)
4. Altenhofen, M, Schaper, J: Flexible Instructional Strategies for e-learning, Proceedings of the 35th Hawaii International Conference on System Sciences (2002)
5. Apache: Apache Xindice, http://xml.apache.org/xindice/ (2003)
6. Barrit, C.: Reusable Learning Object Strategy version 4.0, Cisco Systems, Inc. (2001)
7. Brusilovsky P., Nijhavan H.: A Framework for Adaptive E-Learning Based on Distributed Re-usable Learning Activities, Proceedings of World Conference on E-Learning, E-Learn 2002, Montreal, Canada, October 15-19, (2002) 154-161
8. Co-operative Learning Object Exchange: http://cloe.on.ca/
9. Degwekar, S., Su, S. Y. W., & Lam, H: Constraint Specification and Processing in Web Services Publication and Discovery, to appear in Proceedings of the International Conference on Web Services, San Diego, CA, U.S.A. (2004)
10. Eduworks, O.K.I. Leadership: OKI White Paper: What is the Open Knowledge Initiative?, http://web.mit.edu/oki/product/whtpapers/whatis.html
11. EOE (The Educational Object Economy Foundation): http://www.eoe.org/
12. IMS Global Learning Consortium Inc.: http://www.imsglobal.org
13. Johnson, L. F.: Elusive Vision - Challenges Impending the Learning Object Economy, New Media Consortium, Macromedia® white paper, (2003)
14. Lee, M., Su, S. Y. W., Lam, H.: A Web-based Knowledge Network for Supporting Emerging Internet Applications, the WWW Journal, Vol. 4, No. 1/2 (2001) 121-140
15. MERLOT: http://www.merlot.org/Home.po
16. OASIS. Universal Description, Discovery, and Integration (UDDI), http://www.uddi.org/
17. Su, Stanley Y. W., Lee, Gilliean: A Web-service-based, Dynamic and Collaborative Learning Management System, Proceedings of World Conference on E-Learning, E-Learn 2003, Phoenix, AZ, USA, Nov. 7-11, (2003)
18. W3C: Simple Object Access Protocol, http://www.w3.org/TR/SOAP/
19. W3C: Web Services Description Language (WSDL) 1.1, http://www.w3.org/TR/wsdl
20. York, B. et al.: A teacher for every learner. http://www.cra.org/Activities/grand.challenges /slides/education.pdf (2002)

Implementation Issues on the Quality Evaluation of Web-Based Courses and Digital Learning Resources

Xia Teng[1,2], Brandon Muramatsu[1], JianWei Zhang[3], Joseph G. Tront[4], Flora McMartin[5], and Alice Agogino[1]

[1] NEEDS, University of California, Berkeley,
3115 Etcheverry Hall, Berkeley, California, 94720-1750 USA
xteng@newton.berkeley.edu, mura@needs.org, agogino@needs.org
[2] Chinese E-Learning Technology Standards Committee, Beijing, China
zhangjw@tsinghua.edu.cn
[3] Institute of Educational Technology, Tsinghua University, Beijing, China
[4] Virginia Polytechnic Institute and State University,
359 Durham Hall, Blacksburg, Virginia, 24061-0111 USA
jgtront@vt.edu
[5] MERLOT, California State University,
Long Beach, 1250 Bellflower Blvd., PSY-100 Long Beach, California, 90840-0901 USA
mcmartin@merlot.org

Abstract. The emergence of the Web as a delivery mechanism for education has led a number of organizations to develop and implement quality evaluation criteria for digital learning resources and Web-based courses. The Chinese E-Learning Technology Standardization Committee is developing a specification for evaluating Web-based courses. This paper introduces the background on the standard, CELTS-22, and its guidelines for use. Further, this paper explores critical implementation issues through a case study of two similar evaluation criteria and systems that are used by NEEDS – A Digital Library for Engineering Education and MERLOT – the Multimedia Educational Resource for Learning and Online Teaching in the United States.

1 Introduction

The Chinese E-Learning Technology Standardization Committee (CELTSC) is chartered by the Chinese Information Technology Standards Committee and sponsored by the Chinese government (www.celtsc.edu.cn). Its goal is to develop standards for enabling interoperability and reusability of e-learning technologies, and for managing the quality of educational services. It is also responsible for developing the compliance test software for content delivery platforms and authoring tools.

As one of the important standard in development within the framework of CELTS, The CELTS-22 specification describes quality characteristics of Web-based courses and defines corresponding evaluation criteria [1]. Following the standard development process, the framework of CELTS-22 was initially established, a consensus building phase was then carried out using the Delphi Method, which is to collect and distill feedback from a group of experts in the design, development and management of

W. Liu et al. (Eds.): ICWL 2004, LNCS 3143, pp. 379–385, 2004.
© Springer-Verlag Berlin Heidelberg 2004

instructional technologies [2], where the necessity and importance for each proposed dimensions and their respective subcomponents of quality characters web-based courseware were examined. Although reliability and validity of the evaluation results should be discussed, this paper aims to explore different critical implementation issues through case study of similar evaluation criteria and systems.

2   CELTS-22 Specification

The specification provides guiding principles for evaluating Web-based courses for various constituencies including:

- Providers: such as content, delivery platform and authoring tool vendors that design and develop Web-based courses.
- Consumers: such as organizations, institutions and individuals to select, acquire or use Web-based courses.
- Third party organizations: such as organizations that evaluate, support or maintain Web-based courses.

The CELTS-22 specification is intended for Web-based asynchronous courses that can be taken independently. Typically these courses are a relatively complete learning experience that includes structured content with specified learning objectives, interactive learning activities and assessment of learning outcomes. The specification evaluates the potential of the contents and features of a Web-based course, not specific instances of the course. It is worth noting that elements of the CELTS-22 specification can be used to evaluate courseware or other digital learning resources that are used to enhance traditional or Web-based courses.

2.1   Quality Framework and Evaluation Criteria

The CELTS-22 framework defines quality characteristics for a Web-based course along four dimensions. Table 1 shows the dimensions (Content, Instructional, Interface and Technical Design) and whether the element is Mandatory (M) or Optional (O). In defining these dimensions and elements, CELTS-22 attempts to minimize overlap between each dimension.

The framework is transformed into evaluation criteria by adding a description of the criteria, an expanded description and criteria indicators and a note with samples of the criteria. A descriptive sample of the evaluation criteria is provided in Table 2.

2.2   Use Guidelines

The CELTS-22 specification provides use guidelines for evaluating Web-based courses. Potential implementers of the specification should:

- Perform a requirement analysis to identify the evaluation needs and scope.
- Define a methodology for the evaluation to specify the appropriate evaluation criteria, data collection method and rating system.
- Conduct the evaluation to measure, analyze and present the results.

Table 1. CELTS-22 Quality Characteristics

Content Design	Instructional Design
1.1 Course Description (M)	2.1 Learning Objectives (M)
1.2 Content-Objective Consistency (M)	2.2 Learner Control (M)
1.3 Academic Quality (M)	2.3 Learner-Content Interactivity (M)
1.4 Defining Content Object (M)	2.4 Communication & Collaboration (O)
1.5 Content Sequencing (O)	2.5 Motivation and Attention (O)
1.6 Hyperlinks (O)	2.6 Presentation and Demonstration (M)
1.7 Resources Extension (O)	2.7 Media Use (M)
	2.8 Learning Guidance (O)
	2.9 Practice with Feedback (M)
	2.10 Tracking (O)
	2.11 Assessment (M)
Interface Design	**Technology Design**
3.1 Style Consistency (O)	4.1 System Requirements (M)
3.2 Layout (O)	4.2 Installation and Uninstallation (M)
3.3 Legibility (M)	4.3 Reliability (M)
3.4 Navigation and Orientation (M)	4.4 Multimedia Technology (M)
3.5 Links Labels (O)	4.5 Compatibility (O)
3.6 Electronic Bookmarks (O)	
3.7 Content Search (O)	
3.8 Responsiveness (O)	
3.9 Operational Help (M)	

Table 2. Sample CELTS-22 Evaluation Criteria

Index	Name	Type	Description	Explanation	Notes
2.1	Learning Objectives	Mandatory	Clear and concrete learning objectives of each learning unit; higher level learning objectives of the main learning unit.	**Description:** There should be a description of learning objectives for each learning unit. **Clarity:** The description should be concrete so as to gain certain knowledge, skill, or practical solution strategy, etc. **Levels:** Higher level learning objectives for the main learning units includes: analysis, summarization, evaluation or application of new knowledge for practical problem solving.	A learning unit is a module in a course, such as a chapter, or a module defined in SCORM.

For Web-based courses to successfully complete an evaluation using the specification, they should:

1. Meet all the defined mandatory (M) criteria.
2. Achieve a minimum score for each dimension (where the actual score is dependent on the purpose of the evaluation).
3. Achieve a minimum overall score (where the actual score is dependent on the purpose of the evaluation).

3   Case Study: Implementing Evaluation Systems

This case study will examine the development and implementation of evaluation systems at the NEEDS – A Digital Library for Engineering Education[1] (www.needs.org) and MERLOT – the Multimedia Educational Resource for Learning and Online Teaching[2] (www.merlot.org) digital libraries in the United States. Although the two examples in the case study focus on courseware and other digital learning resources, as opposed to the whole Web-based asynchronous courses of interest to CELTS-22, they are relevant examples because the criteria are similar (see Table 3) and they aim to accomplish similar goals.

Table 3. NEEDS *Premier Award* Evaluation Criteria[3]

Instructional Design	Software Design	Engineering Content
• Learning Objectives • Interactivity • Cognition/conceptual change • Content • Multimedia Use • Instructional use/adaptability	• Engagement • Learner interface and navigation • Technical reliability	• Accuracy of content • Appropriateness of content

3.1   Customize and Evolve the Evaluation Criteria

Both NEEDS and MERLOT have demonstrated the value in having discipline specific criteria that evolve over time. The evaluation criteria in use by NEEDS and MERLOT have been tested over seven years and five years, respectively. Both organizations recognized that to be successful, their evaluation criteria must be appropriate along a number of dimensions including the discipline and type of material being evaluated.

NEEDS, with the help of content experts, instructional designers and software designers, developed a set of high level categories (Instructional Design, Software Design and Content) and criteria that can be applied to courseware (or relatively large granularity learning objects) used by engineering educators [4-5]. Along with each criterion are statements (sub-components) to help users of the criteria determine how to evaluate the criterion (see Table 4). It is also worth pointing out that NEEDS reviews its evaluation criteria annually to determine how to maintain and improve the criteria's effectiveness and applicability for evaluating courseware. Major revisions were made after the criteria was first introduced in 1997 [6], and most recently in 2003 with a focus on Learning Objectives (see Sample Criteria in Table 4).

---

[1] NEEDS is an educational digital library where both educators and learners can search, access and download digital learning resources via the Web for engineering education [3].

[2] MERLOT is an international cooperative, based in the U.S., for high-quality online resources to improve learning and teaching within higher education.

[3] Full details of the (2003) *Premier Award* evaluation criteria can be found at: www.needs.org/needs/public/premier/2003/2003-criteria-prelim.pdf.

Table 4. Sample Criteria with Sub-Components

Category:	Instructional Design
Criteria:	1.1 Learning Objectives
Sub-Components:	• Learning objectives and goals are appropriate and clearly stated, in the software (preferred), in an instructor's guide or the submission packet. • The presentation and organization of content, as well as related activities, supports the learning objectives and goals. • Learners are aware of learning objectives as they are using the software and participating in the learning experience. • A clear method of measuring achievement of learning objectives and goals is provided within the software or by the learning experience. • Learning objectives and goals can be correlated to ABET[4] accreditation criteria.

MERLOT followed a similar process of bringing together experts to draft a generic set of evaluation criteria[5] applicable across the sciences and humanities in higher education in 1999. These criteria were then used as the basis for "custom" criteria used by each of MERLOT's discipline-based Editorial Boards to conduct peer review. Each discipline, therefore, has criteria customized to the nature of the particular discipline[6].

3.2 "Tiered" Evaluation

During the development of the evaluation criteria used by both NEEDS and MERLOT, it became evident that to be most effective the criteria would require a large investment of time and resources to do a thorough evaluation of digital learning resources. Both organizations balance the time and resource needs by implementing the "tiered" evaluation system described in Table 5. The "tiered" system of evaluation recognizes: (a) the need to develop processes that could scale with the ever increasing number of resources available on the Web and (b) the challenges and resources necessary to conduct detailed evaluations [4].

3.3 Training of Reviewers

A critical element to the consistent application of evaluation criteria has been a structured training process for reviewers applying the criteria. The endorsed and premier levels of the "tiered" evaluation system require teams to evaluate the digital learning

---

[4] U.S. Accreditation Board for Engineering and Technology (www.abet.org).

[5] Full details of the generic MERLOT evaluation criteria can be found at: taste.merlot.org/projects/peer_review/criteria.php.

[6] See the MERLOT-Physics criteria at taste.merlot.org/communities/physics/criteria.php and the MERLOT-History criteria at taste.merlot.org/communities/history/criteria.php for examples of "customized" criteria.

Table 5. Tiered Evaluation System used by NEEDS and MERLOT

Level	NEEDS	MERLOT
Base	NEEDS follows a collection development policy that encourages contributions of a wide range of materials [7].	MERLOT follows a collection development policy that encourages contributions of a wide range of materials. As resources are evaluated for whether or not they should be reviewed ("triage" process), some resources might be removed from the collection. In addition, in many disciplines, most of the resources in that disciplinary area have been reviewed to a lesser degree because they have passed that initial evaluation process.
Base+ Annotation	NEEDS encourages users to provide "Amazon.com"-style *User Comments* to further describe resources in its catalog.	MERLOT has a large number of both "Amazon.com"-style *Member Comments* and *Assignments* that provide context to the descriptive catalog records for each digital learning resource.
Endorsed	NEEDS is collaborating with MERLOT-Engineering to develop, implement and conduct *Peer Reviews* of engineering resources.	MERLOT has focused on *Peer Review* using Editorial Boards with editors and reviewers that apply discipline-customized evaluation criteria. MERLOT is transitioning the *Peer Review* process from one that has been financially supported mainly by MERLOT partners, to that of a "professional" responsibility for educators in each disciplinary area that "volunteer" to serve as reviewers [8].
Premier[a]	NEEDS developed the *Premier Award for Excellence in Engineering Education Courseware* to "recognize high-quality, non-commercial courseware designed to enhance engineering education." The annual *Premier Award* is determined during a one and half day judging session by a panel consisting of content experts, instructional designers, students and publishers. The panel applies the evaluation criteria and examines the detailed documentation[b] to select one or more *Premier Courseware* of the year (and potentially one or more *Finalist Candidates*).	MERLOT has instituted the *MERLOT Awards Program for Exemplary Online Learning Resources* (taste.merlot.org/ awards/) to recognized the "best" digital learning resources annually. MERLOT Editors select the "top" resource in each year and it is named the *MERLOT Classic* in that discipline. MERLOT editors then evaluate all of the *MERLOT Classics* to select one or more *MERLOT Editors' Choice(s)* for the year.

[a] NEEDS and MERLOT have agreed that NEEDS *Premier Courseware* are equivalent the *MERLOT Editors' Choice* selections. In addition NEEDS *Premier Award Finalist Candidates* can be considered equivalent to *MERLOT Classics*.

[b] 2004 *Premier Award* submission guidelines can be found at:
www.needs.org/needs/public/premier/2004/submission/.

resources. In the case of MERLOT there are multiple teams of reviewers both within a given discipline and across disciplinary communities; in the case of NEEDS there is a single group of up to 10 reviewers for each annual judging panel. Goals in training reviewers include: (a) providing a shared understanding among the group of reviewers of the details and methods to apply the evaluation criteria and (b) "standardizing" the process to ensure inter-rater reliability (between individual reviewers and across multiple teams/panels).

4   Summary and Conclusions

The CELTS-22 specification describes the general quality characteristics of Web-based courses and corresponding evaluation criteria for the Chinese educational community. The specification also defines criteria and processes that can be used as a general guideline. A number of critical implementation issues can be identified from the brief case study of NEEDS and MERLOT, the importance of these issues should be recognized when the CELTS-22 specification is to be implemented by an organization. The three issues to consider when evaluating potential use of the CELTS-22 specification can be summarized as:

- Understanding that the specification will be customized and localized by implementers to meet their needs.
- Defining appropriate levels of evaluation (or levels of implementation) that balance resource and social constraints.
- Understanding that training is necessary to enable participants to evaluate Web-based courses using the specification.

References

1. China E-Learning Technology Standards Committee. Specification for Evaluating Web-Based Courses, CELTS-22.1 CD1.0. 2004. URL: www.celtsc.edu.cn
2. Teng, X., Duan, C., Zhang, J., and Wang, X. The Development of CELTS-22: the Standard for Evaluating Web-Based Courses. Modern Educational Technology, 11(1), pp. 5-12, 2003
3. Muramatsu, B. and A. M. Agogino, NEEDS – The National Engineering Education Delivery System: A Digital Library for Engineering Education. D–Lib Magazine, 5(4), 1999. URL: www.dlib.org/dlib/april99/muramatsu/04muramatsu.html.
4. Eibeck, P. "Criteria for Peer–Review of Engineering Courseware on the NEEDS Database," IEEE Transactions on Education, Special Issue on the Special Issue on the Application of Information Technologies to Engineering and Science Education, 39(3), pp. 381–387, 1996.
5. Synthesis Coalition, Quality Workshop. Synthesis Coalition: San Luis Obispo, CA, 1995.
6. Muramatsu, B., P. A. Eibeck, J. L. Stern, and A. M. Agogino, "Effective Processes to Give Engineering Educators Easy Access to Quality–Reviewed Electronic Courseware," Invited Presentation, NSF Engineering Education Innovators' Conference, Washington, D.C., April 8, 1997.
7. Muramatsu, B. NEEDS Collection Development Guidelines. 2003.
8. Hanley, G. and F. McMartin. Scaling the Peer Review Process. NSDL All Projects Meeting, Washington, D.C., October 2003.

Reusable Learning Object
and Its Strategies for e-Learning

Qingtang Liu[1,2], Zongkai Yang[1,2], Kun Yan[1], and Di Wu[1]

[1] Huazhong University of Science & Technology
lqtang@yahoo.com
[2] Central China Normal University, Wuhan, China

Abstract. Sequence, granularity and taxonomy of learning objects are three open problems that will be faced in developing learning system. Concerning these problems and other ideas about educational technological standards and instructional design, the article mainly discusses the reusable strategies of learning objects. Firstly, based on discussing learning objects' characteristics, the article designs the learning object's content structure and programs learning objects' reusable administrative levels. Secondly, the article puts forward two sequence ways of learning objects. At last, the article describes reusable learning object's specific applied methods.

Keywords: learning objects, sequence, hierarchy, granularity, taxonomy

1 Introduction

With the rapid increase of learning resources, how to build an interoperative and reusable content management and application system becomes a studying hotspot in e-learning. Because some training departments in enterprises, colleges and other organizations have respectively designed instructional resources repositories or e-learning platform with different descriptions of learning resources, these systems are difficult to communicate and exchange their resources. In order to solve these problems, many organizations all over the world have begun to study and make use of learning technological standards.

A common model of learning object to develop learning resources is built up based on Learning Object Metadata (LOM) and Content Packaging (CP) specifications, described and bund by extensible markup language (XML). But the model only arranges a basic framework for Content Management System (CMS), instructional design and didactical strategies of learning objects are neglected. The paper mainly discusses the learning objects' model meeting standards as well as instructional technologies. It is carried out in five major sections. In the second, the paper analyses learning object's definition and features, and probes into the problems while designing the learning resources. The third of the paper provides learning object's model based on instructional design and standards for specific subjects. In the forth, it also describes data structure and package of learning objects. The last is to summarize learning object's technologies and give some suggestions.

W. Liu et al. (Eds.): ICWL 2004, LNCS 3143, pp. 386–392, 2004.

2   Learning Objects and Related Work

What is Learning Object (LO)? Learning objects are elements of a new type of computer-based instruction grounded in the object-oriented paradigm of computer science. A typical definition of LO is that a LO is small, reusable digital component that can be selectively applied alone or in combination by computer software, learning facilitators or learners themselves, to meet individual needs for learning or performance support [1]. The fundamental idea behind learning objects is that instructional designers can build small (relative to the size of an entire course) instructional components that can be reused a number of times in different contexts.

2.1   Standards and Questions

To facilitate the widespread adoption of learning objects' approach and assure the interoperability of their instructional technologies, some organizations (e.g. ADL, IEEE LTSC, ARIADNE and IMS) have been developing technical standards to support the broad deployment of learning objects. However, within many standards groups, the main focus is on the financial opportunities that may arise, there is astonishingly little conversation about the didactical or instructional design implications of learning objects [2]. There are mainly three open questions in developing learning objects: sequence, granularity and taxonomy.

One of the purposes of LOM standards is to enable computer agents to automatically compose personalized lessons for an individual learner [3]. This means taking individual learning objects and combining them in a way that makes instructional sense, or in instructional design terminology, sequencing the learning objects. The problem is that no instructional design information is included in the metadata specified by the current LOM standards. Obviously, instructionally grounded sequencing decisions are at the heart of the instructionally successful use of learning objects.

The second difficult problem facing the designers of learning objects is that of "granularity". How big should a learning object be? A too big or a too little LO may not well serve the learning objectives of the module. And a large object could diminish the possibility of learning object reuse. From an instructional point of view, alternatively, the decision between how much or how little to include in learning object can be viewed as a problem of "scope". While reality dictates that financial and other factors must be considered, if learning is to have its greatest chance of occurring, decisions regarding the scope of learning objects must also be made in an instructionally grounded, principled manner.

The discussion of learning object characteristics, such as sequence and granularity, leads naturally to the question, "are there different types of learning objects"? In other words, can types of learning objects be meaningfully differentiated?

2.2   Related Works

A didactical taxonomy of learning objects and a didactical metadata approach for the facilitation of reusable navigation patterns had been discussed by Giselher [4], but the granularity and sequence of learning objects had been analyzed little. Michael et al. had utilized a content aggregation model and meta-tagging learning elements to enable the flexible execution of courses and defined levels of learning objects [5]. But the inner structures of learning objects had no accurately described. Cisco systems had designed and developed reusable learning objects in order to move from creating and delivering large inflexible training courses, to database driven objects that can be reused, searched and modified independent of their delivery media [6]. Its strategies include little sequencing and interoperating information in reusable learning objects structures because common descriptions of learning objects are lacked.

We aim at sequence, granularity and taxonomy of learning objects in the following aspects: reusability, platform independence, and extendibility of learning objects.

3 Design of Reusable Learning Object's Structure

3.1 Hierarchy and Granularity of Learning Objects

One of the major goals in our learning objects' model is to provide a common framework for reusability, share, adaptive delivery and its instructional application. We define a tree-based representation, which groups learning resources into a logical order. This hierarchical tree represents the default order that an author intends for the learner to progress through the material. Content is aggregated in four distinct structural levels where each higher level may contain instances of all lower levels. These levels are enumerated from top to bottom: Course, Unit, Lesson (RLO), Knowledge unit (RKU).

The lowest level of granularity is formed by knowledge units, which represent the smallest indivisible element in a course. Several related knowledge unit are typically assembled into "lesson". The lesson is the logical representation of a distinct, thematically coherent unit. The duration to learn a lesson is about 30~35 minutes. Lessons are still considered small in terms of "size" and are further grouped into larger structural units, so-called "unit". Course is the highest structural level that contains some units, lessons and knowledge units. Generally speaking, RLO stands for "lesson" and RKU is the label of "knowledge unit". A RKU (Reusable Knowledge Unit) that has single learning objective is the smallest instructional item, which is composed of some materials (e.g. text, image, sound, video, assessing object). A RLO (Reusable Learning Object) is an instructional meaning entity, which includes the logic sequencing structure of RKUs, instructional strategies.

3.2 Taxonomy and Structure of Learning Objects

We adopt a two-level hierarchy "RKU-RLO" for our content structure. Each RKU is built upon a single objective, content items, practice items, and assessment items. Each RLO is comprised with an Overview, Summary, Assessment, five to nine (7 ± 2) RKUs [6], and relative instructional strategies (navigation graph) derived from a specific task. We revise the Cisco learning model and redesign the description of learning object. (See Fig. 1)

RKU is self-contained chunk of learning content built around a single learning objective, and it is a small knowledge item. To aid in content standardization, each RKU is further classified as a concept, fact, procedure, process, or principle. To represent the nature of understanding of each RKU, the categories of Bloom's taxonomy of educational objective are adopted. Bloom's taxonomy is originally developed as a means of systematically categorizing educational objectives in a way that facilitates communication among educations. The six major categories of the cognitive domain are shown and mapped to RKU categories in table 1.

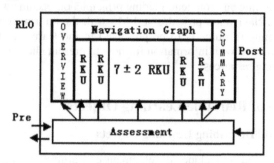

Fig. 1. RKU-RLO Structure

Table 1. Relations of Bloom's Taxonomy and RKU

Category	Description	RKU Type
Knowledge	Remembering learned information	concept, fact
Comprehension	Grasping the meaning of learning content	concept, fact, procedure
Application	Applying knowledge to solve problem	fact, procedure, process
Analysis	Divide substantial whole into its constituent parts	procedure, process
Synthesis	Reasoning from the general to the particular	process, principle
Evaluation	Making judgments based on criteria	principle

A RLO Overview is used to introduce the RLO and act as an advanced organizer for the learner by listing the objective, outline, and prerequisites for this "lesson". The RLO Summary is used to conclude the RLO and tie the scenario and objectives covered in each RKU together. It also offers some suggests for learner to broaden their knowledge and skills in this area. Finally, the Summary is a transition between the RKUS and the final assessment. The purpose of "assessment" is to prescribe RKUS the learner needs to take and to ensure the learner's mastery on all objectives for a given "lesson." Instructional strategies always are contained in learning contents.

3.3   Sequence of Learning Objects

Sequencing strategies must be based not only on domain knowledge but also on teaching style, learning goals and the learners' status. All of these were modeled using conceptual graphs and an inference engine to answer queries about these graphs. This approach is too flexible to ha rdly manageable by ordinary course authors. In contrast to this general approach, we adopt two strategies for the organization of learning objects. These are automated templates and customized templates.

Automated templates are derived from conceptual graph, which is computed according to concept mapping of knowledge units. Sequencing relations between 5~9 knowledge units in a RLO are the part of conceptual graphs. In contrast to automated templates, customized templates allow learners and teachers to adjust their learning contents. Construction of these strategies not only relies on conceptual graphs but also depends on the instructional design's strategies, which includes some descriptions of learners' status, learning environment, guiding principle, or teaching ways.

Sequencing and Navigation provides an LMS with the information it needs to determine what learning resource is to be presented to the learner and when. It also should provide the LMS with information for how to present choices to users to navigate through learning resources.

4   Application of Reusable Learning Objects

4.1   Authoring and Describing Learning Objects

Authoring learning objects includes development of learning resources and metadata description of learning objects. Learning resources come from new contents or existed resources. Description of these resources must be transformed to the standardized format. In our strategies, learning resource sequencing is defined in the content structure and is external to the learning resource. It is the responsibility of the LMS to launch the learning resources in the appropriate defined sequence at run-time. Because learning resource reuse cannot really happen if the learning resource has embedded information that is context specific to the course. As fig.2 shows, it is the authoring tool of learning objects that we have developed. In the authoring tool, we choose XML as the file format to import and export metadata files, we hope these files can be interoperated by other systems because XML technology has been widely applied in the area of data exchange.

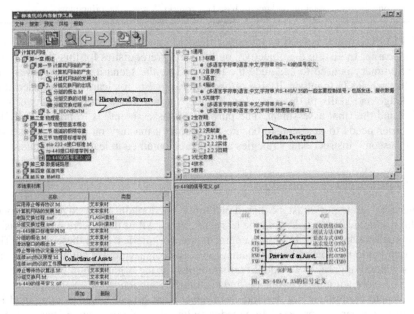

Fig. 2. Authoring Tool of Learning Object

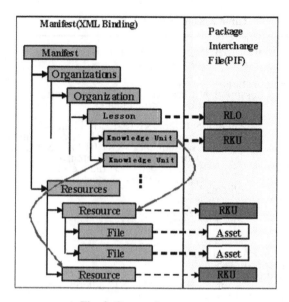

Fig. 3. Content Structure

4.2 Packaging Learning Objects

Content Packaging Information Model describes data structures that are used to provide interoperability of Internet based content with content creation tools, learning management systems, and run time environments. Its purpose is to collect and package instructional contents in some electronic form to enable them efficient aggregation, distribution, management, and deployment [6]. In our authoring tool, the content aggregated model is shown in fig.3. Because of limited space, XML binding of content packaging is represented by Table 2.

5 Conclusion

Strategies of Reusable Learning Objects have some advantages in e-learning. They are of great benefit to learning content modularization, reuse and share, and support flexible learning, just in time learning, and self-paced learning. They also promote cooperation and interaction between learners. In addition, they reduce the cost of developing learning resources.

As discussed above, Learning objects technologies based on standards have some disadvantages. If only we flexibly design the structure of learning objects, effectively organize sequence of learning objects, and accurately classify and describe learning objects, the questions will be improved.

In the paper, we design a model of reusable learning objects according to sequence, granularity and taxonomy of learning objects. And we take account of instructional designing and learning strategies and also probe into applications of model of reusable learning objects.

Table 2. Sample of XML Binding Document

```
<?xml version="1.0"?>
<manifest identifier="MANIFEST1" version= "1.1">
   <metadata> ......        </metadata>
      <organizations>
         <organization>
            <Lesson identifier="RLO01222" identifierref="R_S1">
               <metadata>......</metadata>
               <Overview >......</Overview>
               <item identifier="RKU01231" identifierref="R_S1_1"/>
                  <Prerequisite>RKU01321</Prerequisite>
                  <Subsequence>RKU01243</Subsequence>
                  <Content> ...... </Content>
                  <Practice>......</Practice>
                  <Assessment>......</assessment>
               </item>
               ......
               <Summary>......</Summary>
               <Assessment>......</Assessment>
                  </Lesson>
            ......
            </organization>
         </organizations>
         <resources>
               <resource identifier="R_S1" adlcp:scormtype="rku"
href="Course/ rku1.zip">
                  <file href="Lesson/rku1.htm "/>
                  <file href="Image/pic1.jpg"/>
                  ......
               </resource>
               ......
         </resources>
</manifest>
```

References

1. Available: http://www.fastrak-consulting.co.uk/tactix/features/object/objects.htm, 2003.1
2. Wiley, David A. Connecting Learning Objects to Instructional Design Theory: A Definition, a Metaphor, and a Taxonomy. In: David A. Wiley : The Instructional Use of Learning Objects, 2002, pp.3-23.
3. IEEE P1484.12, "Draft Standard for Learning Object Metadata", Version 6.1, http://ltsc.ieeee.org/wg12/LOM_WD6-1-1_without_tracking.pdf.
4. Giselher. An Educational Taxonomy for Learning Objects, Proceedings of the The 3rd IEEE International Conference on Advanced Learning Technologies, ICALT2003.
5. Michael et al. Flexible instructional strategies for e-learning, proceeding of the 35th Hawaii international conference on system sciences, 2002.
6. Cisco, Reusable Learning Object Strategy, http://www.cisco.com/warp/public/10/wwtraining/elearning/implement/rlo_stratrgy.pdf, 2002.3

An Implementation
of Learning Objects Management System

Wang Xuan[1], Zheng Li[1], and Yang Fang[2]

[1] Computer & Information Management Center, Tsinghua University
Beijing 100084, China
{wangxuan,zhli}@cic.tsinghua.edu.cn
[2] Department of Foreign Languages, Tsinghua University
Beijing 100084, China
yangfang@tsinghua.edu.cn

Abstract. This paper presents a LOMS (Learning Objects Management System) based on the B/S architecture for the support to the reusability and interoperability of various learning objects. After classifying the existing standards, the XML technology is used to support different metadata standards and possible emerging of new standards and standard changes. The system works well with metadata standards IEEE LOM and CELTS-3 now. The work of user input during the metadata generation also has considerably been reduced by the template together with information gathered from the system. The adoption of Xindice – an XML-native database makes the search and retrieval of learning objects effective and easy.

Keywords: learning object, LOM, Learning Object Metadata, metadata, learning resource, XML binding, web-based learning, eLearning, eLearning standards, learning technology, XML-native database

1 Introduction

As web-based Learning being widely used in educating and training, the amount of digital learning resources begin to accumulate. Reusability and interoperability of digital learning resources become one of the major challenges. Transferring traditional courseware into standard computer-based instructional eLearning objects and content packages can greatly enhance the reusability and interoperability of digital learning resource. Thus the cost of courseware development can be lowered through reusing of learning objects.

The main advantage of digital learning objects is reusability. That means learning object developed in one context can be transferred to another context,so learning objects can be stored, and tagged in a course editor tool and they could be reused in other courses on some other occasions. For this purpose, the issue of what exactly should be reusable and how to store and catalogue these learning objects draw much more attention in recent years.

The Internet makes a range of learning resources available to the public. But there is lack of interoperability. Interoperability can be defined as "the ability of two or more systems or components to exchange information and to use the information that

W. Liu et al. (Eds.): ICWL 2004, LNCS 3143, pp. 393–399, 2004.
© Springer-Verlag Berlin Heidelberg 2004

has been exchanged" [1]. Through interoperability contents from multiple sources can be stored in small chunks in a database and built on templates so that data stored in one system can be reused in other systems.

Without reusability and interoperability every courseware has to be developed from scratch. Over the years, the development of learning content is prone to unnecessary repetition, which certainly would be a waste of time and money.

2   The Reusability and Interoperability of Learning Objects

2.1   Break down Learning Contents into Learning Objects

For the reusability and interoperability learning contents should be broken down into chunks. From a pedagogical perspective, each chunk might play a specific role within an instructional design methodology. Such chunks are called learning objects, which are the basic components of the courseware.

The definition of "Learning objects" varies by authors and institutes. An eLearning object is defined as a "small piece of text, visual, audio, video, interactive component, etc. that is tagged, and stored in a database." (Muzio et al, 2002, p.22) Cisco (2001) defines a learning object as "a granular, reusable chunk of information that is media independent." Other terms mentions by Cisco include "educational objects, content objects, training components, nuggets, and chunks."

South and Monson (2001) use the term "media object." They define such an object as "digital media that is designed and/or used for instructional purposes. Such objects range from maps and charts to video demonstrations and interactive simulations." Wiley (2001) defines learning objects as "elements of a new type of computer-based instruction grounded in the object-oriented paradigm of computer science." They allow instructional designers to "build small instructional components that can be used, reused or referenced and which is deliverable over the Internet a number of times in different learning contexts.

2.2   Describe Learning Objects with Metadata

Learning objects should be stored in a database and organized by a management system for easy retrieval and search. For this purpose a small amount of additional information must be provided to describe each learning object. These informations are called metadata. The LOMS is responsible for converting digital learning resources into learning object by adding metadata, storing learning objects in database, search and retrieval them.

In common sense metadata is a label placed on any object, similar to the labels on cans of vegetables and library cards. In e-learning context metadata is the term to describe a package of information about an electronic resource, providing information such as author, title, subject matter, copyright information, and location.

The need for metadata in educational system is self-evident. The full text search approach currently widely used on the World Wide Web proves to be inadequate for the location of high quality resources appropriate to specific learning contexts, levels and styles. Furthermore, a large number of non-text educational materials are produced every day.

2.3 Standardization

It has been recognized that metadata is essential to ensure the accessibility and discovery of information. For reusability and interoperability the metadata model must be standards-based. IEEE Standard for Learning Object Metadata (IEEE LOM) developed by IEEE LTSC (Learning Technology Standards Committee) is a commonly used standard in E-learning. The CELTS-3 (China E-Learning Technology Standards) based on IEEE LOM, "Specification for Learning Object Metadata", has been developed and widely adopted in China. The LOMS represented in this paper is compatible with both IEEE LOM and the CELTS-3.

3 Metadata Usage

As mentioned above, the metadata specified by the IEEE LOM will be used in describing different learning objects, but how to describe the metadata using computers? In other words what is the presentation of metadata in computers? The problem is referred to as the binding for the metadata model. IEEE LTSC has given three different bindings for LOM: ISO/IEC 11404 binding, XML binding and Resource Description Framework (RDF) binding. The XML binding is chosen for our system.

3.1 XML Binding for the Metadata

The LOM metadata model is a hierarchy and XML is perfectly suited for the representation of it. The metadata model could be easily mapped to the structure of an XML document comprised of elements that have contents and attributes.

XML binding for a metadata defines the structure of the XML document, the elements appeared, including the elements' names, attributes and contents and the number of a specific element and order of some elements. For instance, the name of the root element of the XML document for LOM must be "lom". It also defines the value's ranges for some attributes and more for the organization of the XML document.

The conclusion we draw is that the concept of metadata facilitates the reusability and interoperability of learning objects, and the XML binding guarantees the interoperability of the metadata for the XML's portability in the technical layer and it makes metadata operational.

3.2 The Management of Metadata

The XML presentation of metadata should be stored for the management of learning objects. Most work of the LOMS is to generate metadata and store them for the adding of new learning objects, to search the appropriate learning object through searching the metadata. A sub-system called repository serves this purpose.

Xindice is used as the repository in our system, which is a so-called XML-native database. XML-native means that when the XML documents are stored into the database the conversion of the structure of the document into the table-structure used in Relational database is not required and the retrieval of the documents don't need the reverse conversion. Xindice uses the XPath as the query language. It is quite suitable where just the XML binding is used for metadata.

4   Design of the LOMS

4.1   System Objectives

The purpose of the LOMS is the reusability and interoperability of the learning objects. Some characteristics of the system are essential for this.

First, the *usability* of the system is vital to a LOMS. There have been many learning objects available before the creation of a LOMS, so the process of adding them into the system must be simple and easy.

For the most reusability and interoperability, enough metadata standards should be supported and new standards and standards' changes also should be easily adopted by the system. This leads to the second objective of the system - the *extensibility*.

At last, as an option, if the LOMS could be moved smoothly between different operating systems, the adoption of the LOMS may be more extensive.

The LOMS presented takes the extensibility as the first objective, the usability as the second and the cross-platform the last.

4.2   The Architecture of the System

The architecture is based on the B/S (Browser/Server) architecture. Contrast to other Client/Server architectures, B/S is convenient for user, for only a browser is required. In addition, the change of the system doesn't affect the user either.

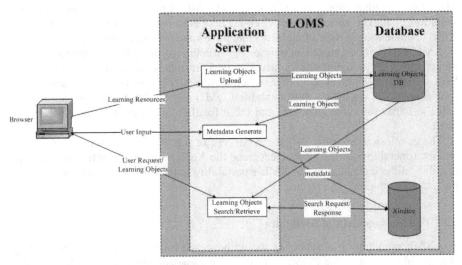

Fig. 1. The overview of the LOMS

The LOMS consists of two sub-systems: application server and the database servers. As Fig.1 shows, the system is distributed on three layers: the presentation layer, the function/control layer and the data layer. The browser on the presentation layer is the entry to the system. Application server focuses on the implementing of the functions of the system, such as the metadata's generating. It is the function/control layer. All the data, including the metadata and the learning objects themselves are stored in different databases, which form the data layer. The metadata is stored in Xindice and the learning objects in file systems.

Three components reside in the application server: *Learning Objects Upload Module* allows a user upload his/her learning resources to the system and stores them into the learning objects database. *Metadata Generate Module* generates the metadata for a learning object. *Learning Objects Search/Retrieve Module* accepts the user's request, finds the appropriate objects and then returns them.

5   More Details for Some Key Features

5.1   Multi-standards Support

Multi-standards support is the most attractive feature of our system, for it greatly enhances the reusability and interoperability of the learning objects. Because of the adoption of the XML binding, this work is easy to carry out, as shown in Fig. 2. However, special considerations need to be taken into account to make the work even more effective and much easier.

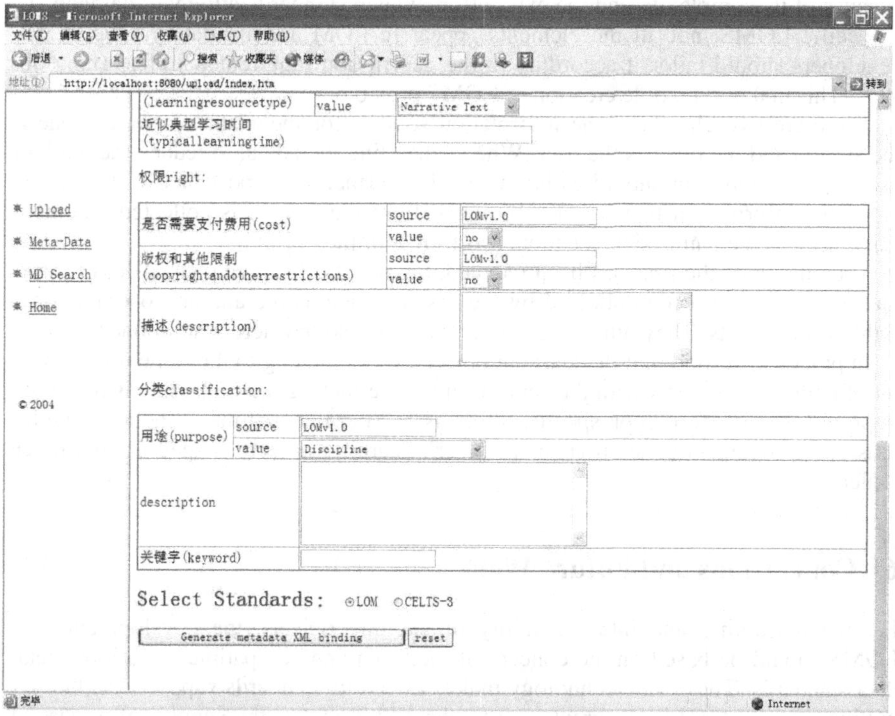

Fig. 2. Metadata generation page. Chinese characters appear for the support to CELTS-3

First, the existing standards are classified into different classes. The main issue is to understand the relationship among them. If one standard, CELTS-3, for instance, is similar to the other standard IEEE LOM, they belong to the same class. This is the case of our implementation, but it is not accidental. The close relationship among various standards has been observed while diving into XML bindings for these standards, such as IEEE LOM, IMS Learning Resource Meta-Data Information Model, CanCore, etc.

As to the concept of classes, in our system only the metadata XML binding for the LOM is generated, and the metadata XML binding for CELTS-3 is converted from the former one through the XSLT (eXtensible Stylesheet Language Transformations) according to a specific transformation schema. A JavaBean named *MetaDataGeneration* is devised for this work, which generates the XML binding for LOM and CELTS-3 respectively.

As a result, the introduction of new standards and new version of existing standard is simplified. What should be modified in our system may be just the xsl files used for XSLT without changing of the source codes.

5.2 Metadata Generation

In order to clearly describe diverse objects, LOM defines a rich set of elements, but these elements yet frustrate many learning resource developers to adopt the standard because of its complexity and the extra efforts which standardization will demand. To a specific LOMS, not all the elements appear in LOM are mandatory. The LOMS developers should tailor it according to the description requirements of learning objects. This makes a flexible creation of LOMS possible.

There are two classes of the information sources for metadata generation: one is the system and the other is the user. When generating metadata, to reduce the work of user input, the system should gather as much information as possible. In our system all of the information that could be colleted from the system is collected automatically, such as the name, size, location, and format of the object.

The burden of the user has been reduced, but it is far from enough. A lot of information has not yet been collected by the system, such as the author, cost and copyright of the objects. They must be entered by the user somewhere at least once.

In practice, we find that the learning objects, which belong to the same user, have a lot of common elements with the same value in the metadata. A template is thus used to provide these information specific to the user. After the creation of the template for a user, the metadata generation for the user's learning objects is sped up and much easier.

6   Conclusions and Future Work

For the reusability and interoperability of learning objects, the development of a LOMS should be based on the concept of metadata and compatible to various metadata standards. The XML technology makes the multi-standards support feasible. By putting the standards in different classes, the XSLT makes the support of a class of standards simple and extensible.

The other effort made in our system is to make use of the templates in LOMS to reduce the user's work during the process of metadata generation.

Next, the user-defined extension of the standards may be supported in our LOMS, and what is more interesting may be the creation of templates library for different users and objects.

References

1. IEEE Standard Computer Dictionary: A Compilation of IEEE Standard Computer Glossaries, New York: IEEE, 1990.
2. Computer Society/Learning Technology Standards Committee (LTSC), IEEE: Standard for Learning Object Metadata, 1484.12.1-2002, 2002
3. China E-learning Technology Standards Committee: Specification for Learning Object Metadata: Information Model, CELTS-3.1 CD 1.6, 2002
4. Leonid Pesin, Marcus Specht, Karim Adam: A flexible approach for authoring and management of learning object metadata. 3rd Annual Ariadne Conference, Katholieke Universiteit Leuven, Belgium. 2003
5. Muzio, J. A. et al: Experiences with reusable E-learning objects: From theory to practice. In The Internet and Higher Education, Vol. 5/1, 2002, pp21-34.
6. South, J. B., & Monson, D. W. (2001). A university-wide system for creating, capturing, and delivering learning objects. In D. A. Wiley (Ed.), The instructional use of learning objects. Available at: http://reusability.org/read/chapters/south.doc

Specification for Service Quality Management System of e-Learning

Yi Zhang[1], Zhiting Zhu[2], Xiaoyong Hu[2], and Qing Li[2]

[1] Graduate School of Education, Huazhong University of Science and Technology,
430074, Wuhan, China
zhangyilyj@hotmail.com
[2] Department of Educational Information Technology, East China Normal University,
200062, Shanghai, China
ztzhu@dec.ecnu.edu.cn, huxiaoy@hotmail.com, zjliqing@etang.com

Abstract. This specification is aimed to apply gap model of service quality in the context of e-learning. First, a conceptual model of service quality of e-learning is firstly suggested in which a set of elements are identified. Second, a standardized framework and scale for measuring service quality is developed. Third, we will apply principles of TQM and thought of ISO9000:2000 in e-learning service quality management and develop a valid dynamic process management model to ensure service quality of e-learning. Last, we will develop a specification for e-learning service quality management to monitor and review service quality in e-learning to prompt improvement management and instruction of e-learning institution to provide better service.

Keywords: Service quality, e-Learning, Quality Management, Standard

1 Introduction

1.1 Scope

This specification defines a reference model and scale for service quality assessment in the context of e-learning in higher education, profession training and compulsory education to measure and evaluate their service elements as service attitude and related condition in implementing instruction, training and management. This specification develops process elements for e-learning service quality management system according to the scale and a process model. The e-learning institution can improve its service quality by the result of assessment and the specification to ensure learner's proper rights to enjoy high quality service finally.

1.2 Purpose and Justification

As the increasing use of e-learning technology in education and training, service quality assurance is becoming a common concern among different kinds of stakeholders. Though a lot of efforts are found among international bodies in developing specification for quality assurance of e-learning, they mainly focus on Institutional Support, Course Development, Teaching/Learning, Course Structure, Student Support, Faculty

W. Liu et al. (Eds.): ICWL 2004, LNCS 3143, pp. 400–406, 2004.

Support, Evaluation and Assessment etc while few researches are devoted to service quality and its assurance system.

In according to the General Agreement on Trade in Services (GATS) of WTO, education falls into the field of service industry. There are even stronger reasons to consider e-learning as a kind of service, because it enables more freedoms for consumers to choice, ranging from contents and media to strategies. As easily seen by us, e-learning has become a common type of service available over Internet nowadays. In this circumstance, it will be practically useful to propose a specification for service quality assurance of e-learning, usable for e-learning provider to improve their service quality and thus to meet explicit and implicit requirements for a variety of learning users.

The purposes of this proposed specification are the following:

✓ To enable e-learning providers to carry out quality management of e-learning service through following the service quality management system process;
✓ To enable e-learning providers to carry out self-evaluation of their service quality by applying a standardized rubric and management system of service quality;
✓ To enable authentication agency to evaluate levels of service quality provided by e-learning providers according to the specification;
✓ To enable customers to select e-learning providers suitable to their own learning demands so that desirable level of service could be expected.

2 Introduction to Mainframe of e-Learning Service Quality

2.1 Framework for Service Quality of e-Learning

The definition for the service quality of e-learning is the overall collection of implicit and explicit characteristic that the service can satisfy the customer.

The framework for service quality of e-learning has 5 dimensions as the following:

✓ Reliability: e-Learning providers have the ability to perform promised service dependably and accurately.
✓ Responsiveness: e-Learning providers would like to help learners and provide prompt service.
✓ Assurance: Faculty and staff engaging in e-learning are professional and knowledgeable to let the learner trust them and feel them reliant.
✓ Validity of Learning Resource: e-Learning providers can offer credible, effective and rich learning resources.
✓ Empathy: e-Learning providers understand the needs of users and can offer individualized service.

2.2 Elements and Framework

For each element, the base scheme was defined as the following. It includes terms which are the name of the element and explanation which is the definition of the element. The following table defines the structure of mainframe of e-Learning Service Quality.

Table 1. Framework of e-Learning Service Quality

No.	Terms	Explanations
1	**Reliability**	**e-Learning providers has the ability to perform promised service dependably and accurately**
1.1	Reliability of education institution	Promises of education institution are reliable
1.2	Reliability of network system	Delivery ability of instruction network has reliability, veracity, stability and rapidity
1.3	Reliability of question answer	In handling the learner's question, the answers of education institution and teacher are reliable
1.4	Reliability of evaluation	Teacher's comments on the learner's study are impartial and reliable
2	**Responsiveness**	**e-Learning providers would like to help learners and provide prompt service**
2.1	Responsiveness of service request	Education institution can satisfy the learner's service request in time（less than a week we advice）
2.2	Responsiveness of teacher	Answer learner's questions and review their assignments timely. (less than 3 weeks we advice)
2.3	Publishing information in time	e-Learning providers should publish information of instruction, management and service timely as notification for class, exam schedule, scores of exam, etc.
3	**Assurance**	**Faculty and staff engaging in e-learning are professional and knowledgeable to let the learner trust them and feel them reliant**
3.1	Integrity of instruction plan	Education institution should provide instruction plan in detail: including learning object, entrance qualification, learning material, learning contents, instruction schedule, evaluation process, qualification authentication, tuition fee and other expenses, time limitation of study, clause of suspending or postponing study and technology requirements etc.
3.2	Providing related information on courses	Provide all the students a clear and comprehensive information about the course, including course objective, learning requirements, examination methods and information on assessment
3.3	Security of private information	Education institution should secure learner's personal information
3.4	Technology guidance	Provide technology service and guidance to students in course studying, including detailed guidance on hardware and software, practice opportunity before examination and technology staff
3.5	Professional knowledge of the teacher	Teacher has adequate professional knowledge to teach
3.6	Complaint mechanism	Education institution should set up complaint mechanism for students and give them valid reply timely

Table 1. (Continued)

4	**Validation of learning resources**	**e-Learning providers can offer credible, effective and rich learning resources.**
4.1	Scientificity	Learning resource should be credible and valid, excluding any error, prejudice or redundant information and should be expressed impartially
4.2	Accessibility	Learning resource should be organized by reasonable way to make it accessible easily
4.3	Integrity	Learning resources should be integral, can offer information related to the objective in depth and width, as learning pre-requirements, related resources, assessment rubric, etc.
4.4	Real-time	Learning resources should be updated periodically•and also information of person or organization, time and frequency of updating should be pointed out.
4.5	Selection of media	Selection of media and technology category should be integrated with curriculum design and should be helpful to accord with instructions objective and satisfy learners
5	**Empathy**	**e-learning providers understand needs of users and can offer individualized service**
5.1	Convenient learning schedule and facility	Education institution should schedule the time and facility to the convince of all learners
5.2	Assistant service	Provide learners some assistant service, including agenda agent, communication service etc.
5.3	Easy to use	Instruction platform, learning resources etc., should be easy to use and access. Less information is needed for user to input
5.4	Customized service	The teacher should know the individual requirements of the learner to offer customized service
5.5	Care	The teacher should care for every learner, and help them to overcome difficulties in study. Faculties should treat every learner warmly and answer his question patiently
5.6	Comfort environment	Environment of education institution (computer lab, etc.) should be spacious and bright
5.7	Interactivity	During teaching process, the teacher should use many kinds of interactive methods (e-mail, BBS, telephone, etc.)to lead learners into learning activity actively

3   The Process Approach and Model for e-Learning Service Quality Management System

3.1   The Process Approach for e-Learning Service Quality Management System

E-Learning is a process-based activity, in order to ensure service quality of it, subsystem in e-learning service quality management system has to be identified, confirmed and analyzed. This document keeps to the process approach in ISO 9001:2000.

3.2   The Process Model for e-Learning Service Quality Management System

Process model of e-learning service quality management system is application of process methods in e-learning service quality management system. It presents main process of management of e-learning instruction. First, management of e-learning institution shall know the requirement of the learner or interested party on e-learning. The management determines detailed quality management activities, that is by valid resource management to define management responsibility of e-learning institution and realize e-learning process, to provide learning service and let the learner get experience and achievement in study; then keep evaluation and improvement on learning process and result of service quality management system, and satisfy requirements of the learner and the interested party.

Learner and the interested party are important in inputting information into e-learning service quality management system. Monitoring on satisfaction of customer and the interested party needs evaluate their real feeling. This information can present the degree of satisfaction of their needs and expectations.

3.3   e-Learning Service Quality Management System – Requirements

3.3.1   General Requirements

To ensure e-learning institution establish customer focused service quality management system, to improve e-learning service quality management, and to provide e-learning service which satisfy the society, this specification introduces idea, principle and approach in ISO9000: 2000 and establish following elements. E-learning institution shall establish, document, implement, maintain and continually improve a service quality management system in accordance with this specification•and continuously improve its validity.

The creation of e-learning service quality management system in accordance with process approach shall include some processes of management activities, resource provision, service provision and continuous improvement as the following:

✓ Identify management processes and service provision processes needed for the e-learning service quality management system;
✓ Determine the sequence and interaction of these processes;
✓ Determine criteria and methods required to ensure the effective operation and control of these processes;
✓ Ensure the availability of information necessary to support the operation and monitoring of these processes; and
✓ Measure, monitor and analyze these processes, and implement action necessary to achieve planned results and continual improvement of management processes and service quality.

3.3.2   General Documentation Requirements

Documentation in service quality management system are base of its operation. It can communicate idea and unify actions. Content of it shall be suitable for the character, scale, market orientation, management principles and objects, and at the same time requirement of customer and the interested party and regulatory shall be taken into consideration.

The e-learning service quality management system documentation shall include:

- ✓ Quality principle and quality objective for making documents;
- ✓ quality manual;
- ✓ Process of making documents in accordance with this specification;
- ✓ Files needed by e-learning institution for effective operation and planning, implementation and control process;
- ✓ Record required by this specification.

3.3.3 Use of Quality Management Principles

Each major clause in this document is based on the ISO 9000:2000 eight quality management principles, which in the context of the e-learning service quality management system may be formulated as follows: Customer focus, Leadership, Involvement of people, Process approach, System approach to management, Continual improvement, Factual approach to decision making and Mutually beneficial supplier relationship.

4 Process Elements
in e-Learning Service Quality Management System

4.1 Management Responsibility

Top management shall prove their commitment on establishing, implementation service quality management system and improving the system continuously through the corresponding activities. Management responsibility includes *management commitment, customer focus, quality policy, planning, responsibility and management review.*

4.2 Resource Management

Resource is the necessary condition for a organization to establish service quality management system and realize its quality policy and quality objective. The organization shall determine and provide the resource needed to impletemnet and improve the process of the quality management system and to address customer satisfaction. Resource management includes *human resource, infrastructure, instruction resource, learner's information and other resources.*

4.3 Service Realization

Service realization includes planning of realization process, process related to customer, design and/or development, purchasing and service provision.

The organization shall have valid control on e-learning service operation to satisfy needs and expectations of the customer. Every functional department takes charge of control on its service operation, and the department of quality management inspects the operation quality of other departments.

Determine the main service provision processes of e-learning instruction including admission service(as ertering for,tutorship,entrance examination, matriculate), learner status management (as tuition fee,password protection,information encryption, system backup), instruction (as development learner ability of collecting material, analysis, judgement, evaluation),course delivery (including learning objectives, learningre quirement, learning content, learning models, learning methods, examination methods, evaluation rubric and evaluation content), tutorship(as teaching face to face,answering questions by email,phone,forum and BBS), learning resource providing(textbook, CD-ROM,network course,reference material etc.), review and feedback of assignments, examination and score management(as making testing paper, testing, reviewing, inquiring result), technology training and support, maintenance on computer devices, consultant and answering questions, Consultant and answering questions, graduate qualification authentication, profession guidance.

4.4 Evaluation and Improvement

The organization shall monitor, audit, analyze and evaluate service quality of e-learning to ensure the validity of service offered, to ensure the service quality management system can satisfy needs of customer and society and to ensure the validity of continual improvement on the service quality management system. The following shall be considered in planning and implementing monitoring and analysis: *measurement and monitoring, control of nonconformance, analysis of data and improvement.*

References

1. A. Parasuraman,Valarie A.Zeithaml & Leonard L. Berry:Refinement and Reassessment to the SERVQUAL Scale. Journal of Retailing, Vol. 67 Winterb (1991)
2. Carman J M: Consumer Perception of Service Quality: An Assessment of The SERVQUAL Dimensions. Journal of Retailingb (1990)
3. Jan M. Pawlowski: CEN / ISSS Workshop on Learning. Project Team Quality Assurance. CWA Quality Assurance Standards (2002)
4. Kumiko Aoki & Donna Pogroszewski: Virtual University Reference Model: A Guide to Delivering Education and Support Services to the Distance Learner. (1998) http://www.westga.edu/~distance/aoki13.html
5. Ormond Simpson: Supporting Students in Online, Open and Distance Learning. Printed and Bound in Great Britain by Clays Ltd, St Ives Plc (2002) http://www.kogan-page.co.uk
6. CELTSC: Chinese E-Learning Technology Standardization Committee. (2003), http://www.celtsc.edu.cn/index.jsp

Personalized Education:
An Exploratory Study of Learning Pedagogies
in Relation to Personalization Technologies

Apple W.P. Fok and Horace H.S. Ip

Centre for Innovative Applications of Internet and Multimedia Technologies (**AIM**tech)
Image Computing Group, Department of Computer Science
City University of Hong Kong
{applefok,cship}@cityu.edu.hk

Abstract. High potential values drive the commercial sectors towards the rapid development of Personalization Technology. In response to individual needs, personalization in education not only facilitates students to learn better by using different strategies to create various learning experiences, but also caters teacher's teaching needs in preparing/designing varied teaching/instructional packages. Empirical results show that using the technologies without regarding pedagogical concepts frequently lead to failure. This paper provides a detailed examination of the opportunities and necessities of Personalized Education (PE) from the perspective of different learning pedagogies. To optimize the benefits of meaningful personalization technologies, we also propose a Personalized Education System (PES) Framework and introduce several PES features that can support personalized teaching and learning under pervasive computing.

1 Introduction

Personalization Technology (PT) is a fast emerging technology on the web these days. "Building a meaningful one-to-one relationship – Riecken D" [1], "Delivering appropriate content and services to fulfill user's needs – Monica Bonett" [2], and "Understanding where and when to suggest the 'right' things – Oracle" [3]. The ultimate goal is *"User satisfaction"* – getting the right thing at the right time in the right place. And more importantly, it should be *"just enough and just in time"*.

The central aim of education is not to serve as a vehicle for transmitting information but rather to help students learn how to learn. An alternative perspective on the relationship between intrinsic and extrinsic motivation [4]; and the Personal Epistemology Research [5], creates fresh implications for learning and teaching. Although the availability of information increases continuously, we, as an individual user, only interest in a relatively small fraction of it, and only those that would be useful in achieving our goals or fit our aptitude. Users, teachers, especially students, need helps to explore and to filter out their preferences from the myriad possibilities [6]. From the pedagogical point of view, the major requirement for distance learning via Personalized Courses is the flexibility of the system to adapt easily, dynamically and with minimum overhead to the individual student's progress, needs and interests. The subject, the content, the details and the tempo should be dynamically personalized on the flow.

W. Liu et al. (Eds.): ICWL 2004, LNCS 3143, pp. 407–415, 2004.
© Springer-Verlag Berlin Heidelberg 2004

Currently the main momentum of personalization technology development is driven from different directions such as Data Mining Technology, Personalization Index, Agent Technology, Intelligence Search and User Modeling etc. All of them carry the same mission: Create and Provide (Serve/Deliver) the Best Personalized Service. Adequate personalization in education requires more than an attractive personal interface design. We will take an in-depth look at personalization, what is required of it, why we need it with regards to different learning pedagogies, and more importantly, to answer the central research questions, *"To what extent do these newer personalization technologies improve the quality of education"* and *"To what extent does personalization rest on different educational psychologies and therefore, require the development of new and special pedagogies?"*

2 Related Work

Static personalization services provide customized features that require high users' engagement. Dynamic personalization services provide high automation that will serve up individualized pages to the user based on some types of model of which the users need. A thorough review of personalization technologies in general is outside the scope of this paper. Instead, here we will focus our review on personalization as applied to learning.

A recent personalized Adaptive Educational Hypermedia (AEH) system, the INSPIRE [7] addresses the issue of different information processing methodologies that learner perceive and process. The learner model guided the INSPIRE to exploit ways in: curriculum sequencing, adaptive navigation support, adaptive presentation, and supports system's adaptable behavior. Based on several levels of adaptation, the INSPIRE monitors learner's actions, updates accordingly the learner model and adapts its response to learner's progress via interaction. One sophisticated feature is offering learner opportunities to undertake control over the system by intervening in the lesson generation process reflecting on their own perspective. Since it is very difficult to determine the amount and the level of user control, an important point raises is a comprehensive study of the issue of learning styles and their impact on learners preferences and studying attitude in the context of web-based learning systems.

Another interesting perspective of user modeling research is based upon human-computer interaction and the impact of user modeling to make systems more usable, useful and learnable. From the focus on the interfaces to more recently "Learner Control" [8], a paradigms shift to share understanding, explanations, justifications and argumentation about actions. The new essential challenges are finding ways to help users to work, think, communicate, learn, criticize and explain with computers. [9] believes the adaptive hypermedia systems employs more recent AI technologies can make solid progress in identifying new cases of modeling and adapting to user's hyperspace experience that take special consideration on user's interest and individual traits. [10] presented and evaluated five techniques for agent modeling to improve prediction performance. The Dual-model approach takes temporal factors into account achieves significant improvement in prediction rate without significantly affecting prediction accuracy. The Single-tree approach merges multiple trees into a single tree, generates only one decision tree for each student, the simplification makes people easier to understand.

Previous works in this area mainly focus on the application of personalization technologies in adult education and distant learning. We believe that PT has much to offer to the area of school-based education to benefit both students and teachers alike. The following sections examine the opportunities and necessities of Personalized Education (PE) from the perspective of different learning pedagogies; propose a Personalized Education System (PES) Framework; and introduce several PES features that can support personalized teaching and learning.

Fig. 1. The Instruction Taxonomy

3 Personalization Beliefs and Their Relation to Teaching and Learning

In the ongoing debate between constructivist educators and behaviorist educators, instruction has been portrayed as an approach whereby knowledge is given to people, while learning is an approach whereby people obtain knowledge for themselves. Notwithstanding, we simply view instruction as the creation and use of environments in which learning is facilitated. Technology-based learning supports both of them. Teachers, the initial-active-key player, are one of the main instruction resource creators and providers, are faced with changes in curricula, pedagogies and students. Based on different approaches and their applicable designed strategies in teaching/learning, the instruction taxonomy has been illustrated in Figure 1. An instructional design reflects the relationship between teacher's proficiency and expectation and describes students' expected reactions, responses and outcomes. In order to structure the wealth of personalization in education, the discussion will be organized according to the four basic classes of personalization functions distinguished from [11]: *memorization, guidance, customization and task performance support.*

3.1 Memorization

Although this is the simplest form of personalization function, this is the most powerful/supportive function that benefits teaching/learning. Remember who you are, what you are interested in, what have you done and what will you do. With accurate user data acquires from all possible sources explicitly or implicitly, engage users in an enthusiastic environment, offer flexibility in making choices and record users' behavior into the active short-term memory session, adopt scaffolding learning strategy that enhanced users' memory capacity through interacting with the Personalized Education System. High memorization capacity strengthen the potential knowledge transformation covers the full spectrum of instructional learning.

3.2 Guidance

Guidance can be provided through recommendations or adding explanatory content to the web page or online help. With different web usage mining techniques, accurate responses/actions would be given. In response to the Elaboration Theory [12], personalization can provide prescriptions for selecting, sequencing, synthesizing and summarizing instructional content meaningfully. It can also satisfy the Component Display Theory [13] by providing prescriptions for the development of the educational material of the domain concepts tailored to specific performance levels.

3.3 Customization

Standardization to customization is a new trend in instruction, not only focus on presenting material but on making sure that users' needs are met. As the experience shared from [11], offers users with the option to intervene in the lesson generation process, express their opinion about their own characteristics or about the lesson contents, and instructional control over the system would benefit learning. Multiple kinds of learning require multiple methods of instructions. Users/participants modify or adjust their own preferences so as to create an individual teaching/learning philosophy that best fit in individual learning. New learning methodology would be identified/formed/found with the intervention of users, user satisfactory approach.

3.4 Task Performance Support

Personalization in an educational context needs a precise understanding between learner and the tasks that are important to learning. Tailored task models perform numbers of actions and assist the work of the user such as the logic instructional model [15], achievement goal construct hierarchical model [7], collaborative learning model [14] and so on. In particular, the task performance support is the most difficult dimension in personalization because this particular functionality requires more sophisticated methods not only in the design phase/initial stage, but also all along the whole development process. Specific task performance support descriptions with clear elaboration and analyses on each instruction design build the most energetic, dynamic and reusable components support multiple teaching/learning philosophies.

4 Personalized Education (PE)

"Personalized Education" encompasses methods and techniques that can be used to deliver value-added teaching/learning experience to teachers and students by exploiting and integrating web-based personalization technologies. In our definition [18], PE is an open learning environment with supportive tools to stimulate/foster/facilitate/ strengthen teaching/learning. This environment enriches the advanced technologies to shift our paradigm, active and dynamic teaching and learning patterns. It provides not only infinite space, but also delivers "just right" information that addresses the concerns of individual differences. Everyone can get the information when s/he needs and adjusts individual plan according to one's own competence. Rather than maintaining a fixed view of what all users want or need, this asynchronous environment offers greater flexibility and enable greater choice for users by providing PE features that include an automatic diagnosis of each user's knowledge/skill level and preferred teaching/learning style; an array of high-quality, interactive learning materials and activities; individualized (teaching/learning) planner; built-in continuous monitoring/assessment to provide instantaneous feedback; and provide appropriate human interaction when needed. Succeed of PE heavily depends upon the acceptance of the changing views of education and changing methods of teaching. PE can potentially provide tailor-made teaching methodology and learning paradigm that would fit each individual participant.

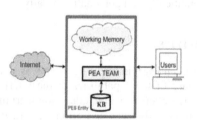

Fig. 2. The PES Architecture   **Fig. 3.** The PES Conceptual Framework

5 An Architectural Framework for Personalized Education

We first introduced the idea and the design of a Personalized Education System (PES) in [18]. PES originally combines several agent technologies with the Argus Center for Information Architecture (ACIA) personalization framework. After careful examination of the use of technologies with individual teaching and learning discriminations, we have further improved the PES framework as shown in Figure 2: The 3-tiers PES Architecture consists of the client browser front end, the application server and the database server; and a more detailed conceptual framework is illustrated in Figure 3. A group of cohesive, competitive and collaborative agents, *the Personalized Education Agents Team (PET/PEA)*, works closely within the personalized education environment. They carry a common goal of seeking the best solution response to the user requests.

How teaching/learning can be efficiently attained? It is important to consider personalization within the framework of varied learning theories and models and thoroughly plan the sharing of personalization tasks between the user and PES. Through the agent-based approach, the ideas of personalization, can be incorporated more easily. Each agent contains its own functionalities and responsibilities to achieve its own objectives (i.e. The Filtering Agent filters the documents with its granted capacities (using various filtering techniques) while the Matching Agent matches the filtered results with user profile with its proficient in matching.) Each of which is an independent problem-solving agent come together to form some coherent whole. At the moment, there is no pre-established architecture or configuration incorporating the PEA members, each of them is being heterogeneous with their individual goals and capabilities. The detail software design of individual agents is outside the scope of this paper. It suffices to note that PEA has a global system goal; they need to coordinate their activities and cooperate with each other, in order to avoid duplication of effort, to avoid unwittingly hindering other agents in achieving goals, and to exploit other agents' capabilities. This division of tasks among several different agents adds flexibility in distributing processing load, changing the flow of information on the fly and distributing tasks across the system boundaries.

To avoid problems of the traditional knowledge-representation and enhance the communication process, PES adapts the idea of Semantic Web using RDF to express meaning and XML to add arbitrary structure to documents. Resources variations will also be standardized by MPEG7. In order to enhance the accuracy, combine the ideas from [19] [20], designed intelligent plan recognizers and several types of validation operators, will be taken into considerations. The meaningful/relevant set of teaching/learning resources would be generated systematically and personalizationally.

6   Personalized Education System Metrics

With our PES design, anyone who wants to learn can learn in his or her own way with gradual satisfaction to succeed. Taking advantages of the capabilities of the Internet and anticipates personalization technologies to create an enjoyable education/learning environment for enriching teaching and learning effectiveness and efficiency. In the following, we would illustrate a possible application to prove how PES adapts several teaching/learning theories/approaches to strive excellent personalization in teaching and learning. The structure of the PES has been illustrated in Figure 4 and the 9 core and 3 supporting applications of the PES in Figure 5.

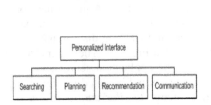

Fig. 4. The Structure of the PES   **Fig. 5.** The PES 9 core and 3 supporting applications

Our PES design incorporates the elementary elements of a general web-based learning system. It broadly supports the main activities that teachers and students perform regularly in a traditional classroom setting. These elements take a balanced view of behaviorist, cognitivist and constructivist beliefs in teaching/learning. The elementary elements include a tidy-working desk with supportive tools – the personalized user-interface. On the desk, a smart/intelligent searching engine assists to recognize/seek for interested/needed information; a personal planner for organizing, scheduling and monitoring individual plan/progress; an intelligent recommender for guiding, advising and evaluating relevant resources; the last most personal tool is the personal communication channel for informing, sharing and collaborating.

6.1   Personalized User-Interface

Holding the benevolence principles [21], the personalized user-interface gives a pleasant, enthusiastic and positive greeting when user starts to work/interact with the PES. Considering the essential difference in the sets of information is presented through a Web browser, PES incorporates the "learning while doing" strategy in the interface design; a collection of specific features for a particular user/user-group should be designed. Concentration is another key factor of effective teaching/learning. Only 4-5 activities will be assigned to a user and only the relevant sets of that information at any one time. The depth of each personalization model will also not be more than 4. Personalized interface offers guidance to individual user at each step of the user's interaction, supports user to use his/her natural intelligence to make choices.

6.2   Personalized Planner

Planning is an essential skill that would ensure the quality of teaching/learning. Only plan cognitively, does not work. The only way that we can make things happen in a way we want is "Plan-Action-Plan". Personal planner helps users to construct personal plan that is matters to them. The system supports automatic generations of personal plans for individual user perform a particular set of applications. For instance, a student wants a study plan so as to master the learning objectives in different learning stages or simply for the examination preparation. Then, the system based on the student query and current profile information to construct a tailored study plan. However, a teacher, most likely is a student, needs an addition planner that can also facilitate his/her teaching plan. The personalized planner must not only be a static information list, functions like notifications, reminders, acknowledgements, recommendations and so on, must also be provided.

6.3 Personalized/Intelligent Search

Unlike searching in the global society, PE focuses on a specific-domain search only cater for two types of users, teachers and students. Educational resources collect and store in the database with particular indexing techniques likes the Semantic Web indexing which supports descriptive instruction search for a particular resource match with a particular objective/learning preference. Customization and personalization search work asynchronously toward in-depth accurate information rather than breath/diverge information. A focus, controlled result set is required rather a portal list of hyperlinks. Filters or advanced classifiers constitute inductive learning strategy with multi-dimensional resources packages.

6.4 Personalized Recommendation Set

Recommendation is another essential personalization feature that helps users to concentrate, retain, or remain on the track and won't get lost in information dissemination. Providing suggestions that effectively prune large information spaces, users are directed toward those recommended resources at the point that best meet their needs and preferences. A variety of techniques have been proposed for performing recommendation, and the selection of a recommendation policy requires a comparative evaluation of the benefit of user policies under different operating conditions. A resource sounds relevant to a particular learning activity/objective only if it has been used frequently. User group and usage group clustering form the fundamental recommendation set. Individual user's usage pattern, single-user policy, is one indicator for getting similar/close related sets of resources. Popularity is another measure of useful resources.

6.5 Personalized Community

A series of teaching professionals handle different aspects of the problem in teaching/learning in one piece of global memory – the PES. Each professional represent a particular aspect of the problem in specific situation. Working and sharing as a community, specialize in specific data, make modification, or add results into the PES, each of this professional can retrieve/use the resources for implementation to do his/her job and add individual result (generate new data and can be used by other experts) effectively and efficiently. Students, the final beneficiary, enjoy their learning through multi-dimensional resources contribute by diverse content providers. Teacher and student develop a tiny learning community, define and create a sense of virtual classroom through their individual workspaces.

7 Conclusion

With regards to the exploitation of personalization in designing a PE system, many questions have to be answered such as evidence about the way learners of specific learning style select and use educational resources that are considered beneficial for their style, the relationship between different navigation pattern with different learning styles, and so on. This paper serves to highlight the pertinent issues that need to be addressed in Personalized Education in relation to established learning pedagogies. A preliminary technical design of PES has been discussed in [18]. We focus here on an analysis of scenarios for the use of PES that has led to a set of system requirements and an architectural framework that guide the design of PES. The close relation between teaching/learning pedagogies and personalization also shed light on the functionality for PES systems that essentially integrate and consolidate the process of personalized teaching and learning.

References

1. Personalized Views of Personalization by Doug Riecken, Guest Editor, Communications of the ACM, August 2000/Vol. 43, No. 8.
2. Personalization of Web Services: Opportunities and Challenges – Monica Bonett http://www.ariadne.ac.uk/issue28/personalization/
3. The Art of Personalization, An Oracle White Paper, August 2003
4. Martin V. Covington and Kimberly J. Mueller, 2001, Intrinsic Versus Extrinsic Motivation: An Approach/Avoidance Reformulation, Educational Psychology Review, Vol. 13, No. 2, P. 157-176.

5. Barbara K. Hofer, 2001, Personal Epistemology Research: Implications for Learning and Teaching, Journal of Educational Psychology Review, Vol. 13, No. 4, P. 353-383.
6. T. Zahariadis and S. Voliotis, 2001, New Trends in Distance Learning Utilising Next Generation Multimedia Networks, Education and Information Technologies 8:1, 67-81, Kluwer Academic Publishers.
7. Kyparisia A. Papanikolaou, Maria Grigoriadou, Harry Kornilakis and George D. Magoulas, (2003), Personalizing the Interaction in a Web-based Educational Hypermedia System: the case of INSPIRE, User Modeling and User-Adapted Interaction 13: 213-267, Kluwer Academic Publishers, Netherlands.
8. Judy Kay, 2001, Learner Control, User Modeling and User-Adapted Interaction 11: 111-127, Kluwer Academic Publishers, Netherlands.
9. Gerhard Fischer, 2001, User Modeling in Human-Computer Interaction, User Modeling and User-Adapted Interaction 11: 65-86, Kluwer Academic Publishers, Netherlands.
10. Frank L and Hans-Peter S, 2000, Recommender Systems for Learning: Building User and Expert Models through Long-Term Observation of Application Use, User Modeling and User-Adapted Interaction 10: 181-207, Kluwer Academic Publishers, Netherlands.
11. Dimitrios P., Georgios P., Christos P., and Constantine D. S., 2003, Web Usage Mining as a Tool for Personalization: A Survey, Kluwer Academic Publishers, User Modeling and User-Adapted Interaction 13: 311-372.
12. Reigeluth C M, and Stein F S, 1983, The elaboration theory of instruction. In: C M Reigeluth (ed.): Instructional Design Theories and Models: An Overview of Their Current Status. Lawrence Erlbaum Associates, Hillsdale, New Jersey, pp. 335-381.
13. Merrill M D, 1983, Component Display Theory. In: C M Reigeluth (ed.): Instructional Design Theories and Models: An Overview of Their Current Status. Lawrence Erlbaum Associates, Hillsdale, New Jersey, pp.279-333.
14. T J Van Weert and A. Pilot, 2003, Task-Based Team Learning with ICT, Design and Development of New Learning, Education and Information Technologies 8:2, 195-214, Kluwer Academic Publishers, Netherlands.
15. Jonas A. Montilva, Beatriz S. and Judith B, 2002, Developing Instructional Web Sites – A Software Engineering Approach, Education and Infromation Technologies 7:3, 201-224, Kluwer Academic Publishers, Netherlands.
16. Phillip L. Ackerman, 1999, Traits and Knowledge as Determinants of Learning and Individual Differences: Putting It All Together, Learning and Individual Differences, Process, Trait, And Content Determinants, the American Psychological Association, P.437-460.
17. Simpson, M. L. and Nist, S. L. , 2000. An update on strategic learning: It's more than textbook reading strategies. J. Adolesc. Adult Literacy 43(6): 528-541.
18. Apple W. P. Fok and Horace H. S. Ip, 2004, Personalized Education (PE) – Technology Integration for Individual Learning, Proceedings of Third IASTED International Conference on Web-Based Education, pp.48-53, Innsbruck, Austria, February 16-18, 2004.
19. Bauer, M., Machine Learning for User Modeling and Plan Recognition, German Research Center for Artificial Intelligence (DFKI). In V. Moustakis J. Herrmann, editor, Proc. ICML'96 Workshop "Machine Learning meets Human Computer Interaction", pp. 5-16, 1996.
20. Adomavicius, G., and Tuzhilin, A., Expert-Driven Validation of Rule-Based User Models in Personalization Applications, New York University, 2001. In the Proceedings of the 5th ACM SIGKDD International Conference on Knowledge Discovery and Data Mining (KDD-99).
21. Nuno D., Jaime S.S., and Helder C., 1999, On being responsible: how to be individualistic and smile benevolence to the others, In: Proceedings of the 3rd European Conference on Cognitive Science, ECCS99, Sienna, Italy, P. 57-62.

Guidelines towards Effectively Sharable LOs

Emanuela Busetti[1], Giuliana Dettori[2], Paola Forcheri[1], and Maria Grazia Ierardi[1]

[1] Istituto di Matematica Applicata e Tecnologie Informatiche del CNR, Genova, Italy
{busetti,forcheri,ierardi}@ge.imati.cnr.it
[2] Istituto di Tecnologie Didattiche del CNR, Genova – Italy
dettori@itd.cnr.it

Abstract. LOs ask teachers to present didactical material in an objective form so to make them easily re-usable by their colleagues. This is a complex task which entails the development of a methodological approach apt to support producer-teachers' work. For this sake, we present guidelines for the design of didactical modules. This proposal aims to help teachers 1) to reflect on how to make explicit their own pedagogical intentions; 2) to detect methods apt to help write sharable LOs, without adding constraints on the choice of the pedagogical approach. This can constitute a starting point to enrich LOs' metadata with more effective pedagogical information, so to meet teachers' needs and use a language familiar to them.

1 Introduction

The interest of the education community in taking advantage of the web's potential to share high quality pedagogical material arouse already in the first years of its existence, as it is witnessed by the realisation, at institutional level, of web sites aiming to facilitate and guide the access to educational resources on the web (see, for example, the Italian INDIRE (Istituto Nazionale di Documentazione per l'Innovazione e la Ricerca Educativa), http://www.bdp.it/, addressed to the school world, from pre-primary to secondary). The scope of such initiatives mainly regarded the diffusion of information, ideas and crafted products, while only limited hints were given to systematically develop re-usable resources. They did not aim explicitly to decreasing production costs so to render technology-based education efficient and economically competitive.

In order to address this aspect, the concept of *learning object* (LO) was created [20], that is, a chunk of self-consistent educational material viewed as instructional component suitable to be used in a variety of contexts. In order to implement this concept, learning materials must be catalogued as concerns content, educational objectives, technical characteristics, etc. The specification of these aspects, called meta-data, have been widely analysed and debated, in order to develop international technical standards [1]. This has determined a shift from a voluntary and non-standardised approach to the systematic production of educational material to be shared over the web.

Teachers, however, still appreciate in limited measure the use of technological artefacts in education [11], so that LOs have so far been used more for enterprise training than in school education. Sharing didactical material, moreover, is not a straightforward task, but requires of teachers a good amount of labour both to integrate in their own lessons other people's material or to prepare new one in a form that can be

W. Liu et al. (Eds.): ICWL 2004, LNCS 3143, pp. 416–423, 2004.

of use for other teachers. Hence, it is proper to wonder whether the introduction of the LO approach can really become successful and widespread in the educational context, that is, if there is sufficient motivation for teachers to put their time and effort in its implementation and diffusion. In this paper we point out the main issues related with the use of LOs in school education and give some guidelines towards making this paradigm more effectively useful for teachers, so to motivate its use and help teachers to reflect on their own teaching activity.

2 Issues Related to the Use of LOs in Education

The research has emphasised the potential advantages of making use of LOs, in terms of decreasing production costs, exploiting experience and saving time [8]. It has also highlighted, though, several problems related to the use of this paradigm in education, of two different kinds, analysed below.

2.1 Issues of Conceptual Nature

The concept of LO has been created and worked out more by technologists than by experts in education. As a consequence, the educational implications of the LO approach have been scarcely analysed, and some points which are relevant from a pedagogical point of view have not been given sufficient attention:

- The construction of LOs has been seen as production of software rather than production of learning; hence, the point of view of teachers who build the educational material have been considered only in limited measure, as well as their need for suitable technical tools and training [3].
- Technologists and teachers have different focus and aims, and even use different technical languages [13].
- There isn't, at present, a unique definition of LO [19]. Several different ones are currently in use, each of which is focused on some relevant aspect of pedagogical resources, such as: intention, facility of use in different times and contexts, educational integrity, importance of the experience with respect to the context (see Table 1). This gives some ambiguity to the concept of LO.
- LOs are not fit to represent material of constructive nature, thus disregarding the currently most promising pedagogical trends [25, 22].
- Metadata are not in line with the current didactical practice. Educational metadata include information which is of limited use from the didactical point of view [7], such as the "semantic density" and the "interactivity degree" in the IEEE LTSC LOM [12]. On the other hand, currently used metadata do not give enough explicit information on the educational model underlying the development of a LO. This is, though, relevant information, since the use of didactical material can result more or less effective in relation with its consistence with the pedagogical and epistemological choices underlying the material itself [18]. Finally, standard international metadata are not apt to take into consideration the peculiarities of national educational systems [16]. We remark, however, that the variety of needs and points of view which should be taken into consideration by on-line material makes it complex to devise a standard set of metadata able to combine simplicity of production with easiness of resource detection [6].

Table 1. Examples of different definitions of LOs, with main focus and characterization

LO definition	Focus	Characterization
"Any entity -digital or non-digital- that may be used for learning, education or training" [12] "A wide variety of entities used to support learning, including but not limited to digital resources [...] and non-digital resources" [24]	Intention	Explicitly didactical The resource is independent of the mode of use
"Relatively small content components that are meant to be reusable in different contexts." [17]	Possibility of re-using in different times and contexts	Re-use of educational resources in contexts which differ from the original ones
"Components of online content (animations, video clips, texts, URLs or sequences of such assets) that have educational integrity" [10] "[LOs] are much smaller units of learning [than a course], ranging, for example from 2 to 15 minutes" [5].	Educational integrity	Granularity and presence of educational value
"A computer mediated or delivered module or unit that stands by itself, which provides a meaningful learning experience in a planned learning context" [14]	Relevance of the experience with respect to the context	Computer's use in the educational context where the LO repository is created Didactical value easy to recognize

In order to make the LO paradigm conceptually suited to the school context, it is, thus, necessary to develop methodologies to integrate the technological point of view with a more strictly pedagogical one [9, 15, 23]. It is also necessary to support teachers in developing a new vision of teaching and learning processes.

2.2   Issues of Practical Nature

All teachers know that re-using parts of lectures in other contexts than that in which they were created is not straightforward, since it is necessary to work out connections to the new context conditions. Even more work can be necessary for recycling, that is making use of some elements for a different task. The same problem obviously applies also to the re-use or re-cycling of LOs.

Producing LOs entails that teachers split their lessons into self-contained and consistent parts (that we call here didactical modules), so to favour their later re-use, by the producers themselves or by other people. As observed by Feldstein [8], this is not easy at all. Mutual references and bindings between modules are essential components of teaching organisation, the ingredient that helps students to build a unitary mental framework of each considered topic. Yet it is obvious that modules explicitly related with each other could hardly be re-used in different contexts and combined with modules from different sources.

Though all teachers appreciate to have at disposal some reference material as support to their teaching activity, at present most of them are not used to produce reusable didactical modules. This is due mainly to the fact that the intuitive aspect is usually prevalent in the didactical planning, since this process must be adjusted based on the student's feedback, and this can not be known a priori. Moreover, the need to adapt anyway their own previous lessons to the context of each class does not encourage teachers to construct modules clearly and completely defined, and independent of each other.

For these reasons, often teachers do not reflect in depth on what determines their didactical programming, and are rather used to rely on their practical experience to fill the gaps or incompleteness possibly existing in it. In such conditions, inexperience appears particularly a handicap for novice teachers. On the other hand, didactical programming would turn to advantage not only of novice teachers, but also of experienced ones, in that it can lead to more homogeneous and consistent teaching, help teachers to evaluate more carefully one's own activity based on objective elements, as well as to meaningfully compare one's own work with that of other teachers.

3 LOs as Tools Helping Teachers Reflect on Their Own Activity

As concerns the conceptual issues outlined above, some proposals have been made towards their solution. Some authors suggest, from a technological point of view, to give the concept of LO a pedagogical perspective, describing it by means of some modelling language [21]; other authors suggest, based on a didactical orientation, to investigate teacher's attitudes and training issues related to LOs, in order to detect strategies for the design and construction of them [2, 8].

We consider the issues from an educational perspective. In order to encourage the teacher's community to reflect on the opportunities given by the LO technology, criteria for the construction of educational modules should be given, that make the production and use of LOs a learning activity for teachers. To this aim, such criteria should take into consideration the following needs:

1. To start from a teacher-centred view, reflecting on what kind of material teachers build and use, and which approach they are used to apply in lesson planning. It is necessary to keep into consideration that often in practice a didactical plan makes use of different didactical approaches (hence, of different types of modules, yet preserving self-consistence).
2. To favour the construction of modules according to characteristics which communicate as clearly as possible the educational intention of the constructor, so to improve usability. Understanding the intentions of the constructor helps the user to reflect, to analyse strong and weak points, to make comparisons and to find analogies.
3. To help the teachers reflect on their own didactical activity; this would favour the use of a module also as the starting point of a pedagogical discussion, to be shared by constructor and user.

Moreover, such criteria should help to devise modules' metadata so to include (teacher-oriented) information on the pedagogical intentions of the constructor-teachers, as well as a description of whatever could be relevant to help their didactical application. These choices would make LOs become a learning tool not only for the user-teachers, who can take advantage of their colleague's experience, but also for the producer-teachers themselves, who would be forced to straighten up and make explicit their own pedagogical approach and design.

Based on the above considerations, we worked out some criteria to guide the construction of didactical modules. These criteria aim to: encourage a rigorous didactical design; help teachers perform an evaluation consistent with their educational activity; ease the pedagogical usability; support user's learning; stimulate reflection on intentions; limit practical obstacles to re-use; ease integration.

3.1   Teacher Oriented Criteria for the Design of LOs: A Proposal

From the point of view of teacher's learning, these criteria, summarized in Table 2, can be organized in 2 classes. The first class aims to help the producer-teachers to reflect on their didactical proposals; the second one aims to help user-teachers to fully take advantage of the shared material.

Table 2. Suggested criteria to guide the construction of didactical modules

For the producer-teachers			For the user-teachers
Educational type	**Pedagogical frame-work**	**Didactical usability**	**Re-use**
Illustrative Active Evaluative Receptive Explorative Supportive	Aim Pre-requisites Cognitive goals	Self-consistency Multifacetedness	Pedagogical support Lack of implicit assumptions

Educational type. This group refers to the main approach used in a module; it aims to lead teachers to reflect on what kind of didactical action they want to develop, and what learning approach they want to favour. Teachers are guided to choose the right type for their modules by means of a short description, as well as detailed examples, pedagogical characteristics, type of use. Our choice of these criteria is based on pragmatic reasons, taking into consideration how teachers usually proceed in their educational planning The types that we consider important to include are described below.

Illustrative: Modules to present/illustrate some content or situation which requires students to get the content presented by the teacher. Examples are: a lecture, a solved problem, a case study, a simulation, the description of a situation together with guidelines to tackle it. *Active*: Modules inspired to some learning theory, aiming to make students carry out individual or group activities in some domain. An example is a set of exercises on any topic. *Evaluative:* Modules aiming to verify if a given cognitive level in some domain has been reached, such as: a closed-answer test, a problem to be solved, a project to work out. *Receptive*: Teaching modules aiming to give competence and abilities related with a given domain by means of 1) concepts' presentation, procedures, etc.; 2) the proposal of activities apt to increase some cognitive abilities in the considered domain. What differentiates this type of modules from the *illustrative* ones is that they include some proposals of activity. An example is a tutorial on some theoretical aspects together with related exercises. *Explorative:* Modules based on constructive learning aiming to stimulate reflection and to ease the construction of knowledge by the students; usually include some qualitative evaluation. *Supportive:* Material to be used as example or as support to the use of some other didactical module.

Pedagogical Framework. This group aims to make teachers reflect on the expected results (in terms of abilities and skills to be learned), as well as on the conditions apt to reach them and to support the adoption of criteria for consistent assessment. Three pedagogical aspects should be considered: aim, prerequisites, cognitive goals, specifying, for each of them, definition, examples, reasons of the choices made, advantages. We suggest to include these criteria and their characterisation based on the literature most widely accepted in the educational community.

Didactical Usability. These criteria help the producer-teachers to figure out other frameworks of use than that for which the module was conceived, as well as encourage and stimulate them to propose multiple perspectives, representations, levels of deepening.

Re-use. These criteria refer to the characteristics of a module which could induce other teachers to re-use them, and possibly give rise to a discussion on innovative pedagogical approaches.

As concerns *pedagogical support*, we wish to point out that a main issue related to an effective re-use of didactical modules, especially of those of constructivist nature, lies in a full understanding of their epistemological foundations. It is, thus, fundamental to give pedagogical guidelines for such tools, which allow user-teachers to understand the module's actual nature and evaluate if it is consistent with their own educational approach. Hence, they should help turn the use of a module into a learning moment for the users.

Lack of assumptions on the users' knowledge means that this kind of criteria must include indications on all technical features necessary to make a module easily reusable, e.g., give glossaries for the terms used, complete diagrams and tables with all the information necessary to understand them, such as measure units, legends, etc. It is important to explicitly specify all technical aspects since in the school world, unlike in enterprises, there is no widely accepted standard for notations, graphical presentations, technical language, etc.

4   Concluding Remarks and Future Work

An effective introduction of LOs adds another step to the change started, within the school system, with the introduction of ICT in education, with obvious implications on the necessary teacher preparation. An effective implementation of teacher-oriented guidelines, like those we propose in this paper, implies that teachers be able to make a conscious analysis of their own didactical and epistemological choices. Without such ability, the introduction of LOs in teaching will not result into effective innovation, but just be a different way to present old technology-based attempts of changing the educational system. A successful implementation depends also on the ability of teachers to overcome the discrepancies of terminology which currently characterize the school world and make communication difficult not only between teachers and technologists but also among teachers of different educational settings.

The criteria presented here have been developed as a basis for the design of LOs within the Project 'TIGER-Telepresence Instant Group for Higher Education in Robotics', partially supported by the Italian Ministry of Education, University and Research. We currently carry out parallel work to analyse what role the experience gained by teachers dealing with educational material could play in the re-using decisions. This analysis aims at working out learning objects which model the evolving nature of educational material, as well as the co-operative process that underlies the formation of pedagogical meaning [4].

References

1. Anido, L.E., Fernandez, M.J., Caeiro, M., Santos, J.M., Rodriguez J.S., Llamas M.: Educational metadata and brokerage for learning resources. Computers & Education 38 (2002) 351-374
2. Boskic, N.: Learning objects design: What do educators think about the quality and reusability of learning objects? Proceedings of the 3rd IEEE International Conference on Advanced Learning Technologies (2003) 306-307
3. Bratina, T. A., Hayes, D., Blumsack, S. L.: Preparing Teachers to use Learning Objects. Faculty and staff development, November/December 2002, (2002) http://ts.mivu.org
4. Busetti, E., Forcheri, P., Ierardi, M.G., Molfino, M. T.: Repositories of Learning Objects as Learning Environments for Teachers. Proceedings of ICALT 2004. (2004) (in print)
5. Chitwood, K., Bunnow, D.: Learning Objects: Resources for Learning. Proceedings of Distance learning 2002, 18th Annual conference on distance teaching and learning, 14-16 August 2002, Madison, Wisconsin, (2002) 67-70
6. Duval, E., Forte, E., Cardinaels, K., Verhoeven, B., Van Durm, R., Hendrikx, K., Wentland Forte, M., Ebel, N., Macowicz, M., Warkentyne, K., Haenni, F.: The Ariadne knowledge pool system. ACM Communications, 44 (5) (2001) 72-78
7. Farance, F.: IEEE LOM Standard Not Yet Ready For "Prime Time". Learning Technology 5 (1) (2003) http://lttf.ieee.org/learn_tech/issues/january2003/index.html
8. Feldstein, M.: Tutorial: How to design recyclable learning objects. eLearn, Vol. 2002 Issue 7, (2002) http://portal.acm.org/portal.cfm
9. Friesen, N.: Three Objections to Learning Objects. In: McGreal, R. (ed.): Education Using Learning Objects. London: Routledge/Falmer (2004) (to appear) see preliminary version on: http//phenom.educ.ualberta.ca/~nfriesen/
10. Friesen, N., Mason J., Ward N.: Building Educational Metadata Application Profiles. Proceedings of International Conference on Dublin Core and Metadata for e-Communities (2002) 63-69
11. Koppi, T., Lavitt, N.: Institutional Use of Learning Objects Three Years on: Lessons Learned and Future Directions. Learning Objects 2003 Symposium: Lessons Learned, Questions Asked 24 June 2003, Honolulu, Hawaii (2003) http://www.cs.kuleuven.ac.be/~erikd/PRES/2003/LO2003/index.html
12. IEEE Draft Standard for Learning Object Metadata, (2002) http://ltsc.ieee.org/wg12/files/LOM_1484_12_1_v1_Final_Draft.pdf
13. Ip, A., Morrison, I., Currie, M.: What is a learning object, technically? Proceedings of WebNet2001 Conference, (2001)
14. Ip, A., Young, A., Morrison, I.: Learning Objects: Whose are they? Proceedings of the 15th Annual Conference of the National Advisory Committee on Computing Qualifications, (2002) 315-320

15. Littlejohn, A.: An incremental approach to staff development in the reuse of learning resources. In Littlejohn, A. (ed.): Reusing on line resources: a sustainable approach to e-learning. Kogan Page, London (2003) 221-233
16. Mason, J., Ward, N.: The Le@rning Federation Metadata Application Profile. Learning Technology 5 (1) (2003) http://lttf.ieee.org/learn_tech/issues/january2003/index.html
17. Neven, F., Duval, E.: Reusable Learning Objects: a Survey of LOM-Based Repositories. Multimedia'02 (2002) 291-294
18. Noss, R.: Thematic Chapter: Computers as Commodities. in diSessa A.A., Hoyles C., Noss R. (Eds): Computers and exploratory learning, Springer Verlag, Berlin Heidelberg New York (1995) 363-381
19. Polsani, P. R.: Use and Abuse of Reusable Learning Objects. Journal of Digital information 3 (4) (2003) http://jodi.ecs.soton.ac.uk
20. Quinn, C. Hobbs, S.: Learning Objects and Instruction Components: Formal discussion summary. Educational Technology & Society 3 (2) (2000)
21. Rawlings, A., van Rosmalen, P., Koper, R., Rodríguez-Artacho, M., Lefrere, P.: Survey of Educational Modelling Languages (EMLs). CEN/ISSS WS Learning Technologies Workshop, (2002) http://sensei.lsi.uned.es/palo/eml-version1.pdf
22. Redeker, G.: Learning Objects- Instructional Metadata and Sequencing. Proceedings of e-Learn 2002 (2002) 798-805
23. Richards, G.: The Challenges of the Learning Object Paradigm. Special issue on Learning Objects, Canadian Journal of Learning and Technology 28 (3) (2002) http://www.cjlt.ca/content/vol28.3/
24. Suthers, D., Johnson, S., Tillinghast, B.: Learning Object Meta-data for a Database of Primary and Secondary School Resources. Interactive Learning Environments 9 (3), (2002) 273-289
25. Wiley, D. A.: Connecting learning objects to instructional design theory: A definition, a metaphor, and a taxonomy. In Wiley, D. A. (ed.): The Instructional Use of Learning Objects (2000) http://www.reusability.org/read/chapters/wiley.doc

Articulation of Learners Requirements for Personalised Instructional Design in e-Learning Services

Lily Sun, Khadidjatou Ousmanou, and Shirley Williams

Informatics Research Centre, The University of Reading, UK
Whiteknights, Reading, RG6 6AF, UK
{lily.sun,k.ousmanou,shirley.williams}@reading.ac.uk

Abstract. As e-Learning environments evolve, learners have become increasingly demanding on personalised learning which allows them to build their own knowledge pathway. This significant change in learning requirements imposes a new learning paradigm which ensures one-to-one learning with flexible mode of content configuration, and adaptive delivery and assessment. Although in the past years, Learning Management Systems (LMS) providers have upgraded system functionality to support instructional design for e-learning package, incorporating individual learners' personal learning requirements in content design still remains challenging. To involve learners in the content design requires identification of their personal learning requirements. This paper presents a method for articulating individual learners' learning requirements (e.g., learning styles, and prior knowledge), and representing them in a set of computable parameters in Learner's Profile. These parameters will then be mapped onto instructional design strategies which determine a selection of suitable learning content and sequencing of content with adequate instruction in a learning package.

1 Introduction

Learning Management Systems have the capabilities of creating, fostering, delivering, and facilitating learning at anytime and anywhere. It is generally argued that these learning tools have not yet fully realised the potential of employing Information and Communication Technologies (ICT) and learning standards [1], [2], [3] for delivering customised learning materials. There is an urge for systems that provide just-in time and just-enough learning materials tailored to individual needs and enable them to achieve effectively their personal learning goals.

There are efforts from industry and research community on rationalising learning resources management which serve as the fundamental basis for learning content packaging. This offers opportunity to satisfy stakeholders' demand, e.g., learners will have more choices on requesting learning content, and content designers will have more choices when designing learning content. On the other hand, this opportunity imposes challenges to the stakeholders, in particular content designers. With the advantage of a large pool of learning resources available, content designers would have difficulties to select and sequence suitable learning content without knowing individual learners' requirements. Therefore, it is important to capture specific learner's requirements which are derived from the personal learning preferences (i.e., learning

W. Liu et al. (Eds.): ICWL 2004, LNCS 3143, pp. 424–431, 2004.
© Springer-Verlag Berlin Heidelberg 2004

styles and prior knowledge) and the educational model at the early stage of instructional design.

Many instructional design practices for e-learning in Higher Education still adopt a one-to-many approach when the learning content is constructed and delivered. This approach meets the educational requirements from an instructional design point of view, but ignores each individual learner learning style. Our research has developed a method for articulating individual learners' learning requirements (e.g., learning styles, and prior knowledge), and representing them in a set of computable parameters. To assist the content design these parameters together with the specific educational requirements are encapsulated in a Learner's Profile. These parameters can then be mapped onto instructional design strategies which determine a selection of suitable learning content and sequencing of content with adequate instruction in a learning package.

2 Learning Paradigms and Their Influence on Instructional Design

E-Learning technologies create an effective learning environment where learners are involved interactively. It is recognised that learners achieve their learning goals at different levels of success when supported with same learning content. A main reason is that individual learner interprets meaning and constructs knowledge from the learning content differently. This is proved by learning theory. Constructivism [4], [5], [6] and Semiotics paradigms [7], [8], [9] provide a framework for resolving challenging issues of personalised instructional design that meets learners' needs.

Constructivism expresses a different view on learning and instructional design by encouraging a user-centered approach over course-driven design. Constructivists advocate that learning is an engaging process in which learners construct new ideas or concepts based upon their current or past knowledge. Learners are guided to conduct and manage their personalised learning activities in a collaborative and cooperative manner for critical thinking and problem-solving. Learners select, transform information, construct hypotheses and make decisions relying on a cognitive structure such as mental models [10]. They can actively impose organisation and presentation of the learning content and construct knowledge in the process.

Semiotic paradigm emphases that understanding is a subjective process where the prior knowledge affects the interpretation of a given sign, and vice versa. The process of Semiotics enables learners to structure their experiences and reveal the nature and culture of their understanding. Signs as codes of experience are related to social settings where learning takes place; learning is never a private act. The constructivist approach notes that living systems survive by fitting with one another and with other aspects of the surrounding medium. It is difficult to assume that learners will derive a similar association between a sign and an object, as it involves issues such as meaning, cognition, behaviour, culture and social context. In order to facilitate the acquisition of knowledge in a certain domain, instructional designers need to present it in an authentic context, i.e., settings and applications that would normally involve that knowledge. Learning strategies such as simulations and role-playing are most useful for situated learning where learners learn best topics that have immediate relevance and value to them.

Adopting semiotics and constructivist paradigm have a tremendous impact on instructional design for courseware in e-learning environments. However, the application of these paradigms in e-learning still remains a difficult task faced by instructional designers for two significant reasons: 1) it involves identification and articulation of individual learners' learning requirements and also customisable educational requirements to enforce knowledge construction; 2) the capture of learners' information in a profile; 3) it entails adequate learning content design skills to ensure flexibility, reusability and interoperability to meeting learners' requirements [11]. We believe an understanding of individual learners' needs and instructional design strategies are fundamental concerns in e-learning.

3   Learning Objects for e-Learning Courseware Design

The application of sound learning paradigms and appropriate instructional design strategies are essential for achieving quality learning content design that meets learning requirements. Instructional design strategies facilitate instructional designers to adopt and adapt e-learning standards such as Reusable Learning Objects (RLO) [2], [12]. A RLO is based on a single learning or performance objective, built from a collection of static or dynamic instructional content and practice activities. Any RLO can be tested through assessments that measure the learning or performance objective.

The use of RLO has revolutionised the way instructional content are designed in e-learning. This new paradigm shift enables big chunk learning material to be broken down into small component objects. These objects possess the provision of meaningful tailored, flexible, and personalised learning experiences. Cisco has successfully implemented the concept of RLO for training courses in industry [13]. However, the adoption of their techniques for courseware design in HE is still challenging as far as pedagogy is concerned. A conceptual model of instructional design for HE (see Figure 1) has been developed and used in courseware design in the University [11].

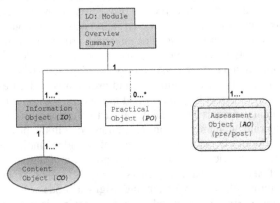

Fig. 1. A conceptual model for instructional design

In this model, a learning object represents a module, which includes the *overview, summary*, and associated *Information Objects (IO)*, *Assessment Objects (AO)* and *Practical Objects* (PO) The *overview* and *summary* components contain general information and direction for next steps about the module respectively. *IO* comprises *Content Objects (CO)* which are aggregated based on the educational requirements specified in the learning objects. *PO* and *AO* are integrated components with the *Information Objects*. The former can be optional and offline depending on the module requirements while the latter is compulsory for assessing learners' mastery over a subject matter.

Learning content can be technically assembled by taking the advantages of learning objects, but providing appropriate personalised learning content to meet individual learners' needs is still the issue. To address this issue, it requires understanding of individual learner's learning behaviour in a learning process, e.g., how they receive and response to information for their knowledge construction. These personal requirements should be captured as part of the learning requirements before instructional design takes place.

4 Modelling a User Profile

Without considering personal learning needs, a learning package is normally constructed based on educational requirements (*ER*), which are specified in a module descriptor. It is suitable for one-to-many learning. E-Learning promotes a one-to-one learning as opposed to one-to-many learning. Personalisation, therefore, becomes an issue in instructional design for courseware. In order to address individual needs and expectations, instructional designers must understand learners' personal learning requirements, i.e. preferred learning styles and level of background knowledge, by which they construct knowledge and solve problems [14].

4.1 Identification of Personal Learning Requirements

They are several classifications of learning styles found in the literature. A theory of psychological type from Jung [15] asserts that everyone is either extraverted or introverted in orientation, and prefers one way of responding to information (sensing or intuition) and one way of deciding on action (thinking or feeling). MBTI, developed by Myers and Briggs [16] is a well-tested instrument in both industry and academia for assessing learners' learning style. The MBTI provides data on the four Jungian dimensions or sets of preferences, which in turn result in 16 learning styles.

Dimension 1 of *Access* (A) identifies learners as judger or perceiver depending on their preferred way of accessing leaning materials. A judger likes learning step-by-step while a perceiver prefers a random, global way of getting information.

$$A = \begin{pmatrix} Judger \\ Perceiver \end{pmatrix}$$

Dimension 2 of *Orientation* (O) categorises learners has Introvert or Extrovert. Introvert learns from watching fist while extrovert learns by taking part in a collaborative manner.

$$O = \begin{pmatrix} Introvert \\ Extrovert \end{pmatrix}$$

Dimension 3 of *Decision on Action* (D) enable the classification of learners as feeler or thinker based their problem-solving aptitude during problem-based learning. Feelers tend to make decisions based on

$$D = \begin{pmatrix} Feeler \\ Thinker \end{pmatrix}$$

personal experiences whereas thinkers decide based on rational thoughts. Feelers like holistic approach at surface level whereas thinkers prefer to go in depth in search of patterns or dissimilarities.

Dimension 4 of *Response* (R) indicates learners' responsiveness to information. Sensing learners prefer to learning facts and things that have apparent connections to reality whereas intuitive learners tend to discover possibilities and relationships.

$$R = \begin{pmatrix} Sensing \\ Intuitive \end{pmatrix}$$

A learner normally falls into a combination of four elements from each dimension. For instance the combination of *Extrovert*, *Sensing*, *Feeling* and *Judging* describes someone who is actively involved and prefers collaborative and practical work. Another most commonly adopted learning style is the perceptual style, which refers to the preferred sensory modality for receiving information. This category named Sensory modality constitutes our fifth dimension for determining learn-learners' preferences.

Dimension 5 of *Sensory Modality* (*Sm*): In general learners prefer a Visual, Auditory, or Tactile mode, although most use a combination of perceptual strategies for selecting and processing information.

$$Sm = \begin{pmatrix} Visual \\ Auditory \\ Tactile \end{pmatrix}$$

Visual learners may think in pictures and learn best from visual displays. Auditory learn best through listening to verbal directions. Tactile or kinaesthetic learner learns best only if there is a given opportunity to interact with new information.

These five dimensions are considered as important personal learning requirements in e-learning. They contribute to instructional design strategies which determine learning content selection and sequencing for individual learners. The finding and experiment from our research [17] show that the learning requirements are incomplete without an indication of a learner's past experience, i.e., prior knowledge. If one's prior knowledge is known before the learning content is packaged, learning can be maintained with interests and motivation.

Dimension 6 of *Prior Knowledge* (*Pk*) is required for capturing knowledge and skills gap. Learner are classified as having none, slight, modest or enough prior-knowledge of the subject to be taught. Each level of knowledge would be reflected during the selection and sequencing of learning content.

$$Pk = \begin{pmatrix} None \\ Little \\ Modest \\ Enough \end{pmatrix}$$

A, O, D, R, Sm and *Pk* can be defined as taxonomy of learning styles and prior-knowledge. This will form the basis for representing learners' preferences, which are encapsulated in a learner's profile.

4.2 Learner Profile and Its Information Categories

There have been several attempts to standardise the creation of learner profile. The two most important examples of such standards are IEEE Personal and Private Information (PAPI) [18] and IMS Learner Information Package (LIP) [19].

PAPI profile distinguishes *personal, relations, security, preference, performance* and *portfolio* information. In the present context of our work, the *preference* and *portfolio* categories are the most crucial ones since they store information about learning styles and prior-knowledge respectively. IMS LIP contains an *accessibility* category for general accessibility to learner information by means of language capabilities, disabilities and learning preferences. The *competency* category represents skills, experiences and knowledge acquired.

To build a richer learner's profile which captures personalised learning requirements, *preference, portfolio* from PAPI and *accessibility, competency from LIP* are adapted in this research work, because they will be important for instructional design and learning experience monitoring.

5 A Method for Learning Requirements Articulation

A personalised learning package is constructed based on learning requirements (*LR*) which include personal learning requirements (i.e., learning styles and prior knowledge) and *ER* specified in an *overview* of the learning object (i.e., a module descriptor). The learning requirements will then be transformed into instructional design strategies (*IDS*) which determine technically 1) selection of learning objects and associated IOs, AOs and POs; 2) sequencing these objects with personalised learning instruction; 3) technical requirements for suitable media to present learning package. These requirements are not merely essential for the design of learning package. They will be evaluated after the learning package is delivered for necessary improvements. Therefore, we create a learner's profile for each of learners where their specific learning requirements are encapsulated and maintained. To elicit the learning requirements involves learners themselves. In general, the *ER* are captured when a learner is enrolled for a module, e.g., C Programming at level 2 (2nd year undergraduate). We devise a technique to allow learners to express their personal requirements by attending a pre-test (Table 1).

Table 1. Sample questions in a pre-test

Q1. Are you more satisfied with
  (a) planned and scheduled activities
  (b) spontaneous or unplanned activities

Q2. When tackling a new problem do you
  (a) try to solve it first and learn by doing it
  (b) like to watch and learn first before solving it

Q3. When observing things, do you look at
  (a) similarities, wholes
  (b) patterns, differences

Q4. Would you rather see
  (a) concepts and principles first before examples
  (b examples and practical first before concepts

Q5. I prefer information which contains more
  (a) pictures, diagrams, graphs, maps
  (b) oral directions, sounds
  (c) text

Q6. What programming language have you used before
  (a) assemblers, LISP, Prolog,
  (b) C, Pascal, Delphi
  (c) C++, Java
  (d) none of the above

Questions 1 to 4 correspond to the elements of the four Jungian's dimensions of learning style *A, O, D* and *R* respectively. Question 5 indicates the means by which learners would grasp best new information, e.g., they prefer illustrative learning content as oppose to all text. With regard to prior-knowledge for our course in programming, Question 6 reveals the learner's prior-knowledge related to C programming. The answers from the pre-test will be articulated based on their weight scores and represented as $P(x)$ in the learner's profile. The parameters in $P(x)$ may have values such as A_2, O_2, D_1, R_1, Sm_1 and Pk_3

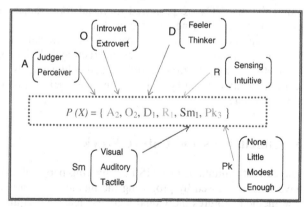

Fig. 2. Personal learning requirements

(see Fig 2). An integration of the $P(x)$ and the *ER* will compose a full set of learning requirements, such as $LR = P(x) \cup ER$.

The *LR* will then contribute to fomulate *IDS* for optimisation of content selection and sequencing. Fig 3 visualises a mapping between the *LR* and *IDS* for a configuration of the learning content. $Pk_3 \cup ER$ determines the suitable learning objects for the learner with the prior knolwedge of C Programming at the Modest level. When the LO is selected, its level of difficulty shoud not be for beginners.

The *IDS* for sequencing involved at the IO, PO, AO requires $Pk_3 \cup A_2 \cup ER$ which indicates a preference for accessing information in a global way with flexible navigation across IO. Whatever the value of *A,* if the prior-knowledge is Pk_1, then *IDS* opt

for a *default sequencing,* which means a selection and sequencing of the learning content based on the rule derived from the *ER.* However if $\neg Pk_1$, then IO are customised accordingly to the value of A.

The *LR* can further assist to make a decision at the CO level by $Pk_3 \cup R_1 \cup ER$. R_1 requires learning the subject starting with the concepts and principles, and then learning the examples and finally attempting the practical to consolidate

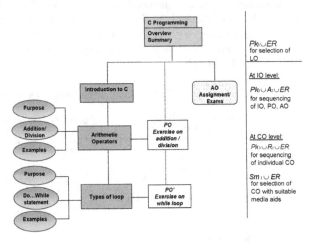

Fig. 3. Mapping the *LR* onto the *IDS* for configuration of the learning content

the understanding. This is a typical default-sequencing rule in the instructional design. In a case of R_2, a *customised-sequencing* rule is applied which means that the navigation on the COs will be entirely up to the learner. To assist learners learn, Sm_1 determines that the COs are preferred in visual form rather than in text form. This is an important factor influencing effective learning.

The parameter *O* and *D* are part of the personal learning requirements, but they have a minimum influence on the instructional design of courseware. *O* and *D* are useful for tracking learning activities and achievements of individual learners so that learning behaviour can be analysed and feedback can be generated to support personalised learning.

6 Conclusions and Future Work

The current limitations of LMS in delivering personalised learning experiences in HE have been addressed by proposing the method for learning requirements articulation. The method captures individual learners' learning requirements (e.g., learning styles, and prior knowledge) and the specific educational requirements in the learner's profile. The instructional design strategies can then be determined for construction of a personalised learning package.

This method has been evaluated through our C Programming and Systems Analysis and Design courses at the University. Future work will concentrate on developing a set of techniques using Agent technology and web semantic languages to assist the formal representation of learners' profile and the automation of the mapping process between these profiles and the Instructional design strategies. The resulted component can be embedded in LMS to improve and facilitate personalisation at all levels.

References

1. SCORM.: Best Practices Guide for Content Developers. Learning Systems Architecture Lab. http://www.lsal.cmu.edu/lsal/expertise/projects/ (2003)
2. IEEE.: Standard for Learning Object Metadata. Learning Technology Standards Committee (LTSC). http://grouper.ieee.org/LTSC/wg12/ (2003)
3. IMS.: IMS Open Specifications for Interoperable Learning Technology. http://www.imsglobal.org/ (2003)
4. Reiser, R.A., Dempsey J. V.: Trends and Issues in Instructional Design and Technology. New Jersey Merrill Prentice Hall (2002)
5. Schuman, L.: Perspectives on instruction. http://edweb.sdsu.edu/courses/edtec540/Perspectives/Perspectives.html (1996)
6. Honebein, P.C., Duffy T., Fishman B.: Constructivism and the Design of Learning Environment: Context and Authentic Activities for Learning. In: Duffy, T.M., Lowyck, J., Jonassen, D. (eds.): Design Environments for Constructivist Learning. Springer-Verlag, New York (1993) 87-108
7. Peirce, C.S.: Collected Papers of Ch.S, Peirce, 1931 - 1935, edited by Hartshorne, C., Weiss, P. (1960) Cambridge, Mass (1932-35)
8. Liu, K.: Semiotics in Information Systems Engineering. Cambridge University Press, Cambridge (2000)
9. Liu, K., Sun, L.: Applying Semiotics in Constructivist Learning. Keynote Paper. International Conference on Teaching and English Translation in the 21st Century, Marco Politechnique Institute, Marco (2002)
10. Bruner, J.: Toward a Theory of Instruction. Cambridge, MA: Harvard University Press (1966)
11. Sun, L., Williams S.: An Instructional Design Model for Constructivist Learning. Association for the Advancement of Computing in Education (AACE), Switcherland (Accepted for publication) (2004)
12. Wiley, D. A.: Connecting learning objects to instructional design theory: A definition, a metaphor, and a taxonomy. In: Wiley, D. A. (ed.): The Instructional Use of Learning Objects. http://reusability.org/read/chapters/wiley.doc (2000)
13. Cisco Systems, Inc. White Paper.: Reusable Learning Object Strategy v4.0. http://business.cisco.com (2001)
14. O'Connor, T. O.: Using learning styles to adapt technology for higher education. www.indstate.edu/ctl/styles/main.html (1999)
15. Jung, C. G.: Psychological Types, Translation by H. Godwyn Baynes (1923) http://psychclassics.yorku.ca/Jung/types.htm (1921)
16. Briggs, K. C., Myers, I. B.: Myers-Briggs Type Indicator Form G question booklet and response form (1976)
17. Sun, L., Williams S., Ousmanou K., Lubega J.: Building Personalised Functions into Dynamic Content Packaging to Support Individual Learners. 2nd European Conference on e-Learning 2003, Glasgow, Scotland, ISBN: 0-9544577-4-9 (2003)
18. IEEE PAPI.: PAPI Learner Specification. http://edutool.com/papi/ (2002)
19. IMS LIP.: Learner Information Package specification. http://www.imsglobal.org/profiles/index.cfm (2001)

Comparison of Pronunciation Scores
in Spoken Language Learning System

Weiqian Liang, Jia Liu, and Runsheng Liu

Tsinghua University, Beijing 100084, China
weiq_liang00@mails.tsinghua.edu.cn, liuj@tsinghua.edu.cn

Abstract. An interactive language learning system should provide prolonged practice and feedback on individual problems. One of the challenges for such a system is to evaluate the learners' input speech for not only correctness but also appropriateness. In this paper we report on the state-of-the-art speech recognition technology for the assessment of pronunciation quality. Using nonnative data from Mandarin Chinese college students, we discuss five kinds of confidence based pronunciation scores such as likelihood, likelihood ratio, duration probability, posterior probability and modified likelihood ratio. Results obtained from the experiments show that these scores are helpful for students to improve their spoken language skills.

Keywords: Pronunciation scoring, nonnative English, speech recognition, computer-assisted language learning

1 Introduction

CALL, computer-assisted language learning, integrates multimedia and web technologies to make it practical to create a self-paced environment for foreign language learning. In this area, the technology of automatic speech recognition (ASR) has been widely used to assess the pronunciation quality of speakers speaking a foreign language and teach correct pronunciation to the learners. Some well-known examples are the WebGrader^{TM} system [1], the Europe ISLE (Interactive Spoken Language Learning) project [2], the IBM's Watch Me! Read [3], and the PLASER (Pronunciation Learning via Automatic Speech Recognition) system [4].

The key to teaching pronunciation successfully is the corrective feedback, especially a type of feedback that does not rely on the student's own perception. We have proposed an ASR-based language learning system for Chinese college students to improve their English speaking ability. In this system, we discuss a number of pronunciation assessment algorithms which can evaluate the learner's overall pronunciation as well as localize and correct detail errors. The pronunciation scores consist of hidden Markov model (HMM) duration normalized log likelihood, duration normalized log likelihood ratio, speech rate normalized duration probability, frame based log posterior probability and n best based modified log likelihood ratio.

W. Liu et al. (Eds.): ICWL 2004, LNCS 3143, pp. 432–439, 2004.

The rest of this paper is organized as follows. We give a broad overview of the present system in section 2. In section 3 we discuss the acoustic models, the recognition network and the confidence-based pronunciation scores and in section 4 the comparison results of these scores are given. Section 5 gives a brief conclusion of this paper.

2   System Overview

The interactive language learning system has four main components: the teaching materials, the teacher side application, the student side application, and the speech processing engine.

The teaching materials cover four levels according to difficulties. Each level is divided into different units in term of topics, and each unit consists of some lessons. These lessons are all organized in multimedia forms. *The teacher side application* is used to help teachers to update the teaching materials, label the text scripts, build the pronunciation dictionary, and design and modify the learning flow. *The student side application* is implemented on a Windows PC with direct audio input/output ability. A general learning course can be described as follows. Students are asked to repeat or read a given sentence in the content database. Hence the overall score is calculated by comparing the input speech with the standard pronunciation models. If the score is beyond a predefined threshold, the judgment of word level pronunciation quality and feedback of sentence level prosodic errors are given. Through provision of these feedbacks, the computerized teacher can bring students to focus on specific individual problems, which stimulates them to attempt self improvement. *The speech processing engine* consists of four modules: HMM based speech recognizer, sentence level stress detector, sentence level intonation detector and the time scale modification program. Among them the speech recognizer is the most important component and will be discussed in detail hereinafter.

3   ASR-Based Pronunciation Assessment Algorithm

In our system, a speech recognizer is used to extract speech feature, align the student's speech to the sentence text by Viterbi search, and compute the confidence-based pronunciation score. The ASR-based pronunciation assessment algorithm can be illustrated in Fig. 1.

3.1   Acoustic Models

The reliability of the assessment results depends on the quality of the used acoustic models. Since the native speaker performance always represents standard pronunciation, it is reasonable to use native speech to train the acoustic models. However nonnative speech is characterized by dissimilar formant structures compared to native speech [5]. In order to reduce accent effect of nonnative

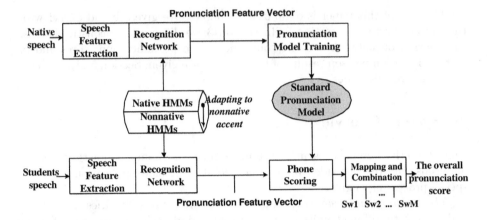

Fig. 1. Flowchart of the proposed pronunciation assessment algorithm

speakers, we offline use the speech of nonnative speakers to adapt the pre-trained native HMMs. These speakers have good pronunciation performance according to English teachers' subjective evaluation.

First, training data (DARPA TIMIT acoustic-phonetic continuous American English speech corpus) are pre-processed to extract 39 element acoustic vectors including static MFCCs, log-energy, deltas and accelerations. Speech is sampled at 16kHz, and features are calculated on frames of 20 msec, in 10 msec intervals. In order to reduce the complexity of the HMM model, we finally utilize a 26 features set, $[C_{1-10}, \Delta C_{1-8}, \Delta^2 C_{1-5}, E, \Delta E, \Delta^2 E]$, [6]. We also map the original used 61 phonemic symbols into 41 phonemic symbols in the cmudict.0.4 [7]. The monophone and tied-state triphone (1185 physical models and 491 states) HMM models are trained on TIMIT by using standard Baum-Welch algorithm. Furthermore we use the global transformation matrix MLLR (maximum likelihood linear regression) and MAP (maximum a-posterior) algorithm (several iterations) to implement the nonnative accent adaptation.

3.2   Recognition Network

In our system, the transcription of the utterance is assumed to be known for the student. The recognition network consists of two passes: the forced alignment (FA) pass and the filler recognition pass, as shown in Fig. 2. The FA pass aims to compare the input speech with what a student is desired to speak. The filler pass still consists of two networks: the phone loop (PL) and N-Best (NB) network. The PL network, where each phone can follow the previous one with equal probability, can generate a phone level transcript of the input speech, i.e. it aims to recognize what a student has actually spoken. The NB network has the same length as the FA pass and contains N (N= the number of monophones) context dependent phone candidates (The context of each candidate is the context of the FA-phone.) for each given speech segmentation.

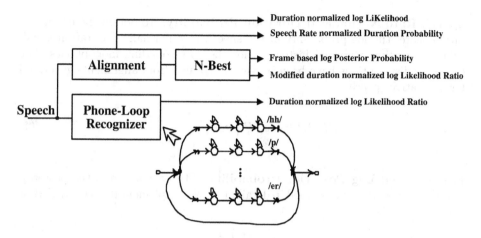

Fig. 2. Baseline recognition network structure

3.3   Pronunciation Scores

By using the recognition network and the statistic results obtained from the native speech database, the pronunciation scores are computed for the input speech at the phoneme level. Because these scores are all based on the phone level information, the result is a flexible (text-independent) system that can easily be customized for new lesson materials by developers. Each of these five phone level scores is described below.

Duration Normalized Log Likelihood.

$$DLK = \frac{\sum_{t=f_s}^{f_s+d_i-1} log\left(p^{FA}\left(\mathbf{X_t}|q_i\right)\right)}{d_i} \tag{1}$$

where d_i is the number of frames in the acoustic segment of the ith phone and f_s is the start frame.

Duration Normalized Log Likelihood Ratio [8].

$$DLR = -\frac{|DLK^{FA} - DLK^{PL}|}{d_i} \tag{2}$$

$$DLK^{PL} = \sum_{j=1}^{N} \frac{\sum_{t=f_{js}}^{f_{je}} log\left(p^{PL}\left(\mathbf{X_t}|q_j\right)\right)}{f_{je} - f_{js} + 1}. \tag{3}$$

where f_{js} and f_{je} denote start and end frame number for the jth phone occurring during the current interval from f_s to $f_s + d_i - 1$ in the phone recognition pass.

Speech Rate Normalized Duration Probability. To obtain the phone duration score, the log-probability of the speech rate normalized duration is calculated by using a normal histogram for the corresponding monophones. The Gaussian distributions have been previously trained from alignments generated for the native speech.

$$SRDP = log \left[P \left(d_i \cdot \frac{N}{\sum_{i=1}^{N} d_i} \right) \right] \tag{4}$$

Frame Based Log Posterior Probability. The calculation of the posterior score has already been described in detail in [9]. We implement it with our N-Best network.

$$FPP = \frac{1}{d_i} \cdot \sum_{t=f_s}^{f_s+d_i-1} log\left(P\left(q_i|\mathbf{X_t}\right)\right) \tag{5}$$

$$P\left(q_i|\mathbf{X_t}\right) = \frac{p\left(\mathbf{X_t}|q_i\right)P\left(q_i\right)}{\sum_{j=1}^{M} p\left(\mathbf{X_t}|q_j\right)P\left(q_j\right)}. \tag{6}$$

Modified Duration Normalized Log Likelihood Ratio. Suppose that the FA-phone is the ith candidate in the N-Best results, $M \leq i < k \leq N$.

$$MLR = -\frac{|DLK_i - \frac{1}{M}\sum_{j=1}^{M} DLK_j|}{|DLK_i - \frac{1}{N-k+1}\sum_{j=k}^{N} DLK_j|} \tag{7}$$

Mapping to Subjective Scores. Subjective scores usually cover finite ranges. Therefore correlation with these human expert scores will be increased by mapping the automatic pronunciation scores into a finite range. We employed a sigma function to do this mapping.

$$M(x) = \frac{1}{1 + exp\left(\alpha \cdot x + \beta\right)} \tag{8}$$

where $\alpha < 0$ ($M(x)$ is an increasing function of x.) and β are empirically selected for each pronunciation score.

Phone Dependent Threshold [8]. A phone-specific acceptance/rejection threshold for the pronunciation quality is computed from 'good' pronunciation score statistics: the threshold for a phone q is defined in terms of the mean μ_q and variance σ_q obtained from the training data of native and good-pronounced nonnative speech.

$$T_q = \mu_q + \alpha\sigma_q + \beta \tag{9}$$

where α and β are determined through experiments.

Sentence Pronunciation Score. Finally the pronunciation score for the target sentence or word is defined as the average phone score.

$$Sentence\ Score = \frac{1}{L} \sum_{l=1}^{L} Phone\ Score\ (l) \qquad (10)$$

where L is the sentence length.

4   Experiments

To evaluate the performance of the proposed pronunciation scores, we collect and hand-transcribe a continuous mandarin-English speech corpus (1, 561 utterances, 31 Chinese college students (16 males and 15 females)). The overall pronunciation quality of each utterance is rated on a scale from 1 to 5 by three English teachers. According to the sentence scores, the speakers are graded on English pronouncing skills. Moreover the speech data of good-pronounced speakers are partially (400 utterances) used to adapt the acoustic models of the speech recognizer. The probability distribution of the average subjective scores is shown in Table 1 and the averaged inter-rater cross correlation coefficient for the three raters is 0.79 at the sentence level. Because of sparse speakers, we do not calculate the speaker level correlation.

Table 1. Probability distribution of the average subjective scores

Score range	1 (1, 2]	(2, 3]	(3, 4]	(4, 5]
%	3.8	15.8	21.3	43.3	15.8

Table 2. Comparison results of the proposed pronunciation scores on the sentence level correlation

Pronunciation scores	Correlation coefficient	Difference ($\frac{Human\ Score - Machine\ Score}{Human\ Score}$%)
DLK	0.46	41.7
DLR	0.65	17.7
SRDP	0.35	55.6
FPP	0.67	15.2
MLR	0.51	35.4
Human Score	0.79	—

We compare these scores on 1, 000 utterances of the nonnative speech database (The data of speakers whose speech is used to adapt HMM models are excluded). From Table 2, we can observe that the frame based log posterior probability and duration normalized log likelihood ratio scores are comparable

Table 3. Correlation Improvement by using nonnative accent adaptation

Pronunciation scores	DLR	FPP
Native HMM	0.56	0.58
Nonnative HMM	0.65	0.67
Improvement ($\frac{Nonnative-Native}{Native}\%$)	16.1	15.6

and outperform other scores. The MLR and DLK scores are in the middle having about 20% lower correlation and the SRDP score is the worst. As illustrated in [8], the reason should be that both the DLR and FPP scores are less affected by changes in the spectral match or acoustic channel variations. The same changes in acoustic match would similarly affect both the numerator and denominator in (2) and (5), making the scores more invariant to those changes and more focused on pronunciation quality. However the distinct dissimilar temporal characters between native and nonnative speech duration should result in the poor performance of the SRDP score.

Table 3 gives the comparison results between native and good-pronounced nonnative HMM Models. We also use the correlation between the English teacher scores and machine scores as the evaluation measure. The native and nonnative HMM models are respectively applied to the pronunciation scoring process. As shown in Table 3, about 16% improvement on the correlation coefficient is achieved by using 'good' nonnative HMM models. As described in [5], speaker accent introduces systemic variance on frequency characteristics. The good nonnative speech is still different with native speech but should be scored as 'goodness'. Accordingly, the nonnative accent adaptation can be justified for pronunciation assessment.

Sentence level correlations are lower than those among humans, suggesting that further work is still needed to improve the performance of automatic scores.

5   Conclusions

Automatic pronunciation assessment is a novel and difficult research task. In this paper, a series of text-independent, even language-independent, pronunciation scores are implemented. Needed for our research a database of nonnative speech has been collected and hand-transcribed at the phoneme level. And various famous robust technologies such as HMM, MLLR accent adaptation and confidence measure, etc. are investigated. Experiments show that the frame based log posterior probability and duration normalized log likelihood ratio scores outperform other machine scores on the correlation with subjective scores. With these assessment algorithms, the computerized language teacher can feedback the judgment on the learner's pronunciation quality immediately. Aided with other speech technologies, such as pitch extraction, time-scale modification and stress detection etc., we have built an web-based interactive English learning system.

References

1. Neumeyer, L., Franco, H., Abrash, V., Julia, L., Ronen, O., Bratt, H., Bing, J., Digalakis, V., Rypa, M.: $WebGrader^{TM}$: A Multilingual Pronunciation Practice Tool. Proc. Speech Tech nology in Language Learning Workshop. (1998)
2. Menzel, W., Herron, D., Bonaventura, P., Morton R.: Automatic detection and correction of non-native English pronunciations. Proc. InSTILL2000. (2000) 49–56
3. Williams, S., Nix, D., Fairweather, P.: Using Speech Recognition Technology to Enhance Literacy Instruction for Emerging Readers. Proc. ICLS2000. (2000) 115–120
4. Brian, M., Manhung, S., Mimi, N., Yik-Cheung, T., Yu-Chung, C., Kin-Wah, C., Ka-Yee, L., Simon, H., Fong-Ho, C., Jimmy, W., Jacqueline, L.: PLASER: Pronunciation Learning via Automatic Speech Recognition. Proc. HLT-NAACL2003. (2003) 23–29
5. Arslan, L., Hansen, J.: Frequency characteristics of foreign accented speech. Proc. ICASSP'97. (1997) 1123–1126
6. Valtchev, V.: Discriminative methods in HMM-based speech recognition. PhD Thesis. the University of Cambridge. (1995)
7. Weide, R.: The Carnegie Mellon Pronouncing Dictionary cmudict 0.4. http://www.speech.cs.cmu.edu/cgi-bin/cmudict. (1995)
8. Silke M. W.: Use of speech recognition in computer-assisted language learning. PhD Thesis. the University of Cambridge. (1999)
9. Franco, H., Neumeyer, L., Kim, Y., Ronen, O.: Automatic pronunciation scoring for language instruction. Proc. ICASSP'97 (1997) 1471–1474

Community Knowledge Building Environment with Concept of KBC

Xinyu Zhang[1], Nianlong Luo[1], XiangCun Wu[1], DongXing Jiang[1],
JianWei Zhang[2], and DongXue Liu[2]

[1] Computer and Information Management Center, Tsinghua Univ., China, 100084
[2] Educational Technology Institute, Tsinghua Univ., China, 100084

Abstract. In the knowledge-based society, the public knowledge building attracts more and more attention. The theory of KBC (Knowledge Building Community) based on the constructivist focuses on the creativity and improvement of the knowledge, discovers the higher substance of knowledge building, and displays the powerful vitality. This paper will make a further study to the KBC theory, propose a new, network-based idea for the design of Community Knowledge Building, introduce the structure of the Community Knowledge Building network system and discuss the practical effects of the newly developed system.

1 Introduction

With the development of the scientific technology, the human society is striding from the industrial society into the information society. The knowledge economy is coming, the public knowledge becomes richer and richer, the renewal cycle becomes shorter and shorter, and the traditional idea of superstition authoritative knowledge is unceasingly receiving the challenge. The knowledge should not be static after proposed by the authoritative scholar, but be evolutive in the process of the development and the consummation of the humanity. In the present era the public knowledge building attracts more and more attention, and shows its huge vitality.

Since 90s in the 20th century, the famous psychologist and educational technologist, Marlene Scardamalia and Carl Bereiter, Toronto Univ., Canada have proposed the theory and model of KBC (Knowledge Building Community). What the theory of KBC concerns is the production and improvement of the public knowledge. Also, it reveals the essential of the knowledge building, and provides an efficacious method for the realization of the community knowledge building [1].

The network technology can provide the people a convenience to construct together the new knowledge using the existing knowledge in the activities of exchanging ideas. Also, it can provide good technological environments and conditions for the realization of KBC. The objective of the present study is to propose a new, network-based idea for the design of Community Knowledge Building, and to develop a Community Knowledge Building network system. Also, we will make a further study to the KBC theory, and discuss the practical effects of the newly developed system.

W. Liu et al. (Eds.): ICWL 2004, LNCS 3143, pp. 440–448, 2004.

2 Theory

2.1 Theory of Knowledge Building Community [2]

The theory of Knowledge Building Community (KBC) proposed by the famous psychologist and educational technologist Marlene Scardamalia and Carl Bereiter, Toronto Univ., Canada is a kind of learning theory and mode of constructivism. And it poses the essential of knowledge construction from both the views of recognition and social cultural, trying to exceed those swallow constructive theories.

The theory of KBC emphasizes the center of knowledge construction. And students should participate and promote the knowledge of the community, which is relative to the community of learners, not to the human community. While they promote the community knowledge, they can develop the knowledge of their own. Not only knowledge construction is a procedure but also it aims at creating some product. And the product is not the tangible physical product but the idealistic artificiality which gets the external existing form so that can be operated, applied, modified and developed by learners. KBC aims at the teaching mode and teaching idea of knowledge creating. And in this sense, in order to differ with the common constructivist theories, Scardamalia and her team use "Knowledge Building", not "knowledge construction", and also point out that "Knowledge Building" may be defined simply as "Creative work with ideas that really matter to the people doing the work" [4].

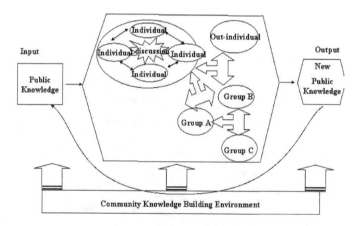

Fig. 1. Process of Community Knowledge Building in web-based environment

3 Idea

3.1 Process of Community Knowledge Building

Fig. 1 shows the knowledge building process in the network-based community knowledge building environment. At the beginning of the knowledge building, the members of the knowledge building community obtain the public knowledge. Then, through the interactive activities among the individuals, among the groups, and between the individuals inside and outside, the public knowledge is added, emended and integrated to become the new constructed public knowledge, which enters into a new round of the knowledge building activity.

3.2 The Community Knowledge Building Ecosystem

The technology acts to help incubate and maintain a new type community knowledge building ecosystem or culture. An ecosystem is always open, in which a variety of species are living. Among the species and between the species and the environment, a dependant and dynamic equilibrium was kept. Though the ecosystem has a certain self-organizing ability and adaptability, it's also apt to be destroyed. The advantage of the new information technology, such as network, is that, it can help to build a new community knowledge building ecosystem, which is entity constructed by the knowledge building community and its physical and virtual knowledge building environment. The members of the community live in this ecosystem, and they have a complex mutual relationship with each other, with the teachers, the researchers and the social culture. Everybody in the ecosystem is the producer of knowledge as well as the consumer of knowledge. The technology, from being as a tool of supporting the individual activity, turns into a tool of supporting the mutual relationship, and help the wise community build a social and distributing "brain" [3].

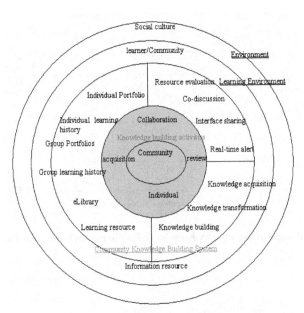

Fig. 2. The Community Knowledge building Ecosystem

The above model illustrates the basic structure of the community knowledge building ecosystem. The community lies in the center of the entire system, and what they face is the community knowledge building ecosystem in which they study and live. The outermost is the outer social cultural environment of the study ecosystem, and adjacent to which, is the study environment faced by the learners. According to the idea of the distributing cognizance, the study environment mainly consists of two aspects, including the study society with which the learners communicate and the information resource with which the learners interchange. Inside is the community knowledge building system, which provides a variety of tools supporting the knowledge building. Members of the community participate in a series of knowledge building activities, such as exchanging ideas and pushing the knowledge forward.

4   Design

4.1   The Structural Map of the System

The learners first login into the community knowledge building system, select a certain kind of study resources represented by a form of files, images, videos etc., and begin a collaborative study by means of E-mail, chat room, forum and electronic bulletins etc. They make a analysis and study on the public knowledge and transform it into the individual knowledge, to which they make additions, emendations and integrations etc. Once the achievements of the building activities are published, they form new public knowledge, which is stored in the system as community knowledge and put back into a new round of building process.

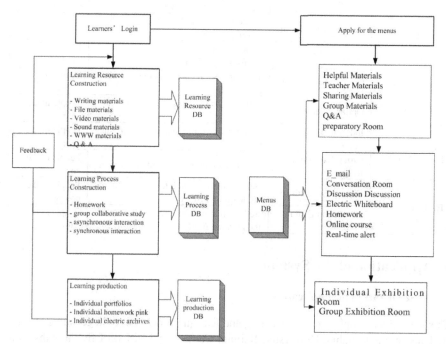

Fig. 3. The structural map of the Knowledge building Community system

4.2 The Composition of Menus

To construct a learning system using the Knowledge Building Community model, so that it can carry a series of learning processes from the stage of understanding problems to the stage of arranging learning, menus need to be composed as shown in Table 1.

Table 1. The composition of menus

Knowledge Construction Model	Menu	Description	Participators
Learning guidance	Helpful Materials	Materials for helping the use of the system	Individual
	Teacher's Materials	Materials for motivation involving and learning	Individual
	Sharing Materials	Materials which were provided by others	Individual
	Group Materials	Materials of the group	Individual
	Q&A	Questions and answers during the class	Individual
	Real-time alert		Individual
	Preparatory Room	Learner preview the course before the class	Individual
Knowledge Building	Homework		Individual or Group
	E_mail	E-mailing among in-learners, out-learners and the teachers	People in the system
	Conversation Room	Learning group to converse about their learning	Group
	Discussion Room	Write learner's opinion on a subject in the from of statement	People in the system
	Electric whiteboard	Learners use the graph or multimedia to communicate	People in the course
	Online Course	Teachers and students interact in real-time class.	People in the course
Knowledge Production	Individual Exhibition Room	Individual learning history and production	People in the course
	Group Exhibition Room	Group learning history and production	People in the course
Evaluation	History Evaluation	Self-evaluation and inter-evaluation of the learning history	People in the course
	Production Evaluation	Self-evaluation and inter-evaluation of the learning production	People in the course

5 Application of the System

5.1 The Duration of Application

This system was applied to the teaching and learning process of college studies for the students in the Tsinghua University, Beijing, China, for a period of five months from September, 2003 to January, 2004.

5.2 The Applied Content

Two classes from the freshmen were selected to be applied in the system: "The multimedia design and implement", and "Programming technology". The community knowledge building system introduced in this thesis was applied to the teaching and learning process.

The teachers of two courses designed the activity of community knowledge building in teaching process and instructed students' learning based on the system of community knowledge building.

The course, "The multimedia design and implement", is an elective course. The learning ability and knowledge level of students in the course is different. At first, teachers submitted the teacher materials and reference papers to "Teacher's Materials", for example, the develop history of PHOTOSHOP software, permitted students to discuss and evaluate these materials, and raised questions to guide student to think; In "Q&A", teachers put out the ordinary questions and answers to help students. Then, teachers divided student into the four-people groups, and offered the reference files in "Group Materials". Based on understanding information and building sense, students utilized "E_mail", "Discussion Room", "Online Course", "Conversation Room" and "Electric whiteboard" to express their opinions. Students made communion in the inter-group or among groups, and evaluated, developed, and integrated idea, and then built sense at deep level, and, finally, it created the conception production (theory's explain and design originality etc.). This production displayed in "Group Exhibition Room". In this process, system could control the learning schedule of students through "Real-time alert".

5.3 The Survey Result about Effect of the System

When the semester was over, a survey was administered to the classes to attempt to gauge the effectiveness of pair programming. The survey was divided into 2 categories: (1) the environment of the system (Table.2), (2) the effects in the study of the students (Table.3).

Of the 168 surveys sent out, 154 (91.7%) were returned. The survey results were entered into a spreadsheet for analysis and the results have been summarized below:

Section1

Table 2. The survey result of the environment of the system

Questions	Strongly agree	Agree	So-So	Disagree	Strongly Disagree
1. The interface of the system is friendly.	12.34%	40.26%	31.82%	12.99%	2.60%
2. The system is easy to operate.	7.79%	31.82%	31.17%	24.68%	4.55%
3. The discussion and interaction to use the system is convenient.	12.34%	34.42%	25.32%	14.94%	12.99%
4. Students like this learning environment.	16.23%	31.17%	35.71%	11.69%	5.19%
5. The function of the system is powerful.	18.18%	31.82%	30.52%	15.58%	3.90%

Summary
From the results of the survey, it appears that the majority of students felt comfortable in studying in the system. Most students appreciate the friendly interface and the simple system operation. 34.42% of the students consider the discussion as "convenient", 12.34% "very convenient" and 12.99% "very inconvenient", which may be explained by the fact that some of the students are not yet accustomed to the network-based study pattern. However, most students enjoy such kind of study environment, and appreciate the powerful system.

Section2
Comparisons with once:

Table 3. The survey result of the effects in the study of the students

Questions	Strongly agree	Agree	So-So	Disagree	Strongly disagree
6. I know how I can obtain the knowledge using the Internet quickly.	35.71%	36.36%	9.09%	9.09%	9.74%
7. I have made good use of the resources provided by the system	28.57%	35.71%	19.48%	6.49%	9.74%
8. I can express my ideas freely	22.73%	43.51%	18.18%	10.39%	5.19%
9. I can fully express my ideas.	28.57%	14.94%	42.86%	7.79%	5.84%
10. I often communicate my idea with others.	37.01%	36.36%	14.94%	7.14%	4.55%
11. I like to consult with others for opinions	12.99%	42.86%	37.66%	1.30%	5.19%
12. My ideas are often different with others	9.74%	28.57%	50.00%	1.30%	10.39%
13. I often rebut others' opinions.	11.69%	34.42%	44.16%	2.60%	7.14%
14. I often review their study method in the study.	18.18%	44.81%	23.38%	3.90%	9.74%
15. I think more deeply than before	25.97%	22.73%	38.96%	8.44%	3.90%

Summary
The results of the survey show that the system has made the following noticeable effects in the learning (change all the others accordingly) of the students:

1. Students are easy to obtain information

Most students agreed that I know how I can obtain the knowledge using the Internet quickly, and among them, 35.71% strongly agreed with the above opinion; and only few of the students expressed their disagreement. Moreover, most of the students claimed that they have made good use of the resources provided by the system.

2. Improving students' self-expression and communication

In the item of "I can express my ideas freely", 22.73% of the students agreed strongly, 43.51% agreed. Further, near half of the students said they have fully expressed their ideas; the total number of these students exceeds that of students who disagreed and strongly disagreed. We can see that the students can freely express their own ideas through the community knowledge building activities.

Most students (37.01%+36.36%) said they often exchanged their ideas with others, and more than half of the students liked to consult with others for opinions. This showed that the students' communicating has been improved in the course of study.

3. Cultivating the students' innovative ideas

The proportion of the students who agreed "my ideas are often different with others'" and "often rebut others' opinions" is greater than that of the students who disagreed, which showed that students can produce the innovate opinion in the study.

4. Making students review their learning strategies

Over half of the students said that they often reviewed their study method in the study. Almost half of the students said "I think more deeply than before". This showed that this building activities improved students review their learning.

It's worthwhile to note the possible constraints of this survey. The reasonability of the design of the questions should be taken more seriously; the range of the investigation should be widened, for the teaching requirements of the courses are different, and the excitations of the students are different.

6   Conclusion

The coming of the information era challenges the authority and certainty of the knowledge, the theory of KBC based on the constructivist focuses on the creativity and improvement of the knowledge, discovers the higher substance of knowledge building, and displays the powerful vitality.

In this work, a Community Knowledge Building environment was designed based on the concept of KBC and a network-based Community Knowledge Building system was built. Supported by the newly developed system, the Community Knowledge Building activities were realized and a Community Knowledge building ecosystem was formed. Our investigation showed that, studying in this environment, learner can bring up these abilities: self-studying, obtaining and using information, expression, communication, creativity, metacognition and higher-level thinking.

References

1. Scardamalia, M., & Bereiter, C. (2002). Knowledge building. In Encyclopedia of education, second edition. New York: Macmillan Reference, USA.
2. Zhang, J. (2001). On Web-based Learning Community. Distance Education in China, Special Issue, 52-54.
3. Chen, Q. & Zhang, J. (2003). A Model of Integrated Learning in the Information Era. Peking University Education Review, 1(3), 90-96
4. Bereiter, C., & Scardamalia, M.. Learning to work creatively with knowledge. In E. De Corte, L. Verschaffel, N. Entwistle, & J. van Merriënboer (Eds.), *Unravelling basic components and dimensions of powerful learning environments*. EARLI Advances in Learning and Instruction Series

5. Scardamalia, M. (2004). CSILE/Knowledge Forum®. In *Education and technology: An encyclopedia*. Santa Barbara: ABC-CLIO.
6. Zhang, J. & Sun, Y. (2004 in press). Constructive Learning: The integrated explorations of learning sciences. Shanghai: Shanghai Education Press.
7. Barab, S., MaKinster, J. G., Moore, J., Cunningham, D., & the ILF Design Team. (2001). Designing and building an online community: The struggle to support sociability in the Inquiry Learning Forum. Educational Technology Research and Development, 49(4), 71-96.
8. Nonaka,I. & .The knowledge creating Company-How Japanese Companies Create the Dynamics of Innovation. Oxford University Press,1995
9. Young, M., Nastasi, B., Braunhardt, L. (1996). Implementing Jasper Immersion: A Case of Conceptual Change. In B. Wilson (Ed.), *Constructivist learning environments: Case studies in instructional design* (pp.121-133). New Jersey: Educational Technology Publications.
10. Zhang XY, Luo NL, Jiang DX, Wu XC. Synchronous Graphic-Interaction in CSCL, ICWL 2003.

Student Participation Index:
Student Assessment in Online Courses

Alan Y.K. Chan[1], Paul Kai-on Chow[1], and K.S. Cheung[2]

[1] Department of Computer Science,
City University of Hong Kong, Hong Kong
{csachan,cspchow}@cityu.edu.hk
[2] School of Continuing Education,
Hong Kong Baptist University, Hong Kong
cheungks@hkbu.edu.hk

Abstract. Online courses have been widely used to support teaching and learning in higher education. It is essential to develop methods to properly assess students in online course usages. This paper proposes a student participation index for assessing students in online courses. The index consists of a number of components, such as pages viewed and forum questions read and posted, and associated weights. It has the benefits of being non-course-specific, non-subjective, extendible and flexible. The development of the index and how it is used to evaluate students are described in the paper. Results indicate that students with higher index usually achieve better grades and vice versa.

1 Introduction

In recent years the proliferation of the Internet and the advancement of its technologies have a significant impact on the adaptation of e-Learning in higher education. Online courses have now become an important component to support teaching and learning in classroom and are widely adopted today as part of the E-Learning initiative in higher education. They are usually delivered on learning management system, such as WebCT and BlackBoard. Online course evaluation is essential in order to improve the quality of teaching and learning. There are several ways to evaluate online courses, such as teacher/student reflection (questionnaires), student performance in assessments (assignments, quiz and examination) and student actions (web server log files and databases).

Understanding student participation in online courses allows instructor to evaluate and assess students. The method for assessing student online participation should be flexible and extensible to allow for enhancement, and should not be based on subjective judgments. This paper proposes a student participation index (SPI) for assessing student in online courses. The index is computed based on student actions, based on what students do in online courses. Data are captured either in a form of web access log files or databases.

The next section discusses the characteristics and functions of online courses and criteria for evaluation. Section 3 describes the methodologies for developing the stu-

W. Liu et al. (Eds.): ICWL 2004, LNCS 3143, pp. 449–456, 2004.
© Springer-Verlag Berlin Heidelberg 2004

dent participation index. Section 4 presents the result and how it is used to evaluate students. Finally, evaluation of the index and possible improvements are discussed in the conclusion.

2 Student Participation

To understand and define student participation in online courses, it is essential to identify the characteristics and functions of online courses. These are discussed in the following sub-sections.

2.1 Characteristics of Online Courses

Online courses provide a flexible learning environment where both instructors and students can teach and learn regardless of time and location. The learning process can be self-paced, independent, collaborative and continuous in online courses. Online courses support high quality learning by offering different kinds of environments such as synchronous or asynchronous or both. Some environments and approaches facilitates student learning while others impede it [1]. A traditional classroom provides a face-to-face learning environment where instructors can direct and take active immediate role in class at a fixed time and place. Online courses provide alternative opportunities for current on-campus students to take classes that they could not take otherwise due to time conflicts with other courses or work [2]. In traditional classroom, it is often instructional where the instructors transfer the knowledge directly to the students. It does not reflect the students' understanding of the knowledge effectively. However, the dynamic nature in the online courses supports better communication such as self-reflections and peer-to-peer reviews. This change in communication transforms the learning process where knowledge is constructed actively by cognition [3].

2.2 Functions of Online Courses

Learning management system is commonly used as a platform for the delivery of online courses. LMS is defined as a distinct, pedagogically meaningful and comprehensive system by which learners and faculty can participate in the learning and instructional process at anytime and any place [4]. Its functions can be categorized into several components such as content delivery (organizer and content pages, URLs, etc), communication and collaboration (chat, whiteboard, forum, mail, calendar, etc), assessment (quizzes, assignments, self-test, etc) and class administration (grade book, syllabus, etc) [5].

2.3 Evaluation of Student Participation

Class attendance and contribution may be considered as student actions which can be used to evaluate student participation in the traditional classroom. In online courses, student actions include accessing course materials, posting and reading discussion forums, taking online quizzes, interacting synchronously in chat room and white board, sharing resources, email communication, etc. They are usually stored in either databases or data files and their transaction log are recorded automatically in web access log files in a specific format.

3 Methodology

The student participation index is an aggregation of various student actions in the online courses. The computation of the index is based on the weight of each pre-defined student action and the median of the students' index scores. Ranking students by the index can be used for grading and comparison purposes. Table 1 below summarizes the constitution and the formula of the student participation index. There are three steps in the development of the index, namely defining the index components and their weights, defining the index formula and ranking the index results. The details are discussed below.

Table 1. Constitution and formula of the Student Participation Index (SPI)

Student Actions	Variable	Weight	Score
Number of pages viewed	A	10%	Score (A) = 10% * A / Max (A)
Number of forum questions read	B	20%	Score (B) = 20% * B / Max (B)
Number of forum questions posted	C	30%	Score (C) = 30% * C / Max (C)
Number of chat sessions participated	D	10%	Score (D) = 10% * D / Max (D)
Number of chat message submitted	E	30%	Score (E) = 30% * E / Max (E)
Total Score			= Score (A) + Score (B) + Score (C) + Score (D) + Score (E)
SPI			= 100 * Total Score / Median Score

3.1 Defining Index Components and Their Weights

As discussed in the previous section, there are different types of student actions in the online courses. In this particular example, the student participation index consists of selected actions such as number of pages viewed, forum question read and posted, chat sessions and chat messages from each individual student. These actions are extracted from the log data in the online course. Each action is assigned a percentage weight. This assigned weighting is based on the subjective importance determined by the instructor. It should be noted that, depending on the course nature, different actions and weights may be included.

3.2 Defining Index Formula

Each student's score is the summation of the score of actions. Each action score is calculated based on the weight, the student value and the maximum value of the action, as shown in Table 1. The maximum value of the action is used to achieve relative scoring. The median can be found after computing all students' scores. It is course-specific and can be used to compute the index. The student participation index for a student is the student score divided by the median and multiplied by 100. If a student's index equals to 100, then he/she is in the median position of the student participation.

3.3 Ranking Index Results

After calculating the student participation index, students can then be ranked for grading and comparison purposes. Instructor can define a score for online participation and students can be graded according to their position in the index.

4   Results

An online course in Java programming has been used as a sample for calculating the student participation index. The course has 72 students and is conducted in the WebCT platform. Results are described and interpreted in the following sub-sections.

4.1 Students by Total Score and Index

Figures 1 and 2 present the total score and the index of each student in descending order. The percentage of each student action constitutes the total score.

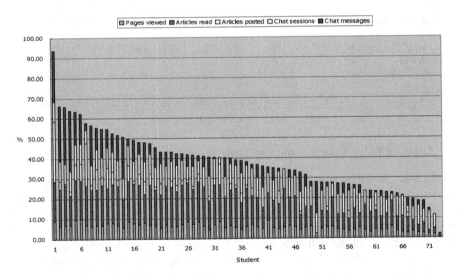

Fig. 1. Student Score

4.2 Sample Calculations

There are 72 students in the sample online course. The highest and the lowest score are 93.61% and 2.15% respectively. The median score is 38.23%. Table 2 below illustrates the calculation of the student participation index for several students.

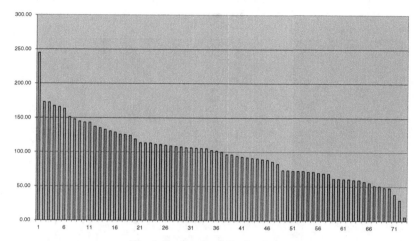

Fig. 2. Student Participation Index

Table 2. Examples of Student Participation Index calculation

Variable	Student 1	Student 2	Student 3	Student 4	Student 5
A	1011	765	717	481	304
B	350	356	320	259	63
C	38	5	2	3	0
D	3	3	3	3	3
E	112	64	43	42	10
Score (A)	8.93%	6.76%	6.33%	4.25%	2.69%
Score (B)	19.61%	19.94%	17.93%	14.51%	3.53%
Score (C)	30%	3.95%	1.58%	2.37%	0%
Score (D)	10%	10%	10%	10%	10%
Score (E)	25.07%	14.10%	9.63%	9.40%	2.24%
Total Score	93.61%	54.75%	45.47%	40.53%	18.45%
SPI	244.85	143.21	118.92	106.01	48.27
Rank	1	10	20	30	69

Notes: Max (A) = 1132, Max (B) = 357, Max (C) = 38, Max (D) = 3, Max (E) = 134

4.3 Comparison by Rank between Student Grade and Participation Index

Figure 3 below is a scatter diagram for the ranking of students by their grades and student participation index. As shown in Table 3 below, student can be categorized into four groups, namely "high grade/high SPI", "high grade/low SPI", "low grade/ high SPI" and "low grade/low SPI". There are more students with high grade/high SPI and low grade/low SPI.

4.4 Assigning Score for Online Participation

Reflecting the flexibility in the index component and depending on the nature of the online course, instructor can define a score relative to the index. This score can be used as part of the student assessment. Here, students are assigned a score out of five according to their index. The score distribution is summarized in table 4.

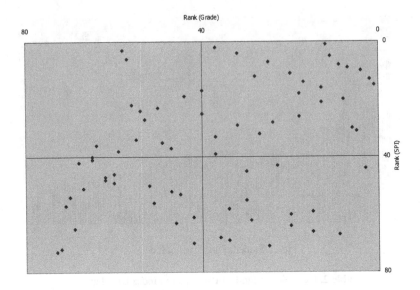

Fig. 3. A diagram of student ranking by their grades and student participation index

Table 3. Number of students in each category of online course participation

	Lower Grade	Higher Grade
Higher SPI	12	27
Lower SPI	20	14

Table 4. Score for Student Participation Index

Score	Rank	Number of Students
5	1 – 10	10
4	11 – 25	15
3	26 – 50	25
2	51 – 69	19
1	70 – 73	4

4.5 Interpretation of Results

For an online course, the relationship between student grades and SPI can have the following interpretation.

Case (i) – High correlation between student grade and SPI: There are more students with high grade/high SPI and low grade/low SPI. Accordingly, there are fewer students with high grade/low SPI and low grade/high SPI. This implies that student participation is a critical factor for better student grade.

Case (ii) – Low correlation between student grade and SPI: The portions of students with high grade/high SPI and low grade/low SPI are not significant. This implies that student participation is not a critical factor for better student grade.

Our online course sample belongs to Case (i), based on the results (the scatter diagram for the ranking of students by grades and SPI) shown in Figure 3. There are relatively more students with high grade/high SPI and low grade/low SPI, implying that student participation is a critical factor for better student grade in the online course.

4.6 Implication of Results

These results have implications on the effectiveness of the online course. For an online course resulting in a high correlation between student grade and SPI, according to the above interpretation, the functions of the online course would have positive effects on the student grades. This implies that the online course is effective in the sense that it contributes to improve the student performance. In contrast, for an on-line course resulting in a low correlation between student grade and SPI, the functions of the online course would not have positive effects on the student grades. This implies that the online course is not effective in the sense that it does not contribute to improve the student performance. However, it should be noted that course effectiveness need to be evaluated among many indicators. The results should be regarded as one useful reference indicator for course evaluation purposes.

5 Conclusion

This paper proposes a student participation index for student assessment in online courses. Student participation is defined from student actions during the use of the online courses. These include web log data on the number of pages viewed, forum questions read and posted, chat sessions participated and submitted. The development of the index involves three steps, namely defining the index components and their weights, defining the index formula and ranking the index results. Students can be assessed by assigning grades based on index ranking. Results from the web log of a sample course indicate that students with higher index usually achieve better grades and vice versa.

The student participation index is non-course-specific, non-subjective, extendible and flexible. Firstly, the index is not limited to any specific course. It is because the use of median during the computation of the index allows the index to be applied to different courses, resulting in an easy articulation of the student participation. Secondly, the index scores are student actions that are gathered from the log data. They are data and not subjective judgments. Thirdly, the index can be extended by adding more student actions to the formula. And finally, it is flexible because the weighting of student actions in the index is defined by the instructor and can be adjusted to fit various situations. These four benefits make the index a useful tool in assessing students in online courses.

Since the log data are collected in batch at the end of the semester, one possible improvement is to gather them regularly during the semester, e.g. weekly basis. Student participation can be evaluated and instructors can continuously assess their students in order to refine teaching and learning strategies. The sample size is limited because the number of students in each course is fixed in each semester. We intend to experiment with other courses in subjects different from programming.

References

1. Lieblein, E., Critical factors for successful delivery of online programs, The Internet and Higher Education, 3(3), 2000, 161-174.
2. Schifter, C., Teaching in the 21st Century, Internet and Higher Education, 1(4), 1999, 281-290.
3. Cheng, C.C., Construction and Evaluation of a Web-Based Learning Portfolio System: An Electronic Assessment Tool, Innovations in Education and Teaching International, 38(2), 2001, 144-155.
4. Dringus, L., & Terell, S., The framework for directed online learning environments, The Internet and Higher Education, 2(1), 1999, 55-67.
5. Coldwell, J., Mapping Pedagogy to Technology – A Simple Model, In Proceedings of the 2nd International Conference on Advances in Web-Based Learning, 180-192, 2003.

Author Index

Lecture Notes in Computer Science

For information about Vols. 1–3038

please contact your bookseller or Springer-Verlag